W9-BNG-879

EIGHTH EDITION

RESEARCH METHODS

A Process of Inquiry

ANTHONY M. GRAZIANO

MICHAEL L. RAULIN

PEARSON

Boston Columbus Indianapolis New York San Francisco Upper Saddle River
Amsterdam Cape Town Dubai London Madrid Milan Munich Paris Montréal Toronto
Delhi Mexico City São Paulo Sydney Hong Kong Seoul Singapore Taipei Tokyo

Editorial Director: Craig Campanella
Editor in Chief: Jessica Mosher
Executive Editor: Stephen Frail
Editorial Assistant: Madelyn Schricker
Director of Marketing: Brandy Dawson
Marketing Manager: Nicole Kunzmann
Marketing Assistant: Jessica Warren
Production Project Manager: Debbie Ryan
Sr. Managing Editor: Denise Forlow
Editorial Project Manager: Maria Piper
Art Director: Jayne Conte
Cover Designer: Bruce Kenselaar
Cover Art: Shutterstock
Media Director: Brian Hyland
Senior Digital Media Editor: Beth Stoner
Full-Service Project Management: Murugesh Rajkumar Namasivayam/PreMediaGlobal
Composition: PreMediaGlobal
Printer/Binder: Courier/Westford
Cover Printer: Lehigh-Phoenix Color/Hagerstown
Text Font: Times LT Std Roman 10/12

Credits and acknowledgments borrowed from other sources and reproduced, with permission, in this textbook appear on appropriate page within text.

Library of Congress Cataloging-in-Publication Data

Catalogue in Publication data available from the Library of Congress

10 9 8 7 6 5 4 3 2 1 V013

Student Edition
ISBN 10: 0-205-907695
ISBN 13: 978-0-205-907694

Instructor's Review Copy
ISBN 10: 0-205-908233
ISBN 13: 978-0-205-908233

CONTENTS

CHAPTER TWO

Research Is a Process of Inquiry 30

CHAPTER THREE

The Starting Point: Asking Questions 58

CHAPTER TWELVE

Factorial Designs 275

CHAPTER THIRTEEN

A Second Look at Field Research: Field Experiments, Program Evaluation, and Survey Research 298

PREFACE

The eighth edition of *Research Methods: A Process of Inquiry* is the latest step in the evolution of this learning package, which now includes the most extensive and integrated website in the market. This package has evolved over more than 25 years of teaching research methods, supervising student research, conducting and reporting our own research, writing other textbooks, and revising earlier editions of this text.

PROGRAMMATIC NATURE OF THE TEXT

Understanding research design is difficult. It requires the understanding and integration of concepts, not merely the learning of a few techniques. Therefore, with every edition, we have emphasized concepts and the integration of those concepts and not cookbook-like strategies. Moreover, we believe that difficult concepts are best taught programmatically. Thus, we introduce complex concepts, such as validity, operational definitions, and statistical inference, early in the text, but only to the degree needed for those introductory discussions. We then systematically reexamine the concepts throughout the text, adding new facets and related concepts. Through that process, we create a coherent model for our students. This programmatic approach makes complex material more accessible and less frustrating for students.

FEATURES OF THE TEXT

This text includes several features designed to enhance student learning and increase interest value, including the following:

Historical Lessons boxes, which use historical psychological and scientific examples to illustrate important principles of research

Costs of Neglect boxes, which provide vivid examples of how badly research can turn out if one does not pay attention to details during the design process

Understanding the Concept boxes, which explain the underlying principles behind various procedures or concepts

Putting It into Practice, which is an embedded feature following the chapter summary that challenges students to take what they have learned in the chapter and apply it to everyday situations. It makes the material more understandable and expands the *critical thinking skills* of students

Go with the Flow boxes, which provide flowcharts to summarize the steps in complex procedures

Classic Studies, which detail studies that changed the field of psychology

We have included the traditional pedagogical features that enhance learning, including chapter outlines, quick-check review questions, chapter summaries, exercises, lists of key terms, and an extensive glossary. We have also included some unique pedagogical features, including a decision-tree flowchart system for selecting appropriate statistics and a research design checklist to pull all of the concepts of the text together for the student. There is an extensive list of examples to illustrate concepts. Finally, we have embedded all of our discussions in an understanding of science, its history, and its approach to knowledge.

Our focus throughout the text is on a conceptual flow of topics, with emphasis on concepts and extensive use of illustrative examples. Secondary topics are covered outside of the chapter in an extensive set of appendices and in a thoroughly integrated website of support topics and hands-on activities. The appendices cover (1) how to use the textbook website, (2) APA style, (3) library research, (4) selecting appropriate statistical procedures, (5) a research design checklist, (6) meta-analyses, (7) a table of random numbers, and (8) answers to the quick-check review questions in the chapters.

The integrated website for the textbook is by far the most extensive in this field. It provides students with a comprehensive list of learning resources. Many of these features are interactive, and others walk students through procedures with animations of what they will be doing. We list the chapter-relevant website resources at the beginning of each chapter and with icons throughout the chapter. The website promotes active learning. Recent research suggests that adding such an active learning component to a course can substantially raise student performance (Schaffhauser, 2008).

A COHERENT MODEL OF THE RESEARCH ENTERPRISE

This text organizes the research process around a coherent descriptive model. This model integrates inductive and deductive reasoning, empirical observation, concepts of validity, and the phases of research (the basic steps through which each research project progresses). The model also introduces the concept of levels of constraint, which refers to the degree of control that the researcher exercises over the research process. We believe it is important to emphasize that valuable research can be conducted at any level of constraint. Experimental research (covered in Chapters 8 to 12) is the most rigorous and allows us to answer questions of causality. However, other research questions are also important, such as questions about the strength and direction of the relationships among variables, about differences between existing groups, and about individuals and their response to manipulations. Furthermore, low-constraint scientific observations can suggest causal hypotheses that we can test with higher-constraint research. We want students to learn that appropriate scientific research design depends largely on the nature of the questions asked and that research at all levels of constraint, whether naturalistic, case study, correlation, differential, quasi-experimental, or experimental, is appropriate and useful.

The text builds a conceptual foundation for all levels of research by developing each level of constraint, thereby providing students with a full spectrum of research knowledge and skills. We have devoted three chapters (6, 7, and 13) to nonexperimental research procedures, which we believe are valuable tools for researchers.

RESEARCH ETHICS

Because of the importance of ethical issues, we have addressed this topic in every chapter of the text. It is covered extensively early in the text (Chapter 3) and, consistent with the text's organization, is revisited repeatedly for more detailed discussions. Our aim is to foster students' sensitivity to ethical issues and to teach the skills needed to address these issues. Those ethical discussions, when taken together, provide a primer on research ethics for our students.

TREATMENT OF STATISTICS

This is a research design text, not a statistics text. However, because research design and statistics are so closely connected, we do cover basic statistical concepts. In addition, we include extensive discussion of statistical concepts and tutorials on computing statistics in the integrated website for the course.

Choosing an appropriate statistical procedure is often confusing for students. We teach that the choice of appropriate statistical analyses follows systematically from the design characteristics of the study. Appendix D presents a unique addition to research methods texts—flowcharts that lead the student step-by-step through the characteristics of any basic research design to the choice of appropriate statistical analysis procedures. A functional version of the flowcharts is programmed into the website, helping students to identify the appropriate statistical procedure and linking them to detailed descriptions of how to compute the statistic.

This organization gives instructors maximum flexibility, allowing them to cover as much or as little statistical material as they wish. We hope that you will take a few minutes to explore the website to see the extensive resources available for you and your students.

THE INTEGRATED WEBSITE

This eighth edition includes both MySearchLab with eText (www.mysearchlab.com) and a Student Resources Website that is thoroughly integrated with the text (www.graziano-raulin.com). *Our goal is to provide the most comprehensive set of student learning resources of any research methods textbook on the market*. MySearchLab contains an eText that students can access anywhere they have an Internet connection, including tablet devices, making it easier for them to study on the go. Interactive glossary flashcards and practice tests help them prepare for exams. MySearchLab also includes Simulations of classic experiments and research inventories, giving students firsthand experience with common research methodologies. The Simulations anonymously track participant data that can be downloaded by instructors and distributed to students for analysis. Chapter 1 outlines the elements of the Student Resource Website and how to access them.

One of the major challenges of the Research Methods course is engaging students in the subject matter and promoting critical thinking. MySearchLab also includes Operation ARA, a critical thinking game developed by Keith Millis, Art Graesser and Diane Halpern. Operation ARA is a role play game that uses a "save the world" storyline to engage students as they learn scientific thinking and research methods. Students progress through three levels in the game, from Basic Training, where they learn the skills, to the Proving Ground, where they demonstrate their mastery of the skills, to Active Duty, where they must apply their skills to stop the world from certain destruction. A separate Instructor's Guide is available to adopters.

The Chapter Resources of the Student Resource Website provide practice for mastering concepts and developing hands-on research skills. This website also provides examples, exercises, and extended discussion of both central and supplemental topics. It includes an interactive Study Guide/Lab Manual, several research skills tutorials (many with flash animations to enhance their effectiveness), coverage of statistical theory and statistical computation, a random number generator program, and dozens of supplementary resources for the student.

MySearchLab is available for purchase standalone, or it can be packaged at no additional cost with the textbook. There is also an unbound Books a la Carte edition that is available with MySearchLab at a significant savings to students.

ADDITIONAL SUPPLEMENTS

In addition to MySearchLab, the adoption package includes an Instructor's Manual, a computerized test bank, a program to construct exams, and basic PowerPoint lectures. You can download any or all of these resources from the instructor's website. Instructors can obtain the necessary authorization to access that website from their local sales representative. (If you do not know who your sales representative is, you can find out by visiting www.pearsonhighered.com/educator and clicking on "Find a representative.")

The Instructor's Manual provides extensive resources for novice and seasoned research methods instructors, including learning objectives, chapter summaries, lecture outlines, lecture launchers and discussion topics, key terms, website resources, and an extended bibliography.

In addition to the Instructor's Manual, there is a computerized test bank, which you can access using the MyTest Program. This program allows instructors to select from 2,500-plus multiple-choice items, modify or write new items, and construct examinations. It is available online at http://pearsonmytest.com and is compatible with most standard web browsers. Since the tests are saved online behind an instructor password, they are more secure than offline test banks, and an instructor can access their tests from any computer.

Finally, a complete set of PowerPoint lectures is available for download from the instructor's website. These lectures include both basic coverage and supplemental slides that instructor's can use if desired.

NEW IN THE EIGHTH EDITION

We continue to improve the text and expand the resources for the text with each edition. Some of the major changes in the eighth edition include:

- More than 100 content changes within the text, including:
    - More than a dozen new topics, such as an operational definition of causation, goals of science, the Belmont Report, the effect of habituation on measurement reactivity, qualitative research, and the impact of restriction of range on correlations
    - Two dozen new figures to explain concepts
    - Updated examples and references

    - Expanded treatment of research ethics
    - An extensively edited glossary
    - Extensive rewriting and reorganization for improved clarity
- Updating several feature boxes and creating two new features for the text (**Go With the Flow** boxes to lead (or take) students through decision processes and **Classic Studies** boxes to illustrate how landmark studies changed the direction of psychological research)
- An updated test bank
- Updated and expanded PowerPoint lectures

ACKNOWLEDGMENTS

A project of this scope would not be possible without the valuable assistance of many people. In past editions, 45 research methods instructors have provided extensive feedback that has helped to improve this text, many of them reviewed several editions. We thank all of them for helping to shape this book. We also wish to acknowledge the feedback and suggestions of our reviewers on this eighth edition, including Natalie Ceballos, Texas State University; Brian Dowling, Hunter College; Michael Dudley, Southern Illinois University Edwardsville; Matthew Jerram, Suffolk University; Justin Oh-Lee, Central Michigan University; Daniel McConnell, University of Central Florida; James Morris, University of Virginia; and Anna Petursdottir, Texas Christian University.

Finally, we want to thank the many editors, production editors, copy editors, assistants, and support staff from the publisher who have shepherded this book through so many editions and so many mergers. In this edition, we want to acknowledge our editor, Stephen Frail, his capable assistant, Madelyn Schricker, production project manager, Debbie Ryan, our production editor, Murugesh Rajkumar Namasivayam, and our copy editor, Suraj Mylapore. Without their help, a project like this would be impossible.

AUTHOR'S STATEMENT

We hope that this text, the integrated website, and the resources available to instructors on the instructor's website will meet your teaching needs. We understand that this is a challenging course to teach and have tried to provide helpful resources. Feel free to send us your comments, questions, and evaluations of this text. You can contact us through e-mail (amgraz@earthlink.net; MikeRaulin@gmail.com).

Anthony M. Graziano

Michael L. Raulin

REFERENCES

Schaffhauser, D. (2008, April 8). University of Houston study: Hybrid courses more effective for students [Preface]. *Campus Technology*. Retrieved from www.campustechnology.com/articles/60481

CHAPTER ONE

CURIOSITY, CREATIVITY, AND COMMITMENT

Among scientists are collectors, classifiers, and compulsive tidiers-up; many are detectives by temperament, and many are explorers; some are artists, and others artisans. There are poet-scientists, philosopher scientists, and even a few mystics.

—Peter Bryan Medawar, *The Art of the Soluble,* 1967

WEB RESOURCE MATERIAL

See the following sections on the website for expanded material.

01:01 A Primer on Logic
01:02 History of Science
01:03 History of Psychology
01:04 Evolution and Psychology
01:05 APA Divisions
01:06 PASW Tutorials
01:07 Study Guide/Lab Manual
01:08 Links to Related Internet Sites

For us, research is the most fascinating, engaging, challenging, and rewarding part of psychology. Perhaps you might not share our enthusiasm and are even a little wary of a course on research methods. However, consider this idea: you conduct informal psychological research every day. Each time you observe people and try to figure out what they are thinking and what they are going to do next, you are conducting psychological research. Whenever you try a new strategy to lose weight, improve your study habits, or impress someone, you are conducting informal psychological research. Think about it.

In this course, you will learn about the formalized research strategies that psychologists use to answer questions about behavior, and you will discover that research questions are endless. For example, Darley and Latané (1968) wanted to know when people are most likely to come to the aid of someone in need of help. Ainsworth (1993) asked how parents could build a secure relationship with their children. Barlow (2002) wanted to know who is most likely to develop a panic disorder. Mroczek and Avron (2007) asked if increasing neuroticism in older men is related to a lower survival rate. Damisch et al. (2010) asked if common superstitious behavior, like knocking on wood, helps to improve performance. Lammers et al. (2010) wondered if moral hypocrisy increased with elevated social power, and van Kleef et al. (2008) asked if elevated social power makes people less compassionate toward others.

These are only a few of the thousands of issues studied by psychologists. You could create your own interesting questions. Try it. What questions are interesting to you?

Darley and Latané (1968) opened a classic line of research that was stimulated by a particularly gruesome crime with a shocking twist. The crime, the twist, and the research are discussed in Classic Studies 1.1 as an illustration of the kinds of questions addressed in psychological laboratories.

CLASSIC STUDIES 1.1 | KITTY GENOVESE AND BYSTANDER APATHY

She was a young lady simply walking home when she was attacked. She was stabbed repeatedly and died. It was a senseless tragedy that on its own would have warranted psychological scrutiny. But it was not the murder that shocked people, which by itself might say something about our society. It was the fact that at least 38 known witnesses observed the attack, which took place over several minutes, and not one person came to Ms. Genovese's aide. No one even called the police. Most of the witnesses were in their own apartments, safe from the knife-wielding attacker and just feet from a telephone. Moreover, there was no evidence that the witnesses were callous; no evidence that they thought Ms. Genovese got what she deserved; in fact, many were terribly distressed by that event. Yet no one even called the police. Why?

Admittedly, this is a more dramatic question than the ones typically faced by psychologists. It is also a more puzzling one, defying common sense, and it may have been the unfathomable idea that so many people could have ignored the fate of this young lady that cried out for an answer. If you cannot be safe with so many people around, you can never be safe.

As you think about this event and try to understand it, you will likely find yourself with lots of questions and no basis in your own experience to begin to answer those questions. You are likely to come back to the number of 38—the number of known witnesses who did nothing.

One you might understand; even 2 or 3, but 38?

It was that fact that intrigued two psychologists: Darley and Latané. Logic might dictate that the more people around to help, the higher the probability that someone in need will get help. Surely some of those 38 people would be good Samaritans. But Darley and Latané (1968) wondered about that logic, and they used the science of psychology to test some of their speculations. What they found in a series of studies was counterintuitive, but not without its own logic. Instead of the probability of getting help increasing when the number of witnesses to the event increases, it decreases, and it decreases dramatically. They explained this finding with a concept called diffusion of responsibility. If you are the only one who can help, you are likely to feel a responsibility to help. If there are several other people available to help, you might reason that someone else will help. Unfortunately, everyone is thinking the same way, and so no one helps. It was not an accident that the witnesses to Ms. Genovese's murder were aware that there were many other witnesses. They probably thought that someone else had called for help.

There are so many questions—important questions—for psychologists to address. We will discuss several in this text. We do not just need answers; we need good answers that will help us to understand, and more importantly, help us to overcome problems. As you will learn in this text, good answers are the result of good questions and careful research to answer these questions. Darley and Latané asked the right question; they translated that question into clever, well-designed, and ethical research. They helped us to understand something that seemed incomprehensible. That is why their study is a classic in the field of psychology.

AN OPENING NOTE TO STUDENTS: ACTIVE LEARNING

Before you get into the main content of this chapter, we want to pass on some ideas we have gained over the years about effective studying. Consider this scenario; we have all experienced it. You block out time to study, make yourself comfortable, and start to read a couple of chapters of your psychology text. Over several hours, you dutifully read every page of those two chapters. Shortly after you finish, you realize that you have no idea what you read. You have read every word, and not one sunk in!

Is that a familiar event? So, why did it happen and how can you prevent it from happening again? Let's face it, you do not have study time to waste.

The principle of what happened is simple. By the time you have reached college, you are so good at reading that it has become an overlearned, fully automatic behavior that you can carry out without much thought. Most of us can read automatically, as well as walk, drive, or ride a bicycle. However, when you were learning these things, they were not automatic and so they required a lot of attention. If you are learning a foreign language, you know that reading in your native language may be automatic, but reading in a new language is anything but automatic. The advantage of automatic behavior is that it takes little of our cognitive capacity, and thus, much of that capacity is available to do other things. A good typist thinks the words and they appear on the screen. Weak typists have to think about the words, and hunt for and peck the letters. Because they are using so much cognitive capacity typing, they often lose their train of thought.

We can easily read without thinking, but we cannot learn new concepts without thinking. Sure, you read every word, but that is all you did. You did not think about what you read. You did not learn the material. If instead, you had stopped after each paragraph and asked what you had read, what it meant, and if you understood it, you would have remembered it, or at least remembered more of it. Granted, it takes you longer to read this way, but you will learn far more in each pass.

Students tend to read chapters by skipping over the "unimportant" stuff, which for most students seems to include the chapter outlines, chapter summaries, footnotes, and exercises. The students' reasoning is that these sections are superfluous, containing nothing different from the material in the chapter. However, these sections are there to facilitate active learning.

Before plunging into the chapter, take 60 seconds to go over the chapter outline and you will have a sense of what to expect in the chapter. This preparation gives you a structure for organizing and learning the new material as you read it. If you concentrate on the summaries, carefully asking yourself if you understand every point, you will identify what you do not understand and your studying will be more effective. Take the time to do the exercises, and you will find that you will learn the material at a level impossible to reach by just reading. You will also remember it longer, will be able to recall it in more situations, and will be able to use it, for example, in examinations. How many times have you faced an exam question that you knew you knew, but you could not remember it in time to get the question correct? When you actively use ideas in different ways, you will recall them more easily in different situations.

Active learning has two advantages. The first is that ideas or procedures that seem clear when you read them may not be at all clear later when you try to use them. Active learning can tell us when we really do not understand a concept, thus allowing us to go back to clear up our confusion. The second advantage is that active learning is more dependable. You learn things better, sometimes dramatically better, when you learn actively. We hope that this brief aside at the beginning of this text will help you to use the text more effectively.

SCIENCE

Psychology is the scientific study of behavior, and this textbook covers the research methods of modern, scientific psychology. To understand the science of psychology, you need to know something of science. This chapter offers you a background on the history and philosophy of science and research.

Science Is a Way of Thinking

Science, one of several ways of learning about the world, uses systematic observation and rational processes to create new knowledge. Scientists seek knowledge through a refined process of questioning. We want you to know, right here in the beginning of this text, that in science, knowing how to ask questions is as crucial as knowing how to answer them. Keep this basic idea in mind: **scientific research** is a process of creating specific questions and then systematically finding answers. Science is a **process of inquiry**—a particular way of thinking.

This process of inquiry generates useful tools and products, such as laboratory equipment, statistical procedures, computers, medicines, and consumer goods. Too often, people mistake the tools and products of science for its essence, but that view is inaccurate; the essence of science is the scientist's ways of thinking—the logic used in systematically asking and answering questions. A scientist can operate scientifically while sitting under a tree in the woods, thinking through a problem, and using apparatus no more technical than paper and pencil. It is not the bubbling liquids and laboratory equipment that make a discipline like chemistry scientific. Likewise, knowing how to use an electron microscope or run a computer program does not make one a scientist. The image of the white-coated laboratory worker surrounded by complex machines is a common visual metaphor, but it does not portray the essence of science any more than a skyscraper really scrapes the sky. *The essence of science is its way of thinking and the disciplined ways in which scientists pose and answer questions. Logical processes and demands for evidence, not technologies, lie at the center of science. Keep this in mind: science is an intellectual process aimed at understanding the natural universe.*

Asking Questions

Asking questions is not new. Socrates and his students asked sophisticated questions over two thousand years ago. A question is one side of an idea; on the other side is an unknown—a potential answer. Every question points to an unknown, to some area of human ignorance or uncertainty. Socrates knew, apparently to his delight, that posing sharp questions about religion, politics, and morality could reveal the ignorance and uncertainties of even the most dignified citizens. Unfortunately for Socrates, the good citizens were made so uncomfortable that they executed him as a subversive and corrupter of youth. It was thus established early in history that asking questions could be hazardous to one's health.

Nevertheless, risk taking is part of science. Those who raise questions and expose ignorance create social and political strains, and often these people suffer reprisals. Nicolaus Copernicus (1473–1543) and Galileo Galilei (1564–1642) challenged church dogma concerning the nature of the solar system. Copernicus knew the risk of church reprisals, and he delayed the publication of his work showing that the Earth revolved around the sun. It was finally published after his death, although many scientists already had clandestine copies. Nearly a century later, Galileo was more outspoken and endured years of house arrest by the church for "blasphemy."

In the 1860s, Charles Darwin, Alfred Russel Wallace, and others implicitly challenged the biblical account of creation, asserting that the earth was millions of years old and that creatures evolved over time. However, such conflicts are not limited to the distant past. Consider the trial of John T. Scopes in 1925 (the "Monkey Trial"). Scopes, a public school science teacher, was convicted of violating a Tennessee law that prohibited teaching Darwinian evolution in public schools. The guilty verdict was later voided on a technicality, but the scripture-based Tennessee law remained until 1965. The debate continues. For example, some public school boards and some administrators have tried to suppress the teaching of evolution in high school biology texts (Matus, 2008). In an important decision, however, a federal judge ruled it unconstitutional to teach intelligent design as an alternative to evolution in high school biology classes, arguing that it was a religious belief rather than a scientific theory (Goodstein, 2005).

Governments often try to suppress scientific knowledge. For example, in 2003, the U.S. Department of the Treasury ruled that American researchers could no longer edit scientific papers written by scientists from Iran, although the government later softened this stance (Bhattacharjee, 2003, 2004). Some states, caught up in political controversy, have proposed outlawing some types of stem cell research (Belluck, 2005). More recently, the Union of Concerned Scientists (2005, 2010) has expressed its concerns about governmental interference with science.

Although scientific information upsets some people, scientists thrive on new knowledge. Scientists are pervasive **skeptics**, challenging accepted wisdom in their search for more complete answers. They are willing to tolerate uncertainty, and they find intellectual excitement in raising questions and seeking answers about nature (Sternberg & Lubart, 1992). Asking a question is a creative endeavor, allowing scientists the personal satisfaction of exercising their curiosity. "What," "how," and "why" are critical words in the scientist's vocabulary. Curiosity may have killed the cat, but it sustains the scientist. J. Robert Oppenheimer (1956) said that scientific research is "responsive to a primitive, permanent, and pervasive human curiosity" (p. 128). According to Linus Pauling (1981), winner of two Nobel prizes, satisfying one's curiosity is one of life's greatest sources of happiness. B. F. Skinner (1956), an influential twentieth-century psychologist, agrees, arguing that "when you run into something interesting, [you should] drop everything else and study it" (p. 223).

A scientist's pursuit of curiosity follows unknown paths, sometimes resulting in dramatic and unanticipated discoveries that can appear to be accidental. However, when scientists drop everything to indulge their curiosity, they do so with a **prepared mind**—a disciplined curiosity that makes them sharply alert to the possibility of unanticipated discoveries. As the Nobel laureate Albert Szent-Gyorgyi noted, a discovery is "an accident meeting a prepared mind" (quoted in Bachrach, 1981, p. 3). Louis Pasteur, whose research led to multiple breakthroughs in the treatment and prevention of diseases, was once asked, "Isn't it extraordinary these days how many scientific achievements are arrived at by accident?" Pasteur replied, "It really is remarkable when you think of it and, furthermore, did you ever observe to whom the accidents happen?" (Nelson, 1970, p. 263).

A scientist's curiosity is active, leading to discoveries, not through luck, but because the prepared mind of the scientist recognized the significance of a curious observation. It is a disciplined curiosity, sharpened by labor, frustrations, and long hours of research. Historical Lesson 1.1 illustrates the importance of a prepared mind.

HISTORICAL LESSON 1.1: THE THREE PRINCES OF SERENDIP

According to the English novelist Horace Walpole, three princes from Serendip (the former name of Sri Lanka) constantly stumbled upon lucky finds. In science, **serendipity** has come to mean unanticipated discoveries. Some call them "lucky" discoveries, accidentally hit upon while the scientist was looking for something else. However, these serendipitous findings are not the "happy accidents" that they appear to be. Scientists might have easily missed them were they not alert to the implication of their observations. Such alertness requires a prepared mind and a sense of curiosity.

There are numerous examples in science of such serendipitous findings (Roberts, 1989). Probably the best-known example of serendipity in science is Fleming's discovery of penicillin after observing the results of an accidental contamination of a specimen by a mold. Penicillin became our first wonder drug. Actually, Fleming was one of several scientists who shared the discovery and development of penicillin (Macfarlane, 1984).

Another example of a serendipitous finding was James Olds and Peter Milner's (1954) discovery of the brain's reward center when the electrode they had intended to implant in the reticular formation of one of their rats missed its target. Surgically implanting a tiny electrode in an area that is smaller than a grain of rice is difficult, and some implanted electrodes missed their mark. Usually, when the electrode missed its mark, nothing much happened. However, Olds and Milner were intrigued by the behavior of one of their rats. The rat kept returning to the place where it had previously received the electrical stimulation, almost as if it wanted more. Alert to the fact that they were observing something new, these investigators began a series of studies of how the brain shapes behavior through reward (Olds, 1958).

Another example comes from the Princeton laboratory of Charles Gross (2008). Gross was studying visual processing in the monkey brain, measuring the response of individual neurons to a standard set of visual stimuli (dots, lines, and colored squares). After hours of fruitless testing with one neuron, the researchers finally gave up. As they were about to shut down the apparatus, Gross waved good night to his monkey, and the neuron they were studying immediately responded. Puzzled but intrigued, Gross began a series of systematic studies into this chance finding. He and his colleagues (e.g., Michael Graziano & Gross, 1993, 1998) had discovered that individual neurons could be sensitive to complex stimuli, such as hands, faces, and even images of food. This discovery stimulated highly significant research into this brain area.

What do these examples have in common? Scientists' curiosity is not idle, but is active and always questioning. These were not lucky discoveries. Each of these scientists knew that they had discovered something interesting, although initially they were uncertain what it was. They had prepared minds, which they nurtured through long hours of research. Without such prepared minds, they would have never realized the importance of their puzzling results and would have dismissed them as meaningless. The best scientists all have this kind of disciplined curiosity.

Science and Art

Curiosity, creativity, skepticism, tolerance for ambiguity, systematic thinking, and hard work are universal in scientists. However, those characteristics are also well developed in poets, sculptors, painters, composers, philosophers, writers, and others. All engage in a mix of artistic and intellectual endeavors, indulge their own curiosity, and explore their worlds with skeptical questioning and sharp observations. They attempt to answer their own questions and to represent nature through their particular medium, whether it is color, shape, sound, or language. A combination of curiosity and creativity compels them to identify relationships in nature and contribute their findings to the public domain, where their work will be viewed, discussed, criticized, accepted, rejected, or worse, ignored.

This is not to argue that science and art are the same, because they are not. Yet each employs variations of the same theme—human curiosity combined with a disciplined process of inquiry to create representations of ideas. Although artists and scientists comprise only a small part of the world's population, they have created an enduring array of knowledge and products that have significantly affected the world.

There is a common belief that art and science are so different that artists and scientists are alienated from each other. People often describe a poet, musician, or actor as the "artistic type," implying that the person has no aptitude for science or math. Alternatively, they may assume that a scientist or mathematician cannot appreciate art and literature. These assumptions are false.

Consider the 40 national winners of the annual high school–level Intel Science Talent Search. Many of these young people, who have demonstrated high achievement in science, mathematics, and technology, are also talented in other creative activities, such as music, writing, and the visual arts. This should not be surprising. As you will see, the same pool of human skills generated art, science, and technology early in civilization. Historical Lesson 1.2 shows how science and art can complement one another, as illustrated by the incredible work of Leonardo da Vinci.

HISTORICAL LESSON 1.2: LEONARDO DA VINCI

The Renaissance was Europe's transition from medieval to modern life. It included severe upheaval of the old, religious values of the Middle Ages. Humanism flourished, and the celebration of life was pursued through momentous developments in art, science, literature, architecture, commerce—virtually all aspects of human creativity.

It was in this setting that Leonardo da Vinci (1452–1519) blended his science and art, demonstrating their natural affinity. His education was ordinary, but he did have solid training in natural sciences, mechanics (physics), and music. He even invented a new musical instrument. He apprenticed with the famous painter,

(continued)

HISTORICAL LESSON 1.2: CONTINUED

Verrocchio, and within 10 years was a recognized master himself.

Leonardo studied anatomy to enhance his art. Going far beyond the artistic study of the human body, he developed detailed drawings and knowledge of the major anatomical systems: skeletal, muscular, cardiovascular, respiratory, genitourinary, and embryological. These studies reflect the meticulously detailed observation typical of artist and scientist alike. He also studied comparative anatomy, dissecting animal bodies and making detailed examinations and drawings. Leonardo was the first great medical illustrator (Gross, 1997). In his studies of bird wings, we see the artist recording his observations in detailed drawings. We also see the scientist and engineer trying to understand the mechanics of the articulation of the bird's wing, such as which muscles control which actions and what happens to the particular limbs, joints, and feathers in the action of flying. From his study of bird wings, he sketched plans for a flying machine—over 500 years ago!

Leonardo was a creative genius in science, technology, and art. As a military engineer, he designed fortifications, tank-like war machines, an underwater breathing apparatus, a submarine, and a crop irrigation system. Yet, he found time for other pursuits. He sculpted a huge model for an equestrian monument, which he never completed because bronze was needed to make cannons. He drew plans for buildings and monuments, pursued studies of mathematics and anatomy, and made detailed observations of fossils, river movements, and rock strata, leading him to brilliant conclusions that modern paleontologists would not develop for another 300 years (Gould, 1997). As if this were not enough, this incredible scientist also created magnificent works of art, including the *Last Supper* and the *Mona Lisa*.

Leonardo's work wove together science and art using mathematics, anatomy, mechanics, painting, and sculpture. His artistic labor alternated continuously with his scientific inquiry. Although much of his work has been lost, more than 5,000 pages of drawings and notes survive (Gross, 1997). He exemplified the affinity of art and science in understanding nature. There were no arbitrary divisions between science and art in this Renaissance genius.

Quick-Check Review 1.1: Science

1. What is the essence of science?
2. How can a scientist practice science while sitting under a tree?
3. What is meant by a prepared mind in science?
4. What are some of the major characteristics of scientists?
5. What do art and science have in common?

ACQUIRING KNOWLEDGE

To learn about nature, scientists employ systematic thinking and they place heavy demands on the adequacy of their information and on the processes they apply to that information. Science is one way of acquiring knowledge. Others are tenacity, intuition, authority, rationalism, and empiricism (Helmstadter, 1970). These methods differ in the demands they make on the adequacy of the information and on how they process the information. *Science, which combines rationalism and empiricism, is the most demanding method for acquiring knowledge, whereas tenacity, intuition, and authority make few demands on information and require minimal processing.*

Tenacity

Tenacity is a willingness to accept ideas as valid knowledge despite contrary evidence and/or a lack of supporting evidence. Ideas that have long been accepted or often repeated may acquire an aura of unquestioned truth. An example from the history of psychology is the powerful belief, held by early twentieth-century psychologists, that women were not as intelligent as men (Shields, 1982). Perhaps due in part to this belief, women were excluded from the all-male university programs and professions well into the 1930s. Male psychologists of that era probably did not question their tenacious beliefs, and they ignored contrary evidence.

Tenacity also operates in modern political campaigns, in which candidates or political commentators repeat distorted ideas so incessantly that voters accept them as true. Advertisers do the same thing, calculating that consumers will accept mindless repetition as truth. *When tenacity operates, there is no demand to check the accuracy of ideas, no serious consideration of alternative ideas, and no testing of the ideas through skeptical, critical, and objective review.*

In a provocative book on how people influence others, Robert Cialdini describes a possible mechanism behind tenacity (Cialdini, 1993). People, he says, generally strive to be consistent in their behavior. They view inconsistency as a negative trait because it suggests that a person has not thought through the issues at hand. Hence, once people act, they often have a strong need to continue to act in the same way, even if the initial action was ill advised or the situation has changed so that the action is no longer appropriate. For many, it is better to have a tenacious, but incorrect, position than to be inconsistent.

Intuition

Intuition is the (supposedly) direct acquisition of knowledge without intellectual effort or sensory processing. Examples include extrasensory perception (a contradiction in terms), which self-styled psychics claim to possess, and knowledge received directly from God, claimed by people who have powerful religious experiences. Mysticism, spiritualism, and even drug-induced altered states of consciousness can lead people to the absolute conviction that they have found truth and knowledge.

Apparent intuition is common in everyday life. We may instantly like or dislike another person we have just met. We seldom examine our reactions rationally; we just "feel" them. People commonly have hunches or gut feelings. These serve us well in many situations, but they also lead to errors. Intuitive responses are rapid assessments based on unexamined experiences, attitudes, and feelings (Myers, 2004). What makes these experiences appear to be intuitive is that people accept the information rapidly, without rational thought or examination.

Scientists also employ hunches, making conceptual leaps without examining the facts. These hunches are often productive in advancing research. However, when they are wrong, the process of science will weed them out.

Authority

Authority is the acceptance of ideas as valid knowledge because a respected source, such as the Bible, the Qur'an, Aristotle, the Supreme Court, Freud, or the president, claims they are valid.

Tenacity, intuition, and authority make few demands on the adequacy of information and the processes used to evaluate that information. These methods share uncritical acceptance of information. They assert that an idea is true because (1) people have "always" accepted it as true, (2) it feels true, or (3) an authority says it is true.

These methods can have value in smoothing personal lives. You might, for example, accept religious teachings intuitively or on authority and experience personal satisfaction. You might accept an urge to have pasta for dinner, without any need for further evaluation. However, would you also uncritically agree to saunter across a busy highway with your eyes closed because a psychic says that he knows you will be perfectly safe, despite the six lanes of vehicles hurtling by from both directions at 75 mph? Clearly, for some decisions, the information and the processes employed to gather and test the information need to be more adequate. Both rationalism and empiricism provide a stronger basis for accepting information as knowledge.

Rationalism

Rationalism is a way of acquiring knowledge through reasoning. Existing information is carefully stated and logical rules are followed to arrive at acceptable conclusions. Consider this classic deductive syllogism:

All crows are black. (major premise)
This is a crow. (minor premise)
Therefore, this crow is black. (conclusion)

The conclusion is derived logically from the major and minor premises. The same logical processes would lead to the rejection of the following conclusion:

All crows are black.
This is black.
Therefore, this is a crow.

In the rationalistic approach, the conclusion is reached through **logic**—systematic rules that allow us to draw accurate conclusions from a basic set of facts or statements.

Rationalism is a more reliable way to acquire knowledge than tenacity, intuition, or authority. However, rationalism has its limitations. Consider this syllogism:

All four-year-old children develop fears of the dark.
Lisa is a four-year-old child.
Therefore, Lisa has developed fears of the dark.

The logic is clear and the conclusion is correct, unless of course Lisa has not developed fears of the dark. What is the limitation? Rationalism is a powerful tool for analysis of propositions or theories. However, its weakness lies in its application to external events. Suppose that it is not true that all four-year-old children develop fears of the dark, or suppose that Lisa is actually seven and not four, or suppose that Lisa is a yacht and not a child. The major limitation of rationalism is that the premises must be true, as determined by some other evidence, to arrive at the correct conclusions. The accuracy of conclusions depends on both the reasoning process and the accuracy of the premises. Unfortunately, when the purely rationalistic approach is applied to external events, there is no provision for assessing their accuracy. (See the Student Resource Website for a primer on logic.)

01:01

Empiricism

Empiricism involves gaining knowledge through observation—knowing something by experiencing it through our senses. For the empiricist, it is not enough to know through reason (or tenacity or intuition or authority) alone. It is necessary to experience the world—to see, hear, touch, taste, and smell it. "I won't believe it unless I see it!" is the empiricist's motto. We are good empiricists when we notice a dark sky and hear distant rumblings of thunder and decide to take an umbrella. Our senses are telling us something.

However, empiricism also has limitations. There are two types of empiricism: **naïve empiricism** and **sophisticated empiricism**. The statement "I won't believe it unless I see it!" is an example of naïve empiricism. Suppose you have never seen Hong Kong, Prague, Nyack, or Chippewa Falls; does this mean that these places do not exist? Because you have never seen gravity or the measles virus, should you conclude that you will never fall down or contract measles? Suppose your empirical observations lead you to assert "I have never been run down while walking along the middle of a highway"; does that mean you can continue walking down highways with impunity? How about when you see something clearly that turns out to be an illusion, as in Figure 1.1?

Sophisticated empiricism goes further. People cannot see heat or gravity or, with unaided eyesight, the measles virus. However, they can observe the rise of the mercury in a thermometer as they turn up a heat source, watch an object fall to the ground, and view a virus through an electron microscope. Empirical observations in science are not limited to direct observations; we can also observe phenomena *indirectly* by observing their impact on other objects, like thermometers.

Empirical observations (i.e., facts) are critical in science. However, if scientists did nothing but collect observations, they would achieve only long lists of facts. They would know nothing about how the facts go together or what the facts mean. Facts are most useful when people can think about them, organize them, draw meaning from them, and use them to make predictions—that is,

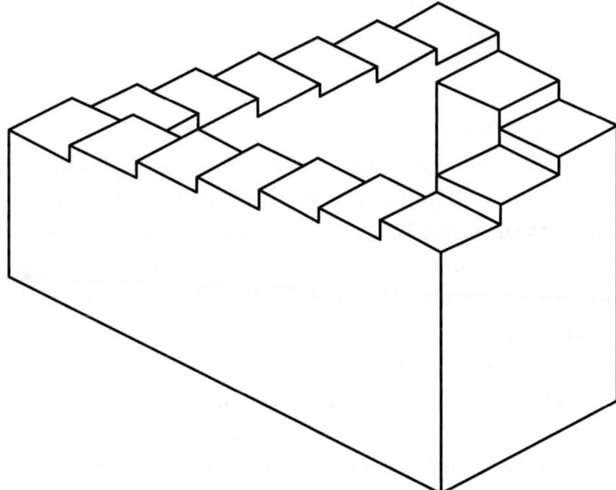

FIGURE 1.1 Reality or Illusion? You cannot always trust what you see.

Source: Penrose, L. S., & Penrose, P. R. (1958). Impossible objects: A special type of visual. *British Journal of Psychology, 49*, 31–33.

when facts are carefully inserted into the logic of rationalism. *We need to integrate empiricism with rational thinking so that the two work together. This is what science does.*

Science

Science brings together rationalism and empiricism, employing rational logic and checking each step with empirical observation. Scientists constantly shuttle between empirical observation, rational thought about general principles, and further empirical observation. This repeated return to empirical observation in an otherwise rationalistic process characterized the sixteenth century's surge into science. Much of the progress in science since then has focused on strengthening the empirical component by developing better observational procedures.

Science is a way of thinking that involves a continuous and systematic interplay of rational thought and empirical observation. Observed events, such as the movements of planets or the behavior of children, are the facts of science. The empirical observation of events and identification or listing of facts, while useful, is not sufficient in modern science. Scientists must go beyond observable facts to construct general principles and to make new predictions about nature based on those principles.

Quick-Check Review 1.2: Acquiring Knowledge

1. What are the common methods of acquiring knowledge?
2. Which two methods does science incorporate?
3. What is naïve empiricism? sophisticated empiricism?
4. What are the limitations of rationalism? . . . of empiricism?
5. What are the "facts" of science?

EMERGENCE OF SCIENCE

The rapid development of science through the fifteenth and sixteenth centuries may suggest that science suddenly emerged and that there was no science before Copernicus, Galileo, or Newton. However, science has been one of Western civilization's methods of acquiring knowledge since the Greeks of 2,400 years ago, and its antecedents date back 8,000 years. Not until the Renaissance did science become independent enough to develop into the powerful social movement that it is today. This section reviews the historical bases of science. (See the Student Resource Website for a more detailed History of Science overview.)

01:02

Early Civilization

Over millennia, humans developed a broad array of skills that enabled a remarkable surge of progress from the late Neolithic period of polished stone tools into the age of metals, about 6000 to 4000 B.C. Urban settlements grew; technological, social, and intellectual tools accumulated; and societies spread around the eastern Mediterranean. The magnificent civilizations of the Babylonians, Egyptians, and others flourished. Their skills included architecture, agriculture, animal husbandry, food preparation, mining, smelting, and tool manufacturing. Their commerce depended on long-distance land and sea navigation, weights, measures, counting, written records, and accurate calendars. By 4000 B.C., there were books on astronomy, medicine, surgery, and mathematics. These remarkable advances coexisted with mystical beliefs about a universe filled with gods, demons, and spirits.

By 1000 B.C., there was a rich legacy of practical skills in agriculture, mining and metallurgy, manufacturing, and commerce. From such concrete, practical skills and knowledge, abstract concepts were gradually developed (Farrington, 1949a, b). For example, early farmers observed weather phenomena, moon phases, sun positions, and other changes in the sky for clues to help in farming. These observations led to the development of accurate calendars. Farmers also learned about fertilizers and plant growth and developed practical mathematics to measure plots and set boundaries. Artisans learned to recognize various ores. They knew that heat transformed solids into liquids; they could measure by weighing; and they understood proportionality, allowing them to reproduce the particular mixtures needed for various alloys. These skills required an abstract understanding of nature gathered and refined through generations of empirical observations and concrete manipulations. Apprentices of the day may not have studied abstract astronomy or mathematics, but early elements of these disciplines were embedded in their crafts. In these early Mediterranean civilizations, the components of modern science developed within the arts, crafts, and trades. Science, art, and technology were inseparable in practice.

Science rests on the **orderliness belief** (Whitehead, 1925), which is the assumption that the universe operates in an orderly manner. To apply their skills in a reliable manner, early artisans and tradesmen had to expect orderliness. How else could they depend on *this* type of rock, when heated, to release *that* kind of metal, which will always have *these* properties, regardless of the different pieces of the rock used?

Greek Science

Empirical science dates to the pre-Socratic Greek period (c. 600–c. 400 B.C.). Thales (c. 625–547 B.C.) was the first Greek philosopher to combine empirical and rational views of the universe. He lived in Ionia, a Greek colony, whose citizens developed impressive commercial skills. The Ionians were pragmatic realists—primarily artisans, farmers, and tradespeople. Empirical knowledge was basic in their culture, and when some, like Thales, turned to philosophy, they developed an empirical view of nature.

Thales' philosophy rejected mysticism and stressed the observation of natural events in a natural universe. He speculated about a natural cosmology in which water was the basic substance from which all else developed and to which all will ultimately return. He studied Babylonian astronomy and predicted the solar eclipse that occurred on May 25, 585 B.C. His observations were careful and painstaking (Whitehead, 1925). Thales founded abstract geometry and Ionian philosophy, and many historians consider him the father of science.

Thales's naturalistic speculations inspired others. Anaximander's (610–547 B.C.) observation that sharks had mammalian characteristics led him to propose that higher-order creatures, including humans, developed from fishes. Xenophanes (c. 560–c. 478 B.C.) observed rock imprints of fish and seaweed on mountains and proposed a theory of geological change over time. Hippocrates (c. 460–c. 377 B.C.) taught that demons and gods played no part in disease, and that prayers and exorcisms would not heal a sick person. The Hippocratic physician relied on careful observations of patients and on rational thought in trying to understand illness.

From Thales through Hippocrates, Ionian science rejected mysticism and emphasized the observation of naturally occurring events in an orderly universe. A later Ionian, Strato (d.c. 270 B.C.), developed the next important step—making the scientist an active observer who manipulates and controls the conditions of observations. Strato, a successor to Aristotle, taught that the best method of acquiring knowledge was empirical manipulation and observation, that is, **experimentation**. He experimented on air and water, demonstrating many of their properties and developing general explanatory principles about nature.

However, by Strato's time, Ionian empirical science was already in decline. The mystical views of religious authorities and the philosophical views of Plato and Socrates were displacing Strato's scientific view. Then, as now, these views conflicted, leading to the near total suppression of early empirical science for almost 1,900 years.

After Socrates, the highest ideals were religion, politics, and rationalistic, mystical philosophy. Practical skills were maintained, but were left to slaves, laborers, artisans, farmers, and tradespeople. Upper-class scholars pursued pure reason and abstract ideas. As a result, scholars taught theology and philosophy and preserved their knowledge in writing, whereas empirical skills, not admitted into the realm of scholarship, remained an oral tradition. Social stratification was not the only factor contributing to the suppression of empiricism. Religious leaders used their increased social power to attack the Ionians' natural philosophy as atheistic, inaccurate, and subversive. Does this echo from 2,000 years ago sound a bit familiar? How about some of today's science-religion conflicts?

The genius of the early Greeks created an empirical science that described an orderly universe operating according to a few basic principles. Greek philosophy was one of humanity's major intellectual achievements. Yet, at the height of this achievement, Plato and Socrates led the movement away from empiricism with a focus on the pursuit of pure reason. As Farrington (1949a) noted, "When Plato died (c. 347 B.C.), he left behind a mystical view of the universe set forth in his dialogues in a unique combination of logic and drama. Its weakness was not that it lacked supports in argument, but that it was not open to correction from experience."

After 400 B.C., Greek philosophy became increasingly mystical, altering the way people viewed discoveries. For example, philosophers argued that the regularity of number relationships and the orderliness observed in astronomy were evidence that divine intelligence controlled nature. This led to a shift in the goals of philosophy and science. Earlier investigators wanted to understand and control nature, but later philosophers sought to illustrate divine intelligence through their study of nature. Science was beginning to be used in the service of religion, a role that continued for 2,000 years.

Medieval Science

By the end of the fourth century, Christianity was the Roman Empire's state religion, remaining a major social and political power for the next 1,000 years. Medieval Christian scholars continued the Greek reliance on intuition and reason, arguing that divine intelligence controlled the universe and the scriptures were the ultimate source of truth.

Theology, the study of God and God's relationship to the universe, dominated scholarship. Revelation, rationalism, and authority were the primary sources of knowledge. Some Christian scholars continued empirical studies in astronomy, optics, and zoology, but these studies were always secondary to theology and in the service of religion (Nagel, 1948).

Eventually, theological scholars, such as Thomas Aquinas and Roger Bacon, rediscovered empirical methods (around the thirteenth century). Bacon repeated optical experiments performed earlier by Islamic scientists. Dietrich of Frieberg used water-filled glass balls to experiment with the visible light spectrum; Jordanus DeNemore experimented with levers and weights on inclined planes; and Peter the Stranger of Maricourt published sophisticated experiments with magnets. Reflecting upon this renewed empiricism, Dietrich of Frieberg noted that "one ought never to renounce what had been made manifest by the senses" (cited in Clagett, 1948, p. 119).

The twelfth and thirteenth centuries saw great changes in politics, art, commerce, and exploration. People focused more on the world around them, which led to a revival of ancient Greek, Greco-Roman, and Islamic scholarship. Europeans expanded trade around the Mediterranean, encountering works of Islamic scholars who had been part of the Moorish high civilization in Spain. They translated Arabic versions of classical works into Latin. By the end of the twelfth century, medieval scholars knew Hippocratic and Galenic writings in medicine, Euclid's mathematics, Ptolemy's astronomy, Archimedes' physics, and Hindu mathematics. Medical schools, largely based on these traditions, were established across Europe, and the empirical study of medicine, mathematics, and physics was revived. This rebirth of empirical science remained within the bounds of theology, where, for a while, there was room for it to grow. However, science ultimately challenged theology and, by the seventeenth century, began to escape from its constraints.

Christian theologians adopted two constraints on empirical science that Greek scholars had established centuries before. The first was that empirical science must not contradict theological dogma. In any dispute between knowledge gained through the senses and knowledge gained through revelation or church authority, the resolution was simple: truth lay with theology, and any contradictory ideas were false. The second constraint was that science was to be used only in the service of religion. However, scientists challenged both constraints, arguing, for example, that science could improve human life on earth by combating sickness. The church tolerated this application of science to humanity as long as it did not challenge church dogma. Eventually, however, that challenge did occur.

The Scientific Revolution

By the thirteenth century, science dominated the new medical centers, and scholars began to recognize the *value of science in the service of humanity*. This was a novel idea for most people—using knowledge to help people in *this* world instead of exclusively focusing on the "next world." The idea of service to humanity was part of the great humanitarian revolution that was gathering. It would eventually become a major theme in science. However, science remained largely under the control of religion well into the fourteenth century.

During the thirteenth through sixteenth centuries, science increasingly conflicted with religion. For example, Catholics and Protestants condemned René Descartes (1596–1650) because he questioned the concept of the soul and argued for objective observation and study of consciousness. In 1633, the courts of the Inquisition forced Galileo (1564–1642), an astronomer, philosopher, and mathematician, to recant his support of the Copernican concept that the Earth orbits the sun.

However, the scientific revolution, fueled by Copernicus, Bacon, Galileo, Kepler, Newton, and others, had already begun. Churchmen vigorously battled against what they saw as scientists' attack on religion. However, by the start of the nineteenth century, science had regained the independence it had lost to religion nearly fifteen hundred years earlier. Scientific centers flourished in universities and industries, and governments actively recruited scientists. By the twentieth century, science had become a well-established major social movement.

Science developed rapidly during the twentieth century and continues to do so in the twenty-first century. For example, developments in high-energy physics provide insights into the building blocks of matter. In biology, the ability to read and manipulate DNA structure has led to breakthroughs offering new ways to solve many difficult problems. Neuroscience, which integrates psychology, biology, neurology, and molecular genetics, created new technologies, such as magnetic resonance imaging (MRI). The development of high-temperature superconducting materials and faster computer chips has enormous potential for future applications.

Modern science depends on a heavily endowed social structure. We now have networks of scientific societies with annual meetings and specialized scientific journals in which scientists communicate with colleagues. It is also important to communicate with the public, and scientists do so through newspapers, magazines, radio, television, books, and the Internet, although some have argued that science should do more to communicate with the public to promote better understanding and acceptance (e.g., Lilienfeld, 2011).

Scientists have created specialized disciplines, such as biology, chemistry, psychology, each with its own content and procedures. The phenomena studied differ from one discipline to another, and methodological procedures vary according to the phenomena studied, the questions asked, and the technologies associated with each discipline. Whatever their specialization, scientists share curiosity about nature and a commitment to the combined use of empiricism and rationalism as their way to understand nature.

Science is not new, but people think it is because many equate science with technology, and technology is constantly changing. Science and technology are closely related, but they are not the same. Technology is one of the practical products of science—useful tools based on scientific principles that solve problems or open new opportunities. Science is a way of thinking; technology is a solution to a problem. Science seeks understanding; technology uses that understanding to improve our lives. Science could exist without technology; technology, at least the impressive technology of today, could not exist without science. Technology changes quickly as new insights lead to new products, but the method of science is remarkably stable, building on the knowledge base, yet relying on the same core processes of empiricism and rationalism.

The pace of science-based technological development has been astounding. Consider the development of aircraft. In 1903, after years of research, Orville Wright flew for 12 seconds in the world's first powered, piloted, heavier-than-air flight. When Orville died in 1948, Chuck Yeager had already broken the sound barrier in a jet-propelled airplane and the first manned flight into space was only 13 years away. Could Orville have imagined at the turn of the twentieth century that such dramatic developments would occur in such a short time? In less than 100 years, humans have walked on the moon and have lived in space for periods as long as 14 months. Airplanes have been built that fly over mach 3 (2,000+ miles per hour) or carry over 800 people. Many commercial planes are longer and have wing spans that are greater than the length of the first flight by the Wright brothers.

The Goals of Science

Scientists indulge their curiosity and search for answers to interesting questions, but the goals of science go well beyond those of individual scientists. The overriding goal of science is to acquire knowledge about the universe—to understand natural phenomena. In the pursuit of scientific knowledge scientists follow the trails of several critical subgoals, including observation and description, prediction, discovering causation, explanation, and application.

Scientists generally start with observation and **description**, in which they identify and observe phenomena and carefully record their details. Description alone does not constitute understanding, but it does provide information that will help in designing new, more sophisticated studies.

Prediction involves finding relationships that are dependable enough that we can make an educated guess about what will happen to one factor if we know what happened with another factor. Prediction brings us closer to understanding, but, as you will see in Chapter 7, we are able to make reliable predictions even without fully understanding why our predictions work.

Establishing **causation** is a step beyond prediction, because it allows us to not only say what will happen, but gives us the power to make it happen—that is, we know what will "cause" a change in a phenomenon. At this stage, we usually do not know why the factor can cause a change; we just know that it can.

Explanation takes us to the next step of understanding how certain factors can change other factors. What are the mechanisms by which those changes occur? Here is where the development of scientific theory is particularly important. (We will discuss theory in later chapters.) By putting our information into theories and attempting to explain phenomena, we move closer to understanding phenomena and to the goal of acquiring knowledge. Some would maintain there are two overriding goals of science: the acquisition and the application of knowledge, that is, to understand natural phenomena and to apply that understanding to the solution of practical problems. As we will discuss in Chapter 3, these goals are often thought of in terms of basic research and applied research.

The goal of **application** involves using our new knowledge to solve real-world problems. It is worth noting that scientists routinely develop applications long before they fully understand phenomena. If you can make predictions, you can use those predictions to make better decisions, such as who is most likely to do well on a job. If you know that a factor can cause a change in another factor, you can use that information to change the environment, even though you may not understand how your causal factor works. Any scientist, whether focusing on basic or applied research, understands that acquiring knowledge and applying that knowledge are the two main goals of science.

Quick-Check Review 1.3: Emergence of Science

1. How did the early practical skills of artisans contribute to modern science?
2. What contribution did Thales make to science?
3. What was the relationship between science and theology during the Middle Ages?
4. Distinguish between modern technology and modern science.
5. What is the orderliness belief, and what does it have to do with science?
6. Why was Galileo put under arrest?

PSYCHOLOGY

Psychology is the science of behavior. This section provides you with a brief overview of the history of psychology. More information is available in several excellent texts (Benjafield, 2005; Benjamin, 2007; Goodwin, 2008; Hergenhahn, 2009; Pickren & Rutherford, 2010; Schultz & Schultz, 2008). (See the Student Resources Website for the History of Psychology Overview.)

01:03

The History of Psychology

Nineteenth-century physiology and the philosophies of romanticism, rationalism, and empiricism provided the context for the emerging discipline of psychology. Romanticism fueled the nineteenth-century humanitarian reform movements, while rationalism and empiricism were the major supports of modern science. The earliest psychological research focused on neurophysiology, including studies of reflex action and localization of brain function.

Scientific psychology was profoundly influenced by Darwin's evolutionary theory, with its concept of **phylogenetic continuity**—the similarity of structure and function between humans and other animals. That idea suggested that studying non-human animals could help scientists to understand human functioning. However, it ran counter to religious and philosophical thought that humans were unique from other animals. The evolutionists' emphasis on adaptation of organisms to their environments highlighted the importance of studying function as well as structure. Darwin's use of data from many sources—geology, paleontology, archeology, biology, naturalistic observations—legitimized the use of diverse data sources and methodologies. The concept of natural selection emphasized individual differences, which helped to set the stage for later psychological work on personality, intelligence, and psychological testing. The influence of evolutionary theory on modern psychological science has been enormous. (See the Student Resource Website for a discussion of evolution and psychology.)

01:04

Pre-scientific psychology dates to Aristotle, but the scientific study of psychology did not begin until the mid-nineteenth century, evolving from philosophy, biology, mathematics, physiology, physics, and even astronomy. Ernst Weber (1795–1878) and Gustav Fechner (1801–1887) were among the first researchers to study perceptual processes objectively. They presented carefully measured stimuli to people under controlled conditions and recorded the participants' responses, an approach known as **psychophysics**.

The early history of psychology was dominated by a series of *schools* or movements. Each school of psychology discussed below defined itself by a central focus, a set of underlying assumptions, research methodologies, and a general philosophy about human functioning and the best ways to study it.

Structuralism. Wilhelm Wundt (1832–1920) established the world's first psychological laboratory in 1879 in Leipzig, Germany, and dominated psychology during the late nineteenth and early twentieth centuries. Wundt studied the structure of consciousness—hence, his school of thought was called **structuralism**. His primary method was **introspection**—asking participants to report on their mental experiences as they performed various tasks.

Functionalism. By the turn of the twentieth century, American psychologists shifted the attention from the structure of the mind to its functioning, creating what was known as **functionalism**. Functional psychologists were interested in practical questions of education, training, treatment, and child rearing. For example, E. L. Witmer (1867–1956) educated children who had cognitive deficits and/or emotional disorders. Witmer established the world's first psychological clinic (in 1896) and created the field of clinical psychology (Witmer, 1907).

Psychodynamics. **Psychodynamic theory** viewed behavior as a function of complex and often contradictory internal influences, many of which were believed to be unconscious and thus not within the awareness of people. In contrast, structuralism assumed that psychological processes were conscious and thus could be accessed through introspection. Sigmund Freud (1856–1939) developed psychodynamic theory based on the work of others going back to the early 1800s. Darwin's evolutionary theory influenced Freud's ideas, including his work on unconscious processes, the importance of dreams, the child-to-adulthood continuity of emotional behavior, and sex as a basic human biological drive (Ritvo, 1990; Schultz & Schultz, 2008; Sulloway, 1979).

Gestalt Psychology. **Gestalt psychology** originated in Germany about 1912. Its founders (Koffka, 1935; Kohler, 1926; Wertheimer, 1945) believed that the structuralists' efforts to divide consciousness into separate parts lost sight of the "wholeness" of experience. Especially with perception, Gestalt psychologists argued that the whole is greater than the sum of its parts; the perceptual system detects lines, edges, and movements, but the brain puts these together and we see meaningful objects and activities.

Behaviorism. **Behaviorism**, which emerged in the United States around 1912, criticized psychology as too mentalistic and subjective. John B. Watson (1878–1958) rejected all mentalistic concepts like mind and consciousness as meaningless carry-overs from pre-scientific psychology. Watson argued for replacing the psychology of consciousness with an objective psychology of observed behavior.

Animal psychology was a major factor in modern behavioral psychology. Behaviorists, such as Ivan Pavlov (1849–1936) and B. F. Skinner (1904–1990), studied animal behavior to understand such complex processes as learning. An application of behavioral principles is **behavior modification**, which therapists now use extensively in clinics, hospitals, and schools.

Humanistic Psychology. **Humanistic psychology** emerged in the mid-twentieth century and was briefly influential (Schultz & Schultz, 2008). It focused on human conscious experience, creativity, and personal growth and assumed there was a natural tendency toward self-actualization—the full expression of human potential. These ideas were consistent with the values of an egalitarian American democracy and, consequently, resonated with many people.

Cognitive Psychology. **Cognitive psychology** is the study of perception, memory, and learning. It grew from early work on perceptual processes and verbal learning. Once almost exclusively an academic discipline, cognitive psychology now also routinely addresses applied questions. Modern cognitive psychology crosses into the broader discipline known as **cognitive science**, which bridges the once separate disciplines of psychology, behavioral neuroscience, computer science, neurophysiology, and linguistics.

Women and Minorities in Psychology

The late nineteenth century and first years of the twentieth century were exciting years for the emerging discipline of psychology. However, like most professions at the time, psychology was a field dominated by white males. Women and minorities were not allowed to enroll in colleges until nearly 1835, and then only as undergraduates. The few women who earned degrees and attained important positions in the early twentieth century did so against great prejudice.

For example, Christine Ladd Franklin (1847–1930) at Johns Hopkins and Mary Whiton Calkins (1863–1930) at Harvard were both refused doctoral degrees despite completing all degree requirements (Schultz & Schultz, 2008). Both eventually obtained their degrees, but only years later and after they had achieved national prominence in their field. Calkins was the first female president of the American Psychological Association.

Edward B. Tichener, one of the most influential of America's early psychologists and an advocate for women's rights, nevertheless barred women from his weekly research meetings at Cornell. His graduate student, Margaret Floy Washburn (1871–1939), was the first woman to earn a doctorate in psychology. She later became president of the American Psychological Association and the first female psychologist elected to the National Academy of Science. Yet, despite Tichener's support of her work, he never allowed her into those research meetings.

Helen Thompson Woolley (1874–1947) studied sex differences for her 1903 doctoral dissertation. She found that males and females did not differ on intelligence or emotional functioning and that women scored slightly higher than men in memory and sensory perception. For this work, she was strongly criticized for her "bias" in failing to find the expected superiority of men.

Largely barred from academic positions, women with doctorates in psychology worked in schools, clinics, and hospitals, where they made important contributions to applied psychology.

While women were the largest group that faced academic discrimination, other minorities were also targets of prejudice. At the turn of the century, some prestigious universities excluded Jews from faculty positions, and well into the 1960s, there remained quotas for Jewish applicants to many graduate schools (Schultz & Schultz, 2008).

For African Americans, the prejudice was even more severe. From 1920 to 1966, only 8 of more than 3,700 doctorates awarded by the ten most prestigious psychology departments went to black scholars (Russo & Denmark, 1987; Schultz & Schultz, 2008). Francis Cecil Sumner (1895–1954) was the first African American to be awarded a Ph.D. in psychology. He had studied at Clarke University under G. Stanley Hall, who was among the few who encouraged women and minorities to apply to graduate schools. Sumner went on to become Chair of the Psychology Department at Howard University.

Kenneth Clark (1914–2005), whose application for graduate admission had been rejected at Clarke University "on the basis of race" (Clark, 1978), earned his Ph.D. at Columbia University. Mamie Phipps Clarke (1917–1983), also a Ph.D. psychologist, faced similar discrimination and was barred from university positions. In the early 1940s, the Clarks, husband and wife, carried out research with black children on racial identity and self-concept. Their research heavily influenced the 1954 U.S. Supreme Court decision ending racial segregation in public schools. In 1971, Kenneth Clark became the first African American President of the American Psychological Association.

Things have changed dramatically. Although most doctoral-level psychologists are men, most psychology students are women, and minorities are well represented in undergraduate and graduate psychology programs (Pate, 2001).

Modern Psychology

Prior to 1940, psychiatry, a medical discipline, dominated mental health programs, and psychoanalysis was the major psychotherapeutic model. World War II brought academic psychologists, with their objective, laboratory-based procedures, into the armed forces to help with selection, training, and treatment of military personnel. The success of psychology during World War II challenged the dominance of psychiatry and psychoanalysis, opening the way for the tens of thousands of clinical psychologists who now provide diagnosis and treatment for a wide range of emotional disorders.

There have also been major changes within the general field of psychology. For example, the clashes between the philosophical schools of psychology that were common in the first half of the twentieth century have dissolved, and we now integrate ideas from different schools. An example is **behavioral medicine** and **health psychology**, which have brought together behavior modification, medicine, nutrition, and health. Cognitively oriented clinical psychologists have integrated behavioral learning theory and cognitive psychology, bringing consciousness back into behaviorism. **Behavioral neuroscience** incorporates such diverse disciplines as cognitive and physiological psychology, neurology, and language development. There is a growing collaboration between cognitive science and neuroscience, as scientists learn to monitor the brain in action using advanced technology. Psychologists are now able to integrate psychological experiences with biological mechanisms, producing a sophisticated understanding of psychological concepts that only a few years ago seemed too complex to unravel (e.g., Sutton & Davidson, 1997).

In clinical psychology, this growing understanding of psychological and biological mechanisms has led to effective individualized treatments for dozens of specific conditions (Barlow, 2008; De Los Reyes & Kazdin, 2008). Social psychologists are now increasingly interested in personality development and psychopathology, topics that bring together aspects of social and clinical psychology. Today's psychologists are unlikely to be strong adherents of any particular school. Rather, most represent **mainstream psychology**, drawing from many psychological theories and areas of research.

Psychology is now an independent scientific discipline, with its roots clearly in the natural sciences. Psychology is one of the seven "hub sciences": mathematics, physics, chemistry, earth sciences, medicine, psychology, and social sciences (Cacioppo, 2007). A **hub science** is a highly influential body of scientific knowledge from which other sciences and non-scientific agencies draw heavily (Boyack, Klavans, & Borner, 2005).

Psychology is a large, diverse discipline. The American Psychological Association (APA) has 53 divisions and 152,000 members, and the Canadian Psychological Association has 6,775 members (American Psychological Association, 2010c; Canadian Psychological Association, 2010). Other large associations include the Association for Psychological Science, the Association for Behavioral and Cognitive Therapies, the Psychonomic Society, the Society for Neuroscience, and the Society for Research in Child Development. (See the Student Resource Website for a current list of the divisions within the American Psychological Association, which give an indication of the diversity of professional interests within psychology.)

01:05

The Science of Psychology

Why is science so critical in psychology? People observe the world, themselves, their actions, the behavior of others, and they try to make sense of it all. In effect, most people are amateur psychologists. However, psychology is a field in which amateurs perform poorly. For example, people think that "seeing is believing," but the science of psychology demonstrates that human perceptual systems are limited, biased, and subject to all kinds of distortions. People believe that they remember past experiences, but the science of psychology demonstrates that their memories are fragile at best, usually biased, and capable of changing from one memory into an entirely different memory. People know how their experiences have changed them, shaping their current personalities, but the science of psychology shows that such events seem to have little impact on later behavior and that genetics plays a strong role in shaping people's behavior. People believe that the more people nearby, the more likely that someone will help them when they need it. The science of psychology shows that just the opposite is true: the more people available to help, the less likely that one will get help from anyone. What most people "know" to be true about the psychological world is often false. The scientific study of psychological phenomena often uncovers surprises.

Even more critical, the science of psychology protects us from the pseudoscience of psychology. Most scientific disciplines have some related pseudoscience. Astrologers use the language of astronomers in their claims to foretell the future; self-styled counselors on television and radio use the language of psychology to sound convincing; so-called creationist science uses the language of biology to justify its beliefs. However, psychology is burdened with more forms of pseudoscience than any other discipline. Collectively known as pop psychology or psychobabble, almost all of this pseudoscience comes from people who are not psychologists. People who would never offer a thought about nuclear physics are perfectly willing to offer theories about personality, psychopathology, social behavior, and child development. Some of these theories are reasonable; others are silly and simplistic; and some are destructive. Nevertheless, the popular press often reports them as if they were established facts (Lilienfeld et al., 2003, 2008, 2010). Some of this pseudopsychology is benign and does little harm, but some of it is far from benign (Lilienfeld, 2007; Lilienfeld et al., 2005). Often the people behind these theories are well-meaning individuals who are scientifically naïve. The major problem occurs when they put such ideas and theories into action and cause harm to unsuspecting persons. As the philosopher Goethe (1749–1832) noted, "Nothing is [more] terrible than ignorance in action."

One example involves the theory of recovered memories of childhood sexual abuse (Bass & Davis, 1988, 1994, 2002; Loftus & Ketcham, 1994; Loftus & Polage, 1999; Lynn et al., 2003). Research suggests that childhood sexual abuse is more common than most people think and is a major social problem. However, some therapists saw sexual abuse, and even satanic ritualistic abuse, in a surprising number of their clients. Parents, grandparents, teachers, and family friends were accused of such abuse after the patients, with the help of a therapist, "recovered" their memories of the abuse (Lambert & Lilienfeld, 2007).

Few people doubted that the therapists involved were well meaning and caring, but scientific research shows that the methods that these therapists used to help their clients almost certainly *created* memories of events that may never have occurred. Not long ago, these therapists were telling other people how naïve they were to not realize the extent of sexual abuse. More recently they have told juries why they should not be found guilty of malpractice for not knowing basic scientific facts about human memory—facts that would certainly have discouraged them from using their techniques (Danitz, 1997). The first rule of any treatment is *primum non nocere* ("first, do no harm"), and this technique violated that rule (Lambert & Lilienfeld, 2007; Lilienfeld, 2007).

Another example is *facilitated communication* in the education of nonverbal students with autism. The student uses a keyboard with the assistance of a facilitator, such as a teacher. People with severe autism, who for all of their lives had been uncommunicative and considered cognitively impaired, suddenly began to communicate, typing complex messages. Professional excitement soared as some 2,000 speech therapists and special education teachers rushed to learn this new technique. Hundreds of people with autism were enrolled in facilitated communication programs; parents were overjoyed because their children were communicating with them. However, controlled experimentation revealed that the students were not producing the communication. Rather, the facilitators, unknowingly, were subtly guiding the student's responses (Jacobson, Mulick, & Schwartz, 1995).

Why were so many parents and professionals so gullible? Because they wanted to believe that their children did have clear and complex thoughts, but just had not been able to express them until now. Perhaps for that reason they had failed to be skeptical. They failed to recognize one of the most elementary ideas in scientific research: *every phenomenon has more than one explanation, and only controlled research can eliminate alternative explanations.* In this case, there were two explanations: (1) the student is communicating through the keyboard, and (2) the facilitator is communicating through the keyboard. Because they wanted to believe their children were communicating, they chose explanation (1) and failed to apply the most basic evaluation. (Their problem, perhaps, was that they had not taken a good course in scientific research methods.)

Pseudoscience in psychology may not be deliberately malicious, but it can easily cause harm. Being muddleheaded can be every bit as dangerous as being malicious when you are dealing with people's lives (Lilienfeld et al., 2005). The science of psychology has taught us that people's impressions are not always correct. It has provided real solutions to critical problems, including better teaching methods, more effective treatments, and better ways to solve social problems. The pseudoscientific nonsense that masquerades as psychology on the airwaves and in the newspapers and magazines presents simplistic explanations for complex phenomena, giving people confidence in ideas and actions that they should view with skepticism. Pseudoscience has never provided real solutions to real psychological problems (see Cost of Neglect 1.1). In contrast, the hardheaded scientific research of dedicated psychologists has led to hundreds of improvements in everyday lives (Donaldson et al., 2006). This is why psychological research is so important and is the reason for this course and this textbook.

COST OF NEGLECT 1.1: SCIENCE AND PSEUDOSCIENCE

Pseudoscience uses methods, theories, assumptions, and conclusions that pretend to be scientific. Pseudoscience practitioners wrap their ideas in distorted, erroneous science, but with enough of the trappings of science to convince many people. The intent of pseudoscience is to be convincing, not to be true. Believing such claims can lead people to engage in behavior and activities that are, at best, ineffective, and may even be harmful.

Among the most common practitioners of pseudoscience are television advertisers, with their obvious attempts to cloak their products with the trappings of science. The scene is a physician's office or a science laboratory, with a nurse or a lab assistant working in the background. The actor is everybody's idea of the mature and dependable scientist or physician—a well-groomed, professional man, wearing a white lab coat and possibly with a stethoscope hanging from the pocket. Some colorful but meaningless charts are on the wall. This spokesperson holds up a package of the product and in a smooth, professional voice tells us how effective it is. Even if the spokesperson never mentions the words "science" and "research," the carefully staged set conveys the false idea that science backs the product. Unfortunately, many people fall for it.

Pseudoscience can appear convincing, but you can learn to recognize it. To identify pseudoscience, ask three questions:

1. What is the nature of the evidence for the claims?
2. In what forms is the evidence reported?
3. What are the affiliations of the supposed scientists?

Typically, the evidence for pseudoscience is a recitation of personal testimonials and use of "authority figures" (like the phony physician on TV). All the evidence is anecdotal, designed to be convincing and uncritically accepted by the public. Anecdotal evidence can be useful starting points for legitimate research, but in

(continued)

COST OF NEGLECT 1.1: CONTINUED

pseudoscience, it is usually the only evidence. The problem with anecdotal evidence is that it is highly selective, carefully chosen from many possibilities, and not gathered under controlled conditions. In pseudoscience, to show that a product or idea really works, you need only to put forth some cases in which it did seem to work and ignore all of those cases in which it clearly did not.

Pseudoscience almost never presents data in mainstream science journals, in which there is quality control through peer review by other scientists. Rather, data are reported in popular magazines, in newspaper articles, on the Internet, on television, in radio broadcasts, or just in the commercials for the product. Unlike scientific journals, these outlets do not provide the details needed to evaluate the validity of the claims and procedures.

Pseudoscientists rarely practice their science in academic or industrial settings, where their work would be subjected to review by other professionals. Many are freelance individuals or private businesses with impressive-sounding titles, or obscure, self-proclaimed institutes.

Be alert to pseudoscience; be careful about uncritically accepting anecdotal evidence. Practice some healthy skepticism! A good reference is *Voodoo Science: The Road from Foolishness to Fraud* (Park, 2002).

Quick-Check Review 1.4: Psychology

1. What were some of the more influential schools of psychology?
2. What is the nature of modern mainstream psychology?
3. Why is it critical that psychology be scientific and objective?
4. How can we tell science from pseudoscience?

CARTOON 1.1 Pseudoscience may not be accurate, but it is often popular and accepted by many people who fail to recognize the weakness of its arguments.

ETHICAL PRINCIPLES

This section is our introduction to ethical principles in scientific research. We will expand our discussions of research ethics in each subsequent chapter.

The development, application, and teaching of research ethics has become a critical part of contemporary science. It brings together philosophy, ethics, science, technology, public policy, business, and even politics, forming a loosely knit, complex, and sometimes conflicting, interdisciplinary mix. At the center of every scientist's work there exists the reality that *each individual scientist, in each research project, must make thoughtful judgments of how best to contribute to science and to humanity.*

As you learn about research methods in this course, you will begin to step into the scientists' role. One of the first things you must learn is that *it is the personal responsibility of each researcher to conduct his or her work so as to enhance both scientific understanding and human welfare—that is, to conduct research in an ethical manner.* That personal responsibility falls into two basic categories:

- Protect those who participate in research;
- Conduct and report research accurately and honestly.

These ethical categories are covered in a detailed code published by the American Psychological Association, *The Ethical Principles of Psychologists and Code of Conduct* (American Psychological Association, 2010a). You can access this code of ethics at www.apa.org. We recommend that you download and read it carefully.

Scientists have a mix of goals, motivations, and rewards. However, research is not primarily for the benefit of the researcher, the profit of a company, or the political aims of government. Unfortunately, those competing goals too often take precedence and distort the ideal values of research (i.e., the enhancement of science and humanity).

Ethical principles help to guide researchers through often complex and difficult issues. All of us are consumers of research; some of us are also producers of research. Almost everyone's life is affected by scientific research. Therefore, it is essential for researchers to understand, respect, and practice their ethical obligations and for students to learn about them.

For these reasons, we have included discussions of research ethics in every chapter of this text. These sections, taken together, will help you to understand the importance of research ethics and to apply those ethics in your own research.

We realize that the following lines are repetitious, but please stay with us as we summarize the main points of this brief introduction.

- Each scientist must make thoughtful judgments about how best to contribute to science and to humanity.
- It is each scientist's personal responsibility to conduct his or her research in an ethical manner.
- That personal responsibility includes protecting those who participate in research and conducting and reporting research accurately and honestly.

Quick-Check Review 1.5: Ethical Principles

1. What is the major idea at the heart of research ethics?

USING THE RESOURCES OF THIS TEXT

The eighth edition of this text provides you with two special teaching aids: a Student Resource Website and a publisher's website called MySearchLab.

Exploring the Student Resource Website

Look at the Student Resource Website now (www.graziano-raulin.com). There you will find a wealth of helpful information, including a Study Guide with exercises and test questions, a Lab Manual, and tutorials on APA writing style, library usage, and statistical computations. All of the material on this website is integrated with the textbook. It is provided free by your textbook authors.

Remember our discussion earlier of *active learning*, in which you manipulate and play with the concepts you are trying to learn. We want you to do some active learning right now with the Student Resource Website. The Welcome Screen is shown in Figure 1.2. Take a few minutes to

FIGURE 1.2 Welcome Screen for the Student Resource Website. The opening screen of the Student Resource Website lists the resources and includes a navigation menu on the top of the screen that will allow you to locate quickly each resource.

examine this screen and see what is available on the website. You can access the resources of the website through the menu bar near the top of the screen. Spend some time exploring the Website. Access several sections and look through them. You need not study them right now, but just practice moving around in the website, going from the menu to various sections. Try this: click the Help menu item and select How to Use This Website. There you will find brief instructions on how to access the many features on the Student Resource Website.

Note that at the beginning of each chapter in the textbook there is a brief list of the website resources for that chapter. You will also find these resources identified with an icon and code number in the margin at the point where that resource would be relevant. Click on Chapter Resources in the menu, select a chapter, and you will see the complete list of resources for that chapter with links to each of those resources. These resources will help you to learn the material in the chapter more effectively.

Continue browsing through the website and you will see that it includes many resources. Click on the Study Resources menu item and select Study Guide/Lab Manual, select a chapter in it, and take a close look at it. Several sections of the Study Guide are interactive, giving you immediate feedback and sometimes even giving hints when you are stuck. It is like having a personal tutor.

Select the tutorials menu item and select Library Research. Browse through the tutorial. Note that there are detailed animations that walk you through how you would search for specific information using a computerized database. There are also tutorials to show you how to set up computerized statistical analyses and how to use various web browser programs.

There is another website provided by the publisher, called MySearchLab (www.mysearchlab.com). This resource can be bundled with selected Allyn & Bacon texts, and your instructor may have arranged for this bundling. If not, you can purchase access to the site by going to MySearchLab.com. This site provides several study resources for research methods and statistics classes.

Quick-Check Review 1.6: Using the Resources of This Text

1. What are some of the resources available on the Student Resource Website?
2. What is the name of the publisher website for students using this text?

SUMMARY

- Science is a way of thinking, of asking and answering questions.
- Science involves a systematic interplay of rational thought and empirical observation.
- Serendipity happens! … to scientists with disciplined curiosity and a prepared mind.
- People gain knowledge through tenacity, intuition, authority, rationalism, empiricism, and science.
- Science is the best way of addressing some kinds of questions.
- Science may seem new, but its roots go back to early Greece. Unfortunately, scientific thought was suppressed for nearly 2,000 years, before reemerging late in the Middle Ages.
- Evolutionary theory is a critical foundation for biological and psychological sciences.
- Psychology is the science of behavior; its research methods derive mainly from the natural sciences.

- Psychology is one of the seven modern hub sciences.
- Pseudoscience is a problem in all sciences, but is especially problematic in psychology.
- Ethical principles are critical in psychology and therefore will be covered in every chapter of this text.

Putting It into Practice

Recall our discussion at the beginning of the chapter on active learning? Here are some additional comments on that topic.

Each chapter in this text begins with an outline, which will give you the organization of that chapter. However, it would be a very good idea to create your own organizational system for the course. Take 30 minutes and page through the text. Your goal is just to see what topics are covered and when, not to learn all the material in the book. This half-hour preview of the text will help you to organize and learn the material throughout the course. Take another 30 minutes to explore the resources on the Student Resource Website (www.graziano-raulin.com). You will find that the website has several tutorials, extended discussion of topics, and useful study resources, such as the online Study Guide.

Students often mistakenly believe that the way to study is to read everything in the text. That may be a good start, but learning involves organizing information and concepts. Take an hour now to create a structure for this course in your mind, and that investment will pay huge dividends as you work to master the material in this text.

EXERCISES

1.1. Define the following key terms. Be sure that you understand them. They are discussed in the chapter and defined in the glossary.

psychology	sophisticated empiricism	psychodynamic theory
science	orderliness belief	Gestalt psychology
scientific research	experimentation	behaviorism
process of inquiry	theology	behavior modification
skeptic	description	humanistic psychology
prepared mind	prediction	cognitive psychology
serendipity	causation	cognitive science
tenacity	explanation	behavioral medicine
intuition	application	health psychology
authority	phylogenetic continuity	behavioral neuroscience
rationalism	psychophysics	mainstream psychology
logic	structuralism	hub science
empiricism	introspection	pseudoscience
naïve empiricism	functionalism	

1.2. Explain this statement: For some types of decisions, most of the common ways of knowing are insufficient, and we need the precision of science.

1.3. Your Aunt Sally and Uncle Richard are firm believers in astrology. You decide to set them straight about science and pseudoscience. Explain to them how to recognize pseudoscience. Give them examples of pseudoscience in popular culture. Tell them some of the dangers posed by pseudoscience.

1.4. Your roommate, a physics major, argues that psychology is a social science and therefore not a true science at all. How would you defend the proposition that psychology is a true science?

1.5. Think about the problems that women and minorities had in entering universities and professions in the early twentieth century. Consider these problems in the light of our world today. Are there comparable barriers to groups today? If so, what barriers? which groups?

1.6. "I'm the artistic type," Aunt Linda says. "Artistic types and scientific types are different kinds of people. A science type can't appreciate art, and an artistic type can't understand science and math!" You are going to enlighten Aunt Linda. What will you tell her?

CHAPTER TWO

RESEARCH IS A PROCESS OF INQUIRY

Science is built up with facts, as a house is with stones. But a collection of facts is no more a science than a heap of stones is a house.

—Jules Henri Poincaré, 1854–1912

WEB RESOURCE MATERIAL

Research is a systematic search for information—a process of inquiry. We can carry out research anywhere—in libraries, laboratories, schoolrooms, hospitals, factories, in the pages of the Bible, on street corners, or in the wild, studying a group of elephants. We can study any phenomena, and anyone can do research. Scientists, rabbis, and head chefs can all carry out systematic inquiry in their own domains.

All research is a systematic process of inquiry, but not all research is scientific. Religious scholarship is a systematic process of inquiry, but, with a few exceptions, it is not, nor is it meant to be, scientific. What distinguishes scientific research from other research is its integration of empirical and rational processes. This chapter introduces the assumptions of science, the concepts on which science is built, and theories, which are the scientist's most powerful tool.

THE SCIENTIFIC PROCESS

Scientific research is a way of thinking. In some ways it is similar to everyday thought, but it is much more formalized, more deliberate, systematic, and therefore, more accurate and reliable.

Basic Assumptions of Science

Science, like every discipline, is built on **assumptions**—ideas that are tentatively accepted as being true without further examination. Science makes few assumptions, preferring to subject most ideas to rational and empirical challenges. All scientific disciplines share basic assumptions about nature:

1. A physical universe exists.
2. There is randomness and thus unpredictability in the universe, but it is primarily an orderly and predictable system.
3. We can discover the principles of this orderly universe through scientific research.
4. Knowledge of the universe is always incomplete. New knowledge will alter current ideas and theories. Therefore, all scientific assumptions, knowledge, and theories are tentative.

Note the assumption that theories and knowledge are tentative. Scientists can discover how the world works, but no scientist has the wisdom to create the perfect theory. In time, research will expose the flaws and limitations of every theory, and better theories will be developed.

Some aspects of the universe, such as gravity, are not directly detectable through human senses. However, even concepts about unseen factors like gravity must conform to the constraints of rationalism and empiricism. Only concepts that have survived scientists' repeated empirical challenges reach the level of "generally accepted scientific theory." Even then, scientists will challenge an accepted theory by (1) discovering its flaws through research and/or (2) proposing better theories that explain current research findings and predict new phenomena.

Observation and Inference: Facts and Constructs

At minimum, scientific research involves the following:

1. Posing a question
2. Developing procedures to answer the question
3. Making empirical observations
4. Rationally interpreting the empirical observations
5. Using those interpretations to predict other events
6. Communicating the research findings

Scientists carefully observe events, consider possible reasons for those events, and then make predictions based on the ideas developed during this reasoning process. Scientists interweave the elements of empirical observation and rational abstraction to create a coherent understanding of the phenomena. They refer to empirical observations as collecting **data**, which are the facts of research.

Facts are those events that we can observe directly and repeatedly; each scientific discipline has its particular kinds of facts. In psychology, facts include the physiological structures of participants, the physical conditions around them, the behaviors of other organisms (including the researcher), and, of course, the participants' own behaviors. Most facts observed in psychology are **behaviors**: verbal and nonverbal behavior, physiological activity, social behavior, and so on. Scientists can observe the behaviors of children at play, shoppers in stores, workers at machines, senators in debate, and animals in the laboratory and in their natural environments. We can observe and record all those behaviors. **Observation** is the empirical process of using one's senses to recognize and record facts.

In addition to studying behavioral facts, psychologists study memory, emotion, intelligence, attitudes, creativity, thinking, perception, humor, and so on. These are not directly observable behavioral events; they are not facts. We cannot directly observe intelligence, thinking, or perception, but we can observe behaviors that we believe are related to these unobservable concepts.

Consider some early research with children with severe autism (Graziano, 1974). We observed that the children frequently exhibited highly explosive behavior, often injuring themselves and others and disrupting the therapy program. Their behavior was a fact that we repeatedly observed, measured, and recorded. A therapeutic program reduced the intensity and duration of the disruptive behavior, but not its frequency. That is, the children were "blowing up" just as often as before, but the episodes were shorter and less intense. We had made progress, but we still wanted to reduce the frequency of these outbursts. Continued observation revealed a subtle, but observable, change in the children's behavior just prior to the outbursts. Their activity stopped, their facial expressions became contorted, their limbs stiffened, and the behavior exploded. We could find no external cause for the facial and body changes that reliably preceded the outbursts. Therefore, we inferred that the children were feeling intense internal arousal just prior to their outbursts, which may have cued the explosive behavior. We then reasoned that, to reduce the frequency of the outbursts, we would have to control the inferred internal arousal. But how were we to control a condition that we could not even see? From the behavior therapy research literature, we selected an approach called systematic desensitization (Wolpe, 1958, 1990), which employs relaxation training as a first step. It had been developed for adults, but had never been used with children. Given our inference that the children's aroused states triggered their outbursts, it seemed a reasonable approach to try. We trained the children in relaxation, and soon the frequency of their outbursts decreased to zero.

This example illustrates the distinction between our observations of behavior (the outbursts and the facial expressions that preceded the outbursts) and our inferences of an internal condition (the arousal). The internal condition is not a directly observable fact; we inferred it from the observations of behavior. An **inference** is an intellectual process in which we draw conclusions from observed facts or from other ideas.

Scientists draw inferences from their observations of events, and most psychological research deals with inferences. When psychologists study anxiety, intelligence, or memory, they are working with inferences. Because inferences are largely drawn from empirical observations (the facts), it is critical that the observations be precise. Otherwise, we will have little confidence in the inferences that we draw. In research, we need to use precisely defined empirical methods in order to develop a solid observational base for drawing inferences about events that we cannot directly observe.

We can draw inferences from other inferences, but in science, an important starting point for making inferences is careful observation (i.e., facts). In general, the better the observational base and the more ways scientists tie inferences to that base, the more confidence they will have in those inferences. When making inferences, we should stay close to the data. As Detective Joe Friday used to tell witnesses in the old *Dragnet* television series, "Just give us the facts." He might have added, "We'll draw our own inferences."

When a researcher draws an inference about a research participant, the inference resides in the researcher and not in the participant. The process involves the researcher's rational activity of accepting the data (the observations) as true and then drawing from those observations an idea (inference) about events that the researchers could not observe.

In the autism example, we inferred that a state of arousal existed. The inferred state of arousal was not a fact; it was an idea. The inference was not in the child; it was an idea created by the researchers, who had no direct observation of what was really going on in the child. We should not confuse our inference of an internal arousal with reality; we do not know if it actually exists. We created this inference as an explanatory idea. It helped to explain the observed behavior and to generate a course of action that proved to be effective. This is an important point for you to understand. Inferred events, such as gravity, electricity, intelligence, memory, and anxiety, are all rational ideas constructed by the researcher. Not surprisingly, such ideas are called **constructs**. Scientists use constructs *as if* they exist in fact and *as if* they really have a relationship with observable events—that is, they use them analogically. In the example, the researchers never observed the children's internal states of arousal. They operated *as if* the inferred state (arousal) actually existed. Furthermore, they predicted that if they reduced this inferred arousal with relaxation training, then the frequency of the disruptive behavior would decrease.

Sometimes we use a construct so frequently that we lose sight of its analogical nature and begin to think it is a fact. For example, some people may believe there really is an id, an ego, or a superego inside each of us; these constructs take on a reality that they were never meant to have. Confusing a construct for a fact is a logical error known as **reification of a construct**. Table 2.1 lists several other common logical errors that scientists must avoid.

Scientists constantly use observations and constructs in research. Note the relationship between the construct of internal arousal and the observed facts in the example of children with autism. First, we inferred the construct from observed behavior. Then we used the construct as a basis for predicting new behavior that we could observe—specifically, that reducing the internal arousal would reduce the disruptive behavior. Thus, the construct relates to observed facts in two ways: we derived it from the observations, and we used it as a basis for predicting future observations.

You learned in Chapter 1 that science involves the continual interaction of empirical observation and rational abstractions. Now you can see that this interaction is between observations and constructs. The scientist moves from one to the other and back again, at each step refining constructs from observations and predicting new observations from constructs. This process provides tentative explanations of relationships among facts and constructs. With the autistic children, the relationship between the observations and the constructs provided a potential explanation of the observed phenomenon of disruptive behavior. We then used the construct as if it adequately represented what was really happening, although we could not observe all the details.

TABLE 2.1 Logical Interpretation Errors

Reification of a construct is one of many problems that scientists are trained to recognize and avoid. Listed here are others. You may have used some of these in your everyday thinking. Everyone does. However, fuzzy thinking interferes with the scientific understanding of nature.

Nominal Fallacy	People commit this error when they mistake the naming of phenomena for an explanation of the phenomena. For example, if you recognize that some people consistently behave aggressively, you might appropriately label them as "aggressive." However, you may also be tempted to explain their aggressive behavior by noting that they are aggressive people. The label, based on their behavior, later becomes the explanation for their behavior—an entirely circular argument.
The All-or-None Bias	This is a tendency to see a statement as either true or false, when in most cases in science the statement is probabilistic. Most good theories explain many things, but they almost never explain everything under every condition. Therefore, they are technically false, although scientists tend to view the theory as true because it is often, although not always, true. It is best to remember that no theory is completely true; rather, it provides accurate explanations for a certain range of situations or events.
Similarity-Uniqueness Paradox	This is the tendency to view two things as either similar to one another or different from one another, when in reality they are probably both. For example, two people may be similar in their backgrounds but different in their aspirations. People have a tendency to simplify such comparisons, which can often blind them to important elements.
Barnum Statement	This effect is named after P. T. Barnum of the Barnum and Bailey Circus, who is alleged to have said, "There is a sucker born every minute." Barnum statements appear to be insightful comments about an issue, when in fact they are nothing more than statements that are true for almost all issues, situations, or people. For example, most people readily accept statements like "You try to do what is right, but sometimes find that temptation is strong." They often comment on how perceptive that statement is, but it is not insightful at all. You can say the same thing to 100 randomly selected people, and most will be impressed by your insight.
Evaluative Biases of Language	Science should be nonjudgmental, but the truth is that language often inserts subtle judgments into the descriptions of objective behaviors. For example, if a person cuts off a telemarketer in the first few seconds of a call by saying, "I do not take unsolicited sales calls," is the person being assertive or aggressive? Labeling the behavior as assertive gives a very different impression than labeling it as aggressive.

Inductive and Deductive Thinking

Sherlock Holmes fans may argue that the great detective never said it, but the statement attributed to Holmes has entertained and misled people for years. You know the scene: at the site of the crime, Holmes inspects the room, his keen eyes darting and his nose alert to lingering tobacco smoke. Suddenly, with an explosive "Aha!" he pounces on a partially burnt matchstick cracked in the middle with a small flake of tobacco stuck to its tip. Holmes examines it closely and then announces, "Our culprit, Watson, is 44 years old, 5 feet 8½ inches tall, and 173 pounds. He is right-handed, a veteran of the India conflicts, and still carries a lead bullet in his right calf. He is a gentleman Watson, and had no intention of committing a crime when he entered this room. He left hurriedly by way of that window when he heard us at the door, and, if I am not mistaken, he will return here to confess his crime and will knock on that door precisely . . . now!"

A tentative knocking is heard. Watson opens the door, revealing the man so precisely described by Holmes.

"Egad, Holmes!" says Watson, wide-eyed. "How did you ever know that?"

"Deduction, my dear Watson," Holmes replies, "a simple process of deduction."

Actually, it was not deduction alone. What Holmes should have said was "Induction-deduction, my dear Watson, a simple process of induction-deduction." Assuming that the great detective could, in fact, have drawn such complete conclusions from such limited evidence, his process was one familiar to everyone. He observed some specific clues and inferred (the induction) something he could not directly observe—the type of person who would have committed the crime and had left those clues. Holmes then made the prediction (the deduction) that the man would return.

When we reason from the particular to the general, we are using **inductive reasoning**; when we use the more abstract and general ideas to return to specifics—that is, to make predictions about future observations—we are using **deductive reasoning** (Copi & Cohen, 2009).[i]

Scientists constantly use the rational processes of induction and deduction. A researcher who begins with empirical observations and then infers constructs is engaged in inductive reasoning. Using constructs as the basis of making predictions about new, specific observations is deductive reasoning. A scientist must use both processes to build and validate conceptual models.

Inductive-deductive reasoning is not unique to science; people use these processes constantly in everyday life. When I return from work on a cold winter day and find the front door left open and a single sneaker tossed onto the hall rug, I inductively infer "the kids are home from school." Having drawn that inductive inference I can now deductively predict that the kids are upstairs e-mailing or texting their friends. I can then go upstairs to make observations and check the accuracy of my predictions. From the specific observation to the general idea, from the general idea to the specific prediction, new observations and further inferences—these are the processes of induction and deduction. We have included a primer on basic inductive-deductive logic on the textbook website.

02:01

People have been thinking inductively and deductively all their lives, although not with scientific precision. This last point is important. Although scientists use the same kind of reasoning processes used in everyday life, they must do so with precision rarely seen in everyday life. Indeed, the scientific research enterprise is a framework within which scientists can carry out inductive and deductive reasoning with the greatest precision.

Building on a point made in Chapter 1, the essence of science is its process of thinking, a process that entails systematic inductive-deductive logic. Science, more than any other way of gaining knowledge, bases its inductive reasoning on carefully observed facts. Making the observations or "getting the facts" is a critical component of scientific research. Science obtains the facts with the greatest precision possible and uses the facts to fuel the inductive-deductive process.

[i]Psychologists tend to use the concepts of induction and deduction as discussed here. However, philosophy students will recognize that this distinction is incomplete, distinguishing only one kind of induction from one kind of deduction (Reese, 1996).

Quick-Check Review 2.1: The Scientific Process

1. What are the data in psychology?
2. How do facts and constructs differ?
3. What is reification of a construct?
4. Explain the two ways in which constructs relate to facts.
5. What are the basic assumptions that scientists accept about the universe?
6. What is the difference between inductive and deductive reasoning?

MODELS AND THEORIES IN SCIENCE

A major task in all scientific disciplines is the development and use of theories. *In science, there is nothing more useful and practical than a good theory.*

A **theory** is a formalized set of concepts that summarizes and organizes observations and inferences, provides tentative explanations for phenomena, and provides the bases for making predictions. There are all sorts of theories floating around society. However, *to be scientific, a theory must be testable*; it must make specific predictions that scientists can test empirically. Furthermore, a theory is scientific only if it is possible to contradict the predictions with empirical evidence; that is, *theories must be falsifiable* (Popper, 1959). This concept might seem puzzling, but think about it for a moment. If there is no outcome that would disprove the theory, it means that the theory can explain any possible outcome; a theory that can explain any possible outcome is a theory that says that "anything is possible" and that "there is no way to predict what will happen." Theories that cannot make specific predictions about what will happen are useless in science because they cannot be tested. Once you make a specific prediction (e.g., that A will happen but not B), you open yourself up to the possibility that, when tested, the prediction will be wrong and will therefore falsify your theory.

Scientific theories are not mere guesses or hunches, nor are they flimsy wisps of fancy. A good theory demands a solid empirical base and carefully developed constructs, and these take time and effort to create. Scientists carefully build theories from empirical observations, constructs, inductive and deductive logic, and precise testing for confirmation or disconfirmation. Building theories that organize what we know about nature and that predict natural phenomena is a major task of scientists. An earlier comment is important enough to repeat: in science, there is nothing more useful and practical than a good theory. We have included an illustration of the importance of scientific theories in the form of a fable on the Student Resource Website.

02:02

You might not yet appreciate how important theory is to science. Theory is not necessarily required to discover new facts, but the facts will be more useful and meaningful when placed within the organizing framework of theory. Theory provides a blueprint that organizes facts into ideas and ideas into an understanding of the world.

Good theories are functional, strong, parsimonious, and valid. A functional theory works; it organizes information and explains how events relate to one another. A strong theory makes specific predictions that scientists can confirm or disconfirm through empirical observation. A **parsimonious theory** (literally, thrifty or economical) is relatively simple and straightforward and is preferred over a complex theory if the theories provide equivalent predictive ability. A single theory that explains several different phenomena is preferred over several theories that collectively explain the same phenomena. A good theory must possess **validity**, which means that it makes specific testable predictions that further observation can confirm.

Theories are the glue that holds science together; they provide a framework that enables researchers to build on the work of others. Even the most brilliant scientists could not make significant breakthroughs if they had to reinvent each finding and concept. Science builds on existing science, moving our understanding of nature to the next level. We illustrate this basic principle in Historical Lesson 2.1, which discusses the first successful human-piloted, powered flight of the Wright brothers.

HISTORICAL LESSON 2.1: THE WRIGHT BROTHERS AS SCIENTISTS

A persistent American myth is that the Wright brothers invented the airplane in a burst of Yankee ingenuity, through mechanical tinkering in their bicycle shop, and that their achievements had little to do with systematic scholarship and research. However, the brothers (Wright & Wright, 1908) complained that "nearly every (newspaper) writer has characterized us as mechanics, and taken it for granted that our invention has come from mechanical skill. We object to this as neither true nor fair. We are not mechanics; we are scientists" (Oppel, 1987, p. 18).

The Wrights had spent years studying theoretical principles of flight, developing their knowledge of the many possible forms of aircraft, and learning of the research on flight by their predecessors. They used careful experimentation in their Ohio workshop and on the windy sand dunes near Kitty Hawk, North Carolina.

The Wrights built on the work of others, as all scientists do. More than 100 years earlier, George Cayley had developed mathematical principles of mechanical flight. He built and flew models and full-sized gliders and established the fixed-wing concept for aircraft (Cayley, 1853), a major departure from the earlier flapping-wing contraptions. The Wrights knew of Cayley's work, even though his book, *On Aerial Navigation*, was published posthumously (Cayley, 1910). The Wrights studied Cayley's designs for a future flying machine, including its lift surfaces, stabilizer, engine, and propellers.

Otto Lilienthal (1889), a German engineer, published *Birdflight as the Basis of Aviation*. Lilienthal was the first person to fly in controlled, heavier-than-air flights, making more than 2,000 successful glides in his biplanes and monoplanes. In 1896, with relatively light gasoline-powered engines available, Lilienthal was working on a design for a powered airplane. He died in a glider crash before his powered airplane was completed. Octave Chanute (1899), a civil engineer, continued Lilienthal's work, developed more gliders, published *Progress in Flying Machines*, and generously gave the Wrights his expertise and enthusiastic support.

On hearing of Lilienthal's death, and learning that Samuel Langley, a Smithsonian Institution physicist, was close to success, the Wrights increased their efforts. Building on the work of Chanute, Lilienthal, Cayley, and others, the Wrights perfected their gliders and competed furiously against Langley to be the first to achieve manned, powered flight. However, Langley, with government support and Smithsonian backing, had already successfully flown a small-scale model of a steam-driven airplane in 1896 and a large gasoline-powered model in 1902—the world's first unmanned flights of powered, heavier-than-air machines. All was set in December 1903 for a test of Langley's human-piloted, gas-powered airplane. The Wright brothers had apparently been left far behind. However, Langley's machine and pilot failed, and the press concluded that it would be "hundreds of years" before the world would see heavier-than-air flight. It was just 9 days later at Kill Devil Hill that the Wrights proved them wrong when Orville flew the gasoline-powered biplane, the *Wright Flyer I*.

The Wright brothers' success was based on a long process of scientific and technological advances, including the work of Cayley, Lilienthal, Chanute, Langley, and the Wrights. There was also the early work of Leonardo da Vinci in the 1500s, the successful balloon flights from France to England in the late

(continued)

HISTORICAL LESSON 2.1: CONTINUED

1700s (before the American Revolution!), improved propeller designs by Jean-Pierre Blanchard in 1797, books on the mathematics and physics of mechanical flight published between 1780 and 1900, and the development of the gasoline engine. The Wright brothers achieved powered flight within the context of long scientific and technical development. Building on the work of others, they added the final developments that made powered flight possible. Their experimentation was neither mere tinkering nor solitary invention, but instead was built on their knowledge of all the preceding work. Their achievement is a good example of how science and technology build on previous discoveries to expand scientific knowledge and to create new technologies.

Types of Theories

All scientific theories involve induction and deduction, but they often differ in the degree to which they emphasize one or the other. Theories that emphasize induction, called **inductive theories**, stay close to the empirical data. B. F. Skinner (1953, 1969, 1972) epitomized this inductive method of theory construction. He built his theories on extensive observational data, being careful not to extend the theory beyond the data. Skinner's behavioral theories predicted what would happen under a specific set of reinforcement contingencies. He made these predictions based on previous studies under similar conditions, and he avoided speculating about unseen internal processes like thoughts and emotions. These unseen hypothesized processes are called **intervening variables**. In an eloquent presentation, only days before his death, Skinner (1990) continued to argue that there are serious risks associated with theories that go far beyond the data and involve intervening variables that are not directly observable.

The more traditional theory, the **deductive theory**, emphasizes deductions from constructs. These deductions are hypotheses, which scientists test empirically through research. An example is Meehl's (1962, 1990) theorizing about the underlying cause(s) of schizophrenia. He argued that genetic factors are a necessary, but not a sufficient, condition for schizophrenia. People who inherited these factors are at greater risk for schizophrenia, but whether a given person develops schizophrenia would depend on life experiences. This was a deductive theory because, at the time that it was proposed, many of these concepts were speculative and not yet supported by specific data. Scientists test Meehl's theory by making predictions from the theory and testing those predictions. Unlike the more inductive theories of Skinner, Meehl's deductive theories go well beyond the data, challenging scientists to make new observations to fill in the gaps in the theory.

Most psychological theories are **functional theories**, which place approximately equal emphasis on induction and deduction. All three types of theories (inductive, deductive, and functional) have the same goals: organizing knowledge, predicting new observations, and explaining relationships among events. Good theories put it all together—the facts and the constructs—in an organized whole for the scientists, making it possible to move ahead in the main task of science: understanding nature.

Scientific Models

A fourth type of theory is the **model**. We can represent any phenomenon with a model. The word "model" derives from the Latin *modulus*, meaning a small measure of something. In science, it has come to mean a miniature representation of reality. A model is a description or analogy that helps scientists to understand something usually unseen and/or complex. Models are somewhat less developed than formal theories and are sometimes referred to as "mini-theories."

Picture a model airplane. It has the form and many characteristics of a real airplane, such as wings and rudder. Although these characteristics correspond to those of a real airplane, the model is not an exact replica. It is usually smaller, does not have all the working parts, and is constructed of balsa wood or plastic instead of metal alloys or carbon fiber.

Models represent reality; they do not duplicate it. Models are useful because constructing and examining a model helps scientists to organize knowledge and hypotheses about the reality represented by the model. They can examine a model, observe relationships among its parts, and view how it operates. They can generate new ideas from the model about how the real world is constructed and how it operates. For example, a model airplane in a wind tunnel can give researchers ideas about how a real airplane might behave and lead them to new ideas or hypotheses about the design and operation of real airplanes. The original stealth fighter, the F-117A Nighthawk, started out as a model. The model demonstrated that a plane could be built that was virtually undetectable by radar (Ball, 2003). Likewise, our model of the relationship of internal arousal and disruptive behavior in children with autism led us to new applications of behavior therapy.

We can construct models to represent any aspect of the universe. We can build models of airplanes or the solar system, of atoms or bacteria, of wave motions, neurons, memory, or genetic structure. We can organize our knowledge of any phenomenon into models to represent reality. Furthermore, the models need not be physical in their construction, such as a balsa wood airplane. They can be abstract or conceptual models, which we construct with ideas and express in verbal and/or mathematical language.

Models are often constructed to explain a diverse set of observations and then used to predict areas to explore that might generate new and interesting observations. Let's take memory as an example. On the simple conceptual level, we all know what memory is, but consider the following well-documented observations of memory and the questions these observations raise.

- Why is it that we can remember something that happened months ago but not the name of the person we met less than 5 minutes earlier?
- Why are certain words in a long list (the first few and the last few) more easily remembered?
- Why do people with diseases that affect memory, such as Alzheimer's, forget things they just said but remember details of their childhood.
- Why are names of objects generally easier to remember than other words?
- Why are there individual differences in how well people remember or what types of things they remember best?
- Why do people with amnesia still remember how to drive, cook, or ride a bike?

The classic model of human memory is a good example of an abstract model that seeks to organize these kinds of diverse observations. It assumes multiple levels of memory, with each level having its own characteristics. The sensory store holds extensive information for a very short period (about 1 second). The short-term memory holds information longer (about 15 seconds), but has a restricted capacity. The long-term memory provides the extended, high-capacity storage that people usually think of when they think about memory. Few cognitive psychologists believe such structures exist or that their model is the way information is stored and processed. However, a model does not have to be real or true to be useful. It need only make accurate predictions about relationships between observable events.

The classic model of memory is a strong one because scientists based it on hundreds of independent observations such as the ones listed above. That is, the model is closely tied to the observational base on which it was developed. Furthermore, the model proved it usefulness by correctly predicting new observations that cognitive psychologists later confirmed through scientific study. It is not a perfect model of memory, and it will likely be replaced by better models as research identifies observations that the model cannot predict or explain. Nevertheless, it is convenient and useful and has contributed enormously to our understanding of how individuals remember things.

Models can also be purely mathematical. For example, there are mathematical models in the field of artificial intelligence that describe how learning agents can modify their behavior in response to reinforcement signals and thereby increase the reward they receive (Sutton & Barto, 1998). Built on the mathematics of linear algebra and dynamic programming, these models use a system of simultaneous equations to describe the interaction between a learning agent (i.e., a person, laboratory animal, or robot) and its environment. These mathematical models help us to understand the role of reinforcement in learning.

All models share the following characteristics:

1. Models are simplified representations of phenomena and have point-to-point correspondence with some of the characteristics of the phenomena.
2. Models provide convenient, manageable, and compact representations of the larger, complex, and mostly unknown reality.
3. Models are incomplete, tentative, and analogical.
4. Models, and manipulations of models, help scientists to organize information, illustrate relationships among parts, create new ideas, and predict new observations.

"This is Gronski's new model of the synaptic transmission mechanism. Nobody understands it, but it won third prize in the campus art competition."

CARTOON 2.1 Science and Art. Scientists use models to organize information in an understandable and simplified manner. When done well, models really can be a thing of beauty.

Scientists judge models and theories primarily by how useful they are in organizing information, explaining phenomena, and generating accurate predictions. For example, the theory of Newtonian mechanics has been proved to be wrong, at least at high speeds. When objects move at a velocity approaching the speed of light, they do not behave the way Newtonian mechanics predicts. Einstein's general theory of relativity describes the movement of objects accurately regardless of how fast the object is traveling. Nevertheless, Newtonian mechanics survives, and teachers routinely cover it in school. Why? The reason is simple. Everyday objects hardly ever travel at speeds approaching the speed of light. Therefore, the theories developed by Newton to describe the relationships among motion, acceleration, and force accurately describe the motion of most ordinary objects. The theory survives because it is useful and accurate in a wide range of commonly encountered situations.

Quick-Check Review 2.2: Models and Theories in Science

1. What is a theory, and how is it useful in science?
2. What is the difference between inductive and deductive theories?
3. What is a model, and how is it used in science?
4. Distinguish between observation and inference.
5. Why should we judge theories on both their usefulness and their accuracy?
6. What is meant by falsifiability in science?

A MODEL OF THE RESEARCH PROCESS

We can study any phenomenon scientifically and develop a model to represent it. This text uses a model of psychological research proposed by Hyman (1964). It simplifies the complexity of psychological research and organizes some important aspects of the research process. This model has two dimensions: phases of research and levels of constraint. Like any model, it is not a complete representation of reality, but is useful.

Phases of Research

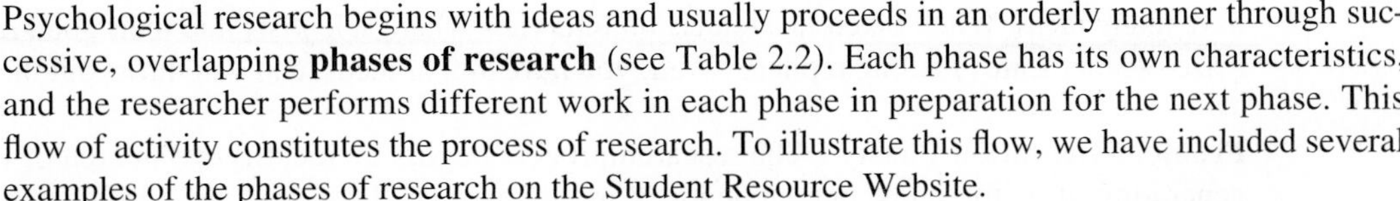

Psychological research begins with ideas and usually proceeds in an orderly manner through successive, overlapping **phases of research** (see Table 2.2). Each phase has its own characteristics, and the researcher performs different work in each phase in preparation for the next phase. This flow of activity constitutes the process of research. To illustrate this flow, we have included several examples of the phases of research on the Student Resource Website.

02:03

Idea-Generating Phase. All research begins with an idea. Suppose that you are a psychological researcher and you are interested in children's reasoning processes, but have no specific idea for a research project. The interest, however, is enough to point you to an area in which you can develop more defined ideas. Your interest in the area will help sustain your work. Remember a point made

TABLE 2.2 The Phases of a Research Study

Idea-Generating Phase	Identify a topic of interest to study.
Problem-Definition Phase	Refine the vague and general idea(s) generated in the previous step into a precise question.
Procedures-Design Phase	Decide on the specific procedures to be used in the gathering and statistical analysis of the data.
Observation Phase	Use the procedures devised in the previous step to collect your observations.
Data Analysis Phase	Analyze the data collected using appropriate statistical procedures.
Interpretation Phase	Compare your results with the results predicted based on your theory. Do your results support the theory?
Communication Phase	Prepare a written or oral report of your study for publication or presentation to colleagues. Your report should include a description of all the preceding steps.

in Chapter 1: a scientist's curiosity is critical in research, both in helping to generate ideas and in sustaining the researcher's efforts.

The **idea-generating phase** can begin with vague thoughts, and initial ideas can emerge in very unsystematic ways. Archimedes supposedly had a flash of creative thought while sitting in a bath. Ideas can be generated while conversing, watching television, walking in the woods, crossing the street, or even while dreaming. However, getting research ideas is not usually so unsystematic, and scientists generate most research ideas in a systematic fashion from other research results. Research ideas vary from unsystematic hunches to highly systematic and precise steps in logical thinking. The former are most characteristic of exploratory research, which occurs in the early history of a research area; the latter are characteristic of research at more advanced levels of a research area.

You do not want to be too quick to criticize initial ideas; premature criticism might destroy an emerging good idea. You should take early ideas seriously and nourish them. Curiosity, interest, hunches, and enthusiasm are important ingredients in science. Once the researcher has identified an area of interest, it is useful to dive right in by reading articles and books and talking with people who work in the area.

We know little about the processes involved in the creative idea-generating phase of research, although this is beginning to change (Leyens, 2006; McGuire, 1997). In fact, this is a good area for research: How do people generate creative ideas? What seems clear is that productive scientists have many ideas. When asked in a television interview where scientists find their good ideas, Nobel Prize–winner Linus Pauling replied, "Well, you have lots of ideas, and you throw out the bad ones."

Problem-Definition Phase. The research process begins by identifying an area of interest and generating ideas for study, but vague ideas are not enough. They must be clarified and refined. In this part of the process, called the **problem-definition phase**, the scientist examines the research literature and learns how other researchers have conceptualized, measured, and tested these and related ideas. This careful examination of the literature (library research) is an important basic part of science. You will find an overview of this process in Appendix C, and a more extensive tutorial on library research in the Student Resource Website.

02:04

The published research literature provides the detailed information scientists need to understand the research problem. Using this information, the scientist continues working on the ideas, clarifying, defining, specifying, and refining them. The goal in this phase is to produce one or more clear questions based on (1) well-developed knowledge of previous research and theory, and (2) the scientist's own ideas and speculations.

Carefully conceptualizing the research question is crucial, because the research questions will largely control the way the researcher carries out the rest of the research in order to answer the questions. The question might involve a precise hypothesis or, if it is exploratory research, a more general question. The activities in the problem-definition phase are rational, abstract processes that manipulate and develop ideas toward the goal of refining those ideas into researchable questions. This rational process leads to the next phase, in which we design the observational procedures.

Procedures-Design Phase. The **procedures-design phase** is systematic and complex. Most research methods courses focus on this phase. Before any data are collected, the researcher must determine which observations to make, under what conditions, how to record the observations, what statistical methods to use to analyze the data, and so on. The researcher also makes decisions in this phase about what participants to include. This introduces concerns for the welfare of participants—questions of research ethics—which will be taken up in the section "Ethical Principles." Completing the procedures-design phase leads into the next phase.

Observation Phase. Making observations (getting the data) is the most familiar phase to beginning students, who often see this as "doing the research." In this **observation phase**, the researcher carries out the procedures that were designed in the previous phase and makes observations of the participants' behaviors under the conditions specified. The observation phase is central in all science. Note that the earlier phases serve as preparation for making the empirical observations, and the remaining phases focus on using those observations by processing, interpreting, and communicating them. *All scientific research revolves around the central aspect of the research process—making empirical observations.*

Data Analysis Phase. In the **data analysis phase**, the researcher processes the data using statistical procedures. Recall that researchers select the data analysis procedures in the design phase, before the data are gathered. As you will see later in this text, many design decisions, such as sample size, will follow from the choice of data analysis procedures. In psychological research, the data will be in the form of a numerical record representing the observations made. Researchers use statistical procedures to describe and evaluate numerical data and to determine the significance of the observations. The statistical procedures might be as simple as counting responses and drawing graphs to show response changes over time, or they may be as complex as a two-way analysis of variance (described in Chapter 12). Whatever the statistical procedures, the important point is that the researcher must choose procedures that are appropriate to the question and to the observational procedures. As we will emphasize later in this text, the nature of the question and the observational procedures determine the choice of statistical procedure.

Interpretation Phase. Having statistically analyzed the data, the researcher interprets the statistical results in terms of (1) answering the research question, and (2) how the answer contributes to knowledge in the field. In the **interpretation phase**, the researcher relates the findings not only to the original questions, but also to other concepts and findings in the field.

This stage represents the other side of the problem-definition phase. When defining the research problem, scientists use theories to suggest important questions. Here the scientists use the answers to their questions to determine how accurately their theories predict new observations. The problem-definition phase uses deductive reasoning, working from the general theory to the specific prediction. The interpretation phase uses inductive reasoning, working from the specific results of the study back to the generality of the theory. For example, the results of a study may suggest ways to expand or modify the theory to increase its usefulness and validity.

Communication Phase. Science is a public enterprise, and communicating our research findings is critical. The **communication phase** includes presentations at scientific meetings and publication in journals, books, and on the Internet. The *APA Publication Manual* (American Psychological

Association, 2010d) provides specific guidelines to organize the information needed in a research
02:05 report. We cover the writing of a research report in APA style in Appendix B and in a tutorial and
02:06 reference source on the Student Resource Website.

Scientific publications must describe procedures in detail, so that other scientists can understand and replicate the research. **Replication** means repeating a study to see if we obtain the same results. If we cannot replicate a research finding, then doubt is cast on the genuineness of that finding. By presenting full accounts of the study's rationale, procedures, findings, and interpretation, the researcher makes the work available for others to evaluate and replicate. The writing of a research report should be clear and concise (unlike Calvin's book report in the *Calvin and Hobbes* cartoon reproduced here).

In the research process, each project can serve as the basis for further questions and further empirical research. Follow-up research may be conducted by the initial researcher or by other researchers. Now we have come full circle, back to the beginning phase of generating ideas. In a developing field of research, the ideas for research are more often than not stimulated by the work of colleagues, whose work raises new research questions. Figure 2.1 illustrates the circular nature of this process.

Calvin and Hobbes by Bill Watterson

CARTOON 2.2 Scientific Writing. This is definitely NOT the way to write research reports!

Source: Calvin and Hobbes, copyright © 1995 Bill Watterson. Distributed by Universal Press Syndicate. Reprinted with permission. All rights reserved.

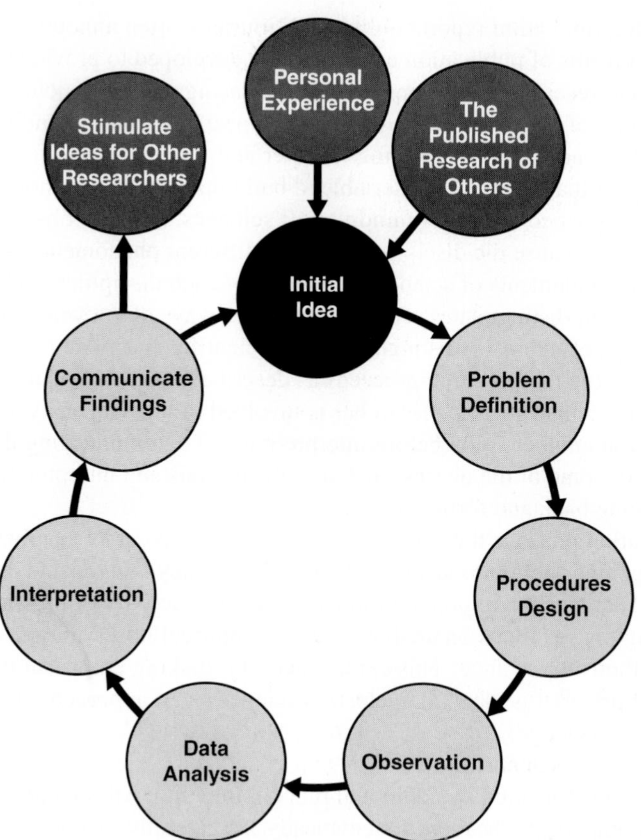

FIGURE 2.1 A Representation of the Process of Conceptualizing and Carrying Out a Research Project. Each research project goes through several phases, from initial ideas to final communication of findings. Ideas for research are generated from sources outside the specific research project and from ideas generated within the research process. Research findings also stimulate new ideas in other researchers.

Scientists use two major avenues for communicating their work: written publications, such as books and scientific journals, and oral presentations at meetings. Books and journals are permanent records of a scientific discipline, preserved by libraries so they can be retrieved and studied by researchers. A disadvantage of written reports is the time-consuming publication process, which usually takes a year or more.

The researchers' presentations at scientific meetings and their informal communication with colleagues are more immediate and interactive than publications. Scientists talk with each other, formally and informally, about their research. They also visit each other's laboratories, exchange letters and e-mail, and so on. Some call this informal communication the "invisible college." It is an important element of scientific communication.

Printed journals are still the major vehicles for disseminating research findings, but most journals are also available online. It will not be long before most journals are published exclusively online because this process controls costs so effectively and speeds up the publication process. Many researchers routinely post prepublication reports online, and journals often announce recently accepted articles. New Internet forms of publication are also being developed to provide libraries and researchers with free access to research articles instead of purchasing expensive journals (Harper, 2004). You can often get a copy of an article months before it appears in print by sending an e-mail request to the researcher. These advances are making it easier and less expensive for scientists to share their work, with the result that science is better able to build upon available knowledge.

The research process described here is common to all sciences. Specific observations vary from one discipline to another, because the disciplines address different phenomena. Nevertheless, the basic processes are common elements of science, regardless of each discipline's subject matter. The process, and not the content, distinguishes science from other ways of knowing; content—the particular phenomena and facts of interest—distinguishes one scientific discipline from another.

Although it is generally true that research proceeds as described here, the sequence of phases is not rigid. New ideas might occur while the researcher is involved in the data analysis phase, and he or she might design and run another study before interpreting and communicating the results of the first. It is also common for some of the phases, such as data analysis and interpretation, to overlap, with the researcher moving back and forth among them.

The empirical observation phase is the center of the research process. Researchers first generate and refine ideas, sharpening them into answerable questions. They then decide on the procedures for answering them. That work is in preparation for the central activity of making empirical observations. The remaining phases focus on analyzing these empirical observations, interpreting them, and communicating their importance. This central activity, making empirical observations within a systematic rational process, is what characterizes science as an approach that is different from other ways of seeking knowledge.

Note that in this process, the scientist moves through a systematic cycle: rational thinking, followed by empirical observations, followed by additional rational thinking. All scientific research revolves around the empirical component. The more systematically and carefully we observe phenomena, the more solid will be the database on which we build an understanding of psychological functioning.

Levels of Constraint

In Chapter 1, you learned the various ways in which people pursue knowledge: tenacity, intuition, authority, rationalism, empiricism, and science. In the order listed, these approaches range from low to high demands on the adequacy of the information and on how that information is processed.

Of these approaches, science is the most demanding. Within science, at the high-demand end of this continuum, there are many approaches to gaining knowledge. Some scientific approaches place fewer demands on the adequacy of the information and the nature of processing it; others place more demands. Thus, within scientific research, some methods are more demanding than other methods, but all have their useful place in scientific research. This continuum of demands on the adequacy of information constitutes the second dimension of our model of research: **levels of constraint**.

Within each level of constraint, the researcher makes decisions about how to develop the research plan. At some constraint levels, the plan may be general, leaving the ideas, questions, and procedures relatively unrefined. This is common in exploratory research undertaken early in the investigation of a phenomenon. At other constraint levels, the plan is detailed and refined, with precise hypotheses, procedures, and statistical analyses. In each, the researcher moves through all the phases, but each is obviously at a different level of refinement. Exploratory research is lower in constraint and makes relatively few demands for precision in each phase. In contrast, highly refined research projects are higher in constraint and make many demands on the procedures.

Suppose that a social psychologist is interested in understanding the psychological techniques that make some salespeople more successful than others. Let us also suppose that little is known about these issues. The psychologist may choose to observe sales representatives at work, perhaps by accompanying them on sales calls. Such observations might reveal that the sales pitch is important, but other factors seem to be even more important. For example, the best sales representatives might be warm and friendly, remembering the names of their customers and following up on past conversations. They might ask about the customer's family or how well a new product is working. Better sales representatives seem to understand the nature of their customers and businesses, and they tailor their sales pitch to each customer. The best are knowledgeable about the products that they sell, but will readily call their company's engineers to verify details of a product, and may even do that when they know the answer already.

These observations may prompt the psychologist to ask sales representatives the reasons for some of their actions. For example, a top salesperson might admit having known the answer to the question asked by the customer, but wanted to demonstrate that the customer had easy access to the experts in the company when needed. Hence, the "spontaneous" call to a company engineer. Similar questions might uncover the fact that the best salespeople are good at listening to the customers and understanding their needs, rather than just launching into a standard sales pitch, like many of the weaker sales representatives.

Note that in this study of salespeople, there was little demand that the question or procedures be precise, complex, or highly structured. If the psychologist notices something interesting and unexpected, the procedure can easily be modified to follow up on this observation. The activities in each phase are flexible. However, as the research questions become more complex and precise, the activities in each phase of research must become correspondingly more precise and controlled. We can see the increased control most readily in the observation phase. As control over the conditions and methods of observation is increased, there are more constraints on the researcher's freedom to be flexible.

In the search for precision, we give up flexibility. In almost all research decisions, scientists are required to make trade-offs, and every design decision has a price associated with it. Beginning students might believe that the best way to conduct research is always to be precise and controlled. However, precision and control may not always be the ideal, because sometimes the loss of flexibility is too great a price to pay.

The concept of constraint provides the second dimension for our model of the research enterprise. The two dimensions are as follows:

1. **The phases of research.** Each complete research project proceeds along this dimension from the researcher's initial ideas to communication of new ideas.
2. **The levels of constraint.** This dimension is one of precision, structure, and control. Projects of the highest precision demand the greatest constraint on activities in each phase; this constraint is most obvious in the controls imposed in the observation phase. Levels of constraint refer to the degree to which the researcher imposes limits or controls on any part of the research process.

These concepts form a two-dimensional descriptive model of research (see Table 2.3). Note that the table gives names to the successive levels of constraint, ranging from the lowest constraint (naturalistic observation) to the highest constraint (experimental research). With the exception of

TABLE 2.3 A Two-Dimensional Model of Scientific Research

This model of the research process includes a range of five levels of constraint, each defined by the precision and/or flexibility of the observational procedures and/or settings. Regardless of the level of constraint, each research project goes through the same phases, from initial idea to final communication. Note that the following table is blank except for the labels for the two dimensions—the phases of research and the levels of constraint. Later chapters will provide the information that defines each of the implied cells in this two-dimensional model.

	PHASE OF RESEARCH						
LEVELS OF CONSTRAINT	**(1) Idea-Generating**	**(2) Problem Definition**	**(3) Procedures Design**	**(4) Obser-vation**	**(5) Data Analysis**	**(6) Interpre-tation**	**(7) Communi-cation**
Naturalistic observation							
Case-study method							
Correlational research							
Differential research							
Experimental research							

differential research, these are all commonly used labels. The term "differential research" represents a broad class of research often overlooked in research methods texts (Hyman, 1964). All the constraint levels in Table 2.3 represent scientific research and combine empirical observation and rational inference.

Some researchers hold the view that only high-constraint methods are scientific. In our model, all of these methods are scientific and effective when used properly. The researcher selects a particular constraint level based on the nature of the question, the precision of the existing knowledge, and practical and ethical constraints. For example, when Jane Goodall (1986, 1988, 2010) was interested in learning about the social behavior of chimpanzees, naturalistic observation was the most appropriate method. Her research produced new knowledge about these animals. Her questions were general and flexible, so the level of research had to be equally general and flexible. High-constraint research would not have been appropriate and could not have given the information sought. The general nature of Goodall's questions was not a flaw in her work. Any scientist breaking new ground might very well start with just such low-constraint questions.

Although all the levels of research in our model are scientific, scientists try to refine their questions so they can answer them using the highest constraint level possible, given both current knowledge and the practical and ethical constraints on the researcher.

Note that Table 2.3 is blank except for the labels for the phases of research and the levels of constraint. This table is essentially the outline for the remainder of the text. Later chapters will provide the information that defines each of the implied cells in this two-dimensional model.

TABLE 2.4 The Levels of Constraint of Scientific Research

Naturalistic Observation	Observing participants in their natural environment. The researcher should do nothing to limit or change the environment or the behavior of the participants.
Case Study Research	Moving the participant into a moderately limiting environment, intervening to a slight degree, and observing the participant's responses.
Correlational Research	Quantifying the strength of the relationship between two variables. The researchers must carefully define and precisely follow the measurement procedures.
Differential Research	Comparing two or more preexisting groups of participants. The setting is usually highly constrained, and the measurement procedures must be carefully defined and precisely followed.
Experimental Research	Assigning participants randomly to groups and then testing each group under a different condition.

Like the phases of research, constraint levels are overlapping rather than sharply categorical. They form a continuum, and the labels (naturalistic, case study, and so on) indicate overlapping bands of the continuum. The number of levels identified for this model of research is not critical in understanding the research activity that the model seeks to represent. The important concept is that constraint ranges from low to high, and that these five labels are adequate for describing most psychological research. Later chapters will discuss the levels of constraint in more detail. We briefly define each constraint level here and summarize them in Table 2.4.

Naturalistic Observation. **Naturalistic observation** requires the researcher to observe the behavior of participants in their natural environment and to not change or limit the environment or the behavior of the participants. The only constraint imposed by the researchers is on their observational methods.

In naturalistic observation, researchers usually are not bound by strong hypotheses that demand a particular set of observational procedures. Therefore, they are free to shift their attention to any behaviors that seem interesting. This flexible approach is common in the early stages of research on a given topic and is useful in generating hypotheses that the researcher can test later in higher-constraint research. Researchers prefer higher-constraint procedures once they become more familiar with an area.

Case Study Research. In **case study research**—the intensive study of an individual—the researcher may observe participants, access records, and actively intervene in the participant's functioning, such as by interviewing and testing. Somewhat more constrained than naturalistic observation, case studies still allow the researcher a good deal of flexibility to shift attention to whatever behaviors seem interesting and relevant. Case study research is not limited to studies of psychopathology or psychotherapy and can be applied to many issues.

Correlational Research. **Correlational research** requires greater constraint on the procedures used to measure behavior. The setting can range from a naturalistic one to the highly constrained setting of a scientific laboratory. However, because researchers are interested in quantifying the relationship between two or more events or characteristics, they must use precise and consistent procedures for measuring each. Testing the relationship between obesity and diabetes or social class and religiosity are examples of correlational research. As you will see, knowing the relationship between two items allows researchers to predict the value of one item from the value of the other.

Differential Research. **Differential research** involves comparing two or more groups of participants, like males and females, democrats and republicans, third graders and sixth graders. Whatever we measure in these groups must be measured in exactly the same way in each group; that is, the settings and observational procedures must be constrained across groups. When done properly, the only thing that is not identical across groups is the characteristic that defines the groups.

In differential research, the aspect that defines the groups is a **preexisting variable** that is not under the researcher's control. Such preexisting variables can include clinical diagnoses, age, IQ, gender, and so on. For example, research that compares males with females, adults born and raised in Canada with adults born and raised in England, Republican voters and Democratic voters are examples of differential research that utilizes preexisting groups.

Experimental Research. **Experimental research** compares the performance of participants under different conditions. A major distinction between differential and experimental research is the way that researchers assign participants to the groups or conditions. In experimental research, the researcher randomly assigns participants to conditions. In differential research, the researcher assigns participants based on a preexisting variable (such as social class or health status) that is outside the researcher's control.

The concept of level of constraint does not represent a single dimension. Some levels differ on the basis of the constraint applied to the setting in which the observations take place; some differ on the basis of the constraint placed on the measurement procedures; others differ on the basis of the constraint placed on the participant selection and assignment. Nevertheless, as researchers move from low-constraint methods to high-constraint methods, they place more constraint on more aspects of the research. In pure naturalistic observation, only the observer is constrained. In experiments, researchers plan every aspect of the study and follow explicit procedures throughout the study; the whole study is constrained.

Once the constraint level of the question has been determined, we must carry out the remainder of the research process at this same level of constraint. For example, it would be a mistake to draw high-constraint conclusions from low-constraint data. In addition, it would be a mistake to try to force high-constraint laboratory methods in an otherwise low-constraint design. Jane Goodall, try as she might, would have had great difficulty and doubtful results had she tried to randomly assign wild chimpanzees to experimental and control groups and to constrain each group of animals to only certain behaviors.

You will understand more about levels of constraint as you proceed through this text. For now, just remember that when we mix constraint levels, we run the serious risk of distorting information.

Moving from One Constraint Level to Another. Low-constraint conclusions drawn from low-constraint research can be the starting points for high-constraint questions and procedures. (That is one of the major functions of low-constraint research.) Let us suppose that you are a clinical psychologist and you observe a pattern of reported childhood trauma in your clients with depression. You have made an interesting observation, so you wonder, "Do the same patterns hold in the general population of depressed persons?" This question could lead you to research using sampling procedures to select participants who represent the general population of depressed people. As a good researcher, you know that concluding that all people with depression have histories of childhood trauma based only on your clinical sample would be an unwarranted leap from your low-constraint data to higher-constraint conclusions. However, by asking the question as posed above, you can move from low- to high-constraint research and adequately answer your question.

Low-constraint research is only one source of ideas that lead to higher-constraint research. Researchers continually make unconstrained, incidental observations, even when they are in the middle of highly constrained experimental studies. You can think of this as informal naturalistic research. These researchers are always open to new observations that might change their thinking on a topic. To use current vernacular, they are able to see and think "outside the box."

In Chapter 1, we noted that serendipity is not the happy accident that many nonscientists think it is. Scientists with prepared minds and an always-observant eye often notice things that others miss. Because of their inherent curiosity, they are alert to events in everyday life and ask what they mean and why they happened. Even in the middle of data collection, they are still watching and wondering, always alert to unexpected phenomena and always willing to take the time to explore such phenomena.

For example, if a researcher noticed a curious response from a participant in an experiment, the researcher might ask the participant about the response after the testing session is over. The participant may or may not be able to provide any insights. Later, the researcher may decide to try out a few ideas in some informal case studies to explore the question and see if it warrants more detailed and systematic study. Depending on what happens in the case studies, the researcher may decide to go on to formal high-constraint research on the phenomenon. This is one way that we can move a research area from lower constraint to higher constraint.

As we move from low- to high-constraint research, the procedures and findings become more precise. However, we also run the risk that the procedures will become more artificial and more removed from the real world, and therefore less relevant. To help to reduce this **precision-versus-relevance problem**, researchers should carry out their research at the highest constraint levels possible and then test the findings in natural settings. For example, there is growing evidence of the dangers of using a cell phone or texting while driving. Research has shown that listening to a radio or CD does not significantly impair driving. However, manipulating equipment, such as dialing a cell phone or adjusting the radio, does interfere with driving (Briem & Hedman, 1995). But what are the effects of actually holding a telephone conversation or texting while driving?

Strayer and Johnston (2001) carried out high-constraint laboratory experiments to simulate cell phone use while driving. The participants manipulated a joystick to track a constantly moving pattern on a video screen. At unpredicted times, a red or green light flashed. At the red light, the participant was to press a "brake button" on the joystick. Strayer and Johnston randomly assigned participants to three groups: radio control, hands-free cell phone, and handheld cell phone. They found that listening to the radio did not disrupt response to the red light, but carrying on a cell phone conversation in both the hands-free and handheld cell phone conditions did disrupt this response. Stayer and Johnson concluded that attention to the cell phone conversation mediated the driving disruption, regardless of whether the driver's hands were actually on the cell phone.

These same investigators followed up this initial study with additional research to pin down exactly what was happening. They found that it was neither holding the phone nor speaking, but rather carrying on a conversation on the phone that distracted the driver (Strayer & Johnston, 2001;

Strayer et al., 2003). In a newspaper interview, these researchers emphasized that conversations on hands-free and handheld phones are equally dangerous (Hafner & George, 2005). Laws that allow hands-free use, they said, are sending the wrong message, because such laws suggest that hands-free use is safe, when it actually is not. Furthermore, they noted that their studies found that the impairment produced by using a phone while driving was as severe as that found in someone driving while legally drunk (Strayer et al., 2006).

Later research showed that cell phone users typically adjust to the distraction by driving slower and responding less to the flow of traffic. This may help avoid accidents, but it can affect thousands of other drivers who are not using cell phones (Strayer & Drews, 2007). In a related finding, Radeborg et al. (1999) found that the disruptive effects may be bidirectional, with driving disrupting the cell-phone conversation.

Such high-constraint research provides precise answers to the question, "Does cell phone use disrupt simulated driving and increase the chance of driver error?" It can serve as a solid basis for making public policy about cell phone use in automobiles. However, as compelling as the research is, we cannot be sure that the laboratory findings would hold in the natural environment. Therefore, it would be useful to design laboratory settings that more closely resemble real driving and to follow up the laboratory findings with research on cell phone use in actual driving conditions. The driving simulator studies clearly address this concern. It would be inappropriate and unethical to test these hypotheses on the highway because of the risks to participants and bystanders. We will cover these and other ethical concerns throughout this text.

Quick-Check Review 2.3: A Model of the Research Process

1. What are the two main dimensions of the model of research presented in this section?
2. Name the phases of research.
3. Define levels of constraint.
4. What is the major difference between differential and experimental research?

ETHICAL PRINCIPLES

Among the decisions made in the procedures-design phase are those concerning human participants and animal subjects. When we engage people and/or animals in research, we subject them to conditions that we select and control. That is an extraordinary responsibility for us to assume; we are making decisions about our use of living organisms in our research. Therefore, we are responsible for the safety and welfare of those human participants and non-human (animal) subjects.

Scientists have developed considerable sophistication about ethical issues and sensitivity for protection of research participants, but that has not always been the case. In this section, we will briefly present some of the factors leading to the current development of ethical principles in research. There are many good sources for more information (e.g., Kimmel, 2007; Lederer, 1995; Nagy, 2011; Sugarman & Sulmasy, 2010).

The rising power of modern industrial technology and science in the nineteenth century alarmed many people. Remember the Frankenstein monster? Written almost 200 years ago, Mary

Shelley's (1818) novel *Frankenstein* has become a classic metaphor for the fears and dangers of unchecked scientific experimentation. By the mid-twentieth century, science had produced nuclear weapons of such power that a single bomb could destroy an entire city in a flash of horror. Investigations following World War II uncovered horrific examples of German doctors working in concentration camps, forcing people into painful, harrowing, inhumane and deadly medical research (Graubard, 1969). At the war's end, these atrocities were investigated and those responsible tried for their involvement; the common defense of so many of those who committed such atrocities was that they were blameless because they were "only following orders." Out of those trials in 1947 came the *Nuremberg Code*—ten ethical principles for the protection of future human research participants (see Katz, 1992). The foremost principle in the Nuremberg Code is that the *voluntary consent of participants* is required. The Nuremberg Code is a primary basis of our ethical research codes today.

What is now considered unethical behavior in research was not confined to Nazi scientists. In the United States, some researchers had deceived people in dangerous medical procedures (Graubard, 1969). One was the notorious Tuskegee syphilis study carried out by the U.S. Public Health Service from 1932 to 1972. Nearly 400 men diagnosed with syphilis were left untreated in order to track the course of the disease and to conduct the eventual autopsies that would reveal how syphilis affects the body (Jones, 1981/1993). These men, all rural, poor, and black, were not told they had syphilis, or that they were subjects in a study, but were told that "bad blood" was their problem. Penicillin, known since 1945 as the treatment of choice, was deliberately withheld so the disease could progress, leaving these men vulnerable to the natural advance of the infection. The men's primary value to the researchers was on the autopsy tables, at which time their bodies would yield the desired data. In their defense, researchers claimed the study had "value to science" and the "subjects" did receive medical attention they could otherwise not afford. Many participating doctors and technicians claimed, echoing Nuremberg, they were blameless because they had been "following orders."

In 1966, researcher Peter Buxton recognized the inhumanity of the study and called for its end. Ignored for the next several years by medical groups and the government, Buxton finally went to the newspapers. In 1972, the *Washington Star* and *New York Times* exposed the project (Heller, 1972). Public and congressional outcries exploded, the project was cancelled, and the remaining participants were belatedly treated. Unfortunately, many had already worsened or died, wives had been infected, and some children had been born with congenital defects related to syphilis. In 1997, President Bill Clinton apologized to those people on behalf of the country.

But years later, questions about the study remained. Reverby (2000), for example, asked why the infected wives and children did not ultimately receive proper treatment, and to what degree did the study reflect the country's racism at the time? During her investigation of the Tuskegee study, Susan Reverby, a medical historian, discovered that one of the researchers, John Cutler, conducted a second and much more ominous syphilis study. In 1946 and 1947, the U.S. Public Health Service, with the approval of the Guatemalan government, conducted research in Guatemala to test if penicillin was effective against sexually transmitted diseases (STDs). The subjects were 699 Guatemalan men and women—prisoners, mental patients, and soldiers—who were *deliberately infected with the STDs* and then treated. None of the subjects were informed of the nature of the study (Minogue & Marshall, 2010; Reverby, 2009, 2011). Faced by Reverby's findings the United States again found itself apologizing for the actions of some researchers (Neergaard, 2010).

There are other examples of such distorted science (Miller, 2010). Those U.S. researchers may have had the good intentions of finding cures for disease, but in our current research environment their actions are grossly inhumane and unethical.

As a result of congressional investigations into the Tuskegee study, the *National Commission for the Protection of Human Subjects of Biomedical and Behavioral Research* was created in 1974. This body produced the *Belmont Report* (1978). It established a uniform set of ethical principles for the protection of human participants and recommended requiring ethics review boards in all research centers.

This scandal awakened professionals and the public to the power and potential abuses of science, and people began to confront the moral implications of scientific research. Philosophers, scientists, and policymakers debated and clarified the complexities of the ethical issues (e.g., American Psychological Association, 2002; Graubard, 1969; International Union of Psychological Science, 2008; Prilleltensky, 1994; Rosenthal, 1994; Sales & Folkman, 2000; Stark, 2007, 2010; Yassour-Barochowitz, 2004). A new international journal, *Ethics and Behavior*, was created in 1991 to continue the discussions of ethics in research and teaching. Scientific organizations began examining their own research practices and creating ethical guidelines for researchers.

The American Psychological Association was one of the first professional organizations to develop ethical guidelines (e.g., American Psychological Association, 1953, 1959), more than two decades before the publication of the Belmont Report. The APA guidelines recognized both the need for research and the rights of research participants. The APA acknowledged that research may involve deception, may make participants uncomfortable, or may seek personal and sensitive information. These and other research procedures place the participants at risk, which means there is a potential for the participants to be harmed by the research.

The ethical principles that professional and governmental organizations developed over decades seek to minimize such risks. The federal government developed policy regarding human participants in research (e.g., Code of Federal Regulations, 2005), and these policies are regularly updated. Federal funding agencies, such as the National Institutes of Health, publish regulations on their websites, and these ethical regulations are constantly evolving. The American Psychological Association has updated its *Ethical Principles of Psychologists and Code of Conduct* several times (American Psychological Association, 2010a). The most recent document sets out five general principles for the conduct of all activities carried out by psychologists and sets out in detail 89 specific standards of conduct, including the 15 standards that apply to research activities. That document, largely rooted in the Nuremberg Code and the Belmont Report, is the current ethics guide for psychologists and has been adopted by other professions. Table 2.5 summarizes the APA ethical principles in research. Take a close look at it; become familiar with it. In subsequent chapters, we will discuss them in more detail.

Every student entering the field of research needs to know that the researcher bears *personal responsibility* to conduct research in an ethical manner and in accord with the guidelines for humane treatment of participants. The National Science Foundation requires, since January 2010, that grant applicants must provide assurance they will educate all students involved in the proposed research (undergraduate, graduate, post-doctoral) in research ethics (Grant, 2009).

When designing a study, the researcher must be sensitive to the ethical principles, must examine the research plans for potential ethical issues, and must take steps to correct those issues *prior to contacting any participants*. The proposed research plan needs to survive ethical evaluation by an appropriate ethics review board; if an ethical problem exists, the researcher needs to modify the plan. Only when the plan can stand up to ethical challenges does the investigator proceed with the next phase, making observations.

TABLE 2.5 The APA Ethical Principles of Psychologists

This summary is based on the *Ethical Principles of Psychologists and Code of Conduct* (American Psychological Association, 2010a). Full text is available at www.apa.org.

GENERAL PRINCIPLES THAT APPLY TO ALL ACTIVITIES OF PSYCHOLOGISTS

1. Psychologists strive to benefit those with whom they work and take care to *do no harm.*
2. Psychologists establish relationships of trust with those with whom they work.
3. Psychologists seek to promote accuracy, honesty, and truthfulness in the science, teaching, and practice of psychology.
4. Psychologists recognize that all persons are entitled to equal access to and benefit from psychological activities and services.
5. Psychologists respect the dignity and worth of all people, and the rights of individuals to privacy, confidentiality, and self-determination.

We repeat from Chapter 1 a critical concept in research. At the heart of research ethics lies the *personal responsibility of each researcher* to conduct his or her work so as to enhance science and human welfare—that is, to conduct the research in an ethical manner.

Quick-Check Review 2.4: Ethical Principles

1. In which phase(s) of research do we need to consider ethical issues?
2. Who bears the responsibility for ethical conduct of a research project?

SUMMARY

- The essence of science is its process of thinking.
- Scientists accept basic assumptions about nature.
- Data gathered through empirical observations are the facts of research, and most facts observed in psychology are behaviors.
- Constructs are ideas created by the researcher, based on facts and/or inferences. We use constructs analogically to generate research hypotheses. As useful as constructs are, scientists must avoid reifying them.
- Induction and deduction are inferential processes.
- A theory is a formalized set of concepts that (1) summarizes and organizes observations and inferences, (2) provides tentative explanations of phenomena, and (3) makes specific testable predictions that researchers can verify or disconfirm.
- Scientists prefer their theories to be parsimonious.
- Theories may be inductive, deductive, functional, or they may be models.
- The two dimensions of the research model proposed here are (1) phases of research and (2) level of constraint.
- Each researcher bears personal responsibility for the ethical conduct of research.

PUTTING IT INTO PRACTICE To appreciate the process of research, you might consider doing a little research project of your own. Look around and find something interesting. For example, notice that some people studying in the library are making faces as they read. You might ask yourself whether this is common and observe other people to find out. You could ask whether there is a gender difference in this phenomenon, or whether the type of material that the person is studying makes a difference. Use the phases of research described in this chapter to guide your informal research. Find something that really interests you to make this exercise fun, and let your curiosity run wild.

EXERCISES

2.1. Define the following key terms. Be sure that you understand them. They are discussed in the chapter and defined in the glossary.

assumptions (of science)
data
facts
behavior
observation
inference
constructs
reification of a construct
nominal fallacy
all-or-none bias
similarity-uniqueness paradox
Barnum statement
evaluative biases of language
inductive reasoning
deductive reasoning
theory
parsimonious theory
validity
inductive theory
intervening variables
deductive theory
functional theories
model
phases of research
idea-generating phase
problem-definition phase
procedures-design phase
observation phase
data analysis phase
interpretation phase
communication phase
replication
levels of constraint
naturalistic observation
case study research
correlational research
differential research
preexisting variable
experimental research
precision-versus-relevance problem

2.2. Think of some issue in your life and try to generate as many general research ideas as you can. You might begin some of your questions with "I wonder what would happen if . . .?" or "I wonder why . . .?" For example, "I wonder why I wake up every morning just a moment or two before my alarm rings?"

2.3. For these brief descriptions of research, identify the level of constraint.

a. A therapist has several clients with similar problems. He compares their statements in therapy to see what might be common among all of the cases.
b. A researcher compares participants' reaction times to visual stimuli in a laboratory setting.
c. Two groups of rats are compared for their accuracy in running a maze. One group is fed just before the maze running, and the other is fed 4 hours earlier.
d. Third-grade and sixth-grade classes are compared based on their taste preferences.
e. A researcher observes prairie dog colonies to learn more about their behavior.
f. A researcher evaluates the relationship between the number of calories consumed and weight.

2.4. Here is a challenge to your creativity! Create a reasonable conceptual model that might explain each of the following phenomena.

a. Huge, centuries-old drawings have been found on the ground in Central America. They are so large that they can be seen only from hundreds of feet in the air. However, there were no aircraft in existence at that time.

b. People who are usually rational and controlled can nevertheless become highly emotional and irrational when in a crowd.

c. Despite the fact that adolescents and young adults know the danger of certain behaviors, such as smoking, many nevertheless continue those behaviors.

d. Many people overeat to the point of becoming obese.

e. Siblings can look, think, and act very differently from one another, even though they have the same parents.

2.5. A radio talk show host argues, "Let's face it folks, evolution is *only a theory; it's not a fact*!" As a scientist, how would you answer that?

CHAPTER THREE

THE STARTING POINT: ASKING QUESTIONS

It appears to me that . . . philosophical . . . difficulties and disagreements . . . are mainly due to a very simple cause: namely to the attempt to answer questions without first discovering precisely what question it is which you desire to answer.

—George Edward Moore, *Principia Ethica*, 1903

WEB RESOURCE MATERIAL

03:01 Library Research Tutorial
03:02 APA Ethical Guidelines for Research with Human Subjects
03:03 Research and Publication Section (APA Ethical Principles, 2002, 2010)
03:04 Guidelines for Ethical Conduct in the Care and Use of Animals
03:05 Study Guide/Lab Manual
03:06 Links to Related Internet Sites

Formulating questions is one of the most creative aspects of scientific research and one of the most difficult to teach. Yet, without good questions, research is pointless. The right questions beg for answers, making the work of conducting research to find those answers difficult to resist. Therefore, in this chapter, we will teach you the skills needed to develop and refine questions.

ASKING AND REFINING QUESTIONS

Research starts with questions, and formulating the right questions is one of the most critical and creative elements of good research. A question is a problem in need of a solution or answer. What are the causes of child abuse? Why are some things difficult to remember? How can we get drunk drivers off the road? Why do some people become depressed? Questions are everywhere; all you have to do is observe and be curious.

Pursuing Your Personal Interests

The most powerful questions often come from our everyday lives. For example, you might be interested in emotions or memory, or wonder about yourself or your family members. You may be puzzled by something you observe and ask, "Why did that happen?" Any of these interests or observations can serve as a starting point for research.

Following Up on the Work of Others

Research often raises more questions than it answers, and those questions can be starting points for more research. Theories and prior research raise questions for new research in two ways: heuristically and systematically. **Heuristic influence** occurs when theories or research findings generate interest, including disbelief or outright antagonism, and suggest further research questions. The work of Darwin and Freud are good examples.

Systematic influence occurs when theories or research provide testable propositions for further research. Research on conditioning, for example, has systematically generated new research. Both heuristic and systematic influences are important in science. Table 3.1 lists a few examples of theories and research that have generated significant psychological research.

The more you know about a research area, the stronger will be your base for generating new research ideas. Beginning students often find it difficult to read primary sources like scientific journals, with their severe space restrictions and technical language. Secondary sources, such as textbooks or review chapters, are often more useful. For example, the *Annual Review of Psychology* publishes review chapters on important research areas in psychology. Textbooks provide background information that makes it easier to understand an area. However, textbooks are a year or two behind the research in review articles and chapters. As you gain sophistication in a research area, journal articles become the major source of information.

Libraries have well-organized, computerized systems for finding relevant research by topic, authors, title, keywords, or other elements. Your reference librarians are knowledgeable and available and can be very helpful in teaching you to use database systems such as *PsycINFO*, *Medline,* and the *Social Sciences Citation Index*. Appendix C covers the basics of library research, and a detailed tutorial is on the Student Resource Website.

03:01

TABLE 3.1 Theories and Research That Generated More Research through Heuristic Influences

- **Freud, S. (1938a, 1938b). Psychoanalytic theory**: Freud maintained that unconscious desires influence much of our behavior.
- **Skinner, B. F. (1938, 1972). Research on learning**: Skinner argued that animals and humans learn in very similar ways and show similar patterns of learning.
- **Miller, N. E. (1971). Studies of motivation**: Miller said that many emotions are shared by animals and humans and are generated by brain mechanisms.
- **Bandura, A. (1969). Research on modeling**: Bandura showed that people can and do learn by merely observing the behavior of others and the consequences those people experience for their behavior.
- **Festinger, L. (1957). Theory of cognitive dissonance**: Festinger maintained that conflicts between values and actions could lead to changes in either to avoid future conflicts.
- **Lovaas, O. I. (1973). Research with autistic children**: Lovaas demonstrated that even severely disturbed children can benefit from learning functional language and will respond to reinforcement contingencies.
- **Seligman, M. E. P. (1974). Depression and learned helplessness**: Seligman argued that both humans and animals respond to a period of uncontrollable stress with behavior that is similar to the behavior found in depression.
- **Gleick, J. (1987). Chaos theory**: Gleick maintained that many apparently random events are actually the result of complex processes (i.e., interacting nonlinear influences) that make long-term prediction virtually impossible.
- **Loftus, E. F. and Polage, D. C. (1999). Repressed memory**: Loftus and her colleagues argued that the concept of repressed memories is likely false and the so-called recovered memories were actually created by the procedures that were designed to recover them.

The disciplined approach that scientists use to address questions tends to produce predictable results. An unusual result, not easily explained by current wisdom, will lead scientists to ask what is happening and why it is happening. As often happens in science, different researchers working from similar theoretical perspectives may well make important discoveries independently. Historical Lesson 3.1 illustrates one of the most famous examples of this phenomenon.

HISTORICAL LESSON 3.1: CHARLES DARWIN AND ALFRED RUSSEL WALLACE

Charles Darwin (1809–1882) was one of the most important scientists in history. His research on facial expressions and human emotion was groundbreaking (Eckman, 2009), and his book *On the Origin of Species* (1859) has had profound effects on science, philosophy, religion, politics, economics, and society.

After completing his famous journeys to the Galapagos Islands, Darwin spent the next 21 years refining his ideas for publication. In June 1858, when his book was still far from completion, Darwin received a manuscript in the mail in which his own thesis had already been written. Another naturalist, Alfred Russel Wallace (1823–1913), had preempted Darwin. Wallace traveled in the Amazon and the South Pacific as Darwin had done many years before (Keith, 1954). Wallace was impressed by the diversity of life he found, and he followed, completely independently, the same line of reasoning as Darwin in making sense of his observations. The result was Wallace's manuscript on the biological operation of natural selection in the origins of species. Wallace mailed his discovery to Darwin for comment.

Who was to be the first to present this momentous discovery to the world? Colleagues arranged to have the two scientists present their work simultaneously at a meeting of the Linnean Society in London on July 1,

1858. The Greeks had developed a concept of evolution over 2,000 years earlier, but it was Wallace and Darwin who gathered the mass of data and recognized that the driving force of evolution was natural selection. The following year, Darwin completed *On the Origin of Species* and became the acknowledged originator of the idea of natural selection and the model that derived from it. Wallace, apparently content with this, made no great effort to share in the subsequent acclaim, and the two men remained lifelong friends. Wallace continued to make important contributions to science and became one of nineteenth century's greatest naturalists (Gross, 2010). However, Darwin is the one who is remembered for this great biological discovery.

Basic, Applied, and Translational Research

Much of the research in psychology is **applied research**—direct attempts to find solutions to practical problems. Questions for applied research in psychology are relatively easy for students to generate. Table 3.2 lists some examples. Try generating some of your own.

Table 3.2 lists examples of basic, applied, and translational research.

TABLE 3.2 Examples of Applied, Basic, and Translational Research

APPLIED RESEARCH

1. Finding ways to train people to be better drivers (Tronsmoen, 2011)
2. Finding ways to reduce shoplifting in department stores (Hayes, 2006)
3. Helping teachers or parents to help an underachieving child to improve academically (Timmermans et al., 2009)
4. Finding the best placement of dials and instruments in a car that will reduce driver fatigue and errors (Matthews, 2002)
5. Finding an effective approach to calming children before and after surgery (Wright et al., 2010)
6. Finding ways to change human behavior on a large scale to reduce the incidence of such diseases as lung cancer and AIDS (Kelly et al., 2010)
7. Finding the most effective treatment for depression (Kiossis et al., 2011)

BASIC RESEARCH

1. Studying the nature of the sleep-wake cycle and the factors that regulate it (Easton et al., 2004)
2. Identifying the mechanisms by which the body regulates food intake (Duva et al., 2005)
3. Studying how cross-cultural language differences can influence the perception of color (Davidoff, 2004)
4. Studying ethnic and educational differences that affect the impact of cortisol on awakening (Bennett et al., 2004)
5. Studying differences in retinal sensitivity to threat-related stimulation (Calvo & Castillo, 2005).
6. Studying arm movement in monkeys to map behavioral repertoire of the cortex (Graziano & Aflalo, 2007)
7. Studying handedness in chimpanzee tool use and its relationship to development of language (Hopkins, Russell, & Cantalupo, 2007)

TRANSLATIONAL RESEARCH

1. Evaluating whether the requirement that all translational research supported by NIH must include training in research ethics is being met (DuBois et al., 2010).
2. Translating the mass of ecological science knowledge about the world to the public in useful forms (Schlesinger, 2010).
3. Translating FDA warnings to the public on prescription drug use (Barry & Busch, 2010).
4. Translating educational research findings for parents—infants learn relatively little from infant media, but many parents mistakenly overestimate the media's success (DeLoache et al., 2010).

Basic research, also known as **fundamental research** or **pure research**, seeks to increase scientific understanding of nature without immediate concern for practical goals. Knowledge is what is sought in basic research, but basic research findings are important foundations for later applied research. For example, a researcher might use information from basic research on children's language development to create training methods for children with language deficiencies.

Unfortunately, it has been more difficult for basic researchers to obtain financial support than for applied researchers. Basic research tends to be long-term and, by definition, has no apparent practical usefulness. Many policy makers do not see the value in basic research with no practical end and, preferring quick solutions, tend to be put off by its long-term nature. For example, in the 1970s the late Senator William Proxmire regularly mocked studies with titles like "Sex Life of a Quail." More recently Senator John McCain, a candidate in the 2008 U.S. presidential campaign, repeatedly derided a study of DNA in bears as wasted money. They and others fail to acknowledge, or perhaps understand, that solving practical problems requires a foundation of basic knowledge, and much of that knowledge comes from basic research.

Research does not divide neatly into basic or applied categories. Many studies contribute to a basic understanding of a phenomenon and also have obvious potential for translating those findings into practical application. The intent is to conduct research in which basic research findings are translated into forms that can be tested and ultimately applied in clinics, schools, hospitals, and industry. Such research has been named **translational research**. Although some scholars consider translational research as an ideal way to encourage both basic and applied research, others view it as a threat to basic research, as discussed in Box 3.1.

BOX 3.1:
THE NEW TRANSLATIONAL RESEARCH MODEL

We have discussed two defining categories of research: *basic research*, seeking fundamental or "pure" knowledge, and *applied research*, seeking current solutions to practical problems. Some research spans the two areas; it is basic research with major potential for near-term practical applications. Over the past decade, this in-between area has been given a name—*translational research* (Breckler, 2006; *Science*, 2010)—and once something has been named, it takes on a life of its own.

Translational research, promoted by the National Institutes of Health, aims at "translating basic research into tools and interventions that can be used to diagnose, treat, and prevent disease" (Zerhouni, 2005, p. 1356). Zerhouni cites modern cognitive behavior therapy (CBT) as an example. Basic animal research in classical, instrumental, and operant conditioning (e.g. Pavlov, Thorndike, Skinner, Hull) was the basis for later clinically and educationally oriented behavior modification research (e.g., Eysenck, 1960; Jones, 1924; Wolpe, 1958). That research merged with new cognitive therapies (e.g., Beck, 1975) and that merger resulted in cognitive behavior therapy (Rachman, 1997). CBT is now a mainstay in applied psychological research and has become a major therapeutic approach—a set of effective data-based clinical treatments for many psychological problems.

That process—discoveries moving from basic research through several translations into ultimate practical application and general acceptance in the community—is what is meant by *translational research*; it is a flowing process from the laboratory to the clinic, schoolroom, factory, and back again.

Translational research is now a high priority in the research world, particularly among the policy makers who decide on public funding for research. It appears to be more than renaming—perhaps a significant restructuring of the entire supporting social network of scientific research. Its planners intend that the new model will encourage basic research, eliminating barriers between basic and applied research and practical application. They also expect it to speed up the development of new treatments and thus enhance the contributions of science to human welfare. By 2012, 60 Translational Research Centers had been developed across the country (Mayo Foundation, 2012a, 2012b). European scientists have also adopted the new model and, more recently, China is showing interest (Wang, Wang, & Marincola, 2011). Each center will link university and private laboratories with schools and hospitals to encourage the flow of discoveries and applications. New journals (e.g., *Clinical and Translational Science, Journal of Translational Medicine*) publish original research, reviews of research, and observations and commentaries on the developing field (e.g. DuBois et al., 2010; Gallagher et al., 2010; Musgrave, 2010).

But there may be a downside. The research community needs to be vigilant. We fear that given the new greater emphasis on applied implications for all research, the fundamental knowledge that is sought through basic research may be jeopardized, weakened, and given lower value, thus reducing significant financial support for basic research. We must be protective of pure basic research that has no obvious practical application in the near term. A critical question for policy makers is this: given the grand scope and considerable promise of the translational research model, how can the goals of basic research be preserved; how can we avoid diluting that core dimension of basic research—seeking knowledge for its own sake?

Refining Questions for Research

Research begins with questions that are gradually refined until they become specific enough to give the researcher a clear direction for answering them. Developing the initial question is critical, because it determines how we will conduct the research. Decisions about the level of constraint, observational methods, or which statistical tests to use depend partly on the nature of the questions asked. Once the initial question is refined, the other decisions follow.

Suppose that you are part of a team of psychologists studying the parenting behavior of elephants in the wild. You want to know how long baby elephants are dependent on their parents or other adults, to what degree the mother and father contribute to a baby elephant's care, and whether other adult elephants also contribute to the care. You and your colleagues begin to refine these questions as follows:

1. In their natural habitat, which adult elephants assist in the birth and early care of infant elephants and in the primary care of the growing young?
2. At what age do young elephants raised in their natural habitat become independent from parents and/or caretakers?

Note two important points about the initial questions. First, the questions specify what behaviors to observe: parenting behavior of the adults and independent behavior of the young. Second, the question also specifies the conditions under which the observations are to be made (the elephants' natural habitat). These specific elements are variables of the study.

A **variable** is any set of events with different values. Height is a variable because organisms and inanimate objects have different heights. Gender is a variable because there are more than one gender. Behavior is a variable because there are many possible behaviors. Any specific behavior, such as aggression, can be a variable because it occurs in different forms and degrees.

We can observe any of these variables and thousands of others. Some variables can be easily manipulated, such as the amount of food eaten or the maximum time allowed for research participants to solve a cognitive problem. Other variables are more difficult to manipulate, such as participants' genetic makeup.

In your study of elephants' behavior, several variables are of interest. We will consider two of them: (1) the setting in which the elephants are observed, and (2) the behavior of the elephants.

You could observe elephants in many different settings, including zoos and natural habitats. This study will focus on the natural habitat of elephants, where the elephants' natural behavior is so variable and complex that the researchers will need to simplify it by establishing broad categories to classify the behavior.

The two initial questions have begun to narrow how the researchers will design and conduct the study. By specifying the natural habitat, you are committed to low-constraint observations in natural settings. Because the questions are about the normal flow of behavior under natural conditions, you will use naturalistic observations of the animals without manipulating the animals' behavior.

In formulating initial questions, researchers proceed through a lengthy process of thinking about their area of interest, posing loosely defined questions, studying the research literature, and gradually refining their ideas into research questions. This process might take researchers far from their starting point, and their refined questions might be very different from the original questions. Theories and research of other investigators guide researchers in this process of refining ideas into researchable questions.

Theories are particularly important in this enterprise, because good theories organize vast amounts of information into a few general concepts. Theories often act like maps of research areas, revealing which areas are well understood and which areas could benefit from additional research.

Once refined, the initial question implicitly helps to identify the major variables of interest and to structure the design and conduct of the research. The level of constraint of a research project, the types of controls, the kinds of observations, and even the kinds of statistical analyses depend largely on the nature of the question.

In general, researchers try to develop the initial question to the highest level of refinement possible given the state of knowledge about the particular area. The more they know about an area, the more refined the questions will be and the more likely that the researchers will use high-constraint research methods to answer it. In areas in which little is known, the initial question will be correspondingly unrefined and less specific, and the procedures will therefore be carried out at lower constraint levels. In the example of your team's study of elephants' parenting behavior, the questions were general, rather than detailed and specific, because little was known about such behavior in elephants. It was impossible to define critical behaviors because there was no way to know which behaviors might be included in the broad category of parenting. You did not want to constrain the observations by trying to be overly specific about what behaviors to observe and how and when to observe them. Doing so might have caused you to miss something important that you had not expected. In this case, you wanted to maintain maximum flexibility, so you placed no constraints on the behavior of the elephants and few constraints on your observational focus, other than to avoid interfering with the elephants. Had more been known about elephants before beginning the research, the questions would have been more specific and your behavior would have been more constrained by this more specific focus.

Quick-Check Review 3.1: Asking and Refining Questions

1. What are the main sources of research questions?
2. How do you distinguish between applied and basic research?
3. What is a variable?
4. How can basic research be valuable in solving practical problems?
5. What is meant by translational research?

TYPES OF VARIABLES IN RESEARCH

Researchers classify variables based on their characteristics as well as on how they are used in research. Table 3.3 summarizes several important ways of classifying psychological variables.

Classifying Variables Based on Their Characteristics

We define three types of variables by their characteristics: behavioral variables, stimulus variables, and organismic variables.

Behavioral Variables. Any observable response of an organism is a **behavioral variable**. This includes a rat running a maze, a chimpanzee opening a puzzle box, a child playing with a toy, a person playing the piano, or people talking to each other. Behavioral variables can be relatively simple behavior, such as a single button press, or complex responses, such as social and verbal behavior. Psychology is the study of behavior; therefore, behavioral variables are of particular importance and are the type of variable most often observed in psychological research.

TABLE 3.3 Classes of Research Variables

VARIABLES DEFINED BY THEIR CHARACTERISTICS
Behavioral Variable—Any observable response of an organism
Stimulus Variable—Environmental factors that have actual or potential effects on an organism's responses
Organismic Variable—A characteristic of an organism that can be used to classify the organism for research purposes
VARIABLES DEFINED BY THEIR USE IN RESEARCH
Independent Variable—A variable that is actively manipulated by the experimenter to see what its impact will be on other variables (manipulated independent variable) or used by the researcher to create groups to study based on preexisting characteristics of the organism (nonmanipulated independent variable)
Dependent Variable—A variable that is hypothesized to be affected by the independent-variable manipulation
Extraneous Variable—Any variable, other than the independent variable, that might affect the dependent measure in a study
A Constant—Any event that is prevented from varying

Stimulus Variables. Behavior always occurs in context. Within a context, those factors that have actual or potential effects on the organism's responses are **stimulus variables**. Stimulus variables may be specific and easily measurable or controllable, such as a flashing light signal in an experiment. They also may be more general, such as the total situation surrounding the participant. Examples of complex stimulus variables are the habitat in which we observe elephants or the condition of a classroom in which we observe a child. Stimulus variables range from simple, such as an auditory signal, to complex, such as social situations. *In psychological research, the researcher typically controls stimulus variables and observes behavioral variables*. As research moves from lower to higher levels of constraint, we increase the level of control over stimulus variables.

Many stimulus variables are internal to the participant—mood, for example. Although some procedures may affect internal stimuli, these internal variables may be difficult to manipulate and are generally not under the experimenter's direct control. Nevertheless, they are part of the participant's environment and can affect behavior.

Organismic Variables. **Organismic variables**, also called **subject variables**, are characteristics of the participants, such as age, gender, racial attitudes, and musical ability. We can directly observe some participants' characteristics, such as gender; these are **observed organismic variables**. Participant characteristics that we cannot observe, such as racial attitudes, are **response-inferred organismic variables**. Although we may not be able to observe them, we can infer the existence of these variables from observable behavior. Response-inferred organismic variables are constructs, which we discussed in Chapter 2.

We can use organismic variables to classify participants. For example, researchers might measure the anxiety level of participants and then divide the participants into three groups: high, moderate, and low anxiety.

Classifying Variables Based on Their Use in Research

In addition to classifying variables based on their characteristics, researchers also classify variables based on how they use the variables in research.

Independent and Dependent Variables. The variables that the experimenter manipulates are the **independent variables**. The participant's responses to these manipulations are the **dependent variables**. For example, suppose that a researcher hypothesizes that verbal criticism and aggression escalate as frustration increases. The researcher randomly assigns participants to three-person workgroups and instructs each group to solve a series of problems. The variables in this study are frustration (the independent variable) and verbal criticism/aggression (the dependent variable). The researcher manipulates the independent variable as follows: One group receives all the information needed to solve the problems easily (the no-frustration condition). Another group has some of the information withheld so that the problems are still solvable, but with difficulty (the moderate-frustration condition). The third group has enough information withheld so that the problems appear to be solvable but, in reality, are unsolvable (the high-frustration condition). In this way, the researcher manipulates the independent variable of frustration and measures the dependent variable of criticism/aggression by recording each group's verbal interactions and later counting all instances of the dependent variable of verbal criticism/aggression. The hypothesis is that the independent variable manipulation will affect the dependent variable; that is, the more frustrated you make people, the more likely they are to show criticism and aggression.

There are two kinds of independent variables: (1) manipulated independent variables and (2) nonmanipulated independent variables.[i] **Manipulated independent variables** are those that the experimenter actively controls, such as the frustration level in the preceding study. With **nonmanipulated independent variables**, also called **classification variables**, researchers assign participants to groups based on preexisting characteristics. The largest category of nonmanipulated independent variables in psychology are organismic variables—preexisting characteristics of the participants, such as IQ, age, and political affiliation. The researcher does not actively manipulate such variables but, rather, assigns participants to groups based on them. For example, suppose that researchers wanted to test the hypothesis that moral problem-solving skills in children vary by age. The researchers would assign children to groups based on their age, and the children would then take a moral problem-solving test. The researchers would then compare test scores of the various age groups to determine whether there were significant group differences.

Researchers often hypothesize a causal relationship between the independent and dependent variables. A **causal relationship** between two variables exists when changes in one variable result in a predictable change in the other. However, as you will see in later chapters, it is difficult to draw causal conclusions without manipulating the independent variable. Thus, conclusions about causal relationships in a study with nonmanipulated independent variables must be tentative.

We will discuss these issues more in later chapters. For now, it is important that you be able to define and distinguish between (1) independent and dependent variables, and (2) manipulated and nonmanipulated independent variables.

Extraneous Variables. **Extraneous variables** are unplanned and uncontrolled factors that can arise in a study and affect the outcome. Consequently, researchers must control extraneous variables to avoid their potential effects.

Suppose that a researcher is studying academic learning and the dependent variable is course grade based on examinations. Distractions during the examinations could be extraneous variables, and it would be wise to hold the examinations in a quiet room to remove this potential extraneous variable.

Variables and Constants. In the broadest sense, research deals with events. When the events vary—that is, occur at different levels or amounts—they are variables. When researchers constrain events to a fixed value, the events become constants. A **constant** is thus a set of events that the researcher prevents from varying.

A variable in one research study might be a constant in another. For example, a researcher might wish to study the effects of hormones on animal learning. Suppose that earlier research suggested that the response to specific hormones varies depending on the age and sex of the animals. The researcher decides to hold these two variables constant and uses only four-month-old male rats. Thus, sex and age are constants in this study, and therefore, they do not affect the outcome of the

[i]Some would disagree with using the term "nonmanipulated independent variable," arguing that an independent variable is, by definition, manipulated. However, the term "independent variable" is typically used more broadly to include organismic variables as possible independent variables. We have made the distinction between manipulated and nonmanipulated independent variables explicit to minimize confusion for students, while acknowledging the broad and somewhat inaccurate general usage of the term.

research. Another researcher might be specifically interested in the effects of age and sex on hormone levels. That researcher would use animals of both sexes and of different ages, making age and sex variables rather than constants.

Quick-Check Review 3.2: Types of Variables in Research

1. Define independent and dependent variables. How do investigators use them in research?
2. Define manipulated and nonmanipulated independent variables.
3. What does it mean to hold a variable constant in research?

VALIDITY AND THE CONTROL OF EXTRANEOUS VARIABLES

Validity is one of the most important concepts in research and a central theme throughout this text. It is a complex idea, and there are many types of validity. In a general sense, they all refer to the quality or precision of a study, a procedure, or a measure—to "how well" each does what it is supposed to do. Some common validity questions follow:

- Does this study really answer the question it posed?
- Does this test measure what we want it to measure?
- What does this laboratory study reveal about the real world?

One fundamental task of research is to maximize the validity of its procedures by including appropriate controls. This section introduces the concept of validity. However, we will revisit that concept repeatedly throughout this textbook, because validity is at the core of the entire research enterprise.

Recall that empirical observation is the midpoint in the scientific research process. Observations in psychological research are usually observations of behavior. Many factors influence behavioral observations—some known and others unknown to the researcher. Some factors may be of theoretical interest, whereas others may be extraneous, distorting the results and making it impossible for the researcher to draw meaningful conclusions. Extraneous variables reduce the validity of the research. Thus, it is important to reduce the influence of extraneous variables on the behavior of research participants.

Controls are the procedures used to reduce extraneous influences in research. The concept of control in research refers to the systematic methods employed by the researcher to reduce threats to the validity of the study posed by extraneous influences on the behavior of participants and researchers. Although such controls are most important in higher-constraint research, they are part of the procedures at all levels. For example, in a case study, we might want to observe problem solving in zoo-raised monkeys by testing each animal individually. What controls might we apply? The researcher would find a quiet place for the testing so that other monkeys or gawking visitors would not distract the monkey. Even in this low-constraint research, controlling the observational setting reduces the effects of extraneous variables.

The control of extraneous variables is the heart of the research enterprise. Without control, we cannot be confident of the research findings. Virtually this entire textbook is devoted to this topic.

You will learn that there are several ways to achieve control. The most powerful is to use research designs that have effective controls built into them. However, researchers can add specific control procedures to any study regardless of the level of constraint.

For now, you need to remember two things. The first is that uncontrolled extraneous variables threaten the validity of research. The second is that effective control procedures exist, and it is the responsibility of the researcher to select the necessary controls and include them in the study in order to enhance validity. In later chapters, you will learn what these controls are, how to select them, and how to implement them.

Quick-Check Review 3.3: Validity and the Control of Extraneous Variables

1. What are extraneous variables?
2. Why must we control extraneous variables in research?
3. What is validity?
4. What do controls have to do with validity?

ETHICAL PRINCIPLES

In the first two chapters, we introduced the importance of ethics in research and the history of why and how formal ethical principles were developed. Here, we cover how these principles are implemented and what systems are in place to assure ethical conduct.

Ethical Principles for Human Research

The first and most basic of all of the ethical principles is that researchers must do no harm. That dictum was set out in the historically important Belmont Report (1978). That report, which outlined basic ethical principles for human research, has been adopted by virtually all research agencies.

The **Belmont Report** proposed that ethical research with human beings rested on the following three principles:

- **Beneficence**: The risk to participants should be minimized and the benefits to participants and society should be maximized. Moreover, any risk to participants should be weighed against the possible benefits.
- **Autonomy**: It is the right of participants to decide whether they will participate, and they must be given sufficient information on which to make that decision.
- **Justice**: Both the risks and the benefits of research should be shared equally by all members of the population.

The Belmont Report argued that participants in research have the right to know what the study involves, and researchers must give them enough clear information so they can freely decide whether to participate. The ongoing concern about these issues has led to rigorous safeguards for participants. These principles are integrated into the APA Ethical Guidelines for Research with

Human Subjects, which is discussed and referenced on the Student Resource Website. The Student Resource Website also includes the ethical guidelines for research publication.

03:02 Psychological research with humans is rarely physically intrusive, and the physical risks to
03:03 participants are not as great as in some biomedical research. Nevertheless, we need to protect our participants. Issues of deception, concealment, invasion of privacy, confidentiality, and participants' right to decline participation still apply to psychological research.

Deception/Concealment involves deliberately misleading participants by giving false information (**deception**) or by withholding some information (**concealment**). Some types of psychological research routinely employ deception or concealment (Hertwig & Ortman, 2008; Pittenger, 2002). Although the use of deception in psychological research has increased (Bower, 1998), it has become more innocuous than in the past (Korn, 1997). Nevertheless, the use of any deception/concealment places participants at risk, and thus researchers must include safeguards. The most common safeguards are (1) the researcher's judgment that the deception/concealment poses no serious or long-term risks, and (2) a **debriefing**, which involves explaining the true nature of the deception/concealment *as soon as possible*, usually immediately following the study. In the debriefing, the researcher informs the participants about the procedures, and identifies and explains the rationale for their use. The debriefing aims to resolve misconceptions or discomfort caused by the deception/concealment. Following the debriefing, the participant signs a statement allowing or denying the use of his or her data. However, some participants become distressed during debriefing on learning that they had been deceived. It continues to be debated whether such negative effects of deception can in fact be reversed through debriefing (Miller et al., 2005).

Potential **invasions of privacy** occur when researchers examine sensitive issues, such as sexual behavior, emotions, private thoughts, and confidential records of hospital patients or students. This is normally private information, and we are asking people to trust us with that information for the purpose of research. We clearly need consent to obtain such information, but the sensitive nature of the information places a serious burden on the researcher. Specifically, the researcher must maintain strict **confidentiality** of the information gathered about participants. To protect participants' confidentiality, researchers commonly label records with code numbers, rather than names.

The most important safeguard built into the APA guidelines is the principle that the *participant decides* whether to take part in a research study (the autonomy principle of the Belmont Report). Each participant has the right to refuse to participate or to discontinue participating in the study at any time, even after having agreed to participate. The ethical researcher is bound to honor this right and can neither coerce participants nor prevent them from withdrawing. Data collection cannot begin until participants give their unequivocal consent. **Informed consent** is a critical basic safeguard. It means that researchers must provide participants with enough information about the research to enable them to make reasonable, informed decisions about their participation.

If the participants are children or have mental or emotional disorders, they may have difficulty in understanding the information or in giving consent. Children, being minors, cannot legally give consent at all. This puts even greater responsibility on the researcher to protect the well-being of research participants. Under these circumstances, one or more people are entrusted to protect the rights of the participants—a parent or school or hospital administrator, for example. They have legal and moral authority to give consent for children's research participation.

At the center of these issues is a genuine conflict of interests and a moral problem. On the one hand, society needs and demands scientific solutions to a large array of problems. On the other hand, searching for solutions may at times violate individuals' rights to privacy. To meet society's demands for new knowledge and for treatments for such physical illnesses as AIDS and cancer, to solve such social problems as poverty or aggression, or to improve education, scientists must be able to carry out scientific research, and this requires the cooperation of participants. It is in the long-term interest of society for people to contribute to scientific efforts. One way is by serving as research participants. Responsible people will consider donating their time, effort, and information as voluntary participants to promote scientific knowledge for its potential benefits to society, even when they do not personally benefit.

A moral dilemma arises because, while research can benefit society, it sometimes exposes participants to risks. In attempting to solve this dilemma, most research agencies, universities, and professional organizations have adopted the following position:

1. Scientific research offers potential benefits to society.
2. It is reasonable to expect that people will behave in a socially responsible manner and contribute to knowledge by voluntarily participating in research.
3. Participants have basic rights when they elect to participate in a research study, including rights to privacy and to protection from physical and psychological harm.
4. Researchers must give participants sufficient information on which to base their decisions about participating in the research project.
5. It is the researchers' responsibility to respect participants' rights and to protect participants from possible harm.

Institutional Review Boards. **Institutional Review Boards (IRBs)** consist of researchers' peers and members of the community at large. Universities, research institutes, hospitals, and school systems establish IRBs to review research proposals to see if they meet ethical guidelines. Every institution that receives federal funding is required to have an IRB. Usually an administrator from the institution appoints the members of the Institutional Review Board. Researchers are responsible for submitting their research proposals to their IRB for review and approval before gathering data.

When it functions well, an IRB is a helpful advisory group that expedites research, advises researchers, suggests improvements, and assists researchers in clarifying and solving potential ethical issues. Even well meaning researchers might make self-serving decisions in their research, blinding them to potential ethical problems. The IRB provides an external viewpoint to reduce this problem. *However, the final ethical responsibility always rests with the researcher.*

Researchers must judge their research in terms of its value to science, the risks it poses to participants, whether potential benefits outweigh those risks, and whether adequate safeguards have been included to minimize the risks (the beneficence principle of the Belmont Report). This process is called a **risk/benefit analysis**. Should risks to participants outweigh potential benefits, the ethical researcher must redesign or discontinue the project. Thus, if the research is badly designed or carried out so that its results are of little or no scientific value, then (1) the potential informational value will be minimal, and (2) participants will have wasted their time and perhaps been exposed to risks in a largely valueless endeavor. The researcher therefore has an ethical responsibility to develop well-designed projects and execute them with care.

TABLE 3.4 Ethical Checks before Beginning the Observations

1. Have we designed the proposed research adequately so that it will be of informational value?
2. Does the research pose risks of physical or psychological harm to participants by using deception/concealment, obtaining sensitive information, or using minors or others who cannot readily give consent?
3. If risks exist, does the research adequately control these risks by including such procedures as debriefing, removing or reducing risks of physical harm, or obtaining data anonymously? If that is not possible, will the study's procedures guarantee that information will remain confidential, and provide special safeguards for minors and participants who may have impairments?
4. Is there a provision for obtaining informed consent from every participant or, if participants cannot give it, from people legally designated to act for the benefit of the participant? Will the researcher provide sufficient information to potential participants so that they will be able to give their informed consent? Is there a clear agreement in writing (the informed consent form) between the researcher and potential participants? The informed consent should also make it clear that the participant is free to withdraw from the experiment at any time.
5. Will participants receive adequate feedback at the completion of the study, including a debriefing if deception is used?
6. Do I accept my full responsibility for the ethical and safe treatment of all participants?
7. Have I submitted the proposal to the appropriate Institutional Review Board for approval?
8. If animals are used, have I included all of the safeguards for the animal subjects?

Ethical Checks. Assume that you are designing a research project with human participants. Once you have an initial design, you need to perform the **ethical checks** listed in Table 3.4. These ethical checks will help you identify and correct most ethical problems. Ethical checks are a necessary final test before you submit your proposal to the Institutional Review Board.

Ethical principles in research continue to evolve as psychologists debate larger issues involving social values and scientific research (Kendler, 1993; Prilleltensky, 1994). The American Psychological Association appointed an ongoing task force to continually review and update ethical principles in research with human participants (Sales & Folkman, 2000). Nagy (2011) is an excellent source for more information on ethical principles and procedures.

Ethics and Diversity Issues in Research. An issue that is related to good research design and to ethical concerns is the diversity of participants. **Diversity** refers to how well the research sample represents various ethnic, cultural, age, and gender groups. In psychological and medical research, researchers have traditionally underrepresented women, children, and many ethnic groups. Consequently, much of our research information might not apply to everyone in our increasingly heterogeneous society. For example, early medical researchers tested the efficacy of some medical treatments almost exclusively on adult Caucasian males. Doctors then applied the treatments to patients in general, on the assumption that the treatment will work for everyone. However, treatments that are effective for Caucasian men might not be effective for women, children, or ethnic minorities, and therefore, these people may have been put at a medical disadvantage.

Early psychological research generally failed to represent population diversity, thus limiting its value and violating the justice principle of the Belmont Report. For example, we never know until we complete the research whether the same psychological findings apply to different ethnic groups. For this reason, funding agencies, such as the National Institutes of Health, now require that researchers actively recruit participants to reflect the diversity of the population, unless it is scientifically justified not to include them (National Institutes of Health, 2005). This means that men, women, children, and members of minority groups must be included. Researchers can exclude groups only if they provide a scientifically valid reason for doing so. However, practical difficulties in recruiting a broad sample of participants are not valid reasons for excluding such groups from the study.

Ethical Principles for Animal Research

Concern for the ethical and humane treatment of animals in research is just as important as concern for human participants. Many biomedical disciplines use animals in research, and large numbers of animals are studied each year (Olsson et al., 2007). Thousands of research psychologists use animals in research (Akins et al., 2005).

The major ethical concerns in animal research involve two issues. First, animals are captive participants and are not capable of providing informed consent. Second, research carried out on animals is generally more invasive than that carried out on humans, and animal participants often incur more serious risks than human participants. Therefore, researchers must assume more responsibility for ensuring that they treat the animals in their research humanely.

03:04

For years, professional and governmental organizations have followed ethical guidelines in the use of animal participants. The APA, for example, has had ongoing professional committees since 1925 to address issues of animal research. Its current set of guidelines is discussed and referenced on the Student Resource Website.

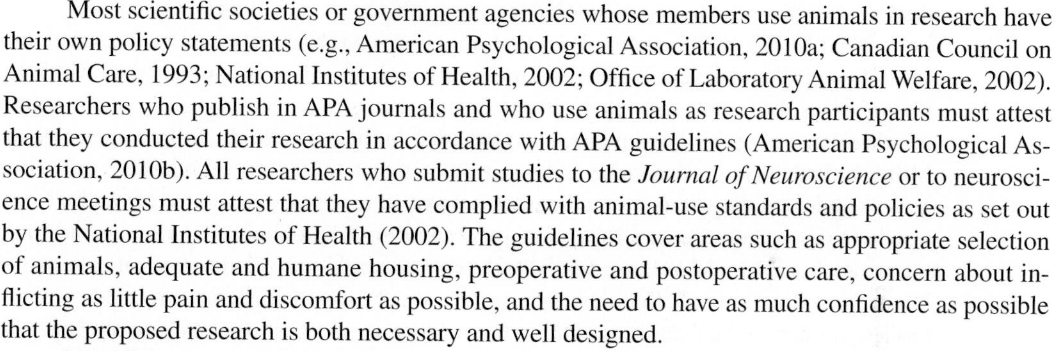

Most scientific societies or government agencies whose members use animals in research have their own policy statements (e.g., American Psychological Association, 2010a; Canadian Council on Animal Care, 1993; National Institutes of Health, 2002; Office of Laboratory Animal Welfare, 2002). Researchers who publish in APA journals and who use animals as research participants must attest that they conducted their research in accordance with APA guidelines (American Psychological Association, 2010b). All researchers who submit studies to the *Journal of Neuroscience* or to neuroscience meetings must attest that they have complied with animal-use standards and policies as set out by the National Institutes of Health (2002). The guidelines cover areas such as appropriate selection of animals, adequate and humane housing, preoperative and postoperative care, concern about inflicting as little pain and discomfort as possible, and the need to have as much confidence as possible that the proposed research is both necessary and well designed.

In addition to the policies demanded by various professional groups, animal research is also constrained by other regulations. Every animal laboratory in the United States, Canada, and Mexico must abide by applicable federal, state, and local laws governing the use and care of animals. In the United States, all laboratories that receive federal funds must have a **Laboratory Animal Care Committee**, which serves the same function as the IRB does for human research. These committees include veterinarians and nonprofessional community representatives, as well as the researcher's professional colleagues. They review and must approve all proposed animal-care-and-use procedures, focusing not only on the specifics of humane care for the animals, but also on the relevance of the proposed research to human and animal health, to the advancement of knowledge, and to society.

Animal researchers must proceed in much the same way as those using human participants. They must thoroughly review the ethical animal-use issues raised by their planned research, must assume full responsibility for the ethical conduct of the research, and must submit the research plan to their local Laboratory Care Committee for evaluation and approval.

Researchers use an estimated 22 million animals each year in the United States, representing a slight decline over the past two decades. Animal use in research has remained constant in Canada over the same period. It has declined in the United Kingdom and some European countries, but the decline in Europe has slowed in recent years (European Science Foundation, 2001).

More than half a century ago, Russell and Birch (1959) argued for alternatives to using live animals in research. An award in their name is now presented to scientists who make significant contributions to reducing live animal research (HSUS, 2011). Scientists continue working to reduce the number of live animals used in research and in training researchers and practitioners. Some institutions involved in this effort are the Johns Hopkins Center for Alternatives to Animal Testing, the Center for Animal Alternatives at the University of California at Davis, the American Veterinary Society, and Psychologists for the Ethical Treatment of Animals. Reductions are being accomplished by sharpening the design of experiments so that fewer animals are needed, using cells cultured in laboratories rather than live animals, substituting mathematical models, computer simulation, and realistic plastic models. However, it is difficult to develop alternatives for behavioral studies because researchers require functioning animals to study behavior and the factors affecting behavior. Nevertheless, many psychologists continue seeking to improve the ethics of animal experimentation (e.g., Blache, Martin, & Maloney 2008; Vogel, 2010).

Animal research has been critically important in medicine. It has facilitated the development of vaccinations against infectious diseases, treatments such as kidney dialysis, organ transplants, and open-heart and heart-valve replacement surgeries, and drug treatments for hypertension and diabetes (Botting & Morrison, 1997; Morrison, 2001).

Neal Miller (1985) pointed out that animal research has also led to the development of successful medical and psychological treatments for such disorders as enuresis (bed wetting), encopresis (losing control of one's bowels during sleep), scoliosis (a severe curvature of the spine), anorexia, life-threatening vomiting in infants, and retraining in the use of limbs following accidents or surgery. Miller and others (e.g., Watanabe, 2007) have noted that animal research has not only contributed to a greater understanding of disease processes, improved services, and reduced risks for humans, but has also led to more humane care for animals and solutions to problems that animals face in natural environments. For example, behavioral research on taste aversion has led to humane alternatives to shooting or poisoning animals that destroy crops or attack livestock. Behavioral and biological research has led to improved habitat preservation for wildlife, to successful reintroductions of Atlantic salmon and other fish to areas where commercial fishing and habitat destruction had killed them off, and to successful treatment for, and vaccination against, many diseases of pets, livestock, and zoo animals.

Concern for humane and ethical treatment of animals in research is legitimate, and few researchers deny its importance. The *Journal of Applied Animal Welfare Science* presents issues and developments in the humane care of animals in research, training, and society in general. Discussions of animal research are frequent in psychological journals. For example, the *American Psychologist* published a series of five articles in 1997 addressing important issues in animal research. There are also several influential books on the ethics of animal research (e.g., Akins et al., 2005). Even animal researchers have challenged past and current practices. Ulrich (1991), for example, argued that misuse and overuse of animals has occurred in research, and that scientists, like everyone else, have been thoughtlessly guilty of our culture's propensity to consume anything, without regard to ecological issues. Ulrich, an animal researcher for many years, writes thoughtfully about scientists' responsibilities to other life forms and the necessity to consider seriously the ethical issues involved in animal research. The concern for animal welfare has also been extended to farm animals, with many psychologists now engaged in research to determine the most humane way to raise animals for food (von Borell & Veissier, 2007).

Research with animals has made enormous contributions to the scientific understanding of nature. As with all research, scientists must balance the costs, in terms of risks to the participants, against the potential benefits to society (Carroll & Overmier, 2001).

Quick-Check Review 3.4: Ethical Principles

1. What is informed consent? How is it obtained, and why is it important?
2. What are Institutional Review Boards? What do they do?
3. What are the major ethical principles applicable to research with animals?
4. What is meant by diversity issues in research?

SUMMARY

- All research involves studying the relationships among variables.
- The nature of the question helps to determine the research procedures.
- Refining the initial question identifies the major variables and helps to determine procedures.
- Psychological research can be classified as basic, applied, or translational research.
- New research ideas can be generated heuristically or systematically.
- The experimenter manipulates the independent variable and measures the dependent variable.
- Validity is critical in research; researchers enhance validity by controlling extraneous variables.
- Ethical researchers must address the issues of informed consent, confidentiality, deception/concealment, debriefing, and diversity in their research with human participants.
- Animal researchers must follow detailed guidelines for the treatment of animals in research.

Putting It into Practice

Can we really find research questions anywhere? You can if you look for them and are open to them. Take a few minutes each day and look around. Perhaps you are sitting in the library studying. Find things of interest to you, and then speculate about why they are the way they are. For example, some people study at open tables while others study in enclosed study carrels. Is one better than the other for studying? Do individual differences determine which type of study environment is optimal for each person? What are the best ways to study?

With a little practice, you will discover that important and interesting questions really are all around us. Once you have learned to see these questions, start to look at them the way a scientist would. Identify the variables you might wish to study, and begin to speculate how those variables relate to one another. If you put a little energy into this assignment, you will find it eye opening and enjoyable. You will rekindle some of the enthusiastic curiosity that you had as a child, and you will begin to realize what it is that drives scientists. It will also make this course easier and more enjoyable.

EXERCISES

3.1. Define the following key terms. Be sure that you understand them. They are discussed in the chapter and defined in the glossary.

heuristic influence
systematic influence
applied research
basic research
fundamental research
pure research
translational research
variable
behavioral variable
stimulus variables
organismic variables
subject variables
observed organismic variables
response-inferred organismic variables
independent variables
dependent variables
manipulated independent variables
nonmanipulated independent variables
classification variable
causal relationship
extraneous variables
constant
controls
Belmont Report
beneficence
autonomy
justice
deception
concealment
debriefing
invasion of privacy
confidentiality
informed consent
Institutional Review Board (IRB)
risk/benefit analysis
ethical checks
diversity
Laboratory Animal Care Committee

3.2. Create five research questions. For each one, identify the major variables involved, the type of variable (stimulus, behavioral, organismic, independent, etc.), and whether the research question represents basic or applied research.

3.3. Identify ethical issues that must be addressed in the research questions you developed in the previous question.

3.4. Think of several examples of variables that could be independent variables in one study and dependent variables in another.

3.5. Create several research situations in which you would use deception. For each one, (a) explain why the deception is needed, and (b) how you would deal with the ethical issues raised by the deception.

3.6. Suppose your Institutional Review Board rejects your research proposal as ethically unacceptable because the design is so flawed that the information from the study would be meaningless. Why is this criticism an ethical issue and not just a design problem?

3.7. Some research situations follow. What are the potential ethical problems in each? Indicate what safeguards you would use.

a. A researcher is going to test third- and fourth-graders to compare boys' and girls' interest in reading.
b. A researcher is studying small-group interactions in adults as participants. The participants, observed in groups of five people, do not know that three of the five members of their group are actually assistants of the researcher and that those assistants are following detailed scripts during the small-group meeting.
c. A researcher wants to examine the files on hospitalized patients with serious depression to obtain basic information about their families.

3.8. Here's a discussion question: Does industry have a responsibility to support basic research, even when there is no obvious profit to be gained?

CHAPTER FOUR

DATA AND THE NATURE OF MEASUREMENT

Since the measuring device has been constructed by the observer ...
we have to remember that what we observe is not nature in itself
but nature exposed to our method of questioning.

—Werner Karl Heisenberg, *Physics and Philosophy,* 1958

WEB RESOURCE MATERIAL

The previous chapter introduced the ideas that observation is the pivotal phase in the research process, that every research project measures and/or manipulates variables, and that the quality of research depends on how well the researcher handles those challenges. In this chapter, you will learn about the measurement process itself.

MEASUREMENT

Every research project includes one or more variables that the researcher manipulates and/or measures. As you learned in Chapter 3, a variable is any characteristic that can take more than one form or value, and any event can become a research variable. Variables such as anxiety and memory are complex events that differ (i.e., vary) from one participant and/or condition to another. If the events of interest are static, with no variation, they cannot serve as research variables. Simply put, *a variable must vary.*

The major task in measurement is to represent the research variables numerically, that is, to assign numbers that represent values of the variable. The measurements for each participant constitute the data, which will later be analyzed and interpreted. You might be puzzled initially about what statistical procedures to use. As you will see in Appendix D, the choice of statistical analyses depends largely on how the dependent variables are measured. In fact, you will learn later that choosing appropriate statistical procedures is relatively easy once you have determined the measurement procedures.

In assigning numbers to a variable, we work with two sets of information: the abstract number system and the variable that we wish to measure. Our task is to bring the two systems together so that the numbers accurately represent the variable. That can become complicated because the two systems do not necessarily function according to the same rules. While the abstract number system has specific and well-defined rules, variables in science are not always so well defined, and they seldom function according to the same clear rules as the abstract number system. Because the two systems do not always match, we must determine how closely the variable we are measuring matches the properties of the abstract number system. That determination is necessary in order to select appropriate statistical methods.

The **properties of the abstract number system** follow:

- **Identity:** Each number has a particular meaning.
- **Magnitude:** Numbers have an inherent order from smaller to larger.
- **Equal intervals:** The difference between units is the same anywhere on the scale.
- **True zero:** A nonarbitrary point indicating a zero level of the variable being measured.

Because of these properties, we can add, subtract, multiply, and divide numbers. However, with some psychological variables, such as intelligence, the number system and the variable do not match exactly. The number system has a true zero point, but the psychological variable of intelligence does not. Zero on an intelligence test is an arbitrary number. There is no living person with zero intelligence. In the abstract number system, 100 is twice as much as 50, but because the psychological variable of intelligence has no zero point, we cannot say that an intelligence test score of 100 shows twice the intelligence as a score of 50.

Let's look at another example. Suppose that you were doing a study of taste preferences. You give your participants samples of drinks, and you ask them to taste and rank the drinks according to which one they liked the most, which they liked second best, which one third, and so on. You assign numbers (1, 2, 3, etc.) to the ranked preferences, with number 1 as the most preferred. Would the difference in preference between 1 and 2 be the same as that between 2 and 3? That is, would this scale have equal intervals?

Suppose, for example, that the drinks were Coke®, Pepsi®, and vinegar. Now, unless they have strange tastes, your participants' rankings would probably be either 1-2-3 or 2-1-3 for Coke, Pepsi, and vinegar, respectively. Clearly, the difference in preference between Coke and Pepsi is much smaller than that between either of those drinks and vinegar, even though the difference in rank orderings is the same. The differences between rank orderings will not necessarily be equal at all points on the scale. Furthermore, it makes no sense to say that the drink ranked 1 is three times as preferred as the drink ranked 3.

In these two examples, the characteristics of the variables do not match the characteristics (properties) of the number system, and so you are limited in the type of mathematical operations that you can perform on the data. In some cases, however, the variable matches the number system nicely. For example, suppose that an educational psychologist wanted to study how many questions children ask of their teacher. The psychologist counts each question and records the total number of questions asked by each child in each school day. Table 4.1 shows sample data for 5 days of observation for 10 children. Because of the nature of the data, all mathematical operations are applicable. We can add the number of daily questions for each child and arrive at each child's total number of questions for the week. If you look across each row in Table 4.1 at the totals for each child, you will see that child 02 asked only 2 questions, whereas child 04 asked 22. We can subtract the totals or divide one by the other and report that, in this particular week, child 04 asked 20 more questions (22 – 2) or 11 times (22 ÷ 2) as many questions as child 02. We can also divide the total for the week by the number of children and report the average number of questions per child for the week. In summary, this number-of-questions variable shows a magnitude in the same direction as the number system, so 22 responses is more than 20 responses. It also has equal intervals, so the difference in response between 4 and 6 is the same as the difference between 10 and 12. Finally, it has a true zero point, which means that a child with a score of zero asked no questions during the

TABLE 4.1 Example of Measurement

We listed the numbers of questions asked in class by 10 students over 5 days.

STUDENT	DAYS					
ID	Mon	Tues	Wed	Thurs	Fri	TOTAL
01	1	2	1	1	1	6
02	0	0	1	0	1	2
03	4	2	3	3	3	15
04	6	4	5	3	4	22
05	1	3	1	0	2	7
06	2	0	2	1	0	5
07	2	3	1	2	2	10
08	2	0	1	1	0	4
09	1	1	0	2	1	5
10	4	3	5	3	3	18
Totals	23	18	20	16	17	94

observation period. Because this variable closely matches the characteristics of the number system, all mathematical operations on the data are legitimate: addition, subtraction, multiplication, and division. This allows researchers to use powerful statistical tests—statistics that the researcher could use only when dependent variables are well matched with the real number system.

Accurate measurement is critical in science and technology. Even an elementary mistake can invalidate an entire project, as illustrated in the infamous case discussed in the Cost of Neglect 4.1.

THE COST OF NEGLECT 4.1: MISSING MARS

It did not really miss Mars. Indeed, NASA's Mars Climate Orbiter most definitely hit the red planet, or at least its atmosphere, with enough force and heat to destroy itself and cost taxpayers more than $125 million. Its mission was to orbit Mars as the first interplanetary weather satellite and serve as a radio relay system for a second vehicle, the Mars Polar Lander, which was scheduled to touch down 3 months later to explore the Martian surface.

What went wrong? After all, this was "rocket science," in which technological precision is routine. It appears that the engineers made an elementary mistake in measurement. The two teams working on this Mars mission, the Jet Propulsion Laboratory in Pasadena and Lockheed Martin Astronautics in Denver, *had used two different units of measurement*. The Denver group based its calculations for the propulsion system on pounds of force, while the Pasadena group based its calculations on the metric system (Stephenson, 1999). The result was that information based on two different measurement systems conflicted, causing navigational errors and sending the orbiter out of control into the Martian atmosphere, where it burned up.

A most elementary error had been committed. The engineers had failed to convert one measurement system to the other and to use consistent measurement units for feeding data into the navigational systems. There is a moral to this sad tale: *Make sure you have your measurements in order before "launching" your research!*

Quick-Check Review 4.1: Measurement

1. What is measurement?
2. Why is accurate measurement so critical?
3. What are the important properties of the abstract number system?

SCALES OF MEASUREMENT

Some variables used in psychological research closely match the number system, whereas others do not. To identify the closeness of match, Stevens (1946, 1957) classified variables into four levels or **scales of measurement**.[i] The scales, arranged from the least to the most closely matched with the number system, are nominal, ordinal, interval, and ratio scales. Coombs et al. (1954) and Roberts (1984) provide more detailed discussions of these scales of measurement. We have also included several examples of each scale of measurement on the Student Resource Website.

04:01

[i]Some people disagree with Stevens, challenging his distinction between scales of measurement on mathematical grounds (Gaito, 1980; Michell, 1986). Although we are sympathetic to these arguments, we believe that Stevens' approach is still a useful teaching and organizational tool for a textbook at this level.

Nominal Scales

Nominal scales are at the lowest level of measurement; they do not match the number system well. Nominal scales are "naming scales," and their only property is identity. Such dependent variables as place of birth (Chicago, Toronto, Tokyo, Nyack, Chippewa Falls), brand name choice (Ford, Honda, Volvo), political affiliation (Democrat, Republican, Socialist, Green Party, Independent), and diagnostic category (panic disorder, schizophrenia, bipolar disorder) are nominal scales of measurement. The differences between the categories of nominal scales are qualitative and not quantitative.

In nominal scales, we can assign numbers to represent different categories. For example, we could label Chicago as 1, Toronto as 2, Tokyo as 3, Nyack as 4, and Chippewa Falls as 5, but the numbers are only arbitrary labels for the categories. Except for identity, these numbers have none of the properties of the number system, and therefore, we cannot meaningfully add, subtract, multiply, or divide them. Is Chicago, with its assigned number of 1, to be understood as only one-fifth of Chippewa Falls, with its assigned number of 5? Nominal scales have no zero point, cannot be ordered low to high, and make no assumption about equal units of measurement. In fact, they are not numbers at all, at least not in the sense that we usually think of numbers. Nominal scales classify or categorize participants. With nominal scales, we count the frequency of participants in each category. We call the data from nominal scales **nominal data** or **categorical data**.

Ordinal Scales

Ordinal scales have the property of magnitude as well as identity. They measure a variable in order of magnitude, with larger numbers representing more of the variable than smaller numbers. How much more is unclear in an ordinal scale. For example, using socioeconomic class as a variable, we could categorize participants as belonging to the lower, middle, or upper socioeconomic class. There is a clear underlying concept here of order of magnitude, from low to high. Other examples of ordinal scales are measurements by rankings, such as a student's academic standing in class, or measurements by ranked categories, such as grades of A, B, C, D, or F. Data measured on ordinal scales are called **ordered data**.

Ordinal scales give the relative order of magnitude, but they do not provide information about the differences between categories or ranks. Student ranks indicate which student is first, second, and so on, but we cannot use the ranks to determine how much each student differs from the next. That is, the numbers provide information about relative position, but not about the intervals between ranks. The difference in academic achievement between students ranked 1 and 2 might be very small (or large) compared with the difference between students ranked 12 and 13.

As illustrated in the example of ranking Coke, Pepsi, and vinegar on taste preference, the intervals in ordinal scaling are not necessarily equal. In fact, we usually assume that they are unequal. Therefore, it is inappropriate to analyze ordered data with statistical procedures, that implicitly require equal intervals of measurement.

Interval Scales

When the measurements convey information about both the order and the distance between values, we have interval scaling. **Interval scales** have the properties of ordinal scales in addition to equal intervals between consecutive values on the scale. Thus, interval scales come close to matching the number system, but still do not have a true zero point.

The most commonly used example of an interval scale is the measurement of temperature on either the Fahrenheit or the Celsius scale. The units of the thermometer are at equal intervals representing equal volumes of mercury. Therefore, 90° is hotter than 45°, and the difference in temperature between 60° and 70° is the same as the difference between 30° and 40°. However, the zero point on this scale is arbitrary and not a true zero point; that is, a temperature of 0° does not indicate a total absence of heat.

We measure most variables in psychology on interval scales or near-interval scales, including IQ test scores, neuroticism scores, and attitude measures. With an IQ test, for example, we can report that the measured IQ difference between two people with IQs of 60 and 120 is 60 IQ points. However, because there is no true zero point on the IQ scale, we cannot say that the second person is twice as smart as the first.

Most test scores are not true interval scales, but by convention, we treat them as interval scales, because they are closer to being interval scales than ordinal scales. The scales of measurement, much like the levels of constraint, are overlapping rather than discrete.

We refer to data measured on interval or ratio scales as **score data**.

Ratio Scales

Ratio scales provide the highest level of measurement and are the scientist's "measurement ideal" (Kerlinger & Lee, 2000). Ratio scales have all the properties of the preceding scales (identity, magnitude, and equal intervals) as well as a true zero point. Ratio scales provide the best match to the number system, which means that all mathematical operations are possible on ratio scales. Such physical dimensions as weight, distance, length, volume, number of responses, and time are measured on ratio scales.

We call them ratio scales because dividing a point on the scale by another point on the scale (taking a ratio of values) gives a legitimate and meaningful value. For example, a person who runs 10 miles is running twice as far as a person who runs 5 miles and 5 times as far as someone who runs 2 miles. The true zero point and equal intervals give the ratio scale this property.

Data measured on either interval or ratio scales are called score data. Although we can measure many variables in psychology on ratio scales, some can be measured only on nominal, ordinal, or interval scales.

04:02

Table 4.2 summarizes the characteristics of the various scales of measurement and gives examples. The Student Resource Website provides an interactive flowchart that will help you to decide what statistical procedures to use based on the scale of measurement for your variables and the questions you want to ask.

Quick-Check Review 4.2: Scales of Measurement

1. List and define the four scales of measurement.
2. What type of data does each scale produce?
3. What are the properties of each scale of measurement?
4. What is the concept of true zero? What is its importance in measurement?

TABLE 4.2 Some Aspects of Scales of Measurement

	LEVELS OF MEASUREMENT			
	Nominal	**Ordinal**	**Interval**	**Ratio**
Examples	Diagnostic categories; brand names; political or religious affiliation	Socioeconomic class; ranks	Test scores; personality and attitude scales	Weight; length; reaction time; number of responses
Properties	Identity	Identity; magnitude	Identity; magnitude; equal intervals	Identity; magnitude; equal intervals; true zero point
Mathematical Operations	None	Rank order	Add; subtract	Add; subtract; multiply; divide
Type of Data	Nominal	Ordered	Score	Score

Note: We could give many more examples of each scale.

MEASURING AND MANIPULATING VARIABLES

Now that you have learned about the different types of variables, scales of measurement, and types of data, you can learn how to measure and manipulate variables. A simple example involving the effects of food intake on weight will illustrate several aspects of measurement. Food intake is the independent variable (the variable we manipulate in the study). The question is this: What effect does manipulation of food intake (the independent variable) have on participants' weight (the dependent variable)? The hypothesis is that weight fluctuations will depend on manipulations of food intake.

Measurement Error

Consider measuring your weight by standing on a standard scale. Leaning against the wall will distort the measurement; wearing heavy boots one time and sandals the next will yield different weights. Such factors are sources of **measurement error**. Measurement error distorts the scores so that the observations do not accurately reflect reality.

Another source of measurement error is **response-set bias**—the tendency to respond in specific ways regardless of the situation or your experiences. A powerful response-set bias is **social desirability**—the tendency to respond in a socially acceptable manner. For example, suppose that you were studying the relationship between level of food intake and weight in a weight-loss program. Have you ever cheated when you were on a diet? If you did, would you always be willing to admit it? There is a good chance that you would not admit it, because you would find it embarrassing. In this case, some participants might underreport their food intake, because they do not want to admit to the socially undesirable behavior of cheating on a diet. This social desirability response set would affect the validity of the measurement and create measurement error.

Minimizing measurement error is critical. The best way to accomplish this is by developing a well-thought-out operational definition of the measurement procedure and by diligently using the operational definition in the research.

Operational Definitions

Here you are, weighing yourself in the morning. By stepping on the scale and reading the numbers, you are operationally defining the concept of weight. Think of it this way: concepts like weight, gravity, intelligence, or aggression are ideas—abstract, theoretical statements that exist on an intellectual level. To carry out empirical research on such concepts, we need to translate them from the abstract level to a concrete level in order to manipulate and/or measure them. We do that by developing operational definitions. An **operational definition** is a definition of a variable in terms of the procedures used to measure and/or manipulate it (Kerlinger & Lee, 2000). When you step on that scale that records weight in pounds or kilograms you have created an operational definition of your weight. You have translated the abstract concept of weight into an empirical event. This is the core of an operational definition; it brings theoretical abstractions to an empirical level, and describes exactly how we will measure the theoretical abstraction. An operational definition is like a recipe that specifies exactly how to measure and/or manipulate the variables in a study. All research requires operational definitions. Even for simple measures like weight, every step of the measurement procedure should be planned carefully to avoid confusion and sloppiness in running the study.

The best ways to measure specific variables can usually be found by examining the research literature. For example, we know from past research that food intake is measured in terms of calories and foods differ in their levels of calories. By knowing the caloric value of each type of food and the amount of food consumed, we can compute the total calorie intake. We can be reasonably sure that this approach to measuring food intake is effective, because it is based on considerable research and theory that is available in the literature.

Researchers often aim to create a particular response in participants, such as increasing their motivation or anxiety, factors that are within the participants and are therefore not directly observable. However, we can study them by operationally defining a set of procedures for manipulating them. In a study discussed earlier, we taught children with autism how to relax to see if relaxation would reduce disruptive behavior. We operationally defined this manipulation as follows:

> A corner of the room was labeled the "quiet spot" and used exclusively for relaxation training. Lights were dimmed, and the children were asked to lie down on a mat. The therapist said in a soft, calm voice, "Close your eyes; nice and comfortable; that's it. Breathe slow and easy; good job; nice and easy." She continued the soothing instructions, and gave immediate verbal reinforcement for all approximations of relaxed behavior.
>
> The first training session lasted less than one minute, and increased daily to a criterion of five consecutive minutes of relaxation for 12 consecutive sessions. Relaxation involved the child being quiet, without talking or squirming, and with no perceptible rigidity or muscle tension. (paraphrased from Graziano, 1974, p. 170).

This operational definition describes the relaxation procedures, giving a clear set of instructions to define the independent variable relaxation training. A good operational definition defines procedures so that other researchers can replicate them by following the description.

The dependent variable, disruptive behavior, was operationally defined as follows:

> Disruptive behavior is any observed, sudden change in a child's behavior from calm, quiet, and appropriate behavior to explosive behavior, including attacks on people, throwing objects, throwing oneself into walls or the floor, self-abuse such as head-banging and biting, which is carried out in a

wild "frenzied" manner. Each incident will be considered to have ended when the child has returned to the previous level of calm, appropriate behavior for at least three consecutive minutes.

Frequency: Each occurrence of disruptive behavior is recorded as a single event. The frequency score per child is the total number of disruptive behaviors.

Duration: The observer times each disruptive event with a stopwatch from the observed beginning to its end.

Intensity: The observer rates the peak intensity of each disruptive event on a three-point scale (low, moderate, high) immediately after the event is over.

Developing an operational definition involves drawing on past research, as well as making arbitrary decisions about how best to measure a variable from both a theoretical and a practical sense. For example, the decision to set the relaxation criterion at 5 consecutive minutes for 12 consecutive sessions is an arbitrary, but reasonable, criterion. The instructions to use a "soft, gentle, calm, voice" leave room for interpretation by others who may want to replicate the study, but still provide a clear idea of how to conduct the relaxation session.

Operational definitions vary in constraint. Under some conditions, it is difficult to create precise operational definitions. Under other conditions, we can operationally define variables precisely. In any study, we need to operationally define the independent and dependent variables as clearly and precisely as possible.

We can operationally define most concepts in several ways (see Table 4.3). Each definition can lead to different procedures and thus to different research projects. Suppose that you are studying how

TABLE 4.3 Examples of Operational Definitions

Researchers should define independent and dependent variables in terms of how they will measure and/or manipulate them. A variable can be operationally defined in different ways, and different operational definitions of the same concept lead to different procedures and thus to different studies. Several examples follow.

VARIABLE	OPERATIONAL DEFINITION
Anxiety	1. A physiological measure, such as heart rate or palmar sweating 2. A self-report of anxiety level 3. Behavioral observation of avoidance behavior
Aggression in children	1. Ratings of aggressive behavior made by a child's teacher 2. Direct observation during play periods of the number of times a child hits, pushes, or forcibly takes toys from other children 3. A child's rate of hitting a punching doll in an experimental situation 4. The number of acts of aggression in stories created by participants in response to pictures
Obesity	1. The pinch test, a measure of fat folds at the waist 2. The volume of water displaced by a submerged participant 3. Comparison of a participant's height-weight ratio against standard charts
Intelligence	1. Score on a standardized IQ test 2. Judgment by others of a person's ability to solve problems 3. Number of school grades completed before dropping out of school

hunger affects mood. You randomly assign participants to three groups (high hunger, moderate hunger, low hunger) and measure their moods. You must operationally define two variables: the independent variable, hunger, and the dependent variable, mood. You can operationally define each in several ways. Hunger can be defined (1) as the number of hours since the previous meal, (2) as the number of calories consumed when food is made available, (3) as physiological measures associated with hunger, or (4) as a score on a questionnaire about how hungry the participant reports feeling. Likewise, you can operationally define mood in several ways. (Think about how you might measure mood.)

04:03 The Student Resource Website includes many examples of operational definitions in psychological research.

There are advantages to having several operational definitions for each concept:

- By defining the concept in different ways (e.g., physiologically, behaviorally, or cognitively), different aspects of a complex phenomenon can be studied.
- When many studies using different operational definitions produce a common finding, we have **convergent validity**—multiple lines of evidence supporting the same conclusion. This use of multiple measures of a single concept is called the **multimethod approach**. Researchers often employ this multimethod approach to give them more confidence in the outcome of studies.
- By examining the literature, any researcher can select and use operational definitions that have been useful in prior research.

Sometimes when we measure variables in divergent ways, we do not find the convergent validity that we expect, but what we do find often gives us a greater appreciation for the complexity of a psychological construct. Take anxiety, for example. We all have a good idea of what anxiety is and could probably name several ways in which we could measure it. Anxiety is a feeling that we could report; it involves such physiological changes as an increased heart rate or sweaty palms; and it drives certain behavior, such as withdrawing from the anxiety-provoking situation. Peter Lang (1985) has shown that these three approaches to measuring anxiety reflect different aspects of anxiety. People can show the physiological arousal of anxiety without being aware of it, or they can be very aware of their anxiety and still not withdraw from the anxiety-provoking situation. Understanding that anxiety is not a simple concept and that each of these possible measures (self-report, physiological, or behavioral) taps a different aspect of anxiety has improved the understanding of anxiety and anxiety disorders, and led to improvements in the treatment of anxiety problems (Barlow, 2002).

Developing operational definitions is one of the systematic elements that make up the overall process of a research project. The researcher narrows a broad concept into a detailed and precise statement of exactly how a variable is to be measured and/or manipulated. These are critical steps in research, and they require knowledge of the literature and experience with the process of specifying operations.

Quick-Check Review 4.3: Measuring and Manipulating Variables

1. What is the best way to reduce measurement error in research?
2. How do operational definitions transform theoretical concepts into concrete events?
3. What is social desirability bias in research? How might it affect research?
4. Explain the concept of convergent validity. What is its importance?

EVALUATING MEASURES

Developing measures by operationally defining variables is a critical first step. We must also evaluate the quality of the measures. Such evaluations should be a routine part of any study that uses new operational definitions. Evaluating the quality of measures and publishing these findings gives other researchers information about new measures for their research projects. This section will discuss three important factors in such evaluations: reliability, effective range, and validity.

Reliability

Good measures give consistent results (the **reliability** of the measure) regardless of who does the measuring. In measuring weight, for example, a bathroom scale is reliable if it always gives the same reading when weighing the same object, assuming that the object has not changed in weight. There are three types of reliability: interrater reliability, test-retest reliability, and internal consistency reliability.

Interrater Reliability. If a measure involves behavior ratings made by observers, there should be at least two independent observers to rate the same sample of behavior. To rate independently, both raters must be **blind** to (unaware of) each other's ratings. This type of reliability is **interrater reliability**. If two raters always agree with one another, then the interrater reliability is perfect. If their ratings are unrelated to one another, then the interrater reliability is zero. The actual level of reliability is likely to be somewhere in between. The concept of interrater reliability is illustrated in Figure 4.1. Researchers typically use a correlation coefficient (discussed in Chapter 5) to quantify the degree of reliability, although there are more sophisticated indices available (see Nunnally & Bernstein, 1994; Raykov & Marcoulides, 2010).

Test-Retest Reliability. Variables that remain stable over time should produce similar scores if we test participants at two different times (**test-retest reliability**). If you change the labels in Figure 4.1 from "rater 1" and "rater 2" to "time 1" and "time 2," you will have a graphical representation of test-retest reliability. Test-retest reliability is usually quantified with a correlation coefficient and is

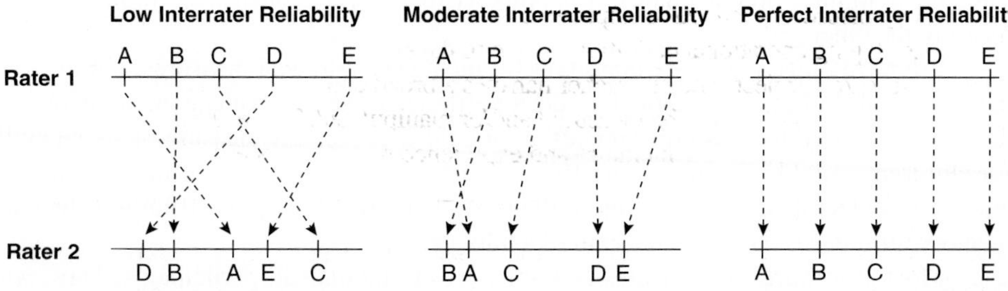

FIGURE 4.1 Interrater Reliability. This illustration has two raters (1 and 2) and five participants (A, B, C, D, and E). Each horizontal line represents the scale that each rater used to rate the participants. If the interrater reliability is perfect, the raters are in perfect agreement on the scores for each participant, as shown in the rightmost figure. The more the raters disagree on scores for participants, the lower the interrater reliability.

reported with both the observed correlation and the length of time between testings. For example, you might report, "The test-retest reliability for the measure over 10 weeks was .74."

Internal Consistency Reliability. The third type of reliability, **internal consistency reliability**, is used when several observations are made to obtain a score for each participant—for example, if participants complete a test with several items or if the researcher makes several independent observations of their behavior. Internal consistency reliability is high if each item or behavioral observation correlates with the other observations, which will occur if all the items are measuring the same thing. An internally consistent scale measures one construct with several independent observations.

Discussing all details of internal consistency reliability is beyond the scope of this book, but we want to mention one principle. Generally, *the more observations we make to obtain a score, such as a classroom test or behavioral observations, the greater will be the internal consistency reliability of the score*. A classroom test with many questions covering all the different topics in the course should give consistent indications of how much students know. Similarly, multiple observations of behavior should give consistent indications of behavioral tendencies. Using only one or two questions or behavioral observations will not provide the same level of consistency.

Why is measurement reliability so critical in research? The reason is simple; if the measures are unreliable, the study cannot produce useful information. The factors that contribute to reliability include (1) the precision and clarity of the operational definition of the construct, (2) the care with which the researcher follows the operational definition, and (3) the number of independent observations on which the score is based (Anastasi & Urbina, 1997; Raulin & Lilienfeld, 2009).

04:04

The Student Resource Website explains how you measure each of the different types of reliability.

Effective Range

Another factor in measuring variables is the **effective range** of the scale. If we are interested in weight changes in people, a normal bathroom scale will usually have sufficient range. However, weighing very large or very small things, such as elephants or mice, would require scales that could accurately measure weight in whatever range is necessary. Although the concept of weight is the same for both mice and elephants, it is unlikely that a scale constructed to measure one can also measure the other.

Effective range issues are important for most psychological measures. For example, a test of mathematical skill sensitive enough to detect differences among college math majors would be too difficult to be used to detect differences among third-graders. A measure of social skills designed for children would be inappropriate for use with adults. A measure of memory ability sensitive enough to detect differences among college students would be too difficult to be used to detect memory differences among brain-injured adults.

Most procedures or measures lack the range to include all participants. Thus, when you design or select measures for your research, keep in mind who the participants will be. This will guide you to measures that have an appropriate effective range for that group.

A related problem is **scale attenuation effects**. "Attenuation" refers to restricting the range of a scale. Using a measure with a restricted range—that is, not ranging high enough, low enough, or both—can result in data that show participants bunched near the top or bottom of the scale. For example, suppose that you are conducting a study on changing college students' attitudes toward tobacco use. You administer your pretest of attitudes and find that virtually all participants have highly negative views toward tobacco use. Suppose that you then conduct the attitude change intervention and take post-intervention measures of attitudes. The posttest results cannot possibly show much change toward greater negative attitudes, even if the intervention is effective. Why? Because the participants were already at the top of the scale before the intervention; they have no room to show change toward still higher scores. This type of scale attenuation is a **ceiling effect**.

A scale may also have a restricted lower range, thus creating a possible **floor effect**, in which most participants tend to score near the bottom of the scale only because the scale does not allow a sufficiently low range. A floor effect would occur if an instructor gave an examination that was too difficult for the class and almost all students scored low. If the scale had a greater lower range, the students' scores would probably be more spread out, rather than bunched at the bottom of the scale.

Figure 4.2 illustrates ceiling and floor effects. Figure 4.2(a) graphs the true weights of each of 10 people. Figures 4.2(b) and 4.2(c) illustrate what would happen if there were a ceiling or floor effect, respectively. A ceiling effect might occur if the scale read weights up to only 200 pounds. A floor effect might occur if the needle stuck so that it never read below 120 pounds. Note that both floor and ceiling effects compress the scores and that the scores for people who are in reality outside the effective range are not accurate.

Scale attenuation effects restrict the range of possible scores for participants' responses; that is, they reduce the potential variability of the data. As we will discuss in Chapter 10, restricting variability results in serious errors. Having sufficient variability is essential in research.

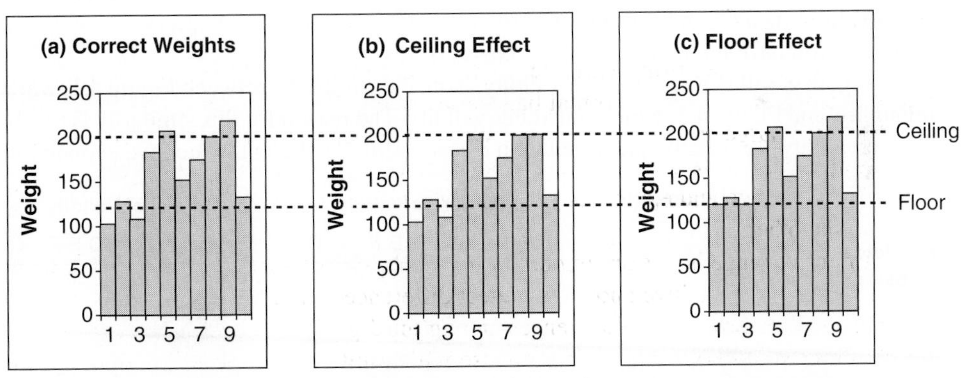

FIGURE 4.2 Floor and Ceiling Effects. Floor and ceiling effects distort the data by not measuring the full range of a variable. Panel (b) shows the impact of a ceiling effect, in which weights above 200 pounds are read as 200. The actual weight of anyone over 200 is underestimated. Similarly, panel (c) shows the impact of a floor effect, in which weights below 120 pounds are read as 120. The actual weight of anyone under 120 is overestimated. With a scale, such effects might occur because the needle is blocked. In psychological measures, the effect is due to the measure having an inadequate range for the participants in the study.

Validity

The third factor to consider in evaluating a measure is its **validity**. To say that a scale designed to measure weight is valid means that the scale measures what it is supposed to measure—weight. Validity is not the same as reliability, which refers to how consistently the weight is measured. A scale for measuring weight, for example, might not be properly adjusted, perhaps giving a reading 10 pounds lighter than the object's true weight. Although this scale would be reliable if it consistently gave that same weight, it would not be valid, because that weight is not the true weight. *A measure cannot be valid unless it is reliable, but a measure can be reliable without being valid.*

Validity, like reliability, is not an all-or-nothing concept. Degrees of validity range from none to perfect. A correlation coefficient is typically used to quantify the degree of validity.

Researchers evaluate the validity of a measure by quantifying how well the measure predicts other variables. For example, a researcher might want to know if SAT scores predict performance in college. This would be referred to as **predictive validity**, because we are evaluating how well our measure predicts a future event. The variable that the researcher wants to predict is the **criterion** (here it would be college grades); the measure used to predict the criterion is the **predictor** (the SAT scores). In other instances, we may want to see if our measure is correlated with a criterion that already exists or can be measured simultaneously. This type of validity is referred to as **concurrent validity**. If we correlated SAT scores with current high school grades, we would be testing concurrent validity. Predictive validity and concurrent validity are two subtypes of **criterion-related validity**, so named because these validities are established by correlating the measure with a criterion measure.

When this concept of validity is used, we must always specify the criterion measure. It makes no sense to say that the SAT test is valid without specifying the criterion measure used in the validity study. For example, the SAT score may be a valid predictor of freshman college grades. It probably is a less valid predictor of whether a student will complete college, because many factors besides academic ability determine this criterion. Finally, the SAT is probably not a valid predictor of a person's happiness.

Validity is a central concept in research. Therefore, in later chapters, we will revisit the concept after you have learned more of the basics of research.

Figure 4.3 illustrates levels of validity. Note the similarity between Figure 4.1, which illustrates reliability, and Figure 4.3, which illustrates validity. The reason for this similarity is that both reliability and validity are usually quantified with a correlation coefficient, which we explain in Chapter 5.

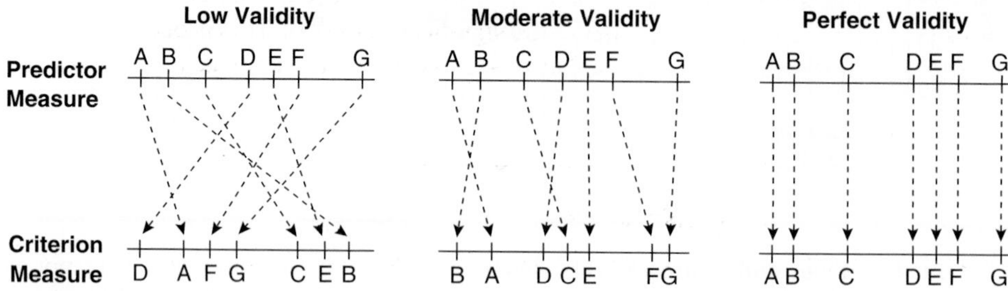

FIGURE 4.3 Validity. This illustration has two measures (the predictor and the criterion) and seven participants (A, B, C, D, E, F, and G). The top horizontal line represents the predictor measure, and the bottom line represents the criterion measure. The more disagreement shown in the rank ordering of participants on the predictor and criterion measures, the lower the validity. The first figure shows extensive disagreement, whereas the last figure shows no disagreement (i.e., perfect correspondence in terms of the rank ordering of participants).

The Need for Objective Measurement

Every science stresses the need for objectivity; but why is objectivity so important? One reason is that subjective measures are researcher specific, and other researchers in the same situation may very well make different judgments.

A hallmark of science is that the laws of nature should hold no matter who tests them. There may be many reasons why two researchers disagree on their subjective impressions of a phenomenon. For example, Ellie might judge a room hotter than Jenne does because Ellie is accustomed to cooler temperatures and so, by comparison, the room seems hot. Another reason for their disagreement might be a differential sensitivity to features other than heat, such as humidity. Yet another reason might be physiological differences in their ability to sense temperature.

Even with something as simple as temperature, subjective impressions pose many problems. If scientists had not developed an objective measure of temperature (the thermometer), most of the physical laws relating temperature to other phenomena would have remained undiscovered. The thermometer measures temperature independently of other variables like humidity. It can measure temperature reliably and across a very wide range. Finally, the thermometer provides at least an interval scale of measurement of temperature. Although this concept may be difficult to grasp based on this brief discussion, it is important to note that an interval scale greatly simplifies the mathematical description of the relationship of temperature to other phenomena.

If so many problems can emerge with subjective measures of something as simple as temperature, imagine the problems that might arise when trying to measure a complicated construct like self-esteem. Many psychological phenomena are events that involve human emotions, which can distort perceptions of the phenomena. For example, researchers who are easily upset by anger might be more sensitive to the presence of anger in a participant who is being frustrated as part of a study on frustration and aggression. Therefore, they might rate the anger as stronger than would researchers who are less sensitive to anger. Good research demands **objective measures** that any scientist can use and that give the same results regardless of who does the measuring.

Statistical procedures are central to modern research because they provide objective ways of evaluating patterns of events. Insisting on the use of statistical analyses for drawing conclusions is an extension of the argument that objectivity is critical in science. Statistics provide an objective and reproducible method for evaluating the significance of data. This is one of the reasons that psychology relies so heavily on statistical analyses to evaluate research data.

Quick-Check Review 4.4: Evaluating Measures

1. Define reliability and list the types of reliability.
2. Can a measure be reliable but not valid? Can it be valid but not reliable?
3. Why must the effective range of a measure be appropriate for the study's sample?
4. What are floor and ceiling effects?
5. How is validity different from reliability?

ETHICAL PRINCIPLES

As we noted in Chapter 1, the researcher has two ethical responsibilities: protection of those who serve as subjects in research and assurance of honesty in conducting and reporting research. The ethical principles that we have discussed thus far apply mostly to protecting participants from harm. Here we will consider the issue of distorting information, including the fabrication of data and plagiarism.

The deliberate fabrication of data and the deliberate presentation of another's work as your own are very serious matters. We are not talking about measurement errors or other inadvertent mistakes that distort data, or a proofreading error that leaves out the quotation marks in a sentence. Such occasional carelessness reduces the value of one's work, but does not constitute serious ethical lapses. Instead, we are talking about deliberate efforts by researchers to manufacture data or to misrepresent authorship in order to serve the researchers' purpose.

It is unfortunate, but our modern society has a high tolerance for the deliberate distortion of facts and ideas in the pursuit of private gain. Advertisers and politicians do this freely and quite creatively, and they are rarely challenged. In our private lives, most of us have at times been guilty of "harmless exaggeration." If we were honest about it, we would admit that we have occasionally pushed some argument beyond complete honesty and accuracy in order to make a point.

In science, however, such distortion is intolerable. Too much of importance in the world depends on accurate scientific information. The willful distortion of data and stealing someone else's work are two of the most egregious ethical offenses that a scientist can commit. In both instances, the misrepresented material is a lie. Presenting information that one knows to be false shows a lack of honesty and responsibility and a willingness to risk the harm to society that such distorted information can cause.

The rigorous peer review processes and/or the failure by other researchers to replicate distorted findings will eventually uncover most such deliberate distortions in academic settings, and those who commit them will suffer reprisals, such as loss of position, ejection from professions, destruction of their very honor and reputation, and, in rare cases, prison sentences. In our view, those people deserve no less. The integrity of scientific disciplines depends upon each scientist's honesty in the use and reporting of research.

It is distressing that some scientists deliberately distort scientific information to serve their own goals. Who perpetrates these distortions, why and how they do it, and what effects these distortions have present a complex and disturbing picture of these ultimate ethical transgressions. Whatever specific form the violations might take, all of them include the deliberate falsification of data and/or authorship in order to mislead others, such as promotion committees, funding agencies, members of Congress, or the public. Their goal is not scientific knowledge, but personal, financial, or political gain. To the best of our knowledge the majority of scientific research is carried out ethically and honestly. However, when scientific misconduct does occur, it threatens the entire scientific endeavor.

Interlandi (2006) reports the case of one university scientist who had published many papers over several years and given lectures based on fraudulent data. The researcher's reports included completely falsified data in his research on obesity, menopause, and aging, and it involved millions of dollars in federal grants. Moreover, many graduate students were snared in this deception. The researcher, who had been awarded prestigious positions and national prizes, was convicted and sentenced to federal prison. In sentencing, Judge William Sessions noted that scientists have positions of trust in society, and when they distort data they put people at serious risk (Interlandi, 2006). Such fraud also puts science at risk. Scientific knowledge is cumulative, gained incrementally as each bit of new knowledge is added to the previous knowledge base. False data breaks that chain of discovery and knowledge (Interlandi, 2006).

While some scientific misconduct cases reported in the media involve individual researchers (e.g., see Harris, 2009; Interlandi, 2006; Kintisch, 2005; Smith, 2001), a particularly ominous form is the distortion carried out by large, powerful organizations. When a powerful industry suppresses, distorts, or makes up scientific data in order to sell its products and protect its profits (Brody, 2007; Eichenwald & Kolata, 1999; Fugh-Burman & Dodgson, 2008; Rensberger, 2005; Santoro & Gorrie, 2005; Smith, 2001) or a government does so for political reasons (Donaghy et al., 2007; Union of Concerned Scientists, 2010a, 2010b) then the lines between independent research and self-interest research are blurred. A serious breach has occurred, with potentially destructive impact on the public.

One highly criticized practice of the pharmaceutical industry, for example, is that of professional medical writers and "guest authors" (Bodenheimer, 2000; Jacobs & Wayer, 2005; Smith, 2001; Wooley, 2006). A company might conduct its own clinical trials of a new drug and will, if the trials are successful, hire professional writers to prepare a research article for submission to a medical journal. To improve the appearance of objectivity, the company will invite a "guest author," usually a physician, who is not associated with the company, to put his or her name on the article as senior author—and offer payment to this guest author. When published in the medical journal, the research and the written report appear to have been carried out by the respected senior author, perhaps at some well-known university or research hospital, but who in fact had nothing to do with the research or the authorship. These and other problems are growing in the scientific community and seem to be related to the increased entanglement of academia with industry (Smith, 2001).

A final note is a caution to students. The ethical principles are guides for you, too. Fudging data in a project, lifting sections out of published books and articles without proper citation (**plagiarism**), and turning in a term paper written by someone else are serious ethical violations. The degree to which they are accepted by students suggests a need for serious concern. Given the complexity and time pressure of, for example, writing a college term paper, it is sometimes easy for students to confuse someone else's ideas and sentences with their own. As inadvertent as that may be, it is still plagiarism if you submit it as your own. *Be careful when taking notes from published sources; clearly label what ideas, words, and phrases are those of others following the guidelines laid out in the APA Publication Manual* (American Psychological Association, 2010d).

Quick-Check Review 4.5: Ethical Principles

1. Why might a researcher be tempted to fabricate data?
2. What are the usual methods for detecting fraudulent data?

SUMMARY

- A variable is any event that can take on different values.
- All research evaluates relationships among variables.
- To measure variables, we apply the abstract number system to the variables.
- The characteristics of variables seldom match the properties of the number system.
- Stevens (1946, 1957) describes four levels of measurement: nominal, ordinal, interval, and ratio.
- An operational definition details the procedures needed to measure or manipulate a variable.
- The appropriate statistical test depends in part on the level of measurement.
- Reliability is an index of the measure's consistency; validity is the measure's effectiveness in reflecting the characteristic measured.
- There are three types of reliability: interrater reliability, which measures the level of agreement between two raters; test-retest reliability, which measures the consistency of a measure over time; and internal consistency reliability, which measures the degree to which multiple items in a measure correlate with one another.
- There are several types of validity. Validity is normally established with one or more criterion-related validity tests, which include tests of predictive validity or concurrent validity. When multiple tests of validity produce consistent results, we say that we have convergent validity.
- A measure cannot be valid unless it is reliable, but it can be reliable without being valid.
- The deliberate misrepresentation of data and/or authorship is major ethical violation.
- The ethical principles for professionals can also guide students in their work.

Putting It into Practice

Psychologists have developed and refined hundreds of measures of psychological variables, and these high-quality measures are available to researchers. However, each measure had to be conceptualized and operationally defined before it could be used.

Take a few minutes each day for the next week to look around and identify psychological variables in the environment. For example, if you see two people arguing, the psychological variables that might be of interest are the degree of anger each feels, how frustrating the actions of one party are to the other party, and how public the argument is. Think about each variable and how you might measure or manipulate it; that is, define it operationally. Try to think of as many ways of measuring it as possible. For example, you can always ask people how angry they are, but are there other ways that you might measure anger that does not involve the self-report of the person?

Finally, think about the ethics of your "eavesdropping." What are the pros and cons of carrying out this exercise? Does it meet the APA's ethical standards?

EXERCISES

4.1. Define the following key terms. Be sure that you understand them. They are discussed in the chapter and defined in the glossary.

properties of the abstract number system
identity
magnitude
equal intervals
true zero
scales of measurement
nominal scales
nominal data
categorical data
ordinal scales
ordered data
interval scales
score data
ratio scales
measurement error
response-set biases
social desirability
operational definition
convergent validity
multimethod approach
reliability
blind
interrater reliability
test-retest reliability
internal consistency reliability
effective range
scale attenuation effects
ceiling effect
floor effect
validity
predictive validity
criterion
predictor
concurrent validity
criterion-related validity
objective measures
plagiarism

4.2. Write two operational definitions for each of the following variables, one that produces ordinal data, and one that produces score data.

a. A potential little league player's baseball skill
b. The strength of one's social support network
c. A lab rat's level of hunger
d. The level of conflict in a business environment

4.3. Following are brief descriptions of research projects. For each one identify (a) which is the independent variable and what type of independent variable it is, (b) which is/are the dependent variable(s), and (c) the level of measurement and type of data for each dependent variable.

a. In a study on the effects of television violence on aggressive behavior, schoolchildren are assigned to two conditions. In one condition, the participants watch a typical half hour of television in which eight violent acts are portrayed (aggressive TV condition); in the other condition, the participants watch a half hour of television in which no violent acts are portrayed (nonaggressive TV condition). Following the TV viewing, the researcher observes the participants in a playroom for aggressive behavior. The hypotheses are that the group exposed to aggressive TV (1) will engage in a greater number of aggressive acts, and (2) will engage in more highly aggressive acts than the participants in the nonaggressive TV condition. The rating will use a five-point rating scale in which the units are not equal intervals.
b. The researcher times college students on how quickly they solve a series of puzzles. The researcher tells one-third of the participants that they will be paid more if they solve the problems quickly and one-third that they will be paid a fixed amount. The last third are not told anything about being paid.

4.4. Identify at least 10 situations in which one might experience problems with a dependent measure because the measure has a restriction-of-range problem.

4.5. Following is a list of possible dependent variables. For each, identify its level of measurement and the type of data it generates.

a. Number of disruptive outbursts
b. Time needed (number of seconds) for a response to occur
c. Place or position of each runner at the end of a race
d. Speed of each runner during the race
e. Annual income of participants
f. Car preference of each participant

4.6. For each of the following variables (a) write an operational definition for a subjective measure of the variable, (b) write a second operational definition for an objective measure of the same variable, and (c) identify potential problems with the subjective measure that might distort the data if it were to be used in an actual study. The variables are as follows:

a. The participants' ambivalence regarding their career goals
b. The degree of frustration experienced while engaging in a laboratory task
c. Competitiveness

CHAPTER FIVE

STATISTICAL ANALYSIS OF DATA

The union of the mathematician with the poet, fervor with measure, passion with correctness, this surely is the ideal.

—William James (1842–1910), *Collected Essays,* 1920

WEB RESOURCE MATERIAL

05:01 Statistical Coverage
05:02 Degrees of Freedom
05:03 Why the Variance Works
05:04 Pearson Product-Moment Correlation Procedures
05:05 Spearman Rank-Order Correlation Procedures
05:06 Linear Regression
05:07 Reliability Indices
05:08 The Standard Normal Distribution
05:09 Independent Samples *t*-Test Computational Procedures
05:10 Correlated *t*-Test Computational Procedures
05:11 ANOVA Computational Procedures
05:12 Effect Size
05:13 Statistical Theory
05:14 PASW for Windows Tutorial
05:15 PASW for Windows Inferential Statistical Analyses
05:16 PASW for Windows Descriptive Statistics
05:16 Study Guide/Lab Manual
05:17 Links to Related Internet Sites

After deciding how to measure variables in a research project (Chapter 4), the next step is to determine how to analyze the data statistically. **Statistical procedures** are powerful tools with two broad purposes: describing the results of a study (descriptive statistics), and helping us understand the meaning of those results (inferential statistics). Without the use of statistics, we would learn little from most studies.

Statistical procedures and research design are closely related. It is early in the research process—in the procedures-design phase—that we make decisions about which statistical procedures we are going to use. That decision is an integral part of the research design, and must be made long before any data are collected.

This chapter provides

- an overview of basic statistical concepts,
- strategies for organizing and describing data,
- an introduction to the logic of statistical decision making, and
- a discussion of inferential statistics.

05:01

We have included more detailed coverage of statistical concepts and procedures in later chapters and on the Student Resource Website.

INDIVIDUAL DIFFERENCES

No two participants or groups will respond in exactly the same manner, and statistical procedures depend on that variability among participants. Suppose, for example, that a researcher predicts that people who receive memory training will perform better on a memory task than those who do not receive such training. The researcher assigns participants to one of two conditions: (1) memory training, or (2) no training. The dependent measure is a memory test that yields scores from 0 to 100.

Table 5.1 presents hypothetical data for this memory study. Note that the groups differ in their mean (average) scores, but there is also considerable variability of scores within each group. The scores in Group A range from 66 to 98, and those in Group B range from 56 to 94. The variation within each group shows that there are **individual differences** in memory skills. Some people, with or without training, remember well; others remember very little; most people fall somewhere in between. All organismic variables studied in psychology show individual differences. Therefore, in the memory study, we cannot be sure if memory training is the reason for the observed group differences. It is possible that participants in the training group had better memory initially and would have performed better regardless of the training.

Here is an important point for you to remember: most of the variables manipulated in psychology make only small differences in how people perform compared with the individual differences that already exist among people. Statistics help researchers to decide whether group differences on dependent measures are due to research manipulations or are the result of existing individual differences.

Research studies generate data (the scores from each person on each of the study's measures). Some of those data sets are large and unwieldy, and we need ways to organize them. Descriptive and inferential statistics provide this organization and complement each other. **Descriptive statistics** summarize, simplify, and describe such large sets of measurements. **Inferential statistics** help us to interpret what the data mean. In the study on memory training, the means (a descriptive statistic) of the two groups are different; as predicted, the trained group shows a higher mean score

TABLE 5.1 Examples of Descriptive Statistics

These hypothetical data are from 22 participants in a memory study, half of whom received memory training, and the other half of whom did not. We ordered the scores in this table from highest to lowest for easier comparison.

STATISTIC	GROUP A (TRAINED)	GROUP B (NON-TRAINED)
	98	94
	93	88
	90	82
	89	77
	87	75
	87	74
	84	72
	81	72
	78	67
	71	61
	66	56
Median	87	74
Mode	87	72
Mean	84	74.36

than the non-trained group. The researcher wants to know whether that difference in means is large enough to conclude that it is due to more than chance variation among participants. That is, is the difference between the groups so large that it probably did not occur by chance, but rather is a real effect? Inferential statistics help to answer such questions.

Quick-Check Review 5.1: Individual Differences

1. What is another term for the differences among people?
2. Define "descriptive statistics" and "inferential statistics."

ORGANIZING DATA

This section introduces two groups of descriptive procedures: (1) frequency distributions, and (2) graphical representations of data. We illustrate these procedures with the hypothetical data in Table 5.2, which represent responses from 24 participants, aged 18 and above, selected at random from the population of a moderate-sized city. The researchers are interested in variables that may relate to voting patterns, and they gathered data from each participant on (1) age, (2) income, (3) number of times voted in the last 5 years, (4) gender, and (5) political affiliation (coded as Democrat, Republican, or other).

TABLE 5.2 Sample Data From 24 Participants

PERSON	AGE	INCOME ($)	NUMBER OF TIMES VOTED IN LAST 5 YEARS	GENDER	POLITICAL AFFILIATION
1	28	32,000	6	M	R
2	46	50,000	4	M	D
3	33	44,000	0	F	D
4	40	45,000	5	M	R
5	21	30,000	1	M	R
6	26	35,000	0	F	O
7	39	42,000	6	M	O
8	23	34,000	0	F	D
9	20	27,000	1	M	O
10	26	31,000	2	M	R
11	29	39,000	6	F	R
12	24	34,000	2	M	D
13	34	44,000	2	M	O
14	35	45,000	3	M	O
15	52	46,000	8	M	O
16	31	39,000	4	F	D
17	30	43,000	6	M	R
18	45	47,000	7	F	D
19	18	28,000	0	M	O
20	29	44,000	7	M	R
21	26	38,000	6	F	D
22	23	37,000	3	M	O
23	47	48,000	7	M	D
24	53	51,000	8	M	D

Note: R, Republican; D, Democrat; O, other.

What type of data does each of these variables generate? Consider the variables age, income, and the number of times the participant voted. Each of these measures has the property of magnitude; 34 is older than 25, $35,000 is more than $28,000, and so on. All three measures have the property of equal intervals; the difference in age between 25 and 20 is the same as the difference between 38 and 33. The variables also have a true zero point; a person whose income is zero does not earn anything; a person who has voted zero times in the last 5 years has not voted in that time. As you remember from Chapter 4, those variables are measured on ratio scales and therefore generate score data. The other two variables, gender and political affiliation, are measured on nominal scales producing nominal or categorical data; there is no meaningful way of ordering the categories in a nominal scale.

Frequency Distributions

Nominal and Ordered Data. For most nominal and ordered data, statistical simplification involves computing **frequencies**: the number of participants who fall into each category. We organize the frequencies into **frequency distributions**, which show the frequency in each category. Table 5.3 shows the frequency distribution of gender for the data from Table 5.2. In any frequency distribution, when we sum across all categories, the total should equal the total number of participants. It is helpful to convert frequencies to percentages by dividing the frequency in each cell by the total number of participants and multiplying each of these proportions by 100, as was done in Table 5.3.

Cross-tabulation is a useful way to categorize participants based on more than one variable at the same time, such as categorizing participants based on gender and political affiliation. Cross-tabulation can help the researcher to see relationships between nominal measures. In this example, there are two levels of the variable gender (male and female) and three levels of the variable political affiliation (Democrat, Republican, and other), giving a total of six (2 × 3) possible joint categories. We arranged the data in a 2 × 3 matrix in Table 5.4, in which the numbers in the matrix are the frequency of people in each of the joint categories. For example, the first cell represents the number of male Democrats. Note that the sum of all the frequencies in the six cells equals the total number of participants. Also, note that the row and column totals represent the **univariate** (one-variable) frequency distribution for the political affiliation and gender variables, respectively. For example, the column totals in Table 5.4 of 17 males and 7 females represent the frequency distribution for the single variable of gender and, not surprisingly, are the same numbers that appear in Table 5.3.

Score Data. The simplest way to organize a set of score data is to create a frequency distribution. It is difficult to visualize all 24 scores at a glance for the voting variable shown in Table 5.2. Some of the participants have not voted at all during that time, and two participants voted eight times, but where do the rest of the participants tend to fall? A frequency distribution organizes the data to answer such questions at a glance. There may be no participants for some of the scores, in which case the frequency would be zero. Table 5.5 shows the frequency distribution for this voting variable.

TABLE 5.3 Frequency of Males and Females in Sample in Table 5.2

	MALES	FEMALES	TOTAL
Frequency	17	7	24
Percentage	71	29	100

TABLE 5.4 Cross-Tabulation by Gender and Political Affiliation

	MALES	FEMALES	TOTAL
Democrats	4	5	9
Republicans	6	1	7
Other	7	1	8
Totals	17	7	24

TABLE 5.5 Frequency Distribution of Voting Behavior in Last 5 Years

NUMBER OF TIMES VOTED	FREQUENCY
8	2
7	3
6	5
5	1
4	2
3	2
2	3
1	2
0	4

If there are many possible scores, then the frequency distribution will be long and almost as difficult to read as the original data. In this situation, we use a **grouped frequency distribution**, which reduces the table to a more manageable size by grouping the scores into intervals. A grouped frequency distribution is required with a **continuous variable**, in which there are theoretically an infinite number of possible scores between the lowest and the highest score. Table 5.6 shows a grouped frequency distribution for the continuous variable of income, which ranges from $27,000 to $51,000. Grouping salary into $2,000 intervals yields 13 intervals.

TABLE 5.6 Grouped Frequency Distribution for Income

INTERVAL NUMBER	ANNUAL INCOME ($)	FREQUENCY
1	50,000–51,999	2
2	48,000–49,999	1
3	46,000–47,999	2
4	44,000–45,999	5
5	42,000–43,999	2
6	40,000–41,999	0
7	38,000–39,999	3
8	36,000–37,999	1
9	34,000–35,999	3
10	32,000–33,999	1
11	30,000–31,999	2
12	28,000–29,999	1
13	26,000–27,999	1

Graphical Representation of Data

A Chinese proverb states, "one picture is worth a thousand words" (Bartlett, 1980), and this is especially true with statistical information. **Graphs** can clarify a data set by presenting the data visually. Most people find graphic representations easier to understand than other statistical procedures. Graphs and tables are excellent supplements to statistical analyses.

We can represent frequency or grouped frequency distributions graphically by using either a **histogram** or a **frequency polygon**. Figure 5.1 shows a histogram and a frequency polygon representing the voting data summarized in Table 5.5. (We generated these graphs in just a few seconds using the *PASW for Windows* data analysis program.) Both the histogram and the frequency polygon represent data on a two-dimensional graph, in which the horizontal axis (***x*-axis** or **abscissa**) represents the range of scores for the variable and the vertical axis (***y*-axis** or **ordinate**) represents the frequency of the scores. In a histogram, the frequency of a score is represented by the height of a bar above that score, as shown in Figure 5.1(a). In the frequency polygon, the frequency is represented by the height of a point above each score on the abscissa. Connecting the adjacent points, as shown in Figure 5.1(b), completes the frequency polygon. To aid in the interpretation of histograms and frequency polygons, it is important to label both axes carefully.

It is possible to display two or more frequency distributions on the same graph so that one can compare the distributions. Each distribution is graphed independently with different colors or different types of lines to distinguish one distribution from the other. Figure 5.2 shows the distribution for the voting variable, graphed separately for males and females.

When group size is small, a frequency polygon or histogram is usually jagged, but will have an overall shape, like those graphed in Figures 5.1 and 5.2. As group size increases, the frequency polygon looks more like a smooth curve. We often describe data by drawing smooth curves, even though such curves are seen only when the group sizes are extremely large.

Figure 5.3 shows several smooth-curve drawings of various distribution shapes frequently found in psychology. Figure 5.3(a) shows a common shape for a **symmetric distribution**: a bell-shaped curve. Most of the participants are near the middle of the distribution. In symmetric

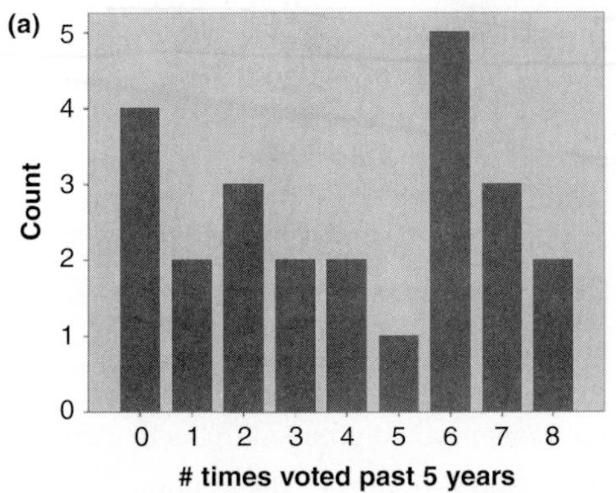

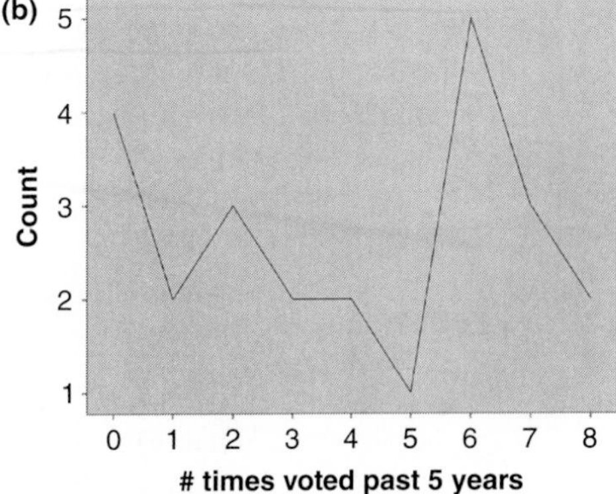

FIGURE 5.1 Histograms and Frequency Polygons. Graphing the distribution of scores with either a histogram or a frequency polygon helps the researcher to visualize the data.

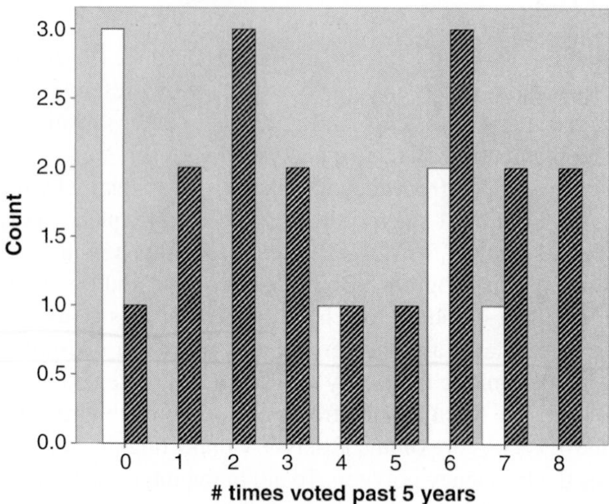

FIGURE 5.2 Comparing Two Distributions. Graphing frequency data from two or more groups on the same histogram or frequency polygon gives a visual representation of how the groups compare.

distributions, the right and left sides of the distribution are mirror images. Distributions with this bell-shape are **normal distributions**. Many variables in psychology form normal distributions, including measures of most human characteristics, such as height, weight, and intelligence.

In **skewed distributions**, the scores pile up on one end of the distribution [see Figures 5.3(b) and 5.3(c)]. The tail of the curve indicates the direction of the skew. In Figure 5.3(b), the curve is **positively skewed**, with most of the scores piled up near the bottom (the tail points toward the high or positive end of the scale). Figure 5.3(c) is **negatively skewed**. We might see a negatively skewed distribution on an easy classroom test, on which almost everyone does well and only a few people do poorly.

In addition to the shape of the curve, we also describe distributions in terms of the location of the middle of the distribution on the x-axis, which is called the **central tendency** of the distribution. We can also quantify the horizontal spread of the distribution, which is called the **variability** of the distribution. *The visual display of quantitative information* (Tufte, 2001) is an excellent book on the graphical presentation of data.

Quick-Check Review 5.2: Organizing Data

1. What are frequency distributions? With what kind of data can we use frequency distributions?
2. Define "cross-tabulation."
3. What is the difference between frequency and grouped frequency distributions?
4. What type of variable requires a grouped frequency distribution?
5. What are the basic shapes of distributions found in psychology?

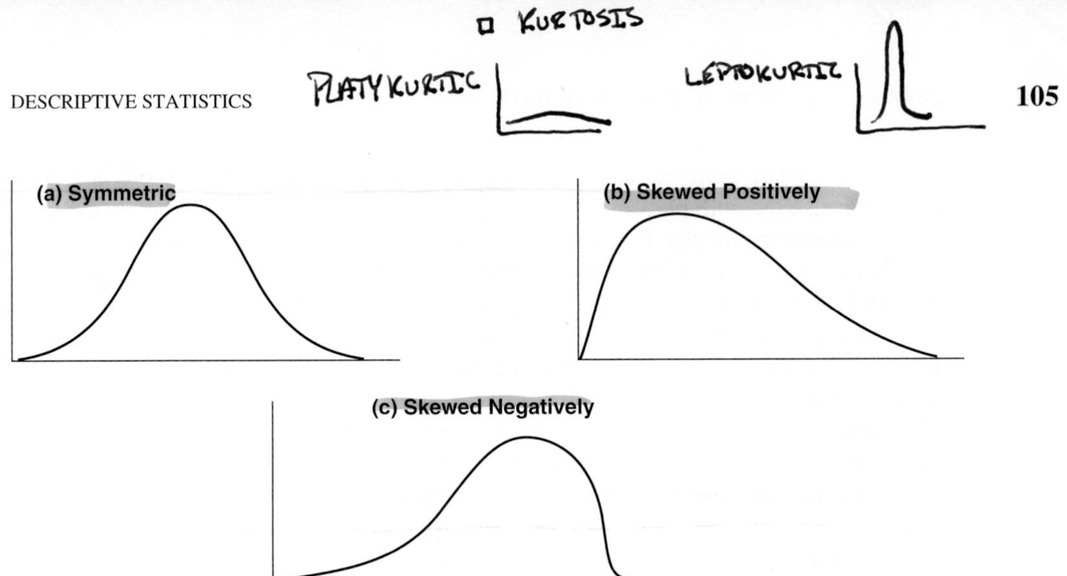

FIGURE 5.3 Symmetric and Skewed Distributions. Many measures yield the classic bell-shaped distribution shown in (a). When scores bunch up at either the bottom (b) or top (c) of the distribution, the distributions are skewed.

DESCRIPTIVE STATISTICS

Descriptive statistics serve two purposes. The first is to describe data with just one or two numbers, which makes it easier to compare groups. The second is to provide a basis for later analyses using inferential statistics. This section covers measures of central tendency, variability, and relationship and introduces the concept of standard scores.

Measures of Central Tendency

Measures of central tendency describe the typical or average score. They indicate the center of the distribution, where most of the scores cluster. Table 5.7 summarizes three measures of central tendency: mode, median, and mean.

The **mode** is the most frequently occurring score in the distribution. In the example shown in Table 5.1, the modes are 87 and 72 for Groups A and B, respectively. In a frequency distribution like the one in Table 5.5, we can determine the mode by finding the largest number in the frequency column and noting the score with that frequency. In Table 5.5, the mode is 6. A distribution may have more than one mode. If there are two, then the distribution is **bimodal**; if there are three, it is **trimodal**.

The mode has the advantage of being easy to compute, but it has the disadvantage of being unstable, which means that it can be affected by a change in only a few scores. We can use the mode with all scales of measurement.

TABLE 5.7 Measures of Central Tendency

Mode	Most frequently occurring score in a distribution
Median	Middle score in a distribution; the score at the 50th percentile
Mean	Arithmetic average of the scores in a distribution; computed by summing the scores and dividing by the number of scores

A second measure of central tendency is the **median**—the middle score in a distribution. The median is also the 50th percentile, which means that half the scores fall below the median. We can easily compute the median if there are few scores and they are ordered from lowest to highest. With an odd number of scores, the median is the $(N + 1)/2$ score, in which N is the number of scores. In Table 5.1, there are 11 scores. Therefore, the sixth score [(11 + 1)/2] will be the median. The sixth score in a group of 11 scores will be exactly in the middle, with 5 scores above it and 5 scores below it. When there is an even number of scores, there will be two middle scores; the median is the average of the two middle scores. In Table 5.1, the median for Group A is 87; in Group B, it is 74. The median can be appropriately used with ordered and score data, but not with nominal data. (To the student: See if you can figure out why the median is not appropriate for nominal data.)

The most commonly used measure of central tendency is the **mean**—the arithmetic average of all of the scores. We compute the mean by summing the scores and dividing by the number of scores as follows:

$$Mean = \overline{X} = \frac{\sum X}{N} \tag{5.1}$$

The term $\overline{X}$ (read "X bar") is the notation for the mean. The term $\sum X$ (read "sigma X") is summation notation and simply means to add all the scores. The mean is appropriate only with score data. (To the student: Why is this so?)

Researchers frequently use the mean and the median to describe the average score. The median gives a better indication of what the typical score is if there are a few unusually high or low scores in the distribution, as discussed in Cost of Neglect 5.1. The mean, on the other hand, is more useful in other statistical procedures, such as inferential statistics.

THE COST OF NEGLECT 5.1: LIES, DAMN LIES, AND STATISTICS

Mark Twain talked about "lies, damn lies, and statistics," and his attitude strikes a responsive chord in many people. However, statistics are not inherently deceptive. Nevertheless, if you do not understand statistics, it is easy for someone to deceive you by selecting those statistics that make their case and ignoring the ones that contradict it. Let's play with some numbers to show how easy this is.

Imagine a five-person company in which everyone, including the owner, makes an annual salary of \$40,000. The mean, median, and mode are all \$40,000. Now suppose that business picks up dramatically and profits soar. The owner of the company decides to take all the additional profit, giving none of it to the employees. So now four people make \$40,000, and the owner makes \$340,000. Table 5.8 illustrates these data.

TABLE 5.8 Average Incomes Example

FIRST YEAR ($)	SECOND YEAR ($)	CHANGE (%)
40,000	40,000	0
40,000	40,000	0
40,000	40,000	0
40,000	40,000	0
40,000	340,000	750

The mode (most frequent salary) is still \$40,000, and the median (the middle salary) is still \$40,000. However, the mean is now \$100,000 (\$500,000/5). The third column of the table reflects the percentage change in the salary for each employee. Both the mode and the median for these salary increases is 0%, but the owner received 750%. If you compute the mean salary increase, you get 150%, which hardly reflects the typical situation in this company.

Because of all this new business, the owner wants to hire new people to continue the growth. To entice new people, the owner offers a starting salary of $30,000, but tells prospective employees that there is plenty of room for advancement, noting that the mean salary is $100,000 and that the average percentage increase in salary in the past year was 150%. Those statistics are all accurate, but do they lie? The answer is actually no. The owner may be lying by presenting a misleading selection of statistics, but the statistics themselves are true.

Statistics don't lie to people who (1) have all the relevant statistics and (2) know how to interpret them. If you apply for a job and are told the mean income for the company, you should ask what the median income is. Almost every company has a few critical people who earn more than most of the rest of the company's employees, so the median will give you a better idea than the mean what the typical salary is. If you are told that the mean salary increase last year was 150%, you might want to ask if that was across the board (meaning everyone got a 150% increase). If not, you might ask what the median increase was. For this hypothetical company, the median increase was 0%.

If you insist on having all the statistics, you cannot be lied to unless the statistics were deliberately falsified. In that case, it is not the statistics that are lying, but rather the statistician who falsified the statistics.

Measures of Variability

In addition to measures of central tendency, it is important to determine the variability of scores. We illustrate the concept of variability in Figure 5.4, which shows two distributions with identical means. However, curve A is narrower; that is, the scores are bunched closer together. They are less variable than the scores of curve B. For example, suppose that you compared the ages of people who attend county fairs with the ages of those who attend pop music concerts. You would probably find that those attending county fairs range from infants to people over 90, whereas pop concert attendees are mostly in their teens and twenties, with few young children or people over 30. Clearly, there is far more age variability at a county fair than at a typical pop concert.

Variability is an important concept and an easy one to understand. Participants differ from one another on many variables. For some variables, there are large differences among participants;

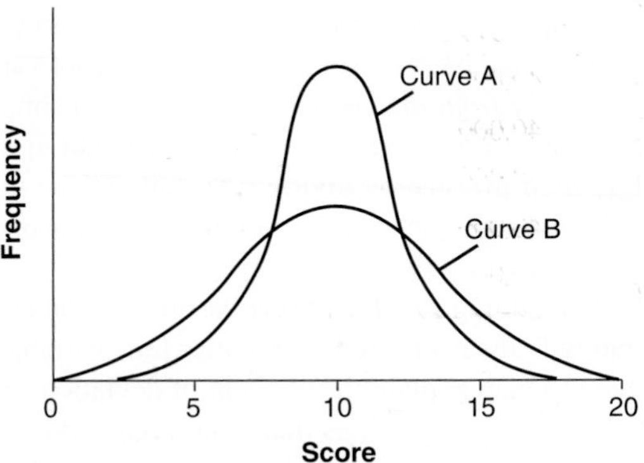

FIGURE 5.4 Two Distributions with the Same Mean but Different Variances. Although both of these distributions have the same mean, they differ in their variability.

TABLE 5.9 Measures of Variability

Range	Distance from the lowest to the highest score in a distribution; may be specified by either giving both the lowest and highest scores or by subtracting the lowest from the highest score and reporting this value
Average Deviation	Arithmetic average of the distance that each score is from the mean
Variance	Essentially the average squared distance from the mean; the variance is computed by summing the squared distances from the mean and dividing by the degrees of freedom (equal to the number of scores minus 1)
Standard Deviation	The square root of the variance

for other variables, the differences are small. There may be many reasons why scores vary among participants, but you need not worry about the reasons at this point. The important ideas to remember are that scores vary and that we can quantify the degree of variability.

Individuals differ from one another on many factors, and these differences affect their responses to stimuli. This variability among participants (thought of as natural variability) often masks the effects of the psychological variables under study. Most research designs and statistical procedures were developed to control or minimize the effects of the natural variability of scores.

Table 5.9 summarizes the measures of variability. The simplest measure of variability is the **range**, the distance from the lowest to the highest score. The range is easy to compute, but is unstable because it depends on only two scores (the highest and lowest), and therefore a single unusually high or low score can dramatically affect the range. For example, the scores for curve A in Figure 5.4 range from 3 to 17 (a range of 14), and the scores for curve B range from 1 to 19 (a range of 18). However, if one more score were added to curve A (a score of 21), the ranges for curves A and B would be equal. Note, however, that even with the addition of this one deviant score, the scores are more tightly clustered (less variable) in curve A than in curve B.

A better measure of variability is the variance. The variance utilizes all of the scores, instead of just the lowest and highest scores. Furthermore, it has statistical properties that make it useful in inferential statistics.

To begin our discussion of variance, suppose that you have a set of scores, and you have calculated the mean of this set. Now suppose that you ask a reasonable question about variability: *On average, how much do the scores in this set differ from the mean of the set?* It is a simple matter to find this value; just subtract the mean from each score (called the deviation), add up these deviations (ignoring the + and – signs), and find their average by dividing the sum of the deviations by the number of scores (called the **average deviation**). The scores in Table 5.10 differ from the mean by an average of 1.6 units.

The plus or minus sign is ignored when adding the deviations because, if the sign is not ignored, the average deviation from the mean will always be zero, no matter how variable the scores.

The average deviation is included here to help explain the concept of deviation. We never use it in statistical analyses, because it lacks the statistical qualities that would make it useful. Instead, the variance and standard deviation are used, both of which use the same concept of variability of scores from the mean. (Be sure you understand what deviation scores are; if it is not clear, go over that material again.)

TABLE 5.10 Computing Measures of Variability

Compute the average deviation, variance, and standard deviation for the following data.

1. Start by setting up three columns labeled X, $|X - \overline{X}|$, and $(X - \overline{X})^2$.

	X	$\|X - \overline{X}\|$	$(X - \overline{X})^2$
	10	2.0	4.00
	7	1.0	1.00
	8	0.0	0.00
	5	3.0	9.00
	10	2.0	4.00
TOTALS	40	8.0	18.00

2. Compute the mean.

$$\overline{X} = \frac{\sum X}{N} = \frac{40}{5} = 8.0$$

3. Compute the average deviation. [Note that $|X - \overline{X}|$ means to take the absolute value of the difference, which means that you should ignore the direction of the difference in computing this value.]

$$\text{Average Deviation} = \frac{\sum |X - \overline{X}|}{N} = \frac{8.0}{5} = 1.60$$

4. Compute the variance.

$$s^2 = \frac{\sum (X - \overline{X})^2}{N - 1} = \frac{18.00}{5 - 1} = 4.50$$

5. Compute the standard deviation.

$$s = \sqrt{s^2} = \sqrt{4.50} = 2.12$$

We calculate the **variance** by squaring the deviations of the scores from the mean to make them all positive. Therefore, the variance is essentially the average squared deviation of each score from the mean. The notation s^2 refers to variance. The equation for variance is

$$s^2 = \frac{SS\ (\text{Sum of Squares})}{df\ (\text{Degrees of Freedom})} = \frac{\sum (X - \overline{X})^2}{N - 1} \tag{5.2}$$

The variance equals the sum of the squared differences of each score from the mean (called the **sum of squares**) divided by the number of scores (N) minus 1 (called the degrees of freedom). The **degrees of freedom** is an important concept in statistics, referring to the number of scores that are free to vary. Understanding the Concept 5.1 explains the idea of degrees of freedom. We provide a more detailed discussion of degrees of freedom on the Student Resource Website.

05:02

UNDERSTANDING THE CONCEPT 5.1: DEGREES OF FREEDOM

"Degrees of freedom," a basic statistical concept used in many statistical computations, refers to the number of scores that are free to vary. Suppose that someone asks you to pick any three numbers. There are no restrictions, and the numbers are completely free to vary. In standard terminology, there would be three degrees of freedom; that is, three numbers are free to vary.

Suppose someone now asks you to choose any three numbers, but they must total 15; in this case, there is one restriction on the numbers. Because of the restriction, you will lose some of the freedom to vary the numbers that you choose. If you choose the numbers 8 and 11 as the first two numbers, the third number must be –4. Two numbers are free to vary, but one is not. In standard terminology, there are two degrees of freedom. In comparison to the first example, in which there were no restrictions and all the numbers were free to vary, we have lost one degree of freedom.

Now suppose that you are to choose three scores in which (1) the total must be 15, and (2) the first score must be 7. Note that there are two restrictions placed on this set of scores. Consequently, two degrees of freedom have been lost, leaving only one degree of freedom. The only score that can vary freely is the second score.

In statistics, the restrictions imposed on data are not arbitrary as they were in these examples. Instead, they are determined by the demands of the statistical procedures. For example, many statistical procedures require that we estimate values, such as the population mean. These estimates constitute restrictions. The more such restrictions there are, the more degrees of freedom we lose. In the computation of the variance, one such restriction is imposed and, consequently, the degrees of freedom are reduced by one. Hence, the denominator is $N - 1$.

To use equation (5.2)

1. compute the mean;
2. subtract the mean from each score and square this difference;
3. sum the squared differences to calculate the sum of squares; [the sum of squares (SS) is short for "the sum of squared deviations from the mean."]
4. divide the sum of squares (SS) by the degrees of freedom ($N - 1$) to obtain the variance. Table 5.10 shows this computation.

05:03

The variance is an excellent measure of variability and is used in many inferential statistics. The Student Resource Website explains why the variance, which is not an intuitive measure of variability for most students, is used so frequently in inferential statistics. Note that the variance is expressed in squared units because we squared the deviation scores before summing them. In contrast, the mean is expressed in the original units of the variable. We can easily transform the variance back into the same units as the original scores by computing the standard deviation. The **standard deviation** (written s) is equal to the square root of the variance. (Note that the variance and standard deviation can be used only with score data.)

$$s = \sqrt{s^2} = \sqrt{\text{Variance}} \tag{5.3}$$

Measures of Relationship

At times, we want to quantify the strength of the **relationship** between two variables, which indicates the degree to which the two scores tend to **covary** (vary together). The best way to index the relationship between variables is with a **correlation coefficient**, also referred to as a **correlation**. There are different correlation coefficients for different types of data.

Pearson Product-Moment Correlation. The **Pearson product-moment correlation** is the most widely used correlation, but it is appropriate only for score data. The Pearson product-moment correlation can range from −1.00 to +1.00. A correlation of +1.00 means that the two variables are perfectly related in a positive direction; as one variable increases, the other variable also increases by a predictable amount. A correlation of −1.00 represents a perfect negative relationship; as one variable increases, the other decreases by a predictable amount. A correlation of zero means that there is no relationship between the variables.

The size of the correlation coefficient indicates the strength of the relationship. For example, a correlation of .55 indicates a stronger relationship than a correlation of .25, and a correlation of −.85 indicates an even stronger relationship. Remember, the sign of the correlation indicates only the direction of the relationship and not its strength. The standard notation for correlation is r. Thus, the correlations above would be noted as $r = .55$, $r = .25$, and $r = -.85$. The Pearson product-

05:04 moment correlation is covered in more detail on the Student Resource Website.

The Pearson product-moment correlation is an index of the degree of **linear relationship** between two variables. What this means is best illustrated by examining a **scatter plot**, which is a graphic technique used to represent the relationship between two variables. To construct one, we label the standard x- and y-axes with the names of the two variables. We have created a scatter plot in Figure 5.5 for the relationship between age and income using data from Table 5.2. As indicated in the figure, participant 1 is 28 years old and earns \$32,000 a year. The point that represents participant 1 is directly above \$32,000 on the x-axis and directly across from 28 on the y-axis. To complete the scatter plot, we plot each person's set of scores in the same way.

The pattern of scores in the scatter plot is informative. For example, the people with the highest incomes are all older; younger people tend to have lower incomes. We could draw a straight line through the middle of the dots from the lower left to upper right of the graph, with most of the dots falling close to that line.

This is a good example of a linear relationship because the points in this scatter plot cluster around a straight line. It is a **positive correlation** because incomes are higher for older participants.

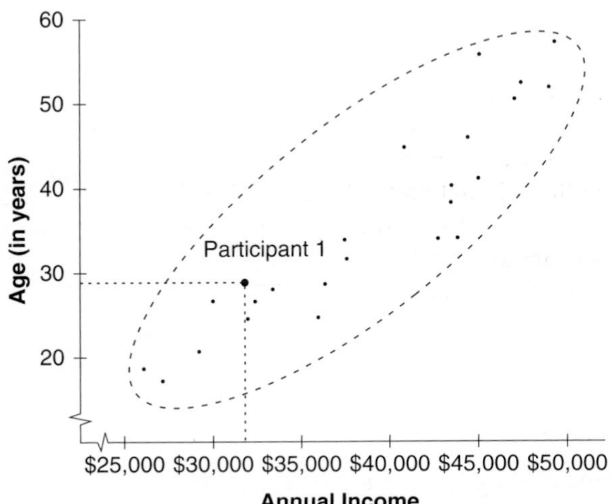

FIGURE 5.5 Scatter Plot for Age and Salary. We construct a scatter plot by graphing each person's data point, which is determined by the two scores for that person.

It is not a perfect correlation. In a **perfect correlation** ($r = 1.00$), all the dots form a straight line, as seen in Figure 5.6(a).

The scatter plots in Figure 5.6 illustrate several types of relationships. Figure 5.6(b) illustrates a strong **negative correlation** ($r = -.92$). Note that the points cluster close to a straight line.

Figure 5.6(c) illustrates a zero correlation ($r = .00$). Figure 5.6(d) illustrates a **nonlinear relationship**, in which the correlation coefficient does not represent the data well. In fact, in this case, the correlation ($r = -.03$) is misleading. The near-zero correlation suggests there is no relationship between the variables, but the scatter plot indicates there is a relationship; it is just not a linear (straight-line) relationship. This is one reason why it is advisable to create a scatter plot to see how the scores cluster, instead of relying on a single number (the correlation coefficient) to summarize the relationship between variables. With modern computer packages, it takes just a few seconds to create a scatter plot.

Other Correlations. If either or both variables are measured on an ordinal scale and neither variable is nominal, the appropriate coefficient is the **Spearman rank-order correlation**. If both of the variables produce nominal data, the appropriate coefficient is **Phi**.

We interpret the Spearman correlation like the product-moment correlation: a correlation of −1.00 is a perfect negative relationship; a correlation of +1.00 is a perfect positive relationship; a correlation of zero means that no linear relationship exists. We interpret Phi a bit differently because

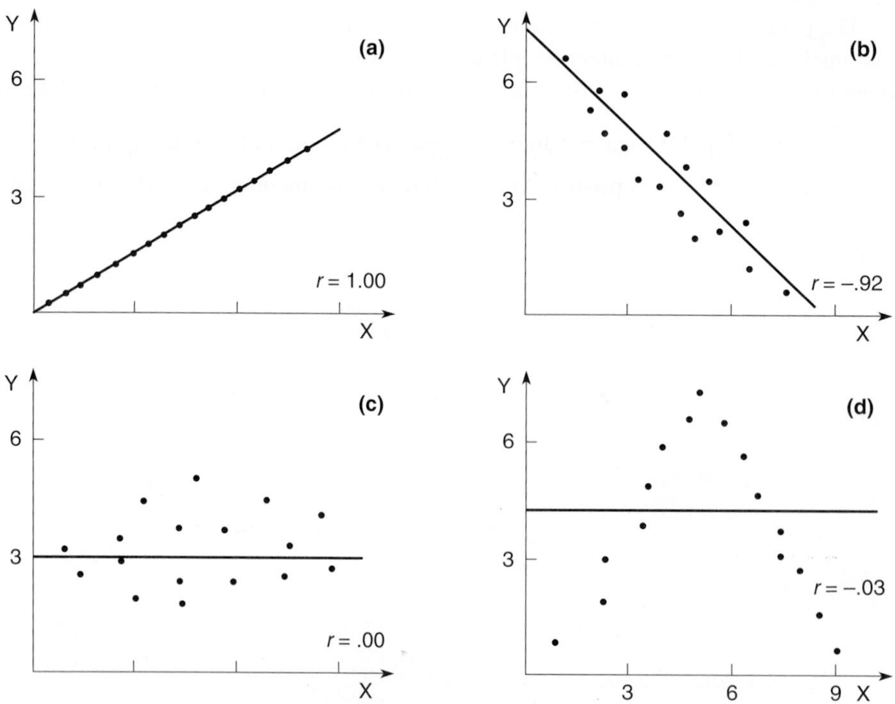

FIGURE 5.6 Scatter Plots and Regression Lines. You cannot always tell what the relationship between two variables is like from the correlation. A scatter plot allows you to see the relationship, including such complex relationships as the one shown in (d) (see text).

there really is no direction to a correlation between nominal variables, which have no natural ordering. Therefore, we interpret only the size of the correlation, again with a correlation of 1.00 indicating a perfect relationship and zero indicating no relationship. The Spearman rank-order correlation
05:05 is covered in more detail on the Student Resource Website.

Regression. Correlation coefficients quantify the degree and direction of relationship between variables. Finding such relationships is a major goal of science. Another goal is to make predictions about events. The correlation coefficient is an important part of this, because a strong relationship between two variables provides information that will help to predict one variable by knowing the values of the other. For example, if there is a correlation between test scores and later job performance, then we have information that may help us to predict future job performance.

"**Regression**" refers to the prediction of the value of one variable from the value of another. We typically assume a linear or straight-line relationship. Nonlinear regression is possible, but the applicable procedures are well beyond the level of this text. You may have noticed that we drew a line in each of the scatter plots in Figure 5.6. This line is the linear regression line for predicting the variable *Y* from the variable *X*. In Figures 5.6(a) and 5.6(b) the points cluster close to the line, suggesting a strong linear relationship. When the correlation is zero, as in Figure 5.6(c), the line is horizontal. In Figure 5.6(d), the regression line, like the correlation, is misleading in that it does not reflect the data well.

Statistical analysis packages can compute a regression line easily for any data set. However, you should always request a scatter plot so that you can see how well the data fit a straight-line function. The Student Resource Website covers both the theoretical aspects of regression and the
05:06 computational procedures.

Reliability Indices. We introduced the concept of reliability in Chapter 4. Correlation coefficients quantify test-retest and interrater reliability. Since these reliability indices are correlations, they behave like any other correlation. They range from a −1.00 to a +1.00, although negative correlations for reliability are unlikely unless something is seriously amiss, such as raters using different rating scales. A correlation of +1.00 indicates perfect reliability, and a correlation of 0.00 indicates no reliability.

The internal consistency reliability index, called **coefficient alpha**, is also a correlation coefficient, although a much more complicated one than those covered in this chapter. Coefficient alpha is an index of the degree of intercorrelation among the items in a measure. The more highly correlated the items are with one another, the higher the coefficient alpha.

The Student Resource Website covers the computation and interpretation of the various reli-
05:07 ability indices.

Standard Scores

The **standard score** (written *Z*; also called the **Z-score**) is a transformation frequently used in research. We compute the standard score by subtracting the mean from the score and dividing the difference by the standard deviation, as shown in equation (5.4). The standard score is a **relative score** because it tells how a participant scored *relative* to the rest of the participants. If the participant scores above the mean, the standard score is positive; if the participant scores below the mean, the standard score is negative. The size of the standard score indicates how far from the mean the participant scored.

$$Z = \frac{X - \overline{X}}{s} \qquad (5.4)$$

Many tests convert the standard score to avoid negative numbers and decimals. For example, the standard score on an intelligence test is converted into an IQ by multiplying the standard score by 15, adding 100, and rounding to the nearest whole number, producing an IQ distribution with a mean of 100 and a standard deviation of 15. The SAT uses a similar conversion to give it a mean of 500 and a standard deviation of 100 for each subtest.

05:08

If the distribution is approximately normal, we can easily convert the standard score into a percentile rank. A person's **percentile rank** tells what percent of the group scored below the person. The details of this transformation are included on the Student Resource Website.

Quick-Check Review 5.3: Descriptive Statistics

1. What are the three measures of central tendency?
2. What are deviation scores?
3. What are the chief measures of variability?
4. Define "correlation" and "regression." How are these used?
5. What is a standard score, and how is it computed?
6. Why is the variance a better measure of variability than the range?
7. Why is the mean a better measure of central tendency than the mode?
8. How does a correlation differ from other descriptive statistics?

STATISTICAL INFERENCE

Using statistics to describe data is the first step in analyzing the results of a research study. The rest of the analysis concerns not so much the specific participants tested, but what the data indicate about a larger group. This section will cover the logic of this process, and the next section will cover the statistical procedures.

Populations and Samples

It is seldom possible to observe whole populations, unless the population is extremely small, like an endangered species that lives in only one specific place. Instead, we select and observe relatively small samples from relatively large populations. The researcher uses a sample as if it adequately represents the population. In human research, a **population** is the larger group to which all the people of interest belong, and a **sample** is a subset of that population. For example, a researcher might select a sample of 100 high school students from the school's total population of 1,000 high school students.

Here's an important distinction to keep in mind: we carry out research projects on samples; but we generalize the results to populations. It is the population that we are interested in, not the sample. We want to draw conclusions about a population based on samples from that population, but how accurate are the samples? How confident can we be in generalizing results from samples to the population? The use of inferential statistics helps us to solve that issue.

No two samples drawn from the same population will be exactly alike. Most samples are reasonably representative of the population from which they are drawn, but sometimes samples are unrepresentative, even though the researcher carried out the sampling procedure flawlessly. This normal variation among different samples drawn from the same population is called **sampling error**. This term does not suggest a mistake, but refers to the natural variability among samples due to chance. Because samples are not perfectly representative of the population from which they are drawn, we cannot be sure that conclusions drawn from samples will apply to the entire population; the best we can do is to calculate probabilities that our inferences are valid. **Probability** provides a numerical indication of how likely it is that a given event, as predicted by our findings, will occur. Probability is a critical concept in inferential statistics, in which the goal is to help us to differentiate between "chance" patterns (like differences and relationships) that are due to sampling error, and "real" patterns that are due to other factors (like our research variables).

Suppose that you are comparing men and women in a study of gender differences in reaction time by recording how quickly participants press a button in response to an auditory signal. The mean reaction times are 0.278 seconds for men and 0.254 seconds for women. The sample means are different, but not very different. However, you are not primarily interested in the samples, but in the population of men compared with the population of women. The aim is to draw conclusions about characteristics of the populations from the results of the samples. Does the observed difference in mean reaction time in these samples suggest that a similar difference exists between the populations, or could the observed difference be a result of sampling error?

Suppose that men and women have the same reaction time. In that case, samples drawn from the populations should have approximately equal mean reaction times. Are the mean reaction times of 0.278 seconds and 0.254 seconds approximately equal? Are they close enough to infer that the population means, which are unknown, are equal? Answering these questions involves testing the null hypothesis.

The Null Hypothesis

The **null hypothesis** states that there is no statistical difference between the population means. Null is from the Latin *nullus*, meaning "not any." If the observed sample means were very different, we would reject the null hypothesis (i.e., of no difference) and conclude that the population means are not equal. The question is, "How different is very different?" The use of inferential statistics gives a probabilistic answer to this question.

Statistical Decisions and Alpha Levels

Researchers use inferential statistics to compute the probability of obtaining the observed data if the null hypothesis is true. If this probability is large, then the null hypothesis is likely to be true. Alternatively, if this probability is small, the null hypothesis is likely to be false. In that case, the researcher would say that the results are **statistically significant**. To say a finding is statistically significant means that it is unlikely that the finding is due to chance alone.

An arbitrary cutoff point called the **alpha level** (written $\propto$) is used for making this decision.[i] Traditionally, researchers set alpha to a small value, such as 0.05 or 0.01. Referring back to the example will help to clarify these important concepts. Let's walk through the steps.

[i]Alpha, as used here, is entirely different from the reliability index of coefficient alpha. It is a historical accident that the first letter of the Greek alphabet was used for these two different statistical concepts.

1. The researcher is interested in the reaction time of men and women.
2. The null hypothesis states that the mean reaction times of the two populations do not differ.
3. The inferential statistical procedure evaluates the size of the observed mean difference between the samples.
4. If the sample means are so different that it is unlikely that the samples could have come from populations with equal means, then we reject the null hypothesis and we infer that the population means must be different.

Type I and Type II Errors

The alpha level guides our decisions about the null hypothesis. When the probability is greater than the alpha level, we retain the null hypothesis; when the probability is equal to or less than the alpha level, we reject the null hypothesis. Of course, there is always the chance that a researcher's decision will be wrong. For example, a researcher might reject the null hypothesis and conclude that the population means are not equal when they actually are equal. In this case, the researcher has made a **Type I error**. (In a Type I error, we conclude that there is a statistically significant difference when there actually is not.) The probability of this error is equal to the alpha level that the researcher selects. The alpha level is the proportion of Type I errors that we can expect to make if we repeat the study many times. If an alpha of .05 is used, Type I errors will occur 5% of the time. If the alpha is .01, Type I errors will occur 1% of the time.

If alpha is the level of Type I error and the researcher decides what alpha to use, why not set alpha to zero to avoid all Type I errors? The reason is that there is another possible error, known as a Type II error. A **Type II error** occurs when we fail to reject the null hypothesis when it is false; that is, when we conclude the population means are equal when they are not. (In a Type II error, we conclude there is no significant difference when there actually is.)

The term "**beta**" (**β**) refers to the probability of making a Type II error. Researchers want to avoid both errors, but because they can never be sure of the real state of nature, there is always the chance for error in the decision. Decreasing the Type I error rate, without doing anything else, will automatically increase the Type II error rate. Therefore, we must balance these two errors against one another. The researcher handles this by selecting a Type I error rate and adjusting the sample size to control the Type II error rate. The procedures for determining the sample size to get a specific Type II error rate are beyond the scope of this text, but we will discuss the principles shortly in our discussion of power. Table 5.11 summarizes the definitions of Type I and Type II errors.

TABLE 5.11 Type I and Type II Errors

	RESEARCHER'S DECISION	
TRUE STATE OF NATURE	**REJECT THE NULL HYPOTHESIS**	**RETAIN THE NULL HYPOTHESIS[a]**
Null hypothesis is true	Type I error	Correct decision
Null hypothesis is false	Correct decision	Type II error

[a]Technically, we never actually accept the null hypothesis. Instead, we "retain" or "fail to reject" the null hypothesis. The interested student should consult an introductory statistics textbook for the reasoning behind this subtle distinction.

Quick-Check Review 5.4: Statistical Inference

1. Distinguish populations from samples.
2. What is sampling error?
3. Define "alpha level," "Type I error," and "Type II error."

INFERENTIAL STATISTICS

We use inferential statistics to draw inferences about populations based on samples drawn from those populations. This section introduces the most common inferential statistics and several statistical concepts, including statistical power and effect size.

Testing for Mean Differences

Researchers use inferential statistics most frequently to evaluate mean differences between groups. The two most widely used procedures are the *t*-test and the analysis of variance.

The *t*-Test. The most commonly used procedure for comparing two groups is the ***t*-test**. The null hypothesis for the *t*-test states that there is no difference between the two population means; that is, the observed difference between the sample means is due only to sampling error.

The general procedure in inferential statistics is to compute the test statistic (*t* in this case) and the probability (***p*-value**) of obtaining this value of the test statistic if the null hypothesis is true. If the *p*-value is less than alpha, we reject the null hypothesis and conclude that the population means are different.

There are two different types of *t*-tests. Which one you should use will depend on the research
05:09 design. We will cover those procedures in Chapters 10 and 11. The procedures for computing these
05:10 *t*-tests are included on the Student Resource Website.

Analysis of Variance. We use an **analysis of variance (ANOVA)** to test for mean differences between two or more groups. The term "analysis of variance" is confusing because the test actually compares the group means, but it compares these means by computing and comparing different population variance estimates. Explaining how this is accomplished is beyond the scope of this book.

ANOVA is one of the most flexible analysis procedures used in psychology. There are many variations. Which variation of ANOVA you should use will depend on the research design. You will learn more about ANOVA in Chapters 10 through 12, including its terminology, interpretation, and what variation of ANOVA to use with each design. The Student Resource Website shows how
05:11 to compute these inferential statistics either manually or by using the PASW statistical software program.

The Power of a Statistical Test

The term "**power**" or "**statistical power**" refers to a statistical procedure's sensitivity to mean differences. Power is the capability of correctly rejecting the null hypothesis when it is false. It is in the researcher's interest to increase the power of the tests (i.e., the tests' ability to recognize when the means differ). Note that if you increase power, you are decreasing the Type II error level.

The primary way to increase power is to increase sample size. The sample size needed to achieve a specified level of power can be computed based on pilot data as part of the procedures-design phase, a process called **power analysis** (Cohen, 1992). Most graduate-level statistics textbooks cover this procedure.

Power is not a function of the statistical procedure or sample size alone, but also depends on the precision of the research design. To understand power, you need to know that *any improvement in a research design that increases sensitivity will increase power.* This includes sampling more precisely, using more precise measures, using better standardization of procedures, and controlling individual differences through the choice of a research design (see Chapter 11).

Effect Size

The primary way to increase power, which is the same as decreasing Type II error, is to increase the sample size. In theory, you can increase the sample size of a study to a level that will detect even the most trivial difference between two populations. You might think that such action would be desirable because the researcher wants to find statistically significant differences in the research, but consider the following.

Suppose research on obesity compares an experimental group that attends a weight-reduction program with a no-treatment control group. After 6 months, the treated group has lost a mean of 2.2 pounds and the control group gained 0.2 pounds, and this difference is statistically significant. However, the *effect* of that weight-reduction program is so small as to be trivial. Although it is statistically significant, is that small weight loss after 6 months of intense effort of any personal significance? Most dieters would say no.

It has become a standard procedure for researchers to go a step beyond statistical significance testing and to compute the **effect size** of an experimental manipulation. This is a measure of the size of the difference between the group means expressed in standard deviation units, as shown in equation (5.5). For example, an effect size of 0.5 says the mean difference is 0.5 times the standard deviation. Cohen (1992) proposed a scale for the size of the effect (small, 0.2; moderate, 0.5; or large, 0.8) to guide researchers in interpreting the calculated effect.

$$\textit{Effect Size} = \frac{\overline{X}_1 - \overline{X}_2}{\text{Average } s} \tag{5.5}$$

Now, a little test. Think this through: suppose that research on three different treatments to reduce phobic anxiety shows that all three are effective and the results are statistically significant. The study also reports effect sizes of 0.1, 0.2, and 0.8. What does that information suggest about the three treatments?

As effect size increases—that is, as the difference between populations means increases—power increases. The reason for the increase in power is that it is easier to detect large differences in population means than small differences. Think of it this way: it would be easier to find a shovel in a haystack than a needle, because the shovel is larger and therefore easier to detect. The same is true of effect sizes. If an independent variable has a small effect, it is like looking for a needle in a haystack, but large effect sizes stand out more readily and therefore are easier to detect statistically.

05:12 The details of computing the effect size are covered on the Student Resource Website.

05:13, 05:14, 05:15, 05:16

The Student Resource Website also has a series of tutorials on statistical theory, using PASW for Windows, and computing descriptive and inferential statistics using PASW for Windows. These resources give you maximum flexibility in deciding how much statistical detail you want to cover. Most of these resources will be discussed in more detail later in the text.

Quick-Check Review 5.5: Inferential Statistics

1. Which statistical tests evaluate mean differences? Under what conditions should each of these statistical tests be used?
2. What is power analysis and why is it important?
3. What is effect size? What important information does this measure provide?

ETHICAL PRINCIPLES

We noted in the earlier Cost of Neglect box that it is possible to deceive people by selecting those statistics that support one's position and ignoring contradictory information. Scientists have a particularly important ethical obligation to present their findings and the statistics that summarize those findings in a manner that accurately reflects the data. Selecting data or using statistical procedures that deliberately emphasize some aspects while de-emphasizing other aspects in order to distort the results and mislead people is dishonest and unethical. It is called cherry-picking the data and, like data fabrication and plagiarism, is grossly unethical scientific behavior. It falls into the ethical responsibilities category of honestly and accurately obtaining and reporting data and authorship.

Cherry-picking is not limited to scientific data but occurs throughout society. In fact it is so common that most people, it seems to us, do not recognize it when it occurs, even when we do it ourselves, such as "stretching a point" in discussion with a friend. In effect, it has become commonly accepted practice. When elected officials tell us about the improvements their economic program has created, presenting only supportive data and failing to mention the costs and other negatives, they are cherry-picking. When advertisers present television testimonials about how successful a product is, but fail to give equal time to the failures and dissatisfied customers, they are cherry-picking. When we see and hear such things, we tend to say, "Well, of course they say that. They're only putting their best foot forward. It's natural for them to do that." But it is also telling a lie by selectively distorting the data—presenting some information and hiding other information—twisting it until it looks the way they want it to look.

In science, we cannot allow the "best foot forward" ethic to take precedence over the honest reporting of data. Some politicians and advertisers seem to be "in the business" of presenting biased information, and they do it quite well. However, we cannot tolerate the same conduct in science.

Scientists are subject to the same expectations and biases that characterize all human beings. (We will discuss those biases in later chapters.) Scientists, however, have a particular responsibility to identify their biases and select procedures that reduce or eliminate them. In analyzing data, the intellectually honest scientist will respect ethical obligations and will be objective about how well the data support his or her own theory and/or the theories of other researchers.

Quick-Check Review 5.6: Ethical Principles

1. What is the responsibility of scientists with regard to presenting their statistical data?
2. What is meant by cherry-picking the data?

SUMMARY

- Statistical procedures depend on variability among participants.
- Statistics are tools that help researchers to interpret the results of studies.
- Frequency distributions and graphs summarize sets of data.
- Descriptive statistics include measures of central tendency, variability, and relationship.
- Inferential statistics, such as the *t*-test and the analysis of variance, help to interpret data.
- Inferential statistics are used in making decisions about populations based on samples drawn from those populations.
- Sampling error is the natural variation among different samples drawn from the same population.
- The appropriate statistic(s) depend on the nature of both the data and the research questions.
- The null hypothesis states that there is no statistical difference between the population means.
- Statistical power refers to the sensitivity of a statistical procedure to the hypothesized mean differences.
- Effect size is an indication of the difference between group means expressed in standard deviation units.
- Ethical researchers should always use statistics to represent their research results accurately and fairly.

Putting It into Practice

Data show that individual differences exist everywhere. Open a newspaper and look at baseball players' batting averages, housing prices, or stock listings. Pick one of these and prepare a frequency distribution and a graph of the distribution. If you have access to a data analysis program, such as *PASW for Windows*, input the data and compute descriptive statistics. Based on your computations, look at individual ball players, houses, or stocks and see how they compare. For example, what is a typical batting average and what batting average is truly exceptional? What is the median housing price in your community? What is the average price of a stock? Taking time to do this exercise will give you a feel for how descriptive statistics can help you visualize what would otherwise be an overwhelming amount of data.

EXERCISES

5.1. Define the following key terms. Be sure that you understand them. They are discussed in the chapter and defined in the glossary.

statistical procedures
individual differences
descriptive statistics
inferential statistics
frequencies
frequency distribution
cross-tabulation
univariate
grouped frequency distribution
continuous variable
graphs
histogram
frequency polygon
x-axis, or abscissa
y-axis, or ordinate
symmetric distribution
normal distribution
skewed distribution
positively skewed
negatively skewed
central tendency
variability
measures of central tendency
mode
bimodal
trimodal
median
mean
range
average deviation
variance
sum of squares
degrees of freedom
standard deviation
relationship
covary
correlation coefficient, or correlation
Pearson product-moment correlation
linear relationship
scatter plot
positive correlation
perfect correlation
negative correlation
nonlinear relationship
Spearman rank-order correlation
Phi
regression
coefficient alpha
standard score, or *Z*-score
relative score
percentile rank
population
sample
sampling error
probability
null hypothesis
statistically significant
alpha level
Type I error
Type II error
beta
t-test
p-value
analysis of variance (ANOVA)
power (statistical power)
power analysis
effect size

5.2. For each of the following data sets (a) graph the data, (b) compute the measures of central tendency, and (c) compute the measures of variability.

a. 10 exam scores: 8; 6; 4; 3; 9; 5; 7; 8; 5; 5
b. 15 IQ scores: 104; 121; 91; 107; 81; 96; 100; 96; 102; 11; 87; 101; 91; 114; 111

5.3. Draw each of the following: a positively skewed curve, a negatively skewed curve, and a symmetrical curve.

5.4. Draw approximate scatter plots for correlations of .22, .50, −.73, .02, −.02, 1.00.

5.5. What kind of statistical test would answer each of the following research questions?

a. Is the weight of sixth-grade boys related to their aggressiveness?
b. Are girls better than boys at fine-motor coordination?
c. Will the behavior of laboratory animals change as the level of noise increases?
d. Do fourth-, fifth-, and sixth-grade children differ in their animal welfare concerns?

CHAPTER SIX

FIELD RESEARCH: NATURALISTIC AND CASE STUDY RESEARCH

[Scientists] must acquire an extensive portfolio of methods . . . and must apply their skills aided by an immense base of shared knowledge about the domain and the profession.

—David Klahr and Herbert Simon, 2001

WEB RESOURCE MATERIAL

06:01 Applied Research Strategies
06:02 For what is a Scientist Remembered? (Sociology of Science)
06:03 Examples of Naturalistic and Case Study Research
06:04 Making Observations
06:05 Study Guide/Lab Manual
06:06 Links to Related Internet Sites

The term "**field research**" applies to a variety of research methods, ranging from low to high constraint. They generally focus on observing naturally occurring behavior under largely natural conditions—that is, observing behavior "in the field." Table 6.1 describes six types of field research. This chapter covers the lower-constraint field-research methods of naturalistic observation, archival research, and case studies. After you will have learned about higher-constraint research, Chapter 13 takes a second look at field research, covering surveys and the higher-constraint field-research methods.

Naturalistic and case study methods are flexible approaches that allow the researcher to take advantage of unexpected occurrences and new ideas developed during the observations. These methods focus on the natural flow of behavior without controls or manipulations by the researcher. Naturalistic research is carried out in natural environments, such as an animal's habitat, a schoolroom, or a workplace. Case study research is slightly higher in constraint, with the researcher intervening to some degree to create situations that are likely to produce interesting information. The Student Resource Website discusses applied research strategies used in a variety of natural settings.

06:01

THE CHALLENGE OF LOW-CONSTRAINT RESEARCH

You might think that low-constraint methods are easy to carry out because researchers impose few controls and make observations in a flexible manner. As in all research, however, care and effort are required. Indeed, the lack of high-constraint procedures adds a burden, because researchers cannot depend on the many supports provided by laboratory settings.

Examples of Naturalistic Observation

The defining characteristic of naturalistic observation is that the researcher observes and systematically records naturally occurring events and later develops hypotheses about why they occurred.

TABLE 6.1 Categories of Field Research

Naturalistic Observation—Observation of events as they occur in natural settings
Archival Research—Studying information from existing records made in natural settings
Surveys—Asking direct questions of people in natural settings
Case Studies—Making extensive observations of an individual or small group of individuals
Program Evaluation—Conducting evaluations of applied procedures in natural settings
Field Experiments—Conducting experiments in natural settings in order to understand causal relationships among variables

Note: Surveys, program evaluation, and field experiments are covered in Chapter 13.

This section illustrates these characteristics with examples drawn from the fields of biology, ethology, sociology, and psychology.

Biology. Naturalistic observation has a long history in science. For example, Darwin's (1859) naturalistic observation of animals and plants is generally considered the most important research in all of biology (Trefil & Hazen, 2007). Darwin recorded detailed observations of hundreds of species of plants and animals and then devoted years to trying to understand the processes that might account for the patterns that he observed. From his observations, Darwin developed his concept of natural selection. He also contributed a pioneering study of child development, recording detailed observations of his son's infancy and childhood (Darwin, 1877). Darwin's work illustrates how powerful naturalistic observation can be in the hands of gifted scientists, as discussed in Historical Lesson 6.1.

Ethology. **Ethology** is the study of organisms in their natural environments. For example, Jane Goodall's (1986, 1988) and Christophe Boesch's (Boesch, 2009; Robbins & Boesch, 2011) naturalistic studies of chimpanzees in the forests of Tanzania produced new knowledge about the

HISTORICAL LESSON 6.1: NATURALISTIC RESEARCH AND EVOLUTION

Naturalistic observation may be the lowest-constraint scientific research, but it is a valuable and powerful tool in the hands of gifted scientists. During their separate journeys, many years apart, Charles Darwin and his contemporary, Alfred Russel Wallace, made extensive observations of plants and animals, carefully recording their observations with written descriptions and drawings. Their studies took place long before the development of photographic equipment and recording devices. Nevertheless, they recorded sufficient detail that each was independently able to recognize what looked like clear patterns in their data.

Both Darwin and Wallace found that species were not random, but formed categories that shared a remarkable number of features. They asked the critical question of how such a pattern might have occurred. Remember our discussion of inductive and deductive reasoning in Chapter 2? Darwin and Wallace used inductive reasoning to ask what kind of process would have created these patterns of species characteristics. Both came to the same conclusion: geographically separated groups will gradually diverge, because the members in each isolated group that are most adapted to the specific demands of the local environment are more likely to survive and mate. In time, each isolated group from this single species will experience so much genetic drift that the two groups will diverge into separate, although obviously related, species.

As groundbreaking as the theory of evolution was, it would have been little more than a footnote in history if it were not for the deductive reasoning of tens of thousands of scientists over the next 150 years of research. These scientists took the theory and derived specific predictions, which they tested in research studies. Most importantly, the data supported the vast majority of those predictions (Larson, 2004). When the predictions failed, that information pointed scientists toward refinement of the theory of evolution (Trefil & Hazen, 2007).

Evolution is the most thoroughly tested theory in the history of science. The tens of thousands of independent research studies in more than a dozen different scientific disciplines have established evolutionary theory as the best-validated theory in all of science. But it was the low-constraint naturalistic observations of Darwin and Wallace, coupled with their brilliant insights, that created the theory that changed biological science (Wynn & Wiggins, 1997).

highly social nature of chimpanzees. Boesch (2005) and Boesch and Boesch-Acherman (1991) observed chimpanzees using stone tools and hunting cooperatively—behaviors considered to be major steps in social evolution. McGrew (1992, 2004) identified 19 different kinds of tools used by chimpanzees. Whiten and Boesch (2001) identified distinct cultural differences between groups of chimpanzees that they passed on to the next generation through instruction. All of these naturalistic observations illustrate the amazing capacity of chimpanzees.

Sociology. A classic example of naturalistic observation is Adeline Levine's (1982) sociological study of the Love Canal disaster, in which a thousand residents abandoned their homes that had been built over a toxic waste dump. Levine (1982) wanted to understand how that catastrophe affected residents and how community leaders responded. She reviewed historical records, met with residents and officials, attended public meetings, and monitored newspaper reports and news broadcasts, documenting the events and their psychological, social, and financial impact. Levine's research is enormously important and could only be carried out using naturalistic research methods.

Another sociological example is Phillip Davis's research on corporal punishment of children (Davis, 1997). More than 80% of American parents report use of some forms of corporal punishment, such as hitting, spanking, whipping, and shaking (Graziano et al., 1996; Taylor et al., 2010). Most studies of corporal punishment use surveys, but there are obvious problems in simply asking parents, "How often and how severely do you hit your kids?"

Davis chose to observe the behavior of parents, children, and bystanders in public places like shopping malls. He watched for adults hitting children, and unobtrusively observed them. The following is an example of one of the 250 hitting incidents he observed.

> Two men, a woman, and a boy (about six) shop in a department store, one man trying out a treadmill. When the boy gets on (another) treadmill the man snaps "… you don't get down, I'm gonna whip you in two seconds!" The boy gets astride a bicycle on display and the man on the treadmill tells the others to do something. The other man pulls the boy from the bike, but the bike nearly topples and the man gives the boy a swat on the bottom. He directs a few hushed words at the boy [then] sees the boy making a face at him. He grabs furiously at the boy's jacketed shoulder with a muffled thud and clutches a handful of collar. Twisting the jacket hard in his fist and jerking the boy forward, he leans into the boy's face and angrily snarls something under his breath. Then he spins the boy around, holds him steady, and hits his bottom hard. As the group is about to leave, the man ... on the treadmill snaps at the boy "One more time and you're OUT!" They stroll away, but the boy gets on a stair step machine. The treadmill man tries to take the boy's arm and the boy pulls back slightly. As though offended by the little show of resistance, the man spanks the boy's bottom five times. He says a few angry words and casually walks away. Frozen and mute at first, the boy breaks into a soft cry before bustling after the group. (Davis, 1997, p. 7)

Psychology. In a now classic study, Rosenhan (1973) investigated the use of psychiatric diagnoses and the experiences of mental patients in hospitals. Eight "pseudopatients" (Rosenhan's research assistants) signed into various mental hospitals with feigned complaints of hearing voices saying "thud, hollow, and empty." The pseudopatients were instructed to display no other signs of mental disorder during their hospital stay. Once admitted, they behaved normally and gave no indication of their supposed hallucinations.

Hearing voices is usually a symptom of psychosis, but without additional symptoms, the person would not qualify for any specific diagnosis. Furthermore, the voices reported by the

TABLE 6.2 Examples of Naturalistic Observation Studies

Athletic drug use patterns in bodybuilders. Auge et al. (1999) went undercover as participant observers to study the use of performance-enhancing drugs by bodybuilders. The data revealed a far greater use of drugs and more extensive communication and support among the athletes than was formerly believed.

Aggression among young adults in bars. Graham and Wells (2001) observed incidents of aggression in bars between midnight and 2:30 A.M. They found that most involved small groups of men.

Children with autism. Toomey and Adams (1995) observed the spontaneous verbalizations of children with autism during social conflict situations and positive social interactions. Their observations suggested that social conflict might actually be a significant vehicle for the development of social competence in these children.

Young children doing mathematics: observations of everyday activities. Ginsburg et al. (1999) observed children in free play and recorded instances in which the children engaged in mathematical explorations well beyond the children's developmental levels. The authors concluded that such observations can serve as the bases for higher-level education in mathematics for young children.

pseudopatients were not typical for patients with psychotic disorders. The eight researchers were admitted to 12 different hospitals, and apparently none of the hospitals' staffs discerned that they were not real patients, although some of the other patients did. Most of the pseudopatients were diagnosed with schizophrenia. Once admitted, they unobtrusively observed hospital conditions and the behavior of staff and patients. As in the Levine study, naturalistic methods were not only appropriate, but were the best way to investigate the issue.

Naturalistic methods are used to study human behaviors in a variety of public places, such as smoking, drinking, driving, shopping, and children in classrooms. Table 6.2 lists additional examples of naturalistic studies.

Examples of Case Study Research

Case-study research imposes mild constraints on the procedures. For example, case studies are not typically carried out in natural environments, but in settings selected by the researcher. In addition, the researcher selects the behavior to be studied, rather than focusing on the total context and natural flow of behavior. By imposing constraints, case studies narrow the focus, but retain the essential interest in participants' natural behavior. This section briefly describes the classic case-study research of Freud, Witmer, and Piaget, and some contemporary case studies of two puzzling clinical phenomena.

Sigmund Freud. Starting in the late nineteenth century, Freud interviewed patients within the mild constraints of his office. Most of these early patients reported physical symptoms, but with no physical basis for those symptoms. As the patients talked of their early lives, dreams, fears, and fantasies, Freud noted patterns, drew inferences about their subjective functioning, and gradually developed psychoanalytic theory and treatment. He believed that case studies, rather than laboratory research, were best for understanding his clients and their problems. Focusing on the psychology of unconscious processes, he popularized an alternative to the then-dominant laboratory-based psychology of consciousness.

E. L. Witmer. At the turn of the twentieth century, E. L. Witmer treated children with learning and behavioral problems and created the world's first psychological clinic at the University of

Pennsylvania (Brotemarkle, 1966). Witmer used medical and psychological examinations of each child to assess whether the child's problems were due to brain pathology or to inadequate teaching and learning. Relying on careful measurements, he tried to determine what treatments would be successful. Witmer developed a case-study, treatment-educational approach that he called "psychoeducation." He also coined the term "clinical psychology" and is widely viewed as the father of clinical psychology.

06:02

It is interesting to compare the impact of people like Freud and Witmer and how each approached the scientific questions they studied. The Student Resource Website compares these two giants of clinical psychology.

Jean Piaget. Whereas Freud and Witmer used case-study methods to treat persons with psychological problems, Piaget studied the normal cognitive development of a small number of children over several years. Presenting specific questions and tasks, he observed how each child solved practical problems, and he drew inferences about their developing thought processes. His case-study approach allowed him the flexibility to alter methods and take advantage of ideas or observations that occurred during his studies. His hypotheses about cognitive development have held up well under examination in later, higher-constraint research.

Contemporary Case Studies. Several case studies describe two puzzling and rare clinical disorders, both of which include severely distorted perceptions of one's physical body. Katherine Phillips studied people with body dysmorphic disorder, the irrational belief that one is ugly and disfigured (Phillips, 2004; Phillips et al., 2007). A related disorder is body integrity identity disorder, which is a desire to have one or more body parts amputated (Bensler & Paauw, 2003; Large, 2007; Levy, 2007; Money et al., 1977). The descriptive case studies of these recently recognized disorders provide hypotheses to be tested in higher-constraint research and suggestions for treating these disorders (e.g., Braam et al., 2006). Because research is fairly new in these areas, low-constraint case studies are appropriate procedures.

06:03

Case study methods are not limited to clinical, educational, and scientific areas, but are used in many others, including business (e.g., Yin, 2009). The Student Resource Website has many other examples of naturalistic and case study research.

Quick-Check Review 6.1: The Challenge of Low-Constraint Research

1. What made the research of Darwin and Goodall naturalistic research?
2. Why is the work of people like Freud and Piaget classified as case studies?
3. Differentiate case study research and naturalistic research.

THE VALUE OF LOW-CONSTRAINT METHODS

This section discusses the value of low-constraint research, when to use these techniques, and what can be learned from them.

Conditions for Using Low-Constraint Research

Exploratory Research. Low-constraint research is appropriate when the questions concern the natural flow of behavior in natural and man-made settings, such as jungles, ocean depths, airports, bars, and workplaces. One productive use of low-constraint methods is at the early stages of a research area (called **exploratory research**). For example, adults can organize their behavior with reference to time, but can children do so? Suppose that you are studying this question by observing young children in a nursery school. You would look for evidence in the child's behavior that indicates an awareness of time. Perhaps it will be tussling over a toy, arguing, "I saw it first!" This suggests a concept of sequencing of events and some idea of time, although the child may be simply echoing an argument successfully used by an older child. Such observations stimulate hypotheses that can be tested later at higher constraint levels.

Creative Starting Point for Research. Low-constraint research is often the creative starting point for new research, facilitating leaps to the next levels of discovery. Such low-constraint research is not only useful but is necessary in contemporary science. Klahr and Simon (2001) note that scientists routinely employ both "strong" and "weak" methods. The strong, high-constraint methods allow valid testing of causal hypotheses. The weak methods include thinking by analogy, recognition of patterns, and making conceptual leaps, all of which are central in low-constraint research. They allow an unfettered, wide-ranging search for contingencies. The best scientists routinely employ both high- and low-constraint methodologies (Dunbar, 1994; Thagard, 1998).

Gifted scientists do not simply collect data in their studies. Even while the data are coming in, those scientists watch for unexpected events that might provide new insights. In a Historical Lesson box in Chapter 1, we noted chance findings in science, suggesting that they were not quite so random. Scientists need to maintain a "prepared mind," constantly looking for interesting phenomena, whether they are walking through a park or monitoring the collection of data. If you are that scientist, you will raise your eyebrows and perk up your ears whenever something out of the ordinary happens. You will immediately want to know what happened and why. For the best scientists, such alertness is as natural as breathing.

Familiarize Oneself with a New Research Area. Another use for naturalistic observation is to familiarize us with events, participants, or settings that are new to us. Suppose that you have little experience in studying young children, but want to extend some part of Piaget's work on cognitive development. It would be useful for you to spend a day simply observing young children in a nursery school, getting some general idea of how those children behave in that setting.

Demonstrating Feasibility. You can also use low-constraint procedures to demonstrate a new research or treatment technique. Here you are not attempting to test a prediction or develop new hypotheses, but only to see whether some method is feasible. For example, to study children's cognitive development, you need to be certain that children will find the research tasks interesting enough that they will cooperate. Thus, it would be useful to try out the tasks with a few children before beginning the actual study.

Testing Generalizability. Case study and naturalistic research can also enhance the generalizability of research findings, especially in areas in which the research has been conducted in

UNDERSTANDING THE CONCEPT 6.1: THE THERAPIST AS SCIENTIST

A widely accepted model for the training of clinical psychologists is the **scientist-practitioner model**. This model holds that therapists require extensive training in the scientific method and the thought processes that are part of that method. Understanding the way scientists gather information and draw conclusions is believed to sharpen clinicians' skill in information gathering and treatment planning.

The case study is a useful research strategy; for the therapist, every client is a case study. A therapist must gather information and generate hypotheses about the reasons for a client's behavior. The effective use of case studies, especially the methods of inference, is an important skill for the effective therapist.

The phases of research presented in Chapter 2 are applicable to the therapy session. The therapist generates ideas about the client's problems, how they developed, and how they might be corrected. The initial information might be vague, suggesting several ideas. The clinician then translates these ideas into specific hypotheses and develops plans for testing them. The observation phase may involve asking the client questions and closely observing how the client responds to situations. The analysis phase relies less on statistics and more on rational inferences, and the analysis and interpretation phases are difficult to separate. Therapists record their observations in progress notes so that the information will be available to them or to other clinicians who might work with the client in the future. The important point is that clinicians, in gathering the information necessary for treatment planning, are operating like research scientists.

The scientist-practitioner model dominates the training of clinical psychologists in most accredited programs. The best therapists, we believe, think like scientists, and scientific training is essential in their education.

laboratory settings. In this context, **generalizability** refers to how well laboratory findings predict events in real-world settings. The advantages of laboratory research are enormous, but can we be sure that the laboratory behavior is what we would observe in the natural environment? Naturalistic research methods, and to some degree case study research, can be used to test the generalizability of the theories developed or refined in laboratory studies. Psychologists have frequently used low-constraint research to test the generalizability of laboratory findings. It is reassuring that most studies from psychological laboratories generalize quite well to the real world (Anderson et al., 1999).

Case study research is particularly valuable for studying specific individuals when there is no concern for generalizing results to a population. This is especially relevant for clinical psychologists, who want to understand individual clients and the causes of each client's problems. The ideal education for clinical psychologists is training to be both scientists and therapists, as discussed in Understanding the Concept 6.1.

Information Gained from Low-Constraint Research

Identifying New Information. Low-constraint observations provide descriptive information. For example, Goodall's (1978) finding that a group of chimpanzees in the wild attacked and killed another group was the first observation of chimpanzee behavior that resembled warfare. These observations could not explain the event or determine what caused it. However, her observations did establish a new fact and, in the process, raised interesting questions. For example, what triggers the chimpanzees to cooperate with allies and engage in aggression toward opponents, and what cognitive abilities are necessary to engage in such activities?

Negating a General Proposition. One of the most valuable functions of low-constraint research is that it can negate a general proposition. Suppose that prior to Goodall's observation we had believed the general proposition that "chimpanzees do not engage in group aggression resembling warfare." Goodall's observations show that this general proposition is incorrect. It takes only a single counterexample to negate a general proposition.

Another example of negating a general proposition involves the statement, "Man's superiority over other creatures is due to the fact that man is the only tool-making and tool-using animal." Again, Goodall's naturalistic observations refute this general proposition. She observed chimpanzees selecting twigs, stripping off the leaves to fashion a flexible rod, inserting the twigs into the narrow tunnels of a termite nest, waiting a moment, and then withdrawing the twig and licking off the termites clinging to it. This was purposeful and sophisticated behavior. The chimpanzees selected and modified natural objects, preparing them for use as food-gathering tools.

A final example involves some early research with autistic children. Psychologists who had pioneered the use of relaxation in behavior therapy believed that neither children nor psychotic adults could learn relaxation (Wolpe, 1958). Graziano and Kean (1968) succeeded in training four autistic children in relaxation skills—training that has been repeated many times with other children (e.g., Mullins & Christian, 2001; Reese et al., 1998). This case study negated the general proposition that children cannot learn relaxation skills.

Although low-constraint research can negate a general proposition, it cannot establish one. We cannot conclude from Goodall's observations that all chimps engage in warfare or from the Graziano and Kean study that all children can learn relaxation skills. We never know if the low-constraint observations are representative of the larger population. This limitation is related to issues of sampling, which we will cover in more detail later in this chapter and again in Chapter 9.

Identifying Contingencies. All research seeks to identify and understand relationships among variables. The type of relationship studied differs from one level of constraint to another. Experimental research identifies causal relationships among variables. In low-constraint research, we cannot make such causal inferences, but we can obtain other useful information. For example, the ethologist Niko Tinbergen (1963) observed that the parent herring gull provided food for its chick when the young bird pecked a red spot on the adult's bill. When the spot appears, the chick usually pecks at it; when the chick pecks at the spot, the parent usually provides food (i.e., when X occurs, then Y will probably occur). Note that this does not state that X causes Y, but only that there is a high probability of one occurring when the other is present. This describes a probabilistic relationship between two variables. This type of probabilistic relationship is a **contingency**.

Low-constraint research can identify contingent relationships among variables, and these contingencies can stimulate higher-constraint research. This is exactly what Tinbergen did once he noticed the contingent relationship between the chick's pecking and the adult's feeding behavior; he followed up this observation by conducting systematic experiments. Contingent relationships observed in low-constraint research can be an important source for hypotheses for scientists to test with higher-constraint research.

Table 6.3 summarizes the value of low-constraint research.

Qualitative Research Methods

One use of low-constraint methods is in qualitative research. In higher-constraint research, we rely on formalized control procedures to increase the validity of research. In lower-constraint research, validity depends more on the researcher's clarity of thought, and there are always severe limitations

TABLE 6.3 The Value of Low-Constraint Research

NATURALISTIC AND CASE STUDY RESEARCH IS USEFUL

1. as exploratory research at the beginning of a new research area in which little information is available;
2. when the researcher wishes to gain familiarity with typical characteristics of settings or participants before planning high-constraint research;
3. when the questions specifically focus on the natural flow of behavior and/or on behavior in natural settings;
4. when the study is of a single individual, setting, or set of events, and the questions are specific to this person, setting, or set of events;
5. for demonstrating feasibility of a new procedure;
6. as a way of discovering contingencies or other interesting phenomena that can then be used as a basis for higher-constraint questions and research;
7. as a way of evaluating the generalizability of findings from laboratory research to natural environments.

FURTHERMORE, NATURALISTIC AND CASE STUDY RESEARCH CAN

1. describe events, including events never before observed;
2. identify contingent relationships among variables;
3. suggest hypotheses to be tested with higher-constraint research;
4. negate general propositions, although these methods cannot establish general propositions.

on what we can legitimately conclude. The low-constraint methods used in ethology have been extended to education, sociology, business management, nursing, communications, and psychology (see Table 6.2). Known collectively as **qualitative research methods**, their major goal is to describe and analyze functioning in everyday settings, ranging from informal conversations among friends to courtroom proceedings. In many qualitative research projects, the goal is different from quantitative research projects (Berg, 2004; Forrester, 2010; Marshall & Rossman, 1999). Specifically, the goal is to understand the actions from the perspective of the individual(s) under study. More emphasis is placed on the meaning attributed by the subject to his or her situation and the actions that they took in the situation. This philosophy is close to the humanistic perspective discussed in Chapter 1.

Qualitative research methods include naturalistic and participant observation, questionnaires, and analyses of conversations and social networks. Typically in qualitative studies, the researcher makes observations, organizes, interprets, and summarizes them, and then reports the results in a narrative rather than a statistical manner. Note that much of the research so far discussed in this chapter (Freud, Piaget, Davis, Levine, & Rosenhan) is qualitative research.

Quick-Check Review 6.2: The Value of Low-Constraint Methods

1. When should naturalistic research be used? When should case study research be used?
2. What are contingencies, and how are they used in later research?
3. Why does naturalistic research generalize more easily than laboratory research?
4. Explain how naturalistic research can negate, but not establish, a general proposition.

USING LOW-CONSTRAINT METHODS

This section presents the basics of conducting low-constraint research. Space constraints limit our coverage; sources such as Berg (2004) and Ritchie and Lewis (2003) provide more detail.

Problem Statements and Research Hypotheses

As we noted in Chapter 3, problem statements and research hypotheses are most highly formalized at the experimental level of constraint, but they are important at all levels of research, helping to organize the researcher's thinking. The inferences that can be confidently drawn differ depending on the constraint level. At the experimental level, the focus is on questions of causality. At the naturalistic and case study levels, the focus is on contingencies. We cannot address causal questions with these low-constraint methods because these methods lack the control available in experimental research.

Problem statements in low-constraint research are often general, because there might be no basis for generating specific questions. Problem statements also change readily in low-constraint research as we begin to grasp the issues through observation and narrow our focus to specific behavior. For example, suppose that you are an industrial-organizational psychologist called in by a company to evaluate a "communication problem." You know about the dynamics of business organizations and the strategies that might be applied to specific problems, but you do not know the nature of this particular company's so-called communication problem.

Your initial problem statement might be, "I wonder what is wrong." Interviewing several key people will likely unearth some clues. For example, carefully observing interactions among members of the company might suggest an underlying defensiveness as an important factor, and your problem statement might shift its focus in that direction. On the other hand, further observations may suggest that the defensiveness is more likely an effect than a cause of problems in the company. You might then begin to work with two or three narrower problem statements based on your knowledge of what types of situations could create the defensiveness. You might independently evaluate each of these through continued observation, fact gathering, and interviewing. All this might occur in the first day of the investigation, or it might take several days or weeks to get this far.

As you see in this example, low-constraint research can move flexibly from one area to another depending on what is discovered. At some point, you will need to focus on key elements, gather relevant data, and make specific suggestions. But, be careful—closing in on a narrow focus too early in your information gathering might blind you to critical issues and lead to poor recommendations.

As in this example, researchers conducting low-constraint research tend to start with general problem statements and then gradually narrow and focus them as more is learned about the issues. Problem statements gradually evolve into specific hypotheses, which guide the researcher in gathering specific information relevant to the hypotheses. However, this process has its limitations; low-constraint research can provide only so much information. If we want to know with confidence what is causing what, then the researcher must translate the hypotheses into higher-constraint research questions. We are sometimes tempted to draw causal inferences from low-constraint research, but it would be a mistake to do so.

Making Observations

The central phase of any research project is the observation or data-gathering phase. In higher-constraint research, the researcher makes detailed plans for gathering and analyzing the data *before making any observations*. In lower-constraint research, planning is less formal and more fluid. The researcher is free to change hypotheses and modify procedures during the observations. It is common in low-constraint research to design new studies based on initial observations. The Student Resource Website provides additional discussion of this critical task of making observations in low-constraint research.

06:04

Naturalistic research and case studies are low-constraint, but the observational methods might nevertheless include highly sophisticated instrumentation, like precise electronic recording equipment for capturing the behavior of animals in the wild. The research is still low-constraint by design; the technological equipment, no matter how sophisticated, does not define the level of constraint.

How to Observe. There are two ways to gather data in naturalistic observation: as an unobtrusive observer or as a participant observer. As an **unobtrusive observer**, the researcher tries to avoid influencing the participant, such as in the example of Davis's studies on spanking children. In fact, the unobtrusive observer tries to avoid notice by blending into the surroundings.

As a **participant observer**, the researcher becomes a part of the situation and may even contribute to it. This may include making the normal contributions almost anyone would make in the situation, or it might consist of carefully planned and executed changes in the researcher's behavior that tentatively test specific hypotheses. Levine utilized participant observation for some aspects of the study of the Love Canal crisis.

When the observer becomes a participant, the procedure is no longer naturalistic observation, but becomes a case study. One advantage of participant observation is that by manipulating one's behavior as an observer, the researcher is able to test hypotheses by creating situations that are unlikely to occur naturally. For example, Piaget did not passively observe children. Instead, he asked questions, created test situations, interacted with the children, and observed their responses.

The term "**measurement reactivity**" refers to the phenomenon of participants behaving differently than they might normally because they know that they are being observed. Some measures, called **reactive measures**, are particularly prone to such distortions, whereas others, called **nonreactive measures**, are not.

Measurement reactivity is a function of what participants believe is the appropriate behavior in the situation. People have a tendency to behave in ways that they think are appropriate when they know that people are observing them. For example, how much more likely is it that you will use a fork and knife to eat your chicken if you are dining in a nice restaurant than if you are at home alone? So if the observer can blend in and be unobtrusive, it is likely that the participants will show less measurement reactivity.

There are many ways to blend in and be unobtrusive when observing people. Sometimes, it can be as simply as sitting nearby and appearing to be uninterested in the activity. This is the classic unobtrusive observer technique. This is especially effective with naturalistic research. Sometimes, it is just a matter of being around regularly. There is a psychological process called **habituation**, in which organisms gradually reduce their attention and their responsiveness to any stimulus that is routinely present. People can actually habituate to having observers present or having cameras present to record behavior. No matter how it is done, decreasing the awareness in participants that they are being observed will tend to minimize measurement reactivity.

Unobtrusive Measures. **Unobtrusive measures** are measures of behavior that are not obvious to the person being observed and, consequently, are less likely to influence the person's behavior.

They take the concept of the unobtrusive observer, who blends in, one step further by making the measures blend in.

Webb et al. (1966, 2000) described several ingenious unobtrusive measures. For example, suppose that you want to measure interest level in a museum exhibit. You first need an operational definition of level of interest. One operational definition might be people's interest ratings. You ask each of the first 200 exhibit visitors to rate how interesting it is. This is an obtrusive measure because participants are aware that you are measuring their interest level, and this awareness might make the measure reactive. An alternative operational definition of interest level is the number of people who view the exhibit. You could measure this unobtrusively by having an observer count the number of people who approach the exhibit. One advantage of this approach is that the observer can record other information, such as how long people observe the exhibit.

Recording such information is called **coding** aspects of the data because it involves classifying aspects of the participant or the participant's behavior into predetermined research codes. Coding is a frequently used method of organizing participants' responses as a step in data organization. Such organization can make the analyzing and interpreting of the behavior much easier and more productive. For example, in developmental psychology, we might videotape children at play and later have trained research assistants code the children's behavior into categories such as aggressive behavior, withdrawal, cooperation, anxiety, or creativity—whatever behavior is being studied. The categories must be carefully defined with clear criteria, so the coders know what they are looking for.

In another example, using such demographic information as income and education level for each respondent, we might assign the numbers 1, 2, 3, or letters A, B, C, or even descriptive terms, Upper, Middle, Lower, corresponding to three socioeconomic levels. Through the process of coding, the participants are categorized into those three groups. Those participant categories would constitute ordinal data and, as discussed in Chapters 4 and 5, would be analyzed using the appropriate methods for ordinal data.

Coding is used to categorize virtually any observed behavior of animals and people in natural or laboratory settings. It is a mainstay of quantitative research, but it is also a common procedure in qualitative research, such as with **narrative data**, which involves the verbal descriptions of activities, events, or internal feelings.

The unobtrusive observer is effective and has the advantage of being able to collect other coded data during the observations. However, Webb et al. (1966, 2000) argue that sometimes researchers can develop simpler measures to provide the desired information. For example, one could note the degree of wear on the tiles of the floor surrounding the exhibit. Museums have to replace tiles around popular exhibits every few weeks, whereas the tiles around other exhibits last for years. Another method is the nose-print approach, in which the exhibit is arranged in a glass display so that people can get the best view by putting their faces right up to the glass. The researcher cleans the glass at the start of each day and dusts the glass with fingerprint powder at the end of the day. The researcher then counts the number of nose-prints made that day. Of course, not everyone will leave a nose-print, and some people will press their noses to the glass in several places, so this method will not give an accurate count of how many people viewed the display. However, measuring the number of people was not our goal; we wanted to measure how interesting the exhibit was. The number of people who viewed the exhibit is an operational definition of interest. The number of nose-prints is also a reasonable operational definition of interest level and may be superior in some ways to the head-count method.

Counting people who move by a location is now a relatively easy task. There are inexpensive devices, most of them wireless, that use magnetic, thermal, or other invisible light beams to capture such information unobtrusively and send it to a central source. Most of this equipment was designed to monitor traffic patterns in shopping settings, but it is easily adapted to other research questions. Wireless cameras are now small and inexpensive and can capture a wide range of behavioral activity. Of course, the use of such equipment may raise ethical issues involving privacy, but using the equipment in situations that one would not normally have an expectation of privacy may be ethically acceptable.

These examples were designed to help you to think more creatively when developing your own measures. There is nothing wrong with asking people to rate the interest level of museum exhibits, but it is valuable to seek independent data to substantiate the ratings.

Archival Measures. Existing records can provide information about events that have already occurred. **Archival records** include school records, marriage and divorce records, driving records, census data, and military, business, or industrial records. Archival records are usually in the form of printed narratives or numbers, but can also be in other forms, like photographs, drawings, and any type of electronic recording. A wealth of archival data is stored all over the world, just waiting for some enterprising young researcher to come and mine it.

A recent example of the use of archival data is a health-related field study carried out in Ghana by Peters et al. (2010). Their theory was that (1) cognitive, numeric, and decision-making abilities increase with exposure to schooling and (2) those abilities contribute to improved personal health behavior, such as AIDS prevention. This study found from the archival data that, as predicted, as education increased, AIDS prevention behavior also increased.

Governments gather archival data routinely to identify nationwide problems quickly. Statistics computed from archival data, such as the *Index of Leading Economic Indicators*, can accurately predict future events. Data gathered from hospitals about diseases under treatment allow officials to identify new diseases and narrow the range of possible causes of the diseases. Effective use of archival data depends on the quality of the data, their relevance to the research question, and the ingenuity of the researcher.

There are difficulties, however, in using data from archival records, most stemming from the fact that the researcher typically had no part in defining or recording the data. The records already exist and the researcher never had the opportunity to impose any research constraints on the procedures. Research with archival records is thus descriptive in nature. We can use existing records to identify variables, observe contingencies, calculate correlations, and make predictions about future events based on those correlations, but we cannot establish causality.

There is another problem that affects some archival records, called **selective survival**. Some records are faithfully and completely stored. These might include things like birth, death, and marriage records; school records; and weather records. Usually, these records are maintained by agencies for specific purposes, and once recorded, are protected and stored. Other records are less likely to be recorded systematically. For example, some families have thousands of photos and videos of their children growing up, whereas other families are much less likely to create such records. Moreover, families differ dramatically on how faithfully they preserve and maintain those photos and videos. It may well be that those families who preserve those records faithfully are different from the families who allow those records to be lost. Finally, historians are selective about what they consider critical to report, and thus some information is more faithfully passed onto future generations than other information. We talked about this when we discussed ancient Greek science, in which the rationalistic ideals of the great Greek philosophers were more diligently recorded and passed on than the empirical traditions that fueled the work of artisans and tradespeople.

There may also be serious problems with access to some archives. For example, school records might be very useful in a research project, but in many cases, privacy laws protect those records. Also, the archival data that is available might be poorly organized, incomplete, or so extensive as to be overwhelming. To make good use of archival data, we need to have a clear idea of what we are looking for, clear definitions of variables, and hypotheses about expected relationships.

Content analysis can be very useful in archival research. It involves examining records and identifying categories of events. For example, one might analyze political speeches for the occurrence of "patriotic-emotion" phrases. One could also analyze facial expressions in family photos for signs of family discord. A child's clumsy movements in home movies might indicate the presence of a subtle neurological disorder. The transcripts of court proceedings can reveal signs of bias by a judge. All of these measures have been used in published psychological research. Such content analyses require the structure of a well-thought-out research plan with clearly defined variables and objective procedures.

Although content analyses are useful with archival data, researchers can perform such analyses with any data set. For example, a social psychologist might use content analysis to understand the nature of leadership in a controlled laboratory study of small-group dynamics.

It might appear that using archival records is a poor way to measure a phenomenon, but this may not be so. Several sophisticated studies of genetic influences in psychopathology used archival records (e.g., Baker, 1989; Kety et al., 1968; Simonsen & Parnas, 1993; Wender et al., 1986). These investigators used records from many sources to track the rates of psychopathology in both the adoptive and biological families of severely disturbed adults who were adopted as infants. Most of these landmark studies were conducted in Denmark, where such archival records are unusually accurate and complete.

Another series of sophisticated studies used family archives to evaluate the hypothesis that people who develop schizophrenia show signs of subtle neurological problems during an otherwise normal childhood. Elaine Walker and her colleagues (e.g., Walker et al., 1994) used home movies to look for subtle indicators of neurological problems in children who years later developed schizophrenia. They found evidence in those home movies of a consistently higher rate of neuromotor abnormalities and motor skills deficits in the children who later developed schizophrenia compared to their siblings who did not develop this disorder. Later research (Mittal & Walker, 2007) found that a history of such neuromotor deficits predicted which individuals at risk for schizophrenia actually developed the disorder. These home movies provided an objective measure of these subtle abnormalities that would have been prohibitively expensive to gather in any other way (Walker et al., 2010).

Archival measures have a long history of use in psychological and social science research. In this information age, they are likely to continue to contribute to our research, although ethical and legal constraints on privacy will make some personal records off limits to researchers. But many archival records are not personal and are readily available to clever researchers who recognize their value in answering a specific research question.

Sampling of Participants

Deciding on the best way to observe participants is critical, but an equally important task is determining which participants to observe. In low-constraint research, we need to pay particular attention to the **sampling** (i.e., the selection) of participants. The more representative the sample, the more confidence we have in the generalizability of the findings. We cover sampling in detail in Chapters 9 and 13, but we want to introduce here the concept of representativeness and its relationship to generalizability. **Representativeness** refers to how closely a sample resembles the population under study.

In naturalistic and case study research, sampling is rarely under the researcher's control. For example, in psychotherapy research, clients seeking treatment constitute the sample. In a study of the impact of a natural disaster, those who had been present during the disaster constitute the sample. It is doubtful that such naturally occurring samples represent the larger population. For example, people who consult a therapist may have more problems or may be more concerned with their problems than are most people. They may be wealthier than most because they can afford the cost of psychotherapy or have insurance that will cover the cost.

When a sample differs from the general population, the sample is unrepresentative of the population. When that occurs, one must take care in generalizing the research findings. If you **generalize** a finding, you are saying that what was observed in the sample would also be observed in any other group of participants from the population. That is a reasonable conclusion if the sample adequately represents the population, but is much less reasonable if the sample is unrepresentative.

We seldom have the opportunity to select our own samples in low-constraint research. Therefore, we must judge how well the sample represents the population to which we want to generalize. The more representative the sample, the more confident our generalizations can be. However, researchers should always be cautious in generalizing from low-constraint research. Such generalizations are tentative hypotheses that might later be tested with higher-constraint research methods. As you will see later, when researchers control the sampling procedures, they can almost guarantee the representativeness of the sample.

Sampling of Situations

There are numerous ways that the sample of situations can be distorted. Some variables are beyond the researcher's control, and others can be controlled only at great cost or inconvenience.

Suppose that animals in the wild are to be the focus of study. Many animals behave differently during different seasons of the year. They may be active during some seasons and inactive during others. Most animals show diurnal fluctuations in activity; some might hunt at night and rest during the day, whereas others forage all day long. If the researcher observes the animals only during morning hours and only during spring and summer, a distorted picture of animal behavior may emerge. An even worse violation of this principle would be studying animals in zoos because they are easy to find, and then trying to generalize your observations to animals in the wild. Therefore, a good rule of thumb in early studies of any population is to sample situations as widely as possible. The broader the sample of situations and the broader the sample of participants, the more confidence one can have in the generalizability of the findings.

Sampling of Behaviors

Another issue is the importance of adequately sampling behaviors. In any situation, individuals may behave in many different ways. Therefore, a single observation of behavior in a particular situation may lead to an incorrect conclusion about how the individual generally behaves in this setting. For example, a normally patient individual may be having a bad day and so loses his or her temper. If you only see this individual on that one day, you might well get an inaccurate impression. However, by sampling behaviors repeatedly in each situation, it is possible to identify whatever behavioral variability that may exist.

Evaluating and Interpreting Data

Once we complete our observations, we should evaluate and interpret the results of the study, which usually involves statistical analyses. In many low-constraint studies, however, statistical analyses are not possible until we code the data.

Low-constraint studies often involve observing and recording everything that happens. For example, in a study of labor contract negotiations, the data set might be the transcripts of all negotiation sessions. In analyzing the data, the researcher may code the interactions into categories like hostile comments, requests for information, and suggested solutions. Dean Pruitt and his colleagues (e.g., Pruitt et al., 1997; Rubin et al., 1994) have used similar categories in a series of studies of negotiation and conflict resolution.

For lower-constraint studies, the statistical procedures may be no more complicated than descriptive statistics. Some comparisons may be useful, such as between different groups of participants or among the same participants under more than one condition. In the preceding example, we might want to compare the verbal statements of the labor negotiators with those of the management negotiators or compare the negotiation sessions that were fruitful with those that were not. Inferential statistics can address such questions. (Appendix D covers procedures for selecting the appropriate statistical test.)

We need to be cautious when interpreting data from low-constraint research studies because low-constraint research employs few controls. Controls help to eliminate alternative explanations of results, making it easier to draw a strong conclusion. Because such controls are largely absent in low-constraint studies, we seldom are able to draw strong conclusions. Furthermore, even the most sophisticated statistical analyses cannot correct these limitations. *No statistical analysis will create controls that were not part of the original study.*

Quick-Check Review 6.3: Using Low-Constraint Methods

1. What is qualitative research?
2. What are problem statements like in low-constraint research?
3. What are the two types of observers in research?
4. What are unobtrusive measures, and what are their advantages?
5. What are archival records, and how are they used in research?
6. What is the researcher's goal in sampling participants?
7. Why is it important to sample situations broadly in low-constraint research?
8. Explain the concept of measurement reactivity.
9. What is coding?

LIMITATIONS OF LOW-CONSTRAINT METHODS

Although low-constraint research methods are valuable tools in science, they have significant limitations that researchers must recognize.

Poor Representativeness

A major weakness in low-constraint research is poor representativeness. Low-constraint research typically observes already existing and available groups of respondents, providing little basis for generalizing from the studied group to a population. For example, a clinical psychologist cannot confidently generalize observations of her clients to all other clients. Why not? Her clients might be from a particular socioeconomic class that does not represent all clients, or they may have particular psychological problems less common in other client groups. Any natural clinical sample is biased because participants select themselves for therapy. Likewise, if an ethologist studies a group of otters, or a social psychologist studies a group of factory workers, he cannot confidently generalize his findings to all groups of otters or all factory workers. In order to generalize the findings from a particular sample to the larger population, we must carefully select a sample that accurately represents the larger population. Such careful selection of a representative sample is a higher-constraint procedure and is usually not possible in low-constraint research.

Poor Replicability

Another limitation of low-constraint research is related to the very characteristic that gives it its greatest strength—its flexibility. Because observations of naturally occurring behavior are made in settings in which the observer has imposed few constraints on participants, it is often difficult to replicate the research. Different investigators studying the same phenomenon using low-constraint methods may make different observations and therefore draw different inferences. Replication is possible only if researchers clearly state the details of their procedures so others can follow them. In low-constraint research, observational methods can shift during a study, making it difficult to document exactly what procedures were followed and why. Consequently, other researchers cannot replicate the study.

Causal Inference and Low-Constraint Research

Drawing causal inferences from low-constraint research is risky. **Causal inferences** are conclusions that imply that one or more variables brought about the observed state of another variable. For example, suppose that you enter a classroom and observe that a teacher appears to be angry and you learn that a child has been misbehaving. "Aha!" you might be tempted to conclude. "The teacher is angry because the child had misbehaved a few moments ago." You might be correct, but then again, perhaps not. In either event, this is an example of ex post facto (after the fact) reasoning.

Ex post facto conclusions are potential problems in low-constraint research. The fact that two variables are related is not sufficient to infer that one caused the other. In the example above, the child's misbehavior might have had nothing to do with the teacher's anger. Perhaps the teacher was angry with a colleague. Without more information, we cannot rule out that possibility. It is also possible that the teacher's anger stimulated the child's misbehavior, and not the other way around. It is tempting when two events occur at the same time or in close sequence to conclude that one event

TABLE 6.4 Examples of Possible Ex Post Facto Fallacies

The relationships listed below might have validity, but the ex post facto reasoning presented does not establish this validity.

1. Hard-drug users all smoked marijuana before turning to hard drugs; therefore, marijuana use leads to hard-drug addiction.
2. Alcoholics started with beer and wine; therefore, drinking beer and wine leads to alcoholism.
3. Child-abusing parents were often abused themselves as children; therefore, being abused as a child leads to becoming an abusive parent.
4. Most inmates in U.S. urban jails are black; therefore, being black leads to crime.
5. Many NHL hockey players are Canadian; therefore, being Canadian leads to playing professional hockey.
6. Aggressive children watch a great deal of television; therefore, watching a great deal of television leads to aggressive behavior in children.

must have caused the other. People draw this conclusion far too often, but low-constraint research does not provide adequate information to justify such causal inferences.

An **ex post facto fallacy** occurs when we draw unwarranted causal conclusions from the observation of a contingent relationship. Table 6.4 lists several examples of ex post facto fallacies. The logical fallacy is obvious in some of the statements, whereas others seem quite reasonable. Some of these assertions may be familiar, and you may have accepted them without much thought. Ex post facto data are insufficient to establish the causal statements in Table 6.4. Some of these conclusions may in fact be true, but it will take better-controlled research to establish that.

To establish causation, we need to establish three things.

1. Covariation of the events (i.e., the events are consistently related to one another).
2. A time-order relationship (i.e., the cause must precede the effect).
3. Alternative explanations have been ruled out.

In our example, the child's misbehavior and the teacher's anger co-occur, so we have established the first criterion. However, we do not know, because we just walked in and did not see the sequence of events, whether the child's misbehavior preceded the teacher's anger. Moreover, we have so little information about all the events that might have happened that we cannot rule out alternative explanations. In most low-constraint research, we simply do not have sufficient data to meet the three criteria for establishing causation.

Identifying contingencies in low-constraint research is useful in suggesting possible causal relationships. However, low-constraint research never provides the controls needed to rule out the possibility that other factors may have been involved. Clinical case studies, for example, are ex post facto approaches. They lack control over independent variables and are unable to rule out possible effects of other variables. For this reason, we cannot have confidence in any causal inference we might be tempted to draw. We should treat such inferences as speculative hypotheses to be tested with further research. For that purpose, case study methods can be useful.

When we interpret low-constraint findings as if they came from high-constraint research, our conclusions will be suspect. These suspect conclusions damage the credibility of other research, even well-designed, high-constraint research. For example, drinking beer and wine might not lead to alcoholism, but years of research suggest that a combination of heavy drinking and a genetic predisposition to alcoholism increases the risk of alcoholism. If teenagers dismiss the risk of heavy drinking because well-meaning people try to dissuade teenage drinking by presenting the simplistic and easily refutable argument in Table 6.4, teenagers might ignore other research, believing that there is no risk associated with heavy drinking.

Limitations of the Observer

Another issue in low-constraint research concerns the limitations of the observer. When clients talk with therapists, are they giving spontaneous verbalizations or are they saying what they think their therapists want to hear? Do the therapists influence what their clients say? When anthropologists use participant observation, do they influence the behavior of the people they observe? Likewise, when ethologists observe groups of chimps, could their presence alter the animals' normal behavior? These questions involve experimenter reactivity or experimenter bias (Rosenthal, 1976).

Experimenter reactivity is any action by researchers that tends to influence the response of participants. For example, if therapists show more interest in their client's statements about feeling angry than in their statements about feeling happy, clients are likely to talk more about anger than about happiness during sessions.

Experimenter bias is any impact that the researcher's expectations might have on the observations or recording of those observations. Whereas experimenter reactivity affects participants, experimenter bias affects researchers. For example, if a researcher expects males to be angrier than females, the researcher might interpret ambiguous behavior, such as sarcastic comments, as anger in men but as humor in women.

Both experimenter reactivity and experimenter bias distort the measurement process. To obtain natural behavior, the observer must be uninvolved. In case studies, it is difficult for observers to control their own reactivity and biases. However, controls that are available in higher-constraint research can minimize the observer's reactivity and bias.

Going Beyond the Data

Recall Rosenhan's (1973) naturalistic study of mental hospitals. It created quite a stir. Few of Rosenhan's critics argued with his data; instead, they criticized his interpretation of the data. Other interpretations are possible, and some of these alternatives are more reasonable given other available data. For example, Rosenhan argued that it is unreasonable to make a diagnosis of schizophrenia based on the single symptom of hearing voices (11 out of 12 admissions received this diagnosis). However, Weiner (1975) notes that by Rosenhan's own admission (Rosenhan, 1973, pp. 365–366), the pseudopatients showed "concomitant nervousness" and were apparently in serious distress because they had gone to a psychiatric hospital and requested admission. This pattern, plus the fact that the pseudopatients would likely have denied other symptoms and experiences that might have indicated alternative explanations for the hallucinations (Spitzer, 1975), makes schizophrenia the most likely diagnosis.

Rosenhan interpreted the discharge diagnoses as indicating that the doctors never detected that the pseudopatients were not psychotic. However, Rosenhan reported that all the patients were diagnosed as "in remission" at discharge (Spitzer, 1975). It is extremely rare for people with a diagnosis of schizophrenia to ever be given the qualifier "in remission" at discharge. Therefore,

Rosenhan's own data clearly indicate that the pseudopatients were seen by the professional staff to be symptom free at discharge.

Rosenhan's research is still widely quoted. His was a powerful study with interesting findings, but his interpretation of the findings may have been scientifically unjustified. Rosenhan drew strong conclusions from low-constraint research, conclusions that seem unreasonable when you compare his results with other research data, such as typical discharge diagnoses. His study illustrates the strengths (the advantages of studying a natural phenomenon in its natural setting) and the weaknesses (the hazards implicit in interpreting naturalistic data) of low-constraint naturalistic research.

Quick-Check Review 6.4: Limitations of Low-Constraint Methods

1. Why is poor representativeness often a problem in low-constraint research?
2. What aspect of low-constraint research complicates the process of replication?
3. What is an ex post facto fallacy?
4. What is the difference between experimenter reactivity and experimenter bias?

ETHICAL PRINCIPLES

In naturalistic observation, there is no manipulation of variables or random assignment of participants to conditions. Therefore, ethical issues concerning the treatment of participants typically do not occur as they do in experimental research. Instead, ethical concerns focus primarily on issues of confidentiality, researchers' access to sensitive material, and participants' informed consent.

The central ethical demands in research with humans is that participants should have reasonable knowledge about the study in which they participate, must be protected from harm, should be able to give informed consent, and should be free to refuse or withdraw at any time. All of those can be difficult to provide in naturalistic research. For example, in archival research, such as obtaining data from medical or school records, the people whose records are being searched might not even know of the activity. The same applies to use of unobtrusive measures, where the participants are not aware of being observed. How can those people provide informed consent? How can they be protected from misuse of their private or sensitive information?

Wherever possible, the researcher must obtain the informed consent of a responsible person who acts on behalf of the targeted group, such as the hospital administrator, school principal, or some other designated person or committee. Increasingly, access to archival records is controlled by various laws designed to protect people's privacy (Breese et al., 2007). Before obtaining consent from a designated person or committee, the study must be reviewed and approved by an Institutional Review Board (IRB).

To justify using unobtrusive measures, the researcher must show that nondeceptive measures would not work and there is no significant risk of harm from using the measures. It is the researchers' responsibility to assure that the techniques proposed are the only feasible means of obtaining the information and that all data will be kept confidential.

Some naturalistic research is so innocuous that consent may not be necessary. However, that decision should never be solely up to the researcher. An appropriate IRB should review the proposal to see if consent can be bypassed. In general, people have no expectation of privacy in public settings, so observing how people shop or study in the library might not require consent. However, it would be another matter if your observations might make the person uncomfortable. Davis observed adults spanking and punishing children in shopping malls, but presumably made those observations unobtrusively so that those observed were unaffected by his observations. If his approach had been to stand near and obviously take notes, that would be obtrusive, probably make them uncomfortable and therefore would require some form of prior consent.

This research by Davis illustrates an interesting point; as researchers, we have more ethical demands on our behavior than everyday people have. Anyone has the perfect right to stare at someone who is spanking a child in a mall. We even have the perfect right to express either approval or disapproval. However, once we step into the role of researcher, our behavior and its consequences on others becomes a central issue, and we must conform to standards that are designed to protect research participants.

Sometimes the line between research and clinical practice can be unclear. A therapist observes and tests hypotheses about the symptoms that a client reports as part of the diagnosis and treatment of the client. Even though it is a case study, it is not research at that point. However, the therapist may later realize that the case had some unique aspects that make it valuable for teaching other professionals, and therefore, the therapist decides to write the case up for publication. Normally, the therapist would discuss this with the client and obtain the client's written consent to publish the case.

Confidentiality is also a critical issue in low-constraint research because the researcher is often reporting on individuals rather than group means. If the researcher provides too much identifying information in the report, it may be possible to identify the person or persons in the study. With single-case studies, researchers try to mask identities. For example, if the client was a CPA, the case report might describe the client as a dentist or a financial analyst. This would protect the anonymity of the client, yet still give reasonably accurate information about the nature of the person's education, type of work, and social class.

Quick-Check Review 6.5: Ethical Principles

1. Are there any situations in which informed consent may be unnecessary?
2. How might a therapist protect the confidentiality of a client when publishing a case study?

SUMMARY

- Low-constraint field research includes naturalistic observation, case studies, and archival research.
- A major advantage of lower-constraint research methods is their flexibility.
- These approaches place little constraint on the behavior of participants.
- A common problem with low-constraint research is the tendency to overinterpret the results.
- We cannot draw causal inferences from low-constraint methods.
- Low-constraint methods can make new observations, identify contingencies, and negate general propositions, but cannot establish general propositions.
- These methods are particularly useful in exploratory research and in new research areas.
- A major ethical issue in low-constraint research involves informed consent.

PUTTING IT INTO PRACTICE

The nice thing about naturalistic and case study research is that you can carry it out almost anywhere. The next time you are riding on a bus, sitting in the student union, or waiting for a class to start, conduct a little naturalistic research of your own. Watch the people around you, observe their patterns of interaction, and try to understand what is influencing these behaviors. Can you tell the difference between two people who are in a committed relationship or married and two people who are flirting with one another? If you have children, young siblings, or friends with children, you might want to play with the children as Piaget did, carefully observing their actions and thought processes. See if you can probe those thought processes a little with some well-selected questions or activities. Of course, if they are not your children, be sure you have the consent of their parents.

You may find that this kind of informal research on human behavior is addictive. It is hard not to be curious about what makes people tick, and indulging that curiosity will make this course a lot more enjoyable and comprehensible.

EXERCISES

6.1. Define the following key terms. Be sure that you understand them. They are discussed in the chapter and defined in the glossary.

field research
ethology
exploratory research
generalizability
scientist-practitioner model
contingency
qualitative research methods
unobtrusive observer
participant observer
measurement reactivity
reactive measures
nonreactive measures
habituation
unobtrusive measure
coding (coding data)
narrative data
archival records
selective survival (of archival records)
content analysis
sampling
representativeness
generalize
causal inference
ex post facto fallacy
experimenter reactivity
experimenter bias

6.2. Imagine doing groundbreaking research in the areas listed below. Assume that there is no prior research to draw on, so you will need to utilize flexible low-constraint methods. Develop an initial research plan to accomplish these goals.

1. Some people are concerned about the possible effects of televised wrestling on viewers and on society in general. How would you begin to study such an issue?
2. Studies have shown that seat belts dramatically reduce the risk of injury or death. Nevertheless, many people still do not use seat belts. The issue of concern to you is how one might increase seat belt use.
3. Naturalists worry about the welfare of animals in the natural environment, but most people are unconcerned with the impact of hunting, habitat destruction, environmental pollution, and so on. Your research seeks to develop ways to sensitize people so they will have greater concern for wildlife and make greater efforts to reduce human incursions. What research would you develop toward these goals?
4. Shoplifting costs retail businesses and consumers billions of dollars annually. A national retail consortium hired you to study shoplifting and recommend ways to control this problem. How would you begin such a study?

CHAPTER SEVEN

CORRELATIONAL AND DIFFERENTIAL METHODS OF RESEARCH

Ignorance never settles a question.

—Benjamin Disraeli, 1866, *speech given in the House of Commons*

WEB RESOURCE MATERIAL

Science is built on identifying and using relationships among variables. Ideally, we want to know the causal effects that one or more variables have on other variables. However, we cannot always use research designs powerful enough to discover such causal effects. In this chapter, we will present designs that identify relationships among variables that may or may not be causal. Nevertheless, scientists can still use the information about those relationships to either predict later events or test specific hypotheses.

DEFINING CORRELATIONAL AND DIFFERENTIAL RESEARCH METHODS

Correlational Research Methods

Correlational research assesses the strength of relationships among variables. For example, a researcher might want to see if there is a relationship between adolescents' self-esteem and earlier experiences of corporal punishment by parents. She administers a test that measures self-esteem and a questionnaire about the amount of participants' past punishment. A correlation quantifies the strength and direction of the relationship between the two measures. As in naturalistic observation, we do not manipulate variables in correlational research. However, unlike naturalistic research, we always measure at least two variables in correlational research, and our plans for measuring variables are formalized prior to measurement.

A correlation does not establish causality, but it can serve two useful functions. The first is that correlations can be used to predict future events. Prediction is possible, even if we have no idea why the relationship exists. For example, as early as A.D. 140, Ptolemy developed a complicated system to predict planetary motion. Although his predictions were remarkably accurate, he had little understanding of how the planets actually moved. In fact, his model of planetary movement, which posited that all celestial bodies revolve about the Earth, was incorrect. However, the inaccuracy of Ptolemy's model did not diminish the accuracy of his predictions.

A second valuable function of correlational research is to provide data that are either consistent or inconsistent with scientific theories. A correlational study cannot prove a theory correct, but it can negate a theory.

We validate theories by deriving predictions from the theory and then testing the predictions empirically. For example, the question of what intelligence is has been debated for over a century. British psychologist Charles Spearman (1904) hypothesized a general intellectual trait (the *g* or general factor), which he said governed performance in all areas of cognitive functioning. One prediction from the Spearman *g* factor theory is that there should be a strong correlation between different cognitive abilities, because the *g* factor affects all cognitive abilities.

Suppose that we test a randomly selected sample of participants on math and vocabulary skills, and the two are highly correlated—that is, people who score high on math skills also score high on vocabulary. Do these data prove Spearman's theory? No, but they do provide support for it. The data show that one relationship out of thousands of possible predicted relationships exists. To prove the theory, we would have to test every prediction from it, which is often impossible because theories typically make many predictions. This is one reason why scientists are reluctant to use the word "prove." However, a finding that math and vocabulary skills are correlated is consistent with the Spearman *g* factor theory and thus increases our confidence in the theory.

Suppose that we also test reading ability, abstract reasoning, memory, and the ability to solve riddles, and we find that all possible correlations among the measures are large and positive. Does this prove the theory correct? The answer is still no because there remain other predicted relationships that have yet to be tested. However, we would have more confidence in the theory, because all the predictions of the theory that we have tested so far have been confirmed.

Now suppose that we find that memory and math ability are uncorrelated. What do these data mean? If we performed the procedures correctly, we would have to conclude that Spearman's *g* factor theory is incorrect. Just as in naturalistic and case study research, correlational research cannot prove a theory, but it can negate one.

07:01 The Student Resource Website presents several examples of correlational research studies.

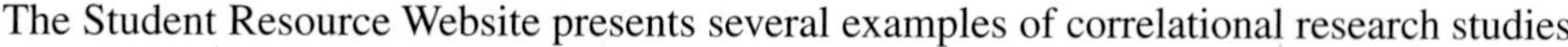

Differential Research Methods

Differential research compares two or more groups that differ on preexisting variables. Qualitative dimensions (e.g., gender, political party affiliation, or psychiatric diagnosis) or quantitative dimensions (e.g., the participant's age or number of years of education) can define the groups. Whether defined qualitatively or quantitatively, the group differences *existed before the researcher conducted the study*. The researcher measures these differences and assigns participants to groups based on them. This classification variable is the independent variable, and the behaviors measured in the different groups are the dependent variables. Independent variables in differential research are nonmanipulated independent variables (see Chapter 3).

Differential research involves measuring variables but not manipulating them and is thus conceptually similar to correlational research. This similarity means that we use the same general principles in interpreting the results from each of these approaches. Specifically, we avoid drawing causal conclusions from either differential or correlational research studies.

Note that there is a structural similarity between differential and experimental research: both utilize different groups defined by an independent variable, and the researcher measures a dependent variable on all participants in each group. Given that similarity, the same statistical procedures are used to evaluate the data from these two approaches. Thus, differential research is similar to both correlational and experimental research. Nevertheless, this similarity between differential and experimental research does not override the admonition that one cannot determine causation from differential research.

Cross-Sectional versus Longitudinal Research. Developmental psychologists often use differential research designs. In a **cross-sectional design**, groups of participants at different ages are compared on a set of variables. For example, the researcher might explore cognitive development by giving groups of three-, five-, and seven-year-olds a set of puzzles. Differences between the younger and older children in performance on the puzzle task provide data about cognitive development. This is a differential research design because participants are assigned to groups based on the preexisting characteristic of age.

As with all differential research, we need to be cautious in drawing conclusions from cross-sectional studies. Suppose that a researcher studies people in their 50s, 60s, 70s, and 80s to understand the aging process better. The researcher must be careful in interpreting the results, because some of the observed differences may be due to other variables besides age. For example, participants in their 80s lived through the Great Depression, whereas participants in their 50s grew up during relatively prosperous years. If the older participants were more cautious about going into debt, it would be unwise to assume that this represented a developmental process, because we could just as easily explain it by differences in life experiences between the groups. The concept that the shared life experiences of people of a given age in a given culture may lead them to behave similarly throughout their lives, but differently from people of other ages or cultures, is known as a **cohort effect**. Those who grew up during the Great Depression shared an experience so powerful that it likely shaped much of their thinking, their expectations, and even their emotional responses.

As you will see later, developmental psychologists use other research designs, such as longitudinal designs and time-series designs. **Longitudinal designs** follow the same people over time to observe developmental changes, thus controlling for cohort effects. However, longitudinal designs have the disadvantage of taking a long time to complete. The aging study described earlier would take 40 years to complete with a longitudinal design. **Time-series designs** are variations of longitudinal designs that involve multiple measurements taken before and after a manipulation. They can be used with individuals or groups and are discussed in Chapter 11.

There is another frequently used design that falls between the pure cross-sectional and pure longitudinal designs. This design uses successive independent samples over time, asking the same questions with each testing, but asking them of a new sample of participants. Pollsters use this design to obtain ratings for things like consumer confidence and ratings of Congress. The poll questions are identical, and they are asked periodically to get longitudinal trends. However, each poll involves taking a new sample or participants.

Artifacts and Confounding. Studying more than one group of individuals forces the researcher to add constraint by standardizing the observational methods. In naturalistic and case study research, we can easily change the procedures in order to study any phenomenon that captures our interest. However, in higher-constraint research, such as differential research, we compare the observations in one group with observations in other groups. That comparison will be useful, however, only if we make those observations in the same way in each group.

Two variables are **confounded** if they vary at the same time—that is, if we fail to keep one variable constant while we vary the other. For example, if we use different observational methods in different groups, then any difference observed between the groups may be real or may be a function of the different observational methods. There would be no way of knowing which explanation is correct. The two variables are confounded; as the group variable changes, the method of observation also changes. Because the two variables change (vary) together, it is unclear which of them is responsible for observed differences in the dependent variable.

The only way to avoid confounding variables is to make sure that they vary independently of one another. To ensure this, we hold constant the variable of least interest and let the variable of greatest interest vary. In differential research, we are less interested in the effects of different observational procedures than in how the groups differ from one another. Therefore, we hold the observational method constant and the group variable is allowed to vary. To do this, the researcher selects in advance the variables to measure and defines how each is to be measured. Once the study starts, the procedures are constrained by these design decisions, and the same measurement procedures must be used for all groups.

Failure to constrain procedures can lead to confounding and artifacts. An **artifact** is any apparent effect of an independent variable that is actually the result of some other variable that was not properly controlled. *Artifacts are the result of confounding.* Therefore, if different measurement procedures were used in the two groups, any observed difference between the groups might actually have been an artifact of changes in the measurement procedure, rather than evidence of real group differences. The problem of confounding will be discussed in more detail in Chapter 8.

Higher-constraint differential research methods are more effective in answering research questions than are lower-constraint naturalistic observation and case studies. The increased effectiveness comes from the ability to compare groups of participants who differ on important variables. However, a price is paid for this additional effectiveness—a loss of flexibility. When there is only one group, as in naturalistic research, we can modify the procedures easily. With more than one group, we must use the same observational and measurement procedures in each group in order to make valid comparisons between groups.

Higher-constraint research requires precise and consistent observational procedures and detailed planning. How can such detailed plans be made before a study even begins? If this is the first study on a topic, detailed planning is impossible. Detailed planning is possible only when we have a reasonable understanding of the phenomenon under study. That is why high-constraint research is seldom used in the early stages of studying a problem. Instead, we use flexible, low-constraint methods, which allow us to explore the phenomenon and to gain a sense of what to expect. Such an understanding is necessary in order to state explicit hypotheses and design appropriate procedures for testing those hypotheses. Research on a particular topic often begins with low-constraint methods and then proceeds to higher-constraint research only after the researcher has a basic understanding of the phenomenon.

Scientists usually study topics that others have already studied extensively, and so they may not need to start with low-constraint research. However, most researchers carry out some low-constraint research to gain familiarity with phenomena that would be difficult to understand solely from reading the published accounts of other investigators.

07:02

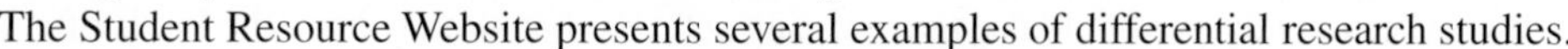

The Student Resource Website presents several examples of differential research studies.

Comparing These Methods

To understand correlational and differential research methods, you need to know how they are conceptually similar, what makes one higher constraint than the other, and when to use each method.

Both correlational and differential research measure relationships among variables, but differential research is higher constraint. One reason is that differential research is structurally similar to experimental research, but by itself, that is not a sufficient reason.

When conducting differential research, we are often interested in causal questions. Researchers should address causal questions with experimental research, but frequently ethical or practical constraints prevent experimental manipulation. For example, it is impossible to assign participants randomly to a group of people with schizophrenia and a group without schizophrenia, but a differential design can compare these already-existing groups. Randomly assigning participants to groups or conditions, as is done in experimental research, tends to equate the groups on potential confounding variables. Without random assignment, the likelihood of confounding is high.

With differential research, we assign participants to groups based on a preexisting variable. However, the groups typically also differ on several other variables. For example, people with chronic schizophrenia tend to be from lower social classes, have fewer relationships in adolescence and early adulthood, and spend more time in hospitals and take more medications than a randomly selected group of people from the general population. These differences are predictable and are well established by past research. Suppose researchers find differences between a group of chronic patients with schizophrenia and a general control group on some dependent measure, such as eye movement abnormalities. There is no way of knowing whether these differences are due to schizophrenia, to social class differences, to social experiences during adolescence, to effects of hospitalization, or to medication. These group differences are potential **confounding variables** that might affect the outcome of a study.

We need to control confounding variables in order to draw strong conclusions. Therefore, instead of selecting a general control group, we should select one or more specific control groups that are comparable to the experimental group on one or more potential confounding variables. For example, suspecting that social class might affect the scores on the dependent variable, we would select a control group that is, on average, of the same social class as the group with schizophrenia (see Raulin & Lilienfeld, 2009). This would ensure that social class could not confound the findings. Active control over sampling is a form of constraint that minimizes confounding and therefore strengthens the conclusions drawn from the study. Correlational research has no comparable control procedure; differential research has more control procedures available and is therefore higher constraint than correlational research.

When to Use These Methods

Differential research designs are most often used when the manipulation of an independent variable is impractical, impossible, or inappropriate. For example, in order to compare the effectiveness of two theories of education, we could set up two separate schools, create a different curriculum for each school, randomly assign students, and then evaluate what the students learn. However, the complexity and expense of setting up such a research program would make the study impractical. Alternatively, we could use two existing schools that already have the kinds of curricula we want to evaluate. This would be a differential research design, because these groups are naturally occurring instead of experimentally manipulated.

Differential designs are also used when an experimental manipulation is impossible to carry out, such as when studying the social development of individuals with superior intelligence. We cannot experimentally raise or lower a newborn's intelligence, so random assignment to normal and superior intelligence groups is impossible. However, we could select children of average and high intelligence and follow their social development.

Finally, some experimental manipulations are technically possible, but unethical to use. For example, one might hypothesize that prolonged separation from parents during the first two years of life would lead to permanently retarded social development. Of course, it would be unethical to select infants randomly and separate them from their parents to test the hypothesis experimentally. However, some children are separated from their parents for reasons that are beyond the researcher's control. Such naturally occurring groups might be suitable populations to study to explore this hypothesis.

A field that often uses correlational and differential research designs, due to ethical considerations, is clinical neuropsychology. A neuropsychologist uses measures of behavior to infer the structural and functional condition of the brain. The neuropsychologist administers tests to people to determine what they can and cannot do. The patterns of such abilities and disabilities can suggest specific neurological problems. Neuropsychologists draw on a wealth of data when they evaluate a person. If they find a particular pattern of abilities and disabilities in people later diagnosed with a specific type of neurological problem, then it is reasonable to predict that another person with that pattern might well be suffering from the same neurological problem. The data gathering in this case is correlational, because the researcher is seeking to identify relationships between behavior and brain dysfunction. Some of the relationships observed in neuropsychology are not easily quantifiable in terms of a simple correlation coefficient, but they are relationships nonetheless. By mapping these relationships, the neuropsychologist can make accurate prediction of brain dysfunction based on a person's test behavior. Remember, prediction is an important goal of correlational research.

Quick-Check Review 7.1: Defining Correlational and Differential Research Methods

1. What is the main purpose of correlational research? of differential research?
2. What information can scientists obtain from correlational research?
3. Can correlational research determine causality?
4. How can correlational research help to validate or invalidate a theory?
5. What type of independent variable do we use in differential research?
6. What are artifacts? How do they affect differential research?
7. How is differential research structurally similar to experimental research and conceptually similar to correlational research?
8. Why do we consider differential research higher constraint than correlational research?

CONDUCTING CORRELATIONAL RESEARCH

Correlational research seeks to quantify the direction and strength of a relationship among two or more variables. The discussion here focuses on the relationships between two variables only. Later in this section, we briefly discuss **multivariate correlational designs**, which employ more than two variables.

Problem Statements

Unlike the flexible problem statements of naturalistic observation and case studies, the problem statements for correlational research are specific. They typically take the following form: "What is the strength and direction of the relationship between variable *X* and variable *Y*?" It is also common to ask, "What is the best equation for predicting variable *Y* from variable *X*?" We call this the regression equation.

Secondary Analyses

The most frequent use of correlational research is for secondary statistical analyses in higher-constraint research to help explain findings. For example, you might conduct a differential research project comparing urban and suburban groups on their fear of crime. Being a good researcher, you routinely collect data on **demographic variables**, which are characteristics of individuals, such as age, education, and social class. Researchers routinely compare the groups on these demographic variables because any of these variables could produce artifacts if the groups differ on them. It is also common to compute the correlation of each of these variables with the dependent measure(s) in the study. These correlations can give considerable insight into the data, and researchers often include them in the research article. The problem statement would likely be this: "What is the correlation of each of the demographic variables with the dependent variable(s)?" Traditionally, we compute these correlations separately within each group, because the relationship might be different in the groups. Thus, if we find in our study of fear of criminal victimization that suburban groups are less fearful of crime than urban groups, we would want to see if there are other differences between these groups that could account for that finding. For example, it might be that the suburban sample is younger and better educated than the urban sample. If either of these variables is correlated with fear of criminal victimization, that might help to explain the group finding.

Measuring the Variables

Developing effective operational definitions of the variables is critical in correlational research. Measurement depends on the adequacy of operational definitions. Researchers must consider every aspect of the measurement process. As in any research study, we need to avoid the possibility of unintentionally influencing participants. This can be accomplished by (1) never allowing the same person to collect both measures on the participant, or (2) never allowing the researcher to know participants' scores on the first measure until after the second measure has been taken.

Two effects need to be controlled: (1) **experimenter expectancy**, the tendency of investigators to see what they expect to see (Chapman & Chapman, 1969), and (2) *experimenter reactivity*, the tendency of investigators to influence the behavior of participants. (Experimenter reactivity was covered in Chapter 6.) We can minimize experimenter expectancy by using objective measures whenever possible, so that little subjective interpretation is necessary. The problem of experimenter reactivity may require the use of two independent researchers or automating the research procedures so the researcher need not be present. Chapters 8 and 9 will cover experimenter effects in more detail.

Another potential problem in correlational research is the participant's influence. Participants like to be consistent, especially when they know that researchers are observing and evaluating them. This is a variation on the measurement reactivity problem discussed in Chapter 6. Such artificial consistency can give the impression of a strong relationship between variables when no relationship or a weak relationship actually exists.

There are several ways of reducing this effect. One is to disguise self-report measures by including filler items so that participants are unsure of what the investigator is studying. **Filler items** are not meant to measure anything, but rather draw the participant's attention away from the real purpose of the measure.

A second method of controlling the participant's influence on the data is to rely on one or more unobtrusive measures. In this way, participants are unaware that they are being observed and are thus less likely to modify their normal behavior.

A third method is to separate the measures from one another, which can be done by taking measurements at different times or by having different researchers take the measurements. The time separation need not be large for this technique to be effective. It is common for researchers to tell participants that they will be involved in two short studies in a single session, when, in fact, the second study is actually part of the first study. This strategy reduces the measurement reactivity because participants believe that the measures taken in the "second study" have nothing to do with their earlier experiences.

Probably the best way to deal with the problem of measurement reactivity is to use measures beyond the control of the participant. For example, anxiety might be assessed with psychophysiological measures rather than self-reports or behavioral observations; most participants have less control over their physiological responses than over what they say or do.

Sampling

A major concern in research is obtaining a sample that adequately represents the population to which the researcher wants to generalize. Another sampling issue, which is unique to correlational research, is whether the relationship between a given pair of variables is the same in all segments of the population. If researchers suspect that such differences exist, they might draw samples from separate subpopulations. For example, if one suspects that males and females demonstrate a different relationship between two variables, either in direction or strength, then separate samples of males and females should be selected and separate correlations computed for each group. In this example, gender is a **moderator variable**—a variable that seems to modify the relationship between other variables. Gender, culture, and ethnicity are commonly used moderator variables.

People raised in one culture may very well react differently to a situation than people raised in a different culture. It is now common in psychology to explore phenomena in other cultures to see how readily the findings generalize across cultures, a procedure called **cross-cultural research**. These are usually differential research studies comparing cultures. Early psychological research often ignored possible cultural influences, but there is now a realization that culture can significantly influence many psychological variables (Sorrentino et al., 2005).

Recognizing potential moderator variables requires a thorough knowledge of the area under study. When in doubt, it is always better to compute correlations for different subgroups. If you find the same relationship in all the groups, you can be more confident that the relationship will hold for the entire population sampled.

Analyzing the Data

Data analysis in correlational research involves computing the degree of relationship between the variables. Which correlation coefficient is appropriate depends on the level of measurement of both variables. If we measure both variables on at least an interval scale, then we should use a Pearson product-moment correlation coefficient. If one variable is measured on an ordinal scale and the other variable on at least an ordinal scale, then the appropriate coefficient is a Spearman rank-order correlation. If at least one of the variables produces nominal data, a Phi coefficient should be used.

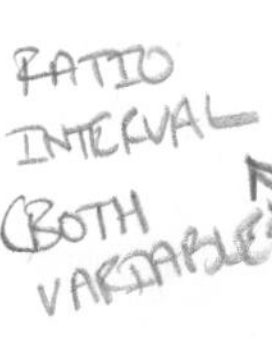

The Pearson and Spearman correlation coefficients indicate the degree of linear relationship between two variables and range from -1.00 to $+1.00$. A -1.00 means a perfect negative relationship exists (as one variable increases, the other decreases in a perfectly predictable fashion). A $+1.00$ means a perfect positive relationship exists. A correlation of 0.00 means there is no linear relationship between the two variables.

It is always wise to produce a scatter plot for the correlation instead of relying on the correlation alone. (See Figures 5.5 and 5.6 for examples of correlation scatter plots.) Scatter plots can detect nonlinear relationships that are not represented accurately by simple correlations.

07:03

The Student Resource Website presents the computational procedures for the various correlations.

The Pearson, Spearman, and Phi correlations quantify the relationship between two variables. However, some research situations demand more complicated correlational analyses, such as correlating one variable with an entire set of variables (**multiple correlation**), or one set of variables with another set of variables (**canonical correlation**). It is also possible to correlate one variable with another after statistically removing the effects of a third variable (**partial correlation**). Analytical procedures, such as **path analysis**, can test the strength of evidence for a specific causal model using correlational data (Raulin & Graziano, 1995). Detailed discussion of these more sophisticated analytic procedures is beyond the scope of this book (see Loehlin, 2004; Myers et al., 2010; or Nunnally & Bernstein, 1994). The Student Resource Website presents a more detailed discussion of the more complex correlational procedures.

07:04

Interpreting the Correlation

The first step in interpreting a correlation is to note its direction and size. Is the correlation positive or negative? Is the relationship small (close to 0.00) or large (close to +1.00 or −1.00)?

The next step is to test for the statistical significance of the correlation—that is, whether the observed correlation is large enough to convince the researcher that there is a nonzero correlation in the population. To state it another way, the researcher is testing the null hypothesis that the variables are uncorrelated in the population.

Computer programs routinely compute the p-value for each correlation. This p-value is the probability of achieving a correlation this large or larger if the correlation in the population were actually zero. If this probability is low, it means that there is little chance that the population correlation is zero. In that case, we would say that the correlation is *statistically significant*. Traditionally the probability must be quite low (usually .05 or even .01) before researchers declare their findings to be statistically significant. For example, if the correlation between two variables is .67 with a p-value of .035, we would conclude that a significant relationship exists, because the p-value is less than the traditional alpha of .05. (See Chapter 5 for a more detailed explanation of this terminology.)

When using correlation coefficients, one should also calculate the coefficient of determination, rather than just rely on the statistical significance of the correlation (Nunnally & Bernstein, 1994). The **coefficient of determination** is the square of the correlation. If the correlation is .50, then $r^2 = .25$. You can convert .25 to a percent by multiplying by 100 ($100 \times .25 = 25\%$). A correlation of .50 indicates that 25% of the variability in the first variable can be accounted for, or predicted by, knowing the scores on the second variable. Statisticians usually shorten this statement by referring to r^2 as the "proportion of variance accounted for." This procedure allows researchers to estimate how useful the relationship might be in prediction. However, it is appropriate to take r^2 seriously only if there is a good-sized sample (a minimum of 30 participants is a generally accepted rule of thumb). Smaller samples do not provide stable estimates of population correlations.

Quick-Check Review 7.2: Conducting Correlational Research

1. What is the difference between experimenter expectancy and experimenter reactivity?
2. What are moderator variables?
3. What are the three most commonly used measures of correlation? Under what conditions should each be used?
4. What is the coefficient of determination? What does it indicate?

CONDUCTING DIFFERENTIAL RESEARCH

Researchers use differential research to compare existing groups when experimental procedures for testing group differences cannot be used for practical or ethical reasons.

Problem Statements

Problem statements for differential research are among the most challenging in all of research. However, on the surface they appear to be straightforward: "Does group *A* differ from group *B* on the dependent variable(s)?"

We could create an infinite number of such problem statements by comparing every possible group with every other possible group on any conceivable dependent measure. Why not ask, "Do balding college professors differ from laboratory rats in their preference for music?" Obviously, it makes little sense to ask such a question; the comparisons that we make should have theoretical significance. Picking two groups and comparing them on something is easy; picking the right groups and the right dependent variable to advance scientific understanding is much more difficult, but that should always be the goal in differential research.

What makes a comparison in differential research theoretically significant? A theoretically significant differential research study will tell us something about factors that affect the dependent variable, rather than just revealing differences between two groups. No one would be surprised to find a difference in music preference between college professors and lab rats. In fact, we would expect to find differences on many variables, such as weight, eye color, diurnal cycle, and social skills. Suppose we find differences on all these variables, as well as on music preference. What would it mean? Who knows, or cares for that matter?

With this comparison, the two groups differ on so many variables that there is no way of knowing which variables are relevant. *The first rule of thumb, therefore, is to develop problem statements that focus on comparing groups that differ on only one variable.* If you are interested in gender differences, do not compare balding professors (presumably male) with a group of fifth-grade girls. These groups differ not only on gender but also on age, education, social class, and the experiences that they have had. If you found a difference, you would have no idea what caused it. A better comparison might be fifth-grade girls and fifth-grade boys. However, you still should be cautious in drawing conclusions about the role of gender based on this one comparison.

This leads us to the second rule of thumb: *use several comparisons when trying to draw a conclusion about the effects of a factor from differential research studies.* If you find similar results in comparisons of fifth-grade girls and boys, college males and females, male and female business people, male and female college professors, and male and female truck drivers, you can be more confident in your hypothesis that gender differences account for all these findings. Even with this whole series of findings based on comparing groups that appear to differ only on gender, you have to be careful in drawing a causal conclusion.

Finally, good problem statements in differential research focus on group differences on theoretically relevant dependent measures. If you were interested in studying self-esteem, you would focus on variables like success, social support, childhood experiences, and cognitions. These variables are likely to affect, or be affected by, self-esteem. Variables like hat size, finger-tapping speed, visual acuity, and the make and model of one's car are less likely to be theoretically relevant.

In summary, good problem statements for differential research compare two or more theoretically relevant groups on a theoretically relevant dependent measure, in which the groups ideally differ on only a single dimension. Because we rarely can achieve the ideal of groups differing on only a single dimension, multiple comparisons are used in drawing conclusions about the influence of group differences on the dependent measure.

Measuring the Variables

In differential research, researchers distinguish between the independent variable and the dependent variable. We measure rather than manipulate the independent variable in differential research. Suppose that we are interested in using educational level as a nonmanipulated independent variable, and we plan to have two groups: high school graduates and high school dropouts. The researcher needs a procedure to measure the education of participants. This seems simple enough, but it can quickly become complicated. For example, in what category would you put someone who obtained a GED (general education diploma), which is a high school equivalency degree? Where do you get the information? Do you ask the person or check with the school that granted the diploma? You need to decide on all these issues before you begin the study. This set of procedures would be the operational definition of education level. (Note that the issues involved in creating operational definitions for the dependent variable are the same in measuring nonmanipulated independent variables.)

Although the nonmanipulated independent variable in differential research is usually a discrete variable, it is always possible to take a continuous variable, such as education level, and break it into discrete intervals, such as high school dropout, high school graduate, some college, college graduate, and so on. This process converts a correlational research design into a differential research design.

Selecting Appropriate Control Groups

The researcher must decide which groups to include in a differential study. In some cases, the decision is simple. If we wanted to study gender differences, gender would be the independent variable, and in most psychological research we consider only two possibilities, male and female. (For the sake of this discussion, we will ignore the rare situation in which a person's gender is androgynous—having both male and female characteristics.) Because the minimum number of groups required in differential research is two, we would use both a male and a female group. However, such is not the case with other independent variables. If the study is about psychopathology, there are dozens of psychiatric disorders. Researchers must choose which of these disorders to compare using a theoretical framework.

A **control group** is any group selected in differential research as a basis of comparison with the primary or **experimental group**. Note that calling the primary group the experimental group is an unfortunate historical choice of terms, because it implies that we are conducting an experimental study. However, in differential research, we do not experimentally manipulate the independent variable.

Recall that we try to select control groups to reduce the effects of potential confounding variables. A variable can have a confounding effect in a differential study only if (1) it affects the scores on the dependent variable(s), and (2) there is a difference between the experimental and control groups on the potential confounding variable. For example, suppose that you want to study gender differences in the ability to perceive details in visual scenes. You know that visual acuity affects performance on the task. Therefore, visual acuity is a potential confounding variable. However, if males and females do not differ on visual acuity, then it cannot differentially affect performance in the two groups and, therefore, cannot be a confounding variable in this study.

We must select the control group with care if it is to be an effective control. The ideal control group is identical to the experimental group on all variables except the independent variable that defines the groups. For example, if we are studying the effects of exposure to toxic chemicals on cognitive performance, the experimental group might consist of people who work in industries that expose workers to such toxins. An ideal control group would include workers of about the same age, social class, and education level who do similar kinds of work, but in an industry that does not expose them to these toxins. A group of office workers from the same company as the plant workers in the experimental group might be a convenient control group, but not a very good one. The office workers would probably differ from the plant workers on a number of important variables, such as education level, age, and the ratio of males to females. Any of these differences could affect cognitive performance and thus constitute potential confounding variables.

Consider another example of selecting a control group. Suppose that the researcher is studying schizophrenia. The experimental group consists of people with schizophrenia. What is a good control group to compare with this experimental group? The choice will depend on the dependent measure and the confounding variables that might affect it. As noted earlier, a variable can have a confounding effect in a differential study only if (1) it affects the scores on the dependent variable(s), and (2) there is a difference between the experimental and control groups on the potential confounding variable.

To select an appropriate control group, we must identify variables that affect the dependent measures. These represent potential confounding variables, but they will not actually confound the results unless the experimental and control groups differ on them. Therefore, it is essential to select a control group that is comparable to the experimental group on these potential confounding variables.

For example, if you want to measure thought processes in people with schizophrenia, you need to identify variables known to affect performance on such measures. Those variables are usually found in the research literature. Past research using the same or similar dependent measures often reports correlations with potential confounding variables. We noted earlier that most correlational research is included in higher-constraint studies as a routine part of the analyses. The reason for this routine inclusion is that it tests for possible confounding variables and it provides information to other researchers regarding variables to be concerned about in planning a research study.

After identifying the potential confounding variables, you can select a control group that is unlikely to differ from the experimental group on these variables. Potential confounding variables might include amount of education, age, and total amount of psychiatric hospitalization. To reduce the threat of these potential confounding variables, select a control group that is similar to the experimental group on these variables, or at least as many of these variables as possible. If you can find a comparison group that does not differ from the experimental group on these potential confounding variables, the variables will not confound the results.

It is rare to find an ideal control group. Instead, researchers usually try to find a group that controls some of the most important and most powerful confounding variables. A confounding variable is powerful if it is likely to have a large effect on the dependent measure. In the hypothetical study of the thought processes of people with schizophrenia, a powerful confounding variable might be education. The researcher can identify education as a powerful confounding variable because the research literature shows that education is highly correlated with measures of cognitive performance.

Another way to deal with the problem of finding an ideal control group is to use multiple control groups. Each control group typically controls for one or more of the major confounding variables, but no group controls for all potential confounding variables. If each of the comparisons of experimental and control groups gives the same results and leads to the same conclusions, then the researcher can be reasonably confident that the independent variable, and not one of the confounding variables, is responsible for the observed effect. Most of the research in medicine and the social sciences relies on such multiple comparisons. Because it is not always feasible to include all possible comparison groups in one study, research often involves multiple studies by different researchers in different laboratories, each using slightly different procedures and control groups. If the phenomenon under study is stronger than the potential confounding variables, each researcher will reach the same conclusion.

Researchers sometimes select multiple comparison groups for strong theoretical reasons. For example, psychologists have recognized for over a century that anhedonia (the inability to experience pleasure) is a central characteristic of schizophrenia (Bleuler, 1950). Anhedonia also occurs in other psychiatric disorders, such as depression. Therefore, it makes theoretical sense to ask if there are differences in the anhedonia experienced by people with schizophrenia and that found in people with severe depression. Blanchard et al. (2001) did just that. Their primary dependent measure was a scale to measure social anhedonia, or the failure to experience pleasure from social interactions (Chapman et al., 1976; Eckblad et al., 1982). They speculated that the difference between the anhedonia in schizophrenia and the anhedonia in depression is that the pleasure deficit comes and goes in depression, but remains constant in schizophrenia.

To test this hypothesis, Blanchard et al. (2001) sampled three groups: people with schizophrenia, people with severe depression, and people with no psychiatric disorder. The group of people with no psychiatric disorder provided a baseline—a measure of normal levels of social anhedonia. These researchers minimized possible confounding by selecting the groups so that they would be approximately the same age, education, and ratio of males to females. They also tried to match their samples on ethnicity and marital status, although they found it more difficult matching on these variables. They then tested their participants, waited a year, and retested them. Depression tends to come and go, so many of the people with severe depression were much less depressed at the retest.

The findings, shown in Figure 7.1, were consistent with their hypothesis. Anhedonia remains high in people with schizophrenia. They also found that it is unaffected by the level of the schizophrenic symptoms. In contrast, anhedonia varies in people with depression, and the level of depression affects the level of anhedonia. Interestingly, the level of depression did not affect the level of anhedonia in people with schizophrenia. People with schizophrenia, like other people, are depressed at times and not depressed at other times. These findings suggest that failure to experience pleasure in social relationships may be a different phenomenon in different psychiatric disorders, although determining the exact nature of the difference will require more research.

Chapter 10 will discuss experimental research designs, in which groups are created through random assignment. Random assignment controls most of the problems described in this section. Our advice to students interested in studying areas in which experimentation is unethical or impossible is to realize that drawing strong conclusions is difficult at best.

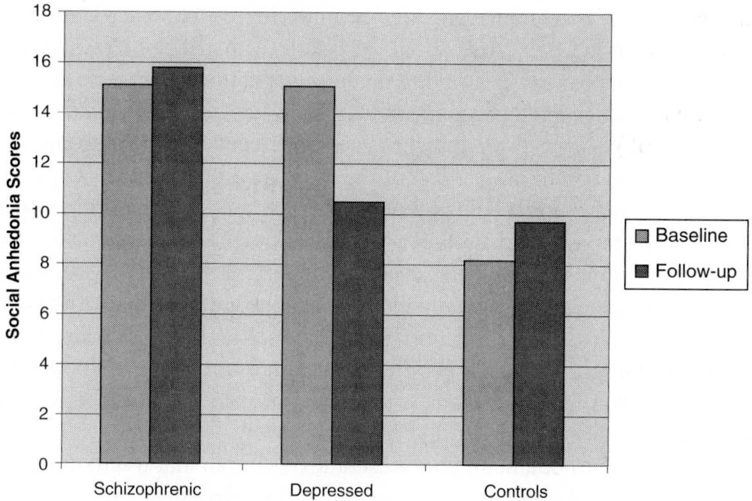

FIGURE 7.1 Anhedonia in Schizophrenia and Depression. Blanchard et al. (2001) found that social anhedonia was a consistent characteristic in people with schizophrenia, but was present in people with depression only during the depressive episode. Furthermore, they found that the level of depression predicted the level of anhedonia in people with depression but not in people with schizophrenia. This combination of results suggests that the anhedonia in schizophrenia may be different from that found in depression and may have a different cause.

Source: Adapted from Blanchard et al. (2001).

Sampling

Regardless of the type of research, the same issues of sampling always apply. To be able to generalize to a larger population, researchers must sample randomly from the population. Random sampling is a procedure for selecting participants from a population so that each participant has an equal chance of being selected. To study people with Alzheimer's Disease, researchers should ideally sample randomly from all people with Alzheimer's, but the ideal is impossible to attain in practice. Usually, the researcher selects a sample from all the available participants. Unless there is reason to believe that participants from one part of the country are different from participants from another part, the sample need not be from the whole country for us to generalize to the whole country.

A serious threat to generalizability is the subtle bias that can occur when a researcher has access only to certain groups. For example, if in a study of Alzheimer's all participants are from one nursing facility, the sample might be unrepresentative because nursing facilities specialize in the kinds of individuals they treat. Some facilities handle primarily Medicaid patients. That sample would under-represent people with more money, who probably have better education and enjoyed better health care most of their lives. In fact, choosing participants from any nursing facility might result in a biased sample. Some people with Alzheimer's may have received care at home for years if they have a supportive family or if their personalities are such that they are cooperative despite their symptoms.

Researchers studying other populations must also be sensitive to sampling biases. For example, a particular school might not have a representative sample of children. Depending on the location of the school, the children might come from higher or lower socioeconomic backgrounds than children in general. The sample might overrepresent or underrepresent some ethnic groups, levels of intelligence, or socioeconomic levels. Any of these variables can affect the results of a study.

Even when researchers appear to be sampling randomly, it is important to be sensitive to subtle biases. For example, is a random sample of people in a shopping center representative of the population? A shopping center on a city's west side may have very different customers from a similar shopping center on the east side. The time of day or day of the week might also affect sample composition. A sample taken on a weekday afternoon would probably overrepresent homemakers, people who work evenings or weekends, the unemployed, kids playing hooky, or people on vacation. To obtain a representative sample, it is best to sample people from several locations, on different days and times. Finally, a sample drawn from any shopping center would underrepresent people who do not like to shop.

Researchers may also make subtle discriminations that bias a sample. Because no one likes to be turned away, researchers might approach people who seem more likely to cooperate and avoid those who seem in a hurry. To the extent that the people approached are different from the ones avoided, the sample could produce biased results.

The point is that it is easy to obtain an unrepresentative sample that might threaten the generalizability of a study. This is a problem with any research and is particularly relevant in differential research. Because the groups in differential research already differ on a preexisting variable, the likelihood is high that they will differ on other variables that might affect the research outcome. We must be careful when sampling participants in differential research and must take care to assure the representativeness of the sample. When a representative sample is not possible, which is often the case, extra caution is needed in interpreting the findings.

In differential research, especially differential research of diagnostic groups, sampling is only one factor affecting the generalizability of the study. The number of participants who drop out can dramatically affect generalizability. Many people with physical or psychiatric disorders might not have the concentration to complete a long and demanding study. To the extent that these people are different from those who do perform the task, we cannot generalize to the larger population.

We will discuss sampling in more detail in Chapter 9.

Analyzing the Data

In some respects, differential studies resemble experimental studies. In both, scores are obtained from each participant in each group, and the scores of the experimental group(s) are compared with the scores of the control group(s). The type of statistical analysis used depends on the number of groups and the scale of measurement of the dependent variable(s). If the dependent measure represents score data and there are two groups, a t-test for independent groups is typically used. If there are more than two groups and score data, an analysis of variance (ANOVA) is used.

07:05 Appendix D covers a selection of the appropriate techniques, and the Student Resource Web-
07:06 site implements this flowchart and links to sections that describe the computation of the statistics .

Interpreting the Data

Whatever statistical test is used, we interpret the results the same way. We compare the p-value (i.e., probability) produced by a statistic with the predetermined alpha level to decide whether we should reject the null hypothesis. The null hypothesis is that the population means are equal. Rejecting this hypothesis suggests that at least one population mean is different from at least one other population mean. This process is illustrated in the Go with the Flow 7.1 flowchart.

GO WITH THE FLOW 7.1 | DETERMINING STATISTICAL SIGNIFICANCE

We determine statistical significance with the same general procedure for each statistical test. A statistics program will compute both the test statistic and the *p*-value associated with that test statistic. Comparing that *p*-value with our selected alpha level tells us whether we have statistical significance. Shown here is a flowchart that illustrates this process for deciding on whether two groups are significantly different from one another.

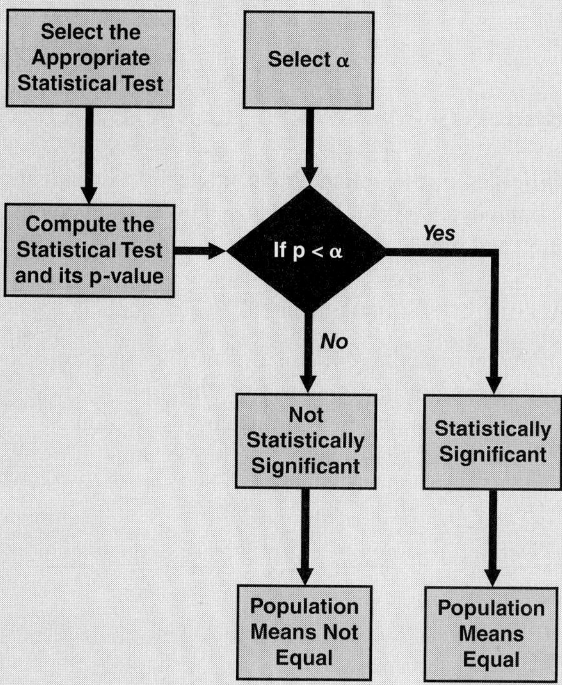

Drawing the proper conclusion from the null hypothesis is the easy part of interpreting data in differential research. The difficult part is taking into account possible confounding factors. In addition, if we suspect that the groups might not be representative, then we must be cautious in generalizing the results. If the control groups are inadequate to control for possible confounding, we should acknowledge this fact in the report of the study.

Confounding variables are so common in differential research that it is difficult to draw solid conclusions based on a single research study. Especially in differential research, we should interpret results in the context of findings from other studies. Therefore, it is critically important for each investigator to describe the research in detail. Whenever possible, the researcher should measure and report on potential confounding variables. For example, any study of psychiatric disorders should routinely report the diagnoses of the clients/patients and the procedures used to obtain them, as well as such variables as participants' average age, education, social class, amount of hospitalization, and any other variables relevant to the interpretation of the study. In this way, future investigators will have the information needed to interpret their studies in the context of your study.

Quick-Check Review 7.3: Conducting Differential Research

1. When should researchers use differential research?
2. Why is it important to develop problem statements that focus on groups that differ on only a single variable?
3. What is a nonmanipulated independent variable?
4. Why is careful selection of the control groups so critical in differential research?

LIMITATIONS OF CORRELATIONAL AND DIFFERENTIAL RESEARCH

Correlational and differential research methods are useful research strategies that can answer many types of questions, but they also have limitations. This section covers two limitations: problems in determining causation and problems with confounding variables.

Problems in Determining Causation

Caution is necessary when drawing conclusions from correlational and differential research. Remember, a correlation does not imply causality. Students might wonder why we emphasize this point so frequently. In the abstract, the point is simple. If A and B are correlated, then three possibilities exist: (1) A causes B; (2) B causes A; or (3) some third factor, C, causes both A and B. Figure 7.2 illustrates these possibilities. In the abstract, any of these possibilities could be true. However, in real life, one or more of the possibilities might appear implausible, and so the researcher might feel justified in drawing a strong causal conclusion.

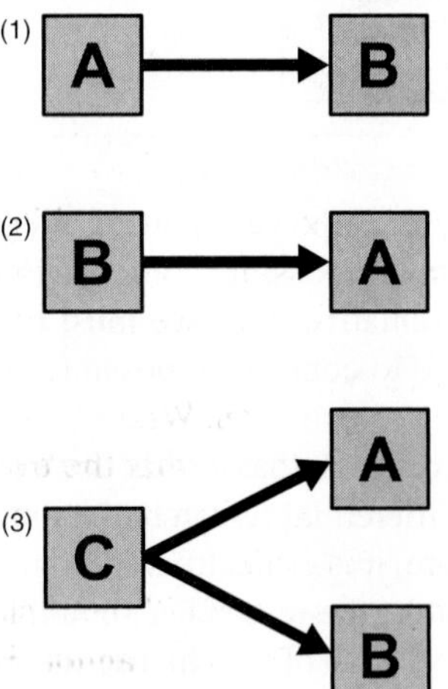

FIGURE 7.2 Correlation and Causation. When two variables (A and B) are correlated, there are three possible interpretations: (1) A causes changes in B; (2) B causes changes in A; or (3) a third variable, C, causes changes in both A and B.

Suppose, for example, that a researcher finds that reading and arithmetic abilities are highly correlated. How should we interpret that finding? We could interpret the finding as being consistent with Spearman's theory that some third factor (in this case, the *g* factor) is responsible for both reading ability and arithmetic ability. However, there are other possible interpretations. Can arithmetic ability cause reading ability? It might, but it would be difficult to imagine a mechanism for how arithmetic skills could lead to better reading skills. Therefore, we might be tempted to dismiss such an interpretation as unlikely.

Consider the reverse causal chain. Can reading ability cause arithmetic ability? How did you learn about arithmetic? Your teacher in elementary school taught you basic arithmetic, and you *read about it* and practiced it from your arithmetic textbook. If you had poor reading skills, you might have been less able to learn other skills, including arithmetic. Therefore, this is a plausible causal chain that could explain how better reading skills can lead to better arithmetic skills.

We should also consider another explanation for a strong correlation between arithmetic and reading abilities. What does a strong relationship between reading ability and arithmetic ability mean? We are not asking you to interpret this relationship but, rather, to define what it means in operational terms: that is, how did we quantify this relationship? In this case, we asked a sample of people to take tests of reading ability and arithmetic ability. What do the scores on the tests really mean? Suppose that the arithmetic test includes the following question:

> *John goes to the market and buys five tomatoes. If tomatoes sell for $6 per dozen, how much change should John receive if he gives the clerk a $10 bill?*

Clearly, this question measures the ability to multiply, divide, and subtract. If tomatoes are $6.00 per dozen, they are $0.50 each, and therefore five tomatoes would cost $2.50. The change that John should receive (assuming no sales tax) is $7.50. It seems simple enough. However, this question could well measure more than it appears to measure. Consider the following example:

> *Jean va au marché et il achete cinq tomates. Si les tomates se vendent á $6 la douzaine, combien de monnaie Jean doit-il recevoir s'il donne á la vendeuse un billet de $10?*

Unless you read French, you probably found this question considerably harder to answer, yet it is the same arithmetic question. The example illustrates how important reading ability is in tests, regardless of what we are testing. Therefore, a correlation between reading ability and arithmetic ability may actually be an artifact of the phenomenon that reading ability is required to perform well on either test.

People tend to overlook another point when interpreting a correlation. When we say that both A and B may be caused by some third variable C, we are not specifying what the third variable might be. In fact, variable C might be anything, so we do not have three interpretations to choose from, but rather hundreds. Suppose that you believe that you can eliminate the possibility that arithmetic skills cause reading skills and the possibility that reading skills cause arithmetic skills. Could you then conclude that Spearman's *g* factor is responsible for both? No, you cannot. Spearman's general intelligence factor is only one of many possible third-factor variables that could account for the observed correlation. General test-taking ability might be a relevant factor. Anxiety level during the testing might be a relevant factor. For example, have you ever taken an exam during which you panicked? The amount of distraction during the testing session might be important, or the level of motivation of participants, or the general quality of their education, or any one of a dozen other variables. Most likely, each of these variables contributes to the observed correlation. Yet it is tempting to conclude that the causal factor that you are interested in is the one that led to the observed relationship.

Now that we have stated that correlations do not imply causality, we want to acknowledge that some theorists disagree with this statement. There are sophisticated correlational designs, well beyond the scope of this textbook, that are sometimes used in disciplines in which direct experimentation may be unethical, such as in medicine or clinical psychology. Some researchers argue that the right combination of correlational studies can so effectively exclude other interpretations of a complex data set that a causal interpretation is reasonable. Even though this may be true, the research literature is littered with hundreds of examples of top scientists drawing what later proved to be incorrect causal interpretations from complex correlational data. Therefore, we believe that the best rule to follow is: *Do not draw causal inferences from correlational data!*

Confounding Variables

As noted earlier, another limitation of differential and correlational research methods is that it is often difficult or impossible to avoid confounding variables. In differential research in particular, confounding is more the rule than the exception. We may be able to control some potential confounding variables with a carefully selected control group, but we rarely are able to eliminate confounding completely. Such problems will always make interpretation difficult, although some researchers choose to think of them as simply making the task more challenging.

Quick-Check Review 7.4: Limitations of Correlational and Differential Research

1. What is the major limitation in interpreting correlational and differential research?
2. What are the reasons for this major limitation?
3. What are confounding variables? Define and explain the concept.

ETHICAL PRINCIPLES

At its most basic level, an experiment is a test of a causal relationship between two variables. The independent variable is manipulated and the effects of the manipulations on the dependent variable are measured. Often, however, experimentation cannot or should not be used. In some situations, the independent variable is too large, complex, or elusive to be manipulated. Natural disasters, such as floods and hurricanes, are examples. We might want to know what psychological problems are caused by such events, but how can we manipulate variables like hurricanes?

Ethical constraints can also limit experimentation. For example, is there a causal link between mercury and childhood autism? No ethical scientist today is going to directly test that hypothesized causal connection with an experiment. However, not long ago this was the major ethical problem in the research that we noted in Chapter 2, known as the Tuskegee study, in which men with syphilis were left untreated in order to compare them at their autopsies with data on noninfected men (Jones, 1981). The ethical issue of allowing known or probable biological harm to the participants was compounded because the subjects were not informed about the nature of the study nor given the opportunity to provide informed consent. In the Tuskegee study, the men were not told that they had syphilis, nor were they told when a treatment was developed years later. That treatment, penicillin, was deliberately withheld. The men in this study were led to believe they were medical patients receiving treatment, but were actually subjects in a research study and were being monitored until they died. With our current ethical sensitivity for the safety and rights of our participants, it is difficult to imagine that those researchers had no qualms about their conduct.

Three of the many important lessons here are as follows: (1) know that the ethics of research are of extreme importance; (2) learn the ethical concerns, the dangers, and the corrections; and (3) understand that your vigilance is constantly required because strong pressures in our society continue to try and weaken ethical constraints in order to satisfy other needs like personal ambition, political goals, and commercial gain. Unfortunately, fraud in science, although committed by a minority of researchers, is a continuing, serious issue (Goodstein, 2010). One of the problems is that scientific research is increasingly carried out in collaboration among scientists in different countries, and the monitoring criteria are not standardized across the world. A good deal of work is needed to address this issue.

Although we cannot or should not do experiments in some situations, we can still carry out good research and gain valid and reliable information. When faced with such ethical or practical constraints, we can use lower-constraint research—correlation and differential methods—which do not require the manipulation of independent variables. Although these methods will not tell us about causality, they can still provide much useful information. Correlation studies can measure the degree of relationship between exposure to toxic substances, such as in the air and soil of neighborhoods, and the occurrence of childhood disabilities, such as asthma. Differential studies can compare children with asthma and those without asthma on the level of various substances in the body and that information contributes to the development of models of toxicity and disabilities. Such lower-constraint research has become sophisticated in, for example, public health and environmental studies, and has produced important information.

In Chapter 13, we will discuss another group of designs (quasi-experimental designs) that can be effectively used when ethical constraints prevent the use of experiments.

Quick-Check Review 7.5: Ethical Principles

1. How can correlational and differential research studies provide information when experimental studies would be unethical to conduct?

SUMMARY

- In correlational and differential research, we measure, but do not manipulate, variables.
- Correlations express the strength and direction of relationships among variables.
- Differential designs test the differences between groups.
- We cannot easily draw causal conclusions from correlational or differential research.
- Correlational and differential methods are useful when we cannot use experimentation.
- Confounding variables are particular problems in differential research.
- When ethical or practical constraints prevent experimental studies, correlational and differential research can provide useful information to guide action.

Putting It into Practice

By this point in the course, you are probably designing your own research studies, and many of the principles in this chapter will be helpful. However, these principles are valuable in other ways as well, such as helping you to interpret published research findings or improving your critical thinking skills.

Here are two exercises that you might make a routine part of your life. When you read research articles, which you will do frequently in psychology, use the critical thinking skills covered in this text to identify potential sources of confounding. The more you practice these skills, the better you will get. You will find critical thinking extremely helpful to your education.

The second exercise is to listen carefully to arguments people make and the data on which they base those arguments. If you ask yourself whether the data support the argument and only that argument, you may be surprised. Many political and business pundits are willing to make strong statements with only the weakest of data to support them. The ability to see through such weak arguments will do much more than earn you good grades; it will give you an advantage in your professional and personal lives.

EXERCISES

7.1. Define the following key terms. Be sure that you understand them. They are discussed in the chapter and defined in the glossary.

cross-sectional design
cohort effect
longitudinal designs
time-series designs
confounded
artifact
confounding variable
multivariate correlational designs
demographic variables
experimenter expectancy
filler items
moderator variable
cross-cultural research
multiple correlation
canonical correlation
partial correlation
path analysis
coefficient of determination
control group
experimental group

7.2. Interpret each of the following correlations for (a) statistical significance, (b) proportion of variance accounted for, and (c) conceptual interpretation.

1. A correlation of .41 (p = .007) between age and height in grade school girls.
2. A correlation of .32 (p = .074) between rank on a depression scale and rank order of activity level on the ward in a group of hospitalized psychiatric patients.
3. A correlation of .20 (p = .04) between two different measures of assertiveness.

CHAPTER EIGHT

HYPOTHESIS TESTING, VALIDITY, AND THREATS TO VALIDITY

Nothing is more dangerous than an idea when it is the only one we have.
—Émile-Auguste Chartier, 1868–1951, *Libre propos*

WEB RESOURCE MATERIAL

08:01 Library Research Tutorial
08:02 Functional Statistical Flowchart
08:03 Identifying Confounding Variables
08:04 Study Guide/Lab Manual
08:05 Links to Related Internet Sites

The main goal of this chapter is to integrate concepts covered earlier in this text and to introduce a few new concepts. We will also expand several concepts introduced in earlier chapters. The chapter systematically lays out issues that researchers must address in designing experiments, which is the focus of Chapters 8 to 13.

HYPOTHESIS TESTING

A crucial part of scientific research is developing and testing *research hypotheses*. Developing good research hypotheses involves several steps. First, the researcher refines an initial idea into a *statement of the problem*, drawing on initial observations of the phenomenon and a thorough review of previous research. The statement of the problem is converted into a research hypothesis by translating the *theoretical concepts* in the problem statement into specific procedures for measurement and manipulation—that is, into *operational definitions* of the concept. Go with the Flow 8.1 illustrates this process, which we discuss in this section.

An experimental research hypothesis is a specific prediction about the effects of a specific, operationally defined independent variable on a specific, operationally defined dependent variable. But experiments are not the only studies that include research hypotheses. Research hypotheses are part of all scientific research. In lower-constraint research, the initial hypotheses are vague, often little more than "I wonder how things work." That vagueness is fine, because the role of lower-constraint research is to generate hypotheses, which are then tested with higher-constraint research. However, by the time we reach correlational and differential research, and especially when we

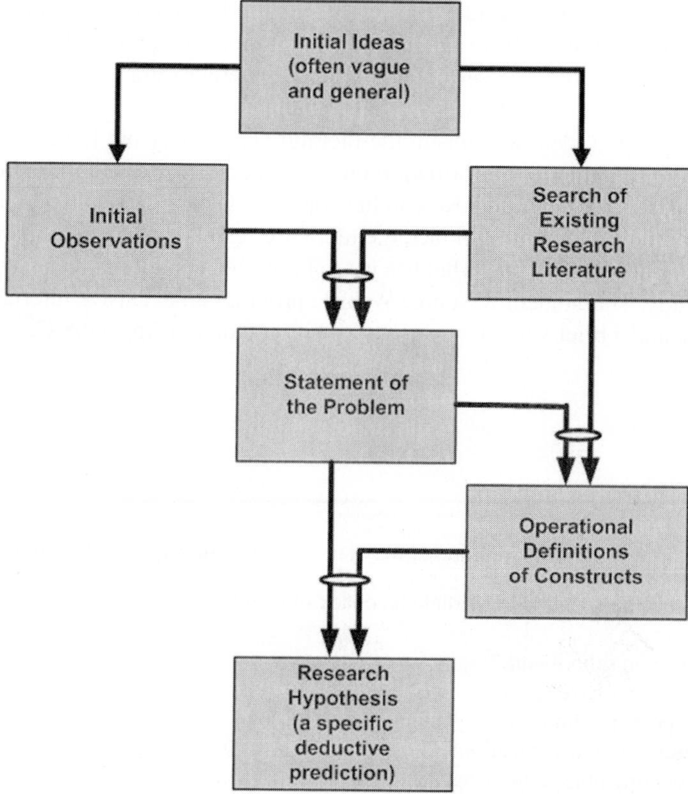

GO WITH THE FLOW 8.1 Generating Research Hypotheses. Initial ideas are refined into a statement of the problem, which is then transformed into a research hypothesis by operationally defining the variables.

conduct experimental research, we are testing clearly specified hypotheses. The form of the hypothesis varies depending on the level of constraint, as shown below.

- The typical wording for hypotheses in correlational research is "*there is a significant (positive or negative) relationship between variables A and B.*"
- The typical wording for hypotheses in differential research is "*there is a significant difference between the groups on the dependent variable.*"
- The typical wording for hypotheses in experimental research is "*the independent variable will have a significant effect on the dependent variable.*"

Note that at the experimental level, the research hypothesis can be directional (e.g., predicting either an increase or a decrease in the dependent variable due to the effects of the independent variable) or nondirectional (predicting an effect, but not specifying the direction of the effect). Hypotheses may be tested at other levels of research, but it is only at the experimental level that we can test causal hypotheses and draw causal inferences with confidence.

Starting Research with an Initial Idea

A research study begins with an initial idea that is refined and developed into one or more specific questions and predictions. The initial idea can come from reading the research literature, from personal interests and observation, or from the need for a solution to a practical problem. Initial ideas focus the researcher on specific variables. Table 8.1 lists several examples of initial ideas. Try to pick out the variables identified in each question in this table.

After developing an initial idea, we consult the literature (i.e., carry out library research) for reports of research on similar issues, for information on how others defined and measured the variables, and to find what procedures they used. Researchers modify, discard, or retain their initial ideas based on this examination of the literature. In fact, the literature search is the first of many tests of a research idea. It tells us what is known and what has yet to be studied, and it points us toward promising areas for further study. The Student Resource Website provides an extensive tutorial on how to conduct library research, and a brief version of this tutorial is included in Appendix C.

08:01

TABLE 8.1 Initial Research Ideas

Here are some examples of initial research ideas that a researcher may later translate into specific research studies.

1. Will children do better in school if they receive immediate feedback of examination results?
2. Does cocaine affect learning?
3. Does nutrition affect performance on schoolwork?
4. Is productivity better when employees have stock in the company?
5. Is it true that older people have poorer memory than younger people?
6. Do men and women have different brain organization?
7. What are the neural bases for locating objects in visual space?

Statement of the Problem

Initial ideas that survive the literature search are refined into a statement of the problem, which guides the researcher through the remainder of the research. In experimentation, the problem statement concerns a causal prediction: "Does variable *A* cause a specific change in variable *B*?" For example, the initial idea "I wonder if nutrition affects schoolwork" could become the problem statement "Will good breakfasts improve academic achievement?" We generally shape the problem statement based on the information learned in the literature search. Table 8.2 lists several examples of problem statements.

Problem statements are in the form of questions, which at the experimental level concern causality. Where possible, the direction of the expected effect is stated, for example, "Will immediate informational feedback improve arithmetic performance?" or "Does cocaine use reduce learning?" Most experimental questions are directional, but sometimes a direction cannot be specified. For example, a researcher might suspect that a manipulation will bring about a change in racial attitudes but cannot predict if it will make the attitudes more positive or more negative. Therefore, the experiment will test whether attitudes change in either direction.

The statement of the problem at the experimental level includes (1) a statement about an expected causal effect, (2) identification of at least two variables, and (3) when possible, the direction of the expected causal effects. Formulating a clear statement of the problem points the researcher toward an effective design.

Developing a clear statement of the problem requires skill and creativity. Consider bystander apathy, sometimes called the "Bad Samaritan" effect. A particularly shocking example occurred on a Detroit bridge late in 1995 (Meredith, 1996). Drivers were stuck in traffic and irritated. It is not clear how the incident started, but a man began attacking another driver, a young woman. She screamed and ran; he pursued her, beat her, knocked her to the ground, and ripped off her clothes. He laughed and invited other men who were watching to join in. At least 40 or 50 people watched as she screamed and pleaded for help. No one helped. The beaten, near-naked woman ran frantically from the attacker, jumped onto the railing, and fell, or perhaps was thrown, into the water to her death. In all that time, although many had been within a few feet, not a single person helped the terrified young woman.

TABLE 8.2 Problem Statements

Here are some examples of problem statements for experimental studies. Each of these problem statements addresses a question of causality.

1. Does the presence of male hormones increase aggressive behavior in rats?
2. Does the presence of a mediator increase the likelihood of reaching a compromise in a negotiation setting?
3. Can people learn easily visualized words more readily than words that they cannot easily visualize?
4. Does the presence of a stranger in the room increase an infant's crying?
5. Do stimulants help hyperactive children control their behavior?
6. Does contingent reinforcement improve the accuracy of maze running in mice?
7. Are people more aggressive when they are frustrated?
8. Will sensory deprivation grossly distort thinking and emotional responsivity?
9. Will mandatory arrest and jail time reduce spousal abuse?

This was not the first time such an incident occurred. In 1964, a young woman named Catherine (Kitty) Genovese was stabbed repeatedly for half an hour while 38 of her neighbors watched from their apartments. No one came to her aid. No one even called the police until after she was dead.

Incidents like these raise questions like "How could this happen?" or "Why didn't anyone help her?" These questions are important, but they are too vague for scientists to answer. Darley and Latane (1968) refined the questions into something more manageable. They studied reports of the attack and witness statements. They looked for similar occurrences in police files and in the research literature. In the end, they focused their attention on only one or two factors, which allowed them to create a workable statement of the problem.

The issue in the Genovese case was that none of the 38 known witnesses to the attack came to her aid. Common sense might lead you to believe that the more people present, the more likely it is that someone will help. However, this incident suggests just the opposite—as the number of people present increases, the likelihood that someone will help decreases. Thus, one variable (the number of people present) might affect another variable (the likelihood of someone offering aid). You might develop the idea into the following problem statement: "Will bystanders be less likely to help a victim when there are many people present than when there are only a few people present?"

The statement of the problem can lead to specific research studies. When Darley and Latane (1968) studied the problem, they found that people were indeed less likely to help if other people were present. In fact, they were much less likely to help. People apparently assume that when others are around, someone else will take responsibility.

Composing a statement of the problem is an important early phase in designing research. Kerlinger and Lee (2000) list the following characteristics of a good problem statement.

1. The problem should state the expected relationships between variables (in experimentation, this is a causal relationship).
2. The problem statement should be in the form of a question.
3. The statement of the problem must at least imply the possibility of an empirical test of the question.

In the next few pages, we will bring together the major concepts that we have been discussing, using for our example the autism research that was discussed in earlier chapters (Graziano, 1974). Although completed many years ago, it provides a good example for understanding these concepts. In that research, the major question was this: "Can relaxation reduce the disruptive behavior of children with autism?" The independent variable was relaxation and the dependent variable was disruption. The expected effect was a decrease in disruption brought about by relaxation training.

With the statement of the problem clearly defined, the next step in the development of the research hypothesis is to operationally define the variables suggested by the problem statement.

Operational Definitions

Before measuring the dependent variable or manipulating the independent variable, we must define them conceptually and operationally. The independent variable in this study was relaxation. The concept of relaxation refers to an internal state, a condition presumably without stress or anxiety. We cannot directly observe that internal state, but it can be inferred from behavioral observations.

Therefore, relaxation is not an observed fact but an inferred construct. The conceptual definition of relaxation provides an idea of what to manipulate. The question is how can one manipulate something that is internal to the participant, and thus not directly observable or accessible? How would we operationally define the manipulation of relaxation?

You learned in Chapter 4 (page 84) that the children were relaxed by having them lie down while the researcher encouraged them to relax with a soothing voice and muscle massage. The definition was spelled out by describing how the researcher should set up the room, as well as what should be said and done to relax the participants. Once we created this definition, the term "relaxation training" was understood to mean all these procedures. Because the definition provided detailed instructions, other researchers could replicate the procedure.

We operationally defined the dependent variable, disruption, as explosive tantrums that included a number of specific behaviors. Examples of specific disruptive behaviors clarified the concept and simplified the task of recognizing which behaviors were disruptive. We measured disruptive behavior in terms of its frequency, duration, and intensity (see Chapter 4, pages 84–85). This example shows how operational definitions can help a researcher move a step closer to formulating a research hypothesis.

Research Hypothesis

To evaluate the effects of relaxation on the disruptive behavior of children with autism, we developed the problem statement into a specific, testable prediction, which became the research hypothesis. Note that the problem statement had already suggested one basic way to test it: measure disruptive behavior before and after relaxation training and see whether the predicted difference exists.

This approach is a pretest-posttest design (see Figure 8.1). As you will see in later chapters, a pretest-posttest design has several weaknesses, and better designs are available to test a hypothesis. However, this simple design helps to illustrate the use of operational definitions.

Having operationally defined both the dependent variable (disruptive behavior) and the independent variable (relaxation training), we can now combine the operational definitions and the statement of the problem into a specific prediction, which is the research hypothesis. In the example, the research hypothesis was this: *following relaxation training, the frequency, duration, and intensity of disruptive behavior will be significantly less than at the pretraining baseline.*

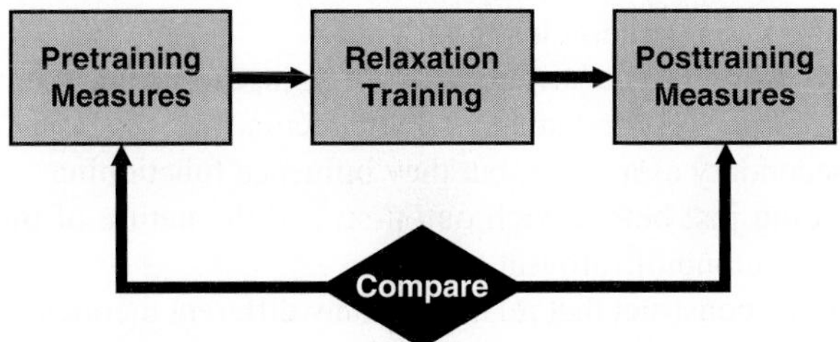

FIGURE 8.1 A Single-Group, Pretest-Posttest Design. This design follows a single group of participants, testing them both before and after a manipulation.

TABLE 8.3 Characteristics of a Research Hypothesis

The following are characteristics of a good research hypothesis:

1. It is a declarative sentence.
2. It is brief and clearly stated.
3. It identifies at least two variables.
4. It states a predicted relationship between at least one variable and at least one other variable.
5. It states the nature of the relationship. [Example: The amount of physical punishment that parents experienced as children will positively correlate with parents' current use of physical punishment on their own children (a correlational hypothesis).]
6. It can state the direction of the relationship if a direction has been predicted by the theory. [Example: Participants in group A will score significantly higher than participants in group B (a directional prediction).]
7. It implies that the predicted relationship can be tested empirically.

A research hypothesis makes a declarative statement about the expected relationship among variables. Remember, even though it is declarative, it is a *tentative* statement to be tested. We summarize the characteristics of a good research hypothesis in Table 8.3.

The Contribution of Theory to the Research Hypothesis

Theory plays a critical role in developing the research hypothesis. Even in a research area that has never been studied before, we usually have implicit theories about how things might relate. Most research involves studying constructs that have been studied extensively, and in such situations, explicit theories guide decisions about the research. Often, several theories guide design decisions. Some of these theories will be mature, with hundreds of research studies providing empirical confirmation of the theory's predictions. Some will be new, with only limited validation, or perhaps so new that it is being tested for the first time in our study. Theories are usually interconnected, and a typical study will provide evidence concerning the validity of more than one theory. This network of theories and established empirical relationships provides a foundation for future studies.

To illustrate this, let's look more closely at the study of relaxation in children with autism. The following are some of the theoretical ideas that contributed to the study.

1. Children with autism have severe functional impairments in emotional development, language, personal relationships, and general learning.
2. Most researchers accept a biological-causation model; that is, the primary condition is a currently unknown brain defect probably related to genetic factors.
3. Environmental factors are secondary as a cause, but they influence functioning.
4. The children's facial grimacing just before each outburst, and the nature of the outbursts, suggest the presence of strong autonomic arousal.
5. Autonomic arousal is a complex construct that relates to many different theories—some physiological, some psychological, and some involving both systems. It involves a coordinated physiological response that increases the readiness of the person to respond rapidly to situations.

6. Several theories imply that arousal and relaxation are mutually exclusive.
7. Thus, inducing relaxation might well reduce the inferred state of autonomic arousal in these children with autism, thus reducing the driving force for the observed outbursts.

This brief review only scratches the surface of the role of theory in this relatively simple study. It is unlikely that all the theories we drew on in developing the research were valid (i.e., that they described accurately all predicted relationships). However, the study provided an answer to the specific question, and that information helped us to evaluate the adequacy of some of the ideas that guided the formulation of the question.

One idea affected by this study was that autism prevents the learning of new skills. However, these children did learn relaxation skills and subsequent research confirmed that children with autism can learn many skills (e.g., Graziano, 2002; McGrath, 2006; Napolitano et al., 2010; Schriebman, 2005).

Testing the Research Hypothesis

The research hypothesis actually encompasses three hypotheses:

1. The null or statistical hypothesis
2. The confounding variable hypothesis
3. The causal hypothesis

To illustrate these three hypotheses, let's look at the simple pretest-posttest design we used to carry out the study of children with autism:

1. We measure the frequency, intensity, and duration of the children's disruptive behavior during a 4-week, pretraining baseline period.
2. We then train the children for 2 months in relaxation to the criteria specified.
3. After training, we again measure the frequency, intensity, and duration of disruptive behavior for a 4-week posttraining period.

Now suppose that, as predicted, there is less disruption after the relaxation training. Can we conclude that the independent variable, relaxation training, reduced the children's disruptive behavior? Not yet, because to answer the research question we must rule out two other hypotheses: the null hypothesis and the confounding variable hypothesis. Go with the Flow 8.2 illustrates the steps in this process.

Null Hypothesis. Before we can conclude that relaxation reduces disruptive behavior, we must determine that the posttraining measures of disruption are *significantly* lower than the pretraining measures of disruption; that is, that the differences observed are not merely due to chance variation.

The first of the three hypotheses that we must test is the **statistical hypothesis**, which we test with an appropriate inferential statistic (see Chapter 5). The *t*- or *F*-tests for correlated groups are appropriate here for two reasons: (1) the dependent measure yields score data, and (2) the measures are correlated (i.e., the same participants were measured before and after treatment). The rationale for selecting the statistical test might be confusing, but for now take our word for it. Appendix D

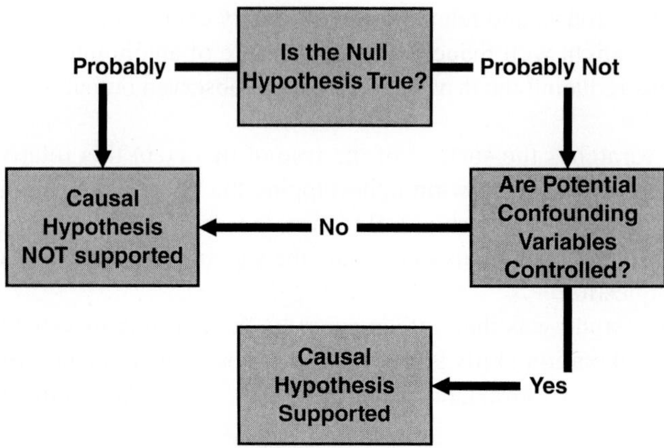

GO WITH THE FLOW 8.2 Evaluating a Research Study's Results. The causal hypothesis that the independent variable affected the dependent variable cannot be accepted until both the null and confounding variable hypotheses have been rejected.

08:02

presents a flowchart system for determining the appropriate statistical procedures in this and most other research, and the Student Resource Website recreates this flowchart with links to the appropriate computational procedures.

As you learned in Chapter 5, the null hypothesis states that there is no difference between the two conditions beyond what we would expect by chance. If we find a difference too large to be a chance difference, we reject the null hypothesis. However, if the differences are within chance limits, we do not reject the null hypothesis. (Note that in Go with the Flow 8.2, the left and right paths are labeled "Probably" and "Probably not," instead of "yes" and "no." Why do you think we did that?)

Suppose that a *t*- or *F*-test discloses that the posttraining measures of disruptive behavior are significantly lower than the pretraining measures, meaning that the differences are large enough that they are not likely to be due only to chance. Therefore, we reject the null hypothesis. Can we then accept the hypothesis that relaxation training is responsible for the observed reduction in disruptive behavior? Not yet; there is still one other hypothesis to consider.

Confounding Variable Hypothesis. Although we have found statistically significant differences in the predicted direction, we still cannot be sure that the observed differences are due to the independent variable of relaxation. They might be due to confounding variables. Rejecting the null hypothesis, while necessary, *is not sufficient to draw a causal inference*. We must also rule out the possibility that factors other than the independent variable have had an effect on the dependent variable. The task here is to rule out confounding variables as explanations of the results. It is best to rule out confounding variables during the design phase, when you anticipate them and design controls to eliminate their effects. (This task will be the focus of the next several chapters.)

The **confounding variable hypothesis** suggests that the observed differences *might* be due to extraneous factors that affected the dependent measures. We accept the finding that there is a statistically significant difference, but being systematic scientists, we are not yet convinced that the difference is due to the independent variable. Rather, we consider the possibility that it might be due to the effects of confounding factors. For example, the relaxation training required 2 months, a long time in the life of growing children, and the observed improvement might have been due to the children's natural maturing processes rather than to the independent variable of relaxation training. That is, the independent variable is confounded with maturation. Therefore, it is unreasonable to conclude that relaxation training is the variable that brought about the improvement.

The confounding variable hypothesis recognizes that relaxation training is only one of several possible explanations for the improvement in disruptive behavior. To have confidence in the conclusions, we must rule out *all* alternative explanations.

Unlike the statistical hypothesis, the confounding variable hypothesis is not tested directly. Rather, we rule out each confounding variable hypothesis by first anticipating potential confounding variables, and then reducing their likelihood by using an appropriate research design and necessary controls. Careful inspection will show where the design is weak and where it is strong. The researcher must judge whether the design is strong enough to rule out the most likely confounding variables.

As you will see in later chapters, some designs are so powerful that they can rule out most confounding variables. Other designs are less effective in ruling out confounding variables, although careful measurement of possible confounding variables might be sufficient to do so.

As you learned in Chapter 7, a variable can confound results only if (1) it affects the scores on the dependent variable, and (2) the groups or conditions we are comparing differ on the variable. If we show that a potential confounding variable is not correlated with the dependent measure, or that the groups or conditions being compared do not differ on this potential confounding variable, we have effectively ruled it out as a source of confounding.

Ruling out alternative explanations is critical in science. We conduct research not only to find evidence to support research hypotheses, but also to rule out alternative explanations, which are also known as *rival hypotheses*. Every uncontrolled confounding variable is a threat to the validity of a study. As you will see in Chapter 10, experimental designs typically rule out most confounding variables.

Causal Hypothesis. The **causal hypothesis** states that the independent variable will have the predicted effect on the dependent variable. Suppose that you tested and rejected the null hypothesis and ruled out confounding variables. (We will discuss how to control or rule out confounding variables in Chapter 9.) You are now ready to return to the research hypothesis: following relaxation training, the frequency, duration, and intensity of disruptive behavior will be significantly less than at the pretraining baseline. Remember that when this research hypothesis was first stated it was a tentative statement to be tested. If you find significantly less disruption after training than before training and can rule out alternative hypotheses, then only one viable hypothesis remains: that the independent variable affected the dependent variable as predicted. Note, however, that the assertion is not absolute, but rather it is a statement of probability. The first hypothesis was the statistical hypothesis, which we tested in terms of probability. Even though the data were sufficiently persuasive to convince us to reject the null hypothesis, there was always the possibility of a Type I error (see Chapter 5).

It is wise to remember that there are so many complicated steps from initial conceptualization to running the study to interpreting the results that we must always be cautious in our interpretations. We can have confidence, but not certainty, in the results of a well-run study. We should consider every finding in science as tentative and subject to change based on new observations. This is one reason why scientists wince when they hear the term "prove" and they rarely use the term.

Another important point about developing research hypotheses is that we can often develop several different research hypotheses from a problem statement. Again, recall that the problem statement in the research on children with autism was "Can relaxation reduce the disruptive behavior of children with autism?" In the study just described, we operationally defined the manipulation of relaxation in terms of procedures used to train the child to slow down, and we defined disruption as the frequency, duration, and intensity of each disruptive behavior. These definitions led to this specific research hypothesis: following relaxation training, the frequency, duration, and intensity of disruptive behavior will be significantly less than at the pretraining baseline.

Now, suppose that we study another aspect of the relaxation-disruption hypothesis, and we operationally define relaxation in terms of the pharmacological effects of a particular drug. Each child is given a drug that is known to have relaxing effects. Now we are testing a different research hypothesis, because the manipulation of relaxation is being operationally defined in a different way. This second study uses the same pretest-posttest design, but now uses drugs, instead of relaxation training, to induce relaxation. We are still evaluating the same statement of the problem, but with a different interpretation, expressed as a different research hypothesis.

Other changes can be made in translating the statement of the problem into a research hypothesis. For example, instead of using the pretest-posttest design, we could use a *two-group, posttest-only design,* as shown in Figure 8.2. Each child would be randomly assigned to one of two groups. One group is given the relaxation drug, and the other is given no drug. We then measure the disruptive behavior of all participants and compare the mean level of disruption in the two groups. (We will discuss this research design, and other commonly used research designs, in Chapter 10.)

The wording of this new research hypothesis is different from that of the previous example, because the independent variable and the research design have been changed. Here is the new research hypothesis: children with autism who receive drugs that relax them will show less disruptive behavior than those who do not receive the drugs. Thus, we can combine the same problem statement with different operational definitions of the independent and dependent variables and different research designs. This results in the generation of several different research hypotheses and, consequently, several different studies. In essence, the researcher is able to investigate the same basic problem in different ways by testing different facets of the same issue.

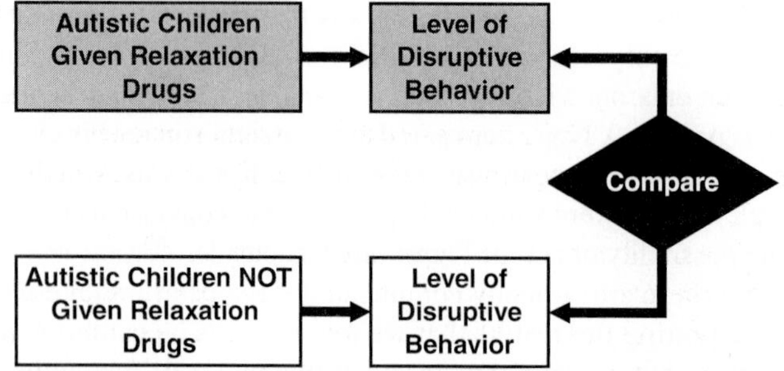

FIGURE 8.2 A Two-Group, Posttest-Only Design. This design used two groups, only one of which received the relaxation drugs. The level of disruptive behavior is then measured in each group and these levels compared.

To summarize, an experiment involves the following steps:

1. We refine initial ideas into the problem statement.
2. The problem statement identifies variables, implies causality, and indicates the direction of the expected causal effect.
3. We operationally define the variables and construct a research hypothesis by combining these operational definitions with the problem statement.
4. The research hypothesis states a specific testable prediction about the relationship between specific variables.
5. Testing the research hypothesis involves several hypotheses: the null or statistical hypothesis, the confounding variable hypothesis (which is often a set of hypotheses), and the causal hypothesis.
6. We accept the causal hypothesis only after the null and confounding variable hypotheses are rejected.
7. Testing the null hypothesis evaluates the likelihood that the findings were due to chance.
8. We can develop several research hypotheses from each problem statement that lead to several different studies, thus examining different facets of the problem.
9. Statistical tests show only whether there is a significant difference between groups, but not whether the difference is due to the independent variable. To draw that conclusion, we must identify and rule out competing interpretations.

Quick-Check Review 8.1: Hypothesis Testing

1. Describe the process of refining initial ideas into a problem statement.
2. What concepts do we combine to produce the research hypothesis?
3. What is the function of the research hypothesis?
4. What three hypotheses must be tested to evaluate the research hypothesis?
5. Why is ruling out potential confounding variables so important?
6. Describe how we can develop several research hypotheses from one problem statement.

VALIDITY AND THREATS TO VALIDITY

A major concern in research is the validity of the procedures and conclusions. The term "validity" has several meanings, the most basic of which refers to methodological soundness or appropriateness; that is, a valid test measures what it is supposed to measure, and a valid research design tests what it is supposed to test.

Validity is relevant at all levels of constraint, but it is especially important in experimental research, which addresses questions about causality. There are many potential threats to the validity of an experiment, and the researcher must (1) anticipate them, and (2) create procedures to eliminate or reduce them. This section outlines the broad concept of validity. It follows closely the classic organization of Campbell and Stanley (1966) and Cook and Campbell (1979), who distinguished among four types of validity: statistical validity, construct validity, external validity, and internal validity (summarized in Table 8.4).

TABLE 8.4 Types of Validity

TYPE OF VALIDITY	DESCRIPTION
Statistical	The accuracy of the *p*-value on which a statistical decision is based
Construct	The degree to which the theory or theories behind the research study provide(s) the best explanation for the results observed
External	The extent to which the results of a particular study generalize to other people, places, or conditions
Internal	The extent to which we can be confident that the observed changes in the dependent variable were due to the effects of the independent variable and not to the effects of confounding variables

Statistical Validity

When statistical procedures are used to test the null hypothesis, the researcher is asking whether the results are due to systematic factors (ideally, the independent variable) or to chance variations. Rejecting the null hypothesis is a necessary first step in testing the effects of the independent variable. **Statistical validity** addresses the question of whether these statistical conclusions are accurate.

Several possible threats to a study's statistical validity must be controlled. One threat is the possibility that the measures used to assess the dependent variable are unreliable. Another threat is the violation of the assumptions that underlie the statistical tests. Each statistical procedure makes assumptions about the nature of the data. Statistics textbooks normally list the assumptions of each statistic. Violating these statistical assumptions distorts the *p*-value for the statistical test, and therefore the statistical decision is undependable.

Statistical validity does not address whether the statistical decision accurately reflects reality. Remember, a statistical decision is based on probability. If alpha is set at .05, it means that we will reject the null hypothesis if there is less than a 5% chance of the decision being correct. This still means that we will be rejecting the null hypothesis incorrectly 5% of the time, as discussed in Chapter 5.

Construct Validity

Scientists construct every research hypothesis within a theoretical context of ideas. **Construct validity** refers to how well the study's results support the theory or constructs behind the research and whether the theory supported by the findings provides the best available explanation of the results. To help to reduce threats to construct validity, a researcher should use clearly stated definitions and carefully build hypotheses on solid, well-validated constructs. The theoretical bases for the hypothesis must be clear and well supported, with rival theories carefully ruled out.

An example of a construct validity question is the continuing debate in psychology over the nature-nurture issue (Ridley, 2003). This question has been raised in many different research areas, from questions about the causes of psychological disorders (e.g., Erlenmeyer-Kimling et al., 2004; Suomi, 2008) to investigations of why males usually score higher than females on math skill measures (Casey, 1996; Dar-Nimrod & Heine, 2006). On the latter, researchers debate how much of the difference is innate and how much is the result of environmental effects (Lubinski & Benbow, 1992).

Environmental variables alone could shape the differences if males receive more training than females in math, or if teachers are more likely to tell males that learning math is important to success. The issue is whether the data support the idea that an innate, genetically determined characteristic is responsible for the observed gender differences (nature) or whether the environment shaped the gender differences (nurture).

We are often tempted to interpret data as being consistent with our own preconceptions and ignore other explanations for the data. For example, the finding that men tend to take more math courses than women would seem to be consistent with the nurture hypothesis that males are better at math because they get more training in it. However, we could interpret this finding to mean that men take more math courses because they tend to be good at math and choose courses in which they know they can excel. Therefore, the data are consistent with both a nature and a nurture hypothesis, and the construct validity of any one interpretation would be in doubt.

External Validity

In its strictest sense, the results of an experiment are limited to those participants and conditions used in the particular experiment. However, when researchers test college students' memory ability, for example, are they interested in how well these particular 20 freshmen did? Not really. They are interested in memory functions in general. They want to generalize the results beyond the specific participants and conditions to other, similar participants and conditions. **External validity** refers to the degree to which researchers are able to generalize the results of a study to other participants, conditions, times, and places.

To make statements about the overall population based on the findings of a particular sample, we must select the sample so that it adequately represents the population. The process of inferring something about a population based on findings from a sample is called **generalization**. The best way to control problems of generalization from a sample to a population is to select participants randomly from the population, as you will learn in Chapter 9.

In similar fashion, the researcher must be careful about generalizing across times, places, and conditions; to do so, the researcher must sample across those times, places, or conditions. If your research study shows that encouragement improves performance in fourth-graders who are having difficulty learning to play a new game, that does not mean that the same will be true for eighth-graders or adults. It does not mean that the same will be true for school or work activities, and it does not mean that it will be true regardless of the pressure or incentives in a situation. Most theories in psychology predict behavior in specific settings, for specific individuals, and under specific conditions. Much of the research in psychology is geared to determining when the theory works (i.e., accurately predicts the results) and when it does not work. We call this process establishing the **limits of generalization**. It would be foolish to assume that any psychological theory applied to all people, all settings, and all conditions.

The term "**ecological validity**" is used to refer to the appropriate generalization from the laboratory to real-life situations (Neisser, 1976). Questions of how laboratory-derived information will generalize to the real world and how much it can help scientists understand real-world issues will depend on how realistically the research captures the critical elements of the real-world scenario. This issue was raised in Chapter 6, where we discussed how naturalistic research can be used to see whether laboratory findings apply to real-world settings. Now you can see that such an evaluation is really checking for the ecological validity of the findings.

An example is Michael Graziano's (2009) descriptions of his many trips to the Bronx Zoo to observe primates that were, if not in natural environments, at least in much less constrained settings than in his laboratory. He wanted to make sure that the overt movement behaviors he worked with in his laboratory were, indeed, naturally occurring in the animals' behavioral repertoire, and not artifacts created by the laboratory environment or experimental procedures. He was making naturalistic observations to assess ecological validity.

External validity is always an issue in research, because ethics require that we use only participants who have given informed consent. That means that no sample will ever be completely random unless everyone we select agrees to participate, which rarely happens. However, it is far better to accept that there will always be some limitations on external validity than to compromise ethical principles of research.

Internal Validity

Internal validity is of major concern to researchers because it involves the very heart of experimentation: the demonstration of causality. It concerns this question: "Was the independent variable, and not some extraneous variable, responsible for the changes in the dependent variable?" An experiment is internally valid when the answer to this question is "yes." Any factor that weakens our confidence that the independent variable accounted for the results is a threat to the internal validity of the study.

As you learned in Chapter 7, the variables that might threaten internal validity are *confounding variables*. These are variables that change at the same time that the independent variable changes. Consequently, when we see a change in the dependent measure, we do not know whether it is a result of the change in the independent variable or an uncontrolled confounding variable. The next section will cover the most common confounding variables. Unless we control all of these confounding variables, we will be unable to draw causal conclusions from our research.

Quick-Check Review 8.2: Validity and Threats to Validity

1. What is validity?
2. Define the various types of validity.
3. Which type of validity is concerned with the accuracy of conclusions about the effects of the independent variable on the dependent variable?

MAJOR CONFOUNDING VARIABLES

Cook and Campbell (1979) identified several confounding variables, which are summarized in Table 8.5 and discussed here.

Maturation

In longitudinal research, especially with children, participants grow older between the pretest and posttest measures. As they age, they may also become more sophisticated, experienced, bigger, or stronger. This process of natural change or growth over time is called **maturation**.

TABLE 8.5 Major Confounding Variables.

CONFOUNDING VARIABLE	DESCRIPTION
Maturation	Changes in the dependent variable that are due to the normal maturation of the participant
History	Changes in the dependent variable that are due to historical events that occur during the study but that are unrelated to, and cannot be controlled by, the study
Testing	Any change in a participant's score on the dependent variable that is a function of the participant having been tested previously
Instrumentation	Any change in the calibration of the measuring instrument over the course of the study that affects the scores on the dependent variable
Regression to the Mean	The tendency for participants who are selected because they have extreme scores on a variable to be less extreme in a follow-up testing
Selection	Any factor that creates groups that are not equivalent at the beginning of the study
Attrition	The loss of participants during a study; differential loss is problematic because the participants who drop out are likely to be different from those who continue
Diffusion of Treatment	Change in the response of participants in a particular condition because of information that the participants gained about other research conditions from participants in those other conditions
Sequence Effects	Effects on a participant's performance in later conditions that result from the experience that the participant had in the previous conditions of the study

Maturation can also occur in participants other than children. Adults placed in a new environment tend to make predictable adjustments over time. Diseases tend to have predictable courses. Several types of observed changes may be due to maturational factors, rather than to effects of an independent variable. Researchers must be particularly alert to maturation when studying children, because change and growth are certainties in children and those natural processes are not going to wait around while you do your study.

History

During the course of a study, events that are independent of the study may occur that can affect the outcome; such events produce confounding due to **history**. In general, threats to internal validity due to history increase with longer times between pretest and posttest measurements. Historical factors are most likely when you are measuring dependent variables that are responsive to environmental events. For example, food intake affects weight, but has little effect on height. Therefore, historical factors are more likely to be a confounding variable for studies of weight than for studies of height. Most weight-control procedures would be lucky to hold their own if we evaluated them during the holidays, when high-calorie foods constantly tempt people.

Testing

The repeated **testing** of participants can threaten internal validity because participants gain proficiency through practice on the measuring instruments. These testing effects are most pronounced on measures in which the participant is asked to perform some skill-related task, such as tests of

CARTOON 8.1 Maturational and historical factors can affect any process that takes time, including research studies. The improvement in this client might well be due to one or both of these confounding variables, rather than to the efforts of the therapist.

Source: Reprinted by permission of Sidney Harris, ScienceCartoonsPlus.Com.

memory, IQ, or manual dexterity. Most people do better on the second administration of such a test because the first administration gave them practice.

Instrumentation

Apparent pretest-posttest changes may be due to changes in the measuring instrument, rather than to the independent variable manipulation. This confounding variable, known as **instrumentation**, is particularly relevant when the measuring instrument is a human observer. This is because an observer might become more proficient at making observations or might change his or her criteria over time, often without being aware of the changes.

Regression to the Mean

The concept of **regression to the mean** suggests that whenever we select participants *because* their scores on a measure are extreme (either very high or very low), they will tend to be less extreme on a second testing; that is, their scores will regress toward the mean. For example, consider the top 10% of students based on their first exam. How would we expect these top students to perform on the second exam? We would expect them to do well, but would they all do as well as they did on the first exam? It is not likely. The reason is that some of the students did well on the first exam because they studied unusually hard. On the second test, however, some of these students might not be as diligent. If you took the top 10% of students on the first test and computed their mean scores on both the first and second tests, you would probably find that they scored, on average, closer to the mean on the second test.

How much regression occurs will depend on how much of the test performance is due to unstable factors, such as amount of study, and how much is due to consistent factors, such as skill and study habits. The more the impact of unstable factors on the score, the more regression you can expect to see.

Selection

Confounding due to **selection** occurs when the groups under study are not equivalent before the manipulations begin. Under ideal conditions, researchers would randomly select and then randomly assign participants to different groups. When random selection and assignment are not possible, as in most naturalistic, case study, and differential research, then the possibility of confounding due to selection exists.

Attrition

Sometimes participants drop out of a study; they might go on vacation in the middle of the study, forget their appointments, lose interest, or become ill. If there are no biasing factors, we would expect such dropouts to be evenly distributed across groups, and they will not differentially affect one group more than other groups.

Confounding due to **attrition** occurs when participants are lost differentially, such as when there are more dropouts from one group than from another, or when participants with certain characteristics are more likely to drop out. Researchers must be careful not to create situations or use procedures that will bias some participants against completing the study, thus differentially affecting the outcome. For example, suppose that a researcher realized too late that nearly all the high school seniors failed to return for the second half of a study because it coincided with school parties, excitement, and general preparation for graduation. Their attrition would leave primarily underclass participants in the second half of the study, thus biasing the results.

Sometimes procedures can cause participants with certain characteristics to drop out, leaving a biased sample. For example, in an unpublished study by one of the authors, many sixth-grade boys dropped out because they thought the procedures were "too girlish." Researchers must take care to avoid confounding studies by allowing attrition of participants to have a differential effect on the outcome.

Diffusion of Treatment

When participants in different experimental conditions are in proximity and are able to communicate with each other, earlier participants might "give away" the procedures to those scheduled later. In addition, experimental participants who receive a treatment may communicate with control participants who do not receive that treatment or who may not have known that they were in a control group. Such information exchanges, called **diffusion of treatment**, can erode the planned experimental differences between groups, making the groups more similar because of the information exchange.

Diffusion of treatment can affect studies in many ways. For example, many psychologists use undergraduate participants. Students often hear about studies from other students, and many even select the study based on what they hear. When they participate, the knowledge of what their friends experienced might affect how they respond. To compensate for this problem, many researchers try to make their study look the same to participants in all conditions.

Sequence Effects

In a good deal of psychological research, participants are exposed to more than one experimental condition. We call this approach a *within-subjects design*. Although this design offers important advantages over other designs, it also introduces another confounding factor, **sequence effects**, in which experiences with earlier conditions of the study affect responses to later conditions.

If, in a study with three conditions, the order of presentation of conditions is always condition A followed by condition B followed by condition C, then systematic confounding can occur. For example, performance in conditions B and C might reflect both the effect of the conditions and the effect of having already experienced condition A. We control sequence effects by using more than one order of conditions. Sequence effects and some methods to handle them are discussed in more detail in Chapter 11.

Examples of Confounding

The best way to appreciate confounding variables is to see how they can creep into research studies. Consider our earlier hypothesis concerning the effects of relaxation training on the disruptive behavior of children with autism and the research procedures used to test it. We had trained four children with autism to relax and found that their level of disruptive behavior decreased following this training. Can we conclude with confidence that the independent variable of relaxation training was responsible for the observed reduction in disruptive behavior? Can we be confident about the internal validity of this study?

Consider the basic design of the first study, which tested this research hypothesis: following relaxation training, the frequency, duration, and intensity of disruptive behavior will be significantly less than at the pretraining baseline. To test the hypothesis, we measured the disruptive behavior of the children with autism, then provided relaxation training, and finally measured disruption again. It required 2 months for all the children in the study to reach the criterion of successful relaxation. After relaxation training, the disruptive behavior decreased in frequency and intensity, and the decrease was statistically significant.

It is tempting to conclude that relaxation training was responsible for the decrease in disruptive behavior, but what alternative explanations might there be for the results? That is, what confounding variables might have been operating to produce the results? One possibility is that the children might simply have improved over the 2-month period through natural maturational processes, with relaxation having little to do with the observed improvement. Therefore, *maturation* is one potential confounding variable.

Another alternative explanation for the observed improvement is that some systematic factor in the program itself, other than relaxation, might have been responsible. The children were in a full-day, 5-day-a-week therapy program that included many components. Could some other factor that we consistently applied to the children during the 2 months of relaxation training be responsible for the improvement? This is an example of the confounding variable of *history*; that is, other things that occurred during the course of the research might have produced the findings.

Regression to the mean might also have been operating. Behaviors naturally fluctuate in frequency and intensity, going through ups and downs of severity. Perhaps we started this research at the peak of severity; perhaps it was even begun because the severity was so great. As time passed, the behaviors returned to severity levels that were closer to the mean. It was then that we took the posttraining measures. If regression to the mean was operating, then the relaxation manipulation might have had little to do with the observed improvement in behavior.

Still another possible confounding variable should be considered. In the course of the research, the staff who observed the children's disruptive behavior might have changed the ways in which they observed and measured the behavior. They might have gradually become more accustomed to the children's severe behavior and, in time, tended to record it as less severe. Thus, their criteria for observation—not the behavior of the children—might have changed during the course of the study. Therefore, the confounding variable of *instrumentation* might account for the findings.

There are many possible confounding variables in research, and there might be several in any given study. Their effects might all be in the same direction, thus compounding the errors, or in opposite directions, thus countering one another. If we want to draw valid conclusions about the effects of one variable on another, we must anticipate and control potential confounding variables to eliminate rival hypotheses, leaving the causal hypothesis as the most likely explanation for the results. The Student Resource Website provides practice in identifying potential confounding variables in research.

08:03

Quick-Check Review 8.3: Major Confounding Variables

1. What is the difference between the confounding variables of history and maturation?
2. If your hometown team wins this year's World Series, what prediction would you make for next year based on the concept of regression to the mean?
3. Suppose that you are interested in gender differences in second-graders, but your procedure is upsetting to girls raised in a single-parent home, and several drop out of your study. What confounding variable would be operating, and what effect might it have?
4. What design has to contend with the confounding variable of sequence effects?

SUBJECT AND EXPERIMENTER EFFECTS

There is a large category of threats to the validity of a study due to subject and experimenter effects. The expectations and biases of the researcher and the participants can systematically affect the results of a study in subtle ways, thus reducing the study's validity. This section describes subject and experimenter effects, and Chapter 9 discusses controls for these effects.

Subject Effects

Every psychological experiment is a social situation in which participants and researchers engage in a common undertaking (Orne, 1962). Each behaves according to his or her understanding of how a participant or a researcher should behave. When participants enter an experiment, they are not entirely naive. They have ideas, understandings, and perhaps misunderstandings about what to expect in the study.

People participate for different reasons. Some do so because it is a course requirement. Others participate because of curiosity or because they will be paid for their participation. Some volunteer because they hope to learn something, perhaps about themselves. Participants enter and carry out their roles with a variety of motivations, understandings, expectations, and biases, all of which can affect their behavior in the research setting. Furthermore, an experiment is an artificial, contrived situation, often far removed from participants' natural environments. When people know they are being observed, they may behave differently than they normally would. This can lead to **subject effects**, which refer to any changes in the behavior of participants that are attributable to being in the study, rather than to the variables under study.

Most participants do their best to be good subjects. This might lead some participants to try to discern the research hypothesis so that they will know how they are "supposed to behave." Participants are often particularly sensitive to cues from the researcher. Furthermore, researchers, with their own expectations and biases, might inadvertently give such cues. Cues given to participants on how the researcher expects them to behave are called **demand characteristics**. Those unintentional cues include characteristics of the setting and procedures and also information and even rumors about the researcher and the nature of the research.

A related phenomenon, the **placebo effect**, can occur when participants expect a specific effect of an experimental manipulation. For example, some participants in a drug study of pain control might enter the study with the clear expectation that the procedures will help, and these participants actually report feeling better and even show physiological changes, all because of the suggestion that the procedure will work. Participants often report improvement when given a placebo treatment, such as a pill that had no active ingredients.

Experimenter Effects

Experimenter effects are any biasing effects in a study that are due to the actions of the researcher. The researcher attempts to carry out the research plan as objectively and as accurately as possible. However, researchers are human and carry their own expectations and motivations into the study.

Experimenter expectancies, as discussed in Chapter 7, are the expectations that a researcher holds about the outcome of a study. These expectancies might lead researchers to bias results in several ways, such as influencing the participant's behavior toward support of the hypothesis (i.e., creating demand characteristics), selecting data that best support the hypothesis, using statistical techniques that best show the anticipated effects but not other effects, and interpreting results in a biased manner. The latter occurs, for example, when the researcher accepts conclusions that are improbable explanations consistent with the research hypothesis, while ignoring more parsimonious explanations that are inconsistent with the hypothesis.

Common to all of these ways of introducing bias is the idea that the researcher will tend to make decisions and choices that favor the hypothesis being tested. This is not to say that researchers deliberately and knowingly falsify data. Rather, they behave in ways that tend to support their own expectations and do so without being aware of it.

For example, suppose that we have randomly assigned participants to two groups to avoid confounding due to selection. We plan to test and time participants in each group on a series of arithmetic problems. The prediction is that, because of the difference in instructions to the two groups, the experimental group will take significantly longer than the control group to complete the problems.

There are several ways that we might inadvertently influence participants. If we know which group each participant is in and know the research hypothesis, then it is possible that our timing of the participants might be biased. We also could influence the results by reading the same set of instructions in a slightly different tone to the two groups, emphasizing speed for the control participants. In either case, we would probably be unaware of this systematic bias and would deny it. However, the bias, accumulated over all the participants in the study, could affect the outcome toward support of the hypothesis.

Much of the scientific understanding of experimenter expectancy effects is due to the research of Rosenthal and his colleagues. Rosenthal and Fode (1963a, 1963b) suggested several ways in which an experimenter might affect a participant's responses and thus bias the results to favor the hypothesis. For example, a researcher might unintentionally present cues by variations in tone of voice or by changes in posture or facial expressions, verbally reinforce some responses and not others, or incorrectly record participants' responses.

Although such experimenter expectancy effects may occur, it has been difficult to demonstrate clearly that they do occur. Consequently, some question how big a problem this is (e.g., Barber & Silver, 1968). Nevertheless, in any research in which experimenter expectancy effects might occur, those expectancies provide alternative explanations for the obtained results. Just raising this possibility is sufficient to cast doubt on the validity of the experiment. If the rival hypothesis could be true, then we cannot assume that the observed differences are due to the independent variable. The researcher would have to repeat the experiment, adding controls to eliminate the rival hypothesis.

Quick-Check Review 8.4: Subject and Experimenter Effects

1. What are subject effects?
2. How can demand characteristics lead to subject effects?
3. How can experimenter expectancies lead to experimenter effects?

ETHICAL PRINCIPLES

Controlling confounding variables and subject and experimenter effects may not seem like an ethical issue, but it is. As we discussed earlier in the text, the decision on how much risk is acceptable is decided in part by what is the likely benefit from the study. A study that fails to control the kinds of confounding effects discussed in this chapter will provide little useful information. Hence, even slight risk would be unacceptable because little information can be gained from the study.

From an ethical point of view, you want to include the best possible controls in a study so that the maximum information can be gained. However, one should never violate an ethical principle to enhance controls. The most sacred of ethical principles is *informed consent*. It is up to the participants to decide whether they want to take part in the study. It is also up to participants to decide if they want to complete a study after they have given consent. Participants always have the right to withdraw from a study. That means that there will always be the potential of confounding due to selection and attrition, but it is a small price for the ethical researcher to pay. To avoid selection and attrition problems, the researcher must design studies that are interesting and unlikely to scare off potential participants.

Quick-Check Review 8.5: Ethical Principles

1. Why is controlling confounding an ethical issue?
2. Why will there always be the likelihood of confounding due to selection?

SUMMARY

- Constructing research hypotheses is critical in all research.
- The most fully developed research hypotheses are found in experimental research.
- Testing the research hypothesis involves three hypotheses: the null hypothesis, the confounding variable hypothesis, and the causal hypotheses.
- Researchers must consider validity and threats to validity in any research study.
- There are four types of validity: statistical, construct, external, and internal.
- The greatest threat to internal validity comes from confounding variables.
- The most common confounding variables are maturation, history, testing, instrumentation, regression to the mean, selection, attrition, and sequence effects.
- Subject and experimenter effects can also produce confounding if not controlled.
- The researcher has an ethical obligation to design strong studies that include proper controls, because without such controls little can be learned from a study, and therefore the risks to the participants will be unjustified.

Putting It into Practice

In the next few chapters, you will learn how researchers control confounding variables. For now, you need to recognize when such variables might be present. Spend some time looking around and observing people's behavior. Formulate a hypothesis about why a given behavior might have occurred; then think of as many alternative hypotheses as you can, which essentially are confounding variables that may have been responsible for the behavior. For example, if you observe someone snapping at other people for something they said, your hypothesis might be that they were upset by what was said. What other explanations might you generate for the observed behavior?

Another exercise is this: the next time someone asserts, "I know why such and such happened" and then proceeds to give his or her explanation, listen respectfully, and give a few alternative explanations for the same event. You can generate some lively discussions this way. To avoid conflict, you may choose sometimes to not share your alternative explanations, but generate them nonetheless.

EXERCISES

8.1. Define the following key terms. Be sure that you understand them. They are discussed in the chapter and defined in the glossary.

statistical hypothesis
confounding variable hypothesis
causal hypothesis
statistical validity
construct validity
external validity
generalization
limits of generalization
ecological validity
internal validity
maturation
history
testing
instrumentation
regression to the mean
selection
attrition
diffusion of treatment
sequence effects
subject effects
demand characteristics
placebo effect
experimenter effects

8.2. Think of five or six experimental research ideas. Create them or obtain them from published reports of studies. For each of these research ideas, (a) develop a clear statement of a problem, (b) identify and operationally define the variables, and (c) combine the problem statement with the operational definitions into a specific research hypothesis.

8.3. Take the problem statements you developed in the preceding exercise, develop different operational definitions, and use them to develop new research hypotheses. Why is it important to be able to do this in research?

8.4. Think of several possible research studies and identify the possible confounding variables that might affect those studies.

8.5. Develop a research project that might need to control experimenter and subject effects.

CHAPTER NINE

CONTROLS TO REDUCE THREATS TO VALIDITY

In the fields of observation, chance favors only the mind that is prepared.

—Louis Pasteur, 1822–1895

WEB RESOURCE MATERIAL

Control procedures counteract threats to validity, thus increasing confidence in the conclusions drawn from a study. Threats to validity and control procedures are two sides of the same conceptual coin. Chapter 8 discussed threats to validity; this chapter discusses methods for controlling threats to validity.

Control is any procedure used to counteract potential threats to the validity of the research. Many control procedures are available, but not every threat to validity is likely to occur in every study. Thus, we do not need every control procedure in every study. Some controls have general control value and, therefore, should be used routinely. Other controls apply to specific situations and are used to counter specific threats to validity. Controls are valuable at all levels of research, but they are most fully developed at the experimental level.

Four types of control are available to the researcher:

1. General control procedures
2. Control over subject and experimenter effects
3. Control through participant selection and assignment
4. Control through specific experimental design

This chapter covers the first three categories. The fourth category, specific experimental design, is introduced here and will be covered in detail in Chapters 10 through 13.

GENERAL CONTROL PROCEDURES

General control procedures can be, and in most cases should be, applied to any research project. They include (1) preparation of the setting, (2) response measurement, and (3) replication.

Preparation of the Setting

The research setting should be structured to eliminate competing variables, simplify the situation, and increase control over independent variables. These steps will increase confidence in the results, because they reduce threats to internal validity. The advantage of the laboratory is that it optimizes control by eliminating many extraneous variables, such as distractions or the influence of other people.

Laboratory settings also have potential disadvantages. For example, the laboratory might reduce external validity if the setting becomes so artificial that it is unlike the natural situation. However, we need not compromise external validity if we make an effort to simulate natural environments in the laboratory. For example, in a children's fear-reduction study, Graziano and Mooney (1982) designed the laboratory as a living room setting in which children were trained in fear-control skills that they would use at home. This home-like setting was designed to enhance generalization of the training.

With modern computer simulation, researchers can create realistic settings almost anywhere (Powers & Emmelkamp, 2007). For example, Krijn et al. (2007) used a realistic computer simulation to help train people to control their fear of flying, and Kurtz et al. (2007) tested schizophrenic patients' adherence to a medication schedule by using a virtual reality apartment. Such technology makes studies involving laboratory and clinic exposure more realistic, making it more likely that treatment and research findings will generalize. Thus, careful preparation of settings in laboratories can enhance both external and internal validity.

Response Measurement

Another general control procedure is the selection and preparation of the instruments used to measure the variables. Using measuring instruments of known reliability and validity improves both statistical and construct validity.

Sometimes we need to create a new measure, and that is not a trivial task. It is the researcher's responsibility to establish the reliability and validity of any new measure created for a study. The quality of measuring instruments can have powerful effects on validity. Unfortunately, in their concern for developing procedures to manipulate the independent variable, researchers sometimes pay less attention to the dependent measures and thereby compromise the validity of the study. On the other hand a researcher might become so involved in creating dependent measures that details of the independent variables might be shortchanged.

Replication

Not everyone considers replication to be a control procedure, but we believe it is. By specifying the laboratory setting, conditions, procedures, and measuring instruments, we make it easier for others to replicate the research.

Successful replication provides important information. If subsequent studies reliably demonstrate a phenomenon observed in an earlier study, we will have more confidence in the original findings. If we cannot replicate the findings, our confidence in those findings will be shaken. Moreover, most replication studies are performed in different locations by different researchers sampling from different populations. If the findings replicate, we have greater confidence in the external validity of the study.

There are three types of replication: exact replication, systematic replication, and conceptual replication, which are summarized in Table 9.1. **Exact replication**, which repeats the experiment as closely as possible to the way it was carried out originally, is rarely done in psychology. Journals seldom publish exact replication studies, and there are no career benefits for scientists to repeat other people's research.

A more common procedure is **systematic replication**—testing theoretical or procedural modifications of the original work. A researcher interested in a particular finding of a colleague's work may tentatively accept the accuracy of the original work and conduct a new study on that topic. If the new predictions prove to be accurate, they will not only extend the theory and/or procedures but also provide a systematic replication.

A third type of replication is **conceptual replication**. Recall that we can develop most problem statements into several different research hypotheses by combining the problem statement with various operational definitions of the research variables, or by using different research designs (see Chapter 8). Thus, we can generate many different studies from the same problem statement. In essence, each of these studies is replicating the concept expressed in the problem statement.

Replication increases confidence in the validity of findings but does not guarantee validity. If, for example, the results of a study were due to confounding factors, then exact replication would

TABLE 9.1 Types of Replication

Exact Replication:	Repeating the study exactly as it was carried out originally
Systematic Replication:	Testing a theoretical or procedural modification of the original procedure that will produce desired results only if the original findings were accurate
Conceptual Replication:	Generating and testing different research hypotheses from the same problem statement

produce the same invalid results as in the initial study. To obtain valid results, the researcher would need to recognize and control the confounding factors.

Quick-Check Review 9.1: General Control Procedures	1. How can preparation of the research setting improve internal validity? What should researchers do to the research setting to maximize external validity? 2. What characteristics should a research measure possess? 3. What is the difference between exact replication, systematic replication, and conceptual replication?

CONTROL OVER SUBJECT AND EXPERIMENTER EFFECTS

Many factors can bias participants and researchers, including motivation, expectations, and information or misinformation about a study. If left uncontrolled, these factors would allow alternative explanations for the results, thus casting doubt on the study's conclusions.

Among the controls for subject and experimenter effects are (1) single-blind and double-blind procedures, (2) automation, (3) objective measures, (4) multiple observers, and (5) deception.

Single- and Double-Blind Procedures

Experimenter effects arise from the researcher's knowledge of (1) the hypothesis being tested, (2) the nature of the experimental and control conditions, and (3) the condition to which each participant is assigned. Such knowledge can subtly affect how the researcher interacts with participants. We can control experimenter effects by reducing the researcher's contact with, and/or knowledge about, the participants. For example, a researcher might employ an assistant to run the study who does not know the condition to which each participant is assigned. In such a case, we would say that the assistant is **blind** to the assignment of participants to conditions. This is a **single-blind procedure**.

A more powerful control is a **double-blind procedure**, in which both the researcher and participants are blind to the assignment of each participant to a condition. Drug studies often use double-blind techniques. The experimental group typically receives the drug in the form of a capsule, whereas the control group receives a capsule, called a **placebo**, which is identical in appearance but has an inert substance in it instead of the experimental drug. Neither the participants nor the researchers know who is receiving the drug and who is receiving the placebo. This is achieved by having a research assistant who is not involved in collecting the data randomly assign participants to conditions and then prepare the capsules for participants.

Using placebo control groups in psychological treatment studies is more difficult than in drug studies. Suppose that a clinical researcher wants to study the effectiveness of exposure therapy for treating adult phobias. The researcher randomly assigns participants to an experimental and a control group. The experimental group receives the exposure therapy, and the control group receives a placebo treatment, but how do we design the placebo treatment?

Placebo treatments must be believable so that participants do not know that they are in the control group. Creating experimentally adequate, ethically acceptable, and believable placebo

CARTOON 9.1 This is taking the principle that it is best to be as blind as possible to avoid expectancy effects just a bit too far.

Source: Reprinted by permission, Sidney Harris, ScienceCartoonsPlus.Com.

manipulations in psychological treatment is a difficult task because of design problems and ethical issues in the use of placebos. For ethical reasons, we must tell participants that they might receive a placebo treatment. However, even with such notice, is it ethical to deny treatment to some participants? For this reason, we do not recommend using true placebos in medical and psychological research when an effective treatment is available. Instead of comparing a new treatment with a placebo, it is advisable to compare the new treatment with the best available treatment.

Having the researcher blind to group membership is also important in differential research. In general, researchers should be blind to each participant's group or condition during data collection, and they should remain blind during the scoring of data, especially when the scoring involves judgments, because knowledge of the hypotheses might affect judgments made during scoring.

In some cases, however, it is impossible for researchers to be blind during certain aspects of the study. For example, in a study of gender differences in aggression, the researcher testing participants will know which participants are male and which are female. In these situations, the researcher should attempt to be blind in as many ways as possible, even if it is impossible to be blind at every stage. If, for example, the measure of aggression is verbal behavior, someone not connected with the study should transcribe the tapes of participants' verbal responses so that auditory cues to a participant's gender are not available when the data are scored. Likewise, someone other than the person who tested the participants should do the scoring. In this study, the people who test participants should ideally be blind to the hypothesis, even if they cannot be blind to group membership. A general rule of thumb is to *test participants and score data as blindly as possible to avoid experimenter biases*.

Automation

Reducing experimenter-participant contact often reduces potential biases. One way to accomplish this is to **automate** the procedures and mechanisms used to deliver instructions and to record responses. For this reason, the use of computers and other electronic equipment in experiments has become standard laboratory procedure.

Automation has other advantages besides reducing experimenter effects. It can test each participant using a precise protocol (i.e., testing procedure). It can even randomly assign participants to conditions, so that the experimenter is blind to this aspect of the study. It can record results in a form that facilitates later statistical analysis, thus saving time and energy and minimizing the possibility of error in entering the data for analysis. Finally, computer-administered experiments can easily control all procedures with split second timing and measure several variables simultaneously. So it is possible to measure not only the response but also variables such as the time that each participant viewed each stimulus or the time it takes the participant to respond.

Using Objective Measures

Using **objective measures** of dependent variables is critical. A measure is objective when it is based on empirically observable and clearly specified events about which two or more people can easily agree. By contrast, a subjective measure involves the impressions of observers, which are often based on poorly specified and/or unobserved events. An example of a subjective measure is an observer's feeling that a person is anxious when asked to speak in public. It is subjective because the observer does not specify what behaviors he or she observed. Thus, it would be difficult for another observer to make the same observations and come to the same conclusions about the anxiety level of the speaker.

Good objective measures precisely define the behaviors to be observed and require minimal judgments on the part of the observer. Consequently, objective measures are less prone to experimenter biases. Such measures usually produce impressive levels of interrater agreement and make replication by other researchers easier. For example, we could operationally define public-speaking anxiety in terms of observable behavior, such as sweating, stammering, rapid speech, and shaky hands (Harb et al., 2003). With objective measures, we know what a score means; with subjective measures, we are never sure.

Multiple Observers

In any research, especially when there might be questions about objectivity, a common control is to employ several observers to record participants' behavior. We then compare the data obtained by the observers for agreement using interrater reliability coefficients or an index of **percent agreement**.

Suppose, for example, that two raters are simultaneously observing a video recording of a group of chimpanzees. At random intervals, the observers are signaled by a variable-interval timer to rate the behavior occurring at that moment as either aggressive or not aggressive. The observers are watching the same video but are kept separate from each other while they independently rate the same behaviors. Ten signals are given, and each observer rates 10 instances of behavior as aggressive or not aggressive. We then compare the two observers' ratings, as shown in Table 9.2, and compute a percent agreement.

TABLE 9.2 Computing Percent Agreement

This hypothetical example illustrates the computation of percent agreement, or the percentage of times two raters agree on an observation.

INTERVAL	RATER 1	RATER 2	AGREE?
1	Aggressive	Aggressive	Yes
2	Aggressive	Aggressive	Yes
3	Not Aggressive	Aggressive	No
4	Not Aggressive	Not Aggressive	Yes
5	Not Aggressive	Not Aggressive	Yes
6	Not Aggressive	Not Aggressive	Yes
7	Aggressive	Aggressive	Yes
8	Aggressive	Not Aggressive	No
9	Not Aggressive	Not Aggressive	Yes
10	Aggressive	Aggressive	Yes

$$\textit{Percent agreement} = \frac{\textit{\# of agreements}}{\textit{\# of observations}} \times 100 = \frac{8}{10} \times 100 = 80\%$$

A more sophisticated index of agreement is **Kappa**, which takes into account the **base rates** (i.e., the relative frequency of the rated behaviors). When two or more observers rate the same behavior, they will agree on some ratings and disagree on others. Some portion of their agreements will be true agreements and some will occur on the basis of chance. By "chance" we mean that the behavior is ambiguous enough that neither rater is sure what rating applies, so each rater makes his or her best guess and they happen to be in agreement for that one instance. The statistic Kappa takes the probability of this chance agreement into account. When calculated, a Kappa of 1.00 indicates perfect agreement and a Kappa of 0.00 indicates only chance agreement. The higher the Kappa, the greater the true agreement. We want our students to know that Kappa exists but using Kappa is beyond the scope of this textbook. The interested student or instructor should consult Cohen (1960) or Raulin and

09:01 Lilienfeld (2009). The Student Resource Website provides procedures on how to compute Kappa.

Having multiple observers also serves a second function. People, including research assistants, tend to be more careful about their work if they know that their performance will be checked. For example, speeders will slow down when driving on a highway known to have many speed traps. The Understanding the Concept Box 9.1 describes a classic research study that illustrates how important this principle is to quality research. This study suggests that there should always be an inter-rater reliability check and that raters should not know which of their ratings will be checked. This gives the raters an incentive to do the best they can on all of the ratings they make.

Using Deception

The most common control for subject effects is obscuring the true hypothesis of the study by using **deception**—that is, deliberately misinforming participants about the study or withholding information that might reveal the hypothesis. Sometimes deception is the only reasonable way to test some

UNDERSTANDING THE CONCEPT 9.1: RELIABLE RELIABILITY

When ratings are involved in research, the accuracy of the dependent measure is a combination of the clarity and objectivity of the scoring manual and the care that individual raters use in applying that scoring manual. Two raters who are conscientious and well trained may produce impressive levels of interrater reliability using a well-designed scoring manual, whereas other less conscientious raters may produce poor interrater reliability. However, Reid (1970) discovered that even well-trained and motivated raters need the pressure of knowing that their work will be checked to produce consistently high interrater reliability.

Reid trained several undergraduate research assistants to use a complex scoring system to rate videotapes of children. During the training, expert raters checked every tape, providing feedback and further training until the undergraduate assistants could use the scoring system reliably. Reid then had these research assistants rate videotapes independently, and another rater checked 20% of their tapes to assess interrater reliability. The raters knew which of their tapes would be checked. What the raters did not know is that, in actuality, all of their tapes were being checked. Therefore, Dr. Reid had measures of reliability from when the raters thought their work was being checked and from when they thought their work would not be checked. He found large differences in interrater reliability in those two conditions. When the assistants knew that their work was being checked, they followed the manual faithfully and produced excellent interrater reliability. However, when they thought that no one would be looking over their shoulders, they were much less consistent in their ratings.

This ingenious study shows that actual interrater reliability is a function of (1) the quality of the scoring manual and the training provided to the raters, and (2) the motivation of the raters. Dr. Reid's assistants were bright and highly motivated undergraduates, virtually all of whom were destined to go onto graduate school. Yet even these highly motivated people produced work that varied dramatically in quality depending on whether they thought they would be observed by someone else. This concept might sound familiar, because we talked about it earlier with respect to research participants. We called it *measurement reactivity*—the tendency for people to behave differently than they might normally because they know they are being observed (see Chapter 6). Individuals who conduct research are no different from individuals who serve as research participants. They all behave differently when they know they are being watched. In this case, we want the research assistants to behave differently, because we want them to do their very best when rating the research data.

There is a simple way to encourage research assistants to maintain high interrater reliability. Instead of telling them which 20% of their work will be checked, you tell them that 20% will be selected randomly and checked and they will never know what work will be checked. That is now the routine procedure for studies using behavioral ratings. This procedure achieves two things. First, it provides an accurate indication of the level of interrater reliability. If Dr. Reid had been evaluating reliability only when he told his assistants that their reliability was being checked, he would have reported an interrater reliability that was much higher than his raters were actually producing most of the time. Second, such random checking of reliability maintains the motivation of raters to do their best work all the time, thus improving interrater reliability at the same time that you are measuring it.

hypotheses. Although usually minor, deception can be elaborate. You learned in Chapter 3 that the ethical standards for research assume that deception places participants at risk. Therefore, plans to include deception must be justified, and the researcher must provide a complete debriefing at the end of the study.

A procedure known as the **balanced placebo design** uses deception to study the effects of alcohol on behavior. More than that, it is designed to tease out the expectancy effects associated

TABLE 9.3 Balanced Placebo Design

This table illustrates the four cells of the balanced placebo design. This design separates the pharmacological effects of alcohol from the expectancy effects.

	PEOPLE LED TO BELIEVE	
ACTUAL SITUATION	**Drinking Alcohol**	**Not Drinking Alcohol**
Drinking Alcohol		
Not Drinking Alcohol		

with alcohol from alcohol's pharmacological effects. The researcher asks participants to drink a beverage that contains either tonic or vodka and tonic (e.g., Kirsch, 2003; Marlatt et al., 1973; Rohsenow & Marlatt, 1981). However, what participants drink and what they are told they are drinking is not necessarily the same thing. Suppose that the study included 100 participants; the researcher would give 50 participants vodka and tonic and 50 tonic. Of the 50 participants who drink tonic, half (25) are told that they are drinking tonic, and the other half (25) are told that they are drinking vodka and tonic. Similarly, half (25) of the 50 participants who drink vodka and tonic are led to believe that they are drinking tonic, and the remaining participants (25) are told that they are drinking vodka and tonic. Table 9.3 illustrates these conditions.

Because vodka is nearly tasteless, it is difficult to distinguish whether it is present by taste alone when mixed with tonic or with something like orange juice. To reinforce the deception that participants are drinking a vodka-tonic mixture instead of only tonic, the drinks are mixed in front of participants. The researcher carefully measures vodka (actually water in the nonalcoholic condition) from what appears to be an unopened vodka bottle, complete with the required tax stamp over the screw top, and adds the tonic. It is equally desirable to have the experimenter blind to participant condition. To accomplish this, the researcher uses a hidden coding system on the bottles. The experimenter knows which bottle(s) to pour the drinks from but does not know what each bottle contains.

More than two dozen research studies used the balanced placebo design to separate the pharmacological effects of alcohol from the expectations of the drinker. In several studies (e.g., Lang & Sibrel, 1989), the behavior of the participants was affected more strongly by whether they thought they were drinking alcohol than whether they actually were drinking alcohol; that is, their expectations were more potent than the pharmacological effects of alcohol.

This is an interesting psychological phenomenon. Normally, we think of the expectations of participants as a source of confounding, and in many research situations, it is. However, a balanced placebo design carefully controls expectations and measures its effects. The results of several studies of alcohol consumption using the balanced placebo design illustrate just how powerful expectations can be, often overwhelming the actual pharmacological effect of the alcohol. It is no wonder that researchers are so concerned about controlling unwanted expectancy effects in psychological studies.

What makes the balanced placebo design work is that the participants can be deceived. As long as the drinks are not too strong or the participants do not drink too much alcohol, the taste and physiological cues are not strong enough for participants to realize they are being deceived. Identifying the parameters that make a deception like this work requires careful pilot testing.

In some cases, a balance placebo or similar deception is possible with some participants but not with others. For example, ten-year-old children with attention-deficit/hyperactivity disorder (ADHD) apparently cannot tell whether they are taking stimulant medication or a placebo, despite the dramatic effects that the medication has on their behavior. In contrast, fifteen-year-old children with ADHD can easily discriminate placebo from stimulant medication (Pelham, 1994; Pelham et al., 1992). In this case, a placebo deception is possible for the ten-year-olds, but not for the fifteen-year-olds.

Quick-Check Review 9.2: Control over Subject and Experimenter Effects

1. Describe the five types of controls for subject and experimenter effects.
2. How do single- and double-blind procedures differ?
3. How is deception used for control? What ethical issues does deception raise?

CONTROL THROUGH PARTICIPANT SELECTION AND ASSIGNMENT

The manner in which researchers select and assign participants to groups can affect both the external and internal validity of a study.

Participant Selection

Participant selection refers to the identification of people asked to participate in a study; it is a form of sampling (specifically, sampling participants). Appropriate participant selection enhances external validity, allowing researchers to generalize their results to the broader population. In most psychological research, the investigator's interest is not limited to specific participants, but rather is focused on the larger, more general group (i.e., the population).

To understand participant selection, you must distinguish among (1) populations and samples, (2) general populations, target populations, and accessible populations, and (3) representative samples, random samples, stratified random samples, and ad hoc samples.

A *population* is the larger group of all people or objects of interest (e.g., laboratory animals) from which the researcher selects a sample. A *sample* is a smaller number of people or objects selected from the population and used in a study as if the sample adequately represented the population.

These concepts were first introduced in Chapter 5, when we described the logic of inferential statistics. In this section, we will consider the sampling process from the standpoint of how it affects external validity.

The **general population** is the group of all organisms, events, and things in which we are interested. The **target population** is the subset in which the researcher is primarily interested, such as subpopulations of grammar-school children, registered voters, and so on. Target populations are not easily available. For example, suppose that you are interested in how well college freshmen understand basic science concepts. You cannot easily sample from all the college freshmen in the

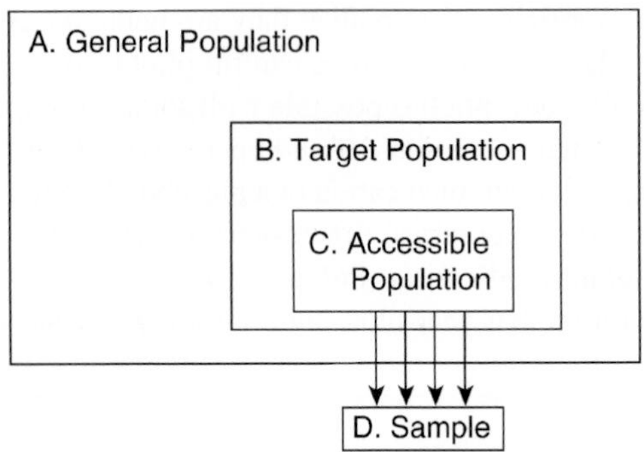

FIGURE 9.1 Populations and Samples.
General population: All events, persons, animals, etc. (e.g., all children).
Target population: All events, persons, etc., of a particular class of interest to the researcher. This is the population to which we want to generalize our findings (e.g., all elementary school children).
Accessible population: The subset of a target population that is available to the researcher (e.g., elementary school children in the local school district).
Sample: The subset of an accessible population on which measures are taken. Note that a sample is rarely drawn directly from a target population.

world (the target population). However, if you have access to the 400 freshmen in local colleges, they become the **accessible population** from which you will select the sample. After completing the study, you can safely generalize the findings from the sample to the accessible population, but you must be cautious about generalizing to the target population. Because most psychological research involves sampling accessible populations, such as introductory psychology students at a particular university, *we must always be cautious about generalizations made to the target population.*

Figure 9.1 shows the relationship among a general population, a target population, an accessible population, and a sample.

Replication can strengthen confidence in broader generalizations, because each replication study is likely to sample different accessible populations. If the results replicate in each accessible population, your confidence in the generalizability of the findings to the target population will increase.

Researchers almost never study populations directly. Instead, they select a sample from an accessible population. They must be careful to select a **representative sample**—a sample that adequately reflects population characteristics—if they want to generalize their findings to the broader population. The basic idea of representativeness is simple. If the sample is representative, then the characteristics found in the population will be found in the sample in the same proportions as in the population. These characteristics might include such variables as gender, age, intelligence, socioeconomic class, ethnicity, attitudes, political affiliations, and religious beliefs. Although the concept is simple, actually obtaining a representative sample can be challenging. Furthermore, small samples often do not adequately represent populations. In general, large samples are more likely to represent the population adequately, because large samples tend to reduce the effects of sampling error. The rationale behind this principle is discussed on the Student Resource Website.

09:02

Sampling of participants is a critical issue in social science research. Researchers have developed methods to solve the problems of obtaining representative samples. We will consider three solutions to the problem of selecting a representative sample: (1) random sampling,

TABLE 9.4 Types of Sampling

Random Sampling:	Drawing the sample so that (1) every member of the population has an equal chance of being selected, and (2) the selections do not affect each other.
Stratified Random Sampling:	Drawing separate random samples from each of several subpopulations.
Ad Hoc Sampling:	Drawing participants randomly from an accessible population.

(2) stratified random sampling, and (3) ad hoc samples. These are discussed below and summarized in Table 9.4. Other methods are beyond the scope of this book.

Random Sampling. **Random sampling** from a population involves drawing the sample so that (1) every member of the population has an equal chance of being selected, and (2) the selections do not affect each other (i.e., the selections are independent). With random sampling, there are no systematic biases that lead some members of the population to have a greater chance than others have of being selected. If the selection of participants is truly random, then we can expect the characteristics of the population, such as age, ethnicity, and intelligence, to be distributed in the sample in roughly the same proportion as in the general population.

The best way to draw an unbiased sample from a population is to draw a random sample. This is rather like picking numbers out of a hat. In actual practice, researchers usually draw numbers, not from a hat, but from a **table of random numbers** (see Appendix G) or using a **random-number generator** (a computer program). The Student Resource Website includes a random-number generator program and instructions on how to use it for sampling from a population.

09:03

Both random-number tables and random-number generators meet two criteria: (1) each number has the same chance of being selected, and (2) each selection is independent of the others. Suppose that you want to draw a sample of 60 participants from the accessible population of 400 freshmen in local colleges. You would list all 400 freshmen and assign each a number from 001 to 400. You would then use the table of random numbers or a random-number generator to get random numbers from 001 to 400 until you have a total of 60 unduplicated numbers. This process is illustrated in Go with the Flow 9.1. In addition, the Student Resource Website covers the process of taking random samples in more detail.

09:04

Random numbers are useful for making any decision based on the principle of randomness. For example, later in this chapter you will learn about using random numbers for assigning participants to experimental conditions.

Stratified Random Sampling. In **stratified random sampling**, we draw separate random samples from each of several subpopulations. The subpopulations are defined in advance based on one or more critical organismic variables. We focus on the organismic variables that are most likely to influence scores on the dependent measures, because small variations in the distribution of these variables in a sample can have a large effect on the results. For example, you might suspect that age is strongly correlated with the dependent measure of political preference. Therefore, you consider it critical that the sample represents the distribution of age in the population studied. Rather than rely on random sampling, you divide the population into subpopulations based on age. You then create

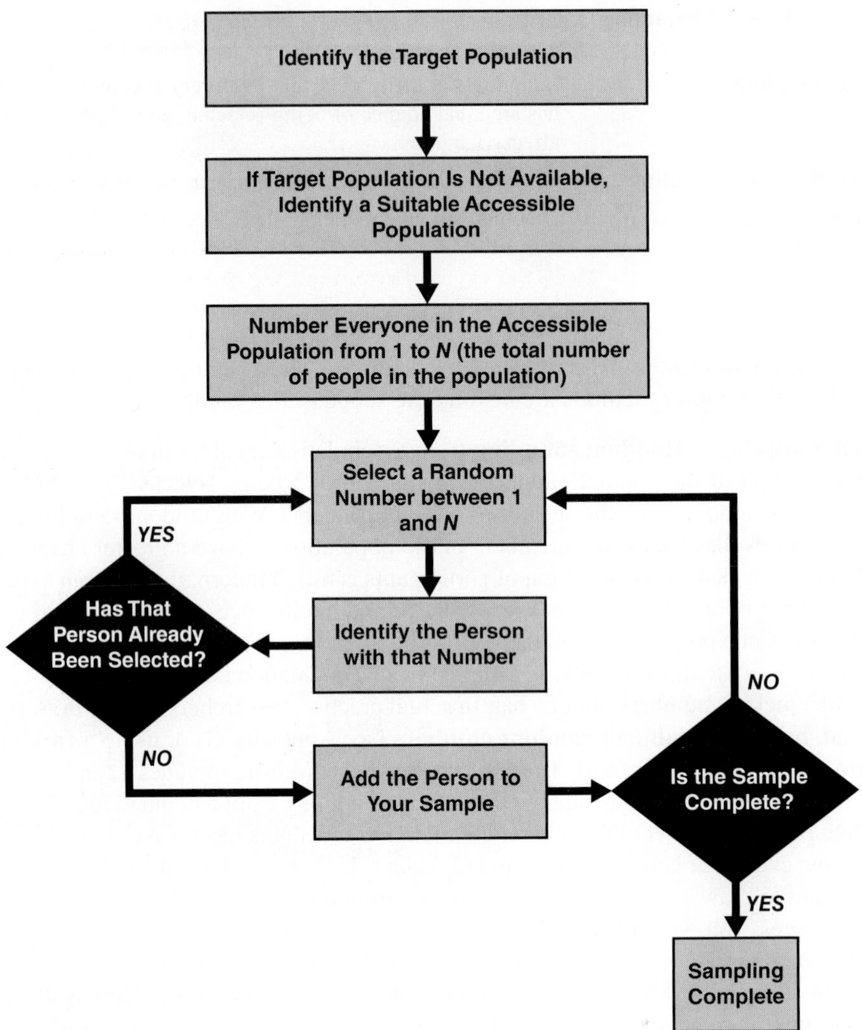

GO WITH THE FLOW 9.1 Random Selection. This figure illustrates the steps for drawing a random sample from an accessible population.

a total sample by randomly selecting the appropriate proportion of participants from each subpopulation. If 16% of the population is between the ages of 20 and 30, you select randomly from that subpopulation the number of participants it would take to make up 16% of the total sample. If the sample were 200 participants, you would select 32 participants from the 20 to 30 age group. We can stratify on any variable, including, for example, socioeconomic level, education, gender, and ethnic identification.

Political pollsters use stratified random samples extensively. With this technique, samples as small as 1,000 people can so closely represent the population that the outcome of elections involving several million voters can be accurately predicted.

Ad Hoc Samples. Although random sampling is a major control for threats to external validity, psychological research rarely employs random sampling from a target population. Target populations are often difficult to access. For any large population, target or accessible, listing and numbering every individual to prepare for random selection are sizable tasks. Random and stratified random samplings from a target population are important in some research, such as in political surveys, but most psychological research does not employ random selection. Instead, psychologists usually draw participants from an accessible population, such as introductory psychology students or children from local schools. This type of sample, called an **ad hoc sample**, is used in most psychological research. Furthermore, ethical considerations require that participants be volunteers. Those who do not volunteer are not included, so any resulting sample may be biased toward persons who are willing to participate. The ethical demand that participants be volunteers makes it difficult for researchers to obtain entirely random samples of any population.

How can researchers generalize results from samples that are not randomly selected from a target population? The answer is twofold: we should generalize (1) cautiously, and (2) only to groups that are similar to the sample. That is, *we must not generalize beyond the limits of the sample*. The population to which one can safely generalize is defined by the characteristics of the sample.

To generalize beyond ad hoc samples and yet maintain external validity, we must know the characteristics of the participants and keep the generalizations within the limits of these characteristics. Thus, when using ad hoc sampling, researchers need to obtain such descriptive data as participants' ages, physical and psychological characteristics, and families' socioeconomic data. The more completely the sample is described, the more secure we can be in establishing the limits of generalization, and the more confidence we can have in making generalizations.

When possible, it is valuable to obtain descriptive information on the people who are invited to participate but who decline, as well as people who drop out before the study is completed. Comparing these participants with those who complete the study helps to pinpoint potential biases in participant selection and attrition that would limit generalization. (However, do you see ethical issues in trying to obtain descriptive information on persons who decline to participate?)

You should draw a random sample whenever it is feasible. In most instances, it will not be feasible, and you will instead use an ad hoc sample. When you do, you should obtain sufficient descriptive information about the participants to establish the limits for generalization.

Participant Assignment

After selecting participants, you should next assign them to experimental conditions. Unbiased **participant assignment** is critical. For example, suppose that you want to test the effectiveness of a new computerized program for teaching statistics to college students. In the experimental condition, students will have statistics lessons and assignments presented on the computer using a variety of animations. In the control condition, students will have statistics lessons and assignments presented by a human instructor, using classroom lectures and demonstrations. There are two levels of the independent variable: computer presentation and teacher presentation. Suppose that you select 120 students as participants and plan to assign 60 to each condition. You need to avoid assigning the best math students or the most motivated students to the same condition. Random assignment will make it likely that the groups are comparable on these variables.

Take another example: In a study of office working conditions, six groups of data entry clerks are compared on their typing speed (number of words per minute) and accuracy (number of errors)

TABLE 9.5 Types of Participant Assignment

Free Random Assignment:	Assigning participants to conditions in a random manner, so that the assignment of any one participant does not affect the assignment of the other participants.
Randomization within Blocks:	Randomly assigning participants in blocks of conditions so that we have one participant in each condition before we move on to assign participants to the next block of conditions.
Matched Random Assignment:	Matching participants on a relevant variable and then randomly assigning the matched participants to groups, with one matched participant per group.
Other Matching Procedures:	Matching by group characteristics rather than by individual characteristics; equating groups by holding the variable constant; building in the variable as another factor.

under six different room temperatures: 55°, 60°, 65°, 70°, 75°, and 80°. We select a sample of 48 typists and randomly assign eight participants to each of the six groups. Random assignment makes it unlikely that all the best typists would be in one group. Therefore, it satisfies a very important basic principle, the **principle of initial equivalence**, which holds that all groups in an experiment must be equivalent at the start of the experiment. Random assignment automatically meets this requirement. Of course, the groups are never *exactly* equivalent. Rather, group differences are no more than would be expected from sampling error. Remember from Chapter 5 that sampling error refers to the small differences among groups randomly sampled from the same population. Therefore, we say that the groups are **statistically equal**, which means that the inferential statistics used will take into account the small differences among the groups that can be expected from sampling error.

The ideal experiment would include (1) random selection of participants from a known population, and (2) random assignment of participants to conditions. The ideal, however, is seldom achieved. As noted earlier, random selection is rare in psychological research. Therefore, caution is needed when generalizing results. *Of far greater importance in an experiment is random assignment of participants to conditions.* Random assignment is a powerful control procedure that helps to reduce both known and unknown threats to internal validity (i.e., confounding variables). There are three ways to achieve random assignment: free random assignment, randomization within blocks, and matched random assignment, which are summarized in Table 9.5.

Free Random Assignment. **Free random assignment** involves assigning participants to conditions in a random manner, so that the assignment of any one participant does not affect the assignment of the other participants. We achieve this by using a table of random numbers or a random-number generator as follows: In the experiment on typing speed and working conditions, the 48 participants can be randomly assigned to six conditions. We would select 48 random numbers between 1 and 6. The first random number determines the assignment of the first participant. For example, if that number is 5, the participant is assigned to the fifth condition. We continue this process for all 48 participants.

Free random assignment works well, especially when there are a large number of participants to assign. One problem with free random assignment is that it is unlikely that each condition will have the same number of participants. If we wanted to be sure that we assign the same number of participants to each group, we should randomize within blocks.

Randomizing within Blocks. When we **randomize within blocks**, we use random assignment to allocate blocks of participants to each of the available groups. In our typing speed example, there are six groups, so we would randomize participants to groups in blocks of six. One way to achieve this is for the researcher to number the participants from 01 to 48. Using a table of random numbers or a random-number generator, the researcher assigns the first participant number encountered to the first condition, the next participant number to the second condition, and so on. After one participant is assigned to each of the six conditions, the researcher starts over until all 48 participants are assigned to the six conditions.

Matched Random Assignment. Researchers often use **matched random assignment** of participants to conditions when conducting small-sample research. This procedure involves matching participants on a relevant variable, such as age or IQ, and then randomly assigning the matched participants to groups, with one matched participant per group. This procedure is explained below and is illustrated in Go with the Flow 9.2.

Many psychological studies use small numbers of participants, and researchers are often faced with the task of assigning a small number of participants to two or three conditions. Free random assignment or randomizing within blocks works best with large samples, but with a small sample of participants, groups formed through random assignment can be unequal on important variables. For example, suppose that you are interested in investigating the effects of a motor-skills training program on high-tech-assembly workers in an electronic equipment factory, but you have the time and resources to study only 12 workers. Your research hypothesis is that those who receive the motor-skills training (the experimental group) will improve their work performance. Specifically, they will show greater productivity, fewer errors, and an increase in job satisfaction compared with those who do not receive the training (the control group).

Free random assignment, or even randomizing within blocks, of so small a number might result in unequal groups on important variables due to normal sampling error. You might find, for example, that you have assigned most of the females, or perhaps the workers with the most years of work experience, to the same group. Thus, the experimental and control groups would not be equivalent on potentially important variables at the start of the study (recall the concept of initial equivalence). If the groups are not equivalent at the start of the study, the results might reflect the original differences between the groups, rather than the effects of the independent variable of motor-skills training. There would be confounding; the groups differ on both the independent variable manipulation and other important variables. This is always a potential problem. If the sample sizes are large, however, random assignment is very effective in producing similar groups. With small samples, we cannot be as confident that the groups will be comparable prior to the independent variable manipulation.

Matched random assignment will mitigate the problems inherent in working with small numbers of participants. To use matched random assignment, you must first decide what variables are the most important potential confounding factors. Suppose that you decide that the gender of the worker is not likely to be a confounding variable. However, you suspect that the number of years worked might confound the results, because more experienced workers are likely to be more proficient than less experienced workers. To carry out the matching, you would first obtain the needed information for each participant—in this case, how many years each has worked. Then you would

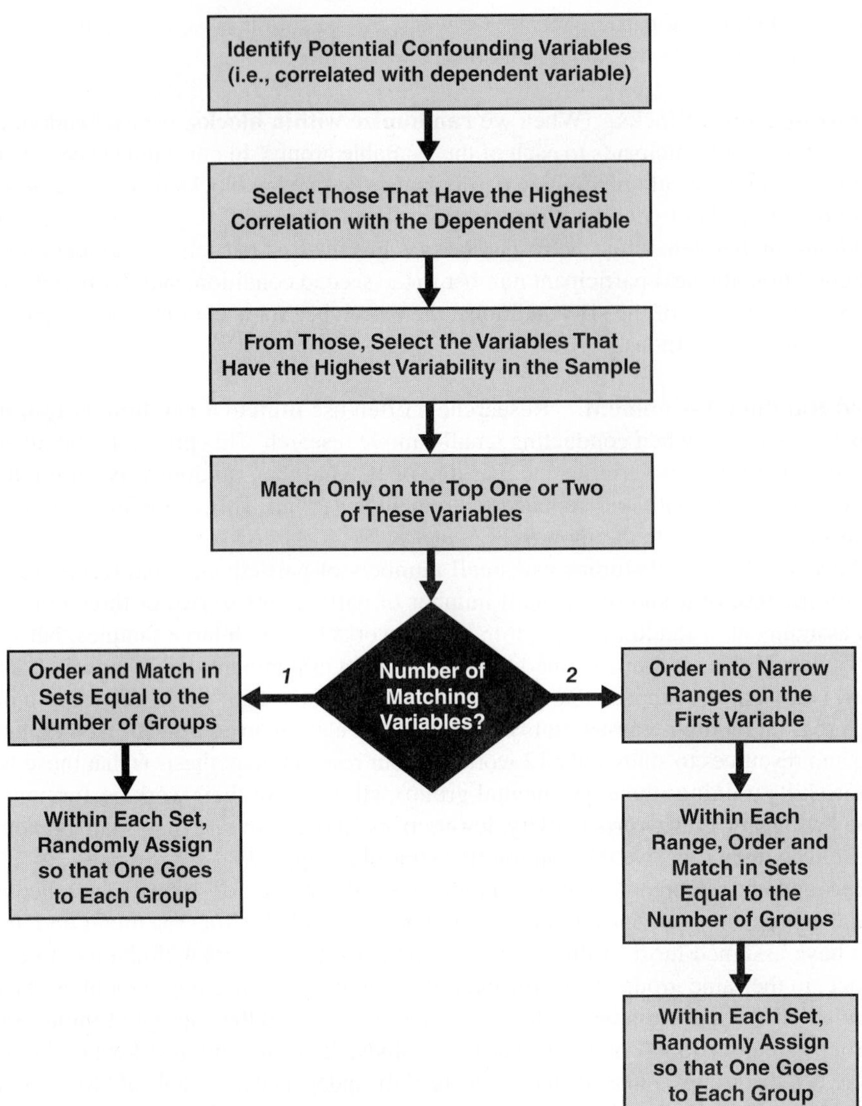

GO WITH THE FLOW 9.2 Matched Random Assignment. This figure illustrates the steps in the matched random assignment process for matching on either one or two variables.

list the workers in order of years of experience, as shown in Table 9.6. Finally, you would match them on this variable by taking the workers in pairs, successively down the list. Smith, the most experienced, would be matched with the next most experienced, Jones; Franks would be matched with Ordell; and so on.

You can now assign the participants to two groups by using a table of random numbers or by tossing a coin. Using the random-number table, you assign the first participant of each pair to group 1

TABLE 9.6 Preparing for Matched Random Assignment

In this example, we start by ordering the people available for a study based on their number of years of work experience and then pairing them. At the assignment stage, we randomly assign one member of each pair to the first group, and the other member is assigned to the second group.

NAME	SEX	NUMBER OF YEARS WORKED
Smith	F	15.7
Jones	M	13.8
Franks	M	12.2
Ordell	M	11.4
Samuels	F	11.0
Collucci	F	10.6
Spero	M	9.5
Kling	F	9.3
Ruiz	F	9.0
Barker	M	8.6
Stanton	M	4.3
Harringer	M	2.4

if the number is odd or to group 2 if the number is even. If a coin toss is used, heads or tails determines group assignment. Whatever method you use, the second participant in each pair is assigned to the other group. This procedure might result in the assignment of participants shown in Table 9.7.

The mean number of years of work experience for the two groups shown in Table 9.7 is close (9.86 years and 9.60 years). Because the groups are comparable on years worked, this variable cannot confound the results. Note that the groups do not have equal numbers of males and females. However, the difference is small, and it is not clear that gender is a potential confounding variable in the study. If prior research suggested that gender was a potential confounding variable, the researcher might have decided to match on gender as well as experience.

Matching increases the sensitivity of small-group research to the effects of the independent variable. It does this by assuring that potential confounding variables are equally distributed among the groups. We can match on more than one variable. However, it is generally not feasible to match on several variables simultaneously because the task becomes cumbersome and difficult. It is usually more efficient to test more participants and assign them to groups randomly.

Researchers need to identify and measure the variables used for matching. How does a researcher determine which variables are most important to match? Think about it. We will want to match on variables that will have the largest effect on the dependent variable. This is precisely why these variables need to be controlled. This issue will be addressed in detail in Chapter 11.

The Student Resource Website provides more details on the process of random assignment to
09:05 groups.

TABLE 9.7 Workers Matched on Experience

We randomly assigned the matched participants from Table 9.6 to produce the groups shown here. Note how this produces closely matched groups on years of work experience.

	GROUP 1			GROUP 2		
	NAME	SEX	YEARS WORKED	NAME	SEX	YEARS WORKED
	Jones	M	13.8	Smith	F	15.7
	Franks	M	12.2	Ordell	M	11.4
	Collucci	F	10.6	Samuels	F	11.0
	Kling	F	9.3	Spero	M	9.5
	Ruiz	F	9.0	Barker	M	8.6
	Stanton	M	4.3	Harringer	M	2.4
% Females			3/6 = 50%			2/6 = 33%
Mean Years Worked			9.86			9.60

Other Matching Procedures. An alternative to participant-by-participant matching is matching preexisting characteristics of groups (see Chapman & Chapman, 1973). This procedure is more commonly used in differential research, but it can be useful in some experimental studies. In such research, we need to identify the variables on which we will match the groups and measure those variables for each potential participant. Using a randomization procedure, we then assign participants to one of the two groups and calculate this group's mean and standard deviation on each matching variable. We then select the second group of participants so that it has a comparable mean and standard deviation on those variables. The result is that the two groups are equivalent on the matching variables, but we will not have matched the individuals in one group with individuals in the other group. Nevertheless, because the groups are comparable on the matching variables, there is little possibility of confounding, at least from the variables on which we matched.

A variation of matching is to equate groups by holding the variable constant. For example, to match on age, you could use only participants of approximately the same age. If there is little or no variability on this factor between the experimental and control groups, this factor cannot be a source of confounding.

One disadvantage to matching by holding the variable constant is that it reduces external validity because it reduces the ability to generalize the results of the study to the larger population. For example, if you used only adult participants, you would be unable to generalize with confidence to adolescents.

Another matching procedure is to build the variable into the study. This creates a *factorial design*, which we will cover in Chapter 12. Suppose that you want to evaluate how the manner of dress affects social class ratings among high school students. You ask student participants to rate social class for a dozen students that they have never met and about whom their only information is a 2-minute video sequence of a hallway conversation among friends. The independent variable is the manner of dress of the students to be rated. The dependent variable is the social class rating.

However, you are concerned about confounding due to differences in age and social development of your participants. For example, freshmen might view the concept of social class differently from seniors. To control for this, you make the academic class variable (freshman, sophomore, junior, senior) a part of the study. In the language of factorial design, academic class would be a second factor (or independent variable) in this study. This strategy not only controls the academic class variable but also allows us to see how much of an effect it has on the dependent variable, as you will see in Chapter 12.

Advantages of Random Selection and Assignment

Randomization is a control method used for both participant selection and assignment. *Randomization is the most basic and single most important control procedure*. It has several major advantages:

1. It can be used to control threats to internal and external validity.
2. It can control for many variables simultaneously.
3. It is the only control procedure that can control for unknown factors.

When we randomly assign participants to groups or conditions, potential confounding variables are distributed without biases, even if the variables have not been specifically identified and are thus not known. Other control methods are effective with known extraneous variables that threaten the study's validity, but randomization is effective in reducing the bias of unknown variables. This is an extremely important point. No researcher can identify all the variables that might affect the dependent measures. However, by randomly assigning participants to conditions, the researcher can distribute the unknown confounding factors evenly among conditions.

Note that random assignment controls for subject variables, such as age and IQ. It does not control for environmental or setting variables, such as time of day, room temperature, or background noise. For these variables, the general control procedures discussed earlier are used. However, a good general rule for the researcher is *whenever possible, randomize*.

Quick-Check Review 9.3: Control through Participant Selection and Assignment

1. Define "general population," "target population," "accessible population," and "sample."
2. Why is it important that we draw samples carefully from a population?
3. Define each type of sampling discussed in this section.
4. What does matching participants control?

CONTROL THROUGH EXPERIMENTAL DESIGN

Protecting internal validity is critical in experiments because it bears on the very essence of experimentation: the predicted causal relationship between independent and dependent variables. Experimental methods are the best procedures for protecting internal validity.

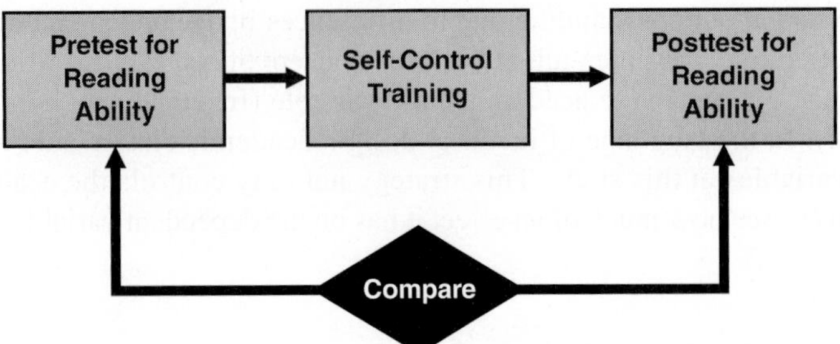

FIGURE 9.2 A Simple Pretest-Posttest Design. In this basic pretest-posttest design, the researcher assesses reading ability before and after the application of the self-control training. The researcher then compares these two measures to see how much change has occurred.

Experimental design refers to the careful arrangement of all parts of the experiment to (1) test the effects of the independent variable on the dependent variable, and (2) protect against threats to internal validity.

Several experimental designs are available. We discuss the basic experimental designs in Chapter 10 and variations on those designs in Chapters 11 and 12. Here we introduce the concept of experimental design by first discussing a nonexperimental design: the pretest-posttest design illustrated in Figure 9.2.

Suppose that a psychologist is studying children with attention-deficit/hyperactivity disorder. These children have an inability to stay focused on a task. Therefore, they often have difficulty learning to read. The psychologist develops a cognitive self-control training program geared specifically to reading tasks. Once trained in a six-step cognitive procedure, the children silently rehearse the steps just before approaching any reading task in school. The researcher tests the effectiveness of the training by using a pretest-posttest design. She first takes pretraining measures of reading ability of five children with ADHD, then trains them in the six-step cognitive self-control procedure, and then again tests them for reading ability.

Suppose that the researcher found a statistically significant difference between the pretest and posttest measures. This finding might seem sufficient to conclude that the training improved reading, but as you learned earlier, it is not. We cannot draw that conclusion because of possible confounding. To avoid confounding variables (in this case, maturation and history), the researcher would have to anticipate them and build suitable controls into the research design. In this instance, a good control would be a no-treatment control group (an equivalent group of ADHD children who do not receive cognitive self-control training). Suppose that there are 20 ADHD children in the program. The researcher could randomly assign 10 of the children to the **experimental group** that receives the treatment and 10 to the **control group** that does not. All the children would remain in the general program and receive the same general treatment. However, only the experimental group would receive the cognitive self-control training. This is the pretest-posttest, control-group design illustrated in Figure 9.3.

The question is whether the experimental group shows significantly greater reading performance than the control group at the posttest. If it does, then the researcher can have considerably more confidence in concluding that self-control training is responsible for the difference, because the confounding variables of maturation and history have been controlled.

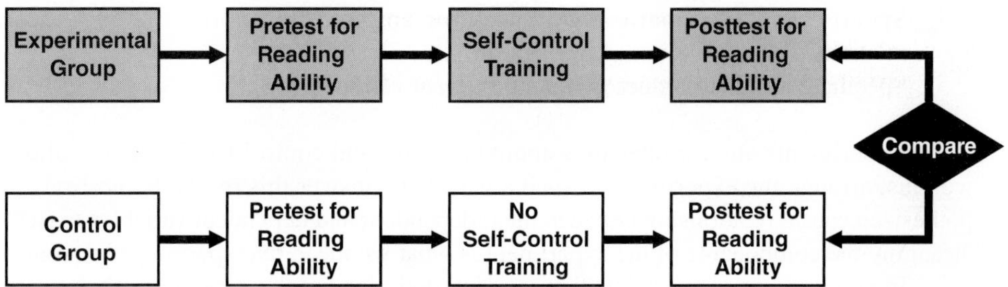

FIGURE 9.3 A Pretest-Posttest Control-Group Design. In the basic two-group comparison design, one group receives the treatment, while the other does not. To evaluate the effect of the treatment, the researcher compares the two groups. To make the design a true experiment, the participants need to be randomly assigned to the groups.

How does this design control confounding due to maturation? If the experimental and control groups are equivalent at the start of the experiment because the researcher randomly assigned children to groups, the researcher can expect maturation to occur equally in the two groups. How does the design control confounding due to history? Both groups receive all other treatments in the general program. Thus, if some program factor other than self-control training affects reading performance, it should affect both groups equally.

For the control-group design to be effective, *it is essential that the experimental and control groups be comparable at the start of the experiment*. If the experimental group has more of the most capable, older, or better-adjusted children, then confounding due to selection is present. We can control confounding due to selection by randomly assigning the participants to the two groups. Randomly assigned groups will vary slightly from one another due to sampling error. However, the inferential statistics take into account these expected sampling error differences when evaluating the groups. Routinely including these two basic control procedures—(1) inclusion of appropriate control groups or conditions, and (2) random assignment of participants to conditions—will control most potential confounding.

The independent variable must vary in experiments. In the ADHD study, we had two levels of the independent variable of cognitive self-control training: all or none. There can be more than two levels; the hypothetical study of typists' productivity at different room temperatures included six levels of the independent variable. That design did not have one control group, but six levels of the independent variable, each of which operated as a control for all other levels.

Scientific research is characterized by attention to details. Competent researchers employ carefully reasoned and clearly stated concepts, well-developed operational definitions, inductive-deductive logic, careful measurement of the observed variables, and use of appropriate statistical methods to analyze data. Well-designed experiments display these characteristics in addition to the following five criteria:

1. A clearly stated research hypothesis concerning predicted causal effects of one variable on another
2. At least two levels of the independent variable
3. Random assignment of participants to conditions

4. Specific and systematic procedures for empirically testing the hypothesized causal relationships
5. Specific controls to reduce threats to internal validity

Experiments answer questions about causality and control for threats to validity. To do so, we must arrange the experiment in such a way as to answer this research question: "does the hypothesized causal relationship between the independent and dependent variables exist?" The task of arranging the components of the experiment is what we mean by experimental design.

In essence, experimental design is a detailed plan for the conduct of the experiment. Once researchers formalize the design, they proceed through it step by step as planned. Remember, at the high-constraint level of experimentation, there is no flexibility to alter any part of the design once the study begins. Chapters 10 through 12 discuss a variety of experimental designs.

Quick-Check Review 9.4: Control through Experimental Design

1. What does unbiased assignment of participants to groups accomplish?
2. What are the five characteristics of any experimental design?

ETHICAL PRINCIPLES

Researchers using the balanced placebo design for studying the pharmacological and expectancy effects of alcohol, which we introduced earlier in this chapter, must address a number of ethical concerns. Like other drugs, alcohol has physiological effects and is a legally controlled substance. Therefore, the researcher must take care to avoid harming participants or breaking laws. Participants must be of legal age, have no medical conditions that preclude alcohol consumption, and have no moral objections to, or dependence on, alcohol. Alcohol researchers routinely use a screening procedure to identify and exclude any participants for whom these issues apply. Furthermore, because people who have little or no experience with alcohol may react dramatically to drinking, participation is usually restricted to people with moderate drinking experience.

Alcohol researchers also have an ethical responsibility to protect participants during and after the study. For example, there must be no lingering intoxication that might put the participant at risk. We do not want a participant to leave the lab, get in a car, and have an accident because of impaired functioning. The researcher often accomplishes this goal by having participants remain in the lab for some time after drinking alcohol, sometimes working on tasks that either are or appear to be part of the study. Some researchers simply insist, on the informed consent form, that the participant agrees to remain in the lab until his or her blood alcohol level drops to a specified level, and they provide a comfortable place where participants can pass the time reading or watching television.

Of particular concern in this research is the use of deception—giving false information to participants in order to carry out the experimental manipulations. The balanced placebo design clearly uses deception, but participants are correctly told as part of the informed consent procedure that they may or may not receive alcohol and that whether they receive alcohol will depend on random assignment. That information is entirely accurate, and so the participant is agreeing to be in a study that may involve the consumption of alcohol. However, as you learned in this chapter, there is deception in this design for some participants. Depending upon their assignment to the conditions, some participants are told they are drinking vodka and tonic, when in fact it is only tonic, and others are told they are drinking tonic, when in fact it is vodka and tonic.

Deception is acceptable in psychological research, but its acceptability depends on the situation and how the deception is handled. The American Psychological Association's (2002) position can be summed up as follows:

1. Psychologists do not deceive participants if that deception will cause physical pain or severe emotional distress.
2. Deception may be used only when
   a. it is necessary in order to conduct the research,
   b. it can be justified by the study's potential scientific, educational, or applied value,
   c. effective non-deceptive alternative procedures are not feasible, and
   d. a full debriefing is provided.

Using the above list to evaluate the balanced placebo design, you can see that the elaborate deception is justified. It does not cause physical pain or severe emotional distress; you cannot study the expectancy effects of alcohol consumption independent of the pharmacological effects any other way; the information is scientifically important; and every participant is provided with an accurate debriefing—told at the end of the study exactly what was done and why.

Debriefing is a procedure to give feedback to the participants. It is carried out as promptly as possible. Usually that means immediately after participants complete the study, but in rare cases, it is delayed until all participants have been tested. The psychologist should provide participants with information about the nature, results, and conclusions of the research, correcting potential misconceptions and answering participants' questions.

The psychologist needs to explain the use of deception, making sure the participant understands what the procedures were and why deception was used, and giving participants the opportunity to withdraw their data from the study if they wish. Every attempt is made to correct misconceptions that might have resulted from the deception and to deal with all concerns that may have been caused by it. However, as careful as the researcher may be, it is still possible that some participants might be disturbed when they learn they had been deceived, and the debriefing might not be sufficient to correct or reverse those negative effects (Miller et al., 2005). In the very rare instances that a participant continues to be upset after the debriefing, the researcher must be sensitive and continue to do all he or she can to resolve the participants' concerns.

We strongly recommend that, when planning a new research study, you carefully review the APA ethical principles and standards (American Psychological Association, 2002, 2010a) to identify any ethical issues that might apply to your study. Then you can put into place the steps needed to address those issues.

Quick-Check Review 9.5: Ethical Principles

1. What are some limitations of debriefing?
2. What safeguards should you employ if deception is used in research?

SUMMARY

- The major groups of control procedures are general control procedures, control of subject and experimenter effects, control through participant selection and assignment, and control through experimental design.
- Single- and double-blind procedures, automation, objective measures, multiple observers, and deception will control for subject and experimenter effects.
- Appropriate participant selection, such as random sampling, helps to control threats to external validity.
- Random assignment of participants to conditions helps control threats to internal validity.
- Randomization is the single most powerful control procedure, and it is the only one that controls for unknown confounding variables; whenever possible, randomize.
- Experiments rule out alternative hypotheses and test causal relationships.
- The highest degree of control to protect internal validity is found in experimentation.
- Most threats to validity can be controlled with the use of control groups and random participant selection and assignment.
- Debriefing is a necessary component of any research that includes deception.

Putting It into Practice

When we talk about control procedures and experimental designs, we are talking about trying to represent natural phenomena in the laboratory, where we can exercise sufficient control to assure internal validity. However, ecological validity is also important. It addresses the question of whether the laboratory procedures faithfully represent natural phenomena so the findings will generalize to the real world.

Over the next week, observe psychological phenomena in natural settings and spend some time thinking about how you might recreate those phenomena in the laboratory without losing critical elements. For example, if you observe a mother interacting with her three-year-old, think about what you would have to do to capture various aspects of that interaction in a laboratory. What would you have to do to make the laboratory study natural enough that it is likely to produce findings that accurately reflect what would have occurred in the real world?

EXERCISES

9.1. Define the following key terms. Be sure that you understand them. They are discussed in the chapter and defined in the glossary.

control	single-blind procedure	percent agreement
exact replication	double-blind procedure	Kappa
systematic replication	placebo	base rate
conceptual replication	automation	deception
blind	objective measure	balanced placebo design

participant selection
general population
target population
accessible population
representative sample
random sampling
table of random numbers
random-number generator
stratified random sampling
ad hoc sample
participant assignment
principle of initial equivalence
statistically equal
free random assignment
randomize within blocks
matched random assignment
experimental design
experimental group
control group

9.2. A researcher randomly selects 30 of 473 elementary school children. On completion of the study, the researcher wants to discuss the results in terms of all elementary school children. Identify the various populations and samples involved in this study. What cautions must the researcher be aware of in generalizing the results?

9.3. Assume you have 60 participants for a study. Use the table of random numbers (Appendix G) to assign participants randomly to three conditions with 20 participants in each condition.

CHAPTER TEN

SINGLE-VARIABLE, INDEPENDENT-GROUPS DESIGNS

Observation is a passive science; experimentation is an active science.

—Claude Bernard, *Introduction à l'Étude de la Médecine Expérimentale,* 1865

WEB RESOURCE MATERIAL

This chapter introduces basic experimental designs and their supporting concepts. It revisits the concept of variance introduced in Chapter 5, this time emphasizing that experimental design involves the measurement and control of sources of variance. *Focusing on the control of variance in research provides the link between research design and statistical analysis.*

Scientific research uses highly evolved procedures to find answers to questions. It is a perimental level of constraint that the design process is most completely developed. It is critical for the experimenter to carry out detailed planning of every aspect of the experiment, from the initial ideas to decisions about data analyses. Consequently, the experimenter must complete all planning prior to data collection.

A well-developed experimental design provides a blueprint for the experimenter to follow. We cannot emphasize enough the importance of developing a clear experimental design before beginning observation. Careful planning can build in the controls necessary to have confidence in the results. Therefore, *plan the experiment carefully and carry it out exactly as planned.*

VARIANCE

We previously discussed several concepts that we will bring together in this section, including variance (Chapter 5), internal validity (Chapter 8), and control (Chapter 9). The following material summarizes those earlier discussions and integrates that material into a more detailed understanding of the logic of research design.

As you learned earlier, variation is necessary in experiments. Without variation, there would be no differences to test. Researchers design the manipulation of independent variables to create variation between experimental and control conditions. If the independent variable has an effect on the dependent variable, the variation in the independent variable created by the manipulation will create variation in the dependent variable. Conversely, if the independent variable does not have an effect on the dependent variable, then the average level of the dependent variable should be roughly the same in both experimental and control conditions.

Why is that true? It is true because participants are randomly assigned to groups in experimental research, which makes the groups statistically equivalent before the manipulation (i.e., any small differences are due to sampling error). Random assignment tends to equate the groups on all variables, including the dependent variable. Independent-variable manipulations disrupt this equality among the groups *only if* the independent variable is capable of influencing the dependent variable.

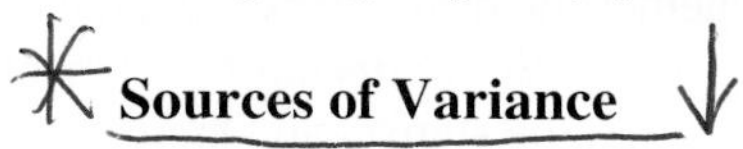

Sources of Variance

There are two major sources of variance in experimental design: (1) systematic between-groups variance, and (2) nonsystematic within-groups variance. We will describe each of these and the factors that influence them.

Systematic Between-Groups Variance. An experiment tests the effects of an independent variable on the dependent variable(s) by

1. setting up at least two levels of the independent variable,
2. testing different groups of participants at each level, and
3. measuring participants' responses on the dependent variable(s).

The researcher predicts that the mean of the dependent variable will differ significantly among the groups if the independent variable has an effect on the dependent variable. Why? The reason is that the differences in the level of the independent variable in each group should change the average level of the dependent measure in each group. That is, we predict significant variability among group means on the dependent measure if the independent variable has an effect. Statisticians refer to this variability among group means as **between-groups variance**.

Suppose that you are a research consultant for a TV production company and you want to test the hypothesis that a recorded laugh track increases viewers' enjoyment of a particular television comedy. You randomly assign 100 people to two groups, 50 in each group. The experimental group views the show with a laugh track, and the control group views the same show without the laugh track. Then all participants rate their enjoyment of the show. Because you randomly assigned participants, you can assume that there is no significant difference between the groups prior to the manipulation, although there may be small differences due to sampling error (as discussed in Chapter 5). The prediction is that the experimental group will enjoy the show more than will the control group. In statistical language, you expect to find significant between-groups variance.

Finding a significant difference between the groups does not necessarily mean that the independent variable is responsible for the difference. This finding indicates only that there are systematic effects that are making the group means different from one another. There are two sources of these systematic effects: (1) the effect of the independent variable (**experimental variance**), and (2) the effects of uncontrolled confounding variables (**extraneous variance**). We call the sum of these systematic effects **systematic between-groups variance**. There is also a small contribution to variability among the means because of the nonsystematic effects of sampling error. Because of sampling error, there are likely to be small differences between the groups even when there are no systematic effects at all.

You learned earlier that *extraneous variables* are uncontrolled variables that can produce confounding. "Extraneous variance" is a similar-sounding term with a different, but related, meaning. *Extraneous variance* is the effect that uncontrolled extraneous variables have on the results of the study. These extraneous variables add to the variability of the means (i.e., the means diverge from one another).

To summarize, the between-groups variance is a function of systematic effects (caused by experimental and/or confounding variable effects) and nonsystematic effects (caused by sampling error). We use an appropriate inferential statistic to test whether the differences are large enough to be taken seriously. If they are, we say the results are *statistically significant* (see Chapter 5). The systematic between-groups variance in an experiment might be statistically significant, thus tempting the researcher to conclude that there is a causal relationship between the independent variable and dependent variable. However, it is possible that the between-groups variance is high only because of confounding variables and not because of the independent variable. Statistical tests can determine only whether there are significant differences among the groups, not whether the observed differences are due to experimental or extraneous variance. If there is any possibility that the group differences are due to extraneous factors, then we cannot draw a causal inference. It is for this reason that we must anticipate and control confounding. This leads us to a basic principle in research: *researchers should maximize the experimental variance (due to the independent variable) and control the extraneous variance (due to confounding variables).*

Nonsystematic Within-Groups Variance. The term "**error variance**" denotes the **nonsystematic within-groups variability**. Error variance is due to factors that affect some participants but not others within a group, whereas systematic variance is due to influences on all members of each group. Error variance may be increased by unstable factors, such as some participants feeling ill when tested, or stable factors, such as individual differences. It can be increa experimenter or equipment variations that cause measurement errors for some participants but not for others in the same group. Because no two participants are exactly alike and no procedure is perfect, there will always be some error variance. Consequently, there will always be a certain degree of natural variability among the means, called sampling error, even in the total absence of systematic effects.

Nonsystematic within-groups influences are random; there should be just as much chance that these influences will occur in one direction as in another or will affect one participant in the group but not another. Thus, if random influences cause some participants to score lower than they ordinarily would, other random influences will cause other participants to score higher than they ordinarily would. The result is that random influences tend to cancel each other. Some participants score too high, others score too low, but the means of the groups are not affected. However, these effects will increase the variability of the scores within groups. In contrast, systematic between-groups factors influence most participants in a group in one direction. The effects are not random; they do not cancel each other. As a result, the mean of the group is moved up or down by systematic between-groups factors, depending on the direction of their influence.

In summary, we make a distinction between

1. systematic between-groups variance, which includes
    a. experimental variance (due to independent variables),
    b. extraneous variance (due to confounding variables), and
    c. nonsystematic within-groups error variance, and
2. nonsystematic within-groups error variance (due to chance factors and individual differences).

It is important to repeat that the between-groups variance is a function of both the systematic between-groups variance (experimental and extraneous variance) and the nonsystematic within-groups error variance. Even when there is absolutely no systematic between-groups variance, there will still be small differences between groups due to sampling error. Systematic between-groups variance increases the between-groups variance beyond the natural variability due to sampling error.

Researchers analyze data by comparing the between-groups variation and the within-groups variation. The ratio of these two measures defines the F-test:

$$F = \frac{\text{Measure Based on Between-Groups Variation}}{\text{Measure Based on Within-Groups Variation}} \tag{10.1}$$

Without going into statistical detail, let us consider the principles involved in the F-test. A measure based on the between-groups variation (the numerator) is a function of both systematic effects (experimental variance plus extraneous variance) and effects of sampling error (error variance). A measure based on within-groups error variation (the denominator) is a function only of error variance. In an F-test, these terms are computed in such a way that the error variance is the same value in both the numerator and the denominator of the formula. Therefore, we can write the preceding equation as follows:

$$F = \frac{\text{Sytematic Effects} + \text{Error Variance}}{\text{Error Variance}} \tag{10.2}$$

Suppose that there are no systematic effects. In this case, both the numerator and the denominator would represent error variance only, and the ratio would be 1.00. Whenever the *F*-ratio is near 1.00, it means that no systematic effects are present; that is, the between-groups variation is no larger than we would expect from sampling error alone. On the other hand, suppose that the between-groups variation is substantially greater than what we would expect from sampling error. This would suggest that there are systematic effects. In this case, a researcher would conclude that the groups do differ; we would say that they are statistically significant. This is the basic idea behind the *F*-test.

Controlling Variance in Research

To show a causal effect of the independent variable on the dependent variable, the experimental variance must be high and neither distorted by excessive extraneous variance nor masked by error variance. The greater the extraneous and/or error variance, the more difficult it becomes to show the causal effects of an independent variable on a dependent variable. This idea leads to an expansion of the rule stated earlier: *in experimentation, each study is designed to maximize experimental variance, control extraneous variance, and minimize error variance.*

Maximizing Experimental Variance. Experimental variance is due to the effects of the independent variable(s) on the dependent variable(s). There must be at least two levels of the independent variable in an experiment. In fact, it is often advisable to include more than two levels, because including multiple levels provides more information about the relationship between the independent and dependent variable(s).

To demonstrate an effect, the researcher must be sure that the independent variable really varies. Therefore, it is often useful to include a **manipulation check** in a study to evaluate whether the manipulation actually had its intended effect on participants.

Let's look at a hypothetical example to see how a manipulation check might be used. Suppose that in a study of the effects of anxiety on performance, the researcher manipulates anxiety by changing the feedback given to participants during a training period. The reasoning behind this manipulation is that participants who think that they are doing poorly will be more anxious than participants who think that they are doing well. Therefore, the researcher sets up two conditions. In one, the participants are told that they did well during training and should have no problems during the actual testing (the low-anxiety group). A second group is told that they did poorly during the training and that they must try harder if they want to avoid making themselves look foolish (the high-anxiety group). How do you know whether this manipulation actually affected the anxiety level of participants? One way is to ask participants to rate their anxiety and see if the experimental group was more anxious than the control group. Another might be to monitor physiological processes that are associated with higher anxiety, such as heart rate or sweating of the palms. This assessment of the effectiveness of the experimental manipulation is an example of a manipulation check. If the groups did not differ on anxiety, then the manipulation of anxiety was ineffective. Consequently, the study provides no basis to evaluate the effect of anxiety on the dependent measure.

Figure 10.1 illustrates the importance of a manipulation check. This hypothetical study compared men and women on their responses to an anger provocation. The researcher hypothesized that males typically externalize anger, and therefore react with hostility when provoked, but women tend to internalize anger, and therefore do not become hostile when provoked.

The rationale for this study is the psychodynamic explanation of depression as "anger turned inward." Because women are twice as likely to develop depression as men (Kessler, 2003), our

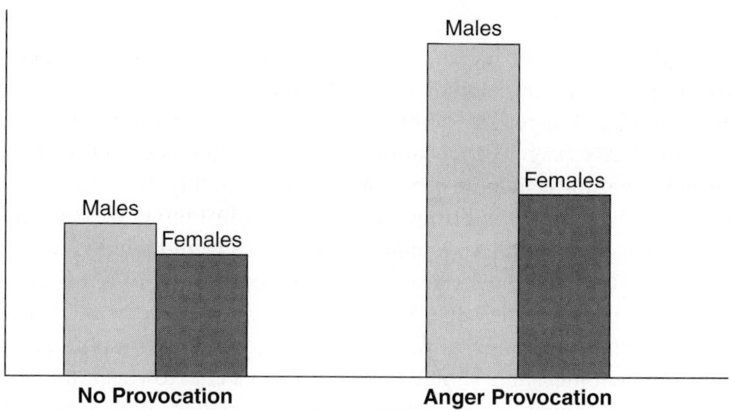

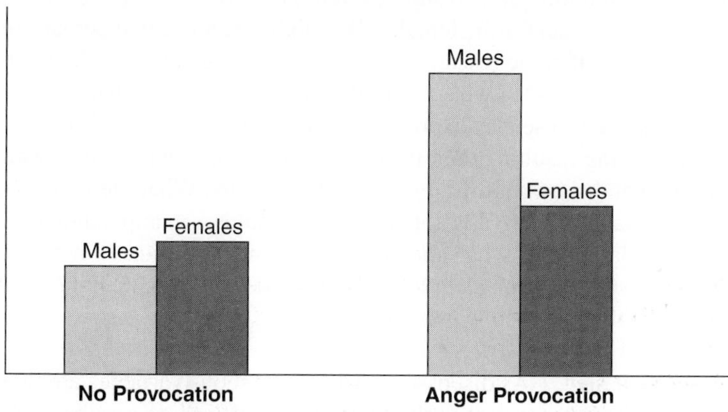

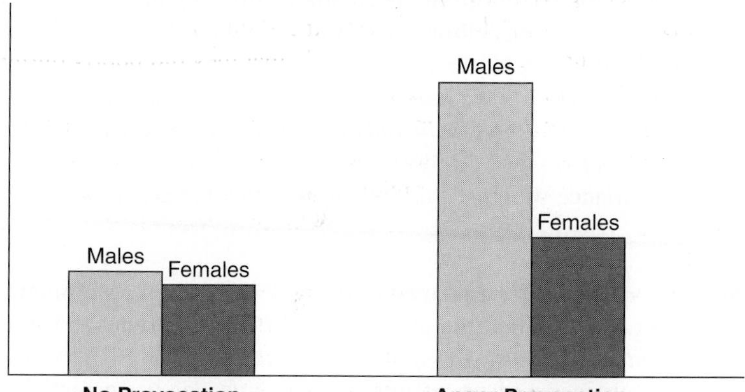

FIGURE 10.1 Importance of Including Manipulation Checks. This hypothetical data set illustrates how manipulation checks can clarify the meaning of data. The hostility data suggest that males do react with more hostility when angered than females, but the manipulation checks suggest that the reason for this pattern is that the anger provocation worked much better for the males than for the females.

hypothetical study looked at a possible mechanism for this gender difference—specifically, that women are more likely to internalize anger, thus increasing their risk for depression.

The researcher manipulated anger by fumbling the research procedure, thus forcing participants to repeat parts of the study (anger provocation). The design included this condition and another condition (no provocation) in which the procedures went smoothly. Both the men and women were randomly assigned to these two conditions. As illustrated in Figure 10.1(a), the results are consistent with the hypothesis. However, two manipulation checks were included, which are shown in Figures 10.1(b) and 10.1(c). These checks looked at the reported level of anger and the level of physiological arousal, respectively. If the anger provocation was effective, these variables should have shown it. Even if women turned anger inward, and therefore did not report experiencing increased anger, the physiological measures should have been elevated. However, the reported levels of anger and the levels of physiological arousal showed the same pattern in men and women as the expressed hostility dependent measure (see Figure 10.1).

How do we interpret such findings? The simplest interpretation is that the anger manipulation worked much better for the males than for the females. We might speculate that perhaps females were more empathetic to the problems that the researcher was experiencing, and therefore not angered by them. What is clear is that it would be unwise to say that this study shows that women internalize anger more than men do simply because they expressed less hostility. Perhaps a different anger provocation procedure, such as making insulting comments about a person's appearance, would have angered both men and women and shown a different pattern of results. What the manipulation check shows is that caution is necessary, because it is not clear that the study's manipulation produced anger in both groups. If the manipulation check had shown that both men and women reported equivalent levels of increased anger and showed equivalent levels of increased arousal, then the study would indicate that men express hostility more than women when they are angered.

Controlling Extraneous Variance. As discussed earlier, extraneous variables are those between-group variables, other than the independent variable, that have effects on groups as a whole, possibly confounding the results. To demonstrate the effects of an experimental manipulation, we must control extraneous variables and keep them from differentially affecting the groups. In this regard, two important goals are basic in experimentation. *First, we must be sure that the experimental and control groups are as similar as possible at the start of the experiment. Second, we must treat each group in exactly the same way except for the independent-variable manipulation (i.e., make sure that the independent-variable manipulation is the only difference in the researcher's treatment of the experimental and control groups).*

To control extraneous variance we must start by ensuring that the groups are equal at the beginning of the study.

1. The best method of controlling for extraneous variance is random assignment to groups, which decreases the probability that the groups will differ on extraneous variables. Thus, *whenever possible, randomly assign participants to conditions.*
2. If a factor, such as age, ethnic identification, intelligence, or gender, is a potential confounding variable, we can control it by selecting participants who are as similar as possible on this variable. For example, we could select only males or only females, or select participants who are within a few IQ points of each other. The cost of using this as a control is that it limits generalizability. For example, using only males or only females limits our conclusions to only one gender.

3. We can control a potential confounding variable by *building it into the experiment as an additional independent variable.* Thus, if gender is a potentially confounding variable, we could add gender as a nonmanipulated independent variable. There would then be two independent variables in the study, a design known as a factorial design (see Chapter 12).
4. We can control extraneous variance also by matching participants (see Chapter 9) or by using a within-subjects design (see Chapter 11).

To achieve the second goal—treating each group exactly the same except for the independent-variable manipulation—we must do the following:

1. Use exactly the same measurement procedures in each group and, as much as possible, rely on objective measures, which will be less likely to be influenced by experimenter bias.
2. Employ blind procedures or automation to avoid subject and experimenter effects that might affect one group more than another.
3. Employ the general control procedures, such as preparation of the setting, on a consistent basis in the groups.

Minimizing Error Variance. Error variance is within-groups variance that is due to chance factors and individual differences. There is always some error variance. However, substantial error variance can obscure differences between conditions due to the experimental manipulations.

One source of error variance is measurement error, which is the result of variations in the way participants respond from trial to trial due to such factors as unreliability of the measurement instruments. To minimize these sources of error variance, we must *maintain carefully controlled conditions of measurement and be sure that the measuring instruments are reliable.*

Often, the largest contributor to error variance is individual differences. Within-subjects or matched-subjects designs, which we cover in Chapter 11, minimize this source of error variance. Although there are problems, such as sequence effects, in using within-subjects designs, the designs are often preferred by researchers because they reduce error variance by eliminating the individual-differences component.

This brief discussion of maximizing experimental variance, controlling extraneous variance, and minimizing error variance is a summary of the earlier discussions of control. Said another way, *control in research is control of variance.*

The general control procedures discussed in Chapter 9 deal with the control of error variance. Other control procedures help to control both error variance and extraneous variance. The most powerful control for extraneous variance is a properly created experimental design in which the researcher randomly assigns participants to conditions.

Figure 10.2 illustrates the principles discussed in this section on variance. It shows the sources of variance and how they are combined in an analysis of variance. The figure provides a visual representation of equation 10.2. It also shows where each of the three principles in controlling variance (maximize experimental variance, control extraneous variance, and minimize error variance) would apply to the statistical analysis of data using an ANOVA.

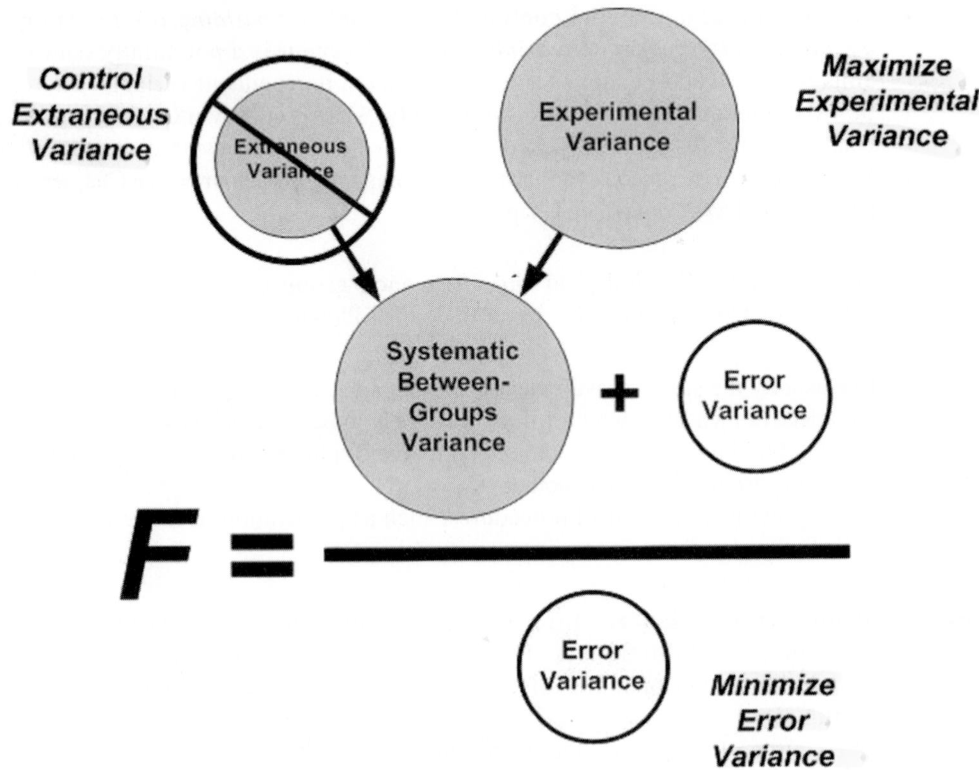

FIGURE 10.2 Controlling Variance in Research. Controlling variance is the concept that links research design to statistical analysis of results. This figure illustrates how different sources of variance affect the *F*-ratio in analysis of variance. Maximizing experimental variance and minimizing error variance increases the sensitivity of the research to effects of the independent variable. Controlling extraneous variance avoids confounding that would make drawing a single conclusion impossible.

Quick-Check Review 10.1: Variance

1. What is systematic between-groups variance?
2. Define "experimental variance" and "extraneous variance."
3. What is error variance?
4. What is the *F*-test? What is it used for?
5. What are the ways of controlling extraneous variance?
6. How do we minimize error variance?

NONEXPERIMENTAL APPROACHES ← KNOW THESE GENERALLY

Now that you understand that the purpose of research designs is to control the sources of variance, we will look at several research designs and see how well they achieve that goal. The primary goal of experimental research designs is to control extraneous variance, although some designs (covered in Chapter 11) also minimize error variance. In this chapter, we will cover single-variable, between-subjects designs, which are designs that have a single independent variable and have different participants in each group.

To appreciate the advantages of experimental designs, you need to understand the limitations of nonexperimental approaches. Therefore, we will begin by discussing the following nonexperimental approaches:

- Ex post facto studies
- Single-group, posttest-only studies
- Single-group, pretest-posttest studies
- Pretest-posttest, natural control-group studies

In this and the next sections, we will consider examples of research, beginning with nonexperimental approaches and progressing to experimental designs. As we progress along this continuum, note that each successive design controls for more sources of extraneous variance. This presentation draws heavily from *Experimental and Quasi-Experimental Designs for Research*, Campbell and Stanley's (1966) classic book.

Ex Post Facto Studies

In an **ex post facto** ("after the fact") **study**, which is illustrated in Figure 10.3, the researcher observes current behavior and attempts to relate it to earlier experiences. For example, a therapist might observe some difficulty in a client and conclude that earlier life events, which the therapist never directly observed or manipulated, caused the problem. This kind of evidence has led many people to conclude that abused children become abusive parents based on the observation that many abusive parents report that they were abused as children.

This is an example of a conclusion that is arrived at in an ex post facto manner. The inferred causal chain might in fact be correct. However, as reasonable as the conclusion seems, we can have little confidence in its validity, because there were no controls for confounding factors. If we cannot control for confounding, then we cannot eliminate rival hypotheses. The simple observation does not rule out the possibility that non-abusive parents are as likely as abusive parents to have been abused as children. Thus, we cannot infer a causal relationship between the independent and dependent variables.

Let us look at another example. Suppose that a researcher suspects that food additives, such as artificial colors, flavors, and preservatives, stimulate hyperactive behavior in some children.

FIGURE 10.3 Ex Post Facto Approach. The ex post facto design makes an observation after a naturally occurring event. There is no manipulation of an independent variable. This design cannot eliminate rival hypotheses, because none of the potential confounding variables is controlled.

Obtaining a sample of 30 hyperactive children, the researcher finds that 28 of them (93%) eat foods containing these additives every day. The number seems high to the researcher, and the findings are consistent with the researcher's suspicion that there may be a relationship between food additives and hyperactivity. The researcher may even formulate the hypothesis for future research that food additives stimulate hyperactivity. However, because the researcher followed an ex post facto procedure, it is unreasonable to infer a causal relationship between food additives and hyperactive behavior.

An ex post facto study can generate hypotheses to test with higher-constraint studies, but it is incapable of testing causal hypotheses. Because no independent variable is manipulated in ex post facto studies, controls to guard against confounding cannot be applied. The researcher cannot know which variable(s) may have affected the results and therefore *cannot eliminate rival hypotheses*. Any of several confounding variables may have been responsible. In our example, the hyperactivity might be due to parental behavior, genetic factors, or the influences of other children, none of which are evaluated or controlled in an ex post facto study. Consequently, results from ex post facto studies should be interpreted with great caution.

Single-Group, Posttest-Only Studies

A **single-group, posttest-only study**, illustrated in Figure 10.4, is at a somewhat higher level of constraint than ex post facto procedures. Here the researcher manipulates an independent variable with a single group and the group is then measured.

Suppose, for example, that a clinician wants to determine whether eliminating foods containing certain additives thought to increase hyperactivity will help hyperactive children. He asks parents of 20 hyperactive children to eliminate these foods from their children's diets for 4 weeks. At the end of the period, he tests the children for hyperactivity, and he finds that now only 8 of the 20 children are hyperactive.

Here there has been an actual manipulation in the form of the dietary change, as well as measurement of posttreatment hyperactivity levels. Nevertheless, there are still several confounding factors, and their existence prevents the researcher from drawing causal inferences. Perhaps the children did not change at all, but because there was no pretreatment measurement, there was no way of knowing this. Perhaps there was a change, but it was due only to the expectation of improvement. That is, children given food with the same additives, who thought they were getting food without the additives, would have also decreased their hyperactivity. Perhaps the children did improve, but the improvement was due to some other uncontrolled factor, such as another program in which the children were involved. Perhaps the children matured over the 4 weeks of treatment, and the lower hyperactivity was due to this maturation. Perhaps they did become less active, but it was only a natural return to their normal activity level. In fact, the parents may have sought treatment

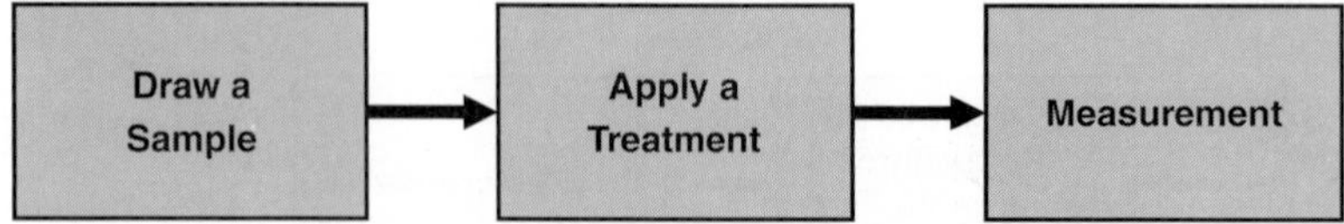

FIGURE 10.4 Single-Group, Posttest-Only Design. The single-group, posttest-only design applies a treatment to a group and then makes a measurement of the dependent variable. This design fails to control the confounding factors of expectation effects, maturation, history, and regression to the mean. (Note: The term "treatment" as used in these figures refers to any kind of manipulation of the independent variable.)

because of a temporary peak in their child's activity level. These examples illustrate that this single-group, posttest-only study does not control for the confounding variables of expectation effects, history, maturation, or regression to the mean. The researcher cannot even be sure if there was any change in activity level.

Single-Group, Pretest-Posttest Studies

A **single-group, pretest-posttest study**, as illustrated in Figure 10.5, is an improvement over the posttest-only approach because it includes a pretreatment evaluation. The researcher in the previous example might (1) select a sample of hyperactive children, (2) observe them for rates of hyperactive behavior, (3) impose the 4-week dietary restrictions, and (4) observe them again for hyperactivity at the end of 4 weeks.

Suppose that the posttest hyperactivity measures are significantly less than the pretest measures. That indicates improvement. However, the single-group, pretest-posttest study still fails to control for several confounding variables. The improvement might have occurred for any of several reasons. For example, the children and parents may have expected improvement (placebo effect), the children may have matured during the treatment period (maturation), some other aspect of the program might have been responsible for the improvement (history), or the pretest measures of hyperactivity were abnormally high and naturally returned to their typical level (regression to the mean). To avoid these confounding variables, an additional control is necessary, as you will see shortly.

The single-group, pretest-posttest study fails to control for maturation. However, in some research, maturation is not a confounding variable but instead is exactly what the researcher wants to study. Developmental psychologists focus much of their research on the process of maturation. They often use designs similar to the pretest-posttest design described here, but without the manipulation. A study that follows the same participants over time is called a *longitudinal design*, which we introduced in Chapter 7. Typically, researchers take multiple measures over the course of a longitudinal study, which is called a **time-series design**. In a developmentally focused longitudinal study, maturation is elevated from a confounding variable to the variable of interest. Thus, the "treatment" shown in Figure 10.5 is actually the passage of time.

History can still confound the study of maturation unless appropriate controls are included. We will discuss this in more detail in the section on time-series designs in Chapter 13.

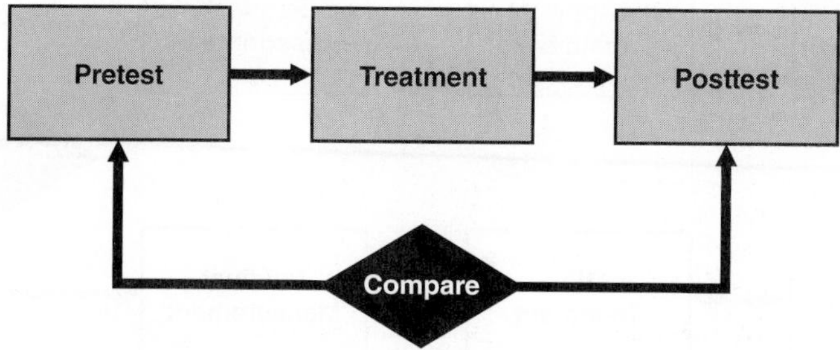

FIGURE 10.5 Single-Group, Pretest-Posttest Design. The single-group, pretest-posttest design measures the dependent variable, applies a treatment to a group, and then measures the dependent variable again. This design can verify that a change occurred, but fails to control the confounding factors of expectation effects, maturation, history, and regression to the mean.

Pretest-Posttest, Natural Control-Group Studies

A good control to add is a no-treatment control group. In a **pretest-posttest, natural control-group study**, illustrated in Figure 10.6, naturally occurring groups are used, only one of which receives the treatment. Participants are not randomly assigned to groups, as they would be in an experimental design. For example, two intact classrooms might be used, with students from one classroom assigned to the first group and students from the other classroom assigned to the second group. Adding this control group significantly strengthens the design.

The natural control-group approach is close to an experimental design. However, this design still has a weakness—there is no procedure, such as random assignment, to ensure that the two groups are equivalent at the start of the study.

Suppose that, in forming the experimental and control groups in the hyperactivity study, the researcher asked parents if they were willing to try the 4-week dietary restrictions. The children of those parents who agreed were assigned to the experimental group and the others to the control group. The serious confounding factor in this procedure is that the experimental and the control groups are different in terms of parents' willingness to try the dietary restrictions. The dietary restriction treatment is confounded by parents' willingness to cooperate.

It could be that parents who are willing to work on the diet are more motivated to help their children to change. Any posttreatment differences between the groups on measures of hyperactivity might be due to either factor: dietary restriction or parental motivation. The children in the two groups may even have been different on the level of hyperactivity before the experiment began. It may be that parents with the most hyperactive children are the most desperate and are therefore the most likely to try *any kind* of treatment, although the pretest in the design would allow a researcher to check this possibility.

When you compare groups of participants at different levels of the independent variable, it is essential that the groups be equivalent on the dependent measures at the start of the study (initial equivalence). Random assignment of participants to conditions is one way of increasing confidence that the groups are equivalent at the start of the study. Such random assignment to conditions is one of the hallmarks of experimental design, which is the topic of the next section.

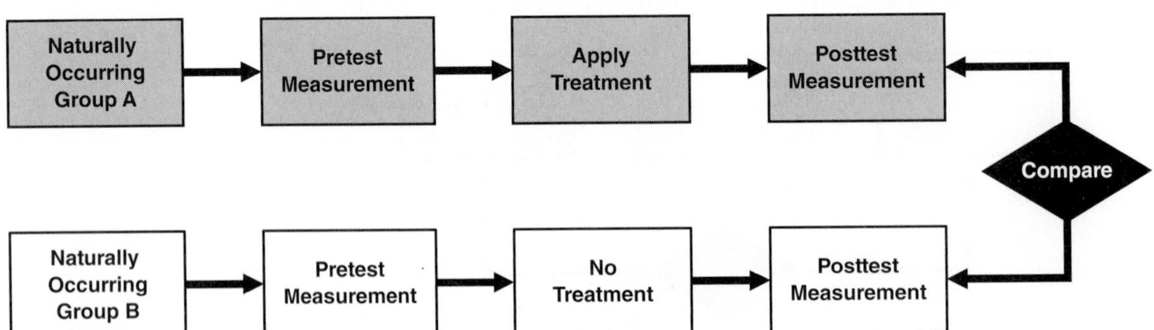

FIGURE 10.6 Pretest-Posttest, Natural Control-Group Design. The pretest-posttest, natural control-group design compares two naturally occurring groups, one that receives the treatment and one that does not receive the treatment. This design fails to control for selection, but provides control for history and maturation.

Quick-Check Review 10.2: Nonexperimental Approaches	1. Identify four nonexperimental approaches. Define each and discuss its limitations. 2. Of these four approaches, which is the weakest? Why? 3. When is maturation not considered a confounding variable? What type of design do researchers use to study maturational processes?

EXPERIMENTAL DESIGNS

Two critical factors—*control groups* and *randomization*—distinguish **experimental designs** from most nonexperimental designs. These two factors control most sources of confounding.

Including proper control groups helps to control for history, maturation, and regression to the mean. The experimental designs discussed here all include at least one control group. To make the control groups effective, the researcher must randomly assign participants to the groups. Control groups do not eliminate confounding factors. Instead, they allow us to control them because the factors should have the same effect in both groups.

Randomization is a powerful tool. Randomly selecting your sample from the population will enhance external validity, and randomly assigning participants to groups enhances internal validity. Thus, a good general rule to follow in designing research is to *randomize whenever possible and when ethically feasible* (as discussed in the Ethical Principles section).

"Well, Professor Gronski, it certainly looks like our growth-enhancement experiment is a complete failure."

CARTOON 10.1 It is important for scientists to be systematic and organized during data collection because it is easy to forget to label your data correctly and completely.

Because there are so many different experimental designs, we will cover them over several chapters. In this chapter, we will discuss designs appropriate for evaluating a single independent variable using independent groups of participants. Chapter 11 focuses on designs for testing a single independent variable using correlated groups of participants. Chapter 12 focuses on designs used for testing more than one independent variable in a single experiment. Finally, Chapter 13 focuses on designs that test causal hypotheses in natural environments.

Although many variations of experimental designs are possible, there are three basic designs to test a single independent variable using independent groups of participants. These **single-variable, between-subjects designs** include the following:

1. Randomized, posttest-only, control-group design
2. Randomized, pretest-posttest, control-group design
3. Multilevel, completely randomized, between-subjects design

Randomized, Posttest-Only, Control-Group Design

Suppose that you want to evaluate the effects of an experimental treatment for disruptive behavior, a special tutorial program for reading skills, stimulus complexity on target detection, or food additives on hyperactivity. In each case, you want to manipulate a variable and measure the effects, but you want to do it in such a way that extraneous variance is controlled. The best approach by far is to conduct an experiment.

The most basic experimental design is the **randomized, posttest-only, control-group design**, which includes randomization and a control group. You start by randomly selecting participants from a general or accessible population or carefully defining an ad hoc sample. You then randomly assign the participants to the experimental (treatment) and control (no-treatment) conditions. Figure 10.7 illustrates this design.

To test the hypothesis that the independent variable significantly affected the dependent variables, you compare the posttest measures from the experimental and control groups. We repeat that it is critical that the two groups be equivalent at the beginning of the study. If they are not, then we cannot know if differences at the posttest are due to the independent variable or to preexisting

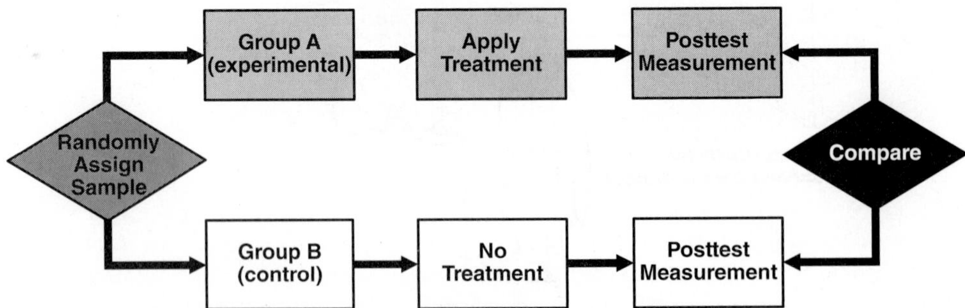

FIGURE 10.7 Randomized, Posttest-Only, Control-Group Design. The randomized, posttest-only, control-group design compares two groups in which the researcher randomly assigned participants to groups, with one group receiving the treatment and one group not receiving the treatment. This is a true experimental design that controls for most confounding variables.

differences between the groups. Random assignment of participants to groups increases the probability that the groups are equivalent at the beginning of the study. Furthermore, when the researcher randomly assigns participants to groups, the small probability that the groups might not be equal is factored into the statistical analysis automatically. After random assignment to groups, the groups are said to be **statistically equal**, because any small differences that might exist are the results of sampling error.

The randomized, posttest-only, control-group design controls several threats to validity. Random selection or ad hoc sample definition protects external validity. The random assignment of participants to groups controls threats to internal validity, from regression to the mean and from selection. Regression to the mean is controlled because, even if the participants were selected because they were extreme, the random assignment assures that both groups will have roughly the same number of extreme participants, and thus both groups should experience the same level of regression. Random assignment assures that the groups are statistically equal on all variables. By including the no-treatment control group, threats to internal validity from instrumentation, history, and maturation are reduced, because these effects should be the same in both groups. Hence, the comparison of the experimental and control group will not be affected by these potential confounding variables.

An experimental design is effective only if the appropriate general control procedures (covered in Chapter 9) are routinely applied. Carefully preparing the setting and using reliable dependent measures will minimize error variance. Using automation and/or single-blind or double-blind procedures will control potential confounding from experimenter or subject effects. An experimental design alone, without using these general control procedures, is not sufficient for ruling out confounding variables.

For example, in the food additive study, a double-blind procedure is needed because both placebo and experimenter effects are anticipated. The no-treatment control group must be indistinguishable from the treatment group for the participants. The researcher could accomplish this by providing specially packaged foods to all participants. The only difference would be that the food given to the experimental group would not contain the additives thought to increase hyperactivity. Ideally, identical packaging and foods that look and taste the same would be used in the two conditions.

Randomized, Pretest-Posttest, Control-Group Design

Recall that the pretest-posttest, natural control-group design discussed earlier in the chapter is not an experiment because it does not include random assignment to groups. In the **randomized, pretest-posttest, control-group design** (illustrated in Figure 10.8), participants are randomly assigned to groups. All participants are tested on the dependent variable (the pretest), the experimental group is administered the treatment, and both groups are then retested on the dependent variable (the posttest). The critical comparison is between the experimental and control groups on the posttest measure.

The randomized, pretest-posttest, control-group design improves on the randomized, posttest-only, control-group design by adding a pretreatment measurement of the dependent variable. Random assignment to groups ensures that the groups are statistically equal. The pretest provides a way to check if they are actually equivalent on the dependent variable at the start of the experiment, thus adding another level of confidence to the results. It also permits calculation of a pretest-posttest difference or change score. However, adding a pretest has some disadvantages, which we discuss later in the chapter.

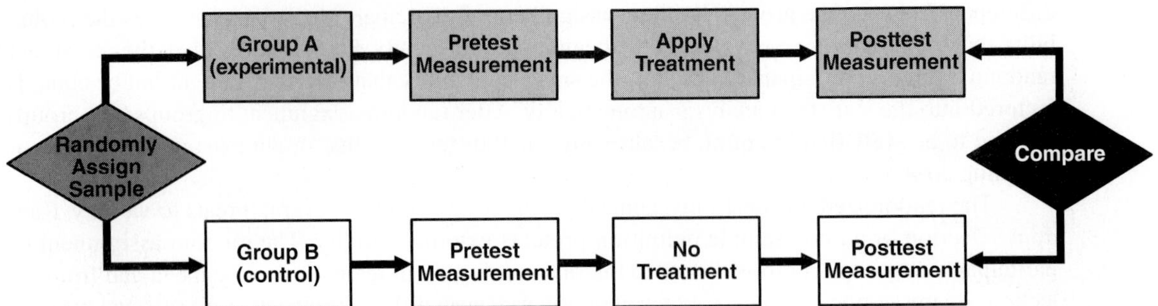

FIGURE 10.8 Randomized, Pretest-Posttest, Control-Group Design. The randomized, pretest-posttest control-group design compares two groups to which participants are randomly assigned: one group that receives the treatment and one group that does not receive the treatment. This is a true experimental design that controls for most confounding variables. The pretest allows you to see the strength of the treatment effect.

Multilevel, Completely Randomized, Between-Subjects Design

The designs discussed so far have had only two levels of the independent variable. The **multilevel, completely randomized, between-subjects design** is a simple extension of the previously discussed designs. Instead of randomly assigning participants to two conditions, the researcher randomly assigns participants to three or more conditions, as shown in Figure 10.9. Pretests may or may not be included, depending on the questions that the investigator wants to answer. Because this design is only an extension of earlier designs, it controls for the same confounding variables as the simple two-group designs.

Recall the study described in Chapter 9, in which the researcher varied room temperature to test its effects on the speed and accuracy of typing. That study used a multilevel, completely randomized, between-subjects design, in which 48 typists were randomly assigned to six groups of eight typists each. Each group of typists was tested at a different room temperature (the independent variable), and their typing speed and accuracy were measured (the dependent variables).

CARTOON 10.2 It may be possible to carry randomization too far, but researchers generally want to use randomization whenever possible.

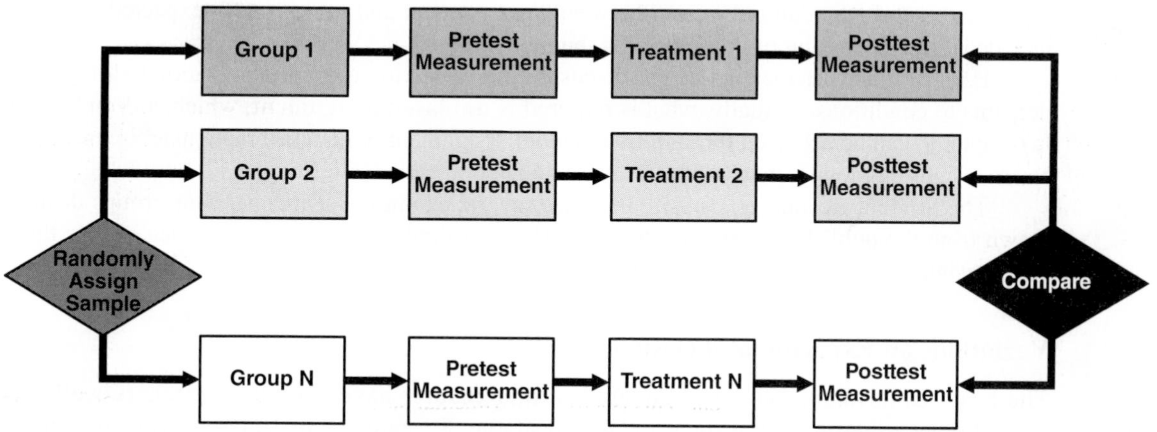

FIGURE 10.9 Multilevel, Completely Randomized, Between-Subjects Design. The multilevel, completely randomized, between-subjects design is an extension of the randomized, pretest-posttest, control-group design to more than two groups. This design may or may not include a pretest.

Pretest-Manipulation Interaction: A Potential Problem

The addition of a pretest improves control in experimental design, but it also creates a new problem: the possibility that the pretest will affect participants' responses to the treatment. We might expect the influence of the pretest to be the same in the experimental and control groups. However, it is also possible that the pretest could interact with the experimental manipulation, producing confounding—that is, the effect of the pretest might not be constant for the groups, but will vary depending on the level of the independent variable.

For example, suppose that a researcher is interested in changing adolescents' attitudes toward cigarette smoking by presenting them with a video about the health hazards of tobacco use. High school students are randomly selected, given a pretest to record attitudes toward tobacco, and are randomly assigned to experimental and control groups. The pretest tells us that the two groups are statistically equivalent at the start of the study on their attitudes toward tobacco use. The researcher shows the experimental group the video and retests both groups on their attitudes toward tobacco use.

However, the pretest of attitudes might sensitize participants to the nature of the research, causing a pretest-manipulation **interaction effect**. When the video is later presented to the experimental group, this sensitization may interact with the new information and change the way the participants respond. The experimenter might erroneously conclude that the observed difference is due only to the video, when it may actually be due to the interaction of the pretest and the video. The video may not have been as effective had there not been a pretest to sensitize participants to the video's message.

One attempt to control such interaction effects is **Solomon's four-group design** (Solomon, 1949). It is a powerful design that combines the randomized, pretest-posttest, control-group design and the posttest-only, control-group design. However, because it requires the resources of two experiments, it is not recommended for routine use. It is best used in research areas in which the hypotheses have already been tested and supported using simpler designs. It is

especially useful when an interaction between the treatment and the pretest is expected. We have included a full discussion of this design on the Student Resource Website.

10:01

Each of the experimental designs discussed in this section uses randomization to assign participants to conditions. Actually, what is required is **unbiased assignment**, which, as you learned in Chapter 9, can be achieved through free random assignment or matched random assignment. We cover designs employing matched random assignment procedures in Chapter 11.

The Student Resources Website includes several examples of independent-groups designs drawn from the published research literature. These examples will give you an idea of how these basic designs are used in actual research.

10:02

Variations on Experimental Designs

The basic experimental designs covered in this chapter have served researchers well, but several other experimental designs are also available. Researchers make two distinctions in experimental research designs. One distinction is between independent-groups designs (also called between-subjects designs) and correlated-groups designs (either within-subjects designs or matched-subjects designs). In **independent-groups designs**, different participants appear in each group. In **correlated-groups designs**, the same or closely matched participants appear in each group.

The second distinction is between **single-variable designs** (also called **univariate designs**) and **multivariable designs** (also called **factorial designs**). Single-variable designs have only one independent variable, whereas multivariable designs have two or more independent variables in a single study. This chapter covered single-variable, independent-groups designs. Chapters 11 and 12 cover correlated-groups designs and factorial designs, respectively.

Quick-Check Review 10.3: Experimental Designs

1. What is the most basic experimental design?
2. Describe the other two experimental designs discussed in this section.
3. How do (a) random assignment of participants to groups, and (b) inclusion of a control group avoid confounding?
4. What problems does the Solomon's four-group design address?
5. Why is it critical that groups be equivalent at the start of an experiment?

ANALYSES OF VARIANCE

This section reviews the statistical analysis of data obtained from experiments. Usually, that means conducting an analysis of variance, although some situations require other statistical procedures. The level of measurement of the dependent variable helps to determine the appropriate statistical procedure (see Appendix D). For example, researchers typically use a chi-square test with nominal data, the Mann-Whitney U-test with ordered data, and a t-test or an analysis of variance (ANOVA) with score data. Most dependent variables at the experimental level generate score data.

Consequently, we will focus primarily on analysis of variance in this section. The Student Resource Website covers several statistical procedures in addition to ANOVA. The coverage includes

10:03

statistical theory, manual computations, and computations using Predictive Analytics Software (PASW), previously known as Statistical Package for the Social Sciences (SPSS).

If we have only two groups and score data, we can use a *t*-test or an analysis of variance. However, many studies are multilevel designs that include more than two groups. For these studies, an analysis of variance is required. In the typist study mentioned earlier, there are six levels of the independent variable of room temperature. A researcher would use a *one-way* ANOVA to test whether any of the six groups is statistically different from any of the other groups. "One-way" simply means that there is only one independent variable in the study.

To introduce how ANOVA works, it is necessary to review some of the earlier discussion of variance. Variance is a relatively simple concept, but it can seem confusing in the context of ANOVA because this procedure calculates more than one variance estimate based on different combinations of the same data.

ANOVA uses both the **within-groups variance** and the between-groups variance. Within-groups variance is a measure of nonsystematic variation within a group. It is error or chance variation among individual participants within a group, and it results from such factors as individual differences and measurement errors. It represents the average variability within the groups. The between-groups variance represents how different the group means are. If all groups have approximately the same mean, the between-groups variance will be small; if the group means are very different from one another, the between-groups variance will be large.

The variance is based on the sum of squares, which is the sum of squared deviations from the mean. In an analysis of variance, there is a sum of squares on which the between-groups variance is based, a sum of squares on which the within-groups variance is based, and a total sum of squares. In the ANOVA procedure, the total sum of squares is **partitioned** into the between-groups sum of squares and the within-groups sum of squares, as shown in the following equation. You need not understand the mathematical details of this process. However, this principle of partitioning the sum of squares is essential in the computation of ANOVA procedures.

$$SS_{\text{total}} = SS_{\text{between-groups}} + SS_{\text{within-groups}} \tag{10.3}$$

Consider the study in Chapter 9 of the effects of room temperature on typing speed, in which the researcher randomly assigned 48 typists to six conditions defined by the temperature of the room in which their typing speed was tested. Table 10.1 shows the data for this study, as well as the mean and standard deviation of typing speed for each group. The first step in doing an ANOVA is to compute each of the sums of squares (between-groups, within-groups, and total).

The next step is to compute between-groups and within-groups variance estimates, which are called **mean squares** in analysis of variance. The mean squares are computed by dividing each of the sums of squares by the appropriate degrees of freedom (df). The between-groups sum of squares is divided by the number of groups minus 1 (in this case, $6 - 1 = 5$). The within-groups sum of squares is divided by the total number of participants minus the number of groups (in this case, $48 - 6 = 42$). The mean square within-groups is referred to as the **error term**; it is a function of both the variability within the groups and the size of the samples. As the sample size increases, the error term gets smaller.

We then compare the between-groups and within-groups mean squares by dividing the between-groups mean square by the within-groups mean square. The result is the *F*-ratio, which we will interpret shortly. These steps for computing a one-way ANOVA are illustrated in the

TABLE 10.1 Typing Speed Study Data

	TEMPERATURE UNDER WHICH TYPISTS WERE TESTED					
	55°	60°	65°	70°	75°	80°
	49	71	64	63	60	48
	59	54	73	72	71	53
	61	62	60	56	49	64
	52	58	55	59	54	53
	50	64	72	64	63	59
	58	68	81	70	55	61
	63	57	79	63	59	54
	54	61	76	65	62	60
Mean	55.75	61.88	70.00	64.00	59.13	56.50
Standard Deviation	5.23	5.69	9.35	5.24	6.66	5.32

Note: The scores in this table are the typing speed in words per minute.

Go with the Flow 10.1 figure. Details of how to compute the ANOVA discussed here are included on the Student Resource Website.

The results of these computations are organized in an **ANOVA summary table** like the one shown in Table 10.2. This table shows the sources of variation, the degrees of freedom associated with each source, the sum of squares, the mean squares, the value of F, and the probability value associated with that F-value. In this basic ANOVA, there are only three sources of variation (between-groups, within-groups, and total). However, as you will see in later chapters, other designs have many more sources of variation and therefore more F-ratios to compute and interpret.

The statistical significance of the ANOVA is based on the ***F*-test** (named after its originator, Sir Ronald Fisher). Fisher's F-test involves the ratio of the between-groups mean square to the within-groups mean square:

$$F = \frac{\text{Mean Square Between-Groups}}{\text{Mean Square Within-Groups}} \tag{10.4}$$

TABLE 10.2 ANOVA Summary Table for the Study of the Effects of Room Temperature on Typing Speed

SOURCE	df	SS	MS	*F*	*p*
Between groups	5	1134.67	226.93	5.51	.0006
Within groups	42	1731.25	41.22		
Total	47	2865.92			

Note: The column heads are standard in ANOVA summary tables. They stand for source of variance, degrees of freedom, sums of squares, mean squares, F-ratios, and probability values.

GO WITH THE FLOW 10.1 | STEPS IN COMPUTING A ONE-WAY ANOVA

The key to doing the manual computations of something as complex as an ANOVA is to be organized and systematic. The Student Resource Website shows how to compute all of the statistical procedures presented in this text, but this Go with the Flow figure shows the steps in a one-way ANOVA.

Conduct Preliminary Computations (ΣX and ΣX^2); See Student Resource Website for Details → Organize the Data into Columns → Setup the ANOVA Summary Table to Put Computations as You Complete Them

Conduct Preliminary Computations → Compute the Degrees of Freedom → Compute the Sums of Squares

Compute the Degrees of Freedom and Compute the Sums of Squares → ANOVA Summary Table

Setup the ANOVA Summary Table → ANOVA Summary Table → Mean Squares Are Computed by Dividing the Sum of Squares by the Degrees of Freedom → The *F*-Ratio Is the Computed by Dividing the $MS_{between}$ by the MS_{within}

10:04

For this discussion, we will assume that the only source of systematic between-groups variance is experimental variance. That would be the case if we used an experimental design that adequately controlled confounding variables and applied all appropriate general control procedures. Figure 10.10 illustrates graphically what factors go into the *F*-ratio and how the relative size of those factors affects the size of the *F*. The size of the circles indicates the relative size of the sources of variance (systematic variance and the error term).

Consider some of the possibilities for the *F*-ratio. If there were no systematic between-groups differences, there would still be some chance differences between the groups due to sampling error. Therefore, if there were no systematic between-groups differences, both the mean square between-groups (based on between-groups variability) and the mean square within-groups (based on within-groups variability) would estimate error variance. In this case, the *F*-ratio should have a value of approximately 1.00. Any factors that increase the size of the numerator relative to the denominator will make the ratio larger. Therefore, as the systematic between-groups variance increases, the *F*-ratio will increase. Furthermore, any factors that decrease the size of the denominator relative to

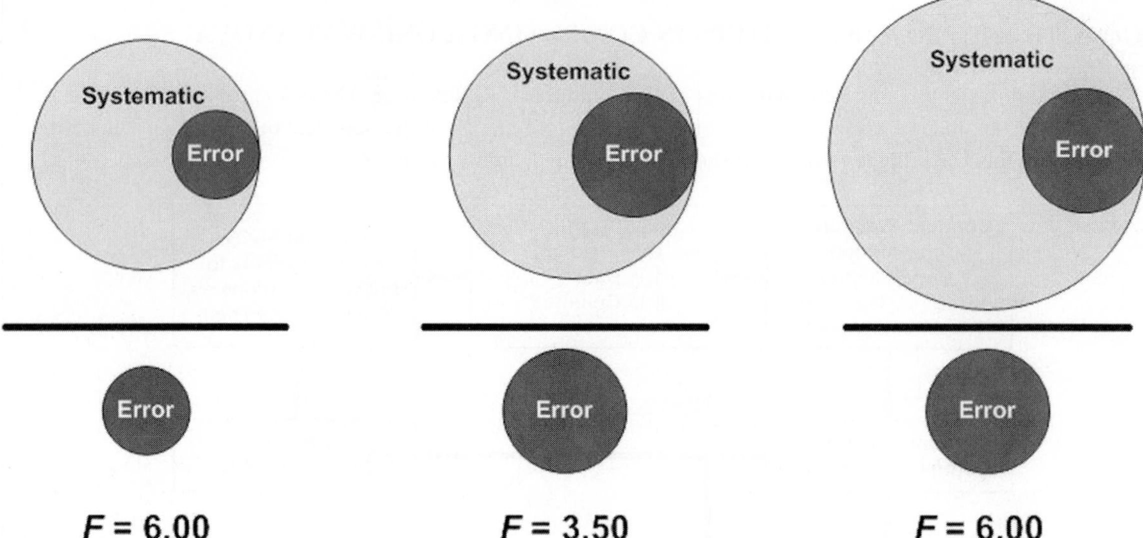

FIGURE 10.10 What Affects the *F*-Ratio. This figure illustrates how changes in the sources of variance affect the *F*-ratio. We have simplified Figure 10.2 by summing the systematic and error variance into a single circle in the numerator. In the middle figure, we have moderate error and modest systematic effects, which produces an *F*-ratio of 3.50. In this figure, the *F* is computed as a ratio of the area in the top circle to the area in the bottom circle. In the left figure, we have cut the error variance in half, which also slightly reduced the circle in the numerator because the error variance is part of the numerator. In the right figure, we have doubled the systematic variance. Both effects increase the observed *F*-ratio and therefore make it easier to detect group differences. The primary way to increase the systematic variance is by making the independent-variable manipulation more dramatic, so that the group differences will be larger if the independent variable has an effect. The primary way to decrease the error variance is to increase the sample size.

the numerator will also make the ratio larger. Thus, we can increase the *F*-ratio by increasing the systematic between-groups variance, by decreasing the nonsystematic within-groups variance, or by a combination of the two, as shown in Figure 10.10.

We can increase the systematic between-groups variance by maximizing the differences between the groups. We can minimize the nonsystematic within-groups variance by controlling as many potential sources of random error as possible, although shortly you will see that there is an easier way to achieve this goal. *Maximize experimental variance and minimize error variance!* This theme should be sounding familiar by now. Add the part about controlling extraneous variance, and you have the guiding principle of research design.

The larger the *F*-ratio, the greater the variance between groups relative to the variance within groups. A large *F* indicates that the experimental manipulation may have had an effect because the group means are very different from one another. In practice, even if there are no systematic effects, the *F*-ratio will sometimes be larger than 1.00. Therefore, we do not reject the hypothesis that there are no systematic differences unless the *F*-ratio is larger than we would expect by chance alone.

Statistical analysis programs routinely compute both the *F*-ratio and the *p*-value associated with it. This *p*-value is the probability of obtaining a specific *F* or larger *F*, which is a function of how different the group means are from one another, if there are no systematic effects. If the

UNDERSTANDING THE CONCEPT 10.1: STATISTICAL POWER

We introduced the concept of statistical power in Chapter 5. As you will see in this box, power is related to the size of the error term of a statistical test; the smaller the error term, the greater the power.

The error terms (i.e., denominators) in both the *t*-test and in the ANOVA procedures are a function of the variance of scores within the groups and the sample size. Remember that one of the goals in research is to minimize error variance, which essentially means to minimize this error term. We noted several ways in which that could be done, including improving the quality of the measurement procedure or using within-subjects designs to control for individual differences.

These procedures do work and researchers routinely use them to control error variance and minimize the error term, thus increasing power. However, by far the most important method for decreasing the error term is to increase the sample size. Larger sample sizes provide better estimates of population parameters, such as population means. Therefore, you do not need as large a difference between your sample means to be convinced that a difference exists in the population means. This concept is called *statistical power*. When we suggest that you want to minimize the error term, we are saying that you want to increase statistical power. The effect is to give you greater sensitivity to any effect that the independent variable might have on the dependent variable.

p-value is less than the alpha level chosen, the researcher rejects the null hypothesis that the groups are equal and concludes that at least one of the groups is significantly different from at least one other group.

Earlier, we suggested that there is an easy way to reduce the size of the denominator in an ANOVA—that is, reduce the error term. Understanding the Concept 10.1 will tell you what it is.

Specific Means Comparisons in ANOVA

Note that the *F*-test indicates whether significant group differences exist, but not which group or groups are significantly different from the others. This is not a problem when we are comparing only two groups. However, when there are three or more groups to compare, an additional step is needed. Specifically, the researcher must **probe** to determine where the significant difference(s) occur(s). Probing is statistically testing the differences between the group means. The best way to carry out these specific comparisons is as a planned part of the research, which are called **planned comparisons** (also called **a priori comparisons** or **contrasts**). Here the experimenter makes predictions about which groups will differ and in what direction based on the theoretical concepts that underlie the experiment; the experimenter makes these predictions before data are collected.

Occasionally a priori predictions are not made, and an ANOVA is carried out to answer the question of whether there are any differences. Under these conditions, if the *F* is significant, we would evaluate the pattern of means using a **post hoc comparison** (also called an **a posteriori comparison** or an **incidental comparison**). Scientific rigor and informational value are generally greater for planned comparisons than for post hoc comparisons. Therefore, researchers usually try to make specific predictions prior to the study to justify planned comparisons based on those predictions.

There are several statistical procedures for specific comparisons, depending on whether they are planned or post hoc. Note that a *t*-test is not an appropriate procedure for doing a post hoc

comparison of means. The *t*-test used as a post hoc probe may indicate that significant differences exist when they do not. Appropriate post hoc tests, such as the Tukey, Newman-Keuls, or Sheffe, have built-in procedures designed to deal with problems with the Type I error level. These problems are too complex to discuss adequately here. The interested student can consult Shavelson (1996) for computational procedures and the rationale. We also cover the basics of these procedures on the
10:05 Student Resource Website.

Graphing the Data

Interpreting the results of a study is a process of making sense out of complicated findings. A useful first step in the interpretation process is to look at the pattern of means. Table 10.1 lists the means for the typing speed study, and Figure 10.11 organizes these means into two commonly used graphs: a bar graph and a line graph. Graphs are usually easier to read than tables and are particularly helpful when there are more than one independent variable.

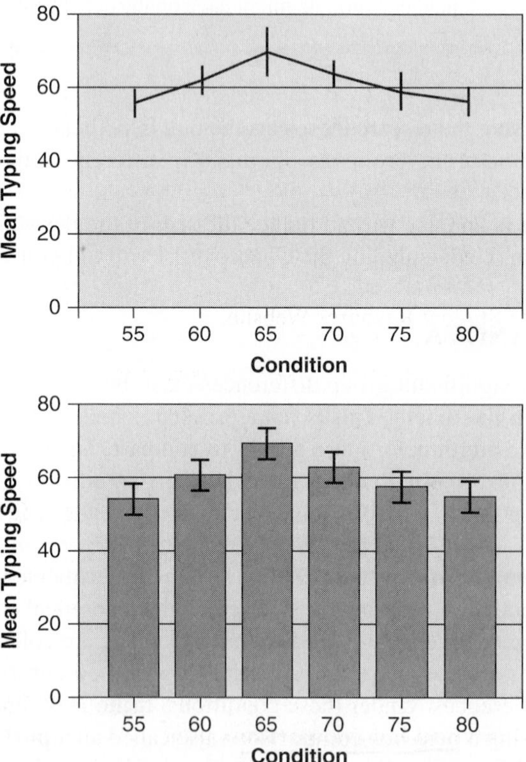

FIGURE 10.11 Effects of Room Temperature on Typing Speed. The graphs of the data on the effects of room temperature on typing speed indicate that optimal typing speed occurs at a temperature of 65°. The top figure uses a line graph, and the bottom figure uses a bar graph to show these data. Which one you use is a matter of preference. The vertical bars at each data point indicate the size of the standard error of the mean.

You learned how to create the graphs shown in Figure 10.11 in Chapter 5. An addition to graphs, called the error bar, is now frequently used in research articles and is recommended or even required by some journals. Each point on a graph typically represents an individual's mean score or the mean of a group. **Error bars** are placed so that the center of the bar is at that point (the mean) and the bar extends above or below the mean to indicate the distribution of the measures. (Under some conditions, the bar extends horizontally to represent more than one variable, but that is beyond this discussion.) The error bar is a graphic depiction of variability for that particular distribution of measures around their mean. Thus, all error bars represent some kind of difference or variability (Belia et al., 2005; Mason & Loftus, 2003). They are indications of statistical uncertainty showing that the true mean of that population falls somewhere within the range represented by the error bar.

Error bars can be based on different measures: the standard deviation of a distribution, the standard error of the mean, or the confidence interval. Although closely related, these measures provide different information, even though the error bars may look the same on a graph. The most commonly used measure of variability for the error bars is the **standard error of the mean** (often simply called the standard error), which is the standard deviation of the distribution we would get if we took every possible sample of a given size from a population and graphed the means of those samples. Unfortunately, there is no agreement on which measure of variability should be used for the error bar. Consequently, you should always indicate in your figure what the error bar represents. Moreover, if you are submitting an article to a journal for publication, you should check to see if the journal wants you to use a particular error bar. Most statistical analysis programs allow you to choose among several options for error bars.

Researchers can look at a graph with error bars and see if the groups are likely to be statistically different. The rule of thumb is that if the error bars overlap, then the groups are probably not significantly different. If the error bars do not overlap, there might be a significant difference between the groups. The error bars allow us a quick visual inspection, but they do not replace the formal statistical test.

10:06 We will not be covering the error bar or the standard error of the mean in detail in the text, but
10:07 we do cover both of these topics on the Student Resource Website.

Quick-Check Review 10.4: Analysis of Variance

1. Under what conditions is the ANOVA most likely used?
2. What information is typically found in the ANOVA summary table?
3. In ANOVA, what does it mean if the F-ratio is significant?
4. What are planned comparisons and post hoc tests?

ETHICAL PRINCIPLES

Experimental design emphasizes control of variance to enhance the validity of the study. One of the most basic and powerful control procedures is randomization. Random selection helps to enhance external validity, and random assignment enhances internal validity. Therefore, we urge our students to *randomize whenever possible.*

However, there are ethical limitations to randomization. Those limitations arise most strikingly in instances in which the researcher attempts to alter something about the experimental group but not the control group. An example is a study of a new drug to treat skin cancer. A straightforward design could be one in which participating cancer patients are randomly assigned to experimental and control groups. The experimental group receives the new drug, which is withheld from the control group.

There are two ethical problems with that design—deliberately withholding treatment from patients, and doing so based on their chance assignment to the control group. The control group is placed at risk; the researcher must counteract the potential risk and protect the well-being of the participants.

The most essential safeguard is informed consent. Participants need to know they will be randomly assigned to treatment and control conditions, and that they will not know their assigned condition until the end of the study. If, knowing that, they agree to participate, then a good portion of the ethical problems will have been avoided. Nevertheless, the researcher still must look out for the well-being of participants. If the results of the study confirm that the treatment is effective, the researcher would have an ethical obligation to then make the treatment available to the control participants.

An added safeguard in such randomized, control-group clinical studies is to provide a "best-treatment" control condition rather than a no-treatment control group. The randomly assigned experimental group would receive the new treatment that is being tested, and the control group would be provided with the standard or most effective treatment currently available. Thus, when giving informed consent, the participants are told they will be randomly assigned to a condition in which they will receive either the new experimental drug or the standard treatment that is currently available. Again, if one treatment proves to be significantly more effective than the other treatment, the ethical researcher would make the most effective treatment available to all participants after the study.

In summary, using randomization whenever it is possible and ethical is a good general rule to follow. However, under some conditions, ethical issues may prevent the use of random assignment. It would be unethical to assign people to experimental conditions that might result in their injury, or to control groups that never receive treatment for a clinical condition. In such cases, lower-constraint methods, like correlational and differential research that do not include random assignment to groups, can provide useful information.

Quick-Check Review 10.5: Ethical Principles

1. What are some ethical limitations to using random assignment?
2. What is the most essential ethical safeguard in research with human subjects?

SUMMARY

- Experimental design focuses on controlling unwanted variance, thus reducing threats to validity.
- Variance includes systematic between-groups variance and nonsystematic within-groups error variance.
- Between-groups variance is a function of both experimental variance (due to the independent variable) and extraneous variance (due to confounding variables), as well as a small effect due to sampling error.

- A major goal in experimentation is to design studies that maximize experimental variance, control extraneous variance, and minimize error variance.
- The key components of an experiment are the inclusion of a control group and random assignment of participants to groups.
- The most commonly used statistical procedure for analyzing experimental studies is the ANOVA, because most experimental procedures use dependent measures that produce score data.
- Although one should use randomization whenever possible in research studies, there are situations in which random procedures may be unethical.

PUTTING IT INTO PRACTICE

You might not be aware of it, but people implicitly use nonexperimental research designs every day as they observe the world and try to make sense out of it. For example, when meeting someone who is obnoxious, we may want to know why that person is that way and may draw ex post facto conclusions based on the limited information we have about the person. We may also take these conclusions and use them to predict the behavior of other people. You have learned in this chapter that such conclusions are often incorrect.

For the next week or so, watch as you observe the world and try to make sense of it. Look at the evidence that is available, and ask yourself how adequate is that evidence? This is a very good habit to get into, one that will prevent you from making numerous mistakes in life based on drawing conclusions from inadequate evidence. See if you can take the principles of this chapter and this text and use them to decide what would constitute adequate evidence for drawing accurate conclusions about the questions you face daily.

This process is called **critical thinking**, and it is perhaps the most important skill a person can develop. You can think of this entire course as a critical thinking exercise applied to psychological research. However, if you also recognize that you can apply the critical thinking skills you learn in this course to many life situations, two things will happen. The first is that you will think more clearly in your everyday life, making better decisions and avoiding many of the mistakes that are so common in life. The second is that the material in this text will be much easier to remember, because you will be able to code the information in terms of concepts that you already know from your daily life experiences. Give it a try.

EXERCISES

10.1. Define the following key terms. Be sure that you understand them. They are discussed in the chapter and defined in the glossary.

between-groups variance
experimental variance
extraneous variance
systematic between-groups variance
nonsystematic within-groups variance, or error variance
manipulation check
ex post facto study
single-group, posttest-only study
single-group, pretest-posttest study
time-series design

pretest-posttest, natural control-group study
experimental designs
single-variable, between-subjects designs
randomized, posttest-only, control-group design
statistically equal
randomized, pretest-posttest, control-group design
multilevel, completely randomized, between-subjects design
interaction effects
Solomon's four-group design
unbiased assignment
independent-groups designs
correlated-groups designs
single-variable design, or univariate designs
multivariable design, or factorial design
within-groups variance
partitioned
mean squares
error term
ANOVA summary table
F-test
probe
planned comparison
a priori comparison
contrast
post hoc comparison
a posteriori comparison
incidental comparison
error bar
standard error of the mean
critical thinking

10.2. You are the teaching assistant for this course and must explain variability to your students. How would you explain the concept, its measure, and its importance?

10.3. Why is it important to minimize the error variance in the *F*-test?

10.4. Define an ex post facto study and explain why it is a weak design.

10.5. What is the relationship among the concepts of confounding variables, threats to validity, and extraneous variance?

10.6. Does a high between-groups variance in an experiment provide sufficient evidence to conclude that the independent variable affected the dependent variable? Explain.

10.7. For each of the following designs (a) give an example, (b) identify the major threats to validity, and (c) state the limits on the conclusions that can be drawn.

- Single-group, posttest-only design
- Ex post facto design
- Single-group, pretest-posttest design
- Pretest-posttest, natural control-group design

10.8. As the course teaching assistant, you are to explain the *F*-ratio. Define all of its components, and explain the logic of the *F*-test.

10.9. For each of the following types of experimental designs (a) give an example, and (b) indicate what threats to validity are controlled.

- Randomized, posttest-only, control-group design
- Randomized, pretest-posttest, control-group design
- Multilevel, completely randomized, between-subjects design

CHAPTER ELEVEN

CORRELATED-GROUPS AND SINGLE-SUBJECT DESIGNS

The real problem is not whether machines think, but whether men do.

—B.F. Skinner, 1969, *Contingencies of Reinforcement*

WEB RESOURCE MATERIAL

Random assignment of participants to conditions, discussed in Chapters 9 and 10, is a cornerstone of experimental design. It assures the statistical equivalence of groups at the beginning of the study, thus making it possible to compare groups under different experimental manipulations.

Randomization is the most basic and single most important control procedure. It can control for threats to internal and external validity, can control several factors simultaneously, and is the only procedure that can control for unknown factors. As we said in Chapter 9, a good general rule in research is, *whenever possible, randomize*.

There are alternatives to free random assignment to groups. One is to use a correlated-groups design. Correlated-groups designs, discussed in this chapter, assure group equivalence by using either the same participants in all groups or closely matched participants. They are called correlated-groups designs because this assignment strategy assures that the participants in one group are correlated with the participants in the other groups.

Some researchers do not consider correlated-groups designs to be experiments because they do not use free random assignment. However, we believe they qualify as experiments because they meet the requirement of initial equivalence of groups and other controls can be applied to eliminate rival hypotheses.

This chapter covers three correlated-groups designs. *Within-subjects designs* (also called **repeated-measures designs**) test participants under all conditions. *Matched-subjects designs* match participants on relevant variables prior to the study and then randomly assign the matched sets of participants, one member of each set to each group. This chapter also covers *single-subject experimental designs*, which are extensions of within-subjects designs.

WITHIN-SUBJECTS DESIGNS

In within-subjects designs, each participant is exposed to all experimental conditions, thereby making the conditions correlated. In essence, *each participant serves as his or her own control*.

Using Within-Subjects Designs

Consider a target-detection experiment. The target is a letter, either T or F. Participants view arrays of random letters on a computer screen, and somewhere in the array is one of the two target letters. The participant's task is to find the target letter in each array and press either the T or F response button. The other letters in the array are distracter items. The question is whether the number of distracter items affects the time that participants take to find a target. Each person is tested under three conditions of distraction: 10, 15, and 20 distracter items. There are 10 trials at each of the three levels of distraction. The dependent variable is the speed of the detection responses, and we sum the 10 trial times to obtain the total search time for each distraction level. The hypothesis is that finding the target will take longer if there are more distracters.

Figure 11.1 illustrates the design of this study. This is a within-subjects design, and the characteristics of within-subjects designs are as follows:

1. Each participant is tested under each experimental condition.
2. Therefore, the scores in each condition are correlated with the scores in the other conditions.
3. The critical comparison is the difference between the conditions on the dependent variable.

Sequence Effects. In within-subjects designs, sequence effects (covered in Chapter 8) are a potential source of confounding. Because each participant is exposed to all conditions, exposure to

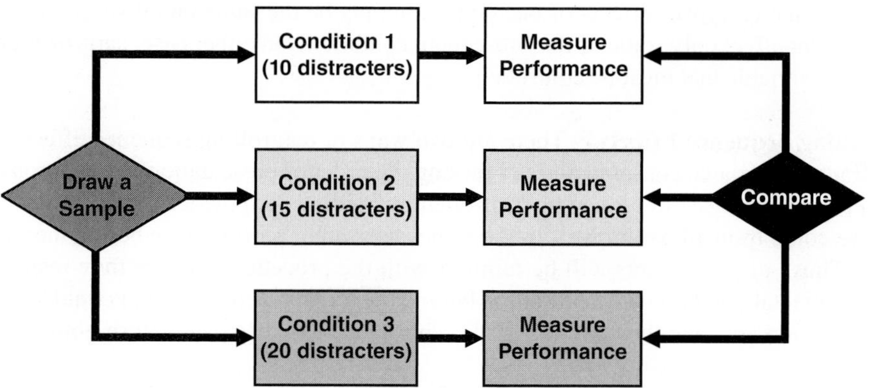

FIGURE 11.1 An Example of a Within-Subjects Design. In a within-subjects design, the same people appear in all conditions. The order of presentation of conditions varies from participant to participant.

earlier conditions may affect performance on later conditions. The within-subjects design is similar to a single-group, pretest-posttest design except that in the pretest-posttest design, each participant responds to the pretest and the posttest in that order. In contrast, in within-subjects designs, the order of presentation of conditions is not necessarily fixed as it must be in a pretest-posttest study.

Subtypes of Sequence Effects. The two most important sequence effects are practice effects and carryover effects. **Practice effects** are due to the growing experience with procedures over successive conditions, rather than to influences of any particular condition on other conditions. If there are five conditions, for example, many participants will perform better in the last two or three conditions because of practice effects. This enhancement of performance on later conditions represents a **positive practice effect**. On the other hand, if the procedure is lengthy or demanding, participants might become fatigued, and their performance will decline in later conditions. This is a **negative practice effect**. Both practice effects can confound a study if not controlled. Because practice effects depend on participants' experience as they move sequentially through the conditions, they occur regardless of the particular sequence of conditions.

Carryover effects are due to the influence of a particular condition or combination of conditions on responses to later conditions. Carryover effects may be greater for one condition than for the others. For example, there may be some aspect of a particular condition (e.g., condition A) that produces an effect on any condition that follows it. Thus, no matter where condition A appears in a sequence, it will influence the next condition.

Suppose that in the target-detection study, the conditions are always presented in the following order: 10-distracter, 15-distracter, and 20-distracter conditions. Furthermore, suppose that the participants are capable of finding the target in the 10-distracter condition by focusing on all 11 items at once (called parallel search), but the 15- and 20-distracter conditions have too many items for the parallel search to work. The best strategy for a search with a large number of distracters is to look systematically at each letter until the target is found (called serial search). If the 10-distracter list always appears first, the participants will learn to try a parallel search, which will hamper target detection in the 15- and 20-distracter conditions and distort the data. If, on the other hand, the 20-distracter list always appears first, the participants will learn to try the serial search first, thus distorting the data for the 10-distracter condition.

Note that carryover effects of one condition may be the same on all subsequent conditions, or they might affect only some of the subsequent conditions. In either case, carryover effects are an extraneous variable that must be controlled.

Controlling Sequence Effects. There are two ways of controlling sequence effects: (1) holding the extraneous variable constant, and (2) varying the order of presentation of conditions.

Positive practice effects can be controlled by holding the practice variable constant. Specifically, we could train all participants to the same criterion of performance before the first condition begins. Thus, all participants will be familiar with the procedures before they respond to any of the experimental conditions. A control for fatigue (negative practice effects) could be the inclusion of a rest period between the conditions, allowing fatigue to dissipate before going on to the next condition.

These procedures minimize practice effects, but the best way to control practice effects is to vary the order of presentation of conditions. Furthermore, varying the order of presentation of conditions is the only way to control carryover effects. The order of conditions can be varied by using either a random or a counterbalanced order of presentation. The logic of both procedures is to control sequence effects by having these effects contribute equally to all conditions.

Random Order of Presentation. In a **random order of presentation**, we randomly assign each participant to a different order of the conditions. Random orders of presentation can be effective if the number of subjects is large, thus producing many random orders. Random orders with large samples tend to cancel out sequence effects, thus equating their effects across conditions. However, when there are only a small number of conditions, you need something that is more systematic, which is counterbalancing.

Counterbalancing. The best control for sequence effects is **counterbalancing**, in which the order of presentation of conditions to participants is systematically varied. In **complete counterbalancing**, all possible orders of conditions occur an equal number of times. The result is that

1. each participant is exposed to all conditions of the experiment,
2. each condition is presented an equal number of times in each position,
3. each condition precedes and follows each other condition an equal number of times.

We discuss sequence effects and their controls more extensively later in this chapter.

Table 11.1 shows the various orders of conditions for the hypothetical target-detection study. Note that this set of orders meets the three conditions outlined above. Table 11.1 also shows hypothetical data for this experiment. The data are the total time (in seconds) required to find the targets at the three levels of distraction. The first column lists the six participants, the second column shows the order of presentation of the stimulus conditions to each participant, and the last three columns show the search times for each of the three experimental conditions.

Counterbalancing can be complete or partial. To calculate how many orders are needed for complete counterbalancing, you calculate *X!* (*X* factorial), in which *X* is the number of conditions. *X!* is calculated by multiplying the integer *X* by all integers smaller than the number. Thus, for the target-detection study, which has three conditions, there are six possible orders ($X! = 3 \times 2 \times 1 = 6$). Table 11.1 shows the six possible orders. Participants are assigned to orders of presentation, with

TABLE 11.1 Hypothetical Data for the Target-Detection Study

		CONDITION (SEARCH TIME IN SECONDS)		
PARTICIPANTS	**ORDER OF PRESENTATION**	**A (10)**	**B (15)**	**C (20)**
1	ABC	18.33	22.39	24.97
2	ACB	15.96	20.72	21.79
3	BAC	19.02	22.78	25.46
4	BCA	25.36	27.48	27.91
5	CAB	19.52	24.64	26.75
6	CBA	23.27	24.96	25.49
Mean scores		**20.24**	**23.83**	**25.40**

an equal number of participants assigned to each order. If there are 30 participants, 5 will be assigned to each of the six orders.

Counterbalancing is very effective with a small number of conditions. With two conditions, there are only two orders of presentation ($X! = 2 \times 1 = 2$). With three conditions, there are six orders of presentation. However, with four conditions, there are 24 orders ($X! = 4 \times 3 \times 2 \times 1 = 24$), and if the experiment has five conditions, there are 120 orders ($X! = 5 \times 4 \times 3 \times 2 \times 1 = 120$). The number of possible orders rises rapidly as the number of conditions increases, making complete counterbalancing impractical. With large numbers of conditions, **partial counterbalancing** may be the best solution. Alternatively, one could use random orders of presentation for each subject, as discussed in the previous section.

What if you have only 10 participants and four conditions and you still want to use a within-subjects design and control for sequence effects? In this case, you could

1. randomize the order of presentation for each participant,
2. randomly select 10 of the 24 possible orders and randomly assign participants to these orders, or
3. use a more formalized partial counterbalancing procedure known as a **Latin square design**.

Latin squares are counterbalanced arrangements named after an ancient Roman puzzle that involves arranging letters in rows and columns so that each letter occurs only once in each row and once in each column. The result is that all letters appear in each position in the sequence an equal number of times, and all letters follow each other letter an equal number of times. Keppel

and Wickens (2004) and Myers et al. (2010) provide more complete discussions of Latin square
11:01 designs. The Student Resources Website provides instructions on how to set up a Latin square.

There is another approach to reducing sequence effects, but it is possible only in some situations. In the target-detection example, each condition consisted of 10 trials. The earlier presentation suggested that all 10 trials would be grouped together, but often that is unnecessary. If, instead, the 30 trials (10 in each of the three conditions) were randomly ordered, then sequencing would be reasonably controlled.

If the researcher did not want to trust randomization completely, trials could be **randomized within blocks**. This would involve arranging the 30 individual trials into blocks of trials (a block includes one trial from each condition) and then randomizing the order of presentation of the trials within each of these blocks. This procedure produces a random order, but without the possibility of one condition tending to have most of the trials either at the beginning or end of the testing. This

11:02 process is explained in more detail on the Student Resource Website.

If strong carryover effects are expected, the within-subjects design is not recommended, even if the preceding controls are included. Carryover effects tend to add error variance to scores, which can offset any increased sensitivity normally expected from a within-subjects design. If strong carryover effects are expected, it is best to use either a between-subjects design or a matched-subjects design.

Sometimes the carryover effects are so strong that it makes no sense to use a within-subjects design. For example, suppose that you want to test two methods of teaching a foreign language. Once you have used one of the methods, the subjects presumably already know the foreign language and therefore would not be appropriate subjects for testing the other method. Physiological studies with animals often employ techniques that destroy specific regions of the brain to determine what behaviors are lost due to that destruction. Once such an action is taken, the animal is changed and it is impossible to use the animal in another condition. In these cases, we have no choice but to use a between-subjects or matched-subjects design.

Analyzing Data from Within-Subjects Designs

The first step in analyzing the results of within-subjects designs is to organize and summarize the data, as shown in Table 11.1. In this hypothetical study, the search times are longest, on average, for the 20-distracter condition, shorter for the 15-distracter condition, and shortest for the 10-distracter condition.

These results suggest that the hypothesis may be correct. But are the differences between conditions large enough to state with confidence that similar differences exist in the populations? That is, are the differences statistically significant?

The appropriate ANOVA for a within-subjects design is called a **repeated-measures ANOVA**. It is similar to the ANOVA discussed in Chapter 10. However, because the conditions are correlated in a within-subjects design, the repeated-measures ANOVA is modified to factor in this correlation. The logic of the repeated measures ANOVA is covered on the Student Resource Website. Note that

11:03 if you have just two conditions in a within-subjects design, you can do either a repeated-measures
11:04 ANOVA or a correlated *t*-test, which is also covered on the Student Resource Website.

You learned in Chapter 5 that statistical power is an index of the sensitivity of a research study to detect small differences between groups, and that this sensitivity is a function of both the statistical procedure and the design. The major advantage of a within-subjects design is that it effectively equates the conditions prior to the experiment by using the same participants in each condition. Therefore, it removes what is often the single largest contributing factor to error variance—individual differences.

What effect does this have on the *F*-ratio? Because within-subjects designs remove the individual-difference portion of the error term, the denominator in the *F*-ratio is smaller and therefore *F* is larger. This means that the procedure is more sensitive to small differences between groups. Statistical power is increased; consequently, you can detect differences between conditions without having to increase sample size to enhance power.

TABLE 11.2 Summary Table (Repeated-Measures ANOVA)

SOURCE	df	SS	MS	*F*	*p*
Between	2	83.69	41.85	32.25	<.001
Subjects	5	95.85	19.17		
Error	10	12.97	1.30		

In repeated-measures ANOVA, the total sum of squares is computed in the same way as in a one-way ANOVA. What is called a between-groups sum of squares in a one-way ANOVA is called a **between-conditions sum of squares** in a repeated-measures ANOVA, or simply a **between sum of squares**.

The within-groups sum of squares in the repeated-measures ANOVA is divided into two terms: subjects and error. The **subjects term** is the individual-differences component of the within-groups variability. The error term is what is left when the individual-differences component is removed. The repeated-measures ANOVA tests the null hypothesis of no differences between conditions by dividing the mean square between (abbreviated $MS_{between}$) by the mean square error (abbreviated MS_{error} or simply MS_e). As in the independent-groups ANOVA, the ratio of mean squares is an *F*-ratio. Table 11.2 presents the results of the analysis of the data from Table 11.1. The Student
11:05 Resource Website presents the computational procedures for repeated-measures ANOVAs.

A significant *F*-ratio in the ANOVA indicates that at least one of the condition means is significantly different from at least one other condition mean. Additional tests must be conducted to determine which means are significantly different from which other means. These tests are conceptually identical to the planned comparisons and post hoc tests discussed in Chapter 10, but different statistical procedures are involved—procedures that take into account the correlated nature of the data. Most advanced statistics textbooks cover the computational procedures for these tests (e.g., Keppel, 2004; Myers et al., 2010). Most computerized statistical analysis packages include these tests as an option.

Strengths and Weaknesses of Within-Subjects Designs

Within-subjects designs have important advantages. First, because the same participants are in each condition, there are no group differences due to sampling error. Participants in each condition are guaranteed to be equivalent at the start of the study, thus eliminating the possible confounding due to selection.

Another important advantage is that within-subjects designs are more sensitive than between-subjects designs to the effects of the independent variable. Why is that true? Remember the design principle: *maximize experimental variance* (variance due to the effects of the independent variable), *control extraneous variance* (variance due to confounding), *and minimize error variance* (variance due to individual differences and chance factors). *A within-subjects design not only minimizes but actually eliminates the variance due to individual differences, thus substantially reducing the error term in the ANOVA and thus increasing the power.*

Therefore, the larger the individual differences in a population, the greater will be the benefit derived from using a within-subjects design rather than a between-subjects design. The greater sensitivity to the effects of the independent variable leads many researchers to prefer within-subjects designs to between-subjects designs when given the choice.

Another advantage is that within-subjects designs require fewer participants. For example, an independent-groups design that has 20 participants in each of three conditions will require 60 participants. Using a within-subjects design that has 20 participants per condition will require only 20 participants. In addition, because of its greater sensitivity, the within-subjects design might require even fewer participants per condition to achieve the same level of statistical power. For example, 14 participants in a within-subjects design might provide the same statistical power as 20 participants per condition in a between-subjects design. Reducing the sample size normally reduces statistical power, but the greater sensitivity of the within-subjects design will balance the loss of statistical power from using fewer participants.

There is yet another advantage of within-subjects designs that further increases efficiency. Because the same participants are tested under several conditions, instructions can be given once instead of at the beginning of each condition, or the instructions may require only slight modifications for each condition. For example, the participants in the target search study have the same task in each condition, so there is no need to repeat the instructions. If the instructions are complicated or if a practice period is part of the instructions, the time-savings can be considerable.

Although within-subjects designs have many advantages, they have one major disadvantage—confounding due to sequence effects, which you learned about in Chapter 8. Sequence effects are strongest when a treatment has a permanent or long-lasting effect on participants. Examples can be found in animal experimentation, when chemical or surgical changes are implemented, or in human experiments, when knowledge or attitudes are changed. A within-subjects design should not be used when the sequence effects are permanent or long lasting. Even if the effects are temporary, there is still the risk of sequence effects.

The ability to control sequence effects is the reason that the within-subjects design qualifies as an experimental design and the single-group, pretest-posttest design is a nonexperimental design. It is not possible to vary the order of presentation in the pretest-posttest design, because the pretest must always precede the treatment and the posttest must always follow the treatment. Therefore, the pretest-posttest design fails to control many sources of confounding. Redesigning it into a pretest-posttest, control group design—that is, adding a separate control group—would solve that problem.

In summary, the within-subjects design is a correlated-groups design in which each participant is tested under each condition. Its major strength is that it equates groups prior to the experimental manipulation and is therefore more sensitive to the effects of the independent variable. Using the same participants in each condition eliminates the single largest contributing factor to error variance—individual differences.

The greater sensitivity of the within-subjects design leads many researchers to prefer it to between-subjects designs. The major disadvantage of this design is sequence effects, which can be controlled by varying the order of presentation of conditions provided the carryover effects are not too strong. The within-subjects design is not recommended if very strong carryover effects are anticipated.

The Student Resource Website presents several examples of within-subjects designs drawn
11:06 from the published research literature.

Quick-Check Review 11.1: Within-Subjects Designs

1. What are correlated-groups designs?
2. What is the major potential confounding factor in within-subjects designs, and how can researchers control it?
3. How do within-subjects designs reduce error variance?
4. What are the strengths and weaknesses of within-subjects designs?
5. What is complete counterbalancing?

MATCHED-SUBJECTS DESIGNS

Matched-subjects designs have many of the strengths of within-subjects designs, as well as some advantages of their own. Instead of using each participant as his or her own control by testing each participant under all conditions, the matched-subjects design uses different participants in each condition, but closely matches the participants before assigning them to conditions. This process of matching before assignment to conditions is referred to as *matched random assignment* (see Chapter 9). The characteristics of matched-subjects designs are the following:

1. Each participant is exposed to only one level of the independent variable.
2. Each participant has a matched participant in each of the other conditions so that the groups are correlated.
3. The analysis takes into account which participants are matched with which other participants.
4. The critical comparison is the difference between the correlated groups, in which the matching procedure creates the correlation.

Although matched-subjects designs are used infrequently, they are valuable. They are most likely to be used when the cost of the study per participant is very high but a within-subjects design is inappropriate because large sequence effects are expected. In such a case, matching increases the sensitivity and statistical power of the study without adding extensively to the cost.

Using Matched-Subjects Designs

Why Use Matched-Subjects Designs. Matched-subjects designs are used when researchers want to take advantage of the greater sensitivity of within-subjects designs, but cannot use, or prefer not to use, a within-subjects design. Matched-subjects designs are most often used when exposure to one condition causes long-term changes in participants, making it impossible for participants to appear in the other conditions. For example, when physiological studies on animals use surgical procedures, the procedures permanently alter the animal, making it impossible to use the animal in another condition.

Another example involves learning. Suppose that the U.S. Air Force wanted to compare two methods of teaching map reading to its navigation students. If one group of participants was successfully taught map reading using method A, then these participants could not be used for testing the effectiveness of method B. A separate group of participants would have to be trained using method B, and then the researcher would compare the two groups. These are examples of extreme forms of carryover effects. Within-subjects designs do not work well when such extreme carryover effects exist.

Another situation in which it would be wise to avoid a within-subjects design is when the demands on participants' time in each condition are excessive, so that it is unreasonable to ask participants to be tested under all conditions. In addition, in some experiments, testing participants under all conditions might allow the participants to discern the study's hypothesis, and thus influence the results through expectancy effects and/or demand characteristics (see Chapter 8). In that case, it is wise to avoid a within-subjects design.

To avoid these problems of within-subjects designs, researchers can choose an independent-groups design and randomly assign participants to each of the various experimental conditions. An independent-groups design relies on chance to equate the groups. It is not as sensitive to small effects of the independent variable as is a correlated-groups design, because statistical tests must take into account the possibility that independent groups of participants may not be equal on the dependent measure before the study begins. Matched-subjects designs provide a solution to this problem; they make it more likely that the groups are equivalent at the beginning of the study by explicitly matching on relevant variables.

Identifying Matching Variables. How do you match participants for a matched-subjects design? You want to match participants on relevant variables, but which variables are relevant? In a within-subjects design, this question is immaterial because each participant serves as his or her own control—that is, the participants in all conditions are the same and therefore are matched on all variables.

Many factors that differentiate one person from another may be irrelevant for a particular study. For example, eye color may be a relevant variable if you are studying ways of increasing attractiveness, but is probably irrelevant if you are studying visual acuity. *A variable is relevant if it is likely to have an effect on the dependent variable in a study*. Participants' eye color may influence the ratings of their attractiveness, but should not influence how well they see.

The more powerful the effect of a variable on the dependent variable, the more important it is to match participants on this variable to assure comparable groups. To use a matched-subjects design effectively, you must identify the relevant variables and match the groups participant by participant on these variables.

This principle for identifying relevant matching variables is similar to an issue we discussed in Chapter 7—confounding in differential research. In that case, confounding could occur only if (1) the potential confounding variable correlates with the dependent measure, and (2) there is a difference between the groups on the potential confounding variable. Variables that correlate with the dependent measure are often problematic in research and therefore require some type of control. Matched-subjects designs ensure that the groups do not differ on potential confounding variables by matching on those variables.

The Process of Matching. The procedure for matching participants and assigning them to groups was described in Chapter 9 in the discussion of matched random assignment. In that example, participants were matched on years of work experience. We then divided them into pairs by selecting the two with the longest work experience, then the two with the next longest work experience, and so on. Finally, we randomly assigned one member of each pair to one of the two groups and automatically assigned his or her partner to the other group. The result was two groups of participants matched on the variable of length of work experience.

It is legitimate during the pairing process to exclude participants for whom a close match is not available. For example, one employee may have worked at a job much longer than anyone else. This employee would be so different from the others that there would be no suitable match, and so this employee would be excluded from the study.

It is possible to extend matching to three or more conditions by matching in sets of three or more participants. The members of the set are then randomly assigned to conditions, one per condition. Of course, increasing the number of experimental conditions to which we want to assign matched participants will also increase the likelihood that potential participants will have to be excluded because enough close matches cannot be found for them.

One can extend the matching procedure to matching on more than one variable. Matching on gender and years of work experience of the participants, for example, is only slightly more complicated than matching on work experience alone, because one of the matching variables (gender) has only two levels (male and female). We could pair participants on work experience, pairing the males only with other males and the females only with other females. Thus, participants in each pair would be similar to each other on both matching variables. We might lose a few more participants than before from the potential sample because appropriate matches could not be found, but the loss should not be too great.

A general rule of thumb is that matching on more than one continuous variable is difficult to accomplish and usually results in significant participant loss. For example, to match on age and IQ, we would order all the participants on one of the variables, such as age, and then divide the participants into small subgroups of narrow age ranges. Within each of these subgroups, we would then order on the second variable of IQ. Next, within each group, we would pair as many participants as possible using the criterion that both members of the pair must have similar IQs. There would probably be several people in each age group with no close IQ match, and they would have to be excluded from the potential sample.

Deciding on the Matching Variables. Now that you know how to match, how do you decide which variables to match? It is best to match on only one or two of the most important and significant variables. So, how do we find those variables?

Start by choosing variables that are strongly related to performance on the dependent measure(s). If age makes little difference in how participants perform on the dependent measure, it makes little sense to match participants on age. Because age does not affect the dependent measure, it cannot confound the results, just as it could not confound the results in differential research.

If you have several variables that could have strong effects on the dependent measure, matching on all of them simultaneously is unworkable. Instead, you should match on those variables that show the greatest variance in the population. The reason is that characteristics that are more variable in the population are more likely to show large mean differences by chance in randomly selected groups. You learned about this principle when we discussed sampling error and the factors that influence it. Therefore, *characteristics that show significant variability in the population should be given the highest priority when deciding on which variables to match in a matched-subjects design.*

For example, if college students are the participants, age is probably not an important variable on which to match, because there is little variability in age among college students, and a difference of 1 or 2 years makes little difference in students' behavior. However, when doing research with young children, age can be an extremely important variable. An age difference in children of even a few months can have major effects on their behavior. Therefore, matching on age is an important control in many research studies with children.

Although it can be difficult to identify the critical variables on which to match, in most cases the needed information is already available in published studies. These studies often report observed correlations of many potential confounding variables with their dependent measures. We noted earlier that correlational research is often included in other research studies to help explain the results or to see whether there might be confounding variables present. If you are using similar dependent measures in your study, these correlations will help you to decide on which variables to match.

Even with the information from past research, you are unlikely to identify all confounding variables for matching. Therefore, it is necessary to assign the matched set of participants randomly to conditions. Random assignment within sets will control for unidentified confounding variables.

We summarize some helpful rules for matching:

1. Match on only one or two of the most important and significant variables.
2. Choose variables that are strongly related to performance on the dependent measure.
3. Match on variables that show the greatest variance in the population.
4. Search the literature to identify appropriate variables for matching.
5. Randomly assign the matched set of participants to conditions.

Analyzing Data from Matched-Subjects Designs

Analyzing data from a matched-subjects design is no more complicated than analyzing data from a within-subjects design. The key is to maintain the ordering of data from the matching of participants at the beginning of the study through the analysis of data at the end. In a within-subjects design, the scores from each condition for a given participant are put on the same line, as shown in Table 11.1. In a matched-subjects design, the scores on a given line represent the scores of different participants tested under different conditions, but all the participants in a given line have been specifically matched with the other participants on that line.

We will illustrate this process using the matched participants from Table 9.6. To refresh your memory, we were interested in evaluating the effectiveness of a motor skills training program for high-tech-assembly workers in an electronic plant. Previous research indicated that experience was highly correlated with job performance in such a setting, so we decided to match our participants on years of experience. We ordered our 12 workers by years of experience and broke them into pairs based on this variable. We then assigned one member of the pair to group 1 (our experimental group) and the other member was automatically assigned to group 2 (our control group). The result was two groups of six workers in each group, with an average of 9.86 and 9.60 years of work experience, respectively.

Table 11.3 shows those 12 workers by name, with the pair on each line matched on years of experience. Also in Table 11.3 are hypothetical performance data (a posttest measure) for the study.

TABLE 11.3 Data on Output Performance Using Groups Matched on Years of Work Experience

These were the matched groups from Table 9.7. To see how these groups were formed, refer back to Chapter 9. The trick to analyzing the matched data is to keep the pairs together for the analyses and to treat the scores from these matched subjects as if they came from a single subject.

EXPERIMENTAL GROUP		CONTROL GROUP	
Name	**Output**	**Name**	**Output**
Jones	87.3	Smith	84.3
Franks	85.9	Ordell	84.0
Collucci	78.8	Samuels	80.1
Kling	80.2	Spero	76.6
Ruiz	79.2	Barker	77.5
Stanton	77.8	Harringer	76.2
Mean Output	**81.53**		**79.78**

Once the data are organized, we analyze them as if all the scores on a given line came from the same participant, instead of from matched participants. Either the repeated-measures ANOVA or the matched-pairs *t*-test (which can be used only if there are two conditions) is used to determine whether the observed mean differences between groups are large enough to infer that real differences exist in the populations; that is, are the differences statistically significant? Note that the mean difference in performance in those two groups is 1.75 points (81.53 – 79.78). That may not seem very large, but even with this small sample of six pairs of subjects (remember that statistical power increases as sample size increases, as you learned in the Understanding the Concept box on statistical power in Chapter 10), that difference is right on the edge of being statistically significant.

If we have carefully matched the participants on relevant variable(s), then the scores for each pair on the dependent measures should be correlated with one another. The correlation, like the inferential statistic, is computed by acting as if the two scores on each line came from a single individual. In this case, the correlation is substantial (+.91), reflecting the fact that the performance of these matched pairs are indeed correlated. These computational procedures for matched-subjects

11:07 designs are discussed in more detail on the Student Resource Website.

Strengths and Weaknesses of Matched-Subjects Designs

Matched-subjects designs have strengths similar to those of within-subjects designs, but have different weaknesses. Both types of design have greater sensitivity to small differences between conditions than do between-subjects designs. Whereas between-subjects designs rely on chance to equate groups, correlated-groups designs use assignment procedures that almost guarantee that groups are equivalent. If we are sure that the groups are equivalent before the study begins, then we do not need large differences after the manipulation to convince us that the independent variable has had an effect. In our earlier example, a difference of about 2% was sufficient to reach statistical significance.

Because matched- and within-subjects designs have greater sensitivity, the researcher can use a smaller number of participants and still be confident about detecting population differences if differences exist. For example, for three conditions with 20 participants in each condition, a between-subjects design will require 60 participants. However, because of the greater sensitivity of the matched-subjects design, we may need only 16 matched participants in each condition to test the null hypothesis with the same confidence that we would have using 20 participants in each condition in the between-subjects design. This is a direct consequence of the increased statistical power or sensitivity of the designs; we can safely reduce the sample size because the design provides a balancing increase in sensitivity.

Another advantage of the matched-subjects design over the within-subjects design is that there are no problems of practice and carryover effects. Therefore, counterbalancing is unnecessary.

However, there are disadvantages to using a matched-subjects design. One is that it requires extra work. The researcher must decide on what variable(s) to match and must obtain measures of this variable from all potential participants. The matching process is tedious, especially when matching on more than one variable. Matching participants in sets can eliminate many potential participants because suitable matches cannot be found for them. We may need to pretest a large sample of participants on the matching variables to obtain a modest sample of matched participants. It may be more efficient to use larger sample sizes in a between-subjects design.

Because matching participants is such a tedious and time-consuming task, it tends to be used only when the cost of evaluating participants is very high. For example, many brain imaging studies cost thousands of dollars per scan, and some research studies require multiple scans. When it costs that much for every participant, adding a few more participants to increase power becomes prohibitively expensive. Matching can increase power without requiring the inclusion of more people in the study.

One final point: matching can also be used in nonexperimental designs, such as differential research. We noted in Chapter 7 how matching can help to control confounding variables in differential designs. Matching can also increase power and sensitivity in such designs. Again, matching tends to be used when the cost of testing more people is expensive. For example, in a study of the genetic influence on schizophrenia, Kety et al. (1968) matched a group of people who were adopted at birth and later developed schizophrenia with a group of people who were adopted at birth but never developed schizophrenia. They matched these groups on nearly a dozen variables (e.g., social class and education of biological and adoptive parents, age at adoption). For each participant in their study, they tracked down all the biological and adoptive relatives and found their medical records in order to determine how many of those relatives had developed schizophrenia. This was a monumentally expensive and complicated procedure at a time when medical, birth, death, and adoption records were not computerized. They literally had to travel all over Denmark (where the study was conducted) to obtain the necessary records. The matching enhanced statistical power and therefore allowed them to use a much smaller sample, saving hundreds of thousands of research dollars. They found that only the biological relatives of individuals who developed schizophrenia showed an increased risk for schizophrenia, suggesting that genes heavily influenced risk for schizophrenia.

In summary, a matched-subjects design increases sensitivity in situations in which a within-subjects design is inappropriate because large carryover effects are expected. Matched-subjects

designs have many of the advantages of within-subjects designs while avoiding the problem of sequence effects. The Student Resource Website presents several examples of matched-subjects
11:08 designs drawn from the research literature.

Quick-Check Review 11.2: Matched-Subjects Designs

1. What major confounding factor found in within-subjects designs is avoided by using matched-subjects designs?
2. What are the characteristics of matched-subjects designs?
3. Under what conditions would we use matched-subjects designs?
4. What are the disadvantages of using matched-subjects designs?

SINGLE-SUBJECT EXPERIMENTAL DESIGNS

Single-subject (or ***N*-of-one**) **experimental designs** are extensions of within-subject designs because each participant appears in each condition of the experiment. They are also variations on **time-series designs** (discussed in Chapter 13), in which repeated measurements are taken over time and manipulations are performed at different points along the time sequence. Single-subject experimental designs have become highly developed alternatives to more traditional group designs. For example, behavior modification researchers routinely use them to evaluate treatment effects (Barlow et al., 2009). They also have played an extensive role in understanding the functioning of the human brain, as illustrated in the Historical Lesson 11.1.

HISTORICAL LESSON 11.1: NEUROPSYCHOLOGY CASES

Neuropsychology is a field that relates the state of the brain to behavior (Saucier & Elias, 2006). This field has advanced dramatically in the last century, often by groundbreaking research involving unusual cases.

One of the most famous cases was Phineas Gage, a railroad construction supervisor who lived in Vermont over a century ago. While using a metal bar to pack explosives into a hole, he accidentally set off the explosives, turning the bar into a deadly projectile that ripped through his left cheek and blew off the top of his skull, taking his left eye and a good portion of his brain in the process. Miraculously, Gage survived, but the accident left him a changed person.

You might think that having a sizable portion of your brain ripped out of your head would leave you a vegetable, but the changes in Gage were more subtle. He went from being a responsible, caring person to one who had little self-control, used profanity constantly, and had little regard for the welfare of others. He had been organized and disciplined, but after the accident, he became disorganized and was unable to complete even routine tasks. Formerly a decisive leader, he could no longer make simple decisions. These and other changes in his behavior and personality gave early neuropsychologists some excellent clues about what role the parts of the brain damaged in Gage's accident played in human behavior.

Another well-known case study in the neuropsychological literature is known by the person's initials: H.M. H.M.'s memory problems developed following surgery to remove brain tissue that was triggering overwhelming seizures. The surgery controlled

(continued)

HISTORICAL LESSON 11.1: CONTINUED

H.M.'s seizures, but had a devastating side effect: H.M. could no longer form new memories, although his old memories were intact. Because H.M. could not form new memories, each time one of his doctors stopped by, H.M. would introduce himself, apparently completely unaware that he had met the doctor many times before.

To test whether H.M could remember anything about his daily encounters, one of his doctors hid a pin in his hand and poked H.M. with it while shaking hands. The next day, H.M. again did not recognize the doctor and started to introduce himself as usual, but H.M. pulled back his hand when the doctor reached out to shake it (Hugdahl, 1995).

What was going on? Was H.M. faking his memory problem, and was this doctor able to unmask that effort with his hidden pin? Not at all. H.M. really did have no memory of his encounters with each of his doctors. What this case study established is that a specific region of the brain (the hippocampus) is critical in forming memories of events. It also shows that there are different kinds of memories and that different brain regions are involved in forming each type of memory. Learning to avoid a painful pinprick is a different type of memory than remembering what you did yesterday, and it involves different brain regions. Those regions were not impaired in H.M., which explains how he could learn to avoid a pinprick without remembering the events that shaped that learning.

Dozens of such case histories in neuropsychology have provided extensive insights into brain functioning. Many cases have been studied for years by neuropsychologists using the single-subject designs discussed in this chapter.

Single-subject experimental designs should not be confused with the case studies discussed in Chapter 6. Case studies are used in clinical research for in-depth clinical *descriptions* of single individuals and *to generate (but not test) hypotheses.* An ex post facto case study is weak because the researcher does not control the independent variable(s); consequently, *alternative hypotheses cannot be ruled out.*

In single-subject, experimental designs, the researcher actually manipulates independent variables and observes their effects on dependent variables. The strength of these designs is in the control of independent variables, which reduces confounding and enhances internal validity. Thus, single-subject designs are experimental in nature and, therefore, can be used to test causal hypotheses.

Single-subject experimental designs are preferable to group comparisons in two situations: (1) evaluating change in a single participant, and (2) obtaining information that might otherwise be lost in a group comparison. Obviously, such designs are appropriate when there is only one participant, such as evaluating the effectiveness of a clinical treatment for a particular client, or determining whether a school program improves a particular child's academic performance. A single-subject experiment is weak in external validity because it includes only one participant. However, it does protect internal validity and provides valid and reliable information about a single individual.

Traditional group-comparison designs summarize a group's performance and, in the process, may lose important information about each individual's performance. For example, suppose that 20 phobic participants are pretested on the intensity of their fears and then randomly assigned to treatment and control conditions. After treatment, the treated group has a significantly lower mean fear score than the control group. Because this experimental design does an excellent job of controlling confounding, the researcher can conclude that the treatment was effective. However, closer examination might indicate that, on average, the treated group reported less fear than the control group, but there is considerable variability within each of the two groups. Additional inspection might show that, while most of the control participants did not improve, some did, and, while most of the treated participants improved, some did not and others deteriorated. Clearly, individuals responded differently to the same treatment. Although the treatment was effective on average, it might not be effective for some participants.

In the 1950s and 1960s, clinical research failed to support the effectiveness of traditional psychotherapy (Bergin & Strupp, 1970). However, closer inspection revealed that some clients improved, some deteriorated, and some remained the same. When taken as a group, the changes tended to cancel out each other. Obscured by group-comparison designs was the improvement of some clients. Sidman (1960) and Bergin and Strupp (1970) suggested studying the improved individuals (1) to determine whether the improvements were due to systematic effects of the treatment or to chance variation, and (2) to identify factors that apparently made psychotherapy effective for some people but not for others. Recognizing the problems of group designs, they argued for the development of experimental methods to study single individuals.

The intensive experimental study of individuals had a prominent place in early psychology for half a century, until the late 1930s, when psychologists began adopting new group-comparison research designs and statistical procedures (Morgan & Morgan, 2001). Sir Ronald Fisher's (1935) book, *The Design of Experiments*, introduced multi-subject, group-comparison designs and statistical procedures, and researchers soon followed Fisher's lead. However, B. F. Skinner (1904–1990) was an influential exception. Skinner (1979) and others continued to develop single-subject experimental designs for the **experimental analysis of behavior**, which were methods for the intensive, systematic, and controlled study of individual participants. New journals appeared (*Journal of the Experimental Analysis of Behavior*, 1958; *Behaviour Research and Therapy*, 1963; *Journal of Applied Behavior Analysis*, 1968; *Journal of Behavior Therapy and Experimental Psychiatry*, 1969; *Behavior Therapy*, 1970; *Behavior Modification*, 1974). The experimental analysis of single individuals became particularly important in clinical psychology, which is now heavily reliant on behavioral treatment methods.

In single-subject experiments, there is no control group. Instead, the researcher uses a controlled manipulation of the independent variable to demonstrate causality. This approach compares the participant's initial pretreatment behavior to his or her post-intervention behavior.

One can make a causal inference in single-subject experimental designs if (1) the person's behavior changes consistently in the predicted direction when the treatment is presented, and (2) we can rule out confounding factors. Several factors are critical in this evaluation, including operationally defining appropriate target behaviors, obtaining baseline measures, applying the treatment manipulation, and monitoring changes in behavior.

The first step is to operationally define the target behavior. For example, a smoking-cessation program might target the number of cigarettes smoked and the intensity of the person's craving for a cigarette. The researcher might measure the number of cigarettes smoked in each 24-hour period and obtain daily ratings from the person of his or her cravings. These may seem like straightforward decisions, but the research literature should be studied to find the best ways to measure these variables. For example, McFall (1970) found that asking people to monitor their own smoking by counting the number of cigarettes actually reduced the smoking from normal baseline measures, and participants were unaware of this behavioral change. That means that having people monitor their smoking is a reactive measure of amount of smoking. This is just one example of why it is so

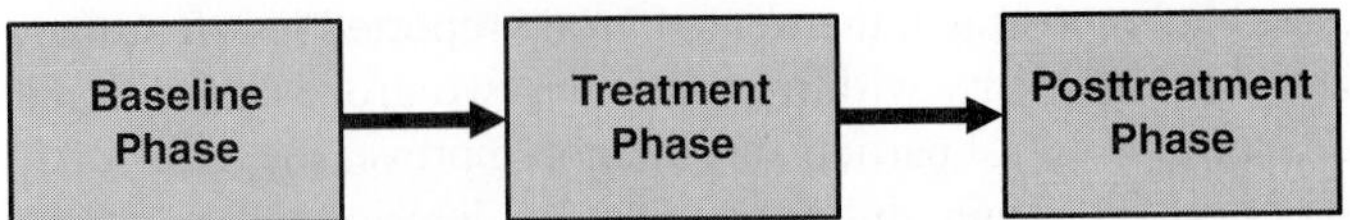

FIGURE 11.2 Single-Subject Experimental Designs. Single-subject experimental designs always include at least a baseline, treatment phase, and posttreatment assessment. In most cases, there are multiple measures taken in each of the phases.

critical to study the research literature on an issue before you try to design studies to investigate the issue.

After operationally defining target behaviors, the researcher selects a **baseline period**. The baseline period is the time from initial monitoring until the onset of the treatment manipulation. The duration of the baseline varies with the nature of the target behavior. Usually, several days or a week is long enough to establish that the target behavior is consistent and representative for the individual. During the baseline of a smoking-cessation study, the number of cigarettes smoked is recorded and the person rates his or her need to smoke at various points during each day.

It is important to avoid an unrepresentative baseline period, when the behavior is momentarily elevated or depressed. If there is a question of whether the baseline period is unrepresentative, it would be best to take a longer baseline period, which will allow the researcher to see the natural variation of the behavior over time.

With some targeted behaviors, it is best for the researcher to carry out the observations. With some participants, such as children and psychiatric patients, the researcher has no choice but to make the observations because the participants will be unable to record the behaviors accurately.

With these baseline data established, the actual treatment can begin. During the treatment phase, the targeted behaviors continue to be monitored and recorded. The treatment will be specific to the nature of the targeted behavior. The independent variable must also be clearly defined operationally. This sequence of a no-treatment baseline, followed by a treatment period and then by posttreatment measures, is the basic manipulation in single-subject experiments. The critical comparison is between the single participant's pretreatment and posttreatment scores on the target behavior. Figure 11.2 illustrates this basic paradigm. This is a time-series design, in which target behaviors (the dependent variable) of a single participant are measured several times before, during, and after the manipulation of the independent variable.

We will cover three variants of this basic paradigm in this section: ABA reversal designs; multiple-baseline designs; and single-subject, randomized, time-series designs. [See Barlow et al. (2009) and Di Noia and Tripodi (2007) for detailed discussions of single subject designs.]

ABA Reversal Design

The **ABA reversal design** evaluates the effects of an independent variable on a dependent variable by measuring the dependent variable several times, during which the treatment is applied and then removed. At a minimum, there is a no-treatment baseline period during which the target behavior is observed, a treatment period in which the manipulation is carried out, and a return or reversal to the no-treatment condition (the ABA design). However, in nearly all instances, the sequence ends with another treatment condition (the ABAB design).

The effect of the independent variable (the treatment) on the dependent variable (the behavior that we hope to change with the treatment) is demonstrated if the behavior changes in the predicted direction whenever the conditions are reversed.

The ABA reversal design is flexible in that it can evaluate treatment programs designed to either increase or decrease behaviors. For example, a common problem in children with mental retardation, autism, or brain injury is self-stimulatory behavior, and the clinical goal is to reduce it. In other situations, behaviors need to be increased. One could, for example, manipulate the attention of teachers to see if shifts in teachers' attention might increase positive behavior, such as attending to the teacher or focusing on the current assignment.

Anglesea et al. (2008) used the ABA reversal design to test a training program for three autistic teenagers with eating problems. Rapid eating is common among persons with developmental disabilities, such as autism. Unfortunately, it can create health problems like severe vomiting and choking. In addition, such behavior is socially unsightly and often stigmatizing for youngsters who already have severe social deficits. However, it is difficult to alter because rapid eating is inherently reinforced more immediately than is normal eating. Anglesea et al. (2008) used a vibrating pager that was hooked on each youngster's belt. The boys were trained to take bites (of snack foods) only when the pager vibrated. Once trained on the snack food, the youngsters' eating behavior of their usual lunches was measured—the time it took them to complete their standard lunch and the number of bites taken during their standard lunch. The measures were made under two conditions—when the pager prompt was absent (condition A) and when it was present (condition B).

Figure 11.3 shows both measures for each of the boys across the ABAB sequence. As can be seen, when the prompt was absent (condition A) the boys ate rapidly. When the prompt was present (condition B) their eating rate slowed. Introducing condition A again brought more rapid eating. Finally, returning to the B condition brought the eating rate down. Note that the number of bites remained the same throughout all conditions; this variable was unaffected by the manipulation. The only thing that was affected was the time between bites. The ABAB reversal design clearly demonstrated that the abnormal rapid eating of the youngsters had come under the control of the prompt (the pager).

Why was the last treatment condition included? The behavior under the B condition was preferable to the behavior under the A condition. Once the effect of the independent variable on the dependent variable has been demonstrated, the researcher has an ethical obligation to use that effect to return participants to the best possible situation.

Although the ABA reversal design is a powerful demonstration of the effects of one variable on another, there are situations in which reversal procedures are not feasible or ethical. For example, suppose that the baseline behavior of a child is injurious or that the researcher succeeds in improving the academic performance of a child in school. In both cases, it is unreasonable to reverse conditions once we have achieved improved functioning. For the first child, a return to baseline could risk injury; for the second, it could disrupt academic performance. Thus, the reversal design might be unacceptable.

The other situation in which the ABA reversal design is problematic is when the treatment creates a long-lasting change. For example, a pain reliever might well end a headache, but you would not expect the headache to come back just because the person stopped taking the pain reliever. On the other hand, pain immediately following major surgery might well come back as soon as the pain medication is withdrawn. A principle in the behavioral treatment of many conditions is that once a change occurs, natural reinforcers will maintain the change (Hartmann & Atkinson,

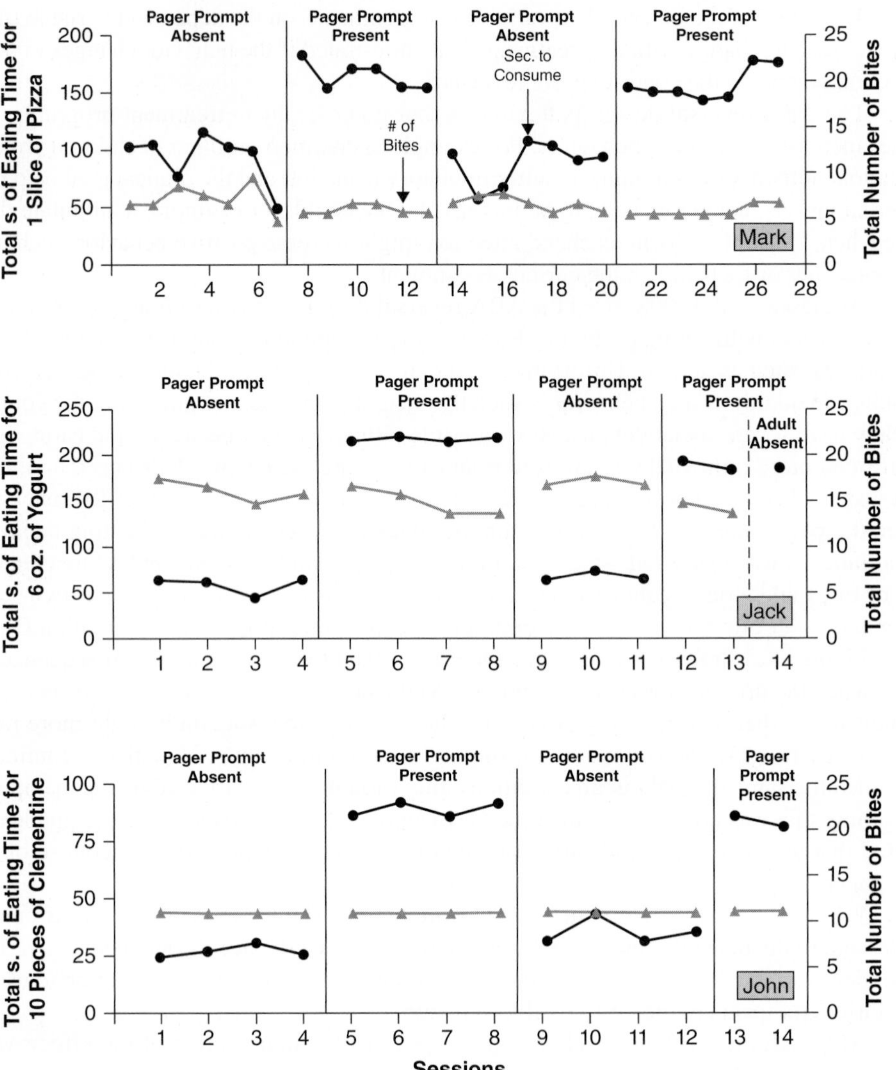

FIGURE 11.3 An Example of a Reversal Design. Anglesea et al. (2008) used an ABAB design with three boys diagnosed with autism to control the pace of eating. Rapid eating is common in such children and it has both health and social consequences. For each child, a vibrating pager prompt was effective at slowing the pace of eating to normal level, with the rapid eating returning as soon as the pager treatment was withdrawn.

Source: Anglesea et al. (2008)

1973). For example, successfully treating a fear of driving would allow the client to do hundreds of enjoyable things that were impossible when the person could not drive, and those enjoyable things reinforce the new behavior of driving. If such natural reinforcers exist, one would not expect the target behavior to return after successful treatment, and therefore another research approach, such as a multiple-baseline design, is needed.

Multiple-Baseline Design

In a **multiple-baseline design**, the effects of the treatment are demonstrated on different behaviors successively. To illustrate, suppose that a fifth-grade boy is doing poorly in math and reading, although he appears to have the ability to achieve at a high level. He is also disruptive and inattentive in class. A psychologist observes the class and sees that whenever the boy acts up, the teacher scolds, corrects, and lectures him in front of the class in an effort to embarrass him. The boy seems to accept the attention with a good deal of pleasure. However, on the rare occasions when he does his academic work, the teacher ignores him. "When he is working, I leave well enough alone," the teacher says. "I don't want to risk stirring him up."

Based on these observed contingencies, the psychologist hypothesizes that the teacher's attention to the boy's disruptive behavior may be a major factor in maintaining this behavior, whereas the teacher's failure to attend to the boy's good academic work may help to account for its low occurrence. The psychologist sets up a multiple-baseline design to test the hypothesis about the importance of teacher attention on both disruptive and positive academic behavior. The independent variable is teacher attention, and the dependent variables are the child's (1) disruptive behavior, (2) math performance, and (3) reading performance. The independent variable is presented at two levels: presence of contingent teacher attention and absence of contingent teacher attention.

Figure 11.4 shows the sequence of phases of the hypothetical study. During baseline, the psychologist measures all three dependent variables, while the teacher continues the usual procedure of trying to punish the disruption and ignore academic behavior. Disruptive behavior is high and math and reading performance are low in this phase. Starting on the sixth day, the teacher's attention to disruptive behavior (punishment) is withdrawn and disruptive behavior is ignored. No change is made in the teacher's behavior for academic performance. However, starting on the ninth day, the teacher focuses on rewarding math performance while both disruptive behavior and reading are ignored. Finally, starting on the eleventh day, the teacher begins to reward reading performance with her attention. The manipulation of teacher attention is applied to each of these variables, but it is applied starting at different times. The pattern of changes in the dependent variables during these manipulations provides evidence for the validity of the hypothesis that contingent teacher attention is an important controlling factor in this child's behavior.

There are three variations of the multiple-baseline design (Barlow et al., 2009).

- **Across behaviors:** In this variation, the researcher studies different behaviors of the same individual, as in the example above.
- **Across individuals:** In this variation, the researcher studies the same behavior in different people, and the same treatment manipulations are applied to test whether the treatment procedure is effective for different individuals.
- **Across settings and time:** In this variation, the researcher applies a treatment to a behavior for one individual in different settings or times. For example, we might want to know if a treatment that is effective in the classroom is also effective at home.

Single-Subject, Randomized, Time-Series Design

A **single-subject, randomized, time-series design** is a time-series design for a single participant with one additional element: the point at which the treatment begins is determined randomly. Time-series designs involve measuring a dependent variable several times over a long period, with an experimental intervention occurring at a selected point during the observations.

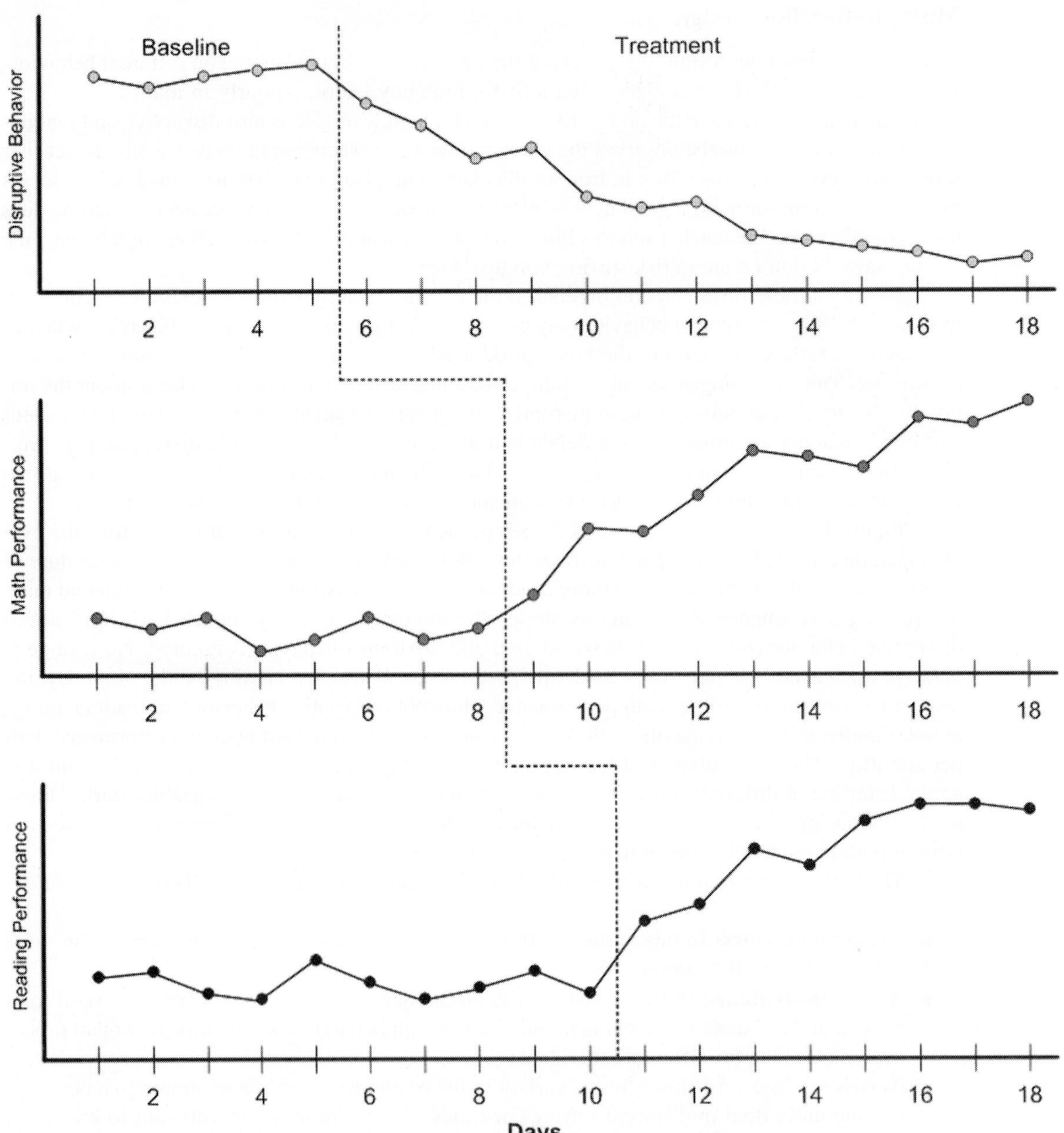

FIGURE 11.4 An Example of a Multiple-Baseline Design. This figure shows hypothetical results of a multiple-baseline design study in which contingent teacher attention decreases disruptive behavior and improves math and reading performance. The dashed vertical lines indicate when teacher attention was manipulated for each of the target behaviors.

CARTOON 11.1 One problem with using a token economy system with your kids is that the kids start to get possessive with their tokens. However, token economies are often effective in improving behavior in both children and adults.

To illustrate the single-subject, randomized, time-series design, suppose that Joey does not complete his work in school. During the 15-minute lesson periods, Joey looks around the room or closes his eyes and does no work. Frequent reminders by the teacher rouse him briefly, but are not enough for him to complete the lessons. The teacher believes that Joey has the skills to do the academic work. How can the teacher help him?

An effective motivational intervention for children is a reinforcement system in which the child receives tokens for desired behaviors. The child can accumulate tokens and spend them for desired items and privileges. The tokens are reinforcements that strengthen the rewarded behavior. If a single-subject, randomized, time-series design is employed, the child's arithmetic achievement might be monitored for 6 weeks (30 school days), which would yield a time graph of 30 measurements. A minimum number of days, perhaps the first 5 and the last 5 (1–5 and 26–30), are devoted to pretreatment and posttreatment measures of arithmetic achievement. This ensures adequate pretreatment and posttreatment measures. Using a table of random numbers, the researcher randomly selects a day between 6 and 25 as the point for introducing the token reinforcement system, and the tenth day is randomly selected. The teacher measures arithmetic performance for 9 days under the usual no-token condition, with the intervention started on the tenth day. The teacher monitors the student's performance for the next 21 days under the token reinforcement condition.

If there is a marked improvement in arithmetic achievement coincident with the randomly selected tenth measurement, as shown in Figure 11.5, we would have convincing evidence of the

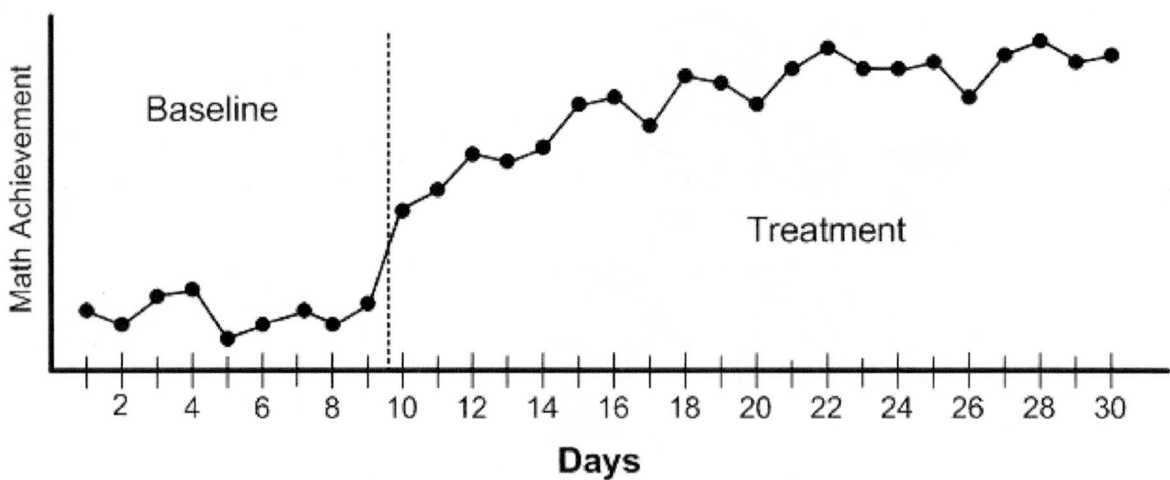

FIGURE 11.5 An Example of a Single-Subject, Randomized, Time-Series Design. This figure shows hypothetical results of a single-subject, randomized, time-series design in which a token economy was effective in improving math performance for this child.

effects of the token system. It is unlikely that such marked improvement would occur by chance at exactly the point at which the *randomly* introduced treatment occurs. It is also unlikely that this particular time-series pattern would be due to maturation, history, or any other confounding variable. (Do you know why?)

Replication in Single-Subject Designs

Our confidence in research findings is strengthened by replication. Replication in single-subject experiments addresses questions about generalization across time, persons, conditions, and target behaviors:

1. **Generalizing across time:** If we repeat the treatment with the same person, will we get the same results each time?
2. **Generalizing across persons:** Will the treatment be effective with other people who have the same problem?
3. **Generalizing across conditions:** Will the treatment be effective under other conditions, such as different therapists or treatment sites?
4. **Generalizing across target behaviors:** Will the treatment be effective for different behavior problems?

These questions about generalization have been studied by using direct replication, systematic replication, and clinical replication. **Single-subject direct replication** means repeating the experiment with the same participant or a series of participants who have the same behavioral issue. For example, in an ABA procedure, each reversal to baseline followed by treatment represents a direct replication.

Single-subject systematic replication carries out the testing still further. Now that we know the procedure works for a particular behavioral issue, we expand the replication by carrying out a series of single-subject experiments with different people in different settings and with new target behaviors. These experiments establish the procedure's effectiveness and reliability for a series of persons with different target behaviors. It is likely that such systematic replication will reveal the limits of generalization, with some interventions working for almost every situation, person, and time, but other interventions effective for only some situations, individuals, or times.

Single-subject clinical replication goes still further. The direct and systematic replications test the effectiveness of one treatment at a time on specific target behaviors. In actual clinical treatment, however, therapists create and test complex treatment packages for multiple problem behaviors using single-subject clinical replication. This involves an integrated treatment package of two or more procedures applied to several people and different clinical disorders. For example, the clients might be adults with depression, and the targeted behaviors might be negative mood expression, low level of physical activity, and social isolation. The treatment package might consist of medication, cognitive therapy, increased physical activity, and graduated desensitization to social activity.

In summary,

1. direct replication establishes the reliability and effectiveness of a single treatment for a single target behavior.
2. systematic replication then establishes the reliability and effectiveness of the treatment with other persons, in other settings, and for other target behaviors (and/or other clinical problems).
3. clinical replication combines two or more treatment elements into a treatment package and tests its reliability and effectiveness for multiple related behaviors, for a succession of clients, and if needed, across different settings. For a more detailed discussion, see Barlow et al. (2009) or Sidman (1960).

Single-subject designs are extensions of within-subjects designs. These designs are usually variations on time-series designs, in which repeated measurements are taken over time and manipulations are performed at different points. Single-subject designs provide alternatives to some traditional designs. They are especially useful in the evaluation of clinical and educational interventions and are used often in research on behavior modification. The Student Resource Website presents several examples of single-subjects designs drawn from the research literature.

11:09

Quick-Check Review 11.3: Single-Subject Experimental Designs

1. What are single-subject designs? For what are they used?
2. How do single-subject experiments differ from the single-case studies?
3. How is internal validity protected in single-subject experiments?
4. Describe reversal; multiple-baseline; and randomized, time-series designs.
5. What are the major strengths and weaknesses of single-subject designs?
6. Why is external validity weak in a single-subject design?
7. What are the major ways of replicating single-subject designs?
8. Explain how causality is determined in single-subject designs.

ETHICAL PRINCIPLES

The single-subject designs discussed in this chapter are particularly useful in clinical and educational settings to evaluate treatment programs. The research questions focus on whether a particular medication, teaching method, or psychological treatment is effective for a given person. The researcher's goals are not only to determine the validity of an experimental manipulation but also to alleviate problems and improve functioning.

The participants are likely to hold more than an academic interest in the procedures and outcome. Indeed, many will have expectations of personally benefitting from the procedure. A basic principle in the APA's position on research ethics is that the psychologist *must do no harm*. When the research is in a clinical setting, that admonition is expanded with the expectation that we must also *do some good*, not only in some general contribution to science and humanity, but in the very specific case of a particular individual. The clinical researcher must not only see that no harm comes to the participants, but has the added ethical responsibility of trying to bring about some positive gain for the participants.

Kazdin (2001) points out that the broad ethical issues that apply here are not limited to psychologists, but apply to all health-related disciplines whenever interventions are used to ameliorate problems—education, medicine, nursing, psychiatry, psychology, and so on. All of those disciplines should have a shared respect for those ethical considerations.

In these research settings, the participant is also the client or patient, and while that does not significantly change the nature of ethical responsibility, it does add another dimension to it. For psychologists, the APA's ethical guidelines (American Psychological Association, 2002) apply here just as in any research. The psychologist must provide the participant or, in the case of minors, a parent or guardian with sufficient information to make a reasoned decision and to provide informed consent. If deception is involved, the psychologist must include a debriefing. If there is any risk of potential harm because of the research, the psychologist must take steps to prevent it.

Concern for the welfare of participants means that the psychologist is ethically bound to return to the treatment condition in the ABA reversal design if the treatment was effective. That is, the researcher has an ethical obligation to use the intervention to return participants to the best possible situation. An additional issue in clinical settings is consideration of the participant's condition—developmental, physical, or psychological—and whether special procedures are needed because of the participant's condition. For example, a fearful individual who has a heart condition may be put at risk with intensive exposure treatment, which is likely to raise the heart rate of the client substantially. The clinician may wish to work with the client's doctor or do the exposure more gradually to avoid excessive strain on the heart.

Quick-Check Review 11.4: Ethical Principles

1. What is the first principle in any treatment research? What is the second principle?

SUMMARY

- Correlated-groups designs include within-subjects, matched-subjects, and single-subject designs.
- In within-subjects and single-subjects designs, the same participants appear in all conditions.
- In matched-subjects designs, different participants appear in each condition, but the participants in each condition are matched with the other participants in the other conditions on one or more relevant variables.
- These correlated-groups designs have greater sensitivity to group differences than do between-groups designs.
- A potential confounding problem in within-subjects designs is that of sequence effects.
- Counterbalancing is a control for sequencing effects.
- Single-subject designs are extensions of within-subjects designs.
- Single-subject designs are particularly useful in the evaluation of clinical and educational intervention for individuals.
- The most commonly used single-subject designs are the reversal design; the multiple-baseline design; and the single-subject, randomized, time-series design.
- The first principle in treatment research is to "do no harm," but such research also has an ethical obligation to at least try to do some good.

PUTTING IT INTO PRACTICE

You may not have realized this, but you have been conducting single-subject experiments much of your life, although you have not been doing them with the precision and formal data collection procedures described here. We would like you to plan and carry out a single-subject experiment focusing on shaping a particular behavior using reinforcement. It might be a practical behavior, such as having your roommate clean the kitchen after using it. It might be an impractical behavior. Students sometimes get together to see how much their professor can be influenced by reinforcement. They decide in advance, for example, that they will pay closer attention and be more responsive whenever the professor moves away from the podium. A class working together can shape a variety of such behaviors, usually without the professor even picking up on what is happening.

Whatever study you decide to do, do it formally. Identify the independent and dependent measures and decide how you will manipulate and/or measure them. Record the data systematically, and see whether your findings suggest a causal connection between your independent and dependent variables.

EXERCISES

11.1. Define the following key terms. Be sure that you understand them. They are discussed in the chapter and defined in the glossary.

repeated-measures design	negative practice effect	counterbalancing
practice effects	carryover effects	complete counterbalancing
positive practice effect	random order of presentation	partial counterbalancing

Latin square design
randomized within blocks
repeated-measures ANOVA
between-conditions sum of squares
between sum of squares
subjects term
single-subject experimental designs
N-of-one designs
time-series designs
neuropsychology
experimental analysis of behavior
baseline period
ABA reversal designs
multiple-baseline design
single-subject, randomized, time-series design
single-subject direct replication
single-subject systematic replication
single-subject clinical replication

11.2. You are the teaching assistant in an introductory research methods course. Explain the particular strength of correlated-groups designs to the students.

11.3. What does it mean when we say "within-subjects designs are experiments that are run on a single group of participants"? How can this statement be reconciled with the requirement that the independent variable must be present at more than one level in experiments?

11.4. Can ANOVA be used to test a null hypothesis in a within-subjects design? If so, are there any special steps that must be taken?

11.5. You have 50 participants to assign to two groups of 25 participants each. Using the table of random numbers or a random-number generator, randomly assign the participants to the two conditions.

11.6. Now assume you have 50 more participants to assign to two groups, but the 50 participants are matched in pairs on IQ. Designate the first pair as participants A_1 and A_2, the second pair as B_1 and B_2, and so on. Use the table of random numbers to assign the pairs to the two groups.

11.7. In counterbalancing, how many possible orders of presentation are there in an experiment with three conditions? five conditions? six conditions? Is counterbalancing feasible with a large number of conditions?

CHAPTER TWELVE

FACTORIAL DESIGNS

In the discovery of secret things and in the investigation of hidden causes, stronger reasons are obtained from sure experiments and demonstrated arguments than from probable conjectures and the opinions of philosophical speculators of the common sort.

—William Gilbert, *De Magnete*, 1600

WEB RESOURCE MATERIAL

The designs discussed in Chapters 10 and 11 have only one independent variable. However, many designs, called **factorial designs**, include multiple independent variables. Factorial designs are particularly valuable because they allow us to study the interactive effects of independent variables on the dependent variable.

FACTORIAL DESIGNS

Suppose that you are developing a treatment program for children who are afraid of the dark. By interviewing children and parents, you learn that the children's fearfulness varies considerably from one night to another. When fearful, the children have difficulty sleeping and they disrupt the entire family. Thus, it appears that, although the children's fears are related to darkness, a condition common to all nights, other variables are also operating.

In further interviews, many of the children report vivid and frightening images of monsters, ghosts, vampires, and burglars when they are in bed and alone in the dark. Can it be that darkness is a necessary, but not a sufficient, condition for fearfulness, and that a combination of being in the dark and having fearful images is what triggers the fear? Perhaps darkness alone, or fearful images alone, may not be sufficient to cause the fear, but the combination of the two is sufficient.

The question about the two variables having effects when they are in combination is a question about their interaction. Our behavior is multiply determined. It is rarely determined by a single variable; instead, it is determined by several factors operating in sequence or simultaneously. Moreover, these factors may interact. An **interaction effect** occurs when the effect of one independent variable differs depending on the level of another independent variable. An interactive effect is greater than simply summing the effects of the variables; it is an enhancement. In our example, the effect of fearful images on the children may be different and more dramatic when the room is dark than when the room is lighted.

The interaction is the single most important issue in factorial research. Consider this example: Accident researchers know that driving faster increases the risk of an accident. The speed at which people drive (the independent variable) has a predictable effect on the accident rate (the dependent variable). Researchers also find that the more slippery the road, the higher the accident rate. Of course, if people drive fast on slippery roads, we would expect an even higher rate of accidents because both risk factors are present. However, this is not necessarily an interaction.

We would say there is an interaction effect only if the increase in the accident rate is more than would be expected if the independent effects of the two risk factors were simply added together. For example, if driving 20 miles per hour faster doubles the risk of accidents, and driving on a slick road triples the rate of accidents, then the additive effects of these two variables might suggest a six-fold increase in accident rates (doubled for driving fast, then tripled for driving on slick surfaces). If, however, we find that driving 20 miles per hour faster on a slick surface increases the accident rate 15 fold, we clearly are getting more than just the additive effects of these two risk factors. We have an interaction, in which the effect of faster driving is greater on slick roads than on dry roads. Driving speed probably interacts with many variables, such as road surface, traffic, the driver's alcohol consumption, and the driver's age. The effect of increased driving speed differs depending on the presence of one or more of these other variables.

In our hypothetical fear-of-the-dark research, we can use a factorial design to study the two independent variables and their interaction (illumination and frightening images). The independent variables in a factorial design are called **factors**. In this experiment, we measure the dependent variable, the children's fear, by measuring heart rate, which has been shown in previous research to reflect fear arousal. We would measure heart rate under two conditions of illumination (lighted condition and dark condition) and two conditions of visual images (fear and neutral images). That is, factor A (illumination) is presented at two levels, and factor B (images) is presented at two levels. The two independent variables, each presented at two levels, produce four treatment combinations, called a **matrix of cells**. The result is a 2×2 (read "two-by-two") factorial design, as shown in Table 12.1.

The **design notation** for factorial studies (e.g., 2×2) shows how many independent variables and how many levels of each variable are included. Each number in the notation represents one independent variable (factor) and denotes the number of levels of that variable. Thus, the notation "3×3" indicates that the design has two independent variables, with three levels of

TABLE 12.1 A 2 × 2 Factorial

	FACTOR A (ILLUMINATION)	
FACTOR B (IMAGES)	**Level A_1 (lighted condition)**	**Level A_2 (dark condition)**
Level B_1 (fearful images)	A_1B_1	A_2B_1
Level B_2 (neutral images)	A_1B_2	A_2B_2

each variable. The notation "2 × 3 × 2" indicates that the design has three independent variables with two levels of factor A, three levels of factor B, and two levels of factor C. (Note that factors are traditionally labeled with capital letters: A, B, C … .) More complex designs produce more cells, require more participants, and are more difficult to interpret. Any number of factors and levels can theoretically be combined in a factorial design, but there are practical limits to the complexity of these designs.

Main Effects and Interactions

A factorial design tests two types of hypotheses: (1) hypotheses about the impact of each independent variable on the dependent variable (**main effects**), and (2) hypotheses about the effects of combinations of independent variables on the dependent variable (interactions). Like single-variable designs, factorial designs can be arranged as between- or within-subjects designs. We will consider first the between-subjects factorial designs, in which the researcher assigns a different group of participants to each cell. The researcher then tests each participant and computes the mean of the scores for each group.

Table 12.2 shows the 2 × 2 matrix for our hypothetical children's dark-fears study and the four groups formed by these factors. The table includes a mean heart rate for the participants in each cell, as well as the row and column means for each variable.

TABLE 12.2 A Hypothetical 2 × 2 Factorial Design

This hypothetical study includes two factors believed to affect children's night fears. Factor A is the level of illumination, and factor B is the type of images.

	FACTOR A (ILLUMINATION)		
FACTOR B (IMAGES)	**Level A_1 (lighted condition)**	**Level A_2 (dark condition)**	**Row Means**
Level B_1 (fearful images)	A_1B_1 (98.3)	A_2B_1 (114.1)	106.2
Level B_2 (neutral images)	A_1B_2 (98.1)	A_2B_2 (99.9)	99.0
Column Means	98.2	107.0	

Note that the matrix is a combination of two studies. Figure 12.1(a) shows that the column means (factor A, illumination) can be compared, just as if one were the experimental and the other the control group in a single-variable design. This comparison can answer the question, "Is there a significant difference in the children's heart rate between the dark and the lighted conditions?" Comparing the two levels of factor B (images), as shown in Figure 12.1(b), is also a comparison of two independent groups. The question answered here is whether there is a significant difference in heart rates between participants in the fear-image and neutral-image conditions.

The comparisons illustrated in Figures 12.1(a) and 12.1(b) are the tests of the main effects of the two independent variables on the dependent variable. In the dark-fears study, we can test whether heart rates differ under lighted and dark conditions (main effect of illumination), and whether they differ under fearful- and neutral-image conditions (main effect of fear imagery).

We could have answered these questions about main effects by conducting two separate, single-variable studies (i.e., with just one independent variable). However, to answer questions about the interaction of the two independent variables, we must combine these independent variables into a single study. When we combine the two separate designs by crossing them, as shown in Figure 12.1(c), the 2×2 matrix is formed, with four cells within which are the data for testing interactions. This allows us not only to investigate main effects but also to address a more complex question: are the effects of one variable different depending on the level of the other variable? This interaction is the major question in our hypothetical dark-fears study. In fact, in most factorial studies, the primary focus is on the interaction. Why is the interest on the interaction? Because designs that allow us to study multiple factors and their interactions bring us closer to the reality that real-life behavior is often determined by several factors working together.

Conducting the factorial experiment is similar to, but more complex than, conducting single-variable studies. The 2×2 factorial, because it is essentially two designs combined into a single study, contains more than one null hypothesis. In fact, in the hypothetical dark-fears study, there are three null hypotheses for each dependent measure. The three null hypotheses are as follows:

1. There is no significant difference in heart rate between the levels of factor A (no main effect for factor A).
2. There is no significant difference in heart rate between the levels of factor B (no main effect for factor B).
3. There is no significant interaction of factors A and B that acts on heart rate.

In factorial designs with more than two factors, there will be even more null hypotheses to test.

Because of the complexity of factorial designs, the potential threats to internal validity are also complex. Suppose that the ANOVA suggests that we should reject one or more of the null hypotheses. As in single-variable designs, the next step is to check for possible confounding to rule out alternative explanations of the findings. If we used an experimental design and randomly assigned participants to the cells, we will have controlled most of the possible sources of confounding. Only if we are convinced that we have adequately controlled confounding can we conclude that the data support a causal interpretation.

The hypothesis-testing procedure in factorial designs is similar to the procedure used in single-variable designs except that the interpretation of interactions is more complex than the

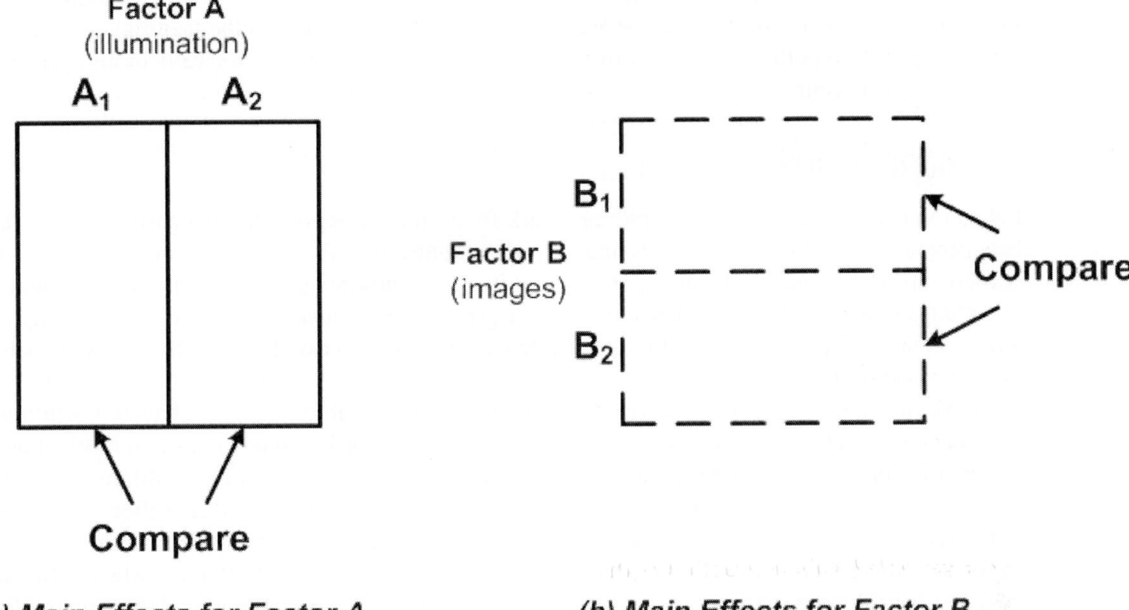

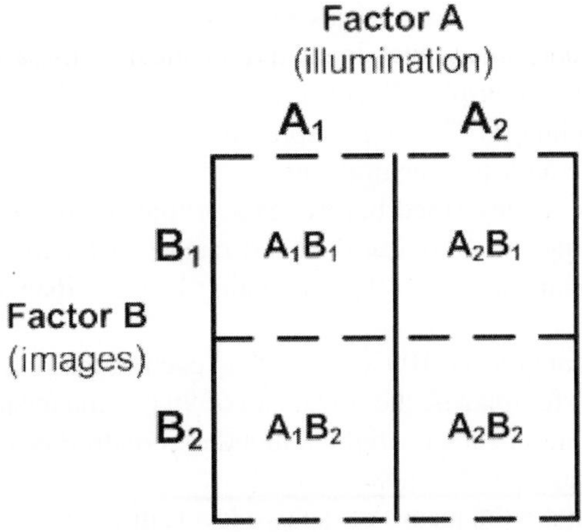

(c) The 2 X 2 Matrix for Testing for Interaction Effects

FIGURE 12.1 Factorial Design as a Combination of Two Studies. You can think of factorial designs as combining two or more studies into a single study. Looking at each factor individually provides a test of the main effects. Combining the factors provides a test of the interaction of the factors.

interpretation of differences in a single-variable study. Nevertheless, the reasoning is identical. The major difference is that, because there are more independent variables in the factorial design, there are several null hypotheses to test rather than only one, and, therefore, there is more chance for confounding to occur.

Running the Children's Dark-Fears Study

Let us return to our hypothetical children's dark-fears study. Suppose that the participants for this experiment are 40 children (20 boys and 20 girls), all afraid of the dark. We randomly assign the participants to the four conditions of the 2×2 matrix (10 children per condition). Random assignment helps to ensure the equivalence of the four groups at the outset of the study. In actuality, we would want to randomize within blocks so that we have exactly five girls and five boys in each of the four conditions.

As shown in Figure 12.1, there are two independent variables (factors). Factor A (illumination) has two levels: a lighted and a darkened condition. Factor B (images) has two levels: fearful and neutral images. The dependent variable is heart rate, a measure of the children's fear. The research hypotheses are that (1) there will be higher heart rates under dark conditions than under lighted conditions, (2) there will be higher heart rates under the fearful-images condition than under the neutral-images condition, and (3) the greatest effects on heart rates will occur when both darkness and fearful images are present. That is, we have hypothesized that there will be a main effect for factor A, a main effect for factor B, and a significant $A \times B$ interaction.

The children are tested individually while seated comfortably facing a projection screen. A small sensor on a finger monitors heart rate. Participants are told that they will be shown 10 slides and will be asked questions about them later. Each slide is shown for 15 seconds with a 5-second pause between slides. Cell A_1B_1 represents the lighted-plus-fearful-images condition. The lights are kept on in the room and the fearful-image slides are presented (e.g., ghostly images or a burglar entering a house). Cell A_2B_1 represents the dark-plus-fearful-images condition. We turn off the lights, and the children are shown the fearful images. Cell A_1B_2 represents the lighted-plus-neutral-images condition, and cell A_2B_2 represents the dark-plus-neutral-images condition. The general procedures in these two conditions are the same as described before, except that the images presented are neutral, such as landscapes and buildings. We monitor the heart rate of each participant during the testing period. Our data will be the heart rates for 40 participants: 10 participants in each of four different conditions.

Table 12.3 shows hypothetical data for the 10 participants in each of the four conditions. The row mean of 106.2 is the mean for fearful images; the row mean of 99.0 is the mean for neutral images; and 98.2 and 107.0 are the column means for lighted and dark conditions, respectively. The individual cell means are in parentheses.

To test for main effects, we compare the means of the two levels of each factor. The means of the two levels of factor A (98.2 and 107.0) are compared to determine whether there is a main effect for illumination [Figure 12.2(a)]. To determine whether there is a main effect for factor B, we compare the means for the fearful and neutral images (106.2 and 99.0) [Figure 12.2(b)]. To determine whether there is an interaction, we compare means of the four cells to see whether the effects of one independent variable on the dependent variable are different depending on the level of the other independent variable. The graph shown in Figure 12.3 suggests that there may be an interaction because the lines are clearly not parallel. As you will see shortly, whenever there is an interaction,

TABLE 12.3 Heart Rates for 40 Dark-Fearing Children

	FACTOR A (ILLUMINATION)		
FACTOR B (IMAGES)	A_1 (Lighted)	A_2 (Dark)	Row Means
B_1 (Fearful)	112	131	
	106	125	
	102	121	
	101	116	
	99	113	
	99	112	
	97	111	
	95	110	
	92	103	
	80	99	
	(98.3)	(114.1)	106.2
B_2 (Neutral)	115	119	
	110	112	
	105	107	
	103	102	
	100	95	
	98	95	
	97	95	
	90	92	
	83	91	
	80	90	
	(98.1)	(99.9)	99.0
Column Means	**98.2**	**107.0**	

the lines of the graph of the data will not be parallel. It is helpful to graph the cell means because it will help you see whether an interaction might exist and whether the mean differences suggest the presence of main effects.

Table 12.3 shows that participants in the dark condition have a higher mean heart rate (107.0) than the participants in the lighted condition (98.2). Moreover, the fearful-images condition has a higher mean heart rate (106.2) than the neutral-images condition (99.0). Finally, the two lines in Figure 12.3 are not parallel. These observations *suggest* that there may be main effects for factor A (illumination) and factor B (images), as well as an A $\times$ B interaction. The A_1 line (for the lighted condition) is virtually flat (98.2 and 98.3). In contrast, the slope of the A_2 line (for the dark

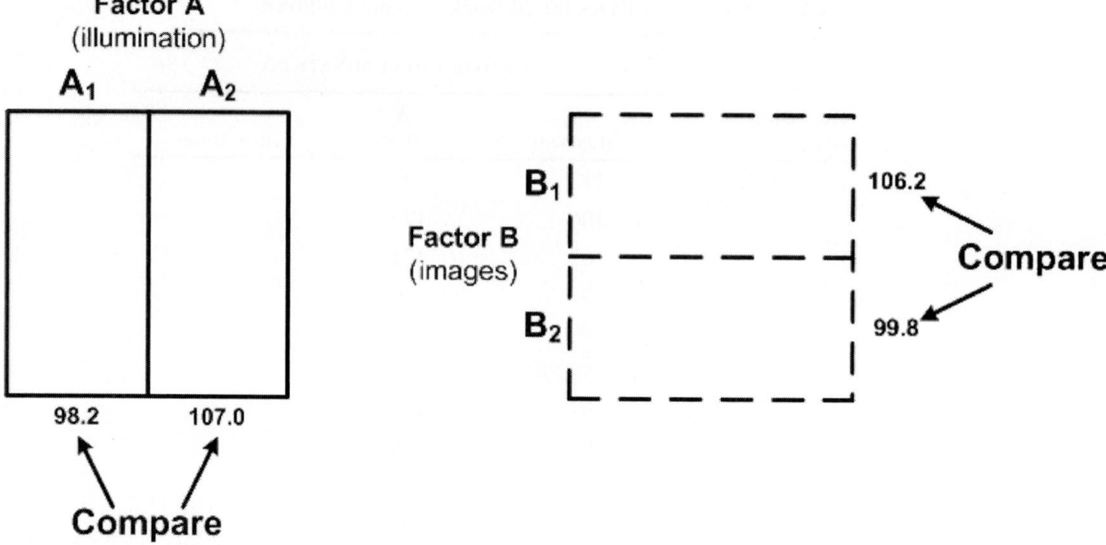

FIGURE 12.2 Testing for Main Effects. We test the main effects by comparing the means for each factor while ignoring the grouping on other factors.

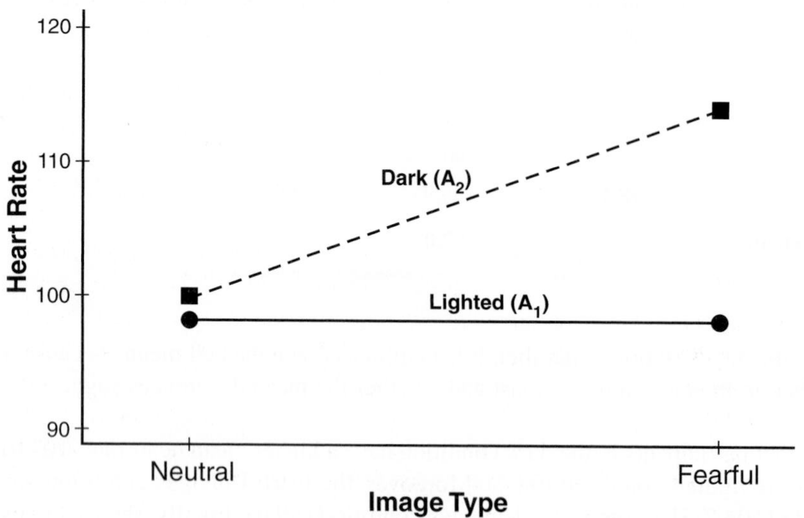

FIGURE 12.3 Graph of Children's Dark-Fears Study. The fact that the lines in this graph of the children's dark-fears data are not parallel suggests the possibility of an interaction. When both main effects and interactions are found, the main effects should be interpreted in light of the interaction.

condition) moves up from 99.9 with neutral images to 114.1 with the fearful images. The slope of this line appears to be due to the elevation of the A_2B_1 cell, in which the dark condition and the fearful images are combined. The mean of this cell is elevated compared with that of the other three cells. This hypothetical study shows that fearful images produce high heart rates, but only in the presence of the dark condition. The A_1 line is nearly flat; that is, the type of images has little effect when the child is sitting in a lighted area.

Possible Outcomes of Factorial Designs

There are many possible outcomes in a factorial study. There may be

- no main effects and no interactions,
- one or more main effects but no interaction,
- one or more interactions, but no main effects,
- both interactions and main effects.

In fact, any combination of main effects and interactions is possible in a factorial.

Figure 12.4 shows several factorial designs. In each, a matrix of hypothetical cell means and a graph showing the same data are included.

In each matrix, you will see the mean score for each cell, and the **row means** and **column means** for each level of each factor. Row means are the means for all the people in a row, and column means are the means for all of the people in a column. In the following discussion, we will assume that (1) there are an equal number of participants in each cell and (2) the cell mean differences are statistically significant. A matrix and a graph provide much the same information but, as you will see, a graph makes it easier to spot a possible interaction.

Figure 12.4(a) illustrates a matrix and a graph for a 2×2 factorial design. At the end of each row and each column you will see the overall means for each level of each variable (i.e., for levels A_1 and A_2, and levels B_1 and B_2). Within each of the four cells is the mean score for the group in that condition. As you see, the means are equal, and there are no differences anywhere in the matrix. Thus, there are no significant main effects for factors A or B and no significant interactions.

On the graph, the levels of variable A are shown on the *x*-axis, and the values of the dependent variable are shown on the *y*-axis. Means for cells A_1B_1 and A_2B_1, identified with small circles, are both 50. The points are connected to show graphically the overall effect of A on the dependent measure at the B_1 level of B. Clearly, there is no effect of A on the dependent measure at level B_1 because the mean values are the same. We have plotted the effects of A at level B_2 in the same way using small triangles. They fall on the same points along the same line, all at the value 50. Again, there is no effect of A at the B_2 level. By inspecting either the table or the graph, we can see that there are no main effects and no interaction.

Look at the 2×2 factorial in Figure 12.4(b). As you see, the overall means for factor A (the column means) are different, but the row means (factor B) are not different. Thus, your inspection of the matrix suggests that there is a significant main effect for factor A, but no significant main effect for factor B. Now, look at the graph. The B_1 and B_2 lines are identical, indicating that B has had no effect. However, the mean of A_2 is greater than the mean of A_1 (see how the line swings upward), indicating an effect for factor A. The 2×2 matrix shows the same results, with the mean for levels B_1 and B_2 equal (at 45) and the means for levels A_1 and A_2 different (30 and 60).

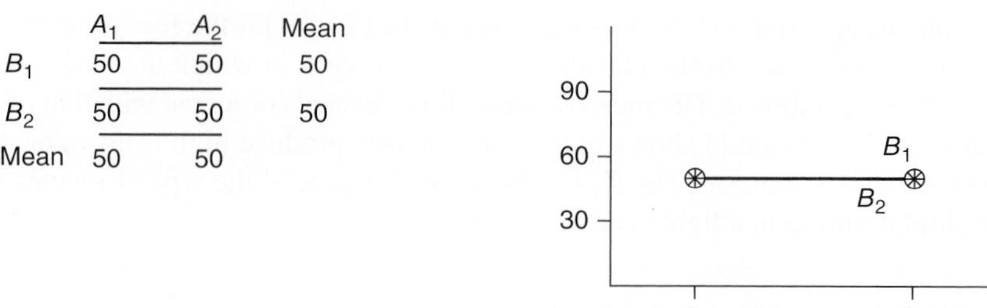

	A_1	A_2	Mean
B_1	50	50	50
B_2	50	50	50
Mean	50	50	

(a) 2 × 2 Factorial (*A* and *B* and the interaction are not significant)

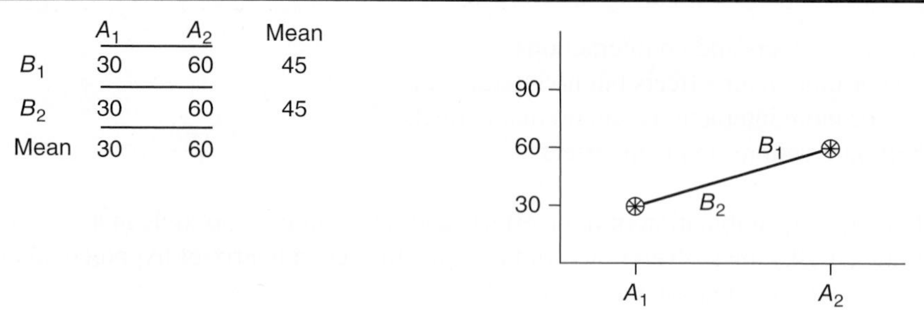

	A_1	A_2	Mean
B_1	30	60	45
B_2	30	60	45
Mean	30	60	

(b) 2 × 2 Factorial (*A* is significant; *B* and the interaction are not significant)

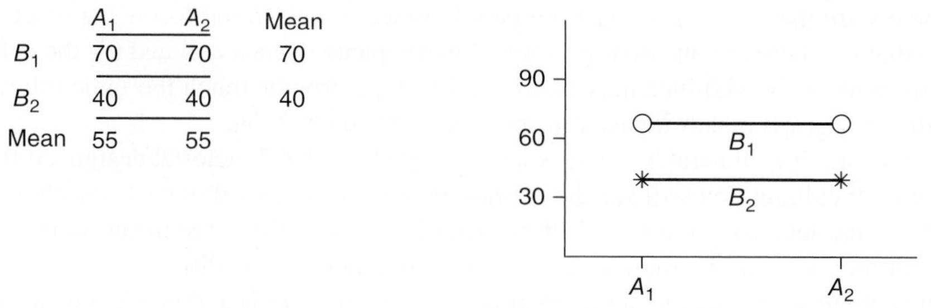

	A_1	A_2	Mean
B_1	70	70	70
B_2	40	40	40
Mean	55	55	

(c) 2 × 2 Factorial (*B* is significant; *A* and the interaction are not significant)

	A_1	A_2	A_3	Mean
B_1	10	30	80	40
B_2	30	50	100	60
Mean	20	40	90	

(d) 3 × 2 Factorial (*A* and *B* are significant; the interaction is not significant)

FIGURE 12.4 Possible Outcomes of Factorial Designs. Eight possible outcomes of a two-factor factorial study.

	A_1	A_2	Mean
B_1	40	60	50
B_2	60	40	50
Mean	50	50	

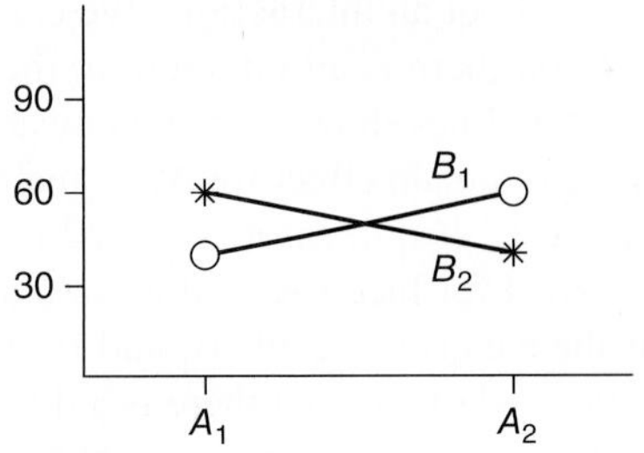

(e) 2 × 2 Factorial (the interaction is significant; *A* and *B* are not significant)

	A_1	A_2	A_3	Mean
B_1	30	40	50	40
B_2	40	40	40	40
Mean	35	40	45	

(f) 3 × 2 Factorial (*A* and the interaction are significant; *B* is not significant)

	A_1	A_2	A_3	Mean
B_1	30	40	50	40
B_2	70	60	50	60
Mean	50	50	50	

(g) 3 × 2 Factorial (*B* and the interaction are significant; *A* is not significant)

	A_1	A_2	Mean
B_1	40	40	40
B_2	40	60	50
Mean	40	50	

(h) 2 × 2 Factorial (*A* and *B* and the interaction are not significant)

FIGURE 12.4 (Continued)

What about an interaction? We can identify interactions most easily in the graph of the cell means. When there is an interaction, the lines are not parallel. In this example, the lines are the same and both lines show the same upward swing from left to right, so there is no interaction effect. Thus, there is a main effect for A, no main effect for B, and no interaction.

Figure 12.4(c) illustrates a 2 × 2 factorial design in which there is a main effect for factor B, no main effect for factor A, and no interaction. The means for levels A_1 and A_2 are the same (55), whereas the means for levels B_1 and B_2 are different (70 and 40). In the graph, the B_1 and B_2 lines are separated, showing that there is a difference between the levels of factor B. The lines are parallel, which suggests that there is no interaction between A and B.

Figure 12.4(d) shows a 3 × 2 factorial, in which there is a main effect for both factor A and factor B, but no interaction. The means are different at each of the three levels of factor A and each of the two levels of factor B. However, the parallel lines in Figure 12.4(d) indicate that there is no interaction.

Figure 12.4(e) illustrates a 2 × 2 factorial with a significant A × B interaction, but no significant main effects. Note that the column means for the two levels of factor A are the same. This indicates that there is no main effect for factor A. The same is true for factor B. Thus, there is no significant main effect for A or B, but when plotted on the graph, the two lines cross; they are not parallel, thus suggesting an A × B interaction.

One of the values of drawing a graph is that interactions become readily apparent. Factor A has a different effect on the dependent measure when paired with B_1 than when paired with B_2. This is a classic interaction, in which one variable systematically influences the effects of a second variable. Note also that the column means and row means in Figures 12.4(a) and 12.4(e) are identical. However, in Figure 12.4(a) the pattern of means within the cells indicates no interaction, whereas the pattern of means in Figure 12.4(e) indicates an interaction. This illustrates that the column and row means provide an indication of main effects only. We must inspect the individual cells on the graph to see an interaction.

Figure 12.4(f) shows a main effect for A and an A × B interaction. *When both a main effect and an interaction occur, we always interpret the interaction first.*

The remaining examples can be read in similar fashion. We also have included a number of exercises in the lab manual on the Student Resource Website to provide additional practice with
12:01 these challenging concepts and procedures.

Analysis of Variance in Factorial Designs

The appropriate statistical analysis for factorial designs is analysis of variance (ANOVA). Typically, statistical-analysis computer programs are used because of the detail and complexity of the computations. Running ANOVAs on your personal computer will take the drudgery out of the calculations.

Knowledge of computer use is critical for researchers, but is not a substitute for understanding the principles of research design and statistical analysis. Remember our admonition in Chapter 1: it is not the technician's manipulation of laboratory equipment, including computers, that defines science. Science is defined by its systematic way of thinking, which guides the use of laboratory techniques.

We will focus in this section on understanding an ANOVA and interpreting the results. Statistical computations for complex ANOVAs are beyond the scope of this text. However, we do cover
12:02 statistical analysis procedures on the Student Resource Website.

TABLE 12.4 ANOVA Summary Table

Here is the summary table for the data shown in Table 12.3.

SOURCE	df	SS	MS	*F*	*p*
Factor A (illumination)	1	765.62	765.62	7.88	.008
Factor B (images)	1	525.62	525.62	5.41	.026
AB Interaction	1	497.02	497.02	5.12	.030
Error	36	3497.50	97.15		
Total	39	5285.78	135.53		

The results of an ANOVA are typically organized in an ANOVA summary table, as shown in Table 12.4. This ANOVA summary table is in the same general format that you learned about in Chapter 10, with columns for source of variance, degrees of freedom, sums of squares, mean squares, *F*-ratios, and *p*-values. The basic difference is that there are more sources of variance in factorial designs, and therefore more rows in the ANOVA summary table. For example, the sources of variance in our dark-fears study include factor A (illumination), factor B (images), the A × B interaction, the within-groups variance (error), and the total variance.

The degrees of freedom (df) for a between-subjects factorial design can be computed using some simple rules.

1. The total degrees of freedom (df_{Total}) are $N - 1$ ($40 - 1$ in our example). N is the total number of subjects.
2. The degrees of freedom for the main effects are equal to the number of levels of each factor minus 1. Therefore, $df_a = (a - 1) = (2 - 1) = 1$, and $df_b = (b - 1) = (2 - 1) = 1$. The typical notation in advanced statistics books, which we have used here, is to use "*a*" to represent the number of levels of factor A and "*b*" to represent the number of levels of factor B.
3. The degrees of freedom for interactions are the product of the degrees of freedom for the main effects. Therefore, $df_{ab} = df_a \times df_b = (a - 1) \times (b - 1) = 1 \times 1 = 1$.
4. The degrees of freedom for the within-groups variance is equal to N minus the number of groups. The number of groups is the product of the number of levels of each factor (in this case, $a \times b$). Therefore, $df_w = N - ab = 40 - 4 = 36$ in our dark-fears study. (Note that if you add the dfs for all the sources of variance, you will get the total dfs.)

12:03

The third and fourth columns list the sum of squares (SS) and mean squares (MS), respectively, for each source of variance. The computational formulas for the sums of squares are complicated, but are covered on the Student Resource Website. We compute the mean squares by dividing each sum of squares by its associated degrees of freedom. The *F*-ratios in the fifth column are computed by dividing the mean squares by the within-groups mean square (the error term). The probability (*p*) of each *F*-ratio is shown in the sixth column. If the *p*-value is less than the chosen alpha level, we reject the null hypothesis and conclude that there is an effect.

Computer programs calculate the *p*-value using an equation. If you were computing the ANOVA by hand, you would look up how large the *F*-value has to be before you would reject the null hypothesis. Again, this procedure is covered on the Student Resource Website, where we show you how to compute the two-way ANOVA by hand or using a statistical-analysis program.

In our ANOVA, there is a significant interaction ($p = .03$, alpha $= .05$). That is, fear, as measured by heart rate, is highest in the condition that includes both darkness and fearful images. The summary table also shows significant main effects for both illumination level and image type, but they should be interpreted in light of the interaction. That is, under the neutral-images condition, the light or dark condition makes no difference; likewise, under lighted conditions, the fearful images do not cause more fear than do the neutral images. The main effects are due to the interaction—to the condition A_2B_1, in which the fearful images and darkness occur together.

When interpreting results that include both an interaction and main effects, we always begin the interpretation with the interaction. The conclusion drawn from this hypothetical study is that neither fearful images alone nor darkness alone appears to be sufficient to stimulate children's night fears, but the two together are a sufficient condition for children's night fears. To accept the finding of a main effect for A without interpreting it in terms of the interaction could lead us to an erroneous conclusion that the darkness itself increases fear.

Quick-Check Review 12.1: Factorial Designs

1. What are factorial designs?
2. Why does a factorial study test at least three null hypotheses?
3. What is an interaction? a main effect?
4. When would you use a factorial rather than a single-variable design?
5. In terms of main effects and interactions, what outcomes are possible in a factorial?
6. Why should one interpret the interaction first when both a main effect and an interaction are significant?

VARIATIONS OF BASIC FACTORIAL DESIGN

Psychological research uses factorial designs extensively because they are better at representing the complex nature of real-world behavior. Many factorial designs are either within-subjects factorials, in which each participant is tested under all conditions, or mixed designs that blend different types of factors into a single factorial study. This section covers both of these variations.

Within-Subjects or Repeated-Measures Factorial

We have already discussed randomized, between-subjects factorial designs, in which the researcher randomly assigns participants to conditions and each participant appears in only one cell. The children's dark-fears study illustrated this basic factorial design. An alternative is the **within-subjects factorial**, also called the **repeated-measures factorial**. If we had employed it in the dark-fears factorial study, then we would have tested each participant under each of the four conditions. The ANOVA carried out to test for statistical significance is a **repeated-measures factorial ANOVA**, which takes into account the correlated nature of the groups.

Recall from Chapter 11 that using a within-subjects design involves disadvantages that stem from the fact that each participant is exposed to each condition. Specifically, sequence effects may confound the results. When potential sequence effects are strong, a within-subjects design should be avoided. However, when not precluded by such strong sequence effects, a within-subjects design has decided advantages over a between-subjects design. Whether a single-variable design or a factorial design, using a within-subjects design can (1) provide greater sensitivity to the effects of the independent variable by reducing the individual-differences component of the error term, (2) assure equivalence of groups at the start of the experiment because the participants in each condition are identical, (3) require fewer participants, and (4) related to the third point, be more efficient.

In the dark-fears study, for example, if we want 10 participants in each of the four conditions, then only 10 participants are needed for a repeated-measures design, while 40 participants are needed for a between-subjects design. This could be a major advantage when participants are difficult to obtain, or when each participant requires extensive preparation. For these reasons, many researchers prefer a repeated-measures design to a between-subjects design.

Mixed Designs

When there is more than one factor, it is possible that the factors will be of different types. For example, one factor may be a within-subjects factor, whereas the other may be a between-subjects factor. Participants would respond to all levels of the within-subjects factor, but be randomly assigned to only one level of the between-subjects factor. This is one type of mixed design.

Researchers use the term "**mixed design**" in two different ways, which can be confusing. It can be used to refer to a factorial that includes both between-subjects and within-subjects factors. It can also be used to refer to a factorial that includes both manipulated and nonmanipulated factors. It is important to distinguish between the two types of mixed designs because they affect the analysis and interpretation of results in different ways.

Between-Subjects and Within-Subjects Factors. When both **between-subjects factors** and **within-subjects factors** exist in the same study, the critical issue is a statistical one. For example, suppose that a study has "level of distraction" as the within-subjects factor and the "amount of potential reward for success" as the between-subjects factor, as shown in Table 12.5. We should assign

TABLE 12.5 One Between-Subjects Factor and One Within-Subjects Factor Mixed Design

		LEVEL OF DISTRACTION (WITHIN-SUBJECTS FACTOR)		
		Low	**Medium**	**High**
AMOUNT OF POTENTIAL REWARD (BETWEEN-SUBJECTS FACTOR)	**Small**			
	Large			

Note: In this design, the researcher randomly assigns participants to either the small-reward or the large-reward condition and then tests the participants under all three levels of distraction.

each participant to one of the potential reward conditions (the between-subjects factor) and test each participant under all levels of distraction (the within-subjects factor). For the within-subjects factor, the order of presentation of conditions should be counterbalanced to control sequence effects.

In this mixed design, the ANOVA formulas will differ depending on which factors are within-subjects factors and which are between-subjects factors. Computation of ANOVAs for mixed designs is beyond the scope of this text. As with most ANOVAs, data from such designs are analyzed using statistical-analysis computer programs.

Manipulated and Nonmanipulated Factors. When both **manipulated factors** and **nonmanipulated factors** are included, the essential issue is one of interpretation of results. In a mixed design in which one factor is a nonmanipulated variable and one factor is a manipulated variable, participants are randomly assigned to the conditions of the manipulated variable, but are assigned to levels of the nonmanipulated variable based on preexisting characteristics. For example, a researcher studying the effects of crowding on aggression could randomly assign participants to one of three conditions (alone, slightly crowded, and crowded) and then observe the level of aggression of participants in each of these conditions. The researcher actively manipulates the variable of crowding.

Suppose, however, that the researcher is also interested in gender differences in response to crowding, suspecting that there is an interaction between gender and level of crowding on the dependent measure of aggression. Gender is a nonmanipulated variable; the researcher places participants in the male or female group based on their gender. Table 12.6 illustrates this design.

Statistical analyses are unaffected by whether the variables are manipulated or nonmanipulated, as they are when we have between- and within-subjects factors. The importance of whether a factor is manipulated or nonmanipulated comes into play when we *interpret* the statistical analysis. Manipulated factors represent experiments that control for confounding variables. We can therefore safely draw causal inferences based on analysis of the main effects of the variables. Research designs using nonmanipulated factors are not experiments. Instead, they represent differential research. Remember that in differential research, we do not assign participants randomly to groups, and therefore, groups may differ on variables other than the independent variable. These potential differences may cause confounding.

Unless we can rule out all potential confounding, we cannot confidently draw causal conclusions. Therefore, caution and careful attention to the likely existence of confounding variables are necessary when interpreting the main effects of nonmanipulated factors. In our example, we need

TABLE 12.6 One Manipulated Factor and One Nonmanipulated Factor Mixed Design

		LEVEL OF CROWDING (MANIPULATED FACTOR)		
		No Crowding	**Slightly Crowded**	**Very Crowded**
SEX OF PARTICIPANT	**Male**			
(NONMANIPULATED FACTOR)	**Female**			

Note: In this design, both factors are between-subjects factors. The researcher randomly assigns participants to the level of crowding (manipulated variable) and assigns participants to male or female groups based on their gender (nonmanipulated variable).

TABLE 12.7 A Design That Is Mixed in Both a Statistical Sense (One-Between, One-Within) and in an Experimental Sense (One-Manipulated, One-Nonmanipulated)

		TYPE OF WORDS (WITHIN-SUBJECTS FACTOR)	
		Neutral	Emotional
DIAGNOSIS (BETWEEN-SUBJECTS FACTOR)	GAD		
	Controls		

Note: In this design, diagnosis is a between-subjects factor, whereas type of words is a within-subjects factor. This will affect the ANOVA formulas used. In addition, diagnosis is a nonmanipulated factor, whereas the type of words is a manipulated factor. This will affect the confidence of causal inference.

to be careful in drawing the inference that gender caused any observed differences in aggression. Furthermore, we should also use caution in the interpretation of any interaction involving a nonmanipulated factor.

Mixed in Both Ways. Finally, it is possible to have a mixed design that is mixed in both of the ways just described. Table 12.7 presents such a situation. In this example, the researcher wants to compare accuracy of recognition of neutral and emotionally charged words in people with generalized anxiety disorder (GAD) and control participants. The researcher arranges a factorial design in which people with GAD and controls view both neutral and emotionally charged words for just a few milliseconds. Note that this is a factorial with one nonmanipulated variable (diagnosis) and one manipulated variable (type of words). Although participants can be randomly assigned to the levels of factor A (type of words), the researcher cannot randomly assign participants to factor B (diagnosis). Note that in addition to being a mixed design in the sense that it includes both manipulated and nonmanipulated factors, this example is also a mixed design in that one factor (diagnosis) is a between-subjects factor, whereas the other factor (types of words) is a within-subjects factor.

In this example, the researcher would first classify each factor on the dimension of between-subjects versus within-subjects factors in order to select the appropriate ANOVA for statistical analysis. Then each factor is classified on the dimension of manipulated versus nonmanipulated factors to interpret the results. Again, we must be especially cautious in drawing conclusions based on main effects and interactions with nonmanipulated factors.

Quick-Check Review 12.2: Variations of Basic Factorial Design

1. What are the major advantages of a repeated measures factorial?
2. What are the two meanings of "mixed design"?
3. Explain the implications of mixed designs for (a) interpretation of results, and (b) statistical analyses.

ANOVA: A POSTSCRIPT

Analysis of variance is one of the most flexible statistical tools available for the evaluation of data. ANOVA compares the variability of the means against a standard based on the variability of scores within groups. If the means are more variable than one would expect based on sampling error alone, the researcher concludes that the independent variable had an effect, assuming that confounding was adequately controlled.

The concept of comparing the variability between groups to the variability within groups is constant in every ANOVA, no matter how complicated it becomes. For example, in within-subjects designs, participants are tested under each condition. The repeated-measures ANOVA considers this fact in computing the error term, but its basic comparison is between the variability of the means between groups relative to the variability within the groups.

With factorial designs, ANOVA is extended still further, examining the effects of each independent variable and the interactive effects of combinations of independent variables. With two factors (A and B), there are three possible effects: the A main effect, the B main effect, and the interaction between A and B. With three factors, there are three main effects (A, B, and C), three two-way interactions (AB, AC, and BC), and one three-way interaction (ABC), for a total of seven different effects. It is important to note that, with factorial ANOVAs, we must take into account which factors are within-subjects factors and which are between-subjects factors.

Although ANOVAs become more complicated as the number of factors in a study increases, extending the logic and the computational formulas of the ANOVAs to factorial designs is not difficult. The formulas themselves can become quite complex, but for the most part, researchers rely

CARTOON 12.1 Interpreting complex interactions can be extremely difficult and very frustrating.

on computers to perform the computation. Because there are many effects, there are many F-ratios, but each F-ratio represents a comparison of between-groups variability with within-groups variability. Furthermore, we interpret the F-ratio in these complex designs the same as in simpler designs; if the p-value is less than the alpha level, the null hypothesis is rejected. The problem lies not with the computation of complex ANOVAs, but in the interpretation stage, in which the researcher must visualize and explain complex interactions.

The consistency in how ANOVAs are used and flexibility of the procedure to analyze data from so many different designs makes ANOVA the most widely used statistical technique in psychology. Given the diversity of ANOVA procedures, it is perhaps not surprising that they have been extended into other designs. These advanced procedures are beyond the scope of this book. We describe them only briefly here, with an emphasis on understanding conceptually what each procedure is designed to accomplish.

Analysis of Covariance

A useful extension of analysis of variance is **analysis of covariance** (**ANCOVA**). Unfortunately, as with other complex research procedures, ANCOVA is easily misused by those who do not understand its nuances (Lord, 1967; Miller & Chapman, 2001).

ANCOVA is used in the same way as ANOVA, with one addition: as part of the analysis, the ANCOVA removes the effects of a theoretically unimportant, but nonetheless powerful, variable. For example, if you want to study the effects of reinforcement strategies on learning in young children, you could set up a study with two or three levels of the independent variable. You could then randomly assign the sample of children to each condition and measure how well they learn (the dependent variable). However, we expect that the age of the children will affect how quickly they learn material.

There are several options to deal with this age issue. These include (1) holding age constant by using only participants who are in a narrow age range, (2) using a matching procedure to make sure that the groups are equivalent on age at the beginning of the study, or (3) creating a factorial design with age as a factor. Yet another alternative is to randomly assign participants to groups and use analysis of covariance to remove statistically the effects of age from the dependent measure. This statistical removal of unwanted variance makes the ANCOVA more sensitive to group differences. This is conceptually similar to the logic of correlated-groups designs, which provide a more sensitive test of hypotheses because the designs remove the variability due to individual differences. Here, control over variability due to individual differences is not built into the design of the study, but rather is built into the statistical analysis. We must caution, however, that ANCOVA is a complicated procedure, with many potential pitfalls. For a detailed discussion of ANCOVA, consult Keppel and Wickens (2004).

Multivariate Analysis of Variance

Another extension of analysis of variance is **multivariate analysis of variance** (**MANOVA**). The difference between an ANOVA and a MANOVA is in the dependent variable. An ANOVA has only one dependent variable, whereas a MANOVA has multiple dependent variables. Statisticians and researchers are still discovering the full power of MANOVA procedures. Just as in ANCOVA, using MANOVA procedures correctly, and interpreting the results appropriately, requires an extensive understanding of the technique.

ANOVA techniques are flexible and powerful procedures for analyzing data from almost any design. With the aid of a computer, the computations are quick and easy. However, researchers still have to understand research design to set up the computer analyses correctly. Even more critical, researchers must understand when ANOVA procedures are appropriate and how to use them. Even for professionals who conduct little research, knowing these concepts is important in understanding and evaluating the research reported by others.

Finally, performing the appropriate statistical analysis is only the first step in evaluating data. The next step is interpreting the meaning of the results, which requires evaluating the entire study on such issues as confounding and the adequacy of control procedures. Statistical procedures, even such ingenuous and useful ones as ANOVA, do not impart meaning to data. Only well-trained researchers, who understand scientific thought, can take this last important step.

Quick-Check Review 12.3: ANOVA: A Postscript

1. What does an analysis of covariance do?
2. How does a MANOVA differ from an ANOVA?

ETHICAL PRINCIPLES

We hope that you have already recognized that the children's dark-fears study described in this chapter presents ethical issues for the researcher. By now, you know that the most basic ethical issue in research with humans is concern for, and protection of, the welfare and rights of the participants. Thus, the researcher must be alert to all of the usual issues: informed consent, right to privacy, confidentiality, and debriefing if deception or distress is involved. A participant's informed consent must be obtained in writing before gathering data. This means providing the participants with enough clear information to make a reasoned decision about whether to participate.

In the dark-fears study, the proposed participants are children, all below the legal age of consent, which means that the children cannot legally give their consent to participate in research. Therefore, the researcher must obtain the informed consent of a responsible person who can legally act for the child in the child's interest. Generally, that person is the child's parent or guardian and, sometimes, a responsible school administrator. However, most school administrators will probably—and wisely—insist on parental consent. Thus, researchers must provide parents with clear information on which to base their decision, provide the opportunity to raise questions, and, even if they consent to their child's involvement, to maintain the right to withdraw the child from the study at any time and for any reason.

However, even with all of that, the responsible adult's consent is not enough. As ethical researchers we need to understand that *children need to be treated with the same degree of respect that we extend to adults*. Thus, we need to explain the study to the child in age-appropriate terms. Children must be told what will be required of them, how long it will take, and so on. The researcher must be reasonably assured that the child has had all questions answered, has understood he or she has the right to decline or withdraw at any time, and assents to the procedure. "Consent" is a legal term, and legally the child is too young to consent. We thus obtain the child's agreement or **assent** to participate. A child's assent carries no legally binding power, but is important to obtain as part of the process of ensuring that the child understands what is being requested.

As we noted in earlier chapters, these ethical requirements for informed consent result in participants who have self-selected to participate. Thus, a truly random selection of participants is hardly ever achieved and generalization of results to the larger population is always somewhat compromised. These ethical realities add to the tentative nature of the results of research with humans.

Issues of consent and assent apply to all children in research, but the dark-fears study raises additional concerns because it exposes children to conditions that may create fear and anxiety. The researcher must be sensitive to those possibilities and be prepared to discontinue procedures and reassure or otherwise assist children who become distressed.

There is another ethical issue that we must address whenever participants are in clinical trials in which procedures have a therapeutic aim, as in children's fear-reduction research. If children are randomly assigned to a treatment or a control group, then the control group must be given the opportunity to also undergo the treatment later. This is particularly important if the results showed that the treatment group did, indeed, improve while the control group did not. Thus, instead of **a no-treatment control group**, there is a **delayed-treatment control group**. The experimental and control groups are compared, and the controls are later provided with the same treatment. This issue is not limited to children, but it does occur often in child-focused clinical research.

12:04 The Student Resource Website discusses these ethical issues in conducting clinical research with children in more detail.

Quick-Check Review 12.4: Ethical Principles

1. What is the difference between assent and consent?
2. How can we solve the problem of a no-treatment control group in clinical trials research?

SUMMARY

- Factorial designs include more than one independent variable.
- They combine information from the equivalent of two or more single-variable studies.
- Their greatest advantage is testing for possible interaction of independent variables.
- Mixed factorial designs include (1) between-subjects and within-subjects factors, (2) manipulated and nonmanipulated factors, and (3) mixed in both of these ways.
- ANOVAs are used for statistical analyses of factorial designs.
- When the analysis indicates that both main effects and an interaction are significant, we should always interpret the main effects in terms of the interaction.
- Two extensions of ANOVA procedures are analysis of covariance and multivariate analysis of variance.
- Children are unable to consent to participate in research because they are too young to give legal consent, and informed consent must be obtained from a responsible adult. However, the researcher must still obtain the children's willing agreement to participate (i.e., the children's assent).

Putting It into Practice

The majority of experimental studies conducted in psychology are factorial studies because almost everything of consequence in the psychological world is influenced by multiple factors, many of which interact with one another. Yet human beings have a natural tendency to try to simplify the world in an effort to understand it. We tend to visualize individual effects on variables and rarely think in terms of interactions.

Identify some issues around you. They could be anything, from what makes people attractive or successful to how traffic jams form. Then identify individual variables that are likely to have an effect on the issue you selected. For example, if you were looking at business success, you might identify variables like education, work experience, tenacity, work ethic, connections, confidence, good communication skills, and even physical attractiveness. Take your time and identify as many variables as you can. Then do a little brainstorming about how some of those variables might interact with one another to influence business success. For example, an individual who possesses both extensive background knowledge and good communication skills might make impressive presentations, which lead people to think that this is someone they want to work with.

It will take you a while to get used to thinking about interactions, but knowledge of interactions will dramatically enhance your ability to understand the complex psychological world.

EXERCISES

12.1. Define the following key terms. Be sure that you understand them. They are discussed in the chapter and defined in the glossary.

factorial designs
interaction effects
factors
matrix of cells
design notation
main effects
row means
column means
within-subjects factorial, or repeated-measures factorial
repeated-measures factorial ANOVA
mixed design
between-subjects factors
within-subjects factors
manipulated factors
nonmanipulated factors
analysis of covariance (ANCOVA)
multivariate analysis of variance (MANOVA)
assent
no-treatment control group
delayed-treatment control group

12.2. For each of the following (a) indicate how many factors are included, and (b) tell how many levels there are for each factor:

a. 2×2
b. 2×3
c. $2 \times 3 \times 2$
d. 4×3
e. $4 \times 3 \times 2 \times 3$

12.3. For each of the above, draw the appropriate matrix and label the factors and levels.

12.4. As the teaching assistant for your course, you are asked to explain the concept of interaction. Organize your presentation, starting by making the distinction between main effects and interactions. Be sure to clarify the distinction between additive and interactive effects.

12.5. As the teaching assistant for your course, you are asked to explain that a 2 × 2 factorial study is, in a sense, two separate studies combined. How would you develop your explanation?

12.6. Given the following cell means and ANOVA summary table, how would you interpret the results?

SOURCE	df	SS	MS	F	p
A	3	121.5	40.5	1.39	n.s.
B	1	93.7	93.7	3.21	<.05
AB	3	288.6	96.2	3.29	<.05
Within	72	2102.4	29.2		
Total	79	2606.2			

MATRIX OF MEANS

	B_1	B_2
A_1	12.1	13.4
A_2	9.5	15.7
A_3	7.5	17.5
A_4	5.9	18.9

12.7. In the children's dark-fears study, suppose that we had found significant main effects for both level of illumination and fearful images, but no interaction. Draw a graph to show how such results would look. How would you interpret the findings conceptually?

12.8. Assume that in the dark-fears study you obtained a significant main effect for fearful images and a significant interaction. What would the graph of the results look like? How would you interpret these results?

CHAPTER THIRTEEN

A SECOND LOOK AT FIELD RESEARCH: FIELD EXPERIMENTS, PROGRAM EVALUATION, AND SURVEY RESEARCH

People don't usually do research the way people who write books about research say that people do research.

—A. J. Bachrach, 1981

WEB RESOURCE MATERIAL

13:01 Examples of Field Research
13:02 Survey Construction Techniques
13:03 Confidence Intervals
13:04 Study Guide/Lab Manual
13:05 Links to Related Internet Sites

The field research introduced in Chapter 6 focused on low-constraint research (naturalistic observation, case studies, and archival research). These methods are useful in gathering facts, observing contingencies, becoming familiar with phenomena, and developing hypotheses for later high-constraint research. However, research in natural settings is not limited to low-constraint methods. This chapter covers higher-constraint field research, including field experiments, program evaluation, and survey research.

CONDUCTING FIELD RESEARCH

Modern society constantly demands the competent evaluation of many social forces, such as the impact of educational and public health programs, natural and man-made disasters, economic recessions, and changing employment conditions. These are questions about causality (e.g., is this new public health program effective?). Low-constraint research cannot adequately answer such questions of causality because, as you learned earlier, it cannot rule out alternative hypotheses.

Conducting experimental research in natural settings is difficult because of the limitations imposed by the settings. For example, it may be impossible to assign participants randomly to groups, precise measures of dependent variables may be impossible, and manipulation of independent variables may be politically or ethically unacceptable. In some studies, such as a study of the psychological effects of a natural disaster, manipulating the independent variable (a flood, hurricane, or forest fire) is impossible. Finally, it is often difficult to maintain projects in the field because decision makers, like politicians and school principals, might—sometimes for good reasons—cancel or curtail ongoing projects. Nevertheless, despite these difficulties, high-quality field research is routinely called upon to address such questions of concern to society. The Student Resource Website gives several examples of research studies conducted in the field.

13:01

Reasons for Doing Field Research

There are three major reasons for conducting experiments in field settings:

1. To test the external validity of laboratory findings
2. To determine the effects of events that occur in the field
3. To improve generalization across settings

Testing External Validity. Experimental research in the laboratory tests causal hypotheses under controlled conditions that maximize internal validity. However, a cost of this improved internal validity may be a reduction of external validity. The more precise and constrained the laboratory, the less natural will be the procedures. This issue is one of ecological validity—the accurate generalization of laboratory findings to real-world settings. Laboratory research might not always generalize to the natural environment.

> Despite the advantages of laboratory control we do not always want to learn about causation in controlled settings. Instead, for many purposes, we would like to be able to generalize to causal relationships in complex field settings, and we cannot easily assume that findings from the laboratory will hold in the field. (Cook & Campbell, 1979, p. 7)

Suppose that we conduct a controlled experiment in a university laboratory school and find that new teaching methods are clearly superior to those traditionally used throughout the state. Is it wise to assume that our new methods will still be successful when taken out of the laboratory and applied in schools that have dramatically different students, faculties, and conditions? The problem is that field situations are usually very different from laboratory situations.

Some researchers maintain that the concern over ecological validity may be overstated (e.g., Anderson et al., 1999). They argue that the ideas of poor ecological validity of laboratory research and poor internal validity of field research are unsupported beliefs rather than empirical facts. These researchers found a significant correlation (.73) between the effect sizes of 38 pairs of laboratory studies and comparable field studies. They concluded that laboratory research does discover phenomena that also exist outside of the laboratory. The strong correlation between the results of laboratory and field studies also suggests that the internal validity of the field studies is strong. The central point here is that well-designed studies, whether in laboratory or field settings, can produce valid information.

Studying Effects in the Field. The second reason for doing field research is to determine the impact of events that occur in real life. There is a growing demand in some quarters for testing the effectiveness of social programs, such as special education programs, public health campaigns, crackdowns on drunk drivers, and tax incentive programs. Each program has an implicit assumption: the educational program will improve literacy; the public health program will reduce drug addiction; the drunk-driving crackdown will reduce highway fatalities; the tax incentives will increase economic growth.

In reality, such assumptions are seldom tested. Social programs, as well meaning as they may be, are too often created for political ends. Their supporters are rarely committed to testing program effectiveness. Politically, it may be better not to subject programs to testing just in case testing reveals that one's costly pet project does not work.

Donald Campbell (1969) argued that developed countries should not rely on political decisions to launch or stop social programs, but ought to carry out social reforms as controlled social experiments. The fate of each program should depend on the objective data. However, such objective evaluations of new programs are not yet routinely carried out.

Improving Generalization. The third reason for conducting field research is to improve generalization. There are three types of generalization:

1. Generalization of results from the participants in a study to the larger population, as discussed in Chapter 9
2. Generalization of the results of the study over time (i.e., testing stability)
3. Generalization of results from study settings to other field settings

The third type of generalization may be enhanced when research is conducted in naturalistic settings. Consider the example given earlier, in which the effectiveness of a new teaching program was tested in a university laboratory school. The high-constraint laboratory setting, high in internal validity, is not necessarily strong in external validity. For example, it may be that the typical teacher in a university laboratory school, in which new ideas are routinely tested, may be very different from the typical teacher in the state's public schools. However, if the new program is found to be superior to other teaching methods when tested in the field, the researcher can have greater confidence that the results will generalize to other, similar classroom settings.

Neisser and Harsch (1992) conducted a clever field study to verify the external validity of a phenomenon that had been well established in the laboratory. Elizabeth Loftus and others had shown that memory is fragile, subject to significant distortion, and that people are often unaware of the distortions (e.g., Loftus & Hoffman, 1989). In 1986, the day after the *Challenger* space shuttle exploded during launch, Neisser and Harsch (1992) asked 44 college students to write down how they heard about the explosion and what they did. They asked these same students again 30 months later. None of these students was entirely consistent in recall a day after the event and at 30 months, and over one-third gave dramatically different accounts at those two times of how they found out about the *Challenger* disaster. More striking is that participants were certain that their memories 2.5 years after the accident were accurate, often describing the memories as exceptionally vivid. Many were astonished when confronted with their own handwritten accounts made the day after the disaster. Participants could not believe that memories that seemed so vivid and accurate could be so distorted over time, or that they would not realize that the memories were distorted.

This field study enhances confidence in the external validity of the laboratory studies of the malleability of memory. It also suggests that these laboratory findings would be relevant to real-world situations, such as eyewitness testimony in courts (Loftus & Ketcham, 1991).

How well do these findings generalize to other situations? The attacks on the World Trade Center and the Pentagon on September 11, 2001 offered psychologists another opportunity to look at this issue. The 9/11 attacks were generally felt more personally than the destruction of the *Challenger* space shuttle, raising anxiety about future attacks. So you might expect memories of the 9/11 attacks to be more intense and more resistant to change over time than the memories of the shuttle disaster. Weaver and Krug (2004) studied the memories of the 9/11 attacks several times over the year following the attack. They found that in the first week, the reports of how people heard about the attack and how they responded did shift from the initial report given the day of the attack, but then the memories seemed to stabilize. They also found that the degree to which the memories shifted was much less than what Neisser and Harsch (1992) had found for the shuttle disaster. Those closest to the events seemed to have the most stable and consistent memories of the events. For example, Paradis and her collaborators (2004) studied New York City residents and found that their memories of the attack were very stable.

These three field studies, as well as others not reported here, collectively indicate that dramatic events create the feeling that we have a strong and indelible memory of the event, but that memory is not always as stable as it feels. However, more emotionally powerful events tend to create memories that are more stable over time than do less emotionally powerful events. These field studies give us confidence that the principles of memory established in the laboratory apply well to most real-world settings, although the presence of extreme personal threat apparently affects memory processes in ways not found in laboratory studies and which would be unethical to recreate in the lab.

Difficulties in Field Research

Ideally, field experiments should be conducted carefully to allow the researcher to draw causal inferences. However, doing so can be difficult. In many field situations, such as schools or when natural events affect a large number of people, we cannot apply laboratory controls or assign participants to groups. For example, suppose that you want to know how much a natural disaster affected residents' physical health. The natural event is the independent variable and the residents' health is the dependent variable. Note that the researcher has no control over the independent variable. How then does the researcher measure the reactions and draw causal inferences?

Take another example: suppose that when studying a population of children, a researcher is unable to assign participants randomly to different groups for treatment because they are all part of a single class in school following a common program. That is, these children are always together, and whatever is applied to one child is applied to all others. Assigning the children to different groups for purposes of the study will seriously interfere with the ongoing program, and the program director will not allow it. The researcher wants to conduct research with as much control as possible in order to draw causal inferences, and yet random assignment might simply not be allowed.

Under such restrictions, how can we evaluate a new treatment? How can we answer questions about causality in natural settings when many manipulation and laboratory control procedures are unavailable?

This chapter discusses two solutions: quasi-experimental designs and program evaluation research. Quasi-experimental designs are research designs that have been developed to answer causal questions in natural settings. Program evaluation research is not a particular design, but rather is an increasingly important research area that includes many designs and strategies for assessing field settings.

Flexibility in Research

We now want to bring up something that all scientists know but rarely discuss in methods courses. This chapter opened with the following quotation: "*People don't usually do research the way people who write books about research say that people do research*" (Bachrach, 1981). Is this true? Well, yes and no. Bachrach was talking about flexibility and creativity in research, much as we did in Chapter 1 in our discussion of serendipity. Good researchers use hunches, flashes of insight, and flights of creativity, and they are alert to interesting and unanticipated events that can crop up. Such alertness—if paid attention to—can open new directions to be explored, help frame old questions in new ways, or suggest new ways of studying things. Creativity and flexibility are especially valuable in field research, in which the controlled environment of the laboratory is not there to help keep everything organized and systematic.

However, Bachrach was not saying that real research is unsystematic. Rather, he points out that there is an important place in the process to engage in the freer flights of research thinking. These free flights are useful precisely because they exist in a total research context that includes the organization, structure, and precision of science. This systematic structure makes it possible to engage in hunches and intellectual leaps without bringing the whole enterprise down in a chaotic jumble. When scientists engage in hypothesis testing, particularly of causal hypotheses, then systematic structure and precision are needed. However, within that structure, opportunities for unanticipated discoveries and hunches may appear, and a good researcher does not ignore them.

So why do we bring this up now, so late in this text? It is important for students to learn the fundamentals of research before they take such free-flight leaps—like the abstract artist who must learn how to draw and paint before beginning to create new and less constrained art forms. Pavlov argued this point when he noted that scientists must master the basics of science before going beyond those basics. With a solid background, the researcher can be more flexible, and such flexibility is often necessary in quasi-experimental designs and field research.

Quick-Check Review 13.1: Conducting Field Research

1. What is field research?
2. List three reasons for conducting field research.
3. What are the major difficulties in conducting field research?
4. What are the three types of generalization discussed in this section?
5. Why is flexibility in field research important?

QUASI-EXPERIMENTAL DESIGNS

Experiments provide the highest degree of control. However, when experiments are impossible, quasi-experimental designs can provide useful alternatives. "Quasi" means "approximately." Thus, a **quasi-experiment** is approximately or almost an experiment, but not quite. Quasi-experiments have the essential format of experiments, and they control for some confounding, but they do not have as much control as experiments. Thus, we must be cautious in drawing causal inferences from quasi-experiments.

Donald Campbell (1969) argued that quasi-experimental designs should be used whenever experiments cannot be carried out. In many field situations, *a quasi-experiment will still provide considerably more useful information than not experimenting at all*. Keep in mind that quasi-experimental designs include experimental control procedures and are thus very different from low-constraint methods.

Quasi-experimental designs include a comparison of at least two levels of an independent variable, but the actual manipulation may not always be under the experimenter's control. For example, in studying the health effects of a natural disaster, you obviously cannot manipulate the disaster. However, you can compare the health records from local hospitals before and after the disaster and compare them to records of people in another part of the state who did not experience the disaster. In this example, participants could not be randomly assigned to groups; indeed, the researcher often cannot assign participants at all, but must accept the natural groups as they exist. Thus, in quasi-experimental designs

1. we state causal hypotheses,
2. we include at least two levels of the independent variable, but cannot always manipulate the independent variable,
3. we usually cannot assign participants to groups, but must accept existing groups,
4. we include specific procedures for testing hypotheses,
5. we include controls for threats to validity.

Compare these characteristics with the characteristics of an experiment (from Chapter 9). A true experiment includes

1. a clearly stated research hypothesis concerning predicted causal effects of one variable on another,
2. at least two levels of the independent variable,
3. random assignment of participants to conditions,
4. specific and systematic procedures for empirically testing the hypothesized causal relationships,
5. specific controls to reduce threats to internal validity.

This chapter focuses on two quasi-experimental designs: the nonequivalent control-group design and the interrupted time-series design.

Nonequivalent Control-Group Designs

The best way to test causal hypotheses is to compare groups that you create through random assignment; random assignment makes it likely that the groups are equivalent at the beginning of the study. The initial equivalence of groups is crucial in experimental design. However, in some situations, we cannot assign participants randomly, and therefore the groups may not be equivalent at the beginning of the study.

There are several designs that attempt to solve the problem of comparing two groups that we suspect are not initially equivalent. We introduced one of those designs (the pretest-posttest, natural control-group design) in Chapter 10, and we emphasized the weaknesses of that design compared with experimental alternatives. However, that design is considerably stronger than many nonexperimental alternatives, as you will see in this section.

Researchers frequently have no choice in field research but to use already existing groups; thus, participants are not randomly assigned to conditions. Even though groups may appear to be similar, we cannot be sure that they are equivalent at the start of the study. The groups may differ on the dependent variable and other potential confounding variables, although a careful researcher may be able to rule out the most likely sources of confounding.

Campbell and Stanley (1966) popularized the **nonequivalent control-group design**, in which groups that already exist in the natural environment are used in research studies. Those groups might not be initially equivalent, but might nevertheless be similar to one another on most relevant variables. The more similar those natural groups are, the closer the design approximates an experiment. Cook and Campbell (1979) extended these ideas to situations in which naturally occurring groups are clearly not equivalent on potential confounding variables. Even in this extreme situation, it is sometimes possible to draw strong conclusions if the researcher carefully evaluates all potential threats to validity. Figure 13.1 illustrates the nonequivalent control-group design.

The research ideal is an experiment in which participants are randomly assigned to groups. If this is not possible, the best alternative is to use naturally occurring groups that give every indication of being similar on most of the relevant variables. Even when this requirement cannot be met, careful analysis of the design and the results can sometimes allow the researcher to draw useful conclusions from what appears to be a weak research design (Cook & Campbell, 1979).

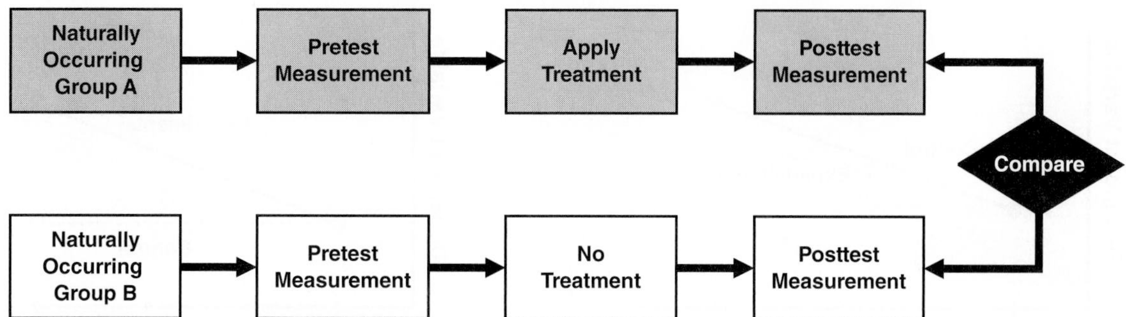

FIGURE 13.1 A Nonequivalent Control-Group Design. The nonequivalent control-group design is essentially the pretest-posttest, natural control-group design.

There are two major problems with nonequivalent groups: (1) the groups may differ on the dependent measure(s) at the start of the study, and (2) there may be other differences between the groups. The basic strategy for addressing the first issue is to measure the experimental and control groups on the dependent measure both before and after the manipulation. The pretest allows us to determine how similar the groups are initially on the dependent variable(s). This similarity is important; the more similar the groups are, the closer the design is to an experiment.

Groups may also differ on variables other than the dependent variable (confounding caused by selection). We need to rule out confounding variables by identifying each potential confounding variable, measuring each, and verifying that the groups do not differ on them. Remember that a variable can confound the results only if (1) it affects the dependent measure, and (2) the groups differ on the variable.

A second strategy, outlined in Chapter 7 in the section "Selecting Appropriate Control Groups," is to select a comparison group that is as similar as possible to the primary group. For example, if we are evaluating the health effects of people who experience a natural disaster, we would want a comparison group that was as similar as possible to the affected group. Since we know that age, education, social class, and income are all related to overall health, we would want to select a comparison sample that was as similar as possible to the affected group on these variables. If we select as a comparison sample an unaffected neighborhood with residents that tended to be younger and more affluent than the affected neighborhood, age and income would be potential confounding variables.

The selection of an effective control group can move this design closer to an experimental design. However, it is still a nonequivalent control-group design because *participants were not randomly assigned to the conditions.* Despite efforts to select a reasonably matched comparison sample, there is always the possibility that the comparison group differs on one or more confounding variables that had not been anticipated.

A full discussion of the principles for identifying confounding variables and interpreting their likely effects on a nonequivalent control-group study is beyond the scope of this text. Students are referred to Cook and Campbell (1979) for a complete discussion.

Figure 13.2 shows six possible outcomes of a nonequivalent control-group design. In Figures 13.2(a) and 13.2(b), the experimental and control groups are equivalent on the dependent measure at

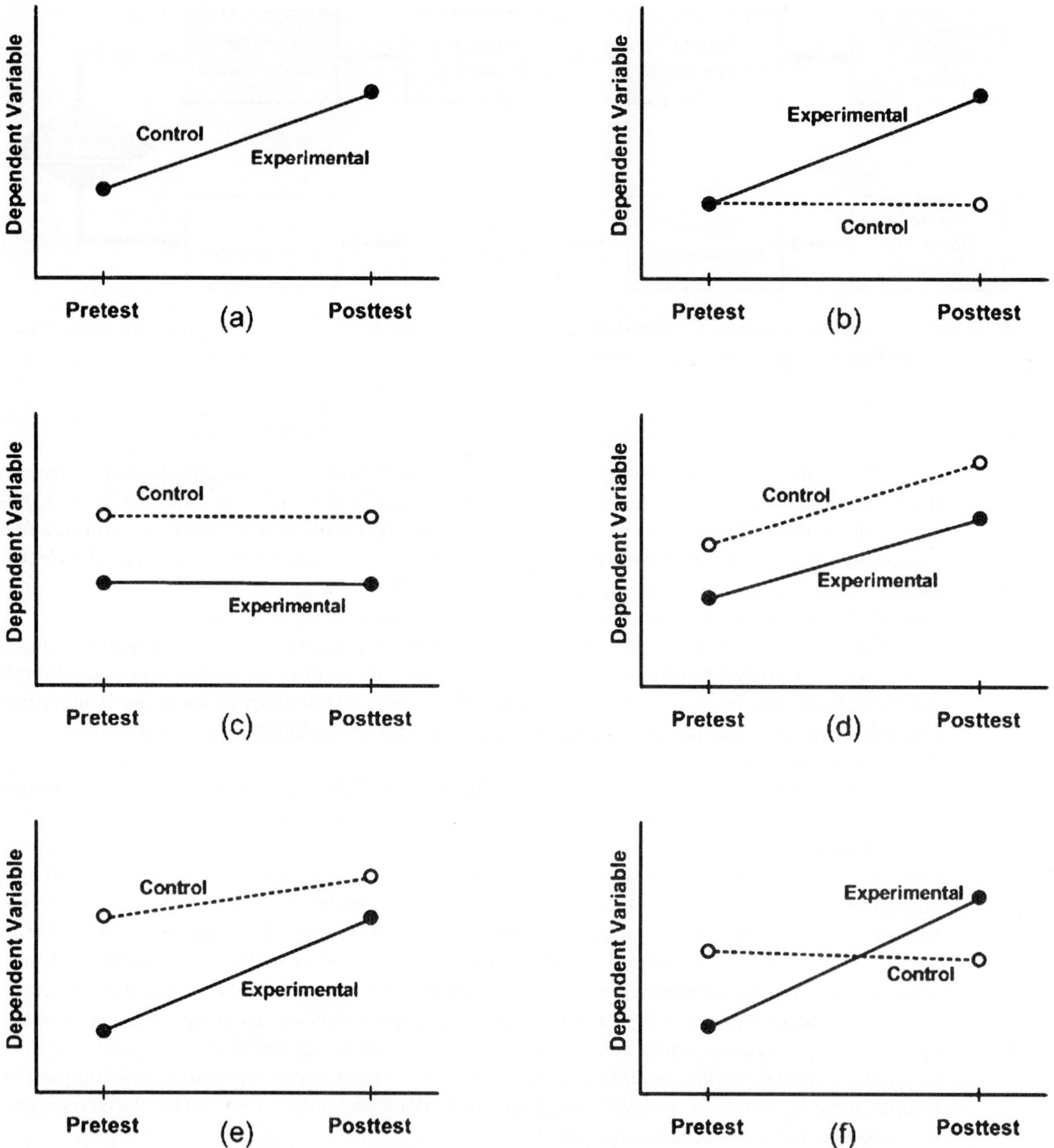

FIGURE 13.2 Interpreting Nonequivalent Control-Group Designs. Some possible outcomes of nonequivalent control-group designs are illustrated graphically. Some outcomes are relatively easy to interpret, whereas others are difficult or impossible to interpret.

the beginning of the study (the pretest). Of course, the groups may differ on other important variables, in which case we must include necessary controls that rule out confounding caused by selection. In Figures 13.2(c) through 13.2(f), the groups differ on the dependent measure at pretest. In these instances, the researcher must include the controls to rule out confounding caused by selection and regression to the mean. For this illustration, we will assume that all changes shown are in the predicted direction.

In Figure 13.2(a), both the experimental and control groups show an increase on the dependent measure from pretest to posttest. The groups are equivalent at the beginning and show equivalent change over time. Thus, there appears to be no effect of the independent variable. The observed changes were likely due to a shared historical variable or maturation.

In Figure 13.2(b), the groups are equivalent on the dependent measures at the beginning of the study. The experimental group shows a large change, whereas the control group does not change from pretest to posttest. There does appear to be an effect of the independent variable. However, before drawing this conclusion, the researcher must still rule out possible confounding caused by selection. For example, the groups may differ on another variable that might account for the different observed rates of change on the dependent measure.

In Figure 13.2(c), neither group changes from pretest to posttest. The obvious interpretation is that the manipulation has had no effect on the dependent variable.

Figure 13.2(d) shows a similar change in both groups from pretest to posttest. However, because both groups changed in the same manner, we cannot attribute the change to the independent variable. It appears more likely that some maturation process or historical event common to both groups may be responsible for the change in scores.

Figure 13.2(e) shows a slight change in the control group but a marked change in the experimental group. Such results suggest an effect of the independent variable. However, there is still the potential for regression to the mean, which limits confidence in this interpretation. Recall from Chapter 8 that regression to the mean is a potential source of confounding whenever we begin an experiment with participants who were selected on the basis of extreme scores. The pretest difference between groups might represent extreme scores for the experimental group, which then regressed toward the mean level represented by the control group. Thus, the change in the experimental group may not be caused by the independent variable.

In Figure 13.2(f), the control group does not change, but the experimental group does, even going beyond the level of the control group. This is called a **crossover effect**. Such results provide considerable confidence in a causal inference. Maturation is an unlikely alternative hypothesis, because the control group presumably matured but did not change. If maturation were responsible, it is unlikely that the effect would be so different in the two groups. Regression to the mean is also unlikely because the experimental group increased, not only to the mean of the control group, but beyond it.

In these examples, the results are fairly easy to interpret. Other situations, however, can be more difficult to interpret. Using nonequivalent control-group designs and correctly interpreting data from them requires considerable expertise, and therefore such designs are not recommended to beginning students. As we said before, an experiment is the best approach. When an experiment is not possible, a quasi-experiment, in which groups are apparently equivalent, is the best compromise. Only if neither of these alternatives is feasible should the researcher consider using a quasi-experimental design with nonequivalent groups.

Interrupted Time-Series Designs

In an **interrupted time-series design**, a single group of participants is measured several times both before and after some event or manipulation (Orwin, 1997). A series of measures is taken over time, is "interrupted" by the manipulation, after which another series of measures is taken. Depending on the nature of the manipulation, the measures may continue even during the manipulation. Time-series designs are variations of within-subjects designs, in which the same participants are measured in different conditions. The time-series design is similar to a simple pretest-posttest design except that multiple pretest and posttest measures are taken.

The simple pretest-posttest design is weak, leaving so many potential confounding factors uncontrolled that we cannot draw causal inferences (see Chapter 10). For example, recall the study of the use of relaxation to reduce the disruptive behavior of autistic children. A major potential confounding factor in this simple pretest-posttest study is regression to the mean. The disruptive behavior may naturally fluctuate over time, displaying considerable variability. The intervention might be applied only at a high point in this natural variation, just before the disruptive behavior decreased again. Thus, the observed improvement might not be caused by the treatment, but instead be only a result of the natural variability of behavior. The reduction might have occurred about that time without the treatment. However, if we include multiple measures both before and after the manipulation, we will have several points of comparison over time, thus allowing us to recognize regression to the mean effects.

To apply the interrupted time-series design in the study of autistic children, we would (1) measure disruptive behavior several times during a baseline observation period, (2) apply the treatment, and (3) measure disruptive behavior several more times after the intervention. This is the design that Graziano (1974) actually used, not the pretest-posttest design that we implied was used in Chapter 8. Disruptive behavior of four autistic children was measured and recorded for a full year as a normal part of the monitoring carried out in the program. The treatment (relaxation training) was applied, and the behavioral measures were again taken for more than a year following the treatment.

Figure 13.3 shows the results. Inspection of the graph shows considerable variation during the 1-year, pretreatment baseline. Following treatment, there was a marked decrease in disruptive behavior, reaching zero and remaining there. The results suggest that the decrease following treatment was not caused by normal fluctuation or regression to the mean. It also seems unlikely to have been caused by maturation of all participants during the same time. Although this study is a good demonstration of the effects of relaxation training, there is still a major confounding factor remaining. Can you identify it? (We will return to this point soon.)

Note in Figure 13.3 the peak of disruptive behavior shortly after training began. Does this suggest that the procedure was not working? Not really. A peak like this is a common clinical phenomenon called a *frustration effect*, which occurs whenever new procedures are initiated. Frustration effects are generally temporary. Again, subtleties like this illustrate how important it is to know the research literature, so that you do not interpret your findings incorrectly.

Interrupted time-series designs are useful in settings in which the effects of an event—naturally occurring or manipulated—may be assessed by taking multiple measurements both before and after the event. These designs can take advantage of data already gathered over a long time. They can also be used in studies in which the presumed causal event occurs for all members of a population. For example, suppose that a state government wants to reduce traffic collisions by reducing the speed limit from 75 to 65 miles per hour. The new speed limit applies to every driver in

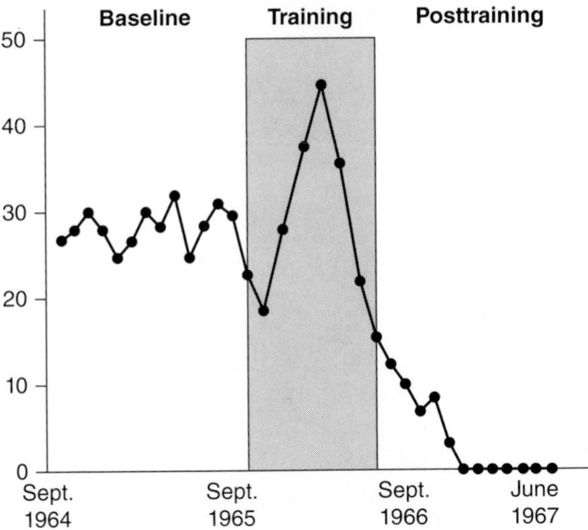

FIGURE 13.3 Relaxation Treatment for Disruptive Behavior. A time-series design using four children with autism demonstrates that relaxation training decreases the frequency of disruptive behavior.

the state; therefore, there cannot be an experimental group of state drivers for whom the new limit applies and a control group for which it does not. This is an ideal situation for an interrupted time-series design. Figure 13.4 shows a hypothetical graph of such a time-series study. The graph shows the variation in the number of serious accidents during the pre-intervention phase, with an overall slight increase throughout the year. Following the new speed limit, there is a sharp reduction, which eventually stabilizes at a new, lower level of accidents.

Are these results sufficient to draw a reasonably confident conclusion that the reduced speed limit is effective in reducing the number of serious accidents? Let us consider the major potential confounding factors. Selection is not at issue, because this is a within-subjects design, and the two groups being compared (the state's drivers before and after the decreased speed limit) were thus equivalent at the start of the study. Testing effects are not critical, because the measures taken are unobtrusive (taken from traffic records and not directly from participants). Maturation is not an issue, because it is unlikely that all the state's drivers suddenly became better drivers at the same time that the speed limit changed. Regression to the mean is not an issue, because the post-intervention decrease in accidents is much sharper, lasts longer, and reaches a lower mean level than the pre-intervention fluctuations. Primarily because of its multiple measures at pretreatment and posttreatment, the interrupted time-series design controls for most potential confounding. It is a far stronger design than a simple pretest-posttest design in which only one measure is taken at each phase.

With time-series designs, however, two potentially confounding factors remain: history and instrumentation. History can confound results in any procedure that requires a long time, because any number of other events might account for changes in the dependent variable. For example, in our hypothetical speed limit study, the state might have also sharply increased the number of patrol cars, the number of speeding tickets, and the severity of penalties for speeding and for drunk driving. Any of these actions may have contributed to the decrease in accidents. Thus, when using the interrupted time-series design, the experimenter must be careful to identify potential confounding caused by history and rule it out. In this example, we must be sure that the state did not initiate

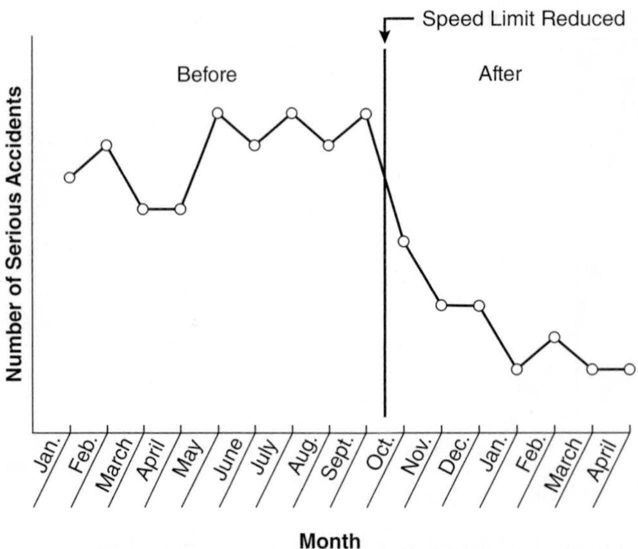

FIGURE 13.4 An Interrupted Time-Series Design. Using an interrupted time-series design, this hypothetical study illustrates the effects of a reduction in the state speed limit on the number of serious accidents.

these actions at the same time that it decreased the speed limit. (Recall a few paragraphs earlier when we asked you to identify the remaining major confounding factor in the time-series design for the relaxation training study. If you identified it as history, you were correct.)

Instrumentation is also a potential threat to validity in time-series designs. When people initiate new approaches or programs, there might also be changes in recording procedures. For example, if the state government was more systematic about collecting accident statistics after the speed limit change, the apparent reduction in accidents might be real, caused by the changes in speed limit, or an illusion, caused by changes in the way the data were gathered. Such confounding due to instrumentation must be ruled out.

In a time-series study, the change must be sharp to be interpreted as anything other than a normal fluctuation. Any post-intervention change that is slight or gradual is difficult to interpret as being caused by the intervention. It should also occur immediately after the intervention, unless there is a theoretical reason to expect a delay. For example, if an intervention by the government is expected to change consumer spending, but only after it has affected other economic variables, the change in consumer spending may be delayed and still indicate an effect of the intervention.

Note two important points about the interrupted time-series design. First, it is a flexible design that can be used in many situations. It can evaluate events that are large or small in scale; that have already occurred or are expected to occur; that are either manipulated (such as the decreased speed limit) or not manipulated (such as a natural disaster). (Think about how you might use this design to evaluate a large-scale natural disaster that has already occurred.)

Second, a time-series design can use existing data, such as official records of auto accidents. Government agencies often use this design to track the effects of new programs.

We can improve an interrupted time-series design by adding one or more comparison groups. In our hypothetical study of the effects of a change in speed limit on the number of accidents, we could compare data from a neighboring state that did not reduce the speed limit. This would help to control such confounding variables as history and maturation. That type of control was used by Guerin and MacKinnon (1985) in their study of a California law that required children under age 4 to be in federally approved child car seats while riding in cars. Using an interrupted time-series design, the authors examined the effects of the new law on child auto injuries. They obtained the number of injuries for children under age 4 from state records for 48 months prior to the start of the new law and 12 months following its initiation. As a comparison, they recorded auto injury data for children between 4 and 7 years old—children not covered by the law. They predicted—and found—a decrease for the younger group, but not for the older group. In addition, they compared the younger group with young children in Texas, where no child car seat law existed. Texas children did not show a decrease during the same period. Adding these two comparison groups increased confidence that the new law, and not other factors, accounted for the reduction in injuries. This was one of the early studies showing the efficacy of the new child safety seats. All states have required their use since 1985.

Graphing the results of interrupted time-series studies provides considerable information, but simply inspecting a graph does not address whether the observed differences are statistically significant. Testing for statistical significance in time-series designs requires sophisticated procedures that are beyond the scope of this book. The interested student is referred to Kazdin (2003) for a more detailed discussion.

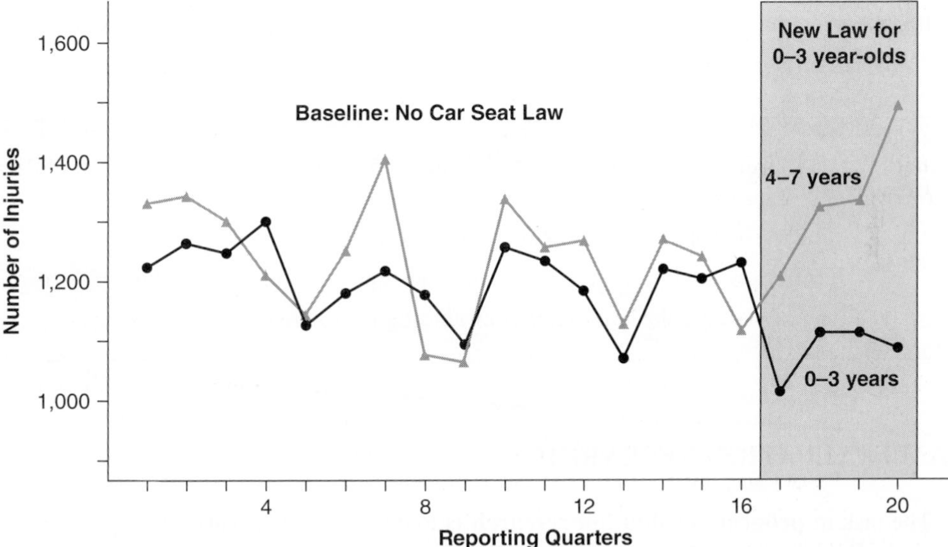

FIGURE 13.5 Effects of a New Child Car Seat Law. These time-series data show that a new car seat law reduced the number of injuries in zero- to three-year-old children in comparison with four- to seven-year-old children, who were not covered by the law.

Source: Adapted from Guerin and MacKinnon (1985)

TABLE 13.1 Research Using Interrupted Time-Series Designs

1. Catalano and Serxner (1992) used an interrupted time-series design to investigate the relationship between employment security and birth weight of children. They found that during periods of employment uncertainty, such as when companies are laying off people, male babies average lower birth weight than during periods when employment is more secure.
2. McKay et al. (1996) used an interrupted time-series approach to study the effectiveness of a treatment procedure for obsessive-compulsive disorder.
3. Stolzenberg and D'Alessio (1997) used an interrupted time-series design to assess the impact of California's "3 strikes and you're out" law on the rate of serious crimes. As a control, they studied petty theft, which was not covered by the law.
4. Campostrini et al. (2006) used an interrupted time-series design to evaluate the effect of changes in the drinking and driving laws in California on the rate of arrests for "driving under the influence."
5. Schwartz et al. (2007) used an interrupted time-series design to evaluate the effectiveness of an educational program for doctors on the proper use of antimicrobial treatment of long-term care patients.
6. Olfson et al. (2008) used an interrupted time-series design to look at the effect of new warnings about the possible suicide risk in adolescents taking antidepressant medications.
7. Grundy et al. (2010) used an interrupted time-series study to evaluate the effects of imposing a 20 miles per hour speed limit in 119,029 road segments in London, England, finding a 41.9% reduction in road casualties (injuries and deaths).

Table 13.1 gives examples of published studies that used interrupted time-series designs. Notice the wide range of educational, medical, psychological, and public safety issues that are studied using this design.

Quick-Check Review 13.2: Quasi-Experimental Designs

1. Define "quasi-experimental design." What is the value of this type of design? What are its limitations?
2. When are nonequivalent control-group designs most effective?
3. How are interrupted time-series designs a variation on within-subjects designs?
4. What are the two major confounding factors in time-series designs?

PROGRAM EVALUATION RESEARCH

The task in **program evaluation research** is to determine how successfully a program meets its goals. For example, researchers may need to evaluate a food stamp program, a state highway speed-control program, or the effectiveness of a rehabilitation program for criminal offenders. In these days of tight budgets, a key concept is accountability. Program evaluation research can provide evidence on whether money spent on a program is accomplishing the program's goals. Such evidence often improves existing programs, making them more effective and targeting them to those who are most likely to benefit, as illustrated in Historical Lesson 13.1.

HISTORICAL LESSON 13.1: FROM HEAD START TO HEADS UP

One of the most prominent aspects of the Great Society Program of the 1960s was the wide range of Head Start Programs that were initiated across the United States (Vinovskis, 2005). The idea behind Head Start was that children who are raised in an environment that lacks intellectual stimulation are likely to be intellectually handicapped for their entire lives. Providing intellectual and social stimulation to preschoolers was an attempt to prevent this handicap.

Actually, at the time that most Head Start programs were introduced, we knew little about how early childhood experiences affected intellectual development, and, consequently, many of the Head Start programs were really experiments. Remember, Donald Campbell (1969) had argued that industrialized nations should routinely evaluate new programs as social experiments, and many of the Head Start programs did indeed have an evaluation component.

The early research on Head Start programs was discouraging. The effects were small and tended to disappear after a few months, although there were exceptions to this pattern. Ramey and his colleagues (1996) looked at this broad pattern of findings and noted that there were important effects discernable in the data. Those effects were often masked by the fact that the Head Start programs were making only a marginal difference in intellectual development for most children. However, for those children whose home environment was extremely deficient, with little social, perceptual, and cognitive stimulation, enrichment programs like Head Start seemed to make a significant difference (Ramey & Ramey, 1998).

Through a series of studies, Ramey and his colleagues discovered that earlier interventions were more helpful and lasted longer (Campbell & Ramey, 1994), presumably because such early intervention provides the necessary stimulation to allow normal brain development. One of the reasons that most Head Start programs had minimal impact is that these early programs focused on children who were almost school age and therefore well past most of the critical periods for brain development. In addition, most Head Start programs targeted children solely on the basis of family income, which is less predictive of intellectual development problems than the level of stimulation in the household (Ramey & Ramey, 1998).

The most effective programs in increasing the intellectual development of children and maintaining the gains are those that (1) begin when children are very young, (2) are intensive (up to several hours per day several days per week), (3) provide the experience directly to the children rather than indirectly through parent training, (4) are broadly aimed rather than focusing on a single cognitive skill, (5) are tailored to individual children, and (6) seek to continue intellectual stimulation after the program ends (Campbell et al., 2002; Ramey & Ramey, 1998, 2004; Pungello et al., 2010).

These findings are based on over 40 years of research, starting with evaluations of the early Head Start programs and continuing with high-constraint experimental studies of the impact of various interventions on the intellectual development of children. Imagine the impact of this research, and the programs that it has stimulated, on children who might have been doomed to marginal intellectual development and the resulting limitations placed on their lives. Clearly, the effective use of program evaluation can improve the world.

Program evaluation research can utilize any of the designs discussed in this text. The best possible research design that permits the strongest conclusions should always be selected. However, special circumstances—dictated by ethical and practical issues—exist in field settings and can restrict our choice of design.

Practical Problems in Program Evaluation Research

High-constraint research brings participants into the laboratory, allowing considerable control. In contrast, program evaluation research involves complex natural settings in which the researcher has little control. For example, program evaluators are interested in how effective a program is in meeting the needs of clients—usually a personal matter for each client. In most cases, the participants have not volunteered for a research study, having joined the program because it addressed their needs. The program evaluator is faced with difficult practical and ethical considerations not found in the laboratory.

Ethical constraints are common in program evaluation, as discussed in the Ethical Principles section in this chapter, but they are not the only restricting issues. In a learning disabilities program, for example, we must accept the possibility that the experimental program might not work—indeed, we are doing the study to find out if it works. Assigning some students to a control condition and denying them access to the experimental program may be ethically acceptable for the researcher because we do not yet know whether the experimental program works. However, it might not be acceptable from the perspective of a school administrator who might believe that it is wrong to deny some students access to the experimental program.

Practical issues also make program evaluations challenging. Unlike controlled studies in the laboratory, a program occurs in a natural setting that is usually not under the control of the evaluator. Staff members want to do their best running the program, and spending time to evaluate it is often a secondary consideration for them. A good program evaluator needs excellent political skills to convince staff to cooperate and to maintain their cooperation throughout. Often, when staff members are involved in an evaluation, they resent the time that the evaluation takes away from their central work: providing services. If the evaluator is not sensitive to these realities, the relationship between the evaluator and program staff can become hostile.

The program evaluator must also be aware of potentially biasing factors in the data. A staff is generally interested in showing the program in its best possible light, not only because it is their program, but also because a program that appears to be ineffective might not get continued funding. Some clients may also have a vested interest in the program if they believe that it has been helpful, and they may therefore inflate their ratings of its effectiveness. On the other hand, some clients may believe that better programs could be implemented; therefore, they deflate their ratings of effectiveness. Such potential biases make it especially important that the evaluator rely on many data sources, at least some of which are objective measures.

Issues of Control

Control in program evaluation research is as important as in any other type of research. Because of the naturalistic nature of the program evaluation setting, it is often difficult to apply controls. Nevertheless, many controls are available, three of which are discussed here.

Selecting Appropriate Dependent Measures. Most programs are developed with several goals in mind. Therefore, the program evaluator needs to use several dependent measures to evaluate the effectiveness of the program in meeting each of the goals. Some measures will focus on actual change in the individuals served by the program, and some will focus on changes outside the program, such as enhanced economic activity in the community. It is useful to include satisfaction measures from the people served by the program as well as from the community in general. Although satisfaction measures do not indicate the program's effectiveness, they may influence future effectiveness. An effective but unpopular program will need to address why it is unpopular or continued funding might be jeopardized.

Minimizing Bias in Dependent Measures. In any research, it is essential to minimize measurement bias. This is particularly important in program evaluation research, in which the possibility of bias is high because the same people who run the program are often responsible for data collection.

Program evaluators try to minimize bias by using objective measures whenever possible, and by using people who are not involved in the administration of the program to gather data. Many broad-based programs are intended to have community-wide effects that can be monitored using routinely available data, such as census data.

No technique for minimizing bias will be effective in all situations. One of the better approaches is to use several dependent measures. If each is a valid measure and they all point to the same general conclusion, you have evidence of convergent validity and the evaluator can be confident of the results.

Control through Research Design in Program Evaluation. As with any research project, the major controls are incorporated into the research design. The strongest program evaluation design is an experiment, with random assignment of participants. If this is impossible, the strongest alternative design should be used.

Typical Program Evaluation Designs

Dozens of research designs have been used for program evaluations, but three or four designs account for most of this research.

Randomized Control-Group Design. The ideal program evaluation design is a control-group design, with random assignment of participants to conditions. This experimental design provides maximum control. The control group may be a no-treatment control, a waitlist control, or some alternative treatment. A **waitlist control group** is a group of people who act as no-treatment controls, but are promised and receive the treatment after they have served as control participants.

Ethical considerations often dictate the nature of the control group. For example, under some conditions it might not be ethical to assign participants to a no-treatment control group. Instead, the best treatment currently available is used as a control against which the experimental procedure is compared.

Nonequivalent Control-Group Design. If a randomized control-group design is impossible, the best alternative is a nonequivalent control-group design. It is often possible to identify a natural control group that is likely to be similar to the group you are evaluating. Our earlier example of evaluating the California Child Passenger Restraint Law used this design with time-series data. The researchers (Guerin & MacKinnon, 1985) selected two control groups: (1) children in the same age range (0 to 4 years) from another state, and (2) slightly older children (4 to 7 years old) from California. Children were not randomly assigned to these groups, but there was no reason to believe that the groups were different on variables likely to affect risk of death or injury from automobile accidents. Even though this was not an experiment, it came very close to an experiment in its ability to rule out confounding variables.

Single-Group, Time-Series Design. If a control group is not possible, the best alternative strategy is a time-series design. Repeated measures on the dependent variables before, during, and after the program can control many threats to internal validity. Depending on the funding source, pretest measures may be difficult to obtain because there is often pressure to begin services as soon as funds are released. Still, this design is flexible and useful in many situations. In fact, even when a control group is possible, using a time-series strategy will increase confidence in the evaluation of the program's effectiveness.

Pretest-Posttest Design. The pretest-posttest design is weak. Unfortunately, it is used much too often in program evaluation research. With only two measures and no control group, few threats to internal validity are controlled. Therefore, the simple pretest-posttest design is not recommended.

Program Evaluation Research: An Example

Managed care is a concept that has quickly become a part of health insurance coverage in the United States. With managed care, the insurance company, or an organization hired by the insurance company, attempts to control health care costs by monitoring health care and authorizing each procedure according to the principle of whether it is "medically necessary." The promise is that managed care will provide quality health care at lower cost by reducing waste and eliminating unnecessary procedures. Critics charge that managed care reduces costs by denying necessary treatment. In a debate of this magnitude, it is surprising that so little data exist on the effectiveness of managed care programs in meeting their stated goals.

Raulin and his colleagues (Raulin et al., 1995a, 1995b) used a nonequivalent control-group design to evaluate the effectiveness of a program to manage mental health benefits. They selected stratified random samples from two insurance plans operated by the same insurance carrier: one that included management of mental health benefits and one that represented the standard insurance policy. The samples were matched on age, sex, and severity of diagnosis, factors that are known to affect the outcome and cost of psychological treatment. Participants were selected from health insurance plans that were matched on their total mental health coverage. Although participants were not randomly assigned to groups, the selection procedure produced groups from the same geographical area that were closely matched on key demographic variables and had equivalent health care insurance coverage.

Participants selected by these procedures were recruited by letter to participate. To increase the likelihood of participation, participants were offered a financial incentive for participation. As is often the case in program evaluation studies, the initial procedures had to be modified because they did not work well. Face-to-face interviews were replaced with a telephone interview to make participation more convenient for participants, and an initial $25 reimbursement rate was raised to $40 because the evaluations took longer than initially expected. Of course, not all individuals who were contacted by letter chose to participate. It would have been unethical to insist that everyone participate. Therefore, the sample may not have been representative of the population because it had a self-selection bias.

The managed care program evaluated in this study was designed to accomplish several things. Therefore, several dependent measures were needed in the evaluation so that it would adequately measure how well the program was functioning. People in treatment were evaluated on (1) symptom level, using several well-validated symptom measures; (2) mood, also using measures with established validity; and (3) satisfaction with their care and their insurance coverage. In addition, cost data were obtained from the insurance carrier for both mental health coverage and for other medical care. The rationale for measuring the cost of other medical care was that previous research had suggested that skimping on mental health coverage increases general medical costs, because people took their mental health concerns to their family physician.

The data suggested that the management of mental health benefits did not decrease the quality of care as measured by the standardized symptom and mood scales and the satisfaction measures used in the study. The mental health care costs were reduced by approximately 50% in the managed care group, and there were no differences between the groups on medical costs.

As with all research, one should be cautious in generalizing from this study to managed care programs in general. This study involved only the management of mental health benefits and therefore indicated little about whether managing general medical benefits would work as well. The managed care firm evaluated was relatively small, operated locally, and was run by an unusually well-qualified clinical director. It is not clear that one could generalize the findings of this study to other managed care operations, which now are almost all large, national operations. Even with these limitations, this study provides useful data for making policy decisions on how to spend health care dollars.

In summary, program evaluation research involves high-constraint research in low-constraint, naturalistic settings. By carefully selecting dependent measures, and by using the strongest research design possible, the evaluation can gather useful information about the effectiveness of programs in meeting their stated goals.

Program evaluation research is a valuable tool in the management of limited resources, because ineffective programs consume dollars that might have been spent on effective programs. The challenges of evaluating field programs are unique and require specific research skills (Posavac & Carey, 2007). Program evaluation research is both a science and an art; one needs good research, political, and communication skills to do it well. More than any other kind of research, program evaluation research depends on the ability of the researcher to gain the cooperation of people who are not necessarily committed to the cause of maximizing the study's internal and external validity.

Quick-Check Review 13.3: Program Evaluation Research

1. What is the major purpose of program evaluation research? What is its importance?
2. What is the major difficulty in conducting program evaluation research?
3. How can internal validity be maximized in program evaluation research?
4. What research designs are used most frequently in program evaluation?
5. Why is program evaluation research both a science and an art?

SURVEYS

Surveys ask participants about their experiences, attitudes, or knowledge. Survey instruments can be used in virtually any type of research, from case studies through experimental studies. Survey research is not a single research design, but utilizes several basic research procedures to obtain information from people in their natural environments.

Surveys can be relatively simple, with just a few questions that can be asked by telephone. They can also be complicated and sophisticated instruments that test hypothesized relationships among variables and require lengthy face-to-face interviews. Surveys often test relationships among variables—a variation of correlational research. This section describes how surveys are used, the types of surveys, the steps in survey research, and how to select and construct an appropriate survey instrument.

Types of Surveys

We will discuss two types of surveys: status surveys and survey research.

Status Surveys. A **status survey** describes the current characteristics of a population, such as voter preferences or teacher satisfaction. Status surveys are commonly used in public health research to determine rates of illness and health-related behaviors. Examples are the status survey of food consumption in the United States (Mosfegh et al., 2009) and adolescents' use of illicit drugs (Johnston et al., 2009).

Survey Research. **Survey research** tries to discover relationships among variables. For example, Serras et al. (2010) surveyed 5,689 college and graduate students looking at self-injurious behavior and its relationship to other variables. Self-injurious behavior is defined as the infliction of physical harm to one's body without suicidal intent, and it is surprisingly common among college students (about 14% engaged in the behavior in the year prior to the study). It includes such behaviors as cutting, biting, or burning oneself, pushing sharp objects into one's skin, or interfering with the healing of a wound. The authors found that self-injurious behavior was associated with depression, smoking, gambling, binge drinking, and drug use, and that the rate of self-injurious behavior seemed to drop with age.

Steps in Survey Research

Surveys are the most familiar and ubiquitous form of research in the social sciences. At first glance, it may appear an easy task to conduct surveys; after all, a survey is simply asking people a few questions. However, as you will see, detailed planning is necessary if surveys are to be successful.

The major goal of a survey is to learn about the self-reported ideas, knowledge, feelings, opinions, attitudes, and behavior of a defined population. Surveys typically include many types of items—demographic, attitude, opinion, knowledge, and behavior items. To carry out a survey, the researcher must carefully work through several overlapping steps as shown in Go with the Flow 13.1.

The first task of the researcher is to determine the informational area to be studied, the population to be surveyed, and the manner in which the survey instrument is to be administered. These decisions guide the construction and administration of the survey instrument. For example, Ahlfeldt et al. (2005) wanted to determine what factors increased engagement in classroom activities (the area of information) in college students (the population) using a group-administered questionnaire (the form of the survey).

Types of Survey Instruments

The survey instrument may be a questionnaire or an interview schedule. In a self-administered **questionnaire**, respondents read the instructions and write or mark their answers to the questions. This is usually done on a pencil and paper form, but increasingly, it is done on a computer or over the Internet. The Serras et al. (2010) study of self-injurious behavior gathered the data over the Internet. In telephone or in-person interviews, the survey instrument is called an **interview schedule**, and the researcher reads the questions to the respondent and records the answers.

The survey instrument lists the questions and provides instructions and methods for answering them. If it is a self-administered questionnaire, it must be a clear guide for the respondent. If it is to

GO WITH THE FLOW 13.1 | STEPS IN SURVEY RESEARCH

Constructing, refining, administering, and interpreting a survey is time consuming, but if you follow these steps, you will create the kind of survey that will answer your questions.

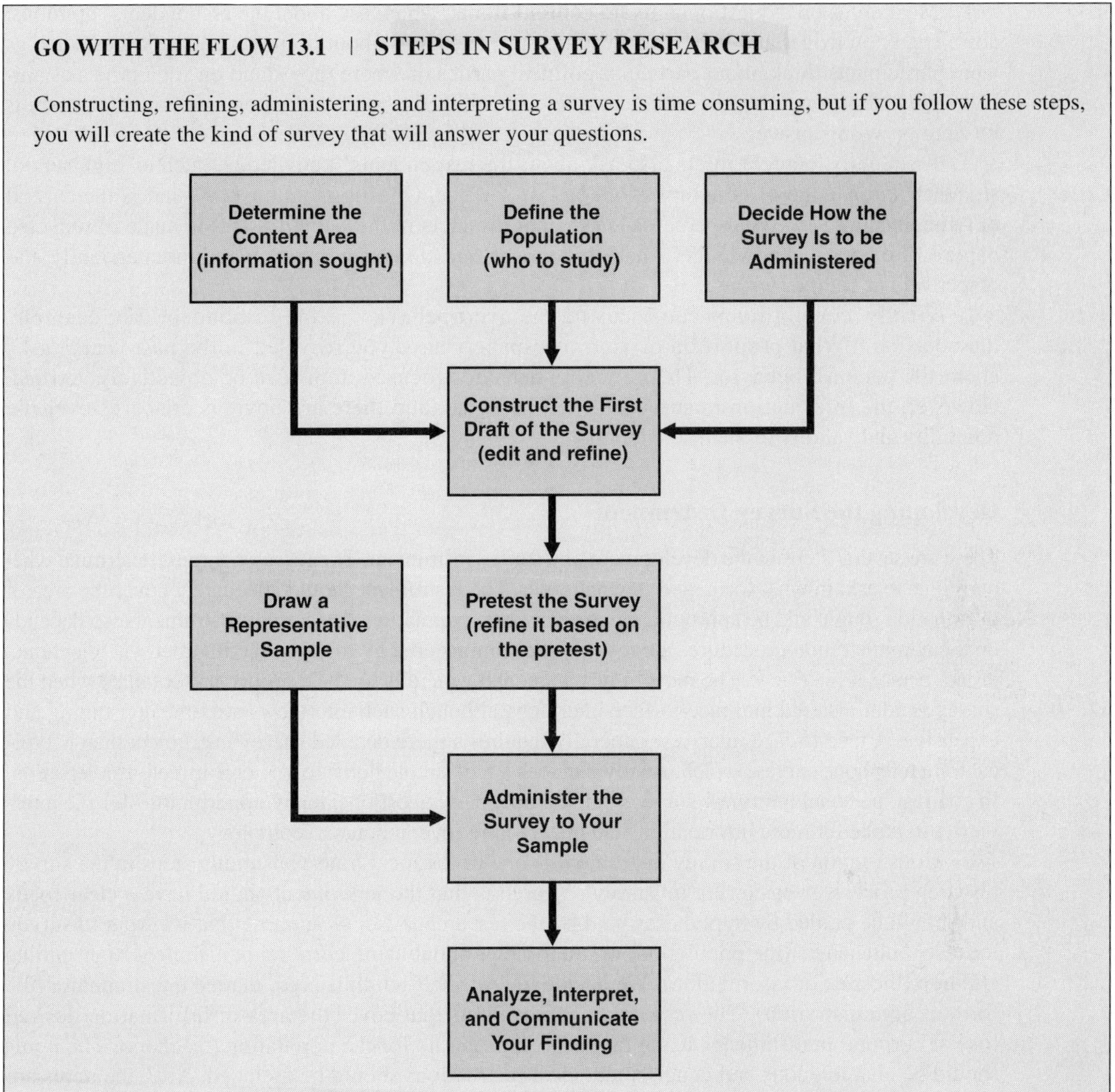

be administered by an interviewer, it must be a clear guide for the interviewer. The language must be unambiguous, concise, and within the reading and comprehension abilities of the respondents.

Questionnaires and interviews begin with an introduction, which explains the purpose of the survey and gives instructions to the respondent. The questions fall into two main categories: demographic and content questions. **Demographic questions** seek descriptive information about the respondents, such as age, gender, occupation, and marital status. These are **factual items**, and they can be verified independently.

Most items on a questionnaire are **content items**, which ask about the respondents' opinions, attitudes, knowledge, and behavior. Responses to questions about opinions and attitudes, such as what participants think about particular political parties or where they stand on such issues as animal rights, abortion, or environmental issues, are subjective and vary among individuals. There is no right or wrong answer.

Frequently, content items also ask about the respondents' knowledge, such as high school students' knowledge of geography, history, or science. Questions that ask, "What is the capital of Afghanistan?" or "What percentage of paper products in the United States is made of recycled paper?" are tests of knowledge. Answers to these questions can be evaluated independently and objectively as right or wrong.

Finally, content items can focus on the overt behavior of the respondent. For example, the question, "What proportion of your newspapers have you recycled in the past year?" asks about the person's behavior. Theoretically, behavior-focused items can be objectively verified. However, the information in surveys is self-reported, and there are obvious concerns over the reliability and validity of such self-reports.

Developing the Survey Instrument

There are several steps in the development of a survey instrument. The researcher must determine what questions to ask, in what form, and in what order. The instrument should adequately cover the area of information sought and be appropriate for the targeted population. The survey instrument also depends on the administration procedure. Surveys can be administered by mail, on the Internet, via telephone, or in a personal interview. The most information, and generally the best results, are obtained when the survey is administered in a face-to-face interview, although such interviews are time consuming and expensive. A face-to-face interview generally requires a more detailed survey instrument than is typical for a telephone survey, which usually includes a few simple items in a 1- or 2-minute conversation. In contrast, personal interview surveys can include many questions, many opportunities for the interviewer to probe for more information, and may require several hours to complete.

Construction of the survey instrument is one of the most time-consuming steps in the survey research process. A basic rule in survey research is that the instrument should have a clear focus and should be guided by hypotheses held by the researcher. Let us suppose that we want to survey local schoolteachers (the population) on their views about using corporal punishment to discipline children (the area of information). We decide to use a self-administered, mailed questionnaire (the form of administration). The researcher writes items that cover the area of information desired (use of corporal punishment), using language appropriate for the population (teachers). The items should be unambiguous and concise, and clear instructions should be included. After the items are written, they should be edited for clarity, pretested, and then refined based on the pretesting. This pretesting is critical because items that may seem perfectly clear to the researcher may be interpreted in more than one way by the subjects who are the focus of the survey.

The items can take several forms: **open-ended items**, **multiple-choice items**, and **Likert-scale items**. In our study, we might ask the following open-ended question:

What do you think of using corporal punishment in disciplining children?

If this were a questionnaire, we would leave sufficient space for the respondents to write their answers. In an interview, we would record answers for later coding and scoring.

An example of a multiple-choice question is

What proportion of parents use corporal punishment to discipline their children?

a. *10%*
b. *25%*
c. *50%*
d. *75%*
e. *100%*

Multiple-choice question have the advantage of being a familiar format that allows the researcher to jump from one question to another without it feeling disruptive to the survey participants.

In Likert scales, we arrange the choices on a continuum, with extreme positions at the endpoints. For example, participants might be asked to indicate the degree to which they agree with a statement:

Corporal punishment is necessary in raising children.

Strongly Agree   Agree   Uncertain   Disagree   Strongly Disagree

13:02

This item could be scored from 1 to 5. A single questionnaire might include items in each format. If so, it is good form to keep items of the same format together. Dawis (1987) and Kerlinger and Lee (2000) provide more details on survey construction. We have included more detail on survey construction techniques on the Student Resource Website.

Sampling Participants

Obtaining an adequate sample is one of the most important factors in conducting surveys. When the identified population is large and diverse, it is impossible to question every member. The U.S. census is an example of such an attempt, but taking a census of this magnitude is expensive and time consuming. Instead, surveys draw a sample of the population and then generalize the findings from the sample to the population. If the sample is drawn properly, one can make confident conclusions about the population. In fact, the U.S. Census Bureau proposed replacing the census of some areas of the country with carefully drawn samples, arguing that they could get a better count from this methodology than the traditional methodology of trying to contact everyone (Duskin, 1999). The proposal was rejected, not on methodological grounds, but on political grounds.

The population in a survey is the larger group about whom we wish to obtain information. Some examples of survey populations might be eligible voters for a presidential election, high school teachers in California, readers of the *National Review*, middle school children in Milwaukee, students at the University of Texas, or Chevrolet owners. In our example, we have taken the first step by identifying the population as local schoolteachers. Now we must be more precise by specifying a geographic area or specific school systems, as well as other characteristics of the population, such as the grade levels of the teachers and/or their areas of teaching expertise (science, social studies, English, etc.). The survey might include all schoolteachers or be limited to grammar school or full-time teachers. We must decide whether to include teachers in private schools or limit the population of study to public school teachers.

Sampling Considerations. Having identified the population of interest, the researcher must also specify the sampling procedures. The heart of survey research is the selection of representative samples. Without it, the results will tell us only about the sample and will not help us learn about a larger population. It can be difficult to achieve this goal, as is discussed in Cost of Neglect 13.1, which discusses the challenges of political polling. It is for this reason that many polls are taken by specialized polling companies or academic groups. By doing polling exclusively, these groups are able to maintain the kind of databases that allow for precise sampling.

THE COST OF NEGLECT 13.1: POLITICAL POLLING AND SAMPLING

Political polling has always been a part of United States history. In a democracy, the will of the people should prevail, and in a technologically advanced democracy, politicians and political pundits increasingly want to know what the people think. However, even with the high technology of the day, it is a challenge to draw the kind of representative samples needed to draw accurate conclusions about the will of the people.

The task of obtaining representative samples is constantly changing and is always a challenge. Most polls are conducted over the phone, because this keeps costs to a minimum. At one point, this produced a significantly biased sample, because phones were expensive and many low-income families did not have phones (Eisenger, 2003). Now most people have phones, so this is less of a problem than it once was. However, there has been a move toward having unlisted phone numbers, and the social demographics of this movement were also a threat to valid political sampling. Specifically, unlisted numbers were more likely to be for families from higher income brackets (Eisenger, 2003). To correct that, pollsters went to random dialing rather than randomly selecting numbers from the phone book. With random dialing, all possible numbers are in the population to be sampled, not just listed numbers.

Another problem arose with the recently enacted Federal Do Not Call law, which allows people to list their phone numbers in a national registry of numbers that are not to be called by telemarketers. However, political pollsters were able to convince Congress that they should be exempt from this rule, or perhaps the politicians in Congress already believed that polling was too valuable to have the Do Not Call Registry interfere with it (Liptak, 2003). It is interesting to note that previous do-not-call legislation on a statewide level did not include a provision to exclude political polling (Bowers, 1997).

The trend toward more use of cell phones, which are generally not listed in phone directories, also complicates polling. Some households now have a half dozen phone numbers, whereas other households may have only one. Random dialing of phone numbers therefore will make some households much more likely to be polled. Cell phones cannot be ignored much longer, because people are increasingly making their cell phone their only phone (Turner, 2004). Furthermore, people may be using caller ID to screen out unwanted calls, including calls from polling companies. In addition, the new laws on portability of local phone numbers mean that the exchange (the three digits between the area code and the last four digits of the phone number) no longer indicates the provider or the type of phone (cell phone or land line). It may not even indicate the community that a person lives in.

When taking polls to predict election results, the problem is to identify who is likely to vote. It does not matter how many of the people favor candidate A; it only matters how many of the people who vote on Election Day cast their ballots for candidate A.

Different polling agencies approach this problem in different ways. Some simply ask if the person intends to vote when taking the poll. Others ask how likely it is that the person will vote and may weight their preference based on their likelihood of voting. People who say they are definitely going to vote are more likely to vote for their preferred candidate than people who say they will probably vote. Other polling agencies ask about the past voting history of their respondents, reasoning that those who have voted regularly in the past are more likely to vote than those who have rarely voted in the past. (How do you handle people who have just reached voting age?)

Despite these problems, the best political pollsters are able to call elections with accuracy. They have developed techniques that sample the voting electorate and predict who among the people they talk to will actually vote on Election Day.

Sampling Procedures. Sampling procedures fall into two major categories: (1) nonprobability sampling, and (2) probability sampling. **Nonprobability sampling** (also called **convenience sampling**) uses respondents who are readily available, with little attempt to carefully represent any population. For example, you might carry out a survey by interviewing the first 50 people you meet on the street or the first 20 people who are coming out of a polling place at election time. Newspaper, television, and radio surveys are often carried out in this way to obtain a quick public response to an issue while it is still a current news item. Nonprobability sampling is convenient, but it is weak because the respondents are unlikely to be representative of the population, and the survey results might therefore be biased.

Probability sampling procedures give us greater confidence that the sample adequately represents the population. The two major probability sampling methods are random sampling and stratified random sampling. We talked about these methods in another context (see Chapter 9).

In *random sampling*, every member of the identified population has an equal chance of being selected, thus reducing selection biases. Random sampling requires a list of all members of the population, but this would be difficult to obtain if the population is large, such as all children in primary and secondary schools. With such large populations, only the largest polling organizations have the resources to use random sampling. If the population is limited, such as all children in a specific school, then creating an initial list (called a **sampling frame**) of all the children is feasible. We could then randomly select from the sampling frame without much difficulty. Thus, random sampling is used for survey research in which population size allows a workable sampling frame from which individuals can be randomly selected.

Stratified random sampling procedures are used when it is important to ensure that subgroups within a population are adequately represented in the sample. The researcher divides the population into subgroups or **strata**, and takes a random sample from each stratum. The number of respondents drawn from each stratum is based on the proportion of the population in the stratum. Thus, we can have confidence that the sample accurately represents the population, at least on the dimensions on which we stratified the sample.

Sample Size and Confidence Intervals. Survey researchers must also determine the size of the sample that will be needed. As a general rule, larger samples represent populations better than smaller samples because larger samples allow a greater chance for the principle of randomness to work (Kerlinger & Lee, 2000). In Chapter 5, we introduced the concept of sampling error, which is the natural variability of samples drawn from the same population. Increasing sampling size decreases sampling error. In inferential statistics, that gives us more power. In surveys, it gives us more precision in estimating the characteristics of the population based on the characteristics of the sample.

We need to determine exactly how large the sample should be for each project. Costs and time are important considerations, but most important is *how large the sample must be to adequately represent the population*, and that will depend on the homogeneity of the population. A **homogeneous** population is one in which the members are similar to one another. In general, if the population is homogeneous, then small sample sizes will represent the population effectively. On the other hand, **heterogeneous** populations have more diversity that must be represented in the sample. Therefore, the sample must be larger to represent the diversity of heterogeneous populations accurately.

We quantify the precision of our survey findings with the **confidence interval**, which indicates a range of scores that is likely to include the population mean. You have seen such confidence intervals reported when professional surveys are reported by news media. For example, political polling might report that 42% of the people sampled say they will vote for a given candidate with a margin of error of ±3. Since we did not sample the entire population, we cannot know what we would get from the entire population. However, we can use those sample numbers to report that there is 95% confidence that the population's support for this candidate is between 39% and 45% (3% above and below the 42% figure from our sample).

Methods for calculating required sample size and confidence intervals are complex and beyond the scope of this text. Interested students are referred to Rossi et al. (1993) or Nardi (2005). We have included more detailed discussion on the Student Resource Website for the interested student. Finally, there are a number of useful sample size calculator programs available on the Internet, although we caution students about using these unless you understand the principles that underlie them.

13:03

Survey Research Design

The next step is to determine the research plan (design) to be used in gathering the survey data. Three basic designs are used in survey research: (1) the cross-sectional survey design, (2) the longitudinal survey design, and (3) the sequential survey design.

Cross-Sectional Design. A **cross-sectional survey design** involves administering the survey once to a sample, obtaining data on the measured characteristics as they exist at the time of the survey. The information can be completely descriptive, such as a status survey, or can involve testing relationships among population characteristics, as in survey research.

Longitudinal Design. The **longitudinal survey design** is a within-subjects survey research design in which the same group or panel of participants is surveyed at several times. Longitudinal surveys make it possible to assess changes within individuals over time. It is often difficult, however, to obtain participants who are willing to be surveyed several times, and frequently large numbers of participants drop out of the study before it is completed.

Sequential Design. A variation that falls between the cross-sectional design and the longitudinal design is the **sequential survey design**. This survey design allows comparisons to be made of population characteristics at different points in time, such as surveying the confidence in the economy in 1990, 1995, 2000, 2005, and 2010 to determine changes over time. This appears to be longitudinal data except that there is no effort to sample the same people at each time interval. So what we have is a cross-sectional survey repeated over time, giving us a sense of how things are changing longitudinally. Businesses and governments are often interested in such surveys to help them to determine the best ways to market products or to address the concerns of their citizens (Howell & Howell, 2008; Sudman & Blair, 1997).

Quick-Check Review 13.4: Surveys

1. Distinguish between status surveys and survey research.
2. What are the major goals in surveys?
3. Describe two forms of survey instruments.
4. What are the types of items that can be used in surveys?
5. What is stratified random sampling?
6. What are confidence limits?
7. Define "cross-sectional designs," "longitudinal designs," and "sequential designs."

ETHICAL PRINCIPLES

Ethical considerations in program evaluation research pose special problems because the research participants are in many cases also recipients of services provided by the program. The programs often have mental health, public health, educational, or training goals. Thus, there is a public welfare aspect that permeates the programs and touches the evaluators and their research. Those who operate the programs often have a sense of mission, of public work, and responsibility to groups of people. The clients may have a proprietary sense of belonging to the enterprise, and have expectations of services, making neither the operators nor the clients objective about the program. The task of evaluating the program may create staff concerns that their competence and the program's success is being questioned, and the clients may feel coerced into compliance, perhaps feeling threatened with the possible loss of services if they refuse to participate or do not give the "right" answers. Coercion violates the cornerstone of ethical research—informed consent (see Chapter 3). Participants have a right to make a reasoned decision, free of coercion, about whether to participate.

Other ethical constraints are common in program evaluation. Many programs are designed to meet urgent needs that cannot be ignored. The most valid experimental research designs would randomly assign participants to conditions, such as a program group and a no-program group. But is it ethical, for example, to deny food stamps to some randomly selected individuals to see whether they really suffer malnutrition more than people who are given food stamps? Is it ethical to deny some children access to a special education program designed to overcome learning disabilities so that the program can be evaluated?

There are also privacy concerns; will the evaluator look into personal records of individuals? What information will be recorded, how will it be recorded, who will have access to it, who "owns" the data, and who determines what will be done with it?

Program evaluators need to be sensitive to issues that threaten the ethical demands of safeguarding the welfare and rights of participants, providing informed consent, and including the right to refuse participation and to withdraw at any time. Good researchers will consider these issues diligently as they design their research. When proposed research raises ethical issues, researchers need to be skillful and flexible to develop alternate procedures that will answer the research questions and correct the ethical problems; they must have acceptable answers and procedures to present to the appropriate Institutional Review Board before commencing the research.

Quick-Check Review 13.5: Ethical Principles

1. What are some of the special ethical issues that are central to program evaluation research?

SUMMARY

- This chapter covered higher-constraint research in naturalistic settings.
- Three major topics in this chapter were quasi-experimental designs, program evaluation, and surveys.
- Quasi-experimental designs include nonequivalent control-group designs and interrupted time-series designs.
- Program evaluation evaluates the effectiveness of programs in achieving their goals.
- Surveys ask questions concerning any issue, from demographic information, to knowledge questions, to questions about attitudes and experiences.
- The heart of the survey is a representative sample.
- Surveys can be carried out as longitudinal, cross-sectional, or sequential studies.
- Program evaluation research raises several ethical issues, including the importance of avoiding any coercion for participation and deciding whether control groups are ethically acceptable.

Putting It into Practice

If you read newspapers or magazines or watch television news, you are often exposed to surveys. Occasionally, the survey results are presented with qualifications that permit you to judge the quality of the information. For example, you learned earlier in this chapter that most political polls give the margin of error; they might report that the figures have an accuracy level of ± 3 points. This figure is based on the sample size and gives you an idea of the confidence limits. In general, such information suggests that the poll was taken by a reputable polling service using generally acceptable polling procedures and scientifically selected samples. However, many of the polls reported by news agencies are far less scientific.

For the next couple of weeks, watch for polls in the paper or on the news. Ask yourself how these polls might be distorted if proper sampling procedures were not followed. Then ask yourself how likely it is that the poll did follow proper sampling procedures and whether one should take the information seriously. You may be surprised by how few of the polls that bombard us daily have information we can trust.

EXERCISES

13.1. Define the following key terms. Be sure that you understand them. They are discussed in the chapter and defined in the glossary.

ecological validity	survey research	probability sampling
quasi-experiment	questionnaire	sampling frame
nonequivalent control-group design	interview schedule	strata
crossover effect	demographic questions	homogeneous
interrupted time-series design	factual items	heterogeneous
program evaluation research	content items	confidence interval
waitlist control group	open-ended items	cross-sectional survey design
survey	multiple-choice items	longitudinal survey design
status survey	Likert-scale items	sequential survey design
	nonprobability sampling	
	convenience sampling	

13.2. How do the research designs discussed in Chapter 6 and those discussed in this chapter differ?

13.3. The following graphs represent results in several nonequivalent control-group designs. How do you interpret each? (Assume differences are statistically significant.)

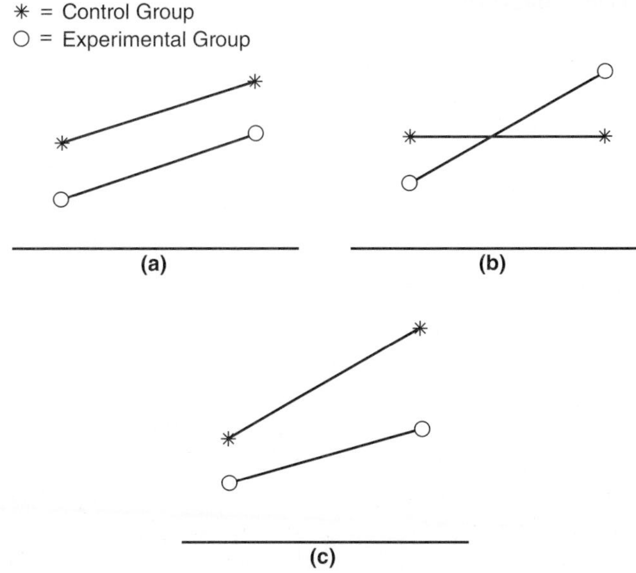

13.4. How would you interpret the following results of time-series designs?

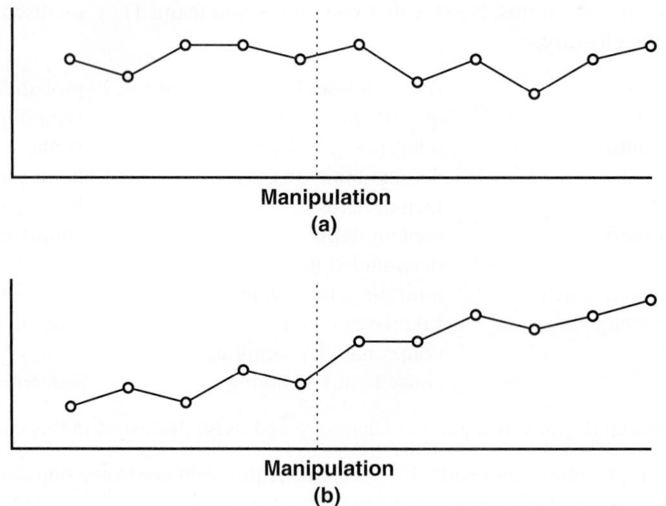

13.5. What are the tradeoffs of doing highly controlled experimental research in the laboratory, rather than doing research in field settings?

A FINAL NOTE TO STUDENTS

The questions we do not yet even have the wit to ask will be a growing preoccupation of science in the next 50 years.

—Sir John Maddox, "The Unexpected Science to Come," 1999

Take a few minutes right now, sit back, relax, and try to imagine what life will be like for you 50 years from now. Will you be retired from work? Perhaps science will have made it more likely that you will continue to work for many more years. Perhaps "retirement" will no longer be an appropriate concept in a future world too remote from us to imagine. Will there be lunar and Martian colonies? Will communication around the world and throughout the solar system be instantaneous (a physical impossibility according to present science) and complete with holographic images? Will the major human problems of aggression, poverty, disease, and ignorance be only memories? Will we be closer to understanding the origins of life and the universe? Will human life expectancy have increased so that you might actually live into the 22nd century? It is tempting to extrapolate to the future and ask, "What will science be discovering in another half-century? What will my life be like?"

The momentous scientific discoveries of the 19th century set the groundwork for a future that people in the 1890s thought they could foretell. In a thought-provoking essay, Maddox (1999) reviewed the major scientific discoveries that changed the 19th century world, including

- John Dalton's confirmation that matter is made of atoms (1808),
- Sadi Carnot's surmise that converting one form of energy to another is inherently limited (about 1830),
- James P. Joule's demonstration of the conservation of energy (1851),
- Charles Darwin's and Alfred Russel Wallace's discovery of natural selection and the eventual Darwinian theory of evolution (1859),
- James Maxwell's mathematical unification of electricity and magnetism (about 1880).

So momentous was that 19th century science, says Maddox, that some people suspected there was little left to learn! Nevertheless, 20th century science developed rapidly and significantly in ways that the earlier scientists and public had never envisioned. The direction of science, Maddox concludes, is unpredictable because new discoveries drive the direction of science. Thus, the discoveries of the 21st century, Maddox suggests, are as unpredictable now as the developments of the 20th century were to people in the 1890s.

Consider the recent research on the human genome (Collins & Jegalian, 1999; Palladino, 2005). Its mapping and sequencing was completed several years ahead of schedule because of breakthroughs during the process. Where will that information lead? Will it tell us about evolution, when and how we diverged from the great apes? Will it explain how and when the human brain and human skills, such as language and art, developed? Will it be the basis for technology that will allow the significant enhancement of future human intelligence? Will degenerative diseases be eliminated? Will we easily re-grow body parts damaged or lost through injury? Will life forms, long extinct, be recreated through future biology? How these and other scientific discoveries will affect the future is unclear, but that they will affect the future is unquestioned (Rose, 2005).

Scientific advances lead us into a complex universe of ideas and technologies, with uncountable twists and turns. Sometimes science opens fruitful new areas one after another; sometimes what seemed fruitful proves to be a dead end. This intertwined mass, like tangled roots in a tropical swamp, presents us with a seemingly impenetrable confusion about the future. How can we predict the direction of each tendril of discovery? We cannot; but the discoveries will be made, wherever they lead.

We will end this text by reminding you of three important ideas:

1. The quality and duration of *your life* will be significantly shaped by science, and the more scientifically literate you make yourself now, the more you will gain in life.
2. Research is tightly woven into modern society, and every research project is, in effect, a mutually beneficial contract with society.
3. Ethical conduct is a central concern in science. As you learn how to conduct scientific research, you must also become sharply sensitive to ethical issues and develop the skills to design ethically appropriate studies.

Finally, we will repeat an idea that we have stressed throughout this text:

The essence of science is its way of thinking.

Scientists systematically combine rational thinking and empirical research to ask and answer questions about nature. The enthusiasm, skepticism, curiosity, hunches, and creativity that characterize scientists, seasoned with a little serendipity, are essential components in the process of scientific thinking. However, the most critical element is the thought process that is at the core of science. To emphasize this point, recall the imagery used in Chapter 1: *a scientist can operate very scientifically sitting under a tree in the woods, thinking through a problem, using apparatus no more technical than a pad and pencil.*

APPENDIX A

USING THE STUDENT RESOURCE WEBSITE

WEB RESOURCE MATERIAL

A:01 Browser Tutorials
A:02 Using the Student Resource Website

This text includes the most comprehensive set of supplementary resources provided for any research methods textbook. These resources are available through two different sites: the Student Resource Website (www.graziano-raulin.com) and publisher's Research Methods Resource website (www.mysearchlab.com). This appendix describes what is available on each of these sites, how to access them, and how to address problems when they arise.

RESOURCES AVAILABLE

Student Resource Website

The Student Resource Website provides (1) an interactive study guide and lab manual, (2) tutorials on library research, statistical analysis, and writing reports in APA style, (3) numerous exercises and handouts, and (4) extensive discussions of statistical theory. We have integrated all of this material with the text and organized it for easy access.

The URL (address) for the Student Resource Website is www.graziano-raulin.com.[i] Figure A.1 shows how to enter this URL on a browser program such as Internet Explorer or Mozilla

[i]The complete address for the website is http://www.graziano-raulin.com/default.htm. Most web browsers allow you to drop the "http://" part; some browsers even allow you to drop the "www." part. The "/default.htm" is the default file that will be accessed and so need not be specified.

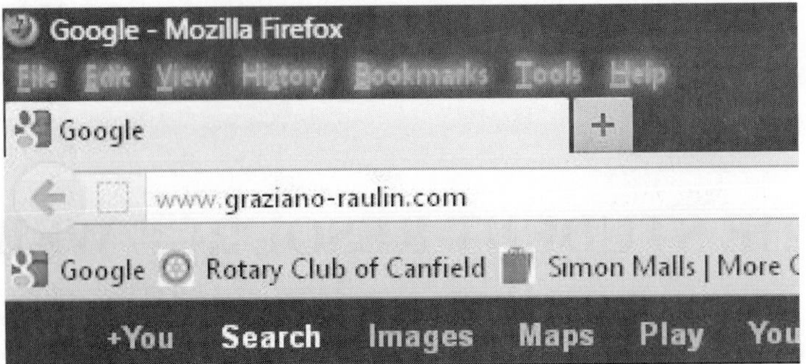

FIGURE A.1 Accessing the Student Resource Website. To access the Student Resource Website, enter the URL as shown here and hit the Enter key.

FIGURE A.2 Student Resource Website Drop-Down Menu. This is a copy of the welcome page from the eighth edition of the text. The menu on the top of the screen will help you to easily navigate the site.

Firefox. This link will take you to the welcome screen shown in Figure A.2. This site does not require a password to access.

If you have not already explored the Student Resource Website, take a few minutes and do so. You can navigate the entire Student Resource Website from the menu at the top of the screen. You are likely to access the Chapter Resources and Study Resources frequently during the course. These options provide materials that will enhance your learning.

We have summarized the chapter resources at the beginning of each chapter. You can access those resources on the Student Resource Website by clicking on Chapter Resources in the menu and then clicking on the chapter number.

MySearchLab Site

In addition to the Student Resource Website, the publisher has produced an extensive resource website called MySearchLab (www.mysearchlab.com). The instructions for its use are included in the preface of your textbook. The first time you access the website from your computer, you will be asked for the password. The password is included in your textbook (usually in the inside front cover or in a separate packet shrink-wrapped with the text). Access to MySearchLab is for your use only. It is part of the package that comes with this textbook. The password will work only on two computers and only for 6 months, so if you give it out to other people, you may not be able to access MySearchLab yourself without purchasing another subscription from the publisher (www.pearsonhighered.com).

WHAT TO DO IF YOU HAVE PROBLEMS

This section lists some common problems in accessing the website, their most likely causes, and how to overcome them.

I PUT IN THE ADDRESS (URL) FOR THE STUDENT RESOURCE WEBSITE AND NOTHING HAPPENED.

1. Did you hit the Enter key after inserting the URL? The web browser does not begin searching for a website until you hit Enter.
2. Are you connected to the Internet? The quickest way to check this is to access a site that should always be accessible, such as www.google.com.

I PUT IN THE ADDRESS FOR THE STUDENT RESOURCE WEBSITE AND THE RESPONSE I GET IS THAT THE SITE WAS NOT FOUND.

1. Check the spelling of the address. It must be entered exactly as follows: www.graziano-raulin.com
2. It may be that there is something wrong at your end—your Internet provider may be temporarily down or your modem may not be connected correctly. Check to see if you can access another site.
3. On rare occasions, the website may be down for maintenance. If this is so, in most cases, you will see a message to this effect, but occasionally, you may just get the message that the site was not found. Try accessing the Student Resource Website again in a couple of hours.
4. The Student Resource Website will be maintained until the release of the next edition. If your textbook is more than 3 years old, it may have been replaced with a new edition. You can check the publisher's website (www.pearsonhighered.com) to see if your current textbook is still in print.

I FOUND THE STUDENT RESOURCE WEBSITE, BUT I AM NOT SURE HOW TO FIND SPECIFIC MATERIAL.

1. The menu for the Student Resource Website is on the top of the screen. Any resource referenced in the textbook can be accessed from the Chapter Resources menu. If all else fails, click on Index to get a complete list the resources of the website.
2. There is a Help button on the Student Resource Website on the far right of the menu. Click Help to get additional instructions on how to use the Student Resource Website.

THE STUDENT RESOURCE WEBSITE JUST STOPPED RESPONDING.

1. This happens frequently on the Internet. Try waiting a minute or so and see if it starts to work again.
2. If the Student Resource Website does not start working again, there are several things that you can do. They are listed here in the order that we recommend them, from the least to the most drastic. It is possible that the problem that is causing the site to not respond is in your computer, or its link to the Internet (i.e., your Internet provider), or even in the computer that runs the Student Resource Website.
   a. Try hitting the escape (Esc) button in the upper left-hand corner of the keyboard a few times. This might free up the program if it is locked.
   b. Try hitting the back arrow key on your web browser. Then hit the front arrow key or hit the refresh button of your browser program.
   c. To determine if the problem is with the Student Resource Website or with your computer, try entering another URL and seeing if that site responds. If other sites can be accessed, you may want to try accessing the Student Resource Website later. Sometimes the traffic at a website is so high that the site just cannot handle it, essentially an electronic traffic jam.
   d. Try opening the Student Resource Website again by entering the URL and hitting the Enter key.
   e. Close your web browser, open it again, and open the Student Resource Website again.
   f. If you have a dialup connection, close it, dial in again, and then try accessing the Student Resource Website again with your browser.
   g. Close all programs and shut down your computer. Then wait a couple of minutes and restart the computer. Open your web browser and access the Student Resource Website again.
   h. You may need to reset your modem. For most systems, that means turning the modem off and waiting a minute or so before turning it on again. Each modem is a little different, so you may need to call the company that provided the Internet connection for more troubleshooting ideas.

GETTING HELP

We have tried in this appendix to anticipate many of the problems that you might encounter while using the Student Resource Website and the publisher's resource website MySearchLab. If you run into a problem not covered here or on the help menu of the Student Resource Website, we recommend the following two-step process.

1. Ask one or two students in your class who are reasonably knowledgeable about computers and have used the Student Resource Website and MySearchLab to help you. You will be surprised how quickly they can spot what you may be doing wrong and tell you how to correct it.
2. If all else fails, email Mike Raulin at MikeRaulin@gmail.com. Detail the problem you are having, including the type of computer, the Internet connection, and the steps you are having difficulty with, and he will try to recreate the problem and work out the solution.

SUMMARY

- This textbook includes free access to a fully integrated companion Student Resource Website, which provides students with resources designed to enhance their research methods course, and a publisher's resource website MySearchLab.
- This appendix provides troubleshooting advice for the most commonly experienced problems, but if you cannot resolve a problem, you can contact the author for help.

APPENDIX B

WRITING A RESEARCH REPORT IN APA PUBLICATION STYLE

WEB RESOURCE MATERIAL

B:01 APA Publication Style Tutorial and Reference Manual
B:02 Improving Your Writing
B:03 Links to Related Internet Sites

Publication is a critical part of the research process. In its most literal sense, publication means "to make public." Making science public serves two purposes. It facilitates building on current knowledge by making it accessible to everyone, and it allows other scientists to review one's logic, procedures, results, and conclusions.

There is much to communicate in a research report, but space is limited. Guidelines are therefore necessary to facilitate concise communication. The American Psychological Association's Publication Manual (2010d) provides the guidelines used by most psychology journals. This appendix summarizes the most commonly used sections of those guidelines. The Student Resource Website provides more extensive coverage of APA style. Psychology majors, particularly those thinking of graduate school, may wish to purchase a copy of the manual.[i]

B:01

[i]The Publication Manual of the American Psychological Association can be purchased directly from the American Psychological Association at nominal cost [www.apa.org]. The American Psychological Association publishes a workbook to help students to learn APA style (American Psychological Association, 2009), and other inexpensive texts are available (e.g., Rosnow & Rosnow, 2008) that focus exclusively on writing reports in APA style.

STRUCTURE OF A RESEARCH ARTICLE

The American Psychological Association (APA) recommends that the body of a research article be organized into four parts: introduction, method, results, and discussion. In addition, the report should include a title page, an abstract (150–250 words), a reference section, and any necessary figures and tables. On rare occasions, there may also be appendices included in the article.

The abstract briefly describes the study and findings, permitting readers to determine if the article is of interest to them. The abstract may also be published in one or more computer databases (e.g., *PsycINFO*, *PsycARTICLES*, *Medline*), which help researchers find relevant research.

The reference section lists each source discussed in the paper and where it can be found. Occasionally, additional attachments are included as appendices. These may contain extended information, materials, or scales that are not readily available elsewhere. Table B.1 lists the major sections of a journal article.

WRITING THE RESEARCH REPORT

The *APA Publication Manual* provides extensive guidance on how to write a research report.

Using Levels of Headings to Organize

A well-written article follows a clear outline. In an article, different levels of headings are used instead of outline indentation to indicate the organization. Table B.2 presents examples of five different levels of headings used in a research report. In a standard article, the Method, Results, Discussion, and References headings would be at a level 1 heading, with subsections under those main headings using level 2 and 3 headings as necessary.

TABLE B.1 Major Sections and Subsections of a Manuscript

1. Title page (includes author note)
2. Abstract
3. Introduction
4. Method
   a. Participants
   b. Materials
   c. Procedure
5. Results
6. Discussion
7. References
8. Appendices
9. Footnotes
10. Tables
11. Figures

TABLE B.2 Five Levels of Headings

This is a Centered, Boldface, Upper- and Lowercase Heading (Level 1)

This is a Flush Left, Boldface, Upper- and Lower Case Heading (Level 2)

This is an indented, boldface, lowercase paragraph heading with a period (level 3).

This is an indented, boldface, italicized, lowercase paragraph heading with a period (level 4).

This is an indented, italicized, lowercase paragraph heading with a period (level 5).

Sections of a Research Report

Title Page. The **title page** includes the title of the article, the list of authors, the institutional affiliations of the authors, and a running head. The title should be concise but descriptive, and no more than 12 words long. Phrases such as "a report on" or "a study of" add no information and should be avoided. A running head is placed at the top of the title page. It is an abbreviated title (no more than fifty characters in length, including spaces). The running head appears at the top of each page in the journal article. Page numbering begins with the title page and continues serially for all pages except those containing figures.

The title page also includes an author's note, which includes information about the authors departmental affiliation, changes in affiliations since the research was conducted, acknowledgements, special circumstances, and the corresponding author and how to contact him or her. There is a detailed structure for each of these items that is spelled out in the APA publication manual (APA, 2010d).

Abstract. The **abstract** summarizes the research paper in 150 to 250 words. Note that each journal sets its own word limit for an abstract, so be sure to check on the journal requirements before submitting a paper for consideration. Enough information should be given so that people who read the research study after reading the abstract will not be surprised by what they find in the article. Even though the abstract appears first, it is usually written last, because it summarizes the work. Although the abstract is one of the shortest sections of the study, it is often the most difficult to write, because so much must be said in limited space. The abstract appears on its own page (page 2).

Introduction. The **introduction** states the research problem and discusses prior research. It begins with a broad or general statement of the research problem and proceeds to narrow the focus to the specific research being reported. A good introduction need not be long, but it must be well organized. You should focus only on prior research that is directly relevant to the current research study; you should not attempt to review all the research in a broad area.

The introduction usually ends with your research hypotheses. A good rule of thumb is that, if the hypotheses seem to follow naturally from everything that precedes them, the introduction is well organized and well structured. If, on the other hand, a reader finds some or all of the hypotheses to be surprising in light of what was stated previously, the introduction is not well focused and fails to provide the rationale for the study.

The introduction starts on a new page (page 3), with the title of the paper at the top. There is no listing of authors on this page, and there is no Introduction heading. Instead, the paper begins right after the listing of the title.

We cite previous research in an article by naming the researcher(s) and the date when the research was published. With this information, the reader can turn to the reference list and find where the work was published. There are two standard forms for citing published work, as shown in the following examples.

> Previous research found the situation to be realistic (Johnson & Hall, 1999).
>
> Johnson and Hall's (1999) participants found the procedure to be realistic.

If you need to cite several studies, you can use the following format:

> Several investigators have found this situation to be realistic for their participants (Johnson & Hall, 1997, 1999a, 1999b; Kelley, 1986; Smith & Rodick, 1994).

These conventions tell the reader what was found, which researchers made the observation, and when. Each citation in a research article must appear in the reference section, and all references that appear in the reference list must be cited in the paper. Note that when there are multiple references in parentheses, you order the references alphabetically by author name and then by date of publication if there are multiple publications by the same author(s).

Method. The **method section** describes how the research was carried out, including who participated and how they were selected, the apparatus, equipment, materials, and procedures. These are typically discussed in separate subsections.

The **participants subsection** describes how participants were selected and their demographic characteristics (such as age, education, and gender), from where participants were obtained (e.g., a college course or a shopping mall), and what inducements were used to obtain their cooperation (e.g., money or academic credit). Many journals now require specific statements in this section, such as "Informed consent was obtained from all participants." The researcher also describes how participants were assigned to groups. If it is differential research, the procedures used to classify participants are described. If participants drop out of the experiment or decline to participate, the number of such participants and the groups that they were in should be reported. There should be enough information to allow a researcher to compare the sample with samples from similar research projects. This section should also include samples sizes and an indication of the level of power provided by the sample size.

The content of the next subsections will depend on the purpose and topic of the study. The goal of these subsections is to provide readers with sufficient information to enable them to replicate the study. Subsection titles like **equipment**, **materials**, **instruments**, or **measures** are common. These subsections describe the physical aspects of the research study. If the study involves equipment, the type of equipment used and the settings of the equipment should be reported. If psychological tests are used, the tests should be described, including information on how to obtain them, which often involves citing the publication that introduced the test. If the tests are unique to the study, they should either be included as an appendix or made available to readers on request.

The **procedure subsection** describes how the study was carried out, including things like testing and scoring procedures or specific instructions to participants. The procedure subsection should tell the reader everything that the participants and the researcher did during the course of the study.

TABLE B.3 Reporting Statistics in a Research Report

REPORTING *t*-TESTS
Boys were found to be significantly more aggressive than girls in the playground situation, $t(28) = 2.33, p = .035, d = .44$, 95% CI [2.34, 3.19].

REPORTING ANOVAs
There was a significant difference in performance between the three distraction conditions, $F(2, 27) = 3.69, p < .05$, est $\omega^2 = .13$.

REPORTING CHI-SQUARES
Psychology majors were significantly more likely to classify themselves as "humanistic" than were engineering majors, $\chi^2(1, N = 60) = 4.47, p < .05$.

Results. The **results section** tells the reader what was found. A statistical description of the results is usually needed, as well as appropriate statistical tests. A standard convention used to report inferential statistics is to report the statistic used, the degrees of freedom, the computed value of the statistic, the *p*-value, the effect size, and the confidence interval as shown in Table B.3. Earlier publications typically stop with the *p*-value, but current APA Style encourages the inclusion of an effect size measure and the confidence interval (when you have two groups).

All non-Greek, single-letter statistical terms (e.g., *F*, *t*, *p*) are italicized. With this format, readers can easily interpret the significance of results, even if they are not familiar with the statistical procedure used, because the *p*-value is interpreted in the same way for all of the tests. Any time *p* is less than .05 (a traditional value of alpha), we conclude that the findings are statistically significant.

Although it is important to express the statistical significance of comparisons, it is equally important to give the reader the information needed to interpret the results, such as the means or frequencies. Often the most effective way of doing this is to organize it in a table or figure. Tables and figures should be carefully labeled for the reader. Tables should give the reader enough information so that the reader can interpret them without information from the text. Each table should be numbered using Arabic numerals, starting with number 1. The first line of the table should read "Table" and the number. The next line should be a brief title, such as *Mean Reaction Times for Distracted and Non-Distracted Participants.* The table title is italicized. If the title is more than one line long, it should be double-spaced. The data in the table are arranged in columns and rows and should be clearly labeled. If additional information is necessary to interpret the table, it should be included as a footnote at the bottom of the table. Table B.4 presents an example of a typical table format.

Figures should also be self-explanatory. The axes should be labeled, and each figure should have a caption. Figures should be numbered sequentially starting with number 1 and should be numbered independently of tables. When submitting a paper for publication, each figure should be submitted as a digital image. Check with the journal to find out the acceptable digital formats for submission of figures. Figure B.1 presents an example.

Tables and figures are placed at the end of the manuscript, and each table or figure should be referred to in the manuscript.

TABLE B.4 A Typical Table in a Research Report

Table 1

Posttreatment Measures for the Three Treatment Approaches

	TYPE OF THERAPY		
Measures	**Behavioral**	**Cognitive**	**Analytic**
Number of activities[a]	4.6	3.8	2.1
Beck scores[b]	16.7	15.3	17.5
Insight ratings[c]	2.0	3.1	3.7

[a]The mean number of recreational activities in a one-week period.
[b]Mean Beck Depression Inventory scores; higher scores indicate greater depression.
[c]Rating based on an independent interview; ratings range from 1 (no insight) to 5 (maximum insight).

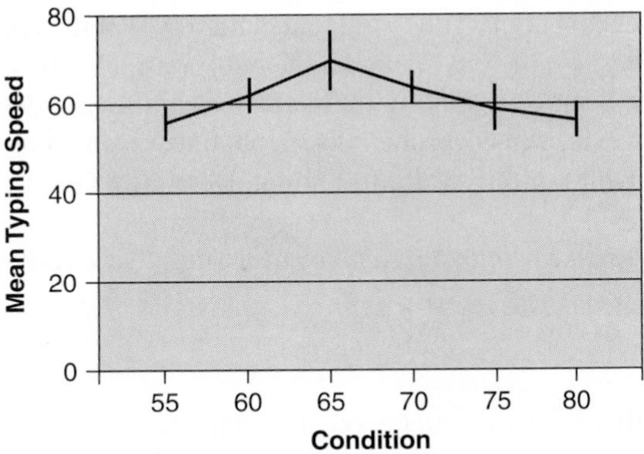

FIGURE B.1 Example of a Line Graph. This is a typical line graph. It appears in Chapter 10 of this textbook.

There is rarely one correct way of presenting the results of a study. It is often useful for the researcher to try to organize results in various ways by testing both tables and figures to determine which method is most effective.

Discussion. The **discussion section** interprets and evaluates the results. It is helpful to begin by briefly summarizing the results in nontechnical language. The interpretation of the results should follow logically from the actual data obtained in the study. If there are weaknesses in the current study, the author should acknowledge them and describe ways to deal with them in the future. It is often helpful to suggest directions for future research. The goal of any research project is to find answers to questions, but the outcome of most research projects is to suggest new questions.

References. The **reference list** provides the reader with the information needed to find articles mentioned in the paper. Each study discussed in the paper is listed in alphabetical order by the last name of the author(s). Works by the same author are arranged chronologically according to publication date. The most common reference is to a journal article. The format for such a reference is to list (1) the author(s), last name first, followed by initials for first and middle names; (2) the year of publication in parentheses; (3) the article title; (4) the journal title and volume in italics; (5) the pages where the article appears; (6) the article's doi (digital object identifier) number if it has one, and (7) whatever retrieval information is necessary to access a journal. Here are two examples:

De Loor, P., Manac'h, K., & Tisseau, J. (2009). Enaction-based artificial intelligence: Toward co-evolution with humans in the loop. *Mind and Machines*, *19*, 319–343. doi:10.1007/s11023-009-9165-3

Collier, R. (1994). An historical overview of natural language processing systems that learn. *Artificial Intelligence Review*, *8*, 17–54. doi: 10.1007/BF00851349

Note that references have a hanging indentation, with the first line not indented but all following lines indented. The easiest way to do this with a word processor is to type the reference as a single paragraph and then format the paragraph to have a hanging indentation.

A similar format is used to reference a book. You list (1) the author(s), (2) the copyright year in parentheses, (3) the book title in italics, (4) the city in which the book was published, and (5) the publisher. Whereas most journals have been converted to online format in the past decade, books still tend to be in printed versions. However, whenever the book is obtained from an online source, you should include the doi (if it is available) or retrieval information. Here are examples:

Kazdin, A. E. (1998). *Research design in clinical psychology* (3rd ed.). New York: Macmillan.

Loftus, E. F., & Ketcham, K. (1994). *The myth of repressed memory: False memories and allegations of sexual abuse*. New York: St. Martin's Press.

The reference section of this textbook provides many other examples.

WRITING STYLE

Good writing is important, whether you are writing a journal article or a letter. It is one of the most difficult things to teach, and it can be learned only through practice. However, there are different kinds of writing. Writing a journal article requires technical writing. Precision, conciseness, and organization are important in technical writing. Flowery adjectives and a poetic style are best left to the creative writer.

The primary purpose of writing a research report is communication, and anything that obscures communication should be avoided. Pronouns should be used sparingly and should never be ambiguous. Abbreviations should also be used sparingly and should always be explained to the reader. Using active voice and simple sentence structure can help a writer to avoid numerous communication pitfalls. Traditionally, the research report is written in the past tense and primarily in the third person (e.g., "The experimenter assigned each participant …"), although first-person narratives are becoming more acceptable. A good way to improve a research report is to have someone not involved in the research review the report. Anything that is unclear to this reviewer will probably be unclear to other readers. Writing manuals such as Strunk, White, and Angell's (2005) *The Elements of Style* or Zinsser's (2006) *On Writing Well* are valuable resources for any writer.

Although some find the writing phase rewarding, many researchers find writing a research report demanding. The task is somewhat easier if the research is carefully planned and well organized. For all researchers, however, telling people about something that they have discovered can be exciting.

B:02 The Student Resource Website includes some more suggestions on how to improve your technical writing skills.

SUMMARY

- The final stage of any research project is the communication of the results.
- The *APA Publication Manual* divides journal articles into the introduction, method, results, and discussion sections, plus an abstract and a list of references.

APPENDIX C

CONDUCTING LIBRARY RESEARCH

WEB RESOURCE MATERIAL

C:01 Library Research Tutorial
C:02 Links to Related Internet Sites

USING THE LIBRARY

C:01

Researchers need to relate their ideas and findings to those of other researchers. University libraries accumulate these findings to facilitate the research of faculty and students. This appendix outlines strategies for library research. The Student Resource Website provides additional details and examples of library searches. In addition, entire texts are devoted to the art of library research (e.g., Reed & Baxter, 2003).

Library Resources

Research studies are found in books, journals, technical reports, and a variety of other media. A small college library may have 250,000 or more books and journals; a major university library may have more than 5,000,000 books and subscribe to more than 10,000 journals. Libraries are increasingly subscribing to online services that provide journal articles so you can access them from any computer, and it will not be long before all recent journal articles will be available online. However, most of those journal articles will be available only through your library and not on the Internet.

In addition, most university libraries will have access to almost any published material through interlibrary loan. When you enter a modern university library, you are in touch with nearly all the information that has ever been published! You should be impressed by this thought and properly respectful of the library and of the professionals who operate it.

The Reference Librarian

The reference librarian knows the smoothest routes through the maze of information. A good reference librarian can help you to track down almost anything. Whether you need to find a particular book or to learn how to use the library's computer search resources, the reference librarian is a valuable consultant. Many university libraries also have courses to help you to master their resources. Although we will be outlining many of the basic sources and strategies for library research in this appendix, we cannot stress enough the importance of utilizing the expertise available in your own library.

HOW RESEARCH MATERIALS ARE ORGANIZED

We make a distinction between primary and secondary sources in the research literature. Primary sources publish research studies; secondary sources publish integrative reviews of broad areas of research. This section describes both.

Primary Sources

Journal Articles. Journals can be both primary and secondary sources of information, although the majority of journals are primary sources that report research studies. A research report typically includes a literature review, the study's hypotheses, the procedures, the results, and a discussion of how the researchers interpreted the results. In the discussion of their findings, researchers relate their results to prevailing models or theories, thus helping to integrate new information and adding to the base on which further research and theory development will rest.

Dissertations. Dissertations are research studies conducted by advanced graduate students as part of the requirements for a Ph.D. Many are eventually published in journals, but you can also get a copy of the original dissertation. Universities maintain copies of dissertations conducted at their own institutions, and any dissertation can be obtained in a few days through UMI Dissertation Publishing, which maintains and sells copies of dissertations from around the world.

Secondary Sources

Secondary sources provide reviews of entire areas of research. However, they are not intended to provide the detail that you will find in the original journal articles. Moreover, the newest research discussed in secondary sources is often at least a year old, reflecting the length of the publication and production cycle. Therefore, you will still have to search current journals to find the most recent research.

Secondary sources summarize, organize, critique, and integrate research areas and identify directions for further research. They are an invaluable source in your literature review and are particularly useful when you need a broad, integrated view of your topic.

Review Articles. Although most journals report the results of research studies, other journals specialize in review articles. Several journals in psychology are devoted completely to reviews (e.g., *Psychological Bulletin* or *Psychological Review*).

Books and Chapters in Books. Reviews of research areas are also published as books or as chapters in books. In fact, edited books are becoming a major secondary source of information in psychology. Fortunately, *PsycINFO* now includes both books and book chapters in its database.

Annual Reviews. This series provides an annual volume in several disciplines, including psychology and neuroscience. You should check recent volumes to see if there is a review of your topic.

FINDING THE RELEVANT RESEARCH

You can find relevant research by using abstracting services, keyword searches, and citation indexes.

Abstracting Services

Computerized abstracting services provide abstracts of articles from thousands of journals, which are organized by title, author, and keywords.

***Psychological Abstracts*.** *Psychological Abstracts* provides abstracts and references for virtually everything relevant to the field of psychology. *Psychological Abstracts* is organized by keywords, which are summarized in a separate publication (*Thesaurus of Psychological Index Terms*). The APA also publishes a series of journals called *PsycSCAN*, which are quarterly compilations of research papers, organized under broad topics (e.g., clinical, applied, or developmental).

Psychological Abstracts has largely been replaced by computerized databases such as *PsycINFO*, *PsycLIT*, *PsycFILE*, *PsycARTICLES*, and *PASAR*. These are far more convenient to use than the bound volumes they replaced.

***ERIC* (Educational Resource Information Center).** *ERIC* indexes and abstracts research in education and related areas. If your topic is related to educational research, you should consult *ERIC* as well as *Psychological Abstracts*.

Subject or Keyword Services

Several indexes reference materials by title, author, and keywords, but do not include the abstract. Even without the abstract, these indexes can be a valuable source for identifying relevant materials.

Library Catalogs. The most familiar index to most students is the library catalog, which lists all the books in the library's collection and indexes them by author, title, and subject. In computerized library catalogs, you may be able to see if the book is available to be checked out. Many computerized catalogs also indicate whether an item is available from another institution for interlibrary loan.

Books in Print. *Books in Print* is a quarterly publication listing all books that are currently in print. Many libraries now have this index available online.

Index Medicus. Just as *Psychological Abstracts* provides an index for literature of interest to psychologists, *Index Medicus* provides an index to biomedical literature. The computerized version is called *Medline* and now includes abstracts.

***Readers' Guide to Periodical Literature*.** This general index covers a wide area of popular literature and provides citations but no abstracts. In many library systems, these citations are linked to a copy of the article.

Literature Citation Indexes

The abstract and keyword services above are helpful in finding material by topic or author. However, there are times when you want to find literature through the citations of previous work. Certain lines of research are so indebted to one or two early publications that you can find virtually every article on the topic by identifying the articles that cite these early publications. The *Science Citation Index* and the *Social Science Citation Index* are two examples of this kind of reference. You can find references to work in psychology in both of these citation indexes.

Table C.1 lists the major indexes for psychological research.

TABLE C.1 Library Resources for Psychological Research

1. Review Articles and Chapters
   a. *Annual Review of Psychology*
   b. *Psychological Bulletin*
   c. *Psychological Review*
   d. *Behavioral Science*
   e. *Clinical Psychology Reviews*
2. Abstract Services and Citation Indexes
   f. *Psychological Abstracts* (bound volumes)
   g. *PsycINFO* (psychological abstracts on computer programs)
   h. *ERIC*
   i. *Books in Print* (bound volumes and computer format)
   j. *Index Medicus* and *Medline* (computer indexes)
   k. *Social Science Citation Index*
   l. *Science Citation Index*
3. Other Important Information Sources
   m. *Thesaurus of Psychological Index Terms*
   n. Library catalog
   o. *Readers' Guide to Periodical Literature*

SEARCH STRATEGIES

Several methods are available for locating relevant research.

Searching by Topic

Identifying Key Terms. How do you find the information you need for your project? Library research needs a clear problem statement and a list of key terms that identify relevant research papers. The right key terms will help you to find exactly what you need. The *Thesaurus of Psychological Index Terms*, published by the APA, lists the key terms used in *PsycINFO* as well as cross-referenced terms that might also identify relevant literature on a topic. Find your topic in the *Thesaurus*, and it will list the index terms under which you will find appropriate references. Many commercially available databases include the *Thesaurus* as part of their service. Use these as your key terms to conduct your library search. Similar publications listing index terms are available for other abstract services.

Computer Searches. Fortunately, most libraries have extensive computer search capabilities. You can access *PsycINFO*, *Books in Print*, *ERIC*, *Medline*, and hundreds of other indexes through computer terminals in the library and elsewhere. Consult your reference librarian to learn how to use these systems.

The procedures for doing computer searches vary from one system to another, but most systems operate under the same general principles. All systems have records (containing the information about a publication) and fields within each record. Each field contains specific information, such as the title, author, journal, keywords, and abstract. You can search a specific field or all fields to find information. For example, if you know that relevant research was published by "Jason Lombard," you can search the author field for that name.

There are many strategies for computer searches, but most people start by searching for keywords. Most indexes will have a keyword field in which a small number of descriptive terms summarize the main content of the paper. Searching this field for specific keywords is adequate for many searches. However, computers are so fast that it is easy to search the entire record to find potentially relevant papers.

Entering keywords to narrow a search is an art that requires some logic. For example, in most systems, entering the term "child" will identify any article that has the terms "child," "childhood," "children," and "child's," because all these terms have "child" in them.

Some keywords identify several thousand potential articles, while others identify just a few. If the list is too large, you will have to reduce it to make it manageable. For example, you might refine the list by limiting it to only those papers published in the last 5 or 10 years.

You probably want to also narrow the list by further restricting the topic. To do this you must understand two Boolean operators: AND and OR. If you are interested in childhood fears, you could use the term "childhood fears" in your search. However, such a search would miss articles that did not use that specific phrase (perhaps use a phrase like "fears common in childhood" instead). The Boolean operator AND will narrow a search by requiring that two conditions be met. Using it to search for "fear AND child" would likely give you a more complete search. Any article that had both the term "fear" and the term "child" in its record would be identified.

In contrast, the operator OR will broaden a search by identifying sources that meet one of several specified conditions. For example, searching for "frontal OR parietal OR occipital OR temporal" would identify any source that mentions one of these lobes of the brain.

Some, but not all, library databases allow you to use a third Boolean operator: NOT. NOT, like AND, allows you to narrow a search. The Boolean operator AND narrows a search by requiring multiple conditions. In contrast, the Boolean operator NOT allows you to exclude items that meet certain conditions. For example, if you were interested in psychogenic amnesia (amnesia due to psychological causes), you might want to search for amnesia using the NOT function to exclude articles that focused on head injuries or brain damage.

Each computer index has its own rules for specifying searches with Boolean operators, although the principles are consistent. Be sure to check the documentation or speak with a reference librarian for details of the system that you are using.

Once you have identified a set of relevant records, you can enter commands to display the records. By reading the titles and/or abstracts you can select those that appear to be most appropriate for your topic.

Now the real work begins. Your list of references is just that—a list. What remains is locating each article, book, or chapter, reading them, integrating the information, and writing your paper or research proposal. As more journals go online, finding copies of journal articles is getting easier, although books and chapters usually have to be retrieved physically from the library. As you proceed, you will eliminate some references as not relevant and you will find more references in articles you are reading. Discussed next are two useful strategies for identifying additional relevant material.

Searching Backward

Every article, chapter, or book reviews relevant research and gives you the references for those studies. This is an invaluable source of relevant material. Of course, not every paper referenced in articles will be relevant to your topic, but some will be. Recently published review articles are especially useful for this strategy. Inspecting the reference list from relevant articles will help to identify other investigators doing work on your topic. Searching the author field for the names of these investigators is often a useful supplementary strategy. These strategies are not a substitute for the topic search, but can be valuable in identifying additional relevant papers.

A note of caution is warranted here. It is bad form to cite a paper that you have not read. It is entirely possible that the description of the paper in another article may be inaccurate.

Searching Forward

The searching forward strategy is possible because of the existence of citation indexes. If virtually all articles on a topic cite one or more classic studies, then one can identify these later articles by using an appropriate citation index. Again, this strategy is not a substitute for searching by topic, but it can be a useful supplement.

Table C.2 summarizes the literature search process.

TABLE C.2 The Literature Search Process

1. Have a clear statement of the problem before beginning your literature search.
2. From this problem statement, identify the key terms for your topic. Use the *Thesaurus of Psychological Index Terms* to help to determine your key terms.
3. Consult with your reference librarian and determine which citation indexes are most likely to include the information you seek.
4. Search the citation indexes using your key terms. *PsycINFO* is probably the most useful for you, although many instructors encourage students to use *PsycARTICLES*, because this database includes every paper that it cites. Look for secondary as well as primary sources. Read the titles and abstracts of the papers and chapters. Narrow your list by deleting those that seem least relevant.
5. Print out the list of remaining references. Find and read the original articles, books, and chapters.
6. As you gain information from your reading, continue to refine your ideas, develop new ideas, and further refine your problem statement.
7. Consult other citation indexes as needed (*ERIC*, *Social Science Citation Index*, *Readers' Guide*, etc.).
8. You can consult your reference librarian at any point in this search process.

SUMMARY

- University libraries archive past research and index it so that you can find it easily.
- This appendix summarized library resources and some of the ways to find relevant background material for a paper. Entire texts are devoted to the art of library research (e.g., Reed & Baxter, 2003).
- The reference librarian at your institution can be an invaluable source of information about how to use the library.

APPENDIX D

SELECTING STATISTICAL PROCEDURES

WEB RESOURCE MATERIAL

D:01 The Decision-Tree Flowcharts
D:02 Functional Decision-Tree Flowchart
D:03 Additional Examples Using the Decision-Tree Flowcharts
D:04 Exercises Using the Decision-Tree Flowcharts
D:05 Post Hoc Tests and Planned Comparisons
D:06 Links to Related Internet Sites

This appendix provides a flowchart system for selecting appropriate statistical procedures. We believe that you will find it useful in your research planning. We suggest that you copy or download the flowcharts from the website, and keep them as guides for your research.

SELECTING APPROPRIATE STATISTICAL PROCEDURES

An important decision in the design phase is determining what statistical procedures to use for the analyses. Recall that we select statistical tests that are appropriate for the data collected and for the questions posed. Like everything in research, systematic procedures simplify the decisions and bring the process under control. Chapters 5, 10, 11, and 12 set the groundwork for this systematic approach by describing several research designs and illustrating appropriate statistical procedures. This appendix will organize this information into a set of flowcharts.

An Initial Example

Appropriate statistical procedures depend upon the characteristics of the research, such as the number of independent variables, type of question, and level of measurement for each dependent variable. We will use the following example as an illustration.

INCIDENTAL LEARNING IN RATS

An experimenter hypothesizes that laboratory rats can learn without specific rewards. Twenty maze-adapted animals are randomly assigned to two conditions. The experimental group is allowed to explore the test maze for 1 hour without any rewards. The control group does not explore the test maze. All animals are then given learning trials in the test maze, and each successful trial is reinforced with food. The experimental and control groups are compared on the number of learning trials needed to reach a criterion of five successive correct trials. The research hypothesis is that the experimental group, having explored the test maze prior to their reinforced learning trials, needs significantly fewer trials to reach criterion than the control group. That is, the animals would learn something about the maze while wandering through it, even though they experienced no reinforcement to shape their learning in this exploration phase.

Our task is to determine the appropriate statistical procedure for this study. The characteristics of the research determine what statistical procedures to use. The preceding description provides all the necessary information. We ask the following questions to identify the characteristics of the research critical to selecting statistical procedures:

1. **What is the level of constraint?** The level of constraint is experimental.
2. **What are the dependent variables, and what type of data does each produce?** The single dependent variable is maze learning, measured by the number of maze-running trials needed to reach criterion; this measure produces score data.
3. **What are the independent variables, what type is each independent variable, and how many levels does each independent variable have?** There is one independent variable, it is a between-subjects factor (i.e., independent groups), and it has two levels (prior exploration and no prior exploration).
4. **What is (are) the research hypothesis (hypotheses)?** There is one research hypothesis (the experimental group will require fewer learning trials than the control group to reach criterion).

We have determined that our study is an experimental design, with one between-subjects independent variable that has two levels. The dependent variable, maze learning, yields score data. The appropriate statistical procedure is one that can test our hypothesis of a group difference. You may recall from earlier discussions that the *t*-test for independent groups or the one-way ANOVA is appropriate. We also routinely include descriptive statistics to summarize data and help us to interpret the results.

In complex research, there may be several research hypotheses and several dependent measures, and we may need different procedures for each hypothesis. In such complex research, the decisions are not so readily apparent, but the procedure to arrive at them is essentially the same. First, we describe the study and ask questions to identify the study's characteristics. Then, we use this information to make decisions about the appropriate statistical procedures. We have incorporated this sequence of steps into a decision-tree model that we will describe.

A Decision-Tree Model

We will now describe a decision-making model for selecting statistical procedure(s). We use a **decision tree**, in which we follow a line of thinking, reach a decision point, make a decision, and then branch off in appropriate directions based on the decision. We have organized these lines of thinking and the branching-off process in a **decision-tree flowchart** system, which is shown in Figures D.1 through D.5. A copy of this decision-tree flowchart system is included on the Student Resource Website, as well as a functional version that links directly to instructions of how to conduct the statistical analyses.

D:01, D:02

You begin by describing the research and its characteristics. Then you proceed through the flowchart to determine the appropriate statistical procedures.

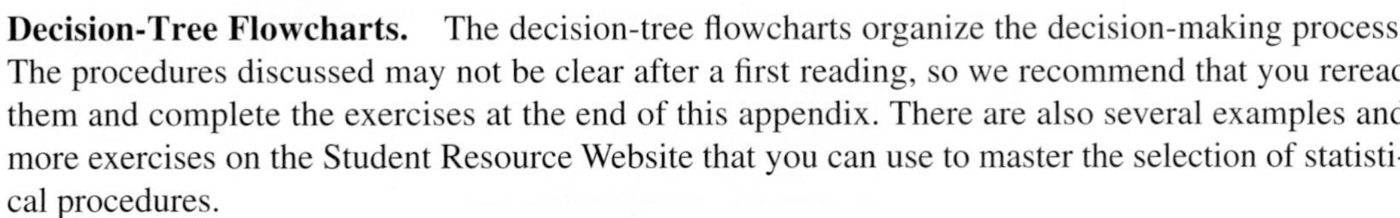

Decision-Tree Flowcharts. The decision-tree flowcharts organize the decision-making process. The procedures discussed may not be clear after a first reading, so we recommend that you reread them and complete the exercises at the end of this appendix. There are also several examples and more exercises on the Student Resource Website that you can use to master the selection of statistical procedures.

D:03, D:04

Most studies test several research hypotheses and include several dependent measures. Therefore, several statistical procedures may be required. You should routinely compute descriptive statistics for all variables in the study, including demographic variables. If there are separate groups, you should compute the descriptive statistics separately for each group. Most computer programs allow the option of having descriptive statistics computed when doing the inferential statistics. We recommend doing this routinely.

In lower-constraint research, you may need only descriptive statistics. In higher-constraint research, however, we typically have refined the questions and designed the study to answer specific questions about differences between groups. In most cases, we cycle through the flowchart several times to determine all necessary statistical procedures.

Although the flowchart may look imposing, it is easy to follow. To use the flowchart, you begin by identifying key aspects of the research. We illustrate this process with a hypothetical study of social problem solving in sixth-grade boys and girls. Unlike the animal-learning study presented earlier, this study tests several research hypotheses. Thus, we need to determine several statistical analyses.

No matter how complex the study may be, the procedures for determining an appropriate statistical analysis are the same.

1. Describe the study.
2. Identify its characteristics.
3. Make systematic decisions using the flowcharts.

Describe the Study. Here is a brief description of the study.

SEX DIFFERENCES IN CHILDREN'S SOCIAL PROBLEM-SOLVING SKILLS

The study compares sixth-grade boys and girls on their problem-solving skills in social situations. From the sixth grade of a local middle school, 20 boys and 20 girls are randomly selected and evaluated on three measures. In the first measure, participants are tested individually. The researcher

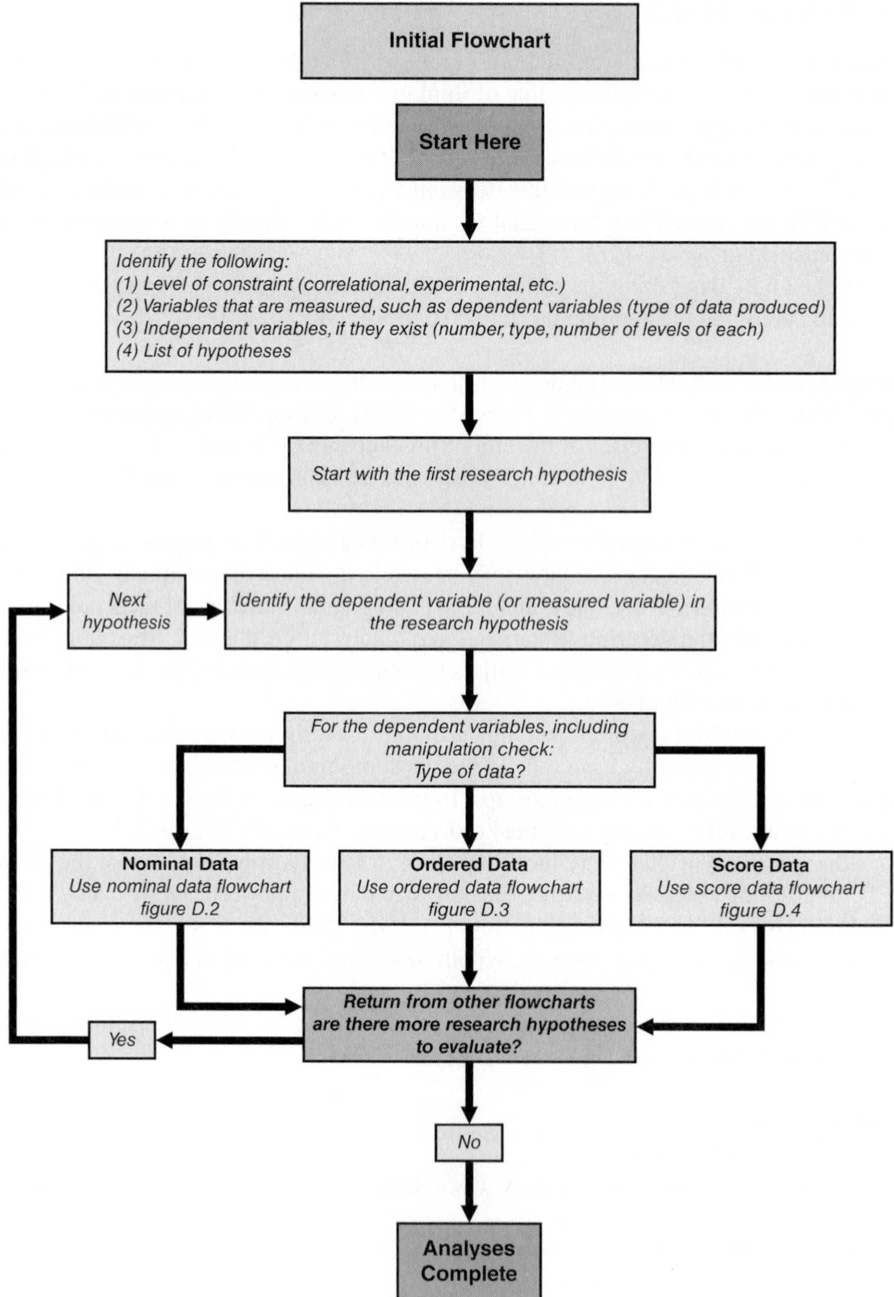

FIGURE D.1 Initial Flowchart. This flowchart system will greatly simplify the task of selecting the appropriate statistical procedures. You start with this flowchart and access the other flowcharts as indicated.

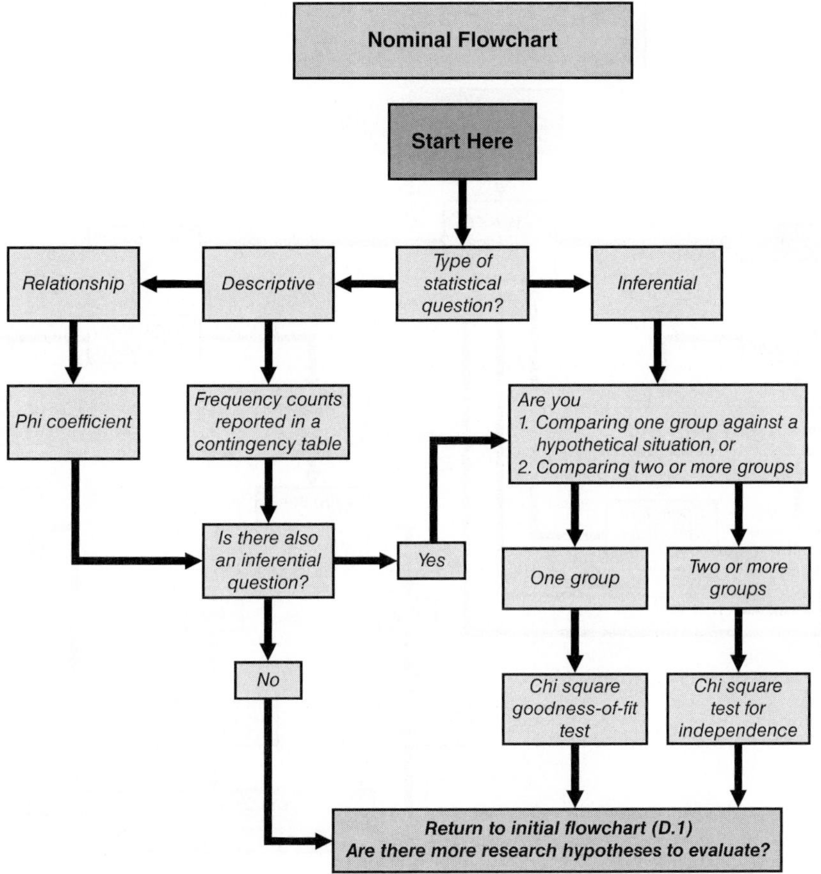

FIGURE D.2 Nominal Data Flowchart. Use this flowchart when the study produces nominal data. Note that one should always include descriptive information.

describes 10 social situations to each participant. Each situation involves a social problem or conflict (e.g., another student pushes ahead in line). The participant selects a solution from a list of three possible ways to solve the conflict (a multiple-choice test). For each problem, one solution is clearly the most socially appropriate and therefore is considered the correct answer. The score is the number of correct choices for the 10 social situations.

The second dependent measure is the teacher's ranking of the children on social competence. The ranking is based on observations of the children's behavior in three settings: the structured classroom, an unstructured social activity within the classroom, and recess.

For the third dependent measure, an independent rater classifies each of the children's problem-solving style based on standardized information provided by the teachers. The styles are avoidance, aggression, and compromise.

The research focuses on sex differences in problem-solving skills. The statement of the problem is, "Do sixth-grade boys and girls differ on problem-solving skills in social situations?" The problem statement leads to three research hypotheses.

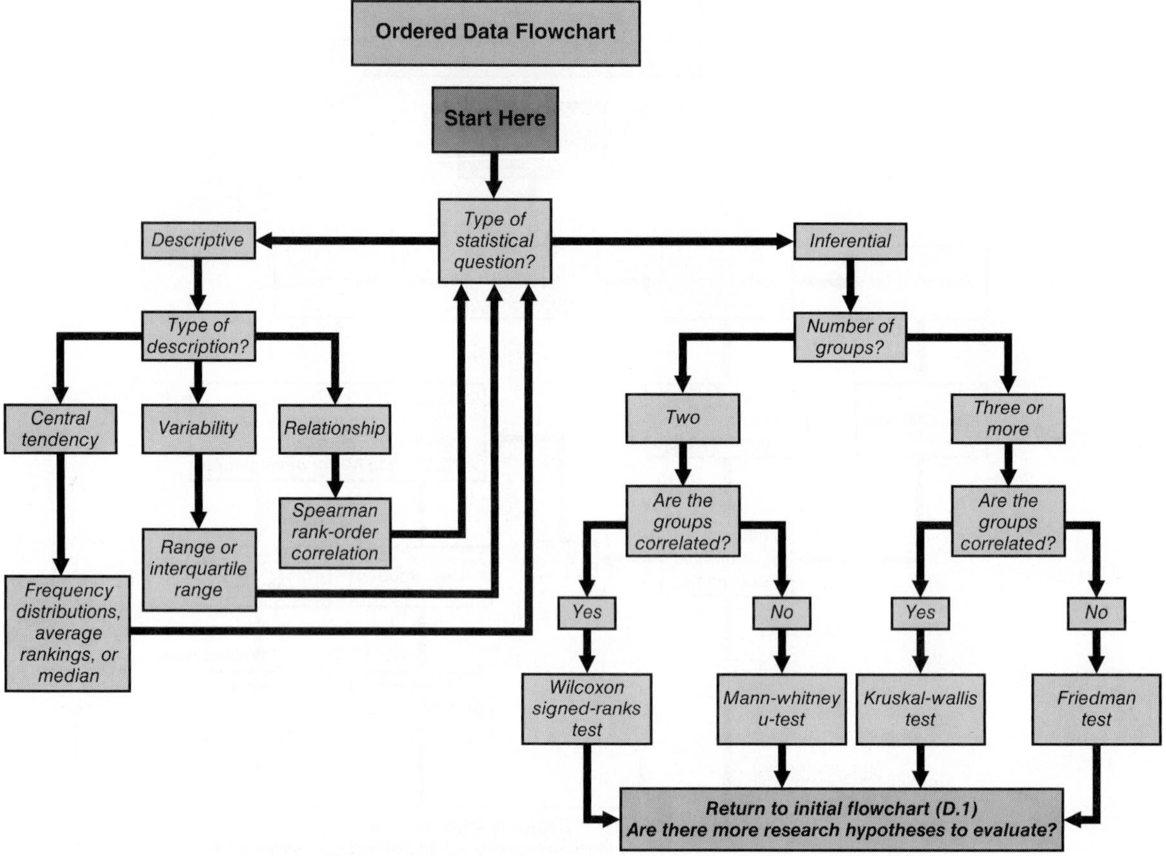

FIGURE D.3 Ordered Data Flowchart. Use this flowchart when the study produces ordered data. Note that one should always include descriptive information.

Identify the Study's Major Characteristics. Having described the study, you should next identify its major characteristics.

1. **What is the level of constraint?** This is a differential study with three dependent variables.
2. **What are the dependent variables, and what type of data do each produce?** The multiple-choice test produces score data; the ranking of students produces ordered data; the judgment of problem-solving styles produces nominal data.
3. **What are the independent variables, what type is each independent variable, and how many levels does each independent variable have?** There is just one independent variable (gender). This is a between-subjects variable with two levels.
4. **What is (are) the research hypothesis (hypotheses)?** There are three research hypotheses.
   a. Sixth-grade boys and girls differ in the identification of the correct social response in a multiple-choice task.
   b. Sixth-grade boys and girls differ in their ranking on social competence based on observations in three behavior settings.
   c. Sixth-grade boys and girls differ in their problem-solving styles.

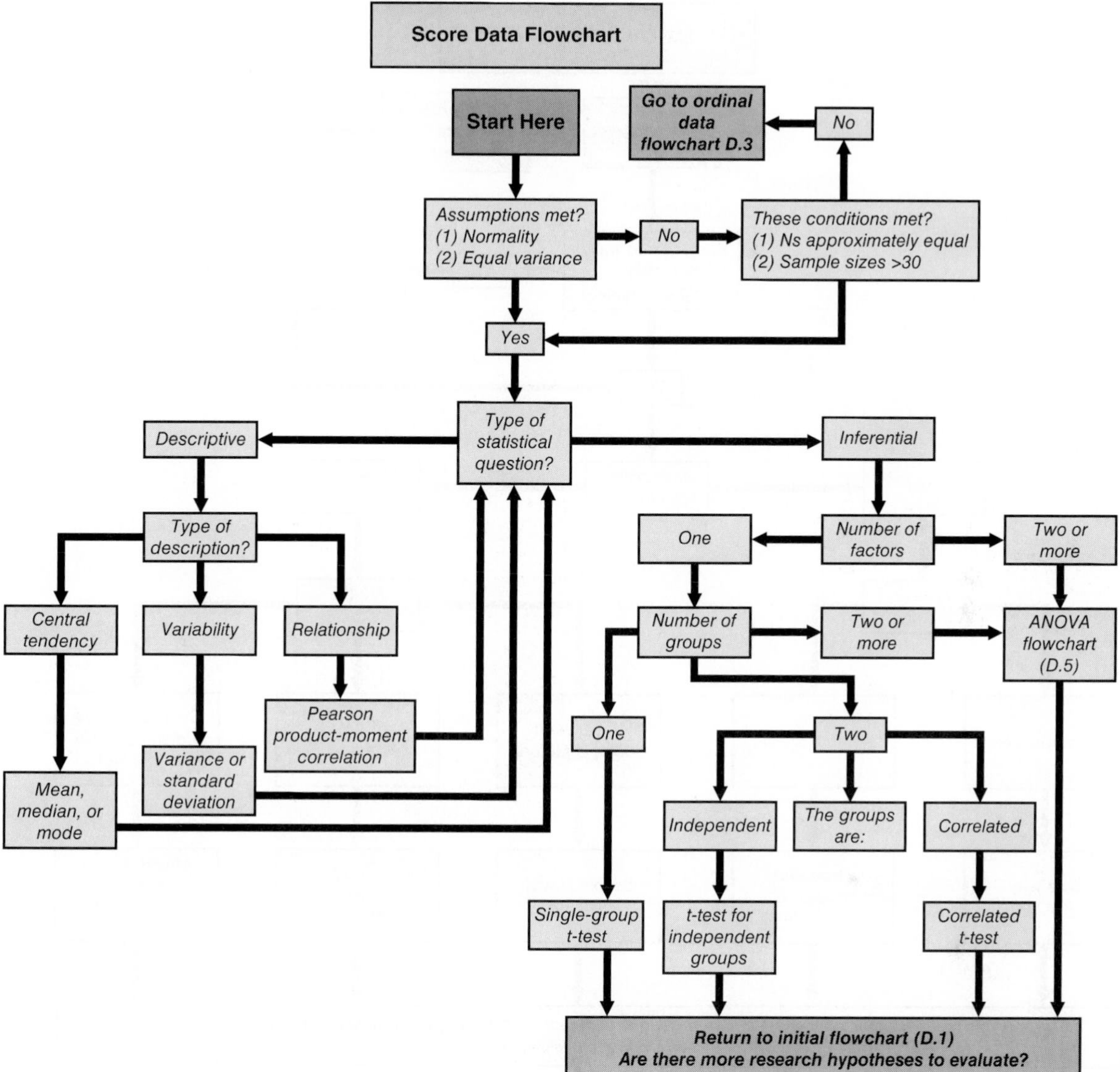

FIGURE D.4 Score Data Flowchart. Use this flowchart when the study produces score data. Note that one should always include descriptive information.

This study is a differential study with two levels of the nonmanipulated independent variable. The dependent measures generate three different levels of data. Therefore, we can expect different statistical procedures will be necessary to test each research hypothesis.

Select Appropriate Statistics. The flowchart system helps us to select appropriate statistics. We have already accomplished the first task described in the initial flowchart (Figure D.1), which is identifying the critical characteristics of the study. Therefore, we begin with the first research

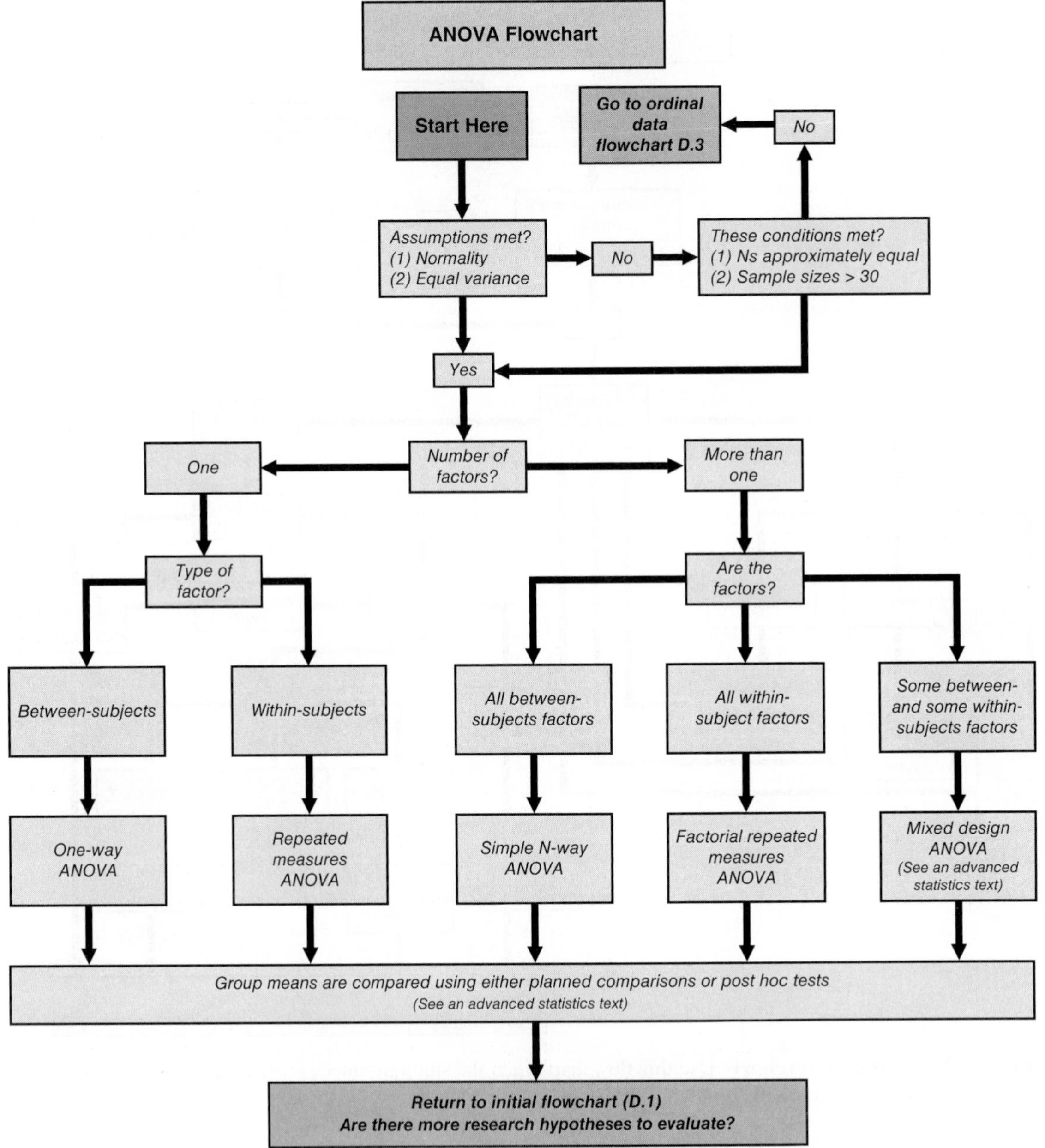

FIGURE D.5 ANOVA Flowchart. This flowchart supplements the score data flowchart, covering the various forms of Analysis of Variance.

hypothesis: that sixth-grade boys and girls differ in the identification of the correct social response in a multiple-choice task. This variable produces score data, so we branch right to the box indicating that we should go to the Score Data Flowchart (Figure D.4).

The Score Data Flowchart begins by asking whether we have met the assumptions of the statistical tests, which include normality of scores and equal variances. If you have, that is fine; you can go on to answer your statistical questions. But if you haven't met these assumptions, you can still use the parametric statistical procedures if you have reasonable sample sizes and approximately equal number of subjects in each group. We will assume that the assumptions are met. You can always check this by using statistical software to print histograms and compute variances.

We always want to include descriptive information on the variables. Therefore, we would follow the arrow that moves to the left to find the "Descriptive" statistics section. Our descriptive statistics should include measures of central tendency (mean, median, and mode) and variability (variance and standard deviation).

Once we select the descriptive statistics, we return to the "Type of Statistical Question?" box and move to the right, to the inferential statistics portion of the flowchart. The flowchart then asks us the number of factors. In this case, we have one factor (gender), with two groups (boys and girls). If you look closely, we actually have two choices, which are equally appropriate. One choice takes us to a new flowchart (the ANOVA Flowchart). The other takes us to a choice between two *t*-tests, depending on whether our groups are independent or correlated. Our groups are independent, so we would select the *t*-test for independent groups and then cycle back to the initial flowchart to find the appropriate analyses for the other hypotheses. If we had followed the link to the ANOVA Flowchart, we would have found that a one-way ANOVA would also be appropriate.

Now we move on to the second hypothesis. We previously determined that the dependent measure in this hypothesis produces ordered data. Therefore, we are directed to the Ordered Data Flowchart (Figure D.3). Again, we should start with descriptive statistics, which suggests that we can use a frequency distribution, median, average rankings, and the range to describe the data. We then return to "Type of Statistical Question?" and move to the right side of the flowchart for our inferential statistics. We have two groups that are not correlated, so we select the Mann-Whitney *U*-test before cycling back to our initial flowchart.

Finally, the third hypothesis generates nominal data, so we are directed to the Nominal Data Flowchart (Figure D.2). The flowchart tells us that the appropriate descriptive statistic is frequency counts in each category, the appropriate correlation is the Phi coefficient, and the appropriate test of group differences is the chi-square test for independence. Use the flowchart and see if you come to the same conclusions.

If our study were a larger one with more research hypotheses, we would continue this process of using the flowchart to select the correct descriptive and inferential statistics for the remaining dependent measures. Most research studies employ more than one measure and test more than one research hypothesis.

Do not forget to analyze the demographic data that you collect for your study to describe your sample and to determine if any of your demographic variables are correlated with your dependent measures. If you have a manipulation check, you would treat it as any other hypothesis, testing whether your manipulation had the intended effect on your subjects.

Although computers can simplify the task of computation, the researcher still needs to decide what statistics to compute, and to label and organize the computer output carefully to avoid later confusion. Our example illustrates the need to be organized, because you need to make many decisions.

Practice using the flowcharts with the research examples at the end of this appendix. With practice, you will become familiar with the rules in the flowchart and eventually will not need to refer to them. Indeed, that is the goal. Initially, however, when you are learning to make decisions, the flowcharts will provide a convenient way to organize information when selecting a statistical procedure. We have included a functional version of these flowcharts on the Student Resource Website that links to the data analysis tutorials.

Secondary Analyses

After completing descriptive and inferential analyses, we often carry out **secondary analyses**, which typically fall into three categories: (1) post hoc analyses or planned comparisons to look at specific mean differences; (2) analyses designed to help to explain the pattern of results; and (3) unplanned exploratory analyses (called **data snooping**).

Post Hoc Analyses. When doing an ANOVA with more than two groups, specific mean comparisons are the logical next step in the interpretation of significant F-ratios. The significant F in a one-way ANOVA, for example, tells us only that at least one of the means is significantly different from at least one other mean. It does not tell us which means are different from which other means. Most often, the interpretation requires this more specific information, which post hoc tests or planned comparisons can provide. We introduced these tests in Chapter 10. The Student Resource Website has additional information about these procedures.

D: 05

Analyses to Help to Interpret Results. Another set of secondary analyses involves looking at variables that may help to explain the results. The differences found may be difficult to interpret because we cannot be sure that some confounding variable was adequately controlled. Experimental research minimizes this problem, but in lower-constraint research, these issues can be serious, and secondary analyses are often essential to interpret data adequately. In many lower-constraint research studies, the secondary analyses may outnumber the primary analyses and be critical in the interpretation of the results. The most common analyses compare groups on potential confounding variables or compute the correlations between the dependent variable and suspected confounding variables. Of course, to compare the groups on these potential confounding variables, we have to anticipate them and include measures of them in the design.

A set of secondary analyses that should be included in the report of any study is descriptive statistics on the demographic characteristics of the sample, such as age, social class, and education level. Specialized populations are likely to have other relevant demographic variables. For example, if you are studying psychopathology, you will want measures of the diagnoses of your participants, the age of onset, and the severity of the symptoms. Such information allows researchers to compare samples from different published studies and provides the information needed to determine the limits of generalizability of the findings.

These are only some of the uses of secondary statistical analyses to help interpret findings of a primary analysis. Some of the analyses in this category are very sophisticated and beyond the scope of this text.

Data Snooping. The third set of secondary analyses is data snooping. Here researchers can play their hunches and see whether, for example, there are unexpected relationships, differences, or interactions in the data. Data snooping is useful in lower-constraint studies in which there may be clues about many potential relationships among variables. Good data snooping is as much an art as a science. If we are appropriately cautious, data snooping can be a rich source of hypotheses for later research. At least one high-level text is devoted entirely to this art (Tukey, 1977).

Caveats and Disclaimers

The flowchart system is a teaching device—a way to organize and formalize what is often a difficult task for students. The inferential statistics portion of this system focuses on the kinds of questions asked most often in psychological hypotheses (specifically, are there mean group differences?). The flowcharts do not cover other questions, such as, "Are there group differences in variability?" For such questions, other reference sources need to be consulted (Keppel, 2006; Myers et al., 2010). However, for most questions investigated in psychological research, these flowcharts identify appropriate statistical procedures to use.

The statistical procedures given in these flowcharts are the ones most commonly used in these situations, but other procedures may also be appropriate. Therefore, the flowcharts are more helpful in finding a statistical procedure to use in a study than in evaluating whether a particular statistical approach used by another researcher is appropriate.

Note that the flowchart takes into account two of the most important assumptions of parametric statistical tests (equal variances and normal distributions). We have covered these assumptions only in passing in this text because our focus has been on research methods and not statistics. However, as the Understanding the Concept D.1 box explains, there is a way for researchers to sidestep virtually all these assumptions in selecting statistical procedures.

UNDERSTANDING THE CONCEPT D.1: THE ROBUST NATURE OF PARAMETRIC STATISTICS

At several points in the text, we noted that statistical tests make assumptions about the data. For example, the *t*-test and ANOVA procedures assume that the distributions are normal and the variances in the groups are equal.

Sometimes, an assumption on which an inferential statistical procedure is based can be violated without threatening the validity of the conclusion drawn from the statistical test. In such a case, we say that the statistical procedure is **robust** to violations of that assumption. For example, many statistical tests were derived mathematically by assuming that scores in the population are distributed normally. If the population of scores is skewed, we have violated this assumption. If the statistical procedure is not robust to this assumption, the violation distorts the statistical test, making conclusions drawn from the statistical analysis suspect.

As it turns out, most statistics are robust to violations of almost all assumptions on which they are based if the sample size in each of the groups is approximately equal and reasonably large ($N > 30$). This conclusion is based on a series of computer simulation studies known as Monte Carlo studies (named after the famous gambling resort). In a **Monte Carlo study**, the computer simulates sampling of participants from populations with known characteristics. In this way, the researcher can see what effect violations of assumptions have on the accuracy of decisions (Levy, 1980). Monte Carlo studies show that most statistics are remarkably robust to violations of assumption when sample sizes are approximately equal and reasonably large. Consequently, we did not emphasize these assumptions in the text, although we did build them into the decision rules of the flowchart. From a design perspective, particularly for the novice researcher, it is a good idea to have approximately equal sample sizes and reasonable size samples.

SUMMARY

- The decision-tree flowcharts can simplify the task of selecting appropriate statistical procedures.
- The flowchart system requires information about the level of constraint, the independent and dependent variables, and the hypotheses of a study.
- Secondary analyses include post hoc analyses, analyses to help interpret results, and data snooping.
- If sample sizes are approximately equal and reasonably large, statistical procedures are robust to violations of underlying assumptions.

EXERCISES

D.1. Define the following key terms. Be sure that you understand them. They are defined in the glossary.

decision tree	secondary analyses	robust
decision-tree flowchart	data snooping	Monte Carlo study

D.2. For each of the following situations, study the research plan and identify

a. level of constraint, dependent variables, data produced by each dependent variable,
b. independent variables (type and number of levels),
c. research hypotheses.

Then use the flowchart to identify (1) the appropriate descriptive statistic(s), and (2) the appropriate inferential statistic(s) for each hypothesis:

1. A researcher randomly assigns 30 hypertensive participants to three groups of 10 each. Group 1 is taught muscle relaxation training; group 2 is taught cognitive relaxation training; group 3 is a no-treatment control. After the manipulation, blood pressure readings are taken on all participants. Blood pressure is represented by two numbers. The systolic blood pressure represents the maximum blood pressure at the point that the heart is actually beating. The diastolic blood pressure represents the minimum blood pressure between beats. Both are measured in terms of the number of millimeters of mercury that can be pushed up in a column by the pressure. The researcher wants to know (a) whether relaxation training reduces hypertension, and (b) whether one type of relaxation training is more effective than the other.
2. A researcher has the following hypotheses: (a) people with phobias are particularly sensitive to minor levels of stimulation, and (b) females with phobias are particularly sensitive. A fear survey questionnaire is given to 300 college freshmen. Of the 300, 50 students have high phobia scores. From the non-phobic participants, 30 females and 20 males are randomly selected. Thus, groups of 50 (30 female, 20 male) phobic and 50 (30 female, 20 male) non-phobic participants are constructed. All participants are tested on their sensitivity, a task that yields a simple score of the number of correct responses.
3. In a study of the effects of teacher feedback on accuracy of performance, 10 children (5 males and 5 females) are tested under three different conditions: immediate feedback, delayed feedback, and no feedback. All 10 children are included in each condition. The order of presentation of conditions is counterbalanced. The children are tested on their reading accuracy (i.e., the number of reading errors is counted).
4. The study focuses on the effects of smiling on children's evaluation of adults and on accuracy of learning and recall. Thirty children (15 males and 15 females) are randomly assigned to

three conditions. Videos of the same teacher reading the same story are created. In the first condition, the teacher smiles 60 percent of the time; in the second condition, the teacher smiles 30 percent of the time; and in the third condition, the teacher does not smile. After viewing the tape, the children are (a) given a learning test scored on the number of correct answers to questions about the story, and (b) asked to provide a rating on a 1–5 scale of how much they like the teacher (assuming an ordinal scale). Two weeks later, the children are tested for retention of material from the story (scored on the number of correct answers to questions about the story).

5. A psychiatric survey is conducted in a large metropolitan area. A random sample of 2,000 residents is selected. Each resident is interviewed and diagnosed into one of six categories as follows: (a) healthy; (b) mild psychiatric symptoms; (c) moderate symptoms; (d) impaired; (e) severe impairment; or (f) incapacitated. The number of people from each social class is calculated for each category.
6. A research study focusing on fear involves 30 parent/child pairs. Three hypotheses are tested in the study: (a) the number of fears reported by the parent is correlated with the number of fears reported by the child; (b) the degree of fear reported by the parent is correlated with the degree of fear reported by the child; and (c) the number of fears and the degree of fear reported by both the parent and the child are reduced by the introduction of a fear-reduction program. Both parent and child are given a fear survey schedule, which measures the number of fears reported. In addition, both parent and child are rated on an index of fear severity with a range of 1–7 (assume the rating scale is an ordinal scale). After the initial measures, parents are randomly assigned to one of two groups. One group receives a fear-reduction program while the other group receives no treatment. At the end of this part of the study, the fear survey schedule and the rating scale of fear intensity are administered again to all parents.

APPENDIX E

RESEARCH DESIGN CHECKLIST

WEB RESOURCE MATERIAL

E:01 The Pre-Data Checklist Tutorial
E:02 Study Guide/Lab Manual
E:03 Links to Related Internet Sites

Research plans are complex. If they are not constructed properly, all the work of collecting and analyzing data will be wasted. Thus, the researcher must be sure that all planning is complete before beginning the data collection. Much like a pilot who makes a preflight check to ensure that the airplane is functioning properly, the researcher should carry out a **research design checklist** to see if the research is "ready to fly." This appendix outlines the steps in the research design checklist; Table E.1 summarizes these steps, and the Student Resource Website has a tutorial on how to use the checklist.

E:01

TABLE E.1 Summary of Research Design Checklist

I. INITIAL PROBLEM DEFINITION

1. Literature review completed?
2. Problem statement developed?
3. Variables identified and operationally defined?

II. RESEARCH HYPOTHESIS

4. Research hypothesis clearly states expected relationship among variables?

III. STATISTICAL ANALYSIS

5. Descriptive statistics planned?
6. Inferential statistics planned?
7. Post hoc or secondary analyses planned?

IV. THEORETICAL BASIS AND OPERATIONAL DEFINITIONS

8. Theoretical base for study clear?
9. Do hypotheses and procedures address issues?

V. INDEPENDENT-VARIABLE MANIPULATION (EXPERIMENTAL RESEARCH)

10. Independent-variable manipulations planned?
11. Manipulations pretested?
12. Manipulation check planned?

VI. DEPENDENT MEASURES

13. Dependent measures operationally defined?
14. Dependent measures piloted?
15. Reliability and validity data available?
16. Procedures to measure reliability included?

VII. CONTROLS

17. Controls for threats to internal validity in place?
18. General control procedures and subject and experimenter controls in place?

VIII. PARTICIPANTS

Participant Selection

19. Sample adequately represents target population?
20. Demographic variables measured?

(*Continued*)

TABLE E.1 (*Continued*)

Sample Size

21. Sample sufficiently large?

Participant Assignment

22. Participants properly assigned to conditions (experimental research)?
23. Groups carefully defined (differential research)?
24. Information on the matching preserved for analysis (matched-subjects design)?

Participant Availability

25. Participants available?
26. Participants scheduled?
27. Participant fee procedures ready?

Research Ethics

28. IRB approval obtained? (human research)
29. Informed consent forms available? (human research)
30. Debriefing and/or feedback procedures ready? (human research)
31. Ethical guidelines checked and research approved? (animal research)

IX. PREPARATION OF THE SETTING

Space and Equipment

32. Adequate space available?
33. Free of distractions?
34. Equipment checked?

Personnel

35. Sufficient research staff?
36. Assistants adequately trained for emergencies?
37. Assistants adequately trained in procedures?
38. Blind procedures in place?

X. ADEQUACY OF PARTICIPANT PREPARATION, INSTRUCTION, AND PROCEDURES

39. Instructions to participants clear?
40. Instructions and procedures piloted?

If all check out, you are ready to go.

INITIAL PROBLEM DEFINITION

Each study begins with a literature review based on your initial ideas. You must refine your statement of the problem, identify the major variables, and operationally define those variables.

1. Has a literature review of initial ideas been completed?
2. Has the problem statement been clearly developed?
3. Are variables identified and operationally defined?

CLARITY OF THE RESEARCH HYPOTHESES

Next, you must check the research hypotheses. The hypotheses predict specific relationships between variables, which may be differential, correlational, or causal. The research hypotheses should indicate the type and, if appropriate, the direction of the relationship.

4. Do the research hypotheses clearly state the type and direction of the relationship among the variables?

STATISTICAL ANALYSIS PROCEDURES

You select statistical procedures before the data are gathered. Select the descriptive and inferential statistical procedures appropriate for each research hypothesis. (Here you can use the flowcharts presented in Appendix D.)

5. Are all descriptive statistical procedures planned?
6. For each hypothesis, are inferential statistical procedures planned?
7. Are you planning post hoc or secondary analyses? If so, what are they?

THEORETICAL BASIS AND OPERATIONAL DEFINITIONS

After you have obtained and analyzed your data, you will have the all-important task of interpreting and communicating the results. These rational processes provide meaning for your research and its discoveries and implications for theory. Your work may stimulate further research and influence practical applications. Thus, it is critical that you have a clear understanding of the theoretical bases for your research. Make sure that your hypotheses and your procedures address the issues that you raised initially.

8. Is the theoretical base for your study clear?
9. Do your hypotheses and procedures address the issues?

ADEQUACY OF INDEPENDENT-VARIABLE MANIPULATION

You must carefully select and carry out the experimental manipulations.

10. Have the independent-variable manipulations been carefully planned (i.e., are experimental and control groups operationally defined)?
11. Have the manipulations been pretested? Are changes needed?
12. Has a manipulation check been planned?

ADEQUACY OF DEPENDENT MEASURES

Dependent measures must be clearly defined, both conceptually and operationally. They should be pilot tested for feasibility, which means using the measures with a small group of people to see that they are understandable and will work in your research. You should evaluate reliability and validity data if available. If these are new measures, they should have been pretested and reliability and validity data obtained.

In either event, be sure that you have included procedures to measure their reliability in your current research. Know how you will score the responses. Piloting helps you to estimate how long the tasks will take and what problems might arise. Problems with the procedures should be resolved before you test a single participant.

13. Are all dependent measures operationally defined?
14. Have they been pretested or piloted?
15. Do you have prior reliability and validity data?
16. Did you include procedures to measure reliability?

ARE ALL CONTROLS IN PLACE?

Check to see that all your controls are in place to protect internal and external validity. You do not want to complete your data collection only to discover that some uncontrolled factor provides an alternative explanation of your results.

17. Are controls for threats to internal validity in place?
18. Are appropriate general control procedures and controls for subject and experimenter effects in place?

PARTICIPANTS

Participant Selection

Do the participants adequately represent the target population? You should know the type of sample that you have (a random sample, a stratified random sample, or an ad hoc sample, for example).

Adequate demographic measures must be included to describe the sample, especially if this is an ad hoc sample. You should include measures of age, sex, socioeconomic class, and similar variables.

19. Will the sampling procedures select a sample that adequately represents the target population?
20. Have demographic measures been included to describe the sample and evaluate how well it represents the population?

Sample Size

There must be enough participants to fill all cells of the design and to provide enough data to meet the needs of the statistical analyses.

21. Is the sample sufficiently large? [This is a complex question having to do with statistical power. The mathematical procedures for defining "sufficiently large" are beyond the scope of this text, but are covered by Cohen (1988). You can often get a reasonable estimate of an adequate sample size by noting the sample sizes of published studies with similar measures. The peer review process will usually weed out studies with inadequate sample sizes, so published studies are a good guideline.]

Participant Assignment

If the research involves group comparison and an experimental manipulation, you must assign participants to conditions. Participant assignments should be carried out according to the research design.

22. Have participants been assigned to conditions according to the research design?
23. If it is a differential design, are there well-defined procedures for measuring the variable that defines the group?
24. If it is a matched-subjects design, has the information on matching been preserved to allow its use in the analysis?

Participant Availability

Procedures should be in place for contacting and scheduling participants, getting their consent, and paying them if funds are available.

25. Are participants available?
26. Have participants been scheduled or is there a procedure for scheduling them?
27. Are participant payment procedures, if required, in place?

Research Ethics Considerations

Ethical issues must be addressed, and participant safeguards must be in place.

28. Has IRB ethics approval been obtained?
29. For human research, are the informed consent forms available?

30. Are debriefing and/or feedback procedures ready?
31. For animal research, have all the ethical guidelines been checked and followed?

PREPARATION OF THE SETTING

Space and Equipment

The research space should be prepared appropriately for the research, and all needed equipment should be in place and functioning correctly.

32. Is adequate space available?
33. Is it free of distracting conditions?
34. Have you checked out all equipment to see that it is working properly?

Personnel

Proper training of research assistants is critical to ensure that the data are collected properly.

35. Are there a sufficient number of research assistants?
36. Are the assistants adequately trained for emergencies?
37. Are the assistants adequately trained in the research procedures?
38. Are single- or double-blind procedures necessary and in place?

ADEQUACY OF PARTICIPANT PREPARATION, INSTRUCTION, AND PROCEDURES

Instructions, procedures, and tests should be prepared and piloted. There should be no surprises for the experimenter; you do not want to "waste" a single participant.

39. Are all instructions to participants clear?
40. Have the instructions and procedures been piloted?

SUMMARY

- The research design checklist helps you to remember all of the critical issues that you must address in the design process.

APPENDIX F

META-ANALYSIS

WEB RESOURCE MATERIAL

F:01 Meta-Analysis

A statistical procedure called meta-analysis has become a significant tool for researchers. Meta-analysis helps to objectify an important process that has long been a central part of science. As you learned in Chapter 2, scientists typically begin their research by examining previous research. They review studies on their topic and summarize their conclusions in review papers. They might compute a box score in these reviews that lists how many of the studies support a given hypothesis and how many do not. The reviewer judges the quality of each study, which indicates how seriously each study should be taken. For example, one well-designed study may carry considerably more weight than three or four poorly designed studies. If all the studies have the same outcome, drawing conclusions is easy. However, it is common to have some studies show one effect, whereas others show a different effect or no effect at all.

LOGIC OF META-ANALYSIS

Meta-analysis is a procedure for statistically combining the results of multiple studies on the same topic (e.g., Abramowitz, 1998; Johnson & Eagly, 2000; Rosenthal, 1998). For example, if 16 published studies employ a cognitive therapy for treating depression, a meta-analysis of those studies would compute an index of treatment effectiveness for each study. These indexes are measures of effect size (i.e., the difference between experimental and control conditions expressed in standard deviation units). For example, an effect size of .5 means that the experimental and control conditions showed a mean difference that was one-half of their average standard deviation.

TABLE F.1 Some Examples of Meta-Analytic Research

- Hollin (1999) found that, contrary to earlier reviews, treatment does reduce recidivism in criminal offenders.
- Irvin et al. (1999) wondered if the cognitive-behavioral methods for relapse prevention that are frequently included in drug-treatment programs really work. Their meta-analysis examined 26 studies, with 70 hypotheses and a combined sample of 9,504 participants. The results indicated that relapse prevention is generally effective, particularly for alcohol problems.
- Concerns have been raised that such frequently used psychological tests as the MMPI (Minnesota Multiphasic Personality Inventory) may be biased against minorities, making individuals who are perfectly normal appear to be pathological based on the test. Hall et al. (1999) conducted a meta-analysis examining 50 empirical studies with a combined sample of 8,633 participants. They compared African-Americans, European-Americans, and Latino-Americans on their MMPI scores. The results showed that the groups do not differ from each other statistically or clinically. The main conclusion is that the tests do not unfairly portray African-Americans or Latinos; they are as accurate at diagnosing pathology in minority groups as they are in Caucasian groups.

These effect sizes are then averaged across studies. The averages are usually weighted by the sample size of each study and sometimes by the quality of the study. So a study with 50 participants would be given more weight in the meta-analysis than a study with 10 participants. A study with strong control procedures and careful measurement would be given more weight than a study with fewer controls and, therefore, more chance of confounding. The overall effect size computed in a meta-analysis indicates how strongly the independent variable affected the dependent variable.

Like any statistical analysis, the value of the analysis depends on the quality of the data. In this case, the data are drawn from several studies, and the quality of the designs and execution of the studies determine how confident we can be in the results of the meta-analysis. Some recent examples of meta-analytic studies are summarized in Table F.1.

Many writers have commented on the drawbacks of significance testing in empirical research and the value of meta-analyses in overcoming them (e.g., Cohen, 1992; Schmidt, 1992; Wilson, 2000). The following discussion reviews these arguments.

LITERATURE REVIEWS

Psychology, like other sciences, routinely assesses the status of research areas. Typically, this is done through formal literature reviews in which previous research is critically examined, findings and ideas from many studies are abstracted and integrated, and conclusions are drawn about the state of that area. These literature reviews are important summary statements, but several researchers have argued that these traditional reviews are flawed and less useful than had been thought (Light & Pillemer, 1984; Hunt, 1997). The problem rests with the nature of the statistical procedures used in psychological research.

ALPHA LEVELS AND KNOWLEDGE

Most research information is based on statistical procedures that use stringent but arbitrary alpha levels in testing the null hypothesis (typically .01 or .05). Thus, when a well-designed study produces statistically significant results, the findings are accepted as valid new knowledge. With an alpha that is small, it is unlikely that the findings are due to chance. If an analysis fails to show statistical significance, it is typically concluded that no new knowledge has been discovered. Studies that fail to find statistical significance are rarely published and therefore are not easily available to the research community. Thus, the accumulated knowledge of a field, such as that presented in traditional literature reviews, is heavily weighted with information that is based on statistically significant findings.

What about those research results that fail to reach statistical significance? Might there be useful information there that is being ignored? Many writers argue that is exactly what is happening; the accumulated scientific knowledge in psychology does not include the information that may reside in studies that were ignored because they failed to reach statistical significance. Consequently, the accumulated knowledge might be drastically limited, hindering the field's progress.

BETA LEVELS AND KNOWLEDGE

Recall from Chapter 5 that setting a stringent alpha (.05 or .01) guards against Type I errors (the tendency to conclude that there is an effect of one variable on another when there actually is none). Minimizing Type I errors increases the probability of Type II errors, which involve concluding that there is no effect when there actually is one. Scientists generally consider Type I errors more serious than Type II errors because a Type I error claims an effect that does not exist. Type II errors *result in the loss of information* but they do not assert a nonexistent effect. Thus, alpha is set low to minimize the more serious Type I errors.

People often interpret significance tests in an either/or fashion: if the results are statistically significant, then *there is an effect of one variable on another*, and if the results are not statistically significant, then *there is no effect of one variable on another* (Oakes, 1986; Schmidt, 1992). In actuality, there might have been effects that were not strong enough to reach statistical significance. Such a result might occur, for example, if the sample is small or participant selection or assignment is biased. Effects lie along a continuum, with some effects being small and not reaching significance and others being large and statistically significant. When small effects are ignored, information on relationships among variables is discarded. That is, the field may be committing a Type II error by failing to recognize real effects. Furthermore, consistently making such Type II errors would significantly truncate the cumulative knowledge in the field (Hunter & Schmidt, 1990). How can science deal with this problem?

META-ANALYSIS AND THE PROBLEM OF TYPE II ERRORS

Meta-analysis deals with the Type II error problem by calculating effect sizes of studies and weighting these effect sizes for qualitative factors, such as the number of subjects and the inclusion of controls. It goes beyond the simple statement of statistical significance and the categorical acceptance or rejection of the null hypothesis to quantify the strength of the effect. For example, studies with large sample sizes may be statistically significant at the .05 level but still have small effect sizes. Conversely, studies with modest sample sizes may fall short of statistical significance and yet have moderate effect sizes.

Literature reviews are critical in science. Reviews based on meta-analyses can mine what we might call the Type II error area to unearth important information previously ignored.

Meta-analytic techniques are fairly new, but they have the potential to significantly influence the direction of research. Indeed, the important breakthroughs in science in the future might not come from individual research reports of single studies, but from the careful meta-analysis of large groups of research (Schmidt, 1992). This possible future for science would include primary and theoretical scientists, with primary scientists conducting individual studies and providing the data and theoretical scientists applying sophisticated meta-analyses to the accumulated studies to "make the scientific discoveries" (Schmidt, 1992, p. 1180). Meta-analysis provides technology for combining results across diverse samples and different measures of outcome.

Although imperfect, meta-analysis is probably better than traditional qualitative methods of summarizing studies in literature reviews. Several informative books are available for students who want additional understanding of meta-analysis, such as Hunt (1997), Light and Pillemer (1984), and Cooper (1998). There is also a more detailed discussion of meta-analysis on the Student Resource Website.

F:01

SUMMARY

- Meta-analysis is a procedure for statistically combining the results of multiple studies on the same topic.
- It objectively sums the effect sizes of studies, providing information beyond simple statistical significance.

APPENDIX G

RANDOM NUMBERS

WEB RESOURCE MATERIAL

G:01 Random-Number Generator Program

To use the table of random numbers, select a starting point and a direction (up, down, left, or right). For example, if you want to assign participants randomly to each of five groups, you might start at the beginning of row 85 and move left to right. Number the groups 1 through 5 and assign the first participant to the group designated by the first digit between 1 and 5 that you encounter; the second participant to the group designated by the next suitable digit you encounter, and so on. By this method, the first 10 participants will be randomly assigned to the following groups: 4, 2, 4, 1, 3, 1, 2, 5, 4, 3.

It is also possible to randomize within blocks, so that the same number of participants is in each condition. For example, if you want to assign the first five participants—one to each of the five groups—and you use the same starting point (beginning of row 85), you get the following assignment: 4, 2, 1, 3, 5. Your second block of five participants is assigned to the following groups: 4, 3, 1, 5, 2.

G:01

We have also included a random-number generator program on the Student Resource Website to automate the tasks of randomly selecting participants and randomly assigning them to groups. That program generated the random numbers that appear in this appendix.

ROW										
001	83118	14731	72347	05185	38446	85974	67889	14058	54841	29718
002	81674	38122	65870	81929	55257	19229	17379	63796	47472	87950
003	22937	52188	99536	54411	21963	33498	38155	41574	39264	26947
004	22829	58431	46591	27214	21701	03593	95248	75216	61897	40229
005	39684	46986	66273	38889	99304	31481	97050	88654	90675	41237
006	45325	13071	57484	77350	70803	81536	65871	81744	02195	12600
007	74780	78335	36516	94590	32226	74922	43020	34888	34870	18298
008	63460	21270	84658	40385	80368	04132	98867	90374	65094	48713
009	69708	58825	25201	25018	36329	37621	52473	91771	33829	88908
010	23016	10773	85210	18148	71764	30821	29660	29905	56811	84112
011	12488	37464	54883	54464	96512	93616	01798	20936	56702	71232
012	73882	22231	64464	64360	11288	58910	81545	82163	03895	18109
013	30945	27042	36199	14144	87799	66926	89889	07591	16374	40290
014	78759	83697	09315	64169	37143	39222	96036	70662	12725	37273

(continued)

ROW (CONTINUED)										
015	81220	53475	64497	05620	98858	79121	42071	67756	10450	60471
016	56360	87714	88118	63224	33404	78568	37903	74596	36066	70407
017	94438	55519	93553	76732	08140	69812	25562	65841	82755	36246
018	79574	38717	07937	47592	98540	96339	76449	04728	43420	19482
019	20376	49792	03224	17401	85150	62736	64881	13145	96148	58475
020	20808	66420	74390	05150	00541	03629	23554	82705	47143	61207
021	96144	20831	65068	13998	96356	51762	20113	76105	39037	44932
022	13392	17257	77582	54479	28127	49782	64648	24239	02955	32839
023	79320	60327	31428	25782	38896	71108	92293	42967	46286	80305
024	59008	92182	18624	48854	95184	29679	49459	24419	34755	39439
025	85970	51575	53312	69378	93930	91596	30312	68294	26209	85517
026	58940	87118	92175	53724	81347	70107	79208	66360	28390	10116
027	18339	51469	93587	79316	83366	12707	22100	94360	56882	79989
028	21653	31764	67860	93719	51818	00292	00049	05552	27347	17163
029	94304	09542	71131	93017	17760	76197	05876	65521	09067	43134
030	68798	27764	57792	42681	62709	62103	01574	92489	58305	15094
031	73938	34353	98486	81835	72741	96778	90877	97094	99993	07317
032	41573	69750	81246	05518	63206	80092	27941	91955	17383	89193
033	14391	69700	30749	01549	88707	76606	29925	41908	19205	93096
034	25710	41477	76631	61902	60259	20928	79292	90245	36502	94500
035	48659	61316	35496	42845	33371	00891	52015	24457	00436	84575
036	87287	92603	09557	61085	95950	30210	79794	08952	92388	90960
037	18360	26766	06166	29883	49595	06885	68738	44573	63970	85737
038	20142	19985	83242	87248	53573	44304	31508	86085	08906	45048
039	17141	44434	83156	67903	99357	66671	50067	74693	80147	71212
040	70158	82947	46691	41988	12066	59837	26886	27920	62156	88619
041	85310	43446	28453	68134	40170	74233	63290	48840	46068	21058
042	29911	70027	00102	56774	80124	49327	70034	65898	23121	42817
043	66713	67891	03696	79832	28902	40379	13806	08082	34467	98521
044	15106	23211	63885	55282	49366	88791	31708	52205	75272	48874
045	50764	72607	73134	99349	68679	08898	90086	08433	61106	49410
046	21630	42677	14249	26227	15171	38228	82702	66842	81562	26293
047	74824	87463	93921	80023	49515	68740	29091	16641	18784	38244
048	40990	22512	33234	99119	49268	59536	91836	00816	00007	75098
049	59580	80386	33937	35199	23532	47753	89891	96523	34600	45307
050	64091	30030	33181	74708	93231	56741	52948	96259	76121	58405
051	31824	78938	30980	49020	62446	80074	43680	81712	52483	79078
052	67969	12622	73680	23983	32074	60639	69857	99973	63132	37061
053	35921	82274	22932	11428	46274	74176	23475	36535	25610	87607
054	84158	72348	38806	68394	42850	03337	17833	71881	51637	72407
055	99737	35440	84944	57599	34108	03142	97967	27293	68134	80787
056	55390	72866	81929	96978	76416	26316	56457	87686	97081	92846
057	01953	19734	52239	25241	15975	93088	23032	58234	95869	32320
058	71277	04995	11835	00247	30771	49833	31264	47941	71120	15224
059	52997	85735	37789	70896	36743	44021	62933	77828	56986	95924
060	55529	47677	22379	73820	43629	15246	57252	94972	23363	53105
061	51961	50692	58110	92174	32326	32253	82722	99770	95444	23743

ROW										
062	22312	54117	33727	40973	32715	68819	17534	10547	89198	80743
063	55368	25767	45743	35073	34917	30118	43828	09625	26040	35459
064	32374	87623	02289	69901	67058	50238	09498	62670	94732	42760
065	40635	41716	72239	86255	59078	49699	74706	60497	79116	32541
066	64856	08694	74107	18926	22729	66481	60972	33396	94773	94499
067	34701	87568	04539	75936	02035	29627	34092	74335	82249	45349
068	87001	15741	88047	62816	57123	69232	88751	35715	11098	19031
069	11435	46068	55361	78347	86149	88025	88531	79671	67168	16110
070	54257	59218	20069	29548	76696	91133	83276	47285	22399	88936
071	95198	30106	39394	37018	41532	28823	89515	95630	38671	29585
072	72017	34748	20191	54815	89082	03586	79140	64774	92552	69922
073	72798	75562	42759	22272	52536	20193	13317	76075	81897	35768
074	45722	07179	34383	01840	95205	80135	46087	74793	53028	63292
075	12889	63858	57215	33854	96933	56439	91606	79486	54367	27520
076	60474	62549	51279	27597	84906	31190	15275	98602	97278	59405
077	36531	73173	28700	35695	79873	33365	87410	01839	06088	03829
078	69676	06790	02620	96835	20949	31179	18258	15658	57156	31779
079	65616	05030	15608	57507	42489	41809	01589	45263	35040	29724
080	29160	86008	07190	36614	32860	20719	83037	08304	53340	66598
081	59588	14659	02715	64045	40206	86131	96766	49273	78492	25791
082	93801	94620	79694	68519	97134	54773	95823	86725	96789	31487
083	24154	30694	71665	70941	18200	67698	01103	05252	83074	11519
084	70888	06573	00667	05785	32631	98007	84191	62914	52041	60811
085	74924	91987	73125	43149	77456	89670	23200	49846	59982	93179
086	49940	09303	92980	24718	91573	65615	17349	15924	96599	77619
087	89613	49600	21383	74997	08075	04288	12174	89777	13928	40755
088	57360	80375	23887	69666	02963	46671	83041	37586	77814	37597
089	95037	16802	43724	78706	09783	35397	95404	79948	50739	73108
090	89622	91889	63293	26165	96836	05735	70768	83833	00481	49366
091	23532	74639	03016	15846	83236	40760	13170	26226	65834	13894
092	20403	89871	44465	38300	47138	86525	01195	85785	44264	18946
093	97753	63450	22935	14547	92885	57640	82705	38544	46209	54291
094	30648	99862	86695	69193	03872	29420	91098	39930	89154	82686
095	72834	03535	60001	07382	77030	65642	22398	93616	16803	36038
096	79783	09152	64407	64089	84663	39960	95258	54710	33018	83122
097	45219	40588	39493	81674	15374	79198	72048	13931	39033	71389
098	45503	97841	18057	18003	83983	55778	48237	74738	17764	88205
099	36778	97647	04573	42126	45961	39496	76514	47502	97612	79768
100	51120	04760	08058	28748	18773	88952	42871	45010	28347	65129
101	25255	76481	41117	90882	11630	51403	11362	11007	00504	23018
102	53953	60218	54847	67236	75583	38424	58217	29313	47506	80910
103	72176	32105	13076	78892	77242	73598	94482	70282	55412	48555
104	49195	32423	43919	20558	71048	95888	21722	38979	83531	44643
105	27011	53804	75190	49931	11222	75341	20564	85031	75038	81461
106	88008	99817	10292	94200	66252	54303	75837	73282	59038	61094
107	10659	38155	58293	07308	11914	75448	75658	71870	31010	82651
108	35740	18568	65113	93178	86534	76698	55280	16662	59460	88946

(continued)

ROW (CONTINUED)										
109	48102	98843	36372	45858	34229	91502	91819	12288	52143	38841
110	77197	82753	64021	94574	47096	42935	44589	20094	25563	83324
111	48992	39559	20380	78597	89753	47522	89571	29643	73374	47473
112	03031	10160	41169	70993	40470	91936	70057	13146	77359	97249
113	55982	09121	48733	76166	31348	03899	03232	17113	44939	72454
114	30687	59552	73286	36661	29328	92119	56983	09420	76055	59392
115	51911	73200	07159	51225	15510	94026	48025	99865	17198	03317
116	32755	67994	17389	77532	18882	06871	12389	53841	32454	68959
117	18590	62076	42117	65999	09611	28952	20484	01072	44431	43796
118	39015	86276	62894	77314	46682	00654	38771	31956	77844	39537
119	48752	60298	78624	40689	73051	36263	46991	65761	77297	48454
120	44217	50954	77320	87296	70543	70854	12364	62358	36633	68399
121	21243	18397	29867	31079	29860	70287	59530	12896	33920	11519
122	14123	97125	99681	54038	45145	19647	71999	72215	64740	65563
123	65089	82496	81262	15650	39272	44864	23323	30033	03205	17789
124	50511	99354	56654	50746	18033	44304	61053	56006	66677	72838
125	27487	99733	95940	02709	19355	82979	72947	78956	76225	30858
126	02168	30432	14158	60658	76393	04204	20108	83740	89710	33124
127	35821	51848	29202	53991	28576	90023	55471	86712	77360	63121
128	49913	30732	36144	47934	76174	89443	70845	62716	32945	86566
129	06826	59517	81599	14261	37053	53652	95978	62068	48837	81194
130	67726	46900	54363	60403	89460	41928	89937	29152	72276	38216
131	04275	01594	32250	65288	50198	03541	74247	19785	88064	78646
132	98966	52997	30708	57162	00223	88104	89127	32357	96899	07006
133	19027	53348	95065	19951	61648	28312	93198	27916	29554	48594
134	96760	91736	17906	28693	41613	13104	24297	02404	12890	57768
135	82122	56424	58942	29923	07444	45429	79177	38336	31258	78013
136	97832	70924	64171	49772	70243	57519	79936	32081	20065	88406
137	21233	22597	48600	06043	09177	41257	34025	40703	61161	45231
138	85928	24009	15291	29180	16737	82598	67825	05780	76185	67168
139	14311	99633	52617	92317	01653	15331	39636	51240	33526	91423
140	66493	63692	57495	16101	24780	94356	92477	46698	41507	86337
141	97545	39274	08335	16941	61924	10546	97574	80311	71330	01153
142	70537	19763	35253	83445	34836	72799	63831	95877	37183	57376
143	24199	21810	06850	53740	92721	47176	36322	47627	35639	57784
144	76990	82225	26824	38655	44098	93369	51602	60490	19842	94941
145	81445	07421	49059	28624	81279	66009	17409	34509	77085	08565
146	71554	95825	25082	39004	50604	75487	30339	42774	38881	26343
147	88883	59512	71443	84140	07557	13915	86176	91566	05148	29691
148	30073	66539	58325	20133	20384	77471	07568	35888	82975	84672
149	40277	30770	07659	63125	82337	68223	66332	24814	46712	01047
150	20842	44544	66012	03807	84905	17077	46816	90997	87097	23645
151	89163	56893	03784	44678	57440	97445	69591	53496	66564	34291
152	66350	21271	39444	84068	99582	21254	34503	35084	58380	11273
153	26845	15059	46445	32688	84496	02705	73544	94403	91046	22445
154	09702	53258	93821	01729	08314	75835	20560	18108	04014	79609

ROW										
155	59997	97465	52495	64878	23572	97085	81466	26729	65060	88862
156	99272	09307	47918	46942	55924	43283	15640	15783	18324	65845
157	41103	98684	63883	44378	37184	57853	13488	12236	34932	62998
158	40487	79441	86361	75056	04931	91260	92374	47920	29337	49917
159	70839	82012	56482	12072	17799	37113	90574	39686	10964	62936
160	11432	27398	77236	05779	12844	83746	58325	85884	44383	68371
161	52200	12168	04587	89810	05516	90950	57756	94841	44441	33640
162	14672	87496	98339	75794	06722	08737	94374	25584	99322	01565
163	20031	21679	57841	97210	77988	05256	65250	81704	33867	85141
164	12823	99801	43537	00685	79519	04736	82797	32687	91791	67722
165	33461	05704	81818	83718	84803	38390	52384	79002	97027	25653
166	54115	44664	31892	40071	83755	86330	15274	85063	34858	85281
167	55233	45371	36391	07741	71163	72204	51945	09099	12894	40060
168	64731	87242	68811	16692	31175	53623	21219	28018	13017	77958
169	06999	44867	02444	99641	31363	04394	17274	07422	00761	43866
170	07504	27709	49077	63878	72558	21585	07914	33214	03321	19785
171	28292	22466	88654	23137	13894	87275	68554	89672	31949	33814
172	07111	08720	12048	53004	14517	90301	93413	58445	09401	46158
173	08859	38995	75808	95176	53361	65917	72708	78862	17047	82962
174	90682	60063	60342	16794	39344	69169	89762	55435	32558	39973
175	55095	58153	77635	91124	27142	23120	97590	29899	50508	26562
176	12564	91616	20992	30608	06172	52284	58880	59058	27908	64790
177	62055	06938	94167	98110	97639	46148	61706	68907	53794	74432
178	35840	35157	38587	79730	74794	37029	32234	94318	00362	60880
179	13868	61497	31772	65411	42674	51355	89586	64028	40757	65433
180	94489	89663	31096	67989	29225	97262	49873	87494	74832	89738
181	27758	55660	07466	76310	71686	08755	87474	59653	31777	91914
182	00332	26697	72170	04327	22163	19567	88833	44998	31824	15560
183	77196	20359	86007	76293	06161	96019	25897	55777	20802	54783
184	46535	90956	70515	43694	29552	24643	85435	50189	69001	35710
185	28489	48643	54263	41304	94704	36970	24093	43693	95752	74289
186	21732	83865	70761	83003	15200	91606	49385	35266	16704	87160
187	04655	48636	11844	47571	14112	91117	81737	36120	16635	55989
188	24469	83255	17519	32932	87926	58084	35797	86268	28686	22755
189	08372	56478	64545	21083	44627	88559	29894	72051	22660	90145
190	12331	39856	45218	10150	72762	72432	39124	18104	52619	97933
191	34687	24872	71119	74212	04600	41207	39447	42290	98949	63776
192	76119	22118	98560	20820	09580	56669	88878	83121	33412	68276
193	37619	76005	05180	39531	73854	42005	96054	37362	32172	31952
194	20569	95523	49314	06753	35953	25661	95765	34399	11379	85105
195	97337	24684	13722	05331	79035	61109	21548	73730	32928	58640
196	29869	83275	51320	31043	93801	82738	16009	13064	01051	69734
197	12418	21848	14560	92262	68467	30405	40452	81182	97125	40914
198	42272	04229	92392	85203	16819	40504	33469	83869	45318	20801
199	41902	60206	46536	84309	56899	54821	40759	65412	43273	30732
200	07596	95996	78689	87458	92356	99471	30110	72670	66514	53078

APPENDIX H

ANSWERS TO QUICK-CHECK REVIEW QUESTIONS

CHAPTER 1

1.1.1 The essence of science is its way of thinking, which combines rationalism and empiricism.

1.1.2 Science is a way of thinking, and it is possible to think scientifically anywhere.

1.1.3 A prepared mind refers to the ability to recognize and react to unexpected findings because the person has a sufficient background in, and understanding of, the phenomena under study.

1.1.4 Scientists are pervasive skeptics who challenge accepted wisdom, are intellectually excited by questions, and are willing to tolerate uncertainty.

1.1.5 Scientists and artists share curiosity, creativity, skepticism, tolerance for ambiguity, commitment to hard work, and systematic thinking.

1.2.1 The common methods of acquiring knowledge are tenacity, intuition, authority, rationalism, empiricism, and science.

1.2.2 Science combines empiricism and rationalism.

1.2.3 Naive empiricism insists on experiencing evidence directly through the senses. In contrast, sophisticated empiricism allows indirect evidence of phenomena, such as the effects of gravity on falling objects.

1.2.4 The limitation of rationalism is that the premises must be correct for the conclusions to be correct. The limitation of empiricism is that, by itself, it does little more than collect facts; it needs rational processes to organize these facts.

1.2.5 Facts are empirically observed events.

1.3.1 The early practical skills of artisans illustrated the advantage of abstract information in solving everyday problems, thus justifying the kind of scientific study that seeks to systematically develop such information.

1.3.2 Thales, considered the father of science, rejected mysticism and studied natural phenomena using empirical observation and rational thought.

1.3.3 During the Middle Ages, science was used to support theological ideas.

1.3.4 Modern technology is the practical application of scientific discoveries, whereas modern science is a way of thinking about and studying phenomena.

1.3.5 The orderliness belief is the idea that the universe operates in a lawful manner. Without this belief, it would make no sense to engage in scientific investigation, because there would be no general principles to discover.

1.3.6 Galileo was arrested for the crime of "blasphemy" for accepting the model that said that the Earth and the planets revolved around the sun, thus arguing that the Earth was not the center of the universe.

1.4.1 Some of the more influential schools of psychology were structuralism, functionalism, psychoanalysis, Gestalt psychology, behaviorism, humanistic psychology, and cognitive psychology.

1.4.2 Modern mainstream psychology tends to be integrative in that its theories and ideas cut across several perspectives.

1.4.3 Psychology needs to be scientific and objective because the subjective impressions of people about psychological events tend to be undependable.

1.4.4. Ask three questions: What is the nature of the evidence for the claims? In what form is the evidence presented? What are the affiliations of the "scientists"?

1.5.1 The major idea at the heart of research ethics is that the researcher has personal responsibility to make thoughtful and ethical decisions to enhance science and human welfare.

1.6.1 The Student Resource Website has an interactive Study Guide/Lab Manual, several tutorials, and an expanded discussion of numerous topics.

1.6.2 The publisher's website for this text is called MySearchLab.

CHAPTER 2

2.1.1 The data in psychology are observations of behavior.

2.1.2 Facts are directly observed, whereas constructs are inferences about unseen mechanisms, drawn to explain observations.

2.1.3 Reification of a construct means believing that the construct is a fact.

2.1.4 Constructs are based on facts and are used to predict new facts.

2.1.5 Science is built on the following assumptions: (1) a true, physical universe exists; (2) the universe is primarily an orderly system; (3) the principles of this orderly universe can be discovered, particularly through scientific research; and (4) knowledge of the universe is always incomplete. New knowledge should alter current ideas and theories. Therefore, all knowledge and theories are tentative.

2.1.6 Going from empirical observations to constructs is inductive reasoning; going from constructs to predictions is deductive reasoning.

2.2.1 A theory is a formalized set of concepts that summarizes and organizes observations and inferences, provides tentative explanations for phenomena, and provides the foundation for making predictions.

2.2.2 Inductive theories depend heavily on empirical observations, whereas deductive theories go well beyond the existing data and encourage the testing of new predictions from theories.

2.2.3 A model is a miniature representation of reality. Scientists construct and examine models to provide insights into natural phenomena.

2.2.4 Observations are the facts of research, whereas inferences are inductive leaps beyond the observations.

2.2.5 Many technically incorrect theories nevertheless make accurate predictions in many situations and therefore are useful in these situations.

2.2.6 Falsifiability is the principle that, for a theory to be scientific, there must be some evidence that, if found, would lead to a rejection of the theory.

2.3.1 The two dimensions in our model of research are (1) levels of constraint, and (2) phases of research.

2.3.2 The phases of research are (1) idea generation, (2) problem definition, (3) procedures design, (4) observation, (5) data analysis, (6) interpretation, and (7) communication.

2.3.3 Levels of constraint refer to a continuum of demands on the adequacy of information and the level of control used during the observation phase.

2.3.4 The groups in differential research are naturally occurring, whereas the groups in experimental research are formed through random assignment.

2.4.1 Ethical issues need to be anticipated and addressed in the procedures-design phase before proceeding any further in the research. We must also remain sensitive to ethical issues throughout the research.

2.4.2 Each researcher bears the major responsibility for the ethical conduct of the research.

CHAPTER 3

3.1.1 The main sources of research questions are your own interests and the research of other investigators.

3.1.2 Applied research is designed to solve specific problems, whereas basic research is interested in finding new knowledge, without a specific application.

3.1.3 A variable is any set of events that may have different values.

3.1.4 Basic research often provides an understanding of natural phenomena, which can later be used to address practical problems.

3.1.5 Translational research is basic research conducted with an eventual goal of "translating" the information into applied uses.

3.2.1 The independent variable is the variable that the researcher manipulates, and the dependent variable is the variable that the research measures and expects will change as a result of the independent-variable manipulation.

3.2.2 Manipulated independent variables are actively controlled by the researcher, whereas nonmanipulated independent variables are defined by preexisting characteristics of participants.

3.2.3 Holding a variable constant involves preventing the variable from varying. For example, the researcher can hold the variable of age constant by testing only those participants who are of a particular age.

3.3.1 Extraneous variables are uncontrolled factors that can affect the outcome of a study.

3.3.2 Uncontrolled extraneous variables can distort research findings.

3.3.3 Validity refers to how well a study, procedure, or measure does what it is supposed to do.

3.3.4 Controls reduce the effects of extraneous variables and thus increase our confidence in the validity of the research findings.

3.4.1 Informed consent refers to a person's agreement to participate in a study after being fully informed about the study and its risks. It is obtained in writing. It is important because it addresses moral issues about violating people's rights by giving people a choice of whether they will participate in a study.

3.4.2 Institutional Review Boards are groups set up at universities, hospitals, and research centers to screen research proposals for risks and ethical safeguards.

3.4.3 Animals cannot give informed consent, and the research carried out on animals is often more invasive than that carried out on humans. The ethical focus is on providing animals with humane care and minimizing discomfort and pain.

3.4.4 Diversity issues in research refer to the need to include a broad representation of people so that results will generalize to broader populations.

CHAPTER 4

4.1.1 Measurement is assigning numbers to represent the level of a variable.

4.1.2 Without accurate measurement, we cannot be confident of the accuracy of the conclusions of our research.

4.1.3 The properties of the abstract number system are identity, magnitude, equal intervals, and a true zero.

4.2.1 Nominal scales are naming scales; ordinal scales order phenomena based on their magnitude; interval scales convey information about both order and the distance between values; ratio scales provide the best match to the number system.

4.2.2 Nominal scales produce nominal or categorical data. Ordinal scales produce ordered data. Interval and ratio scales produce score data.

4.2.3 Nominal scales have the property of identity; ordinal scales have the properties of identity and magnitude; interval scales have the properties of identity, magnitude, and equal intervals; ratio scales have the properties of identity, magnitude, equal intervals, and a true zero.

4.2.4 A true zero means that zero on the scale represents a zero level of the property being measured. When a scale has a true zero, taking the ratio of two measures on the scale provides a meaningful number.

4.3.1 The best way to minimize measurement error is to develop well-thought-out operational definitions and follow them exactly.

4.3.2 Operational definitions transform theoretical variables into concrete events by stating precisely how these variables are to be measured.

4.3.3 Social desirability is participants' tendency to respond in what they believe to be the most socially acceptable manner. Such response tendencies distort measures and therefore threaten the validity of research.

4.3.4 Convergent validity involves multiple lines of research converging on the same conclusions, which increases confidence that the phenomenon is consistent.

4.4.1 Reliability refers to the constancy of a measure. The types of reliability are interrater reliability, test-retest reliability, and internal consistency reliability.

4.4.2 Measures can be reliable without being valid, but cannot be valid without being reliable.

4.4.3 If the effective range of a scale is inadequate, the data will be distorted.

4.4.4 Floor effects occur when the scores bunch at the bottom of the scale, whereas ceiling effects occur when scores bunch near the top of the scale.

4.4.5 Reliability refers to the consistency of a measure, whereas validity refers to its accuracy.

4.5.1 A researcher might be tempted to fabricate data for personal, financial, or political gain.

4.5.2 Most data fabrication is uncovered in the peer review process or because the findings will not replicate in the labs of other scientists.

CHAPTER 5

5.1.1 The differences among people are called individual differences.

5.1.2 Descriptive statistics are used to describe data, whereas inferential statistics help the researcher to draw conclusions from the data.

5.2.1 Frequency distributions show the number of participants with each possible score, and they can be used with any kind of data.

5.2.2 Cross-tabulation involves simultaneously categorizing participants on more than one variable.

5.2.3 Frequency distributions give the frequency for each possible score, whereas grouped frequency distributions provide the frequency for ranges of scores, in which the ranges are of equal size.

5.2.4 Continuous variables require grouped frequency distributions.

5.2.5 The most common distribution shapes are symmetric and skewed. The most common symmetric distribution is the normal distribution.

5.3.1 The three measures of central tendency are mean, median, and mode.

5.3.2 Deviation scores are the distances of each score from the mean.

5.3.3 The measures of variability are range, variance, and standard deviation.

5.3.4 A correlation quantifies the strength and direction of a relationship between variables. Regression uses the relationship to predict one variable from the value of the other variable.

5.3.5 A standard score indicates how many standard deviations a score is above or below the mean. It is computed by subtracting the mean from the score and dividing the difference by the standard deviation.

5.3.6 The variance takes into account all the scores in a distribution, whereas the range only uses the highest and lowest scores.

5.3.7 The mean takes into account all the scores in a distribution, whereas the mode can be unstable, shifting considerably if one or two scores change.

5.3.8 Correlations, unlike other descriptive statistics, describe the relationship among two or more variables.

5.4.1 The population is the larger group of people of interest, whereas the sample is a subset that is drawn from the population.

5.4.2 Sampling error is the natural variation among different samples drawn from the same population.

5.4.3 Alpha level refers to the cutoff point used for making a decision to reject the null hypothesis. Type I error is rejecting the null hypothesis when it is true. Type II error is failing to reject the null hypothesis when it is false.

5.5.1 The *t*-test and ANOVA test for mean differences. The *t*-test is used when there are two groups, and the ANOVA is used with two or more groups.

5.5.2 A power analysis determines how large a sample size should be to detect an existing group difference. It is important because it assures that the researcher has sufficient power before the study is started.

5.5.3 The effect size is an index of the size of the difference between group means expressed in standard deviation units. It tells us the size of the effect, which indicates how much the independent variable shifted the distribution of the dependent variable.

5.6.1 Scientists must present their data and statistics accurately and without bias.

5.6.2 Cherry-picking data means reporting findings that are consistent with your hypothesis while ignoring contradictory results.

CHAPTER 6

6.1.1 Both Darwin and Goodall studied natural phenomena in natural environments without doing anything to influence these phenomena.

6.1.2 Freud and Piaget worked extensively with individuals, observing their behavior, but also asking questions or testing them under various conditions.

6.1.3 Naturalistic research involves observing phenomena in natural settings, whereas case study research involves modifying the settings somewhat to see how the modifications affect the performance of participants.

6.2.1 Naturalistic research is used whenever we are interested in the natural flow of behavior. Case studies are used when one is interested in single individuals.

6.2.2 A contingency is a probabilistic relationship ("If x occurs, y is likely to occur."). It can be used to generate causal hypotheses for higher-constraint research.

6.2.3 Laboratory research simplifies and constrains real-life settings. Such changes may threaten generalizability. In contrast, naturalistic research has no problem with generalizability, because it is conducted in natural settings.

6.2.4 Naturalistic research can negate a general proposition by finding a single counterexample. It cannot establish a general proposition because it does not adequately sample from the population and thus does not represent the population.

6.3.1 Qualitative research is research that describes and summarizes behavior and typically reports its results in a narrative rather than a statistical manner.

6.3.2 Problem statements in low-constraint research are often general, because there may be no basis for generating more specific questions.

6.3.3 Observations may be made by unobtrusive observers or participant observers.

6.3.4 Unobtrusive measures are observations that are not obvious to the person being observed and thus are less likely to influence the person's behavior.

6.3.5 Archival records are existing measures of phenomena that have already occurred, such as course grades or census data.

6.3.6 The goal in sampling is to obtain a sample that is representative.

6.3.7 Taking a broad sample of situations allows the researcher to see if behavior differs across settings.

6.3.8 Measurement reactivity is the phenomenon of participants behaving differently than they might normally because they know that someone is observing them.

6.3.9 Coding is recording data into predetermined categories (e.g., observing children at play and coding their behavior as "aggressive," "cooperative," or "neutral").

6.4.1 Low-constraint research studies available samples, which are often not representative of the population.

6.4.2 Low-constraint research is flexible, allowing the researcher to follow interesting leads. Unfortunately, this also means that it is difficult to describe and is therefore difficult for others to replicate.

6.4.3 The ex post facto fallacy is drawing unwarranted causal conclusions from the observation of a contingent relationship.

6.4.4 Experimenter reactivity is any action by researchers that influences participants' responses. Experimenter bias is any effect that the researcher's expectations might have on observations or the recording of observations.

6.5.1 Observing public behavior may not require informed consent because people have no expectation of privacy in public. However, all research, including observing public behavior, requires an IRB review and approval. In that sense, it may be said that all research with humans requires some form of consent.

6.5.2 Therapists routinely modify descriptive information about a client in a case report to make it difficult for anyone to identify the client from the description.

CHAPTER 7

7.1.1 Correlational research assesses the strength of relationships among variables. Differential research assesses differences between two or more groups that are differentiated based upon a preexisting variable.

7.1.2 Correlations quantify the strength and direction of relationships and can be used for predicting one variable from another variable.

7.1.3 Correlational research cannot determine causality.

7.1.4 Correlational research cannot prove a theory, but it can negate one.

7.1.5 Differential research uses a nonmanipulated independent variable.

7.1.6 Artifacts are apparent effects of independent variables that are actually the result of other variables not properly controlled, thus confounding the research.

7.1.7 Differential research is structurally similar to experimental research in that we compare groups on a dependent measure. It is conceptually similar to correlational research in that we measure two variables and look at the relationship between those variables.

7.1.8 Differential research is considered higher in constraint than correlational research because additional control procedures are available in differential research, which can increase the confidence of the conclusions drawn from studies.

7.2.1 Experimenter expectancy is the tendency of investigators to see what they expect to see, and experimenter reactivity is the tendency of investigators to influence the behavior of participants.

7.2.2 Moderator variables modify the relationship between other variables.

7.2.3 The most common correlations are the Pearson product-moment correlation, the Spearman rank-order correlation, and Phi. A Pearson product-moment correlation coefficient is used if both variables are measured on at least an interval scale; a Spearman rank-order correlation is used if one variable is measured on an ordinal scale and the other variable is at least ordinal; a Phi correlation is used if at least one variable is measured on a nominal scale.

7.2.4 The coefficient of determination is the square of the correlation, and it indicates the proportion of variability in one measure that can be predicted by knowing the other measure.

7.3.1 Differential research should be used whenever we want to know whether groups that are formed based on a preexisting variable are different from one another.

7.3.2 Unless groups differ on only a single variable, it is impossible to determine which variable may have accounted for any observed group differences.

7.3.3 A nonmanipulated independent variable is a variable that existed prior to the study. It is used to assign participants to groups in differential research.

7.3.4 Careful selection of control groups can minimize confounding by forming groups that differ on only a single variable.

7.4.1 Neither correlational nor differential research is capable of determining that a causal relationship between variables exists.

7.4.2 Causal relationships cannot be determined because both of these approaches simply measure and do not manipulate variables.

7.4.3 Two variables are confounded when they vary together. Because they vary together, we cannot know which of the variables is responsible for the observed results.

7.5.1 Even when we cannot ethically or practically manipulate an independent variable to determine a causal relationship, correlational or differential research can provide information that is either consistent or inconsistent with a causal hypothesis. In fact, in some cases, such data may be sufficient to reject a causal hypothesis, although it cannot establish one.

CHAPTER 8

8.1.1 Initial ideas are converted into problem statements based on a search of the literature and/or making initial observations of the phenomenon.

8.1.2 The research hypothesis is a combination of the statement of the problem and the operational definitions of the variables.

8.1.3 The function of the research hypothesis is to state a specific, testable hypothesis that can be evaluated with data.

8.1.4 The research hypothesis includes the statistical hypothesis, the confounding-variable hypothesis, and the causal hypothesis.

8.1.5 We cannot accept the causal hypothesis until all confounding variables are ruled out.

8.1.6 Problem statements can be worded in different ways that imply different research designs. Furthermore, the variables can be operationally defined in different ways, each creating a different research hypothesis.

8.2.1 Validity has several meanings, the most basic of which refers to methodological soundness or appropriateness. That is, a valid test measures what it is supposed to measure; a valid research design tests what it is supposed to test.

8.2.2 Statistical validity addresses the question of whether statistical conclusions are reasonable. Construct validity refers to how well the study's results support the theory behind the research. External validity refers to the degree to which generalization is possible. Internal validity concerns the question of whether the independent variable was responsible for the observed effect.

8.2.3 Internal validity is concerned with the accuracy of the conclusions about the relationship between independent and dependent variables.

8.3.1 Maturation refers to the normal and expected changes that occur over time, whereas history refers to the effect of external events that occur during a study.

8.3.2 Based on regression to the mean, the winner of this year's World Series is unlikely to win the World Series next year.

8.3.3 In this case, the confounding variable of attrition is operating, which might distort your sample so that it no longer represents the target population.

8.3.4 Sequence effects are found only in within-subjects designs.

8.4.1 Subject effects are any changes in the behavior of participants that are due to being in the study, rather than to the variables under study.

8.4.2 Demand characteristics are unintentional cues about how participants are expected to behave that might influence the behavior of participants.

8.4.3 Experimenter expectancies might cause researchers to bias their observations or lead them to produce unintended demand characteristics.

8.5.1 In making ethical evaluations, we must balance risk against potential benefit. If we do not control confounding, the potential benefit is so small that no risk is acceptable.

8.5.2 Because participants have the right to refuse participation, our sample will include only those who agree to be in the study. Hence, we have confounding due to selection.

CHAPTER 9

9.1.1 Careful preparation of the setting can reduce the presence of confounding variables, thus increasing internal validity. External validity can be enhanced by making the laboratory situation as natural as possible.

9.1.2 All measures used in research should be both reliable and valid.

9.1.3 Exact replication is repeating the experiment as nearly as possible in the way it was carried out originally, whereas systematic replication is repeating the study with some systematic theoretical or procedural modification of the original work. Conceptual replication involves repeating the experiment using different operational definitions for the variables.

9.2.1 Blind procedures keep the participants and researchers unaware of to what condition each participant is assigned. Automation standardizes instructions and/or data collection, thus decreasing opportunities for experimenter effects. Objective measures take the subjective component out of measurement. Multiple observers allow an assessment of the reliability of the measures. Finally, deception prevents participants from seeing the purpose of the study and thus reduces potential subject effects.

9.2.2 In a single-blind procedure, the researcher is blind to group assignment, whereas in the double-blind procedure, both the researcher and the participants are blind to group assignment.

9.2.3 Deception reduces subject effects by preventing participants from recognizing what is being studied. Deception is considered to automatically place participants at risk. Therefore, it should be used only when nondeceptive procedures will not work.

9.3.1 The general population is the large group of all persons, whereas the target population is the subset in which the researcher is ultimately interested. The accessible population is the population available to the researcher, and the sample is a group drawn from the accessible population.

9.3.2 Unless samples are drawn carefully, they are unlikely to be representative of the population, thus restricting generalizability.

9.3.3 Random sampling involves drawing a sample so that every member of the population has an equal chance of being selected. Stratified random sampling involves drawing separate random samples from each of several subpopulations. Ad hoc samples are drawn from accessible populations.

9.3.4 Matching controls for individual differences.

9.4.1 Unbiased assignment to groups makes it unlikely that the groups will differ on any variable other than the independent variable.

9.4.2 Experimental designs (1) clearly state a hypothesis concerning predicted causal effects of one variable on another, (2) have at least two levels of the independent variable, (3) use unbiased assignment of participants to conditions, (4) have specific procedures for testing the hypothesis, and (5) include specific controls to reduce threats to internal validity.

9.5.1 Even when properly used, debriefing might not be sufficient to correct the distress of some participants upon learning they had been deceived.

9.5.2 The most important safeguards when using deception is to avoid any procedure that might cause physical or emotional harm and to use a debriefing to explain the procedure and to remove any misconceptions that might upset the participant.

CHAPTER 10

10.1.1 Systematic between-groups variance reflects consistent group differences due to the independent variable, uncontrolled confounding variables, or both.

10.1.2 Experimental variance is due to the effect of the independent variable, whereas extraneous variance is due to the effects of uncontrolled confounding variables.

10.1.3 Error variance is the nonsystematic within-groups variability that is due to random factors that affect some participants more than others or to individual differences.

10.1.4 The *F*-test is an inferential statistical procedure that tests for group differences.

10.1.5 Extraneous variance is controlled by making sure that the experimental and control groups are as similar as possible at the start of the experiment, and by treating all participants exactly the same way except for the independent-variable manipulation. You can assure that groups are similar at the start of the study by (1) randomly assigning participants to groups, (2) selecting participants who are as homogeneous as possible, (3) building potential confounding variables into the experiment as additional independent variables, and (4) matching participants or using a within-subjects design.

10.1.6 Error variance can be minimized through careful measurement and/or using a correlated-groups design to control individual differences.

10.2.1 Four nonexperimental approaches are (1) ex post facto studies, (2) single-group, posttest-only studies, (3) single-group, pretest-posttest studies, and (4) pretest-posttest, natural control-group studies. Ex post facto studies relate observed phenomena to earlier experiences that were not directly observed or manipulated. In the single-group, posttest-only study, the independent variable is manipulated with a single group and the dependent variable is measured. In the single-group, pretest-posttest studies, a single group of participants is measured both before and after a manipulation. Finally, in the pretest-posttest, natural control-group design, one of two naturally occurring groups receives the treatment. None of these designs adequately controls for confounding variables, although the natural control-group design comes close if the groups are reasonably similar at the start of the study.

10.2.2 The weakest design is the ex post facto design, which controls virtually none of the potential confounding variables.

10.2.3 Maturation is not considered a confounding variable in studies of development. Developmental studies typically employ time-series designs.

10.3.1 The most basic experimental design is the randomized, posttest-only, control-group design.

10.3.2 In the randomized, pretest-posttest, control-group design, participants are randomly assigned to experimental and control groups, all participants are pretested on the dependent variable, the experimental group is administered the treatment, and both groups are then tested again on the dependent variable. In the multilevel, completely randomized, between-subjects design, participants are randomly assigned to three or more conditions. Pretests may or may not be included.

10.3.3 Control groups control for history, maturation, and regression to the mean. Control groups are effective only if (1) participants are randomly assigned to groups to assure that the groups are comparable at the beginning of the study, and (2) they are treated exactly the same during the study except for the independent-variable manipulation.

10.3.4 The Solomon four-group design controls for the possible interaction of the pretest and treatment.

10.3.5 If groups are not equivalent at the beginning of the study, observed differences could be due to the manipulation, the initial differences, or both.

10.4.1 The ANOVA is used when two or more groups are compared on a dependent measure that produces score data.

10.4.2 The ANOVA summary table shows the sources of variance, the degrees of freedom for each source of variance, the sums of squares, the mean squares, the *F*-ratios, and the probability values for each *F*.

10.4.3 If the *F*-ratio is significant, at least one mean is significantly different from at least one other mean.

10.4.4 Planned comparisons and post hoc tests are specific means comparisons that are either planned before the research is conducted or performed without such preplanning, respectively.

10.5.1 It would be unethical for researchers to randomly assign participants to conditions that expose them to risk, such as injury or denial of medical treatment.

10.5.2 The most essential safeguard in human research is informed consent.

CHAPTER 11

11.1.1 Correlated-groups designs assure group equivalence by either using the same participants in all groups or participants that have been closely matched.

11.1.2 The major confounding factor in within-subjects designs is sequence effects, which are controlled by counterbalancing.

11.1.3 Within-subjects designs reduce error variance by removing the individual differences component.

11.1.4 The strengths include greater sensitivity, reduction in the number of participants needed, and an increase in efficiency. The weakness is confounding due to sequence effects.

11.1.5 Complete counterbalancing means that an equal number of participants are assigned to every possible order of conditions.

11.2.1 There are no sequence effects to worry about in matched-subjects designs.

11.2.2 The characteristics of matched-subjects designs are that (1) each participant is exposed to one condition, (2) each participant has a matched participant in each of the other conditions, (3) the analysis takes into account which participants were matched with which other participants, and (4) the critical comparison is the difference between the correlated groups, in which the correlation is created by the matching procedure.

11.2.3 Matched-subjects designs are used when researchers want to take advantage of the greater sensitivity of within-subjects designs, but cannot, or prefer not to, use a within-subjects design. Matched-subjects designs are most often used when exposure to one condition causes long-term changes in participants and when the cost per participant is very high.

11.2.4 The disadvantages of a matched-subjects design include the time to do the matching and the loss of participants because no suitable match could be found.

11.3.1 Single-subject designs are extensions of within-subjects designs in which a single individual is tested under multiple conditions. They are used most often in evaluating a treatment program for a single client.

11.3.2 The single-case study is used to describe clients, rather than to evaluate whether a treatment has been effective, which single-subject experimental designs achieve by manipulating the independent variable.

11.3.3 Single-subject experiments control internal validity by controlling the timing of the independent variable manipulation. To demonstrate a causal connection, the dependent variable must consistently change when the independent variable is manipulated.

11.3.4 Reversal designs demonstrate the effects of an independent-variable manipulation by measuring the dependent variable over time, during which the treatment is applied and then removed. Multiple-baseline designs demonstrate the effects of treatment on different behaviors successively. Randomized time-series designs insert a treatment at a randomly determined point in a series of measurements.

11.3.5 The strength of single-subject experimental designs is that they allow researchers to make causal inferences. The weakness is that the data provide little information about the generalizability of the findings.

11.3.6 External validity is weak because a single participant will never adequately represent the diversity in the general population.

11.3.7 Single-subject direct replication involves repeating the study with the same participant or a series of participants. Single-subject systematic replication involves carrying out a series with different people in different settings and with different behaviors. Single-subject clinical replication involves using an integrated treatment package that is applied to a succession of participants.

11.3.8 Causality is inferred when each manipulation of the independent variable results in a predictable change in the dependent variable.

11.4.1 The first principle in treatment research is to do no harm; the second principle is to try to do some good.

CHAPTER 12

12.1.1 Factorial designs are designs with more than one independent variable.

12.1.2 A factorial study must have at least two factors. With two factors, there will be the main effects of each factor and the interaction of the two factors. If there are more factors, there will be even more null hypotheses to test.

12.1.3 An interaction involves two variables in which the effect of one variable differs depending on the level of the other variable. Main effect refers to the individual effect of each factor on the dependent variable.

12.1.4 Factorial designs are used when the researcher is interested in the interactive effects of two or more independent variables.

12.1.5 Any combination of main effects and factorials is possible in a factorial study.

12.1.6 We always interpret main effects in light of the interaction, because the main effects may be present only when some specific combination of the factors is present. The dark-fears study illustrates this point.

12.2.1 The major advantages of repeated measures factorials are that fewer participants are needed and there is a greater sensitivity to the effects of the independent variables on the dependent variable.

12.2.2 Designs can be mixed by having factors that include (1) both within-subjects and between-subjects factors, (2) both manipulated and nonmanipulated factors, or (3) mixed factors in both of these ways simultaneously.

12.2.3 Designs that are mixed in terms of within- and between-subjects factors must take into account the type of factors in setting up the data analysis. Designs that are mixed in terms of manipulated and nonmanipulated factors must take into account the type of factors in the interpretation.

12.3.1 An analysis of covariance (ANCOVA) removes the effects of a theoretically unimportant, but nonetheless powerful, variable from the dependent variable scores as part of the analysis.

12.3.2 A MANOVA includes more than one dependent variable, whereas an ANOVA includes only a single dependent variable in the analysis.

12.4.1 "Consent" is a legal term; only adults who have the ability to understand what is being asked of them can give consent. Assent means agreeing to be part of the study when your age or mental condition would preclude giving legal consent.

12.4.2 The most common way to address the ethical problem of a no-treatment control group is to provide that group with the treatment after the study is completed.

CHAPTER 13

13.1.1 Field research is any research that is carried out in the natural environment.

13.1.2 Field research (1) tests the external validity of laboratory studies, (2) determines the effects of events that occur in the field, and (3) improves generalization across settings.

13.1.3 The major difficulties in field research are that normal laboratory controls may be unavailable and some independent variables cannot be controlled.

13.1.4 The three types of generalization are (1) generalization from participants in a study to the larger population, (2) generalization over time, and (3) generalization from the settings of the study to other settings.

13.1.5 It is common in field research to see things that may indicate something significant. Flexible and observant researchers will recognize the potential importance of such observations and thus plan and carry out further research that will provide more definitive information about the phenomenon.

13.2.1 A quasi-experimental design is almost an experiment, but not quite equal to it. Quasi-experiments test causal hypotheses in natural settings with reasonable control of extraneous variables. Their weakness is that they rarely control all confounding, thus requiring caution in drawing causal inferences.

13.2.2 Nonequivalent control-group designs are most effective when the groups appear to be similar on the dependent variable and potential confounding variables.

13.2.3 In both time-series and within-subjects designs, participants are tested under all conditions.

13.2.4 History and instrumentation are most likely to confound time-series studies.

13.3.1 Program evaluation research assesses the effectiveness of programs, which is critical because money spent on ineffective programs could be used on more worthwhile projects.

13.3.2 Program evaluators often have to rely on the cooperation of those implementing the program. Therefore, excellent political skills are required.

13.3.3 Internal validity is enhanced by (1) selecting appropriate dependent measures, (2) minimizing potential bias in these measures, and (3) selecting the strongest research design possible.

13.3.4 The most widely used designs in program evaluation are the randomized control-group design, the nonequivalent control-group design, and the single-group, time-series design.

13.3.5 Program evaluation research addresses the scientific issues of internal and external validity. It is an art in that it requires political skill to obtain cooperation from those involved with the program.

13.4.1 Status surveys describe the current characteristics of a population, whereas survey research tries to discover relationships among variables.

13.4.2 Surveys seek to learn about the ideas, knowledge, feeling, opinions, attitudes, and self-reported behavior of defined populations.

13.4.3 The survey instrument may be a questionnaire or an interview schedule.

13.4.4 Factual items ask about information that can be verified independently. Content items ask about the respondents' opinions, attitudes, knowledge, and behavior.

13.4.5 Stratified random sampling involves dividing the population into subgroups (strata) and randomly sampling from each stratum.

13.4.6 Confidence limits represent the interval in which we have a specified level of confidence that the population value will lie.

13.4.7 Cross-sectional designs involve administering the survey once, and yield data on the current characteristics of the sample. Longitudinal designs are within-subjects designs in which participants are surveyed several times. Sequential designs involve asking the same questions repeatedly over time to a different sample for each administration of the survey.

13.5.1 Program evaluation researchers must be careful to avoid any coercion or even the appearance of coercion so that individuals are free to give informed consent. Sometimes the urgent need being addressed by a program ethically precludes the use of certain designs.

GLOSSARY

a posteriori comparison: See *post hoc test.*

a priori comparison: See *planned comparison.*

ABA reversal design: See *reversal design.*

abscissa: The x-axis on a graph

abstract number system: The commonly used number system, which possesses the characteristics of identity, magnitude, equal intervals, and true zero.

abstract: A brief description of a research study that appears at the beginning of the paper and is included in online databases, such as *PsyINFO.*

accessible population: The subset of a target population that is available to the researcher and from which the sample is drawn.

ad hoc sample: Sample of participants drawn from an accessible population. The ad hoc sample should be described in detail to define the limits of generalizability.

all-or-none bias: The tendency to see statements as either true or false when, in fact, they are actually probabilistic (sometimes true and sometimes false).

alpha level: Type I error level (probability of incorrectly rejecting the null hypothesis).

analysis of covariance (ANCOVA): Statistical procedure for evaluating mean differences between two or more groups, which statistically removes unwanted variance in the dependent variable and hence increases statistical power.

analysis of variance (ANOVA): Statistical procedure that analyzes mean differences between two or more groups by comparing between-groups and within-groups variance.

ANOVA summary table: Table that organizes the results of an ANOVA. For each source of variation, the degrees of freedom, sums of squares, mean squares, F-ratios, and p-values are listed.

apparatus subsection: The section of a research report that describes the physical aspects of the study (apparatus, measuring instruments, etc.).

application: In scientific research, the goal of application involves using our knowledge to solve real-world problems.

applied psychology: Any use of psychology to deal with real-world problems.

applied research: Research to provide solutions to practical problems.

archival records: Any data source for events that have already occurred.

artifact: Any apparent effect of a major conceptual variable that is actually the result of an uncontrolled confounding variable.

artificial intelligence: Machines that evaluate and respond to situations.

assent: Agreeing to participate in a study when you are under the legal age to give consent or are considered legally unable to give consent due to a severe developmental disability or emotional disorder.

association: Relationship or correlation.

assumptions (*of science*): The basic tenets behind scientific theory and research.

attrition: Loss of participants before or during the research, which may confound the results because the remaining participants may not represent the population.

authority: A way of acquiring knowledge. New ideas are accepted as valid because some respected authority has declared the ideas to be true.

automation: Use of equipment to present stimuli and record participants' responses. Automation increases precision in data gathering and minimizes experimenter bias.

autonomy: Refers to the most basic ethical safeguard, which is the right of participants to decide for themselves whether they will participate in the study.

average deviation: The average distance from the mean.

balanced placebo design: A 2 × 2 factorial design developed in alcohol research, in which the factors are (1) what participants consume (alcohol or no alcohol), and (2) what participants are told they are consuming (alcohol or no alcohol). This design separates the pharmacological and expectation effects of alcohol. See *deception.*

Barnum statement: Any statement that appears to be insightful, but is actually true only because it is true for almost all issues, situations, or people.

base rate: Naturally occurring frequency of an event or condition.

baseline period: Time from initial monitoring of target behavior until the start of the manipulation.

basic research: Fundamental or pure research. Basic research is carried out to add to knowledge, but without applied or practical goals.

behavior modification: A set of teaching or therapeutic procedures that are based on laboratory-derived principles of learning.

behavior: Any observable act from an organism.

behavioral medicine: See *health psychology*.

behavioral neuroscience: A field that relates the behavior of an organism to the brain mechanisms contributing to the behavior.

behavioral variable: Variable representing some aspect of an organism's behavior.

behaviorism: A philosophical perspective that argues that a scientific psychology should base its theories only on observable events.

Belmont Report: Outlined the basic ethical principles for human research that has been adopted by virtually all research agencies.

beneficence: A basic concept in the Belmont Report that in research the risk to participants should be minimized and the benefits to participants and society should be maximized.

beta: The probability of making a Type II error.

between sum of squares: A generic term that usually refers to the between-conditions sum of squares in a repeated-measures ANOVA, but may also refer to the between-groups sum of squares in an ANOVA.

between-conditions sum of squares: The sum of squares used in a repeated-measures ANOVA to compute the between-conditions variance, which is also known as the between-conditions mean square.

between-groups sum of squares: The sum of squares used in an ANOVA to compute the between-groups variance, which is also known as the between-groups mean square.

between-groups variance: Index of the variability among group means.

between-subjects design: Research design in which each participant appears in only one group.

between-subjects factors: Independent variables in which participants are assigned to conditions in such a way that each participant appears in only one condition.

bimodal: A distribution of scores that has two modes.

Biomedical Programs (BMDP): Computer package for statistical analyses.

blind: When the researcher and/or participant are unaware of information that might bias their responses. See *single-blind procedure* and *double-blind procedure*.

canonical correlation: A correlation between two sets of variables.

carryover effects: When participants' involvement in one condition affects their performance in subsequent conditions.

case study level of constraint: Extensive observations of individuals or small groups, using minimal constraints on behavior.

case study research: See *case study level of constraint.*

case study: See *case study level of constraint.*

categorical data: Synonymous with *nominal data.*

categorical variable: Synonymous with *discrete variable*. A categorical variable can have only a finite number of values.

causal hypothesis: States that the independent variable has a causal effect on the dependent variable. To accept this hypothesis, we must reject the null hypothesis and all cofounding-variable hypotheses.

causal inference: Concluding that the change in the independent variable resulted in a change in the dependent variable. It may be drawn only if all confounding variables are controlled.

causal relationship: A relationship between variables in which one variable causes a predictable change in the other variable.

causally related: Two variables are causally related if a change in one variable results in a predictable change in the other variable.

causation: Bringing about a change in a phenomenon.

ceiling effects: See *scale attenuation effects.*

central tendency: Average or typical score in a distribution. See *mean*, *median*, and *mode*.

chi-square: Inferential statistical procedure used with nominal data.

classification variables: Organismic variables used to classify participants and assign them to groups in differential research.

coding data: Process by which scores are assigned to behaviors.

coefficient alpha: An index of internal consistency reliability.

coefficient of determination: The square of the Pearson product-moment correlation. It represents the proportion of variability in one variable that can be predicted based on information about the other variable.

cognitive psychology: A subdiscipline in psychology that studies perceptual processing, memory, and basic thought processes.

cognitive science: A broad field that encompasses several disciplines, including behavioral neuroscience, neurophysiology, computer science, and linguistics, all of which are interested in modeling and understanding brain processes and thought.

cohort effect: Concept that people of a given age and culture behave similarly to one another and differently from people of other ages and cultures due to shared life experiences.

column means: In factorial designs, one factor is usually illustrated as separate columns of data, in which each column represents a different level of the factor.

communication phase of research: Research phase in which the rationale, hypotheses, methods, results, and interpretations of the study are presented.

complete counterbalancing: See *counterbalancing*.

computer-analysis programs: Programs for statistical analyses of data.

concealment: Deliberately misleading participants by withholding some information about the research.

conceptual replication: Repeating a study using different operational definitions.

concurrent validity: Assessing a measure by its correlation with a criterion that has already been measured or can be measured simultaneously.

confidence interval: An interval in which we predict population parameters to fall with a specified level of confidence.

confidentiality: Ethical requirement to protect a participant's sensitive information.

confounded: Variables are confounded if they vary together, so that it is impossible to determine which variable was responsible for observed effects.

confounding-variable hypothesis: States that a confounding variable may be responsible for the observed changes in the dependent measure.

confounding variable: Any uncontrolled variable that might affect the outcome of a study. A variable can confound a study only if (1) there is a group mean difference on the variable, and (2) the variable is correlated with the dependent measure.

constants: Variables that are prevented from varying (i.e., held constant).

constraints: Restrictions applied to increase the precision of the research and enhance the validity of conclusions.

construct validity: Validity of a theory. Most theories in science make many predictions, and construct validity is established by verifying the accuracy of each of these predictions.

construct: Idea constructed by the researcher to explain observed events.

content analysis: Classifying behaviors found in naturalistic research or archival records to create data for analysis.

content items: Content items in surveys focus on respondents' opinions, attitudes, and knowledge, rather than on factual items that can be independently verified.

contingency: A relationship between two or more variables, in which the first event is predictive of the second event.

continuous variable: Variable that can theoretically take on an infinite number of values. Often contrasted with *discrete* or *categorical variables*.

contrast: See *planned comparison*.

control group: A group of participants that serves as a basis of comparison for other groups. The ideal control group is similar to the experimental group on all variables except the independent variable that defines the group.

control in research: Any procedure that reduces confounding.

control of variance: Control of error variance and extraneous variance in research.

control: See *control in research.*

controlled research: Research that employs controls to rule out confounding.

convenience sampling: Also called *nonprobability sampling*. Using respondents who are readily available, with little attempt to carefully represent any population.

convergent operations: A term for the agreement among findings from different studies carried out with different operational definitions of the same concepts.

convergent validity: Occurs when different studies, using different operational definitions, produce similar findings.

correlated *t*-test: Statistical procedure for testing mean differences between two groups in a within-subjects or matched-subjects design.

correlated-groups design: Research design in which participants in one group are related to participants in the other groups, thus controlling individual differences and increasing power. This design is contrasted with an independent-groups design.

correlated-subjects design: See *correlated-groups design.*

correlation coefficient: Index of the degree of linear relationship between variables.

correlation: Degree of linear relationship between two or more variables.

correlational level of constraint: Research designed to quantify the relationship between two or more variables.

correlational research: Research that seeks to measure the relationship between variables. The term is sometimes used broadly to include nonexperimental research, such as differential and quasi-experimental designs.

counterbalancing: Control for sequence effects. With complete counterbalancing, all possible arrangements of conditions are included.

covary: When the values of two or more measures change (vary) together.

criterion measure: The variable that we want to predict in regression.

criterion: The variable that we are attempting to predict in regression.

criterion-related validity: Measures, such as predictive and concurrent validity measures, that are established by correlations with known criterion measures.

critical thinking: Applying the principles of inference discussed in this textbook to everyday situations.

cross-cultural research: Exploring psychological phenomena across more than one culture.

crossover effect: In quasi-experimental research, a finding in which two groups show one pattern of scores before the manipulation and the reverse pattern after the manipulation. The name derives from the crossed lines when the data are graphed.

cross-sectional design: A design that compares performance of people of different ages or at different times in history. Often contrasted with *longitudinal designs*.

cross-sectional research: Research that uses a *cross-sectional design.*

cross-sectional survey design: Surveying a group of people only once.

cross-tabulation: Procedure that illustrates the relationship between two or more nominal variables. A cross-tabulation table shows the frequency of participants who show each particular combination of characteristics.

cursor: Symbol on the screen of a computer that indicates where action will take place. The cursor is moved using a mouse or other pointing device.

data analysis phase: Research phase in which data are analyzed.

data snooping: Secondary analysis of data to generate hypotheses for later study.

data: Plural noun that refers to information gathered in research.

debriefing: Disclosing to participants after the study the full nature of a study that used deception.

deception: Procedures used in research to hide the true nature of the study. Ethical use of deception requires complete debriefing at the end of the study.

decision tree: An organized pathway leading to a defined goal, in which successive decisions are made until one reaches the goal.

decision-tree flowchart: Flowchart model in which answers to specific questions lead to branching to a new set of questions or procedures.

deductive reasoning: Reasoning from the general to the particular, such as when one makes specific predictions about future events based on theories.

deductive theory: A theory that emphasizes constructs and the relationship between constructs and seeks to make predictions from the theory that can be tested with empirical research. Often contrasted with *inductive theory* and *functional theory*.

degrees of freedom (df): A statistical concept in which one degree of freedom is lost each time that a population parameter is estimated.

delayed-treatment control group: See *waitlist control group*.

demand characteristics: Any aspect of the research situation that suggests to participants what behavior is expected.

demographic questions: Questions in a survey or research study about the characteristics of a participant, such as age, marital status, and education level.

demographic variables: Data that describe the participants in a study.

dependent variable: Variable hypothesized to have a relationship with the independent variable.

description: Identifying and observing phenomena and carefully recording their details. One of the goals of research.

descriptive statistics: Statistics that summarize and/or describe a sample of scores.

design notation: A way of indicating the number of independent variables and the number of levels of each independent variable in a factorial design.

difference score: Difference between two scores on a measure.

differential level of constraint: Research in which two or more groups, defined on the basis of a preexisting variable, are compared on a dependent measure.

differential research: Research that involves comparing two or more existing groups.

diffusion of treatment: When participants communicate information to participants in other conditions, thus potentially confounding the results of the study.

direct differences *t*-test: See *correlated t-test*.

discrete variable: A variable that can take on only a finite number of values. Often contrasted with *continuous variables*.

discussion section: The section of a research report in which the researcher interprets the findings in light of other research and theory.

dispersion: How spread out the scores are in a sample.

diversity: How well various ethnic, cultural, age, and gender groups are represented in the research sample.

double-blind procedure: Research procedure in which neither the researcher nor the participant knows to which condition the participant was assigned.

ecological validity: When studies accurately reproduce real-life situations, thus allowing easy generalization of their findings. See *external validity*.

effect size: Index of the size of the difference between groups, expressed in standard deviation units.

effective range: The range over which the dependent measure accurately reflects the level of the dependent variable.

empirical: Based on observed data.

empiricism: System of knowing that is based solely on observation of events.

enumerative data: Synonymous with *nominal data*.

equal intervals: A characteristic of the abstract number system, in which the difference between units are the same anywhere on the scale.

equipment subsection: See *apparatus subsection*.

error bar: An addition made to either histograms or frequency polygons that indicates the size of the standard error of the mean.

error term: A measure of the variability of scores within each group that provides a basis for comparing observed differences between groups.

error variance: Chance variability within a group. Also called *within-group variance*.

ethical checks: A series of questions about the research procedures designed to identify and correct potential ethical problems.

ethology: The study of organisms in their natural environment.

evaluative biases of language: Language has a tendency to blend description and evaluation, which can distort the perceptions of behavior.

ex post facto design: Nonexperimental design in which the current situation is observed and related to reports of previous events.

ex post facto fallacy: Error in reasoning in which we assume that the observed relationship between current and reported historical events represents a causal relationship.

ex post facto reasoning: See *ex post facto fallacy.*

ex post facto study: See *ex post facto design.*

exact replication: Repeating a study by using exactly the same procedure used in the original study. See also *replication.*

experiment: High-constraint research procedure in which participants are randomly assigned to conditions, thus controlling virtually all confounding variables.

experimental analysis of behavior: Procedures for the controlled study of single individuals, which are based on B. F. Skinner's operant conditioning concepts.

experimental design: In experimental design, participants are randomly assigned to groups, and all appropriate control procedures are used.

experimental group: Groups defined by a specified level of the independent variable. Contrasted with a *control group.*

experimental level of constraint: Research in which participants are randomly assigned to groups and are compared on at least one dependent measure.

experimental research: See *experimental level of constraint.*

experimental variance: Variability among the group means in a research study that is due to the effects of the independent variable.

experimentation: Manipulating the independent variable to observe its effects on the dependent variable.

experimenter bias: Biasing effects produced by the expectations of the researcher.

experimenter effects: Behavior of the researcher that might affect the behavior of participants or the measurement of dependent variables.

experimenter expectancies: Expectations of the researcher that may affect the accuracy of observations, especially when judgments are required.

experimenter reactivity: Any action by the researcher, other than the independent variable manipulation, that tends to influence participants' responses.

explanation: Using scientific understanding to develop a statement of the mechanisms of how certain factors can change other factors. One of the goals of science.

exploratory research: Low-constraint research designed to investigate feasibility and to generate, rather than test, hypotheses.

external validity: Extent to which a study's results generalize to the larger population.

extraneous variable: Any variable, other than the independent variable, that might affect the dependent measure and thus confound results.

extraneous variance: Variability due to the effects of extraneous variables.

factor analysis: A variation of multidimensional scaling that is used to identify underlying factors that might account for a wide range of observed characteristics.

factorial ANOVA: Analysis of variance procedure for evaluating factorial designs.

factorial designs: Designs employing more than one independent variable and thus allowing researchers to identify interactive effects independent variables.

factors: Each independent variable in a factorial design.

facts: Empirically observed events.

factual items: Those survey questions that can be independently verified, such as the respondent's age or occupation.

field research: Research conducted outside the laboratory.

fields (in computer files): A computer field represents a variable, which has a score for each participant.

filler items: Questions that are included in the dependent measure, but not scored, in order to distract participants from the purpose of the study.

floor effects: See *scale attenuation effects.*

flowcharts: Organizational device that allows one to reach a decision by following a path defined by answers to particular questions.

***F*-ratio:** An inferential statistic that is the ratio of two variance estimates.

free random assignment: Assigning participants to groups so that the assignment of any given participant has no effect on the assignment of any other participant.

frequencies: The number of objects or participants that fall into a specified category.

frequency data: Synonymous with *nominal data.*

frequency distribution: Organizational device used to simplify large data sets.

frequency polygon: Graph that illustrates a frequency distribution by placing a dot above each possible score at a height that indicates the score's frequency, and then connects the dots.

***F*-test:** See *F-ratio.*

functional theory: Functional theories emphasize both inductive and deductive elements. Often contrasted with *inductive theory* and *deductive theory.*

functionalism: A philosophical perspective that stresses the need to study how the mind functions and adapts to the environment. Often contrasted with *structuralism.*

fundamental research: Another term for *basic research.*

general control procedures: Control achieved through preparation of settings, careful response measurement, and replication.

general population: See *population.*

generalizability: Extent to which research findings are applicable to the outside world.

generalization: The process of assuming that the findings from one's study will also apply to other situations, places, or times.

generalize: To assume that the findings of a study will be found for other participants or in other settings.

genetic algorithms: A computer-based problem-solving procedure largely inspired by biological evolution.

Gestalt Psychology: A philosophical perspective on perception that rests on the concept that the whole is greater than the sum of its parts.

graphs: A means of presenting data visually. See *histograms* and *frequency polygons.*

graphs of factorial data: Graphs that illustrate main effects and interactions.

grouped frequency distribution: Lists the frequency of scores in equal-size intervals.

habituation: A process in which organisms gradually reduce their attention and their responsiveness to any stimulus that is routinely present.

health psychology: An applied discipline that focuses on understanding and modifying behavior that affects a person's physical health.

heterogeneous: A group is said to be heterogeneous if there is considerable variability within the group.

heuristic influence: The nonsystematic impact of research or theory in stimulating new research.

histogram: A bar graph in which the frequency of scores is represented by the height of the bar.

history: Confounding variable that represents any change in the dependent variable that is a function of events other than the manipulation of the independent variable.

homogeneity: See *homogeneous.*

homogeneous: Situation in which participants are similar to one another.

hub science: A highly influential body of scientific knowledge from which other sciences and non-scientific agencies draw heavily.

humanistic psychology: A philosophical perspective that emphasizes subjective experience and the distinctively human qualities of choice and self-realization.

hyperlink: A link between web documents, which allows one to transfer to the linked document with a single mouse click.

icon: Pictures on a computer screen that represent a program, action, or data set.

idea-generating phase of research: First step in any research project, during which the researcher selects a topic to study.

identity: A characteristic of the abstract number system, in which each number has a specific meaning or identity.

incidental comparison: See *post hoc test.*

incidental learning: Learning that occurs without specific reinforcement.

incomplete counterbalancing: See *counterbalancing.*

independent samples: Samples that include different participants in each group, and in which each sample is selected independently.

independent variable: A variable that defines groups of participants on the basis of either (1) a preexisting characteristic (nonmanipulated independent variable) or (2) random assignment (manipulated independent variable).

independent-groups design: See *between-subjects design.*

individual differences: Natural differences among people.

inductive reasoning: Reasoning from the particular to the general. Inductive reasoning is used to generate theories based on observations.

inductive theory: Inductive theories are built on a strong empirical base and stray little from that base. Often contrasted with *deductive theory* and *functional theory*.

inference: Any conclusion drawn on the basis of empirical data and/or theories.

inferential statistics: Statistical procedures that allow us to decide whether the sample data suggest that population differences exist.

informed consent form: A form signed by participants prior to a study indicating that they have been fully informed about the study and have decided to participate.

informed consent: Principle that participants have the right to know exactly what they are getting into before they agree to participate in a research study.

initial equivalence (principle of): The groups to be compared in an experiment must be equivalent at the start of the experiment.

Institutional Review Board (IRB): Formal body that reviews research proposals to determine if they meet ethical guidelines.

instrumentation: Confounding variable involving shifts in the measuring instrument that cause it to give different readings when no change has occurred in participants.

instruments subsection: See *apparatus subsection*.

interaction effects: Combined effect of two or more independent variables, such that the effect of one independent variable differs depending on the level of the other independent variable.

internal consistency reliability: Index of the homogeneity of the items of a measure.

internal validity: Accuracy of a research study in determining the relationship between the independent and dependent variables.

interpretation phase: Research phase in which the results are interpreted in light of (1) the adequacy of control procedures, (2) previous research, and (3) existing theories.

interrater reliability coefficient: A correlation coefficient expressing the degree of agreement of observations made by two or more raters. See *reliability*.

interrater reliability: Index of the consistency of ratings between separate raters.

interrupted time-series design: Research design in which multiple measures are taken before and after an experimental manipulation or event.

interval scale: Scale of measurement in which the distance between adjacent scores is the same anywhere on the scale, but zero is not a true zero.

intervening variable: Inferred factors hypothesized to operate between observed variables such as a stimulus and response, helping to explain their relationship.

interview schedule: A standardized interview that lists all questions to be asked.

introduction: The section of a research paper in which the authors review previous research and theory to provide a framework and rationale for the study.

intuition: Way of acquiring knowledge without intellectual effort or sensory processes.

invasion of privacy: Failure of researchers to protect the confidentiality of records.

justice: The concept in the Belmont Report that both the risks and the benefits of research should be shared equally by all members of the population.

Kappa: Index of interrater agreement that adjusts for chance agreement.

knowledge: Any information about the world.

Laboratory Animal Care Committee: A committee that reviews the ethics of research proposals involving animals.

Latin square design: A counterbalancing procedure that identifies a set of orders that ensures that every condition appears equally often in every position.

levels of constraint: Degree of systematic control applied in research.

levels of headings: Organizational mechanism used in research articles for organizing the report.

Likert-scale items: Rating on a continuum, such as from "strongly agree" to "strongly disagree."

limits of generalization: The conditions in which a theory or scientific finding no longer validly applies.

linear relationship: Relationship between variables that, when plotted in a standard coordinate system, cluster around a straight line.

logic: Set of operations that can be applied to statements, and the conclusions drawn from these statements, to determine the internal accuracy of the conclusions.

longitudinal (panel) design: A research design in which a group of participants is followed over time. This design is often contrasted with *cross-sectional designs*.

longitudinal research: Research that uses a longitudinal research design.

longitudinal survey design: Giving a survey to a group of people several times over time.

magnitude: Characteristic of the number system in which numbers have an inherent order.

main effects: The individual effects of the independent variables in a factorial study.

mainstream psychology: Contemporary psychology that represents an integration of many of the earlier schools of psychology and their theoretical models.

manipulated factors: Independent variables in a factorial design, in which participants are randomly assigned to the different levels of the independent variable.

manipulated independent variable: Type of independent variable in which participants are randomly assigned to conditions.

manipulation check: Procedure designed to verify that the independent variable actually varied in the different conditions.

manipulation: The explicit control of the independent variable by the researcher.

Mann-Whitney *U*-test: A nonparametric inferential statistic used to test the difference between two groups when the dependent measure produces ordered data.

matched random assignment: Experimental procedure in which participants are matched on relevant variables, and a set of matched individuals is randomly assigned so that one member of the set appears in each of the conditions of the study.

matched-pairs *t*-test: See *correlated t-test*.

matched-subjects design: Research design in which participants are matched on a variable that is highly correlated with the dependent measure.

materials subsection: See *apparatus subsection*.

matrix of cells: Structure of cells in a factorial design.

maturation: Potential confounding factor involving changes in participants during the study that results from normal growth processes.

mean square: A variance estimate used in ANOVAs.

mean: Arithmetic average of scores that should be computed only for score data.

measurement error: Any inaccuracy found in the measurement of a variable.

measurement reactivity: Any effect on participant's behavior that results from the participant being aware that he or she is being observed.

measures of central tendency: Descriptive statistics that indicate the typical score.

measures subsection: See *apparatus subsection*.

median: Middle score in a distribution.

mentalistic: Based on the subject experience of a person rather than objective behavior.

meta-analysis: Statistical averaging of results of multiple studies of a phenomenon.

method section: The section of the research report that details the nature of the sample and the procedures used in the study.

Minitab: Computer package for statistical analysis of data.

mixed designs (*between- and within-subjects variables*): Factorial design in which at least one of the factors is a between-subjects factor and at least one of the factors is a within-subjects factor.

mixed designs (*manipulated and nonmanipulated variables*): Factorial design in which at least one of the factors represents a nonmanipulated independent variable, and at least one of the factors represents a manipulated independent variable.

mode: Most frequent score in a distribution.

models: A simplified representation of the complex reality of the real world.

moderator variable: Any variable that has an effect on the observed relationship between two or more other variables.

Monte Carlo studies: Procedure that evaluates the effectiveness of statistical tests by simulating the sampling of participants from a population with known parameters.

mouse: A device for moving the cursor on the screen of a personal computer.

multilevel, completely randomized, between-subjects design: A design with more than two groups, in which each participant is randomly assigned to one group.

multimethod approach: In research, using several measures of a single concept to increase confidence in the results.

multiple correlation: Correlation between a criterion and a set of variables.

multiple observers: Control used to evaluate the accuracy of observations made by two or more independent observers.

multiple-baseline design: A single-subject research design in which several behaviors are monitored, and treatments are applied at different times for each behavior.

multiple-choice items: Questions or items in which participants select an answer from a list of several possible answers.

multivariable designs: See *factorial designs.*

multivariate analysis of variance (MANOVA): Extension of ANOVA in which two or more dependent measures are simultaneously evaluated.

multivariate correlational designs: Correlational designs that include more than two variables.

multivariate techniques: Advanced statistical procedures that are used to evaluate complex relationships among several variables.

naive empiricism: Extreme dependence on personal experience in order to accept events as facts.

narrative data: Verbal descriptions of activities, events, or internal feelings, rather than their quantitative measures

naturalistic level of constraint: Research carried out in natural settings, in which the researcher does not manipulate the environment.

naturalistic observation: Observing the natural flow of behavior in natural settings.

negative correlation: Relationship between two variables in which an increase in one variable predicts a decrease in the other.

negative practice effect: A decrement of performance due to previous exposure of participants to the measurement procedures.

negatively skewed: When scores are concentrated near the top of the distribution.

neuropsychology: A field that studies the relationships of brain functioning to behavior.

***N*-of-one designs:** See *single-subject experimental designs.*

nominal data: Data that are frequencies of participants in each category.

nominal fallacy: Confusing a label of a behavior as the explanation for the behavior.

nominal scale: Scale of measurement in which the scores are categories.

nonequivalent control-group design: Quasi-experimental design, in which two or more groups that may not be equivalent are compared on the dependent measure after a manipulation in one or more of the groups.

nonexperimental designs: Any research design that does not include both a manipulation of the independent variable, a control group, and random assignment.

nonlinear relationship: Any relationship between variables that is characterized by a scatter plot in which the points cluster around a curve instead of a straight line.

nonmanipulated factors: Independent variables in which participants are assigned to groups based on preexisting factors.

nonmanipulated independent variable: The preexisting variable that determines group membership in a differential research study.

nonparametric statistics: Inferential statistical procedures that do not rely on estimating such population parameters as the mean and variance.

nonprobability sampling: Sampling procedure in which some participants have a higher probability of being selected than other participants, or the selection of a given participant changes the probability of selecting other participants.

nonreactive measure: Any dependent measure that provides consistent and accurate scores, even when the participant is aware of being measured.

nonsystematic within-groups variance: Variance due to random factors that affect some participants more than others. Also called *error variance.*

normal distribution: Distribution of scores that is characterized by a bell-shaped curve. Psychological variables tend to show distributions that are close to normal.

no-treatment control group: A control group in a treatment study that receives no treatment of any kind.

null hypothesis: States that the groups are drawn from populations with identical population parameters.

objective measure: Any measure that requires little or no judgment on the part of the person making the measurement.

observation: Collecting data about a phenomenon.

observation phase: Research phase in which the data are gathered.

observational variable: Any variable that is simply observed and not manipulated.

observed organismic variable: Participant characteristic that can be used for classification.

one-way ANOVA: Statistical procedure that evaluates mean differences between two or more independent groups.

open-ended items: Questions that the participant answers in his or her own words.

operational definition: Procedures used to measure or manipulate a variable.

ordered data: Data produced by ordinal scales of measurement.

orderliness belief: Ancient belief that events in nature are predictable.

ordinal scale: Scale of measurement in which the scores can be rank ordered, but the distance between adjacent scores varies.

ordinate: The *y*-axis on a graph.

organismic variable: Any characteristic of the individual that can be used for classification.

outline: The main aspects of ideas and arguments, organized under headings and subheadings.

panel design: See *longitudinal design.*

parametric statistics: Inferential statistical procedures that rely on sample statistics to draw inferences about population parameters.

parsimonious theory: See *parsimony.*

parsimony: A guiding principle in science, which suggests that a simple theory is preferred over a more complex theory if both theories explain the data equally well.

partial correlation: A correlation between two variables, in which the effects of a third variable are statistically removed.

partial counterbalancing: Control procedure in which the order of presentation of conditions is randomly selected for each participant.

participant assignment: Assigning participants to conditions either randomly or on the basis of preexisting variables.

participant effects: See *subject effects.*

participant observer: Any researcher gathering data while being an active part of the setting.

participant selection: Procedures used to select participants for a research study.

participant variable: Synonymous with *organismic variable.*

participants at risk: Participants involved in a research project that poses potential risk.

participants subsection: Section of a research report in which the participants and the methods of participant selection are described.

participants' rights: Guarantees of proper treatment for research participants.

partitioned: Separating the total sum of squares into between-groups and within-groups sums of squares.

path analysis: Procedure that seeks to test causal models by factoring the correlation matrix to see how closely the correlational pattern fits the model.

Pearson product-moment correlation: Index of the degree of linear relationship between two variables in which each variable represents score data.

percent agreement: A measure of interrater reliability in which the percentage of times that the raters agree is computed.

percentile rank: See *percentile.*

percentile: Score that reflects the percentage of participants who score lower.

perfect correlation: Correlation of a +1.00 or a −1.00.

phases of research: The stages of a research project.

Phi: A measure of relationship between two nominal variables.

phylogenetic continuity: An evolutionary concept about the continuity of structure and function between humans and other animals.

pilot testing: Evaluating for feasibility prior to using a measure or procedure in your research project.

placebo: An inert treatment that appears identical to the experimental treatment.

placebo effect: Any observed improvement due to a sham treatment.

plagiarism: The deliberate distortion of information by presenting another person's work as one's own.

planned comparison: Comparison of mean performance between groups that was planned before data collection. Also called a *contrast.*

population: A defined set of objects or events (people, occurrences, animals, etc.).

population parameters: Summary statistics computed on the entire population.

positive correlation: Relationship between two variables, in which one variable increases as the other variable increases.

positive practice effects: Enhancement of performance that results from previous exposure to the measurement procedure.

positively skewed: Distribution in which scores are concentrated near the bottom of the scale.

post hoc comparison: See *post hoc test.*

post hoc test: Secondary analysis that evaluates effects that were not hypothesized by the researcher. Also called *a posteriori comparison* or *incidental comparison.*

power analysis: Procedures that determine the power of a statistical test to detect group differences if those differences exist.

power of a statistical test: Ability of an inferential statistical procedure to detect differences between groups when such differences actually exist.

power: See *power of a statistical test.*

practical significance: Whether the observed group differences are large enough to have a meaningful impact on participants.

practice effects: Any change in performance that results from previous exposure to the measurement procedure.

precision-versus-relevance problem: The concern that higher-constraint laboratory research may be less relevant than lower-constraint naturalistic research and, conversely, that lower-constraint research may be unacceptably imprecise.

prediction: making a statement about what will happen to one factor if we know (or control) what happens with another factor.

predictive validity: The degree to which a measure can accurately identify (predict) a future event.

predictor measure: The variable used to predict the criterion measure.

predictor: See *predictor measure.*

preexisting variable: Any characteristic of the individual that existed prior to the research study.

prepared mind: A disciplined curiosity that makes scientists sharply alert to the possibility of unanticipated discoveries.

pretest-posttest design: Set of research designs, in which participants are tested both before and after the administration of the independent variable.

pretest-posttest, natural control-group design: Design in which preexisting groups are measured before and after the manipulation of an independent variable.

primary sources: Sources of information in the library that report the details of specific research studies.

principle of initial equivalence: The necessity of having experimental groups equal on the dependent measure before any manipulation occurs.

probability sampling: Sampling participants so that each has an equal probability of being selected and the selection of any participant does not change the probability of selecting any other participant.

probability: The ratio of specific events to the total number of possible events.

probe: Testing to see which groups are statistically different from one another.

problem-definition phase: Research phase in which research ideas are converted into precise questions to be studied.

procedure subsection: The subsection within the method section that describes how the study was carried out.

procedures-design phase: Research phase in which the specific procedures to be used in the gathering and analyzing of data are developed.

process of inquiry: The perspective that views research as a dynamic process of formulating questions and answering those questions through research.

program evaluation research: Specific area of field research that focuses on evaluating the effectiveness of programs in meeting their stated goals.

properties of the abstract number system: See *abstract number system.*

pseudoscience: Popular distortions of scientific knowledge and procedures, which appear on the surface to be scientific, but lack critical scientific procedures.

psychoanalysis: Psychological treatment based on Freud's psychodynamic theories.

psychodynamic theory: Freud's theory that behavior is shaped by a complex interaction of internal forces and the constraints of the external environment.

psychology: Scientific study of the behavior of organisms.

psychophysics: Involves the presentation of precise stimuli under controlled conditions and the recording of the participants' responses.

pure research: Another term for *basic* or *fundamental research*. See *basic research*.

***p*-value:** The probability of obtaining the statistic (e.g., *t* or *F*) or a larger statistic by chance if the null hypothesis is true.

qualitative research method: A research approach that seeks to understand psychological operations by observing the broad pattern of variables.

quasi-experiment: A study that is not quite a true experiment.

quasi-experimental design: Research designs that approximate experimental designs, providing experiment-like controls to minimize threats to internal validity.

questionnaire: A list of questions to be asked of participants.

random order of presentation: A way of controlling for carryover effects, in which the order of the conditions is randomly determined for each participant.

random samples: Samples that are drawn using random sampling techniques.

random sampling: Procedure for selecting participants, in which each participant has an equal chance of being selected and the selection of any one participant does not affect the probability of selecting any other participant.

randomization: Any procedure that assigns a value in a random manner.

randomized, posttest-only, control-group design: Experimental design in which participants are randomly assigned to two groups, and each group is tested on the dependent variable after the independent variable manipulation.

randomized, pretest-posttest, control-group design: Experimental design in which participants are randomly assigned to two groups, and each participant is tested on the dependent variable both before and after the manipulation.

randomizing within blocks: A control procedure to reduce sequence effects, which involves using a block of one trial from each condition and randomizing participant assignment to these conditions before going on to the next block.

random-number generator: Computer program that generates random sequences of numbers.

range: Distance between the lowest score and the highest score.

ratio scale: Scale of measurement in which the intervals between scores are equal and the zero point on the scale represents a zero level of the quality being measured.

rationalism: A way of knowing that relies on logic and a set of premises from which logical inferences are made.

reactive measure: Any measurement procedure that produces different scores depending on whether participants are aware that they are being measured.

records (*in computer files*): Each record represents the data for a single participant.

reference list: The listing of sources that contributed to a paper. The *APA Publication Manual* specifies how to list such references.

reference section: The section of a report that lists each paper and article that contributed to the ideas and procedures of the study.

regression: A mathematical procedure that produces an equation for predicting a variable (the criterion) from one or more other variables (the predictors).

regression equation: The mathematical equation that predicts the value of one variable from one or more other variables.

regression to the mean: Confounding variable that occurs whenever participants are selected because they have extreme scores (either very high or very low). When retested, the original extreme sample tends to be less extreme on average.

reification of a construct: Incorrectly accepting a construct as a fact.

relationship: Any connection between two or more variables.

relative score: See *standard score*.

reliability: Index of the consistency of a measuring instrument in repeatedly providing the same score for a given participant. See *interrater reliability*, *test-retest reliability*, and *internal consistency reliability*.

repeated-measures ANOVA: Statistical procedure to evaluate mean differences between conditions in a within-subjects design.

repeated-measures design: Any research design in which participants appear in all conditions.

repeated-measures factorial ANOVA: The statistical procedure for analyzing the results of a factorial study in which all factors are within-subjects factors.

repeated-measures factorials: Factorial design in which all factors are within-subjects factors.

replication: To repeat a study with no changes in the procedure (*exact replication*); small, theory-driven changes (*systematic replication*); or changes in the operational definitions of variables (*conceptual replication*).

representative sample: Sample of participants that adequately reflects the characteristics of the population.

representativeness: Degree to which a sample reflects population characteristics.

research data: See *data*.

research design checklist: An assessment of a research design made prior to data collection.

research ethics: Set of guidelines designed to protect human and animal subjects from the risks of participating in research.

research hypothesis: Precise and formal statement of a research question, which is constructed by operationally defining the variables in the statement of the problem.

research setting: Characteristics of the situation in which a research project is run.

response-inferred organismic variable: A hypothesized internal attribute of an organism that is inferred on the basis of observed behavior.

response-set biases: Any tendency for a participant to distort responses to a dependent measure and thus create measurement errors.

results section: The section of a report that describes the findings and reports on the statistical analyses of the data.

reversal (ABA) design: Single-subject design in which the effects of an independent variable are inferred from observations made first without the independent variable present, then with the independent variable present, and again without the independent variable present.

risk/benefit analysis: Assessing research in terms of the risks it poses to participants, its value to science and society, and whether potential benefits outweigh those risks.

rival hypothesis: Any feasible alternative hypothesis to the causal hypothesis.

robust: A statistical test is said to be robust to violations of the assumptions if the test consistently leads to accurate conclusions despite the assumption violations.

row means: In factorial designs, one factor is usually illustrated as separate rows of data, in which each row represents a different level of the factor.

sample: Any subset drawn from a population.

sample statistic: Index of some characteristic of the sample of participants.

sampling: Process of drawing a sample from a population. See *random sampling* and *stratified random sampling*.

sampling error: Chance variation among samples drawn from the same population.

sampling frame: A list of all participants from an available population.

scale attenuation effects: Any aspect of the measuring instrument that limits the ability of the instrument to make discriminations at the top of the scale (ceiling effects) or the bottom of the scale (floor effects).

scales of measurement: How well scores on a measurement instrument match the real number system. See *nominal*, *ordinal*, *interval*, and *ratio scales*.

scatter plot: Graphic technique that illustrates the relationship between variables.

science: Way of knowing that combines rationalism and empiricism.

scientific research: Research based on a combination of rationalism and empiricism.

Scientific Revolution: Period (fifteenth through seventeenth centuries) in which scientific methods and applications achieved independence from theology and developed rapidly into a generally recognized way of understanding nature.

scientist: Anyone who utilizes the methods of science to study phenomena.

scientist-practitioner model: A model for the training of clinical psychologists, which teaches research and clinical skills in an integrated manner.

score data: Data produced by interval or ratio scales of measurement.

secondary analyses: Analyses that look at questions beyond the original research hypotheses, which may be relevant to understanding the primary analyses.

secondary sources: Sources of information in the library that provide reviews of entire areas of research.

selection: A potential confounding variable that involves any process that may create groups not equivalent at the beginning of the study.

selective survival: The phenomenon in which some stored records are maintained (i.e., survive) while other records are lost due to known or unknown factors.

sequence effects: The confounding effects on performance in later conditions due to having experienced previous conditions.

sequential survey design: A type of survey research design that falls between the cross-sectional design and the longitudinal design. Independent groups are sampled one time and asked the same questions.

serendipity: The process of experiencing unanticipated scientific discoveries.

similarity-uniqueness paradox: The tendency to simplify comparisons between objects by seeing them as either similar to, or different from, one another.

simple random sampling: See *random sampling*.

single-blind procedure: Research procedure in which the researcher is unaware of the condition to which each participant is assigned.

single-group, posttest-only study: Nonexperimental design that involves manipulating the independent variable and then taking a post-manipulation measure on the dependent variable.

single-group, pretest-posttest study: Nonexperimental design in which participants are measured on a dependent variable both before and after the manipulation.

single-subject clinical replication: A specialized form of replication for single-subject designs, which is used primarily in clinical settings.

single-subject direct replication: Repeating a single-subject experiment with the same participant or other participants and with the same target behavior.

single-subject experimental designs: Designs that seek information from studying single subjects. See *reversal design*; *single-subject, randomized, time-series design*; and *multiple-baseline design*.

single-subject systematic replication: Testing for generalization of a procedure to other conditions, persons, and target behaviors.

single-subject, randomized, time-series design: Design in which multiple measures of the dependent variable are taken both before and after a manipulation for a single individual.

single-variable designs: Designs that include just one independent variable.

single-variable, between-subjects design: Designs that include only one independent variable and in which participants are randomly assigned to groups.

skeptic: A person who characteristically applies skepticism.

skepticism: Unwillingness to accept information without documentation to confirm it.

skewed distribution: Any distribution in which scores bunch up at the end of the scale.

skewed negatively: Distribution in which scores are concentrated at the top of the scale.

skewed positively: Distribution in which scores are concentrated at the bottom of the scale.

social desirability: Response set in which participants tend to say what they believe is expected of them.

Solomon's four-group design: Design that combines the randomized, posttest-only, control-group design and the randomized, pretest-posttest, control-group design.

sophisticated empiricism: Accepting indirect evidence for a phenomenon.

Spearman rank-order correlation: Indexes the degree of relationship between two variables, each of which is measured on at least an ordinal scale.

specific means comparison: Testing to see which groups are statistically different from which other groups. See *planned comparison* or *post hoc tests*.

spread: Synonymous with *variability*.

spreadsheet: A mechanism for organizing data in rows and columns.

SPSS for Windows: A computer package for statistical data analysis. Now sold by IBM as PASW.

standard deviation: An index of variability that is the square root of the variance.

standard error of the differences between means: The denominator in a *t*-test.

standard error of the mean: The standard deviation of the sample divided by the square root of the sample size. The standard error of the mean is the standard deviation of a distribution of means for a given sample size drawn from a specified population.

standard score: Score that gives a person's relative standing. It is computed by subtracting the mean from the score and dividing by the standard deviation.

statement of the problem: First major refinement of initial research ideas, in which a clear statement of the expected relationship between variables is made.

Statistica: Computer package for statistical data analysis.

Statistical Analysis System (SAS): Computer package for statistical data analysis.

statistical hypothesis: Synonymous with *null hypothesis*.

Statistical Package for the Social Sciences (SPSS): Computer package for statistical data analysis. Now sold by IBM as PASW.

statistical power: See *power of a statistical test*.

statistical significance: A finding is statistically significant if it is unlikely that it occurred by chance alone.

statistical symbols: Conventional shorthand used to denote statistical terms.

statistical validity: Accuracy of conclusions drawn from a statistical test.

statistically equal: Groups are statistically equal when the small differences that do exist are the result of sampling error.

statistically significant correlation: A correlation that is large enough that we would conclude that there is a non-zero relationship between the variables.

statistically significant differences: A large enough difference among group means that it is unlikely to be a chance occurrence.

statistics: Mathematical procedures used to describe data (*descriptive statistics*) or to draw conclusions from the data (*inferential statistics*).

status survey: Survey that provides a description of the current status of population characteristics.

Statview: A statistical analysis package for Macintosh computers.

stimulus variable: Any part of the environment to which an organism reacts.

strata: Subpopulations from which we draw samples. See *stratified random sampling*.

stratified random sampling: Sampling in which a population is divided into narrow strata, and participants are selected randomly from each strata.

structuralism: A philosophical perspective, popularized by Wundt, in which scientists seek to identify the structure of consciousness.

subject assignment: See *participant assignment*.

subject effects: Any response by participants that is different from the way that they would normally behave. See *placebo effect* and *demand characteristics*.

subject selection: See *participant selection*.

subject variables: See *organismic variables*.

subjective measures: Measures based primarily on participants' uncorroborated opinions, feelings, biases, or judgments.

subjects at risk: See *participants at risk*.

subjects' rights: See *participants' rights*.

subjects subsection: See *participants subsection*.

subjects term: The individual differences component of the within-groups variability in a repeated-measures ANOVA.

sum of squares: Sum of the squared differences from the mean.

summary statistics: Descriptive statistics that provide, in a single number, some general characteristic of the sample.

survey research: Research that uses surveys to find relationships among variables.

survey: A set of questions posed to a group of participants about their attitudes, beliefs, plans, lifestyles, or any other variable of interest.

symmetric distribution: Distribution in which the right half of the distribution is a mirror image of the left half.

systematic between-groups variance: Variability between groups that is brought about by either the experimental manipulation or by a confounding variable.

systematic influence: The stimulating effects of previous research and theories in providing testable hypotheses for further study.

systematic replication: Repeating a study with small, theory-based procedural changes.

table: Organizational device in which information is summarized.

table of random numbers: A table containing randomly generated numbers.

target population: Population to which we hope to generalize the findings.

technology: Physical instruments or tools used by or developed by researchers.

tenacity: Way of knowing based on accepting an idea as true because it has been accepted as true for a long time.

testing: Potential confounding variable that represents any change in a participant's score due to the participant having been tested previously.

test-retest reliability: Index of the consistency in scores over time.

theology: The philosophical tenets and/or study of religion.

theoretical concept: Idea that defines the relationship between two or more variables.

theory: Collection of ideas about how and why variables are related.

time-series design: See *interrupted time-series design*.

title page: The first page of a research manuscript, which lists the authors and their affiliations, the title of the paper, a running head (a shortened title), and the author's note.

translational research: Any research, particularly basic research, that is planned so as to lead to practical applications such as in medicine, education, and industry.

treatment: See *manipulation*.

trimodal: A distribution that has three modes.

true experiment: See *experiment*.

true zero: Characteristic of a measurement scale in which zero represents a zero level of the characteristic being measured.

***t*-test for independent groups:** Statistical procedure that tests for mean differences between two groups, in which participants appear in one and only one group.

***t*-test:** Statistical procedure that tests for mean differences between two groups.

two-group, posttest-only design: A design in which two groups of participants are compared after some manipulation of the independent variable.

two-way ANOVA: Statistical procedure for the analysis of a factorial design with two independent variables.

Type I error: Probability of rejecting the null hypothesis when it is true.

Type II error: Probability of not rejecting the null hypothesis when it is false.

unbiased assignment: Assigning participants to groups or conditions in such a way that the groups are statistically equivalent at the start of the study. The most common unbiased assignment method is random assignment.

univariate designs: See *single-variable designs*.

univariate: Having to do with one variable.

unobtrusive measure: Any measure that can be used without the participants being aware that they are being measured.

unobtrusive observer: Anyone who is able to observe the behavior of participants without the participants being aware that they are being observed.

validation: A process of establishing methodological or conceptual soundness of research findings

validity: Major concept in research that has several meanings (*internal validity, external validity, construct validity, statistical validity*). In general, validity refers to the methodological and/or conceptual soundness of research.

variability: Differences among participants on any given variable.

variable: Any characteristic that can take on different values.

variance: Summary statistic that indicates the degree of variability among participants.

waitlist control group: A group of people in a treatment study who serve initially as a no-treatment control group with the understanding that they will receive the treatment later.

within-groups variance: Variability among participants within a group or condition.

within-subjects design: Design in which individual differences are controlled by having the same participants tested under all conditions.

within-subjects factorial: Factorial design in which participants appear in all conditions.

within-subjects factors: Independent variables in factorial designs in which each participant is tested under all conditions.

***x*-axis (abscissa):** The horizontal axis in a graph.

***y*-axis (ordinate):** The vertical axis in a graph.

Z-score: See *standard score*.

REFERENCES

Abramowitz, J. S. (1998). Does cognitive-behavioral therapy cure obsessive-compulsive disorder? A meta-analytic evaluation of clinical significance. *Behavior Therapy*, *29*, 339–355. doi: 10.1016/S0005-7894(98)80012-9 (F)

Ahlfeldt, S., Mehta, S., & Sellnow, T. (2005). Measurement and analysis of student engagement in university classes where varying levels of PBL methods of instruction are in use. *Higher Education Research and Development*, *24*, 5–20. doi: 10.1080/0729436052000318541 (13)

Ainsworth, M. (1993). Attachment as related to mother-infant interaction. In C. Rovee-Collier & L. Lipset (Eds.), *Advances in infancy research* (Vol. 8). Norwood, NJ: Ablex. (1)

Akins, C. K., Panicker, S., & Cunningham, C. L. (Eds.). (2005). *Laboratory animals in research and teaching: Ethics, care, and methods*. Washington, DC: American Psychological Association. (3)

American Psychological Association. (1953). *Ethical standards of psychologists*. Washington, DC: Author. (2)

American Psychological Association. (1959). Ethical standards of psychologists. *American Psychologist*, *14*, 279–282. (2)

American Psychological Association. (2002). *Ethical principles of psychologists and code of conduct*. Washington, DC: Author. Retrieved from www.apa.org/ethics on May 1, 2012. (2, 3, 9, 11)

American Psychological Association. (2009). *Mastering APA style: Student's workbook and training guide* (6th ed.). Washington, DC: Author. (B)

American Psychological Association. (2010a). *Ethical principles of psychologists and code of conduct: 2010 amendments*. Washington, DC: Author. (3, 9)

American Psychological Association. (2010b). *Guidelines for ethical conduct in the care and use of nonhuman animals in research*. Retrieved from http://www.apa.org/science/leadership/care/animal-guide-2010.pdf on April 14, 2012. (3)

American Psychological Association. (2010c). *Membership statistics*. Retrieved from http://www.apa.org/about/division/index.aspx on April 1, 2012. (1)

American Psychological Association. (2010d). *Publication manual of the American Psychological Association* (6th ed.). Washington, DC: Author. Hard copies of APA electronic publications may be requested from American Psychological Association, Science Directorate, 750 First Street, Washington, DC 20002-4242. (4, B)

Anastasi, A., & Urbina, S. (1997). *Psychological testing* (7th ed.). Upper Saddle River, NJ: Prentice Hall. (4)

Anderson, C. A., Lindsay, J. J., & Bushman, B. J. (1999). Research in the psychological laboratory: Truth or triviality? *Current Directions in Psychological Science*, *8*, 3–9. doi: 10.1111/1467-8721.00002 (6, 13)

Anglesea, M. M., Hoch, H., & Taylor, B. A. (2008). Reducing rapid eating in teenagers with autism: Use of a pager prompt. *Journal of Applied Behavior Analysis*, *41*, 107–111. doi: 10.1901/jaba.2008.41-107 (11)

Auge, I. I., Wayne, K., & Auge, S. M. (1999). Sports and substance use: Naturalistic observation of athletic drug-use patterns and behavior in professional-caliber bodybuilders. *Substance Use and Misuse*, *34*, 217–249. doi: 10.3109/10826089909035644 (6)

Bachrach, A. J. (1981). *Psychological research: An introduction*. New York: Random House. (1, 13)

Baker, L. A., Mack, W., Moffitt, T. E., & Mednick, S. (1989). Sex differences in property crime in a Danish adoption cohort. *Behavior Genetics*, *19*, 355–370. doi: 10.1007/BF01066164 (6)

Ball, R. E. (2003). *The fundamentals of aircraft combat survivability: Analysis and design*. Reston, VA: American Institute of Aeronautics and Astronautics. (2)

Bandura, A. I. (1969). *Principles of behavior modification*. New York: Holt, Rinehart and Winston. (3)

Barber, T. X., & Silver, M. J. (1968). Fact, fiction and the experimenter bias effect. *Psychological Bulletin Monograph Supplement*, *70*, 1–29. doi: 10.1037/h0026724 (8)

Barlow, D. H. (2002). *Anxiety and its disorders: The nature and treatment of anxiety and panic* (2nd ed.). New York: Guilford Press. (1, 4)

Barlow, D. H. (Ed.). (2008). *Clinical handbook of psychological disorders* (4th ed.). New York: Guilford. (1)

Barlow, D. H., Nock, M., & Hersen, M. (2009). *Single case experimental designs: Strategies for studying behavior change* (3rd ed.). Boston, MA: Pearson/Allyn & Bacon. (11)

Barry, C. L., & Busch, S. H. (2010). News media coverage of FDA warnings on pediatric antidepressant use and suicidality. *Pediatrics*, *125*, 88–95. doi: 10.1542/peds.2009-0792 (3)

Bartlett, J. (1980). *Bartlett's familiar quotations: A collection of passages, phrases, and proverbs traced to their sources in ancient and modern literature*. Boston, MA: Little, Brown and Company. (5)

Bass, E., & Davis, L. (1988). *The courage to heal: A guide for women survivors of sexual abuse*. New York: Harper & Row. (1)

Bass, E., & Davis, L. (1994). *The courage to heal: A guide for women survivors of sexual abuse: Featuring "Honoring the truth: A response to the backlash"* (3rd ed., rev.). New York: HarperPerennial. (1)

Bass, E., & Davis, L. (2002). *Courage to heal* [paperback]. Vermilion, OH: Vermilion. (1)

Beck, A. (1975). *Cognitive therapy and the emotional disorders*. New York: International Universities Press, Inc. (3)

Belia, S., Fidler, F., Williams, J., & Cumming, G. (2005). Researchers misunderstand confidence interval and standard error bars. *Psychological Methods*, *10*, 389–396. doi: 10.1037/1082-989X.10.4.389 (10)

Belluck, P. (2005, February 10). Massachusetts governor opposes stem cell research. *New York Times*, p. A14. (1)

Belmont Report. (1978). *Ethical principles and guidelines for the protection of human subjects of research* (DHEW Publication no. (os) 78-0012). Washington, DC: The National Commission for the Protection of Human Subjects of Biomedical and Behavioral Research. (2, 3)

Benjafield, J. G. (2005). *A history of psychology* (2nd ed.). New York: Oxford. (1)

Benjamin, L. J. (Ed.). (2007). *A brief history of psychology*. Malden, MA: Blackwell. (1)

Bennett, G. G., Merritt, M. M., & Wolin, K. Y. (2004). Ethnicity, education, and the cortisol response to awakening: A preliminary investigation. *Ethnicity and Health*, *9*, 337–347. doi: 10.1080/1355785042000285366 (3)

Bensler, J. M., & Paauw, D. S. (2003). Apotemnophilia masquerading as medical morbidity. *Southern Medical Journal*, *96*, 674–676. (6)

Berg, B. (2004). *Qualitative research methods for the social sciences* (5th ed.). Boston, MA: Pearson. (6)

Bergin, A. E., & Strupp, H. H. (1970). The directions in psychotherapy research. *Journal of Abnormal Psychology*, *76*, 13–26. doi: 10.1037/h0029634 (11)

Bhattacharjee, Y. (2003, October 10). U.S. license needed to edit Iranian papers. *Science*, *302*, 210. doi: 10.1126/SCIENCE.302.5643.210b (1)

Bhattacharjee, Y. (2004, April 9). Easing the squeeze on "sanctioned" authors. *Science, 304*, 187. doi: 10.1126/science.304.5668.187a (1)

Blache, D. Martin, G. B., & Maloney, S. K. (2008). Towards ethically improved animal experimentation in the study of animal reproduction. *Reproduction in Domestic Animals* (Special Issue), *33*(S2), 8–14. doi: 10.1111/j.1439-0531.2008.01137.x (3)

Blanchard, J. J., Horan, W. P., & Brown, S. A. (2001). Diagnostic differences in social anhedonia: A longitudinal study of schizophrenia and major depressive disorder. *Journal of Abnormal Psychology*, *110*, 363–371. doi: 10.1037/0021-843X.110.3.363 (7)

Bleuler, E. (1950). The fundamental symptoms. In E. Bleuler (Ed.), *Dementia praecox; or the group of schizophrenias*. J. Ziskin (Trans.) (pp. 14–54). New York: International University Press. (Original work published in 1911) (7)

Bodenheimer, T. (2000). Uneasy alliance—Clinical investigators and the pharmaceutical industry. *New England Journal of Medicine*, *342*, 1539–1544. (4)

Boesch, C. (2005). Joint cooperative hunting among wild chimpanzees: Taking natural observations seriously. *Behavioral and Brain Sciences*, *28*, 692–693. (6)

Boesch, C. (2009). *The real chimpanzees: Sex strategies in the forest.* Cambridge, MA: Cambridge University Press. (6)

Boesch, C., & Boesch-Achermann, H. (1991, September). Dim forest, bright chimps. *Natural History*, *9*(9), 50–56. (6)

Botting, J. H., & Morrison, A. R. (1997, February). Animal research is vital to medicine. *Scientific American*, *276*(2), 83–85. (3)

Bower, B. (1998). Psychology's tangled web. *Science News*, *153*(25), 394–395. (3)

Bowers, D. (1997). Georgia on our minds. *Marketing Research*, *9*(2), 34. (13)

Boyack, K. W., Klavans, R., & Borner, K. (2005). Mapping the backbone of science. *Scientometrics*, *64*, 351–374. (1)

Braam, A. W., Visser, S., Cath, D. C., & Hoogendijk, W. J. G. (2006). Investigation of the syndrome of apotemnophilia and course of a cognitive behavioral therapy. *Psychopathology*, *39*, 32–37. doi: 10.1159/000089661 (6)

Breckler, S. J. (2006). Psychology is translational science. *APA Monitor*, *37*, 22. (3)

Breese, P., Rietmeijer, C., & Burman, W. (2007). Contact among locally approved HIPAA authorization forms for research. *Journal of Empirical research on Human Research Ethics*, *2*, 43–46. doi: 10.1525/jer.2007.2.1.43 (6)

Briem, V., & Hedman, L. R. (1995). Behavioural effects of mobile telephone use during simulated driving. *Ergonomics*, *38*, 2536–2562. doi: 10.1080/00140139508925285 (2)

Brody, H. (2007). *Hooked: Ethics, the medical profession, and the pharmaceutical industry*. Lanham, MD: Rowman and Littlefield Publishers. (4)

Brotemarkle, R. A. (1966). Fifty years of clinical psychology: Clinical psychology, 1896–1956. in I. N. Mensh (Ed.), *Clinical psychology: Science and profession* (pp. 63–68). New York: Macmillan.

Cacioppo, J. T. (2007). Psychology is a hub science. *APS Observer*, *20*(8), 7–42. (1)

Calvo, M. G., & Castillo, M. D. (2005). Foveal vs. Parafoveal attention-grabbing power of threat-related information. *Experimental Psychology*, *52*, 150–162. doi: 10.1027/1618-3169.52.2.150 (3)

Campbell, D. T. (1969). Reforms as experiments. *American Psychologist*, *24*, 409–429. doi: 10.1037/h0027982 (13)

Campbell, D. T., & Stanley, J. C. (1966). *Experimental and quasi-experimental designs for research*. Chicago, IL: Rand McNally. (8, 10, 13)

Campbell, F. A., & Ramey, C. T. (1994). Effects of early intervention on intellectual and academic achievement: A follow-up study of children from low-income families. *Child Development*, *65*, 684–698. doi: 10.2307/1131410 (13)

Campbell, F. A., Ramey, C. T., Pungello, E., Sparling, J., & Miller-Johnson, S. (2002). Early childhood education: Young adult outcomes from the Abecedarian Project. *Applied Developmental Science*, *6*, 42–57. doi: 10.1207/S1532480XADS0601_05 (13)

Campostrini, S., Holtzman, D., McQueen, D. V., & Boaretto, E. (2006). Evaluating the effectiveness of health promotion policy: Changes in the law on drinking and driving in California. *Health Promotion International*, *21*, 130–135. doi: 10.1093/heapro/dak005 (13)

Canadian Council on Animal Care. (1993). *Guide to the care and use of experimental animals*. Ottawa, Canada: Author. (3)

Canadian Psychological Association. (2010). *Annual report for 2010–2011*. Retrieved from www.cpa.ca/home/annual reports. (1)

Carroll, M. E., & Overmier, J. B. (Eds.) (2001). *Animal research and human health: Advancing human welfare through behavioral science*. Washington, DC: American Psychological Association. (3)

Casey, M. B. (1996). Understanding individual differences in spatial ability within females: A nature/nurture interactionist framework. *Developmental Review*, *16*, 241–260. doi: 10.1006/drev.1996.0009 (8)

Catalano, R., & Serxner, S. (1992). The effect of ambient threats to employment on low birth weight. *Journal of Health and Social Behavior*, *33*, 363–377. doi: 10.2307/2137314 (13)

Cayley, G. (1853). *Design drawing for a man-powered flying machine* [Graphic/lithograph]. Jolicouer, pass. Vendome, 25. (2)

Cayley, G. (1910). *On aerial navigation.* London: King, Sell & Olding, Ltd. (2)

Chanute, O. (1899). *Progress in flying machines.* New York: M. N. Forney. (2)

Chapman, L. J., & Chapman, J. P. (1969). Illusory correlation as an obstacle to the use of valid psychodiagnostic signs. *Journal of Abnormal Psychology*, *74*, 271–280. doi: 10.1037/h0027592 (7)

Chapman, L. J., & Chapman, J. P. (1973). *Disordered thought in schizophrenia*. Upper Saddle River, NJ: Prentice Hall. (9)

Chapman, L. J., Chapman, J. P., & Raulin, M. L. (1976). Scales for physical and social anhedonia. *Journal of Abnormal Psychology*, *85*, 374–382. doi: 10.1037/0021-843X.85.4.374 (7)

Cialdini, R. B. (1993). *Influence: The psychology of persuasion* (2nd ed.). New York: William Morrow. (1)

Clagett, M. (1948). The medieval heritage: Religious, philosophic, scientific. In J. L. Blau, J. Buchler, & G. T. Matthews (Eds.), *Chapters in western civilization* (Vol. 1, pp. 74–122). New York: Columbia University Press. (1)

Clark, K. B. (1978). Kenneth B. Clark: Social psychologist. In T. C. Hunter (Ed.), *Beginnings* (pp. 76–84). New York: Crowell. (1)

Code of Federal Regulations. (2005, June 23). Title 45: Public Welfare; Title 46: Protection of Human Subjects. Available from the United States Department of Health and Human Services. Retrieved from http://www.hhs.gov/ohrp/policy/ohrpregulations.pdf on April 6, 2012. (2)

Cohen, J. A. (1960). A coefficient of agreement for nominal scales. *Educational and Psychological Measurement*, *20*, 37–46. doi: 10.1177/001316446002000104 (9)

Cohen, J. A. (1988). *Statistical power analysis for the behavioral sciences* (2nd ed.). Hillsdale, NJ: Lawrence Erlbaum. (E)

Cohen, J. A. (1992). A power primer. *Psychological Bulletin*, *112*, 155–159. doi: 10.1037/0033-2909.112.1.155 (5, F)

Collins, F. S., & Jegalian, K. G. (1999, December). Deciphering the code of life. *Scientific American, 281*(6), 86–93. (FN)

Cook, T. D., & Campbell, D. T. (1979). *Quasi-experimentation: Design and analysis issues for field studies.* Chicago, IL: Rand McNally. (8, 13)

Coombs, C. H., Raiffa, H., & Thrall, R. M. (1954). Some views on mathematical models and measurement theory. *Psychological Review*, *61*, 132–144. doi: 10.1037/h0063044 (4)

Cooper, H. M. (1998). Synthesizing research: A guide for literature reviews. Thousand Oaks, CA: Sage. (F)

Copi, I. M., & Cohen, C. (2009). *Introduction to logic* (13th ed.). Upper Saddle River, NJ: Prentice Hall. (2)

Damisch, L., Stoberock, B., & Mussweiler, T. (2010). Keep your fingers crossed!: How superstition improves performance. *Psychological Science*, *21*, 1014–1020. doi: 10.1177/0956797610372631 (1)

Danitz, T. (1997, December 15). Making up memories? *Insight on the News*, *13*(46), 14–15. (1)

Darley, J. M., & Latané, B. (1968). Bystander intervention in emergencies: Diffusion of responsibility. *Journal of Personality and Social Psychology, 8*, 377–383. doi: 10.1037/h0025589 (1, 8)

Dar-Nimrod, I., & Heine, S. J. (2006). Exposure to scientific theories affects women's math performance. *Science*, *314*, 435. doi: 10.1126/science.113110 (8)

Darwin, C. (1859). *On the origin of species by means of natural selection, or the preservation of favored races in the struggle for life*. London: John Murray. New York: Modern Library, 1967. (3, 6)

Darwin, C. (1877). A biographical sketch of an infant. *Mind*, *2*, 285–294. (6)

Davidoff, J. (2004). Coloured thinking. *The Psychologist, 17*, 570–572. (3)

Davis, P. W. (1997, July). *Naturalistic observations of 250 children hit in public settings.* Paper presented at the Fifth International Family Violence Research Conference, Durham, NH. (6)

Dawis, R. (1987). Scale construction. *Journal of Counseling Psychology, 39*, 481–489. doi: 10.1037/0022-0167.34.4.481 (13)

De Los Reyes, A., & Kazdin, A. E. (2008). When the evidence says "Yes, no, and maybe so": Attending to and interpreting inconsistent findings among evidence-based interventions. *Current Directions in Psychological Science, 17*, 47–51. doi: 10.1111/j.1467-8721.2008.00546.x (1)

DeLoache, J., Chiong, C., Sherman, K., Islami, N., Vanderborght, M., Troseth, G. L., et al. (2010). Do babies learn from baby media? *Psychological Science, 11,* 1570–1574. doi: 10.1177/0956797610384145 (3)

Di Noia, J., & Tripodi, T. (2007). *Single-case for clinical social workers.* Washington, DC: National Association of Social Workers Press. (11)

Donaghy, T., Freeman, J., Grifo, F., & Kaufman, K. (2007). *Atmosphere of pressure: Political interference in federal climate science.* Cambridge, MA: Union of Concerned Scientists, Government Accountability Project. (4)

Donaldson, S. I., Berger, D. E., & Pezdek, K. (Eds.). (2006). *Applied psychology: New frontiers and rewarding careers.* Mahwah, NJ: Erlbaum. (1)

DuBois, J. M., Dueker, J. M., Anderson, E. E., & Campbell, J. (2010). Instruction in the responsible conduct of research: An inventory of programs and materials within CTSAs. *Clinical and Translational Science, 3,* 109–111. doi: 10.1111/j.1752-8062.2010.00193.x (3)

Dunbar, K. (1994). How scientists really reason: Scientific reasoning in real-world laboratories. In R. J. Sternberg & J. Davidson (Eds.), *The nature of insight* (pp. 365–395). Cambridge, MA: MIT Press. (6)

Duskin, M. S. (1999, March). Census 2000 doesn't add up. *Contemporary Women's Issues, 48*(3), 6–11. (13)

Duva, M. A., Siu, A., & Stanley, B. G. (2005). The NMDA receptor antagonist MK-801 alters lipoprivic eating elicited by 2-mercaptoacetate. *Physiology and Behavior, 83*, 787–791. doi: 10.1016/j.physbeh.2004.09.020 (3)

Easton, A., Meerlo, P., Bergmann, B., & Turek, F. W. (2004). The suprachiasmatic nucleus regulates sleep timing and amount in mice. *Sleep: Journal of Sleep and Sleep Disorders Research, 27*, 1307–1318. (3)

Eckblad, M. L., Chapman, L. J., Chapman, J. P., & Mishlove, M. (1982). *The revised social anhedonia scale.* Unpublished test, University of Wisconsin, Madison. (7)

Eichenwald, K., & Kolata, G. (1999, May 17). A doctor's drug studies turn into fraud. *The New York Times*, p. 1. (4)

Eisenger, R. M. (2003). *The evolution of presidential polling.* New York: Cambridge University Press. (13)

Ekman, P. (2009). Giving Darwin his due. *The Observer, 22*(8). Retrieved from http://www.psychologicalscience.org/observer/getArticle.cfm?id=2560 on April 13, 2012. (3)

Erlenmeyer-Kimling, L., Roberts, S. A., & Rock, D. (2004). Longitudinal prediction of schizophrenia in a prospective high-risk study. In L. F. DiLalla (Ed.), *Behavior genetics principles: Perspectives in development, personality, and psychopathology: Decade of behavior* (pp. 135–144). Washington, DC: American Psychological Association. (8)

European Science Foundation. (2001). *The use of animals in research: Policy briefing.* Strasbourg, France: Author. (3)

Eysenck, H. (1960). *Behavior therapy and the neuroses.* Oxford: Pergamon Press. (3)

Farrington, B. (1949a). *Greek science: 1. Thales to Aristotle.* Harmondsworth, UK: Pelican Books. (1)

Farrington, B. (1949b). *Greek science: 2. Theophrastus to Galen.* Harmondsworth, UK: Pelican Books. (1)

Festinger, L. (1957). *A theory of cognitive dissonance.* Stanford, CA: Stanford University Press. (3)

Fisher, R. A. (1935). *The design of experiments.* London: Oliver & Boyd. (11)

Forrester, M. (2010). *Doing qualitative research.* Los Angeles, CA: Sage. (6)

Freud, S. (1938a). The interpretation of dreams. In A. A. Brill (Ed. & Trans.), *The basic writings of Sigmund Freud* (pp. 179–549). New York: Random House. (Original work published 1900) (3)

Freud, S. (1938b). The psychopathology of everyday life. In A. A. Brill (Ed. & Trans.), *The basic writings of Sigmund Freud* (pp. 33–178). New York: Random House. (Original work published 1901) (3)

Fugh-Burman, A., & Dodson, S. J. (2008). Ethical considerations of publication planning in the pharmaceutical industry. *Open Medicine, 2*. Retrieved from http://www.openmedicine.ca/article/viewArticle/118/215. (4)

Gaito, J. (1980). Measurement scales and statistics: Resurgence of an old misconception. *Psychological Bulletin, 87*, 564–567. doi: 10.1037/0033-2909.87.3.564 (4)

Gallagher D., Larson, E. L., Yang, Y.-H. C., Richards B., Weng C., Hametz P., et al. (2010). Identifying interdisciplinary research priorities to prevent and treat pediatric obesity in New York City. *Clinical and Translational Science, 3*, 172–177. doi: 10.1111/j.1752-8062.2010.0021.x (3)

Ginsburg, H. P., Inoue, N., & Seo, K. (1999). Young children doing mathematics: Observations of everyday activities. In J. V. Copley (Ed.), *Mathematics in the early years* (pp. 88–99). Washington, DC: National Association for the Education of Young Children. (6)

Gleick, J. (1987). *Chaos: Making a new science*. New York: Penguin Books. (3)

Goodall, J. (1978). Chimp killings: Is it the man in them? *Science News, 113*, 276. (6)

Goodall, J. (1986). *The chimpanzees of Gombe*. Cambridge, MA: Belknap Press/Harvard University Press. (2, 6)

Goodall, J. (1988). *In the shadow of man*. Boston, MA: Houghton Mifflin. (2, 6)

Goodall, J. (2010). *50 years at Gombe*. New York: NY: Abrams. (2)

Goodstein, D. L. (2010). *On fact and fraud: Cautionary tales from the front lines of science*. Princeton, NJ: Princeton University Press. (7)

Goodstein, L. (2005, December 21). Issuing a rebuke, judge rejects teaching of intelligent design. *The New York Times*. (1)

Goodwin, C. J. (2008). *A history of modern psychology* (3rd ed.). Hoboken, NJ: John Wiley. (1)

Gould, S. J. (1997, May). Leonardo's living earth. *Natural History, 106*, 18. (1)

Graham, K., & Wells, S. (2001). Aggression among young adults in the social context of the bar. *Addiction Research and Theory, 9*, 193–219. doi: 10.3109/16066350109141750 (6)

Grant, B. (2009). *NSF adopts new ethics rules*. Retrieved from thescientist.com/blog/display/55962 on September 3, 2009. (2)

Graubard, S. R. (Ed.). (1969). Ethical aspects of experimentation with human subjects [Special issue]. *Daedalus, 98*, 219–598. (2)

Graziano, A. M. (1974). *Child without tomorrow*. Elmsford, NY: Pergamon Press. (2, 4, 8, 13)

Graziano, A. M. (2002). *Developmental disabilities: Introduction to a diverse field*. Boston, MA: Allyn & Bacon. (8)

Graziano, A. M., & Kean, J. (1968). Programmed relaxation and reciprocal inhibition with psychotic children. *Behaviour Research and Therapy, 6*, 433–437. doi: 10.1016/0005-7967(68)90023-5 (6)

Graziano, A. M., & Mooney, K. C. (1982). Behavioral treatment of "nightfears:" A 2- to 3-year follow-up. *Journal of Consulting and Clinical Psychology, 50*, 598–599. doi: 10.1037/0022-006X.50.4.598 (9)

Graziano, A. M., Hamblen, J. L., & Plante, W. A. (1996). Subabusive violence in child rearing in middle-class American families. *Pediatrics, 98*(4), 845–848. PMD 8885986. (6).

Graziano, M. S. A. (2009). *The intelligent movement machine: An ethological perspective on the primate motor system*. New York: Oxford University Press. (8)

Graziano, M. S. A., & Gross, C. (1993). A bimodal map of space: Somatosensory receptive fields in the macaque putamen with corresponding visual receptive fields. *Experimental Brain Research, 97*, 96–109. (1)

Graziano, M. S. A., & Gross, C. (1998). Spatial maps for the control of movement. *Current Opinions in Neurobiology, 8*, 195–201. doi: 10.1016/SO959-4388(98)80140-2 (1)

Graziano, M. S. G., & Aflalo, T. N. (2007). Mapping behavioral repertoire onto the cortex. *Neuron, 56*, 239–251. doi: 10.1016/j.neuron.2007.09.013 (3)

Gross, C. G. (1997). Leonardo da Vinci on the brain and eye. *History of Neuroscience*, *3*, 347–354. (1)

Gross, C. G. (2008). Single neuron studies of inferior temporal cortex. *Neuropsychologia*, *46*, 841–852. doi: 10.1016/j.neuropsychologia (1)

Gross, C. G. (2010). Alfred Russell Wallace and the evolution of the human mind. *The Neuroscientist*, *16*, 508–518. doi: 10.1177/1073858410377236 (3)

Grundy, C., Steinbach, R., Edwards, P., Green, J., Armstrong, B., & Wilkinson, P. (2010). Effect of 20 mph traffic speed zones on road injuries in London, 1986–2006: Controlled interrupted time series analysis. *British Medical Journal*, *339*, 4469. doi: 10.1136/bmj.b4469] (13)

Guerin, D., & MacKinnon, D. P. (1985). An assessment of the California Child Passenger Restraint Requirement. *American Journal of Public Health*, *75*, 142–144. (13)

Hafner, K., & George, J. (2005, March 3). For drivers, a traffic jam of distractions. *The New York Times*, E1. (2)

Hall, G. C., Bansal, A., & Lopez, I. R. (1999). Ethnicity and psychopathology: A meta-analytic review of 31 years of comparative MMPI/MMPI-2 research. *Psychological Assessment*, *11*, 186–197. doi: 10.1037/1040-3590.11.2.186 (F)

Harb, G. C., Eng, W., Zaider, T., & Heimberg, R. G. (2003). Behavioral assessment of public-speaking anxiety using a modified version of the Social Performance Rating Scale. *Behaviour Research and Therapy*, *41*, 1373–1380. doi: 10.1016/S0005-7967(03)00158-X (9)

Harper, W. (2004, September 29). Publisher for the people: Biologist Michael Eisen hopes to accomplish for science publishing what Linux set out to do for computing. East Bay Express (California). (Available through LexisNexis Academic) (2)

Harris, G. (2009, March 10). Doctor admits pain studies were fabricated, hospital says. *The New York Times*, p. A 22. New York edition.

Hartmann, D. P., & Atkinson, C. (1973). Having your cake and eating it too: A note on some apparent contradictions between therapeutic achievements and design requirements in *N*=1 studies. *Behavior Therapy*, *4*, 589–591. doi: 10.1016/S0005-7894(73)80013-9 (11)

Hayes, R. (2006). Evaluating the effects of EAS on product sales and loss: Results of a large-scale field experiment. *Security Journal*, *19*, 262–276. doi: 10.1057/palgrave.sj.8350025 (3)

Heller, J. (1972, July 26). Syphilis victims went untreated for 40 years. *Washington Evening Star* and *NY Times*. (2)

Helmstadter, G. C. (1970). *Research concepts in human behavior*. New York: Appleton-Century-Crofts. (1)

Hergenhahn, B. R. (2009). *An introduction to the history of psychology* (6th ed.). Belmont, CA: Wadsworth/Cengage Learning. (1)

Hertwig, R., & Ortman, A. (2008). Deception in experiments: Revisiting the arguments in its defense. *Ethics and Behavior*, *18*, 59–92. doi: 10.1080/10508420701712990 (3)

Hollin, C. R. (1999). Treatment programs for offenders: Meta-analysis, "what works," and beyond. *International Journal of Law and Psychiatry*, *22*, 361–372. doi: 10.1016/S0160-2527(99)00015-1 (F)

Hopkins, W. D., Russell, J. L., & Cantalupo, C. (2007). Neuroanatomical correlates of handedness for tool use in chimpanzees. *Psychological Science*, *18,* 971–978. doi: 10.1111/j.1467-9280.2007.02011.x (3)

Howell, R. T., & Howell, C. J. (2008). The relation of economic status to subjective well-being in developing countries: A meta-analysis. *Psychological Bulletin*, *134*, 536-560. doi: 10.1037/0033-2909.134.4.536 (13)

HSUS. (2011). *Scientists apply now for Animal Alternatives Award.* The Humane Society of the United States. Retrieved from forums.alttox.org/index.php?topic=256.0 on April 11, 2012. (3)

Hugdahl, K. (1995). Classical conditioning and implicit learning: The right hemisphere hypothesis. In R. J. Davidson & K. Hugdahl (Eds.), *Brain asymmetry* (pp. 235–267). Cambridge, MA: MIT Press. (11)

Hunt, M. M. (1997). *How science takes stock: The story of meta-analysis*. New York: Russell Sage Foundation. (F)

Hunter, J. E., & Schmidt, F. L. (1990). *Methods of meta-analysis: Correcting error and bias in research findings*. Newbury Park, CA: Sage. (F)

Hyman, R. (1964). *The nature of psychological inquiry*. Upper Saddle River, NJ: Prentice Hall. (2)

Interlandi, J. (2006, October 22). An unwelcome discovery. *The New York Times*. Retrieved from http://www.nytimes.com/2006/10/22/magazine/22sciencefraud.html?_r=1&oref=slogin on April 14, 2012. (4)

Irvin, J., Bowers, C., Dunn, M., & Wang, M. C. (1999). Efficacy of relapse prevention: A meta-analytic review. *Journal of Consulting and Clinical Psychology*, *67*, 563–570. doi: 10.1037/0022-006X.67.4.563 (F)

Jacobs, A., & Wayer, E. (2005). The role of medical writers in developing peer-reviewed publications. *Current Medical Research and Opinion*, *21*, 317–320. (4)

Jacobson, J. W., Mulick, J. A., & Schwartz, A. A. (1995). A history of facilitated communication: Science, pseudoscience, and antiscience science working group on facilitated communication. *American Psychologist*, *50*, 750–765. doi: 10.1037/0003-066X.50.9.750 (1)

Johnson, B., & Eagly, A. (2000). Quantitative synthesis of social psychological research. In H. Weiss & C. Judd (Eds.), *Handbook of research methods in social and personality psychology* (pp. 496–528). New York: Cambridge University Press. (F)

Johnston, L. D., O'Malley, P. M., Bachman, J. G., & Schulenberg, J. E. (2009). *Monitoring the future: National results on adolescent drug use: Overview of key findings, 2008* (NIH Publication No. 09-7401). Bethesda, MD: National Institute on Drug Abuse. (13)

Jones, J. H. (1981/1993). *Bad blood: the Tuskegee syphilis experiment.* New York: Free Press. (Expanded version, 1993) (2, 7)

Jones, M. C. (1924). Elimination of children's fears. *Journal of Experimental Psychology*, *7*, 382–397. doi: 10.1037/h0072283 (3)

Katz, J. (1992). The consent principle of the Nuremberg Code. Its significance then and now. In G. J. Annas & M. A. Gradin (Eds.), *The Nazi doctors and the Nuremberg Code* (pp. 227–239). New York: Oxford University Press. (2)

Kazdin, A. E. (2001). *Behavior modification in applied settings* (6th ed.). Belmont, CA: Wadsworth/Thomson. (11)

Kazdin, A. E. (2003). *Research design in clinical psychology* (4th ed.). Boston, MA: Allyn & Bacon. (13)

Keith, A. (1954). Darwin and the "origin of species." In H. Shapley, S. Rapport, & H. Wright (Eds.), *A treasury of science* (pp. 437–446). New York: Harper and Brothers. (3)

Kelly, J. A., Amirkhanian, Y. A., Seal, D. W., Galletly, C. M., DiFranceisco, W., Glassman, L. R., et al. (2010). Levels and predictors of sexual HIV risk in social networks of men who have sex with men in the Midwest. *AIDS Education and Prevention*, *22*, 483–495. doi: 10.1521/aeap.2010.22.6.483 (3)

Kendler, H. H. (1993). Psychology and the ethics of social policy. *American Psychologist*, *48*, 1046–1053. doi: 10.1037/0003-066X.48.10.1046 (3)

Keppel, G. (2006). *Introduction to design and analysis*. New York: Worth. (D)

Keppel, G., & Wickens, T. D. (2004). *Design and analysis: A researcher's handbook* (4th ed.). Upper Saddle River, NJ: Prentice Hall. (11, 12)

Kerlinger, F. N., & Lee, H. B. (2000). *Foundations of behavioral research* (4th ed.). Fort Worth, TX: Harcourt College Publishers. (4, 8, 13)

Kessler, R. C. (2003). Epidemiology of women and depression. *Journal of Affective Disorders*, *74*(1), 5–13. doi: 10.1016/S0165-0327(02)00426-3

Kety, S. S., Rosenthal, D., Wender, P. H., & Schulsinger, F. (1968). The types and prevalence of mental illness in the biological and adoptive families of adopted schizophrenics. In D. Rosenthal & S. S. Kety (Eds.), *The transmission of schizophrenia* (pp. 345–362). Oxford: Pergamon. (6, 11)

Kimmel, A. J. (2007). *Ethical principles in behavioral research: Basic and applied perspectives*. Malden, MA: Blackwell Publishers. (2)

Kintisch, E. (2005, March 25). Researcher faces prison for fraud in NIH grant application and papers. *Science*, *37*, 1851. doi: 10.1126/science.307.5717.1851a (4)

Kiossis, D. N., Leon, A. C., & Areán, P. A. (2011). Psychosocial interventions for late-life major depression: Evidence-based treatments, predictors of treatment outcomes, and moderators of treatment effects. *Psychiatric Clinics of North America*, *34*, 377–401. doi: 2011-09149-010 (3)

Kirsch, I. (2003). Hidden administration as ethical alternatives to the balanced placebo design. *Prevention and Treatment, 6*, artID 5c. doi: 10.1037/1522-3736.6.1.65c (9)

Klahr, D., & Simon, H. A. (2001). What have psychologists (and others) discovered about the process of scientific discovery? *Current Directions in Psychological Science, 10*, 75–79. doi: 10.1111/1467-8721.00119 (6)

Koffka, K. (1935). *Principles of Gestalt psychology*. London: Lund, Humphries. (1)

Kohler, W. (1926). *The mentality of apes*. Ella Winter (Trans.). New York: Harcourt Brace. (1)

Korn, J. H. (1997). *Illusions of reality: A history of deception in social psychology*. New York: State University of New York Press. (3)

Krijn, M., Emmelkamp, P. M. G., Ólafsson, R. P., Bouwman, M., van Gerwen, L. J., Spinhoven, P., et al. (2007). Fear of flying treatment methods: Virtual reality exposure versus cognitive behavioral therapy. *Aviation, Space, and Environmental Medicine, 78*, 121–128. (9)

Kurtz, M. M., Baker, E., Pearlson, G. D., & Astur, R. F. (2007). A virtual reality apartment as a measure of medical management skills in patients with schizophrenia: A pilot study. *Schizophrenia Bulletin, 33*, 1162–1170. doi: 10.1093/schbul/sbl039 (9)

Lambert, K., & Lilienfeld, S. O. (2007, October/November). Brain stains: Traumatic therapies can have long-lasting effects on mental health. *Scientific American Mind, 18*(5), 46–53. (1)

Lammers, J., Stapel, D. A., & Galinsky, A. D. (2010). Power increases hypocrisy. Moralizing in reasoning, immorality in behavior. *Psychological Science, 21*, 737–744 doi: 1177/0956797610368810] (1)

Lang, A. R., & Sibrel, P. A. (1989). Psychological perspectives on alcohol consumption and interpersonal aggression: The potential role of individual differences in alcohol-related criminal violence. *Criminal Justice and Behavior, 16*, 299–324. doi: 10.1177/0093854889016003004 (9)

Lang, P. J. (1985). The cognitive psychophysiology of emotion: Fear and anxiety. In A. H. Tuma & D. Maser (Eds.), *Anxiety and the anxiety disorders* (pp. 131–170). Hillsdale, NJ: Erlbaum. (4)

Large, M. M. (2007). Body identity disorder. *Psychological Medicine, 10*, 1513. doi: 10.1017/S0033291707001237 (6)

Larson, E. J. (2004). *Evolution: The remarkable history of a scientific theory*. New York: Random House. (6)

Lederer, S. E. (1995). *Subjected to science: human experimentation in America before the Second World War*. Baltimore, MD: Johns Hopkins University Press. (2)

Levine, A. G. (1982). *The Love Canal: Science, politics and people*. Lexington, MA: D. C. Heath. (6)

Levy, K. (1980). A Monte Carlo study of analysis of covariance under violations of the assumptions of normality and equal regression slopes. *Educational and Psychological Measurement, 40*, 835–840. (D)

Levy, N. (2007). *Neuroethics: Challenges for the 21st century*. Cambridge, MA: Cambridge University Press. (6)

Leyens, J. P. (2006). Getting social psychological research ideas from other human sciences. In P. A. M. Van Lange (Ed.), *Bridging social psychology: Benefits of transdisciplinary approaches* (pp. 135–138). Mahwah, NJ: Erlbaum. (2)

Light, R. J., & Pillemer, D. B. (1984). *Summing up: The science of reviewing research*. Cambridge, MA: Harvard University Press. (F)

Lilienfeld, S. O. (2007). Psychological treatments that cause harm. *Perspectives on Psychological Science, 2*, 53–70. doi: 10.1111/j.1745-6916.2007.00029.x (1)

Lilienfeld, S. O. (2011). Public skepticism of psychology: Why many people perceive the study of human behavior as unscientific. *American Psychologist.* (Advanced online publication). doi: 10.1037/a0023963 (1)

Lilienfeld, S. O., Fowler, K. A., Lohr, J. M., & Lynn, S. J. (2005). Pseudoscience, nonscience, and nonsense in clinical psychology: Dangers and remedies. In R. H. Wright & N. A. Cummings (Eds.), *Destructive trends in mental health: The well-intentioned path to harm* (pp. 187–218). New York: Routledge. (1)

Lilienfeld, S. O., Lynn, S. J., & Lohr, J. M. (2003). *Science and pseudoscience in clinical psychology*. New York: Guilford Press. (1)

Lilienfeld, S. O., Lynn, S. J., Ruscio, J., & Beyerstein, B. L. (2010). *Fifty great myths of popular psychology: Shattering widespread misconceptions about human behavior*. Malden, MA: Wiley-Blackwell. (1)

Lilienfeld, S. O., Ruscio, J., & Lynn, S. J. (2008). *Navigating the mindfield: A guide to separating science from pseudoscience in mental health*. Amherst, NY: Prometheus Books. (1)

Lilienthal, O. (1889). Birdflight as the basis of aviation; a contribution towards a system of aviation, compiled from the results of numerous experiments made by O. and G. Lilienthal. London, New York, Longmans, Green. Translated in 1911 from the 2nd ed. by A. W. Isenthal. (2)

Liptak, A. (2003, September 27). No-call list: Hard choices. *New York Times*, p. A1. (13)

Loehlin, J. C. (2004). *Latent variable models: An introduction to factor, path, and structural equation analyses* (4th ed.). Mahwah, NJ: Erlbaum. (7)

Loftus, E. F., & Hoffman, H. G. (1989). Misinformation and memory: The creation of new memories. *Journal of Experimental Psychology: General*, *118*, 100–104. doi: 10.1037/0096-3445.118.1.100 (13)

Loftus, E. F., & Ketcham, K. (1991). *Witness for the defense: The accused, the eyewitness, and the expert who puts memory on trial*. New York: St. Martin's Press. (13)

Loftus, E. F., & Ketcham, K. (1994). *The myth of repressed memory: False memories and allegations of sexual abuse*. New York: St. Martin's Press. (1)

Loftus, E. F., & Polage, D. C. (1999). Repressed memories: When are they real? How are they false? *Psychiatric Clinics of North America, 22*, 61–70. doi: 10.1016/S0193-953X(05)70059-9 (1, 3)

Lord, F. M. (1967). A paradox in the interpretation of group differences. *Psychological Bulletin*, *68*, 304–305. doi: 10.1037/h0025105 (12)

Lovaas, O. I. (1973). *Behavioral treatment of autistic children*. Morristown, NJ: General Learning Press. (3)

Lubinski, D., & Benbow, C. P. (1992). Gender differences in abilities and preferences among the gifted: Implications for the math-science pipeline. *Current Directions in Psychological Science*, *1*, 61–66. doi: 10.1111/1467-8721.ep11509746 (8)

Lynn, S. J., Lock, T., & Loftus, E. F. (2003). The remembrance of things past: Problematic memory recovery techniques in psychotherapy. In S. O. Lilienfeld, S. J. Lynn, & J. M. Lohr (Eds.), *Science and pseudoscience in clinical psychology* (pp. 205–239). New York: Guilford Press. (1)

Macfarlane, G. (1984). *Alexander Fleming: The man and the myth*. Oxford, England: Oxford University Press. (1)

Maddox, J. (1999, December). The unexpected science to come. *Scientific American. 281*(6), 62–67. (FN)

Marlatt, G. A., Demming, B., & Reid, J. B. (1973). Loss of control drinking in alcoholics: An experimental analogue. *Journal of Abnormal Psychology*, *81*, 233–241. doi: 10.1037/h0034532 (9)

Marshall, C., & Rossman, G. B. (1999). *Designing qualitative research* (3rd ed). Thousand Oaks, CA: Sage Publishers. (6)

Mason, M. E. J., & Loftus, G. R. (2003). Using confidence intervals for graphically based data interpretation. *Canadian Journal of Experimental Psychology*, *57*, 203–220. doi: 10.1037/h0087426 (10)

Matthews, G. (2002). Toward a transactional ergonomics for driver stress and fatigue. *Theoretical Issues in Ergonomic Science*, *3*, 195–211. doi: 10.1080/14639220210124120 (3)

Matus, R. (2008, January 24). North Florida weighing in against evolution: Several school boards say they want to teach alternative theories. *The St. Petersburg Times*. (1)

Mayo Foundation. (2012a). *National consortium.* Center for Translational Science Activities, The Mayo Foundation for Medical Education and Research. Retrieved from www.mayo.edu/ctsa/about/national-consortium on April 11, 2012. (3)

Mayo Foundation. (2012b). *Clinical and translational research.* Center for Translational Science Activities, The Mayo Foundation for Medical Education and Research. Retrieved from www.mayo.edu/ctsa/about/clinical-and-translational-research on April 11, 2012. (3)

McFall, R. M. (1970). Effects of self-monitoring on normal smoking behavior. *Journal of Consulting and Clinical Psychology*, *35*, 135–142. doi: 10.1037/h0030087 (11)

McGrath, P. (2006). Psychosocial issues in childhood autism rehabilitation: A review. *International Journal of Psychosocial Rehabilitation*, *11*, 29–36. (8)

McGrew, W. C. (1992). *Chimpanzee material culture*. Cambridge, MA: Cambridge University Press. (6)

McGrew, W. C. (2004). *The cultured chimpanzee: Reflections on cultural primatology.* Cambridge, MA: Cambridge University Press. (6)

McGuire, W. J. (1997). Creative hypothesis generating in psychology: Some useful heuristics. *Annual Review of Psychology, 48,* 1–30. doi: 10.1146/annurev.psych.48.1.1 (2)

McKay, D., Todaro, J. F., Neziroglu, F., & Yaryura-Tobias, J. A. (1996). Evaluation of a naturalistic maintenance program in the treatment of obsessive-compulsive disorder: A preliminary investigation. *Journal of Anxiety Disorders, 10,* 211–217. doi: 10.1016/0887-6185(96)00006-0 (13)

Meehl, P. E. (1962). Schizotaxia, schizotypy, schizophrenia. *American Psychologist, 17,* 827–838. doi: 10.1037/h0041029 (2)

Meehl, P. E. (1990). Toward an integrated theory of schizotaxia, schizotypy, and schizophrenia. *Journal of Personality Disorders, 4,* 1–99. (2)

Meredith, R. (1996, April 30). Man is guilty of murder in death after bridge dispute. *New York Times,* Sect. A, p. 16. (8)

Michell, J. (1986). Measurement scales and statistics: A clash of paradigms. *Psychological Bulletin, 87,* 564–567. doi: 10.1037/0033-2909.100.3.398 (4)

Miller, F. G., Wendler, D., & Swartzman, L. C. (2005). Deception in research on the placebo effect. *PloS Medicine, 2,* e262. Retrieved from http://www.plosmedicine.org/article/info%3Adoi%2F10.1371%2Fjournal.pmed.0020262 on April 14, 2012. (3, 9)

Miller, G. (2010). Misconduct by post docs leads to retraction of paper. *Science, 329,* 1583. doi: 1126/science.329.5999.1583 (2)

Miller, G. M., & Chapman, J. P. (2001). Misunderstanding analysis of covariance. *Journal of Abnormal Psychology, 110,* 40–48. doi: 10.1037//0021-843X.110.1.40 (12)

Miller, N. E. (1971). *Neal E. Miller: Selected papers.* Chicago, IL: Aldine Atherton. (3)

Miller, N. E. (1985). The value of behavioral research with animals. *American Psychologist, 40,* 423–440. doi: 10.1037/0003-066X.40.4.423 (3)

Minogue, K. & Marshall, E. (2010). Guatemala study from 1940s reflects a dark chapter in medicine. *Science, 330,* 137–280. doi: 10.1126/science.330.601.160 (2)

Mittal, V. A., & Walker, E. F. (2007). Movement abnormalities predict conversion to Axis I psychosis among prodromal adolescents. *Journal of Abnormal Psychology, 116,* 796–803. doi: 10.1037/0021-843X.116.4.796 (6)

Money, J., Jobaris, R., & Furth, G. (1977). Apotemnophilia: Two cases of self-demand amputation as a paraphilia. *Journal of Sex Research, 13,* 115–125. doi: 10.1080/00224497709550967 (6)

Morgan, D. L., & Morgan, R. K. (2001). Single-participant research design: Bringing science to managed care. *American Psychologist, 56,* 119–127. doi: 10.1037/0003-066X.56.2.119 (11)

Morrison, A. R. (2001). A scientist's perspective on the ethics of using animals in behavioral research. In M. E. Carroll & J. B. Overmier (Eds.), *Animal research and human health: Advancing human welfare through behavioral science* (pp. 341–356). Washington, DC: American Psychological Association. (3)

Mosfegh, A., Goldman, J., Ahuja, A., Rhodes, D., & LaComb, R. (2009). *What do we eat in America? National Health and Nutrition Examination Survey 2005–2006: Usual nutrient intakes from food and water compared to 1997 dietary reference intakes for vitamin D, calcium, phosphorous, & magnesium.* Washington, DC: U.S. Department of Agriculture, Agriculture Research Service. (13)

Mroczek, D. K., & Avron, S., III (2007). Personality change influences mortality in older men. *Psychological Science, 18,* 371–376. doi: 10.1111/j.1467-9280.2007.01907.x (1)

Mullins, J. L., & Christian, L. (2001). The effects of progressive relaxation training on the disruptive behavior of a boy with autism. *Research in Developmental Disabilities, 22,* 449–462. doi: 10.1016/S0891-4222(01)00083-X (6)

Musgrave, E. (2010). Advancing science across the discipline. *Clinical and Translational Science, 3,* 69–70. doi: 10.11/j.1752-8062.2010.00197.x (3)

Myers, D. G. (2004). *Intuition: Its powers and perils*. New Haven, CT: Yale University Press. (1)

Myers, J. L., Well, A. D., & Lorch, R. F. (2010). *Research design and statistical analysis* (3rd ed.). New York: Routledge. (7, 11, D)

Nagel, E. (1948). The development of modern science. In J. L. Blau, J. Buchler, & G. T. Matthews (Eds.), *Chapters in western civilization* (Vol. 1, pp. 241–284). New York: Columbia University Press. (1)

Nagy, T. F. (2011). *Essential ethics for psychologists: A primer for understanding and mastering core issues*. Washington, DC: American Psychological Association. (2, 3)

Napolitano, D. A., Smith, T., Zarcone, J. P., Goodkin, J., & McAdam, D. B. (2010). Increasing response diversity in children with autism. *Journal of Applied Behavior Analysis*, *43*, 265–271. doi: 10.1901/jaba.2010.43-265 (8)

Nardi, P. (2005). *Doing survey research*. Boston, MA: Allyn & Bacon. (13)

National Institutes of Health. (March, 2002). *Methods and Welfare Considerations in Behavioral Research with Animals* (NIH Publication No. 02-5083). Retrieved from http://www.nimh.nih.gov/research-funding/grants/methods-and-welfare-considerations-in-behavioral-research-with-animals.shtml (3)

National Institutes of Health. (2005). *Grants policy and guidance: Inclusion guidance*. Retrieved from http://grants1.nih.gov/grants/policy/policy.htm (3)

Neergaard. L. (2010, Friday, October 1). U. S. apologizes for 1940s syphilis study in Guatemala. *The Washington Times*, p. 1. (2)

Neisser, U. (1976). *Cognition and reality: Principles and implications of cognitive psychology*. San Francisco, CA: W. H. Freeman. (8)

Neisser, U., & Harsch, N. (1992). Phantom flashbulbs: False recollection of hearing the news about Challenger. In E. Winograd & U. Neisser (Eds.), *Affect and accuracy in recall: Studies of "flashbulb" memories* (pp. 9–31). New York: Cambridge University Press. (13)

Nelson, G. (1970). Interview. In S. Rosner & I. E. Abt (Eds.), *The creative experience* (pp. 251–268). New York: Grossman. (1)

Nunnally, J. C., & Bernstein, I. H. (1994). *Psychometric theory* (3rd ed.). New York: McGraw-Hill. (4, 7)

Oakes, M. (1986). *Statistical inference: A commentary for the social and behavioral sciences*. New York: Wiley. (F)

Office of Laboratory Animal Welfare. (2002). *Public Health Service policy on humane care and use of laboratory animals*. Retrieved from http://grants1.nih.gov/grants/olaw/references/PHSPolicyLabAnimals.pdf on April 14, 2012. (3)

Olds, J. (1958). Self-stimulation of the brain. *Science*, *127*, 314–324. doi: 10.1126/science.127.3294.315 (1)

Olds, J., & Milner, P. (1954). Positive reinforcement produced by electrical stimulation of the septal area and other regions of the rat brain. *Journal of Comparative and Physiological Psychology*, *47*, 419–427. doi: 10.1037/h0058775 (1)

Olfson, M., Marcus, S. C., & Druss, B. G. (2008). Effects of Food and Drug Administration warnings on antidepressant use in a national sample. *Archives of General Psychiatry*, *65*, 94–101. doi: 10.1001/archgenpsychiatry.2007.5 (13)

Olsson, I. A. S., Hansen, A. K., & Sandoe, P. (2007). Ethics and refinement in animal research. *Science*, *317*, 1680. doi: 10.1126/science.317.5845.1680 (3)

Oppel, F. (Ed.). (1987). *Early flight: From balloons to biplanes*. Secaucus, NJ: Castle. (2)

Oppenheimer, J. R. (1956). Analogy in science. *American Psychologist*, *11*, 127–135. doi: 10.1037/h0046760 (1)

Orne, M. T. (1962). On the social psychology of the psychological experiment: With particular reference to demand characteristics and their implications. *American Psychologist*, *17*, 776–783. doi: 10.1037/h0043424 (8)

Orwin, R. G. (1997). Twenty-one years old and counting: The interrupted time series comes of age. In E. Chelimsky & W. R. Shadish (Eds.), *Evaluation for the 21st century: A handbook* (pp. 443–465). Thousand Oaks, CA: Sage. (13)

Palladino, M. A. (2005). *Understanding the human genome project*. Redwood City, CA: Benjamin-Cummings. (FN)

Paradis, C. M., Solomon, L. Z., Florer, F., & Thompson, T. (2004). Flashbulb memories of personal events of 9/11 and the day after for a sample of New York City residents. *Psychological Reports*, *95*, 304–310. doi: 10.2466/PR0.95.5.304-310 (13)

Park, R. L. (2002). *Voodoo science: The road from foolishness to fraud*. New York: Oxford University Press. (1)

Pate, W. E., II. (2001). Analysis of data from graduate study in psychology: 1999–2000. Retrieved from http://www.apa.org/workforce/publications/grad-00/index.aspx on April 1, 2012. (1)

Pauling, L. (1981). Cited in A. J. Bachrach, *Psychological research: An introduction* (4th ed., p. 3). New York: Random House. (1)

Pelham, W. E. (1994, November 3). *Attention deficit hyperactivity disorder*. Colloquium presented at the State University of New York at Buffalo. (9)

Pelham, W. E., Murphy, D. A., Vannatta, K., Milich, R., Licht, B. G., Gnagy, E. M., et al. (1992). Methylphenidate and attributions in boys with attention-deficit hyperactivity disorder. *Journal of Consulting and Clinical Psychology*, *60*, 282–292. doi: 10.1037/0022-006X.60.2.282 (9)

Penrose, L. S., & Penrose, P. R. (1958). Impossible objects: A special type of visual. *British Journal of Psychology, 49*, 31–33. (1)

Peters, E., Baker, D. P., Dieckmann, N. F., Leon, J., & Collins, J. (2010). Explaining the effects of education on health: A field study in Ghana. *Psychological Science*, *21*, 1369–1376. doi: 10.1177/0956797610381506 (6)

Phillips, K. A. (2004). Psychosis in body dysmorphic disorder. *Journal of Psychiatric Research*, *38*, 63–72. doi: 10.1016/S0022-3956(03)00098-0 (6)

Phillips, K. A., Pinto, A., Menard, W., Eisen, J. L., Mancebo, M., & Rasmussen, S. A. (2007). Obsessive-compulsive disorder versus body dysmorphic disorder: A comparison study of two possibly related disorders. *Depression and Anxiety*, *24*, 399–409. doi: 10.1002/da.20232 (6)

Pickren, W. E. & Rutherford, A. (2010). *A history of modern psychology in context*. Hoboken, NJ: John Wiley. (1)

Pittenger, D. J. (2002). Deception in research: Distinctions and solutions from the perspective of utilitarianism. *Ethics and Behavior*, *12*, 117–142. doi: 10.1207/S15327019EB1202_1 (3)

Popper, K. R. (1959). *The logic of scientific discovery*. New York: Basic Books. (2)

Posavac, E. J., & Carey, R. G. (2007). *Program evaluation: Methods and case studies* (7th ed.). Upper Saddle River, NJ: R. G. Carey and Associates. (13)

Powers, M. B., & Emmelkamp, P. M. G. (2007). Virtual reality exposure therapy for anxiety disorders: A meta-analysis. *Journal of Anxiety Disorders*, *22*, 561–569. doi: 10.1016/j.janxdis.2007.04.006 (9)

Prilleltensky, I. (1994). Psychology and social ethics. *American Psychologist*, *49*, 966–967. doi: 10.1037/003-0664.49.11.996 (2, 3)

Pruitt, D. G., Parker, J. C., & Mikolic, J. M. (1997). Escalation as a reaction to persistent annoyance. *International Journal of Conflict Management*, *8*, 252–270. doi: 10.1108/eb022798 (6)

Pungello, E. P., Kainz, K., Burchinal, M., Wasik, B. H., Sparling, J. J., Ramey, C. T., et al. (2010). Early educational intervention, early cumulative risk, and the early home environment as predictors of young adult outcomes within a high-risk sample. *Child Development*, *81*, 410–426. doi: 10.1111/j.1467-8624.2009.01403.x (13)

Rachman, S. (1997). The evolution of cognitive behaviour therapy. In D. Clark, C. G. Fairburn, & M. C. Gelder (Eds.), *Science and practice of cognitive behaviour therapy* (pp. 1–26). Oxford, England: Oxford University Press. (3)

Radeborg, K., Briem, V., & Hedman, L. R. (1999). The effect of concurrent task difficulty on working memory during simulated driving. *Ergonomics*, *42*, 767–772. doi: 10.1080/001401399185441 (2)

Ramey, C. T., & Ramey, S. L. (1998). Early intervention and early experience. *American Psychologist*, *53*, 109–120. doi: 10.1037/0003-066X.53.2.109 (13)

Ramey, C. T., & Ramey, S. L. (2004). Early learning and school readiness: Can early intervention make a difference? *Merrill-Palmer Quarterly: Journal of Developmental Psychology*, *50*, 471–491. doi: 10.1353/mpq.2004.0034 (13)

Ramey, C. T., Mulvihill, B. A., & Ramey, S. L. (1996). Prevention: Social and educational factors and early intervention. In J. W. Jacobson & J. A. Mulick (Eds.), *Manual of diagnosis and professional practice in mental retardation* (pp. 215–227). Washington, DC: American Psychological Association. (13)

Raulin, M. L., & Graziano, A. M. (1995). Quasi-experiments and correlational studies. In A. M. Coleman (Ed.), *Psychological research methods and statistics* (pp. 1122–1141). London: Longman. (7)

Raulin, M. L., & Lilienfeld, S. O. (2009). Studying psychopathology. In P. H. Blaney & T. Millon (Eds.), *Oxford textbook of psychopathology* (2nd ed., pp. 86–115). New York: Oxford University Press. (4, 7, 9)

Raulin, M. L., Brenner, V., deBeaumont, S. M., & Vetter, C. J. (1995a, November). *The impact of managed care on treatment outcome: Initial findings*. Poster presented at the annual convention of the Association for the Advancement of Behavior Therapy, Washington, DC. (13)

Raulin, M. L., de Beaumont, S. M., Brenner, V., & Vetter, C. J. (1995b, June). *Comparing outcome of psychological/psychiatric intervention in managed care and traditional health insurance environments.* Poster presented at the annual convention of the Association of Applied and Preventive Psychology, whose convention is held jointly with the American Psychological Society, New York. (13)

Raykov, T., & Marcoulides, G. A. (2010). *Introduction to psychometric theory*. New York, NY: Routledge Academic. (4)

Reed, J. G., & Baxter, P. M. (2003). *Library use: A handbook of psychology* (3rd ed.). Washington, DC: American Psychological Association. (C)

Reese, R. M., Sherman, J. A., & Sheldon, J. B. (1998). Reducing disruptive behavior of a group-home resident with autism and mental retardation. *Journal of Autism and Developmental Disorders*, *28*, 159–165. doi: 10.1023/A:1026096700607 (6)

Reese, W. L. (1996). *Dictionary of philosophy and religion: Eastern and Western thought*. Atlantic Highlands, NJ: Humanities Press. (2)

Reid, J. B. (1970). Reliability assessment of observation data: A possible methodological problem. *Child Development*, *41*, 1143–1150. doi: 10.2307/1127341 (9)

Rensberger, B. (2005, October). Science abuse: Subverting scientific knowledge for short-term gain. *Scientific American*, *293*, 106. (4)

Reverby, S. M. (2000). *Tuskegee's truths: Rethinking the Tuskegee syphilis study*. Chapel Hill, NC: University of North Carolina. (2)

Reverby, S. M. (2009). *Examining Tuskegee: The infamous syphilis study and its legacy*. Chapel Hill, NC: University of North Carolina Press. (2)

Reverby, S. M. (2011). Normal exposure and inoculation syphilis: A PHS "Tuskegee" doctor in Guatemala, 1946–1948. *The Journal of Policy History*, *23*, 1. doi: 10.1017/S0898030610000291 (2)

Ridley, M. (2003). *Nature via nurture: Genes, experience, and what makes us human*. New York: Harper-Collins. (8)

Ritchie, J., & Lewis, J. (Eds.). (2003). *Qualitative research practice: A guide for social science students and researchers*. Thousand Oaks, CA: Sage. (6)

Ritvo, L. B. (1990). *Darwin's influence on Freud: A tale of two sciences*. New Haven, CT: Yale University Press. (1)

Robbins, W. W., & Boesch, C. (Eds.). (2011). *Among the apes: Stories and photos from Africa.* Berkeley, CA: University of California Press. (6)

Roberts, F. S. (1984). *Measurement theory with applications to decision making, utility, and the social sciences*. New York: Cambridge University Press. (Originally published in 1979 by Addison-Wesley) (4)

Roberts, R. M. (1989). *Serendipity: Accidental discoveries in science*. New York: Wiley. (1)

Rohsenow, D. J., & Marlatt, G. A. (1981). The balanced placebo design: Methodological considerations. *Addictive Behavior*, *6*, 107–122. (9)

Rose, S. (2005). *The future of the brain: The promise and perils of tomorrow's neuroscience*. New York: Oxford University Press. (FN)

Rosenhan, D. L. (1973). On being sane in insane places. *Science, 179*, 250–258. doi: 10.1126/science.179.4070.250

Rosenthal, R. (1976). *Experimenter effects in behavioral research*. New York: Halsted Press.

Rosenthal, R. (1994). Science and ethics in conducting, analyzing, and reporting psychological research. *Psychological Science, 5*, 127–134. doi: 10.1111/j.1467-9280.1994.tb00646.x (2)

Rosenthal, R. (1998). Meta-analysis: Concepts, corollaries, and controversies. In J. Adair & D. Belanger (Eds.), *Advances in psychological science, Vol. I: Social, personal, and cultural aspects* (pp. 371–384). Hove, England: Psychology Press/Erlbaum. (F)

Rosenthal, R., & Fode, K. L. (1963a). The effect of experimenter bias on the performance of the albino rat. *Behavioral Science, 8*, 183–189. (8)

Rosenthal, R., & Fode, K. L. (1963b). Three experiments in experimenter bias. *Psychological Reports, 12*, 491–511. (8)

Rosnow, R. L., & Rosnow, M. (2008). *Writing papers in psychology: A study guide* (5th ed.). Pacific Grove, CA: Brooks/Cole. (B)

Rossi, P. H., Wright, J. D., & Anderson, A. B. (Eds.) (1993). *Handbook of survey research*. San Diego, CA: Academic Press. (13)

Rubin, J. Z., Pruitt, D. G., & Kim, S. (1994). *Social conflict, escalation, stalemate, and settlement*. New York: McGraw-Hill. (6)

Russell, W. S., & Burch, R. L. (1959). *The principles of humane experimental techniques*. London, England: Methuen. (3)

Russo, N. F., & Denmark, F. L. (1987). Contributions of women to psychology. *Annual Review of Psychology, 38*, 279–298. doi: 10.1146/annurev.ps.38.020187.001431 98 (1)

Sales, B. D., & Folkman, S. (2000). *Ethics of research with human participants*. Washington, DC: American Psychological Association. (2, 3)

Santoro, M. A., & Gorrie, T. M. (Eds.). (2005). *Ethics and the pharmaceutical industry*. Cambridge, England: Cambridge University Press. (4)

Saucier, D., & Elias, L. (2006). *Human neuropsychology: Clinical and experimental foundations*. Boston, MA: Allyn & Bacon. (11)

Schlesinger, W. H. (2010).Translational ecology. *Science, 329*, 609. doi: 10.1126/science.1195624 (3)

Schmidt, F. L. (1992). What do data really mean? Research findings, meta-analysis, and cumulative knowledge in psychology. *American Psychologist, 47*, 1173–1181. doi: 10.1037/0003-066X.47.10.1173 (F)

Schriebman, L. (2005). *The science and fiction of autism*. Cambridge, MA: Harvard University Press. (8)

Schultz, D. P., & Schultz, S. E. (2008). *A history of modern psychology* (9th ed.). Belmont, CA: Thompson/Wadsworth. (1)

Schwartz, D. N., Abiad, H., DeMarais, P. L., Armeanu, E., Trick, W. E., Wang, Y., et al. (2007). An educational intervention to improve antimicrobial use in a hospital-based long-term care facility. *Journal of American Geriatrics Society, 55*, 1236–1242. doi: 10.1111/j.1532-5415.2007.01251.x (13)

Science. (2010). Translational medicine: Integrating medicine and science [Whole issue]. *Science, 2*(43). (3)

Seligman, M. E. P. (1974). Depression and learned helplessness. In R. J. Friedman & M. J. Katz (Eds.), *The psychology of depression: Contemporary theory and research*. Washington, DC: Winston-Wiley. (3)

Serras, A., Saules, K. K., Cranford, J. A., & Eisenberg, D. (2010). Self-injury, substance use, and associated risk factors in a multi-campus probability sample of college students. *Psychology of Addictive Behaviors, 24*, 119-128. doi: 10.1037/a0017210 (13)

Shavelson, R. J. (1996). *Statistical reasoning for the behavioral sciences* (3rd ed.). Boston, MA: Allyn & Bacon. (10)

Shelley, Mary Wollenstonecraft. (1818). *Frankenstein; or The Modern Prometheus* (three volumes). London: Lackington, Hughes, Harding, Mavor, & Jones. (Reprinted by Pocket Books (New York) in 2004) (2)

Shields, S. A. (1982). The variability hypothesis: The history of a biological model of sex differences in intelligence. *Signs*, *7*, 769–797. doi: 10.1086/493921 (1)

Sidman, M. (1960). *Tactics of scientific research: Evaluating scientific data in psychology*. New York: Basic Books. (11)

Simonsen, E., & Parnas, J. (1993). Personality research in Denmark. *Journal of Personality Disorders*, *7*, 187–195. (6)

Skinner, B. F. (1938). *The behavior of organisms*. New York: Appleton-Century-Crofts. (3)

Skinner, B. F. (1953). *Science and human behavior*. New York: Macmillan. (2)

Skinner, B. F. (1956). A case history in scientific method. *American Psychologist*, *11*, 221–233. doi: 10.1037/h0047662 (1)

Skinner, B. F. (1969). *Contingencies of reinforcement: A theoretical analysis*. New York: Appleton-Century-Crofts. (2)

Skinner, B. F. (1972). *Cumulative record: A selection of papers* (3rd ed.). New York: Appleton-Century-Crofts. (2, 3)

Skinner, B. F. (1979). *The shaping of a behaviorist*. New York: Alfred A. Knopf. (11)

Skinner, B. F. (1990, August). *Skinner's keynote address: Lifetime scientific contribution remarks.* Presented at the annual convention of the American Psychological Association, Boston, MA. (Available on audio- or videocassette from the American Psychological Association Continuing Education Section) (2)

Smith, R. (2001). Editorial: Maintaining the integrity of the scientific record. *British Medical Journal*, 323, 588. doi: 10.1136/bmj.323.7313.588 (4)

Solomon, R. L. (1949). An extension of control group design. *Psychological Bulletin*, *46*, 137–150. doi: 10.1037/h0062958 (10)

Sorrentino, R. M., Cohen, D., Olson, J. M., & Zanna, M. P. (Eds.). (2004). *Cultural and social behavior: The Ontario Symposium* (Vol. 10). Mahwah, NJ: Erlbaum. (7)

Spearman, C. E. (1904). "General intelligence" objectively determined and measured. *American Journal of Psychiatry*, *15*, 200–292. (7)

Spitzer, R. L. (1975). On pseudoscience in science, logic in remission, and psychiatric diagnoses: A critique of Rosenhan's "On being sane in insane places." *Journal of Abnormal Psychology*, *84*, 442–452. doi: 10.1037/h0077124 (6)

Stark, L. (2007). Toward a broader view of research ethics. *Journal of the History of the Behavioral Sciences*, *43*, 227–228. doi: 10.1002/jhbs.20233 (2)

Stark, L. (2010). The science of ethics: Deception, the resilient self, and the APA code of ethics, 1966–1973. *Journal of the History of the Behavioral Sciences*, *46*, 337–370. doi: 10.10021/jhbs.20468 (2)

Stephenson, A. G. [Chairperson] et al. (1999). *Mars Climate Orbiter Mishap Investigation Board Phase I Report*. Washington, DC: National Aeronautics and Space Administration. Retrieved from ftp://ftp.hq.nasa.gov/pub/pao/reports/1999/MCO_report.pdf on April 14, 2012. (4)

Sternberg, R. I., & Lubart, T. I. (1992). Buy low and sell high: An investment approach to creativity. *Current Directions in Psychological Science*, *1*, 1–15. doi: 10.1111/1467-8721.ep10767737 (1)

Stevens, S. S. (1946). On the theory of scales of measurement. *Science*, *103*, 677–680. (4)

Stevens, S. S. (1957). On the psychophysical law. *Psychological Review*, *64*, 153–181. doi: 10.1037/h0046162 (4)

Stolzenberg, L., & D'Alessio, S. J. (1997). "Three strikes and you're out": The impact of California's new mandatory sentencing law on serious crime rates. *Crime and Delinquency*, *43*, 457–469. doi: 10.1177/0011128797043004004 (13)

Strayer, D. L., & Drews, F. A. (2007). Cell-phone-induced driver distraction. *Current Directions in Psychological Science*, *16*, 128–131. doi: 10.1111/j.1467.8721.2007.00489.x (2)

Strayer, D. L., & Johnston, W. A. (2001). Driven to distraction: Dual-task studies of simulated driving and conversing on a cellular telephone. *Psychological Science*, *12*, 462–466. doi: 10.1111/1467-9280.00386 (2)

Strayer, D. L., Drews, F. A., & Crouch, D. J. (2006). A comparison of the cell phone driver and the drunk driver. *Human Factors and Ergonomics*, *48*, 381–391. doi: 10.1518/001872006777724471 (2)

Strayer, D. L., Drews, F. A., & Johnston, W. A. (2003). Cell phone-induced failures of visual attention during simulated driving. *Journal of Experimental Psychology: Applied*, *9*, 23–32. doi: 10.1037/1076-898X.9.1.23 (2)

Strunk, W., Jr., White, E. B., & Angell, R. (2005). *The elements of style* (4th ed.). Upper Saddle River, NJ: Prentice Hall. (B)

Sudman, S., & Blair, E. (1997). *Marketing research: A problem-solving approach*. San Francisco, CA: McGraw-Hill. (13)

Sugarman, J., & Sulmasy, D. P. (Eds.). (2010). *Methods in medical ethics* (2nd ed.). Washington, DC: Georgetown University Press. (2)

Sulloway, F. J. (1979). *Freud: Biologist of the mind*. New York: Basic Books. (1)

Suomi, S. J. (2008). How mother nurture helps Mother Nature: Scientific evidence for the protective effects of good nurturing on genetic propensity toward anxiety and alcohol abuse. In K. K. Klein (Ed.), *Authoritative communities: The scientific case for nurturing the whole child* (pp. 87–102). New York: Springer. (8)

Sutton, R. S., & Barto, A. G. (1998). *Reinforcement learning: An introduction*. Cambridge, MA: MIT Press. (2)

Sutton, S. K., & Davidson, R. J. (1997). Prefrontal brain asymmetry: A biological substrate of the behavioral approach and inhibition systems. *Psychological Science*, *8*, 204–210. doi: 10.1111/j.1467-9280.1997.tb00413.x (1)

Taylor, C. A., Manganello, J. A., Lee, S. J., & Rice, J. C. (2010). Mothers' spanking of three-year-old children and subsequent risk of children's aggressive behavior. *Pediatrics*, *125*, e1057–e1065. doi: 10.1542/peds.2009-2678. Retrieved from http://pediatrics.aappublications.org/content/125/5/e1057.full.html on April 17, 2012. (6)

Thagard, P. (1998). Ulcers and bacteria I: Discovery and acceptance. *Studies in the History and Philosophy of Biology and Biomedical Science*, *9*, 107–136. (6)

Timmermans, M., van Lier, P. A. C., & Koot, H. M. (2009). Pathways of behavior problems from childhood to late adolescence leading to delinquency and academic underachievement. *Journal of Clinical Child and Adolescent Psychology*, *38*, 630–638. doi: 10.1080/15374410903103502 (3)

Tinbergen, N. (1963). *The herring gull's world*. London, England: Collins. (6)

Toomey, J., & Adams, L. A. (1995). Naturalistic observation of children with autism: Evidence for intersubjectivity. In L. L. Sperry & P. A. Smiley (Eds.), *Exploring young children's concepts of self and other through conversation. New directions in child development* (No. 69, pp. 75–89). San Francisco, CA: Jossey-Bass. (6)

Trefil, J., & Hazen, R. M. (2007). *The sciences: An integrative approach* (5th ed.). Hoboken, NJ: Wiley. (6)

Tronsmoen, T. (2011). Differences between formal and informal driver training as experienced by the learners themselves. *Transportation Research Part F: Traffic Psychology and Behaviour*, *14*, 176-188. doi: 10.1016/j.trf.2010.11.009 (3)

Tufte, E. R. (2001). *The visual display of quantitative information* (2nd ed.). Cheshire, CT: Graphics Press. (5)

Tukey, J. W. (1977). *Exploratory data analysis*. Reading, MA: Addison-Wesley. (D)

Turner, D. (2004, October 26). Polls grow increasingly fuzzy: Cell phones, caller ID pose new challenges. *Buffalo (NY) News*, p. A1. (13)

Ulrich, R. E. (1991). Animal rights, animal wrongs, and the question of balance. *Psychological Science*, *2*, 197–201. doi: 10.1111/j.1467-9280.1991.tb00132.x (3)

Union of Concerned Scientists. (2005). *Political interference in science*. Washington, DC: Union of Concerned Scientists and Government Accountability Project. Retrieved from http://www.ucsusa.org/scientific_integrity/interference/ on May 1, 2008. (1)

Union of Concerned Scientists. (2010). *Science and politics at the Environmental Protection Agency*. Washington, DC: Union of Concerned Scientists and Government Accountability Project. Retrieved from http://www.ucsusa.org/assets/documents/scientific_integrity/interference-at-the-epa.pdf on April 1, 2012. (1)

Union of Concerned Scientists. (2010a). Debunking misinformation about stolen climate e-mails in the climategate manufactured controversy. Retrieved from http://www.ucsusa.org/global_warming/

science_and_impacts/global_warming_contrarians/debunking-misinformation-stolen-emails-climategate.html (4)

Union of Concerned Scientists. (2010b). Scientific integrity: Alphabetical list of case studies. Retrieved from http://www.ucsusa.org/scientific_integrity/abuses_of_science/a-to-z-alphabetical.html (4)

van Kleef, G. A., Oveis, C., van der Lowe, L., LuoKogan, A., Goetz, J., & Keltner, D. (2008). Power, distress, and compassion: Turning a blind eye to the suffering of others. *Psychological Science*, *19*, 1315–1322. doi: 10.1111/j.1467-9280.2008.02241.x (1)

Vinovskis, M. A. (2005). *The birth of Head Start: Preschool education policies in the Kennedy and Johnson administrations*. Chicago, IL: University of Chicago Press. (13)

Vogel, G. (2010). Animal research: Long-fought compromise reached on European animal rules. *Science*, 329, 1588–1589. doi: 10.1126/science.329.5999.1588 (3)

Von Borell, E., & Veissier, I. (2007). Special section: Stress and welfare in farm animals. *Physiology and Behavior*, *92*, 291–292. doi: 10.1016/j.physbeh.2007.01.007 (3)

Walker, E. F., Savoie, T., & Davis, D. (1994). Neuromotor precursors of schizophrenia. *Schizophrenia Bulletin*, *20*, 441–451. doi: 10.1176/appi.ajp.161.11.2021 (6)

Walker, E. F., Shapiro, D., Esterberg, M., & Trotman, H. (2010). Neurodevelopment and schizophrenia: Broadening the focus. *Current Directions in Psychological Science*, *19*, 204–208. doi: 10.1177/0963721410377744 (6)

Wang, X., Wang, E., & Marincola, F. M. (2011). Translational medicine is developing in China: A new venue for collaboration. *Journal of Translational Medicine, 9*. Retrieved from http://www.translational–medicine.com/content/9/1/3. doi: 10.1186/1479-5876-9-3 (3)

Watanabe, S. (2007). How animal psychology contributes to animal welfare. *Applied Animal Behaviour Science*, *106*, 193-202. doi: 10.1016/j.applanim.2007.01.003 (3)

Weaver, C. A., III., & Krug, K. S. (2004). Consolidation-like effects in flashbulb memories: Evidence from September 11, 2001. *American Journal of Psychology*, *117*, 517–530. doi: 10.2307/4148989 (13)

Webb, E. J., Campbell, D. T., Schwartz, R. D., & Sechrest, L. (1966). *Unobtrusive measures: Nonreactive research in the social sciences*. Chicago, IL: Rand McNally. (6)

Webb, E. J., Campbell, D. T., Schwartz, R. D., & Sechrest, L. (2000). *Unobtrusive measures*. (Rev. Ed.) Thousand Oaks, CA: Sage. (6)

Weiner, B. (1975). "On being sane in insane places": A process (attributional) analysis and critique. *Journal of Abnormal Psychology*, *84*, 433–441. doi: 10.1037/h0077126 (6)

Wender, P. H., Kety, S. S., Rosenthal, D., Schulsinger, F., Ortmann, J., & Lunde, I. (1986). Psychiatric disorder in the biological and adoptive families of adopted individuals with affective disorders. *Archives of General Psychiatry*, *43*, 923–929. (6)

Wertheimer, M. (1945). *Productive thinking*. Chicago, IL: University of Illinois Press. (1)

Whitehead, A. B. (1925). *Science and the modern world*. New York: Macmillan. (1)

Whiten, A., & Boesch, C. (2001, January). The cultures of chimpanzees. *Scientific American*, *284*(1), 60–67. (6)

Wilson, D. (2000). Meta-analysis in alcohol and other drug abuse treatment research. *Addiction*, *95*(Suppl. 3), S419–S438. doi: 10.1080/09652140020004313 (F)

Witmer, E. L. (1907). Clinical psychology. *The Psychological Clinic*, 1, 1–9. (1)

Wolpe, J. (1958). *Psychotherapy by reciprocal inhibition*. Stanford, CA: Stanford University Press. (2, 3, 6)

Wolpe, J. (1990). *The practice of behavior therapy* (4th ed.). New York: Pergamon Press. (2)

Wooley, K., et al. (2006). Declaration of medical writing assistance in international peer-reviewed publications. *Journal of the American Medical Association*, *296*, 932–938. doi: 10.1001/jama.296.8.932-b (4)

Wright, K. D., Eisner, A., Stewart, S. H., & Finley, G. A. (2010). Measurement of preoperative anxiety in young children: Self-report versus observer-rated. *Journal of Psychopathology and Behavioral Assessment*, *32*, 416–427. doi: 10.1007/s10862-009-9158-9 (3)

Wright, O., & Wright, W. (1908, September). The Wright Brothers' aeroplane. *The Century Magazine*. (2)

Wynn, C. M., & Wiggins, A. W. (1997). *The five biggest ideas in science*. New York: Wiley. (6)

Yassour-Barochowitz, D. (2004). Reflections on the researcher-participant relationship and the ethics of dialog. *Ethics and Behavior*, *14*, 175–186. doi: 10.1207/s15327019eb1402_5 (2)

Yin, R. K. (2009). *Case study research: Design and methods* (4th ed.). Thousand Oaks, CA: Sage. (6)

Zerhouni, E. (2005). Basic, translational, and clinical sciences [Editorial]. *Journal of the American Medical Association*, *294*, 1356. doi: 10.1001/jama.294.11.1352 (3)

Zinsser, W. (2006). *On writing well, thirtieth anniversary edition: The classic guide to writing nonfiction*. New York: Harper Trade. (B)

NAME INDEX

SUBJECT INDEX

Page numbers followed by "f" denote figures; those followed by "t" denote tables.

Q

R

T

U

V

W

X

Y

Z